HIDDEN IN PLAIN SIGHT

HIDDEN IN PLAIN SIGHT

QUAKER WOMEN'S WRITINGS 1650-1700

edited by

MARY GARMAN

JUDITH APPLEGATE

MARGARET BENEFIEL

DORTHA MEREDITH

with a foreword by
Rosemary Radford Ruether

Pendle Hill Publications

Wallingford, Pennsylvania 19086

Cover by Melanie Watson

October 1995: 1,500
March 2003: 1,000

Library of Congress Cataloging-in-Publication Data

Hidden in plain sight : Quaker women's writings, 1650-1700/edited by
    Mary Garman . . . [et al.] : with a foreword by Rosemary Radford
    Ruether.
        p.   cm.
    Includes bibliographical references and index.
    ISBN 0-87574-957-7. -- ISBN 0-87574-923-2 (pbk.)
    1. Quaker women--England--History--17th century--Sources.
    2. Society of Friends--England--History--17th century--Sources.
    I. Garman, Mary.
    BX7748.W64H533 1996
    289.6'082--dc20   95-33745
                                                           CIP

To our Quaker foremothers
who followed God's call
in spite of the cost

TABLE OF CONTENTS

THEOLOGICAL WORKS
"SPELLING THE WORD WITHOUT KILLING THE SPIRIT"

LETTERS AND EPISTLES
"WEAVING THE WEB OF COMMUNITY"

FOREWORD

by
Rosemary Radford Ruether

It is with great pleasure that I greet the publication of this volume on Quaker women's writings from the second half of the seventeenth century. Though this is a project that I am happy to claim some credit for initiating, it would never have borne fruit without the perseverance of Mary Garman and the other members of the Quaker Women Research Group. This group includes Judith Applegate, Margaret Benefiel, and Dortha Meredith, as well as current and former students at Earlham College and the Earlham School of Religion. The fruit includes this volume as well as a microfilm collection of the more than two hundred Quaker women's writings of this period made available through University Microfilms International.

I spent the Spring of 1986 on sabbatical leave in London researching seventeenth-century English women's religious writings. I undertook this research with the thesis that seventeenth-century England saw the emergence, not only of the first feminists,[1] but also of the first feminist theology. By first feminists, I meant that this period saw the first critique of male domination of culture and society as a conscious movement.

My assumption is that women have long implicitly resisted the pretensions of male superiority and right to rule over them, but their voices have been silenced and remain largely unknown to us. Those women whose writings remain either state their questions in safe and self-deprecating ways or else appear as isolated, marginal figures, often labeled "crazy" and "heretics" by the dominant Western Christian leaders.

It was first in seventeenth-century England that there was enough disruption of the systems of hegemonic cultural control by the dominant society that sub-cultures could emerge, such as the Society of Friends, that could not only organize dissenting movements, but also produce and preserve their writings for the future. Not, of course, that the Society of Friends did not suffer persecution for their dissenting witness, but there was enough social space for their movement that we can read their foundational writings in publications they printed on their own presses in libraries carried down by their Society. We are not left to read between the lines of writings by their enemies, or with only the occasional writing preserved accidentally by other groups or even under other names, as is the case with the "heretics" of the Patristic and Medieval periods.

The Renaissance and Reformation also saw the outbreak of a movement called the *Querelle des Femmes* in which the superiority or inferiority of women was debated, mostly by men, trading texts from the Bible and the classics.[2] A few educated women were able to enter this debate. Here we find some of the first efforts to interpret the biblical texts traditionally used to argue for women's innate moral inferiority, such as Genesis 1-3 and 1 Timothy 2:11-15, in alternative ways that affirmed women's equal worth in the sight of God. The beginning of what we might call 'feminist hermeneutics' can be found in this debate literature.

By the seventeenth century in England, one had not simply what appears to be the isolated female *savant* writing her views, but evidence of movements, circles of women and men, who questioned this inferiorization of women and championed women's right to education, to participation in public leadership, to teaching and preaching. Since the Bible and Christian theology were the main sources to argue for women's exclusion from such public roles, they necessarily had to produce their own alternative readings of these texts and theological arguments to claim women's rights to larger cultural roles in society and in the church. Thus we can speak of the first movement of 'feminist theology.'

Armed with a checklist of some 651 English women's published writings between 1600 and 1700, I set out to substantiate this thesis.[3] Many of these writings were not explicitly religious. Some had to do with housekeeping and medicine. Having made my way through most of the writings in the collection of the British Museum that expressed a theological perspective, I found myself left with a substantial list of almost two hundred titles that were not in this collection. Most had apocalyptic-sounding titles, such as "Oh, Wo, Wo from the Lord" (Esther Biddle, 1659), "A Warning to the Inhabitants of England" (Mary Adams, 1676) and "A Testimony for Truth against all Hireling Priests" (Judith Boulby, 1673).

Suspecting that most of these writings were from Quaker women, I made my way to the Friends House Library in London, and there to my delight found virtually all of these writings carefully preserved in original printed editions. However, when I asked in the bookstore of the Society of Friends in the same building if any of them were available in modern editions, I drew a blank. The bookstore proprietors were unaware of the existence of such writings.

I was able to read a number of these Quaker women's tracts from the second half of the seventeenth century during my visits to the Friends House Library. I was impressed by how readily available they were in well-preserved printed form. I had only to look up a title in the card catalogue and ask for it, and in minutes a courteous librarian was back with it from the archives. And yet these women and their writings seemed so unknown to contemporary Quakers. These seventeenth-century Quaker women's writings were, as the present volume terms it, "hidden in plain sight." It was evident that I had stumbled on a treasure trove for early Quaker history, as well as for the history of women's religious thought and activity.

In the course of my research I formulated the thesis that there were two distinct kinds of feminist movements in seventeenth-century England, coming from different religions, and usually from different class backgrounds. One I called 'humanist women,' usually of the aristocracy and gentility. These women had the opportunity to read the classics, and even learn Greek and Latin, to study these books in family libraries. They did scholarly writings, translations, and poetry and argued for the expansion of women's education. They were usually Anglicans, and their religious piety had affinities with the Cambridge Platonists. They argued for a God-given equality of 'souls,' *qua* intellects, between the sexes, but did not challenge the social or church orders.

The second group I dubbed "prophets." These women rose from the middle and working classes and cultivated dissenting religious groups. Their language was typically apocalyptic, and they saw the dissenting church and political movements against the Anglican church and social establishment as signs of an impending crisis in which God was about to judge the English for their apostasy and was bringing in a new generation of prophets as harbingers of a coming Kingdom of God that would overturn the present social order.

Gender as well as class equality was central to their agenda of the new age to come. Their favorite text came from Acts 2:17-18 (cf. Joel 2:29-29) : "In the last days it shall be, God declares, that I will pour out my Spirit upon all flesh and your sons and your daughters shall proph-

esy . . . yes, on my menservants and on my maid servants in those days
I will pour out my Spirit and they shall prophesy." The writers of these
tracts had no doubt that theirs was the time and they were the 'daughters' and 'maidservants' referred to in this New Testament text.

The first in this period to use this prophetic apocalyptic mode to
argue both that the end times were near and that God was empowering
women to speak as prophets of an age of gender-equality to come were
Baptists during the Civil War period of 1645-53, such as Mary Cary in
her treatises, "A Word in Season to the Kingdom of England" (1647),
"The Resurrection of the Witnesses" (1648), and "The Little Horns
Doom, a New and More Exact Mappe of the New Jerusalem's Glory"
(1651). The heirs of this millennial prophecy in a more disciplined
form would be the Religious Society of Friends in the 1660s. They carried with them also the vision of women's spiritual equality, as well as
the equality of classes in the church, the true community of Christ's
redemption.

The Quaker writers, men as well as women, supported women's
preaching and evangelizing in public, as well as women's participation
in internal church leadership through the women's meetings. In their
tracts, and particularly those by women, an exegetical argument was
developed, showing that equality of the sexes in the image of God was
God's original plan for creation, undone by sin, but continually renewed
and advanced through God's prophetic gifts, fulfilled in the coming of
Christ and the founding of the Christian community. The most developed expression of this feminist hermeneutic is found in the writings of
Margaret Fell, especially her 1666 tract, "Women's Speaking Justified,
according to the Scriptures."

I was charmed by the way Quaker women and men turned on their
heads the arguments from the New Testament against women's right to
preach. Mary Cole and Priscilla Cotton, in their tract written from
prison, "To the priests and people of England, we Declare our Conscience" (1656), argue that the text in I Corinthians 14:34 telling women
to keep silence in church referred only to women who did not yet possess the Spirit. These women were to keep silence in order to hear from
those inspired women and men who had received the Spirit, as evi-
denced by Paul's reference to women praying and prophesying in I
Corinthians 11:5.

Cole and Cotton argue that all Christians, but particularly those
prone to error, such as Bishops(!), who have not yet received the Spirit

should keep silence to hear the Spirit-inspired prophets and prophetesses. The Spirit, on the other hand, was for them an equal-opportunity employer and not only allowed, but demanded that those women, as well as men, upon whom God poured out God's Spirit must speak and speak boldly in public places, including the confronting of "hireling priests" in Anglican church assemblies. That this exegesis was no novelty became evident when I found exactly the same reading of the combined texts of I Corinthians 11:5 and 14:34 in a 1671 Quaker catechism, *Some Principles Concerning the Elect People of God, in Scorn called Quakers*.

My research on seventeenth-century English women, both from the humanist and the prophetic lines of thought, bore fruit in a 1990 article, "Prophets and Humanists: Types of Religious Feminism in Stuart England."[4] But I also felt the need to see that this rich collection of Quaker women's writings became better known, both to all those interested in Christian women's religious history and also to members of the Society of Friends itself. Since seventeenth-century England was not my primary field, and it also seemed like a major project, I thought that a team of people working together should take on the task of making these writings known.

I communicated this concern, and also my readiness to share my findings with a team of women that would research and publish these writings, with my student, Mary Garman, then completing her doctoral degree in the Joint Program in Religious and Theological Studies of Garrett Evangelical Theological Seminary and Northwestern University in Evanston, Illinois. The rest, as one might say, is history or is about to become so. Although she had her own doctoral thesis to complete, Mary Garman did not forget this idea. Once she was established on the faculty at Earlham College in Richmond, Indiana, she gathered around her a team of students and faculty colleagues from Earlham College and the Earlham School of Religion interested in researching these writings.

To complete this volume, members of the Quaker Women Research Group spent time at Quaker archives in England and in North America, and contacted University Microfilms so that most of the writings by early Quaker women are now available on microfilm. In 1990 I travelled to Richmond to served as a consultant when the Quaker Women Research Group met to discuss their research on the writings of early Quaker women. This volume represents one of the fruits of that gathering. It is an important contribution to knowledge of an important body of women's writings in Christian religious history. I look forward to being able to use this volume in my own teaching.

Notes

1. Please see Moira Ferguson, *First Feminists: British Women Writers, 1578–1799* (Bloomington, Indiana: Indiana University Press, 1985).

2. Please see Frances L. Utley, *The Crooked Rib: An Analytical Index to the Argument about Women in English and Scots Literature to the End of the Year 1568* (Columbus, Ohio: Ohio University Press, 1944).

3. Please see the checklist of women's published writings of 1600-1700 in Mary Prior, *Women in English Society, 1500-1800* (London: Methuen, 1985), pp. 242-44.

4. *The Journal of Religion* 70:1 (January, 1990): 1-18.

EDITORS' PREFACE

This anthology of early Quaker women's writings collects documents first written in seventeenth-century England. Dates in the table of contents are those of the printed editions reproduced in this volume. More details of print history can be found in the introductory material.

Dorotha Meredith, of Earlham College, painstakingly entered into the computer all the texts of the original documents. They are reproduced here with very minor editorial changes. She changed the seventeenth-century use of "ſ," "ʃ," and "vv" to the modern usages of "s," "s," and "w." In *7000 Handmaidens of the Lord*, she uniformly capitalized all names. She used the term [*sic*] to indicate words as they appeared in the original texts and pages that were out of sequence.

In sum, however, the hope has been to share these documents as the women who wrote them would have recognized them. Whatever may be sacrificed in enhanced readability, we hope it is more than balanced by the authenticity of the women's seventeenth-century language. The reader will meet vernacular idioms, lengthy sentences, more colons and semi-colons than periods, capital letters within sentences, italicized phrases, and many variant spellings of words and people's names.

Modern literary sensibilities may find this style grandiloquent, awkward, and verbose. We encourage readers to enter the world of the writers by adopting a slow, more meditative reading pace. With this adjustment, the rich language can be savored, and the periodic sentences allowed to build like a series of waves to the fullness of each point. The writing conveys passion of meaning powerfully and often communicates complex ideas brilliantly. If met on their own terms and given time, the texts cry to be read aloud. The voices are prophetic and poignant.

We want to encourage researchers and religious seekers to continue important conversations with common reference to these documents. Though interpretations can give context and digest salient points, we felt wider access to original voices was a more faithful tribute to the power of these women's lives. We hope to join many others in expanding our own interpretations of the significance of this material.

In these writings, we have met passionate, sensitive, and brilliant women. With great pleasure, we are glad to introduce them to others.

Dortha Meredith • Mary Garman • Judith Applegate • Margaret Benefiel

ACKNOWLEDGMENTS

The generosity and help of many people created this book. We would like especially to thank Rosemary Radford Ruether, whose original dream and encouragement were crucial to this project.

Another source of the energy and enthusiasm for this project emerged in the summer of 1990 at the Woodbrooke College of the Selly Oak Colleges in Birmingham, England. Quaker women from all over the world gathered for the first International Theological Conference for Quaker Women, sponsored by the Friends World Committee for Consultation, Woodbrooke College, and the Earlham School of Religion. We feel an enormous amount of gratitude to all the women who took part in that conference, and especially to two of the Conference planners: Pam Lunn and Val Ferguson.

Librarians and archivists helped us to find these documents, made it possible for us to work with them, and encouraged us in many different ways. Thanks are due Malcolm Thomas and staff at Friends House Library in London; Christina Lawson, librarian and curator of the Bevan Nash collection at Woodbrooke; Mary Ellen Chijioke in the Friends Historical Library at Swarthmore College; Elizabeth Potts Brown, Diana Peterson, and Emma Lapsansky in the Friends Collection at Haverford College; Tom Kirk and Tom Hamm in the Quaker Collection at Earlham College. We would also like to thank Liz Kamphausen, currently at Pendle Hill, for her emergency help in transcribing parts of the Katharine Whitton text, and Sara Emmons, for her help in transcribing some writings by Margaret Fell while she was in London on an Earlham program.

Many of our current and former colleagues at Earlham College and the Earlham School of Religion have supported and encouraged us during this long process: Special thanks are due Jerry Bakker, Michael Birkel, Dick Davis, Andy Grannell, Carol Hunter, Paul Lacey, John Newman, Fred Tiffany, Lonnie Valentine, and Dick Wood.

We are most grateful for a grant from the John S. and James L. Knight Foundation, and the Knight Committee at Earlham. This grant financed several stages of our project: the initial trip to London, the student/ faculty collaborative research which involved teams of students in the project, a trip to present our research to the Midwest Regional meeting of the American Academy of Religions, and the consultation with

Rosemary Radford Ruether. We would like to thank the students involved in the Knight project: Leila Eastman, Sara Emmons, Janet Fiskio-Lasseter, and Marie White. Two other groups of students from Earlham and the Earlham School of Religion joined with Margaret Benefiel in studying early Quaker women and their writings. We want to acknowledge especially the hard work of Jennifer Bennage and Pauline Cheek whose efforts made possible the microfilming of most of the Quaker women's writings by University Microfilms International.

Many women from the community joined us in the particularly arduous task of proofreading these documents. We want to thank: Pauline Cheek, Sabrina Falls, Nancy Brewster, Jane Van Vleck, Janet Fiskio-Lasseter, Daniél Rose, Cheryl Cayford, Beth Haywood, Holley Webster, Liz Kamphausen, Kathleen Flanagan, and Ann Petracek. Special thanks are due Jane James and Holley Webster for their work on the Index.

Our editor at Pendle Hill Publications, Rebecca Kratz Mays, has been wonderfully patient throughout this process, and we want also to thank her for her hard work, creativity, and enthusiasm for this project. Thanks, too, go to Eve Beehler for her layout and design of the book to help make the seventeenth-century texts visually appealing and to Melanie Watson for her excellent cover.

Finally, we would like to thank our families who loved us and supported us throughout this project.

HIDDEN IN PLAIN SIGHT

by Mary Garman

Introduction

In the mid-1600s a group of dissenting Christians in England proclaimed
that the experience of God's empowering presence was immediately
available to anyone who chose to live "in the Light." One of the distinguishing characteristics of this group, which came to be called the
"Religious Society of Friends" or "Quakers," is that women in large
numbers joined the movement, preached the gospel, had their writings
published, and were recognized as ministers.

Women were also crucial to the spread of Quakerism around the
world. George Fox, who first gathered Friends together, met and convinced a woman named Elizabeth Hooten in 1647, in the midst of the
turmoil surrounding the English Civil Wars. Hooten became the first
woman Friends minister, travelled widely throughout England and North
America and, like Fox, suffered because of the harsh laws against religious dissent.[1] During the Commonwealth and after the restoration of
Charles II, Friends went to jail charged with (among other things) va-
grancy, blasphemy, and refusal to pay tithes or swear oaths. A series of
laws was enforced which criminalized activities that were central to
Quaker faith, and informing on Quakers became a source of income for
some civil and religious authorities.[2]

In 1659, or shortly thereafter, Quaker women began to meet apart
from the men's gatherings, to plan strategies to meet the needs of Friends
whose lives had been disrupted by the persecutions. For example, they
collected funds for prisoners and the families of those in prison, and
wrote letters of encouragement that were read and then circulated. The
creation of these separate "Women's Meetings" caused controversy
among early Friends, and also provided women with opportunities to
develop their skills in organization and administration.[3]

When they were not in prison during the early decades of the movement, women ministers travelled widely throughout the world. They
wrote tracts, theological treatises, epistles, letters, and journals. After
the Glorious Revolution in 1688, the persecutions of religious dissent-
ers in England began to wane, and the needs of the Quaker community
changed. By 1700 Quaker women were focusing their attention on sus-

taining systems of spiritual nurture and development for families and for religious communities.[4]

Quakerism as a religious movement grew quickly and attracted followers from all social classes.[5] Those who were "convinced" joined a religious society which made rigorous demands on its membership. Friends were expected to examine all aspects of their daily lives, and to be willing to make radical changes. In the earliest days, they met to worship God in homes, not in established churches. They worshipped without any liturgy, prayer book or priest, instead waiting together in silence until one of their number—woman or man, servant or aristocrat—received words from God to speak to all. They refused to participate in any aspect of civil life that infringed on their religious convictions, and established alternative systems for the oversight of marriages, the recording of births and deaths, and the practices of family life. Male and female Friends began to travel as public ministers throughout the country and the world, preaching their views wherever they could.[6] Those who stayed behind cared for family and community life. Early Friends lived their faith, despite the consequences.

Sometimes those consequences were dire indeed. For example, Elizabeth Fletcher and Elizabeth Leavens, two young Quakers, gave witness as Friends in Oxford in 1654 and suffered "savage treatment" from the scholars there. Two other women, Elizabeth Williams and Mary Fisher, received similar treatment at Cambridge in 1654.[7] When Mary Fisher and a different companion, Anne Austin, arrived in Boston in 1656 as the first two Quakers in that town, they were arrested, put in prison, and "stripped naked, under pretence to know whether they were witches, though in searching no token was found upon them but of innocence: and in this search they were so barbarously misused, that modesty forbids to mention it."[8] Katharine Evans and Sarah Cheevers, on their way to Jerusalem, were held in prison at Malta by the Inquisition for three years, where their captors attempted "all the ways they could to frighten and terrify them, to make them submit to their wills."[9] Margaret Fell, known by many as the "Mother of Quakerism," spent long years in prison for her beliefs.[10] These examples are only a few of the many stories of the sufferings endured by Quaker women during the first fifty years of the movement. In the conclusion of the first volume of his chronicle of Friends' sufferings, Joseph Besse listed the names of those who were especially brave and suffered the most "for the sake of their public Testimony to the Truth." He noted especially a number of women whose "excellent Endowment" was "serviceable to the Church in the office of the Ministry, for which they were particularly gifted being esteemed by the Brethren as Fellow-helpers in the Work of the Gospel of Christ, and not unlike the Deaconesses in the first Ages of Christianity."[11]

Friends interpreted the successes of women as ministers and leaders as evidence that God was restoring creation to its state of original wholeness. The persecutions and sufferings of women ministers were seen as evidence of the continued wickedness of the world, the government, and the established church, and the need for redemption. Friends taught that true faithfulness to the Gospel meant living "in the Power" of the original wholeness which had been restored by the coming of Christ, even if it offended prevailing sensibilities, or violated established laws.[12] One way Quaker women offended the established order was by writing, publishing, and distributing tracts, pamphlets, treatises, letters, and epistles.[13]

The documents in this volume were selected from among two hundred or more works by Quaker women written during the first fifty years of the Quaker movement. The insights of Quaker women into the political, sociological, and theological issues of the day reflect diversity of opinions and experiences. These documents have been collected and preserved since the seventeenth century, but almost all have gone out of print. They are seldom found in anthologies of Quaker writings, and are rarely considered in summaries of Quaker thought or practice. As a consequence, the written words of early Quaker women and the unique contributions of women to the formation of Quaker practices are generally overlooked or ignored.

The tracts of warning and proclamation (Part One) are significant because they reflect the immediacy of the earliest days of the movement. In keeping with Quaker traditions, tracts often included challenges to political authorities, who were indicted for not attending to the needs of the poor and oppressed. In my article I maintain that in the midst of the urgency one can also find "the earliest articulations of theological ideas and insights which became central for Quakers during the later, calmer, and more reflective eras (p.19)."

The travel narratives and journals written by early Quaker women (Part Two) were among the earliest Quaker autobiographical writings. These narratives contain insights and information about the day-to-day activities of Friends, and also offer additional models for writing spiritual autobiography. Judith Applegate argues that the journals, in all their variety, offer us "insights into the prophetic ministry of women, the ideal of equality for female and male leadership, and the struggles to maintain that equality in the early movement (p. 151)."

Theological treatises and debate tracts written by Quaker women (Part Three) show the range of views held by Friends during the early decades. Margaret Benefiel presents two Quaker women theologians who entered into the crucial theological discussions of the day and "spoke out in ways which broke down gender barriers and expectations of their time and culture (p. 313)."

The final section of the book (Part Four) focuses on the Letters and Epistles which circulated among Friends women during this era. Here Margaret Benefiel argues that "letters and epistles wove the ties of community both within meetings and throughout the Religious Society of Friends (p.443)." These writings bear testimony to the practical aspects and the hard work of creating a faith community in the midst of persecutions, and the benefits for participants of sustaining such a community with their letters.

Review of the Research

Histories of the beginning of Quakerism rely on certain key documents: George Fox's *Journal* and his collected *Epistles*; the letters and papers exchanged among Friends, which were collected and edited and are known as the Swarthmore Manuscripts; Minutes and Epistles from Monthly, Quarterly, and Yearly Meetings; treatises, tracts, journals, and narratives written by Friends.[14] Also crucial for Quaker research are the two-volume catalog edited by Joseph Besse, which tells of the sufferings of Friends; biographical accounts by other early Friends; a collection of early writings by Friends edited and published by Norman Penney as *First Publishers of the Truth*;[15] and the *Extracts from State Papers* which includes documents written by anti-Quaker civil authorities during the persecutions.[16]

An early history of Quakerism was compiled and organized by William Sewel.[17] His goal was to answer critics of the movement and to portray accurately the sufferings and the stamina of its earliest participants, in the hope that his audience would see in them patterns of virtue for their own lives. He described the earliest years of Quakerism as "hard and difficult, and in the process often sad and dreadful." After summarizing the extent of early Friends' sufferings, he described the virtues of the people who withstood the earliest persecutions, praising their "unfeigned godliness, sincere love, much true-heartedness, extraordinary meekness, singular patience, ardent zeal, undaunted courage, and unshaken steadfastness."[18] Sewel's work forms the basis for subsequent histories of Quakers. Among these, the four-volume history of Quakerism, which is part of the "Rowntree Series," conceived by William Rowntree and written by Rufus Jones and William Braithwaite, published between 1909 and 1912, continues to be considered definitive.

In 1915 Mabel Brailsford published the first history that emphasized the contributions women made to the early Quaker movement. Her book was based on documents written by Quaker women during the first forty years, and told of their courage, creativity, and stamina.[19] In addition to the work by Mabel Brailsford, other biographers have written about Margaret Fell, Elizabeth Hooten, Loveday Hambly, Gulielma Penn and other extraordinary Quaker women of the earliest decades.[20] Shorter works which focused on individuals or specific episodes in the lives of Quaker women also have added to the understanding of the role of women in the early years of the Religious Society of Friends.[21]

Like many historians of women, those who focused on Quaker women discovered that simply adding the stories of exceptional women to the prevailing historical accounts did not fully address the underlying questions. Feminist critiques that developed during the 1960s and 1970s have suggested alternative approaches and methodologies. Adapting some of the methods of social historians, these feminist historians focused their attention on the daily lives of everyday women, and radically re-evaluated their activities in the home, the church, and other areas known as the "private sphere." The contributions made by women were evaluated according to the values and experiences of women, which led to challenging traditional methods of research, ways of dividing up time periods, and interpretation.[22]

Early Quaker women's writings have become important for a number of feminist historians. Catholic feminist theologian and historian Rosemary Radford Ruether, for example, has argued for links between Quaker women and the humanist scholars of the same period. Ruether has suggested that both represent "an early modern feminism."[23] In 1975 the first issue of *Signs: A Journal of Women in Culture and Society* included an edited version of Margaret Fell's letter to women's meetings, with commentary which suggested the significance of Quaker women's activities for modern feminists.[24] Mary Maples Dunn, in her survey article of Quaker women's writings, commented on the admiration contemporary women historians have felt for early Quaker women, so engaged in and committed to their lives of faith.[25] Quaker historian

Margaret Hope Bacon, in her study of Quaker women in the United States, developed further the argument that the leadership skills of nineteenth-century Quaker reforming women can be traced to early Quaker women's experiences in separate women's meetings.[26] Other scholars from a variety of fields, using feminist critiques and insights, have assessed and analyzed the contributions of women to Quakerism.[27]

Historians of Quaker women have gone beyond adding the stories of the accomplishments of exceptional Quaker women to the larger history of Quakerism and of the church.[28] Recently historians have also begun to challenge some of the traditional interpretations of Quaker history. For example, using the writings of early Quaker women, Christine Trevett has analyzed the "fall" of James Nayler.[29] In 1656 Nayler entered the city of Bristol riding on a donkey and accompanied by a crowd of followers crying "Hosanna!" He was convicted of blasphemy because of this episode, and sent to prison. Historians of Quakerism usually identify the Nayler story as a pivotal event in the earliest days of the movement, and suggest that after 1656 the male leaders of the Religious Society of Friends began to develop systems for discipline and oversight of members.

The traditional interpretation of the Nayler events has been that the women followers, such as Martha Simmonds and Hannah Stranger, were "misguided," "extravagant," and generated a "divided spirit."[30] By contrast, Nayler is generally judged to have been guilty mainly of "following his reason in certain small matters,"[31] eventually becoming "unhinged" by "mental overstrain and physical prostration."[32] Trevett argues that historians have been too quick to blame the women around Nayler without considering the role that men played. She urges scholars of the period to consider the Nayler episode as an event which took place in a particular context; that is, in an atmosphere of heightened enthusiasm, potential schism and power-struggle.[33]

Recent biographical studies of Quaker women have offered alternative interpretations which draw on the insights of feminist analysis.[34] Bonnelyn Kunze, in her biography of Margaret Fell, has challenged the use of the term "nursing Mother in Israel," and has suggested that a more appropriate term to describe Fell would be "Mother Superior."[35] Maureen Bell, George Parfitt, and Simon Shepherd have raised questions about the priority that has been given to Margaret Fell in works on Quakerism and on women in the seventeenth century, and have suggested that other more radical Quaker women of the era have thereby been overlooked. They suggest that it is "high time for the texts of

these 'forgotten' Quaker women to be reread, and for their interven-
tion in the history of women's speaking and writing to be inspected."[36]
Questions are being raised about the traditional interpretations of
women's activities in all the periods of Quaker history, about the Society's
attitudes toward women, and even the meaning of gender as a category
for historical interpretation.[37]

As more sources relating to Quaker women have been discovered
and analyzed, studies which consider one region or one particular
aspect of their lives have been published. For example, Beatrice Carre's
article focuses on the region of Lancaster, and especially on the
prominence of widows who were attracted to Quakerism because
of "the degree of individuality and status it accorded to its female
adherents."[38] Scholars continue to concentrate on the particular
experiences of Quaker women in the United States, and have published a collection of articles from a national conference held at Guilford
College in 1979.[39]

In 1989 Elizabeth Potts Brown and Susan Mosher Stuard published
a book which combines primary documents by Quaker women and interpretive articles from a feminist perspective.[40] Other recent publications include works which draw on analytical methods developed by
feminist literary critics and contemporary social historians. For example,
in her introduction to *Visionary Women: Ecstatic Prophecy in Seventeenth
Century England*, historian Phyllis Mack suggested that "many seventeenth-century people would have found post-structuralist theory more
easily digestible than many modern people do," given seventeenth century attitudes toward the power of language and social location to determine human experiences and limitations.[41] At the same time, Mack
also perceived the limits of post-modern approaches for understanding
fully the lives of seventeenth-century Quaker women. She argued instead for an approach that takes seriously the spiritual depths and insights of these "visionary women."[42]

In 1915, Mabel Brailsford commented on the "modern atmosphere
both of thought and effort which surrounds the ancient chronicles,"
and expressed curiosity at "the strange chance which has left [the documents by women] unknown and unexplored, save by experts, for more
than two centuries."[43] Seventy-seven years later, Phyllis Mack, one of
the "experts" who has sought out the words of Quaker women, agreed
that their words and work establish "part of the heritage of modern
feminism," and added that current scholars can also find in them indi-
cations of "some of the movement's deepest problems."[44] This volume

of early Quaker women's writings seeks to continue the process of ex-
ploration, reinterpretation, and deepening of insight.

Conclusion

After surveying the histories of Quakerism written since the seventeenth century, and the more recent research into the roles women
have played in the movement, it is clear that Quaker women have not
been "hidden from history" in the same way as women in other eras or
other faith traditions.[45] The prominence of Quaker women as leaders
in reform movements, the wide range of documents written by Quaker
women, and the long tradition of Quaker women's leadership all testify
to a type of visibility that women in other religious traditions have not
enjoyed. Nevertheless, the paradox remains: most of the documents
written by early Quaker women are available only in archives, and these
copies are rapidly deteriorating.[46] Instead of being "hidden from history," early Quaker women have been "hidden in plain sight." As a
consequence, the writings of Quaker women have not been antholo-
gized along with those of their male counterparts, and their insights—
theological and practical—have not been incorporated into the
on-going interpretations of the significance and developments within
the Quaker movement.

Perhaps Quaker women were "hidden in plain sight" due to the attitude of early Friends toward gender as a category for analysis. One es-
sential aspect of their teaching was that the rigid gender roles assigned
by society were evidence of the fallen state of humanity.[47] How exactly
to move into redemption from that fallen state became a point of conflict among Friends. Achieving the ideal of equality between men and
women within the Religious Society of Friends has proved to be much
more complicated and elusive than was first imagined. Although partnerships between female and male Quakers, in the organization and
work of the Society of Friends and in Quaker families have always been
a distinguishing feature of the movement, historical accounts of those
partnerships have tended to emphasize the roles of men.[48] The presence and activities of women have been noted, but in most cases their
deeds have not been differentiated from those of men, so the significance
of their participation has not been emphasized or fully interpreted.[49]

To resolve this paradoxical state of being "hidden in plain sight," the
words and deeds of early Quaker women need to be brought forward
and emphasized. Historical, literary, and theological analysis of the in-

sights and activities of early Quaker women will encourage future parallel readings with early Quaker writings by males.[50]

In their tracts, narratives, treatises, letters, and epistles these early Quaker women articulated a vision for the Religious Society of Friends and the world that was grounded in their experiences of God's power. They focused on translating those experiences into collective and individual obedience to God's claims on their lives. They expressed themselves in language that was both tender and strident, described their lives and adventures using poetry and narrative, wrote epistles and letters filled with encouragement and advice, and articulated their theological insights with wit, clarity, and brilliance. They lived and wrote as Quakers and as women in the hope of convincing others of the truth they had come to know.

EDITORS' NOTE: **References to page numbers in all the notes refer to the orginial sources named except for the documents reprinted in this anthology. For titles included in this book, we have used the page numbers found in this volume.**

NOTES

1. Braithwaite, William, *Beginnings of Quakerism* (originally published by MacMillan and Co. Ltd., 1912; now distributed by William Sessions Limited, York, England, 1970), p. 44. In the 1911 edition of George Fox's *Journal* (Cambridge University Press), editor Norman Penney commented on the significance of the fact that women were the first ministers in London, at the universities, and in the colonies, pp. 463-64.

2. The Quaker Act enacted in 1661, and the series of Conventicle Acts (1664 and 1668) brought about harsh persecutions of Quakers, including prison sentences, threats of banishment, and confiscation of property. Braithwaite, in *The Second Period of Quakerism* (originally published by MacMillan and Co. Ltd., 1919; now distributed by William Sessions Limited, York, England, 1961), indicates that informers received one-third of the property for their participation in convicting Quakers, p. 67. Braithwaite's narrative of the sufferings of Friends relies on journals, the collection of public documents known as *Extracts from State Papers*, edited by Norman Pinney, and the two-volume chronicle by Joseph Besse: *An Abstract of the sufferings of the people call'd Quakers* (London: Printed and sold by the assigns of J. Sowle, at the Bible in George Yard, Lombard Street, 1733-38).

3. The founding of the women's meetings and their activities during the early decades has been described by Irene L. Edwards, in "The Women Friends of London: The Two-Weeks and Box Meetings," *Journal of the Friends Historical Society* 47 (1955): 2-21. The account written by William Beck and T. Frederick Ball, *The London Friends' Meetings, Showing the Rise of the Society of Friends in London* (London: F. Bowyer Kitto, 1869), stresses the importance to the early Society of the "external work" (345-46) done by the women. Beck and Ball also indicate that the conflicts came from the fact that some Quaker men taught that the women's "assistance . . . in public ministry was rather discouraged than promoted," p. 344. See chapter 3 of Christine Trevett, *Women and Quakerism in the 17th Century* (York: Session Book Trust, The Ebor Press, 1991) where she explores the development and significance of women's meetings.

4. Trevett, *Women and Quakerism*, pp. 130-31.

5. Jones, Rufus, *The Quakers in the American Colonies* (London: MacMillan and Co., Ltd., 1911). He suggests that between 1656 and 1780 "there were times . . . when [Quakerism] seemed destined to become one of the foremost religious factors in the life and development of America," p. xiv.

6. See pp. 152-53 in Applegate article which discusses the tradition of "yoke-mates" among Quaker women travelling ministers.

7. Braithwaite, *Beginnings*, mentions these events several times: pp. 158-59, 189, 294-95, and 445.

8. Sewel, William, *The History of the rise, increase, and progress, of the Christian people called Quakers; with several remarkable occurrences intermixed.* Written originally in Low-Dutch, and also translated into English (3rd edition corr. Burlington, N.J., Printed and sold by I. Collins, 1774), p. 184. The report of this incident is probably based in part on the chronicle by Joseph Besse, 2, pp. 177–78. Mary Fisher also travelled to Turkey between 1658 and 1660 to bring the message of Friends to Sultan Mahomet IV. The possibility that Austin and Fisher, Evans and Cheevers, and other Quaker women were raped while in prison needs to be explored.

9. Whiting, *Persecution Exposed* (London: 1715), p. 472.

10. See the biography written by Isabel Ross, *Margaret Fell, Mother of Quakerism* (London: Longmans, Green, and Co., 1949), as well as Fell's own writings, which were numerous.

11. Besse, *Sufferings, 1*, p. 484.

12. In his "Epistle to All Women's Meetings," dated 1672, George Fox reminded Friends that men and women were "helps meet" to one another in the Kingdom that Christ had restored, and that every woman and ev-

ery man who had seen Christ risen was called to "see that all that have received the gospel, do walk in the gospel, the power of God which they are heirs of" ("Epistle," p. 145). In another "Epistle," dated 1676, Fox developed a long argument based on scripture to support the meetings of women and their public preaching. He concluded with the word that "if there were no Scripture . . . Christ is sufficient, who restores man and woman up into the image of God" (p. 190).

13. See Appendix 3, "Quaker Women Writers," in Maureen Bell, George Parfitt & Simon Shepherd, *A Biographical Dictionary of English Women Writers, 1580-1720* (Boston: G.K. Hall & Co., 1990), pp. 257-63.

14. The Cambridge University Press edition of Fox's *Journal* (published in 1911), includes many helpful annotations and cross-references, as well as additional documents in the appendices. A more modern (and more readable) edition of Fox's *Journal* (edited by John L. Nickalls,) was published in 1975. The *Epistles* of George Fox were edited by Samuel Tuke, and have been republished a number of times since the eighteenth century, most recently in 1979. A guide to the Swarthmore Manuscripts was edited by Geoffrey Nuttall and published in 1952 by the Friends House Library in London. Many documents by early Friends are located in the archives of Quaker institutions in North America and in Britain. Quaker writings of this era are cataloged in Joseph Smith's *Descriptive Catalog of Friends' Books* (London: 1867) and in *The Short-Title Catalogue of Books Printed in England, Ireland, Wales, and British America, 1641-1700*, collected by Donald G. Wing (New York: Index Society, 1945-51).

15. Norman Penney, *The First Publishers of Truth, Being Early Records (now first printed) of the introduction of Quakerism into the counties of England and Wales* (London: Headley Brothers; New York: D.S. Taber, 1907).

16. Friends' Historical Society, *Extracts from State Papers Relating to Friends*, edited by Norman Pinney, (London: Headley Brothers; Philadelphia: H. Newman, 1910-13). Another recent and helpful volume for Quaker research is the *Index to Volume 1 and Volume 2 of "A Collection of the Sufferings of the People Called Quakers" by Joseph Besse* (Fort Lauderdale, Florida: Genealogical Society of Broward Co., 1991).

17. William Sewel, *The History of the Rise, Increase, and Progress of the Christian People Called Quakers*, two volumes, 1722. Sewel acknowledges an earlier history by Gerardus Croese, *The General History of the Quakers, containing the lives, tenets, sufferings, tryals, speeches and letters of all the most eminent Quakers, both men and women* (London: Printed for John Dunton, 1696), but claims Croese "got the chief contents from me" and that his interpretation is "very imperfect and defective," (p. vi.) and not based on the sort of personal knowledge that Sewel claimed.

18. Sewel, *History*, pp. 7ff.

19. Incorporating women's experiences into the prevailing historical narrative presents a number of difficulties. See the argument developed by Ann D. Gordon, Mary Jo Buhle, and Nancy Schrom Dye, who trace this process in "The Problem of Women's History," in *Liberating Women's History: Theoretical and Critical Essays*, edited by Berenice A. Carroll (Urbana, Illinois: University of Illinois Press, 1976), pp. 74-92. Gerda Lerner called for expanded approaches that went beyond existing methods in "New Approaches to the Study of Women in American History" in *The Majority Finds Its Past* (Chicago: University of Chicago Press, 1984), pp. 1-18, and in "Placing Women in History: Definitions and Challenges," in *Feminist Studies* 3:1/2 (1975): 5-14. See also Brailsford, Mabel Richmond, *Quaker Women, 1650-1690* (London: Duckworth, 1915).

20. Ross, Isabel, *Margaret Fell, Mother of Quakerism* (London: Longmans, Green, and Co., 1949). Manners, Emily, *Elizabeth Hooten: First Quaker Woman Preacher, 1600-1692* (London, New York, Toronto: Longmans, Green, and Co., 1947). Hodgkin, Lucy V., *A Quaker Saint of Cornwall: Loveday Hambly and Her Guests.* (London, New York, Toronto: Longmans, Green, and Co., 1927). Hodgkin, Lucy V., *Gulielma: Wife of William Penn*, (London, New York, Toronto: Longmans, Green, and Co., 1947). One area for future research is the large group of female historians of Quakerism who wrote during the period between 1900 and 1940. This group would include the biographers above, as well as Luella Wright, author of *The Literary Life of Early Friends, 1650-1725* (New York: Columbia University Press, 1932); Amelia M. Gummere, author of *Witchcraft and Quakerism: A Study in Social History* (Philadelphia: The Biddle Press, 1908); and Emelia Fogelklou, author of *James Nayler, The Rebel Saint 1618-1660: An Attempt to Reconstruct the Chequered Life History of a Singular Personality from the Age of the Commonwealth*, translated by Lajla Yapp (London: E. Benn, 1931) and others.

21. See, for example, Lydia Rickman, "Esther Biddle and Her Mission to Louis XIV," *Quaker History* 47 (1955): 38-45 and Irene Edwards, "The Women Friends of London: The Two-Weeks Meeting and Box Meetings," *Journal of the Friends Historical Society* 47 (1955): 2-21.

22. A great number of historical works on women which challenge the prevailing methods and interpretations have been published during the past twenty years. Two recent books that reviewed the accomplishments and point toward possible new directions are *Writing Women's History: International Perspectives*, edited by Karen Offen, Ruth Roach Pierson, and Jane Rendall (Bloomington, Indiana: Indiana University Press, 1991), which focuses

on the United States and Europe, and *Expanding the Boundaries of Women's History*, edited by Cheryl Johnson-Odim and Margaret Strobel (Bloomington, Indiana: Indiana University Press, 1992), which focuses on women in Africa, India, Asia, and Latin America.

23. "Prophets and Humanists" by Rosemary Radford Ruether in *Journal of Religion* 70 January (1990): 1-18. See also her "Women in Sectarian and Utopian Groups," (written with Catherine M. Prelinger) in *Women and Religion in America, vol. 1*, edited by Rosemary Radford Ruether and Rosemary Skinner Keller (San Francisco: Harper and Row, 1983), pp. 260-62.

24. Milton D. Speizman and Jane C. Kronick, "A Seventeenth Century Quaker Women's Declaration," *Signs* 1:1 (1975): 231-45.

25. Dunn, "Latest Light on Women of Light," in Elizabeth Potts Brown and Susan Mosher Stuard, eds., *Witnesses for Change* (New Brunswick: Rutgers University Press, 1989), p. 71.

26. Margaret Hope Bacon, *Mothers of Feminism: The Story of Quaker Women in America* (San Francisco: Harper and Row, Publishers, 1986), p. 2.

27. See Elaine Huber " 'A Woman Must Not Speak': Quaker Women in the English Left Wing" in *Women of Spirit: Female Leadership in the Jewish and Christian Traditions*, edited by Rosemary Radford Ruether and Eleanor McLaughlin (New York: Simon and Schuster, 1979); Mary Maples Dunn, "Saints and Sinners: Congregational and Quaker Women in the Early Colonial Period," *American Quarterly* 30 (1978): 582-601.

28. See, for example, Michael Galgano's comparative study "Out of the Mainstream: Catholic and Quaker Women in the Restoration Northwest," in *The World of William Penn*, edited by Richard S. Dunn and Mary Maples Dunn (Philadelphia: University of Pennsylvania Press, 1986), pp. 117-37.

29. Christine Trevett, "The Women Around James Nayler, Quaker: A Matter of Emphasis," *Religion* (1990): 249-73.

30. Braithwaite, *Beginnings*, p. 245-46. A more recent account of these events is found in "Martha Simmonds, a Quaker Enigma," *Journal of the Friends Historical Society* 53 (1972): 31-52. Kenneth Carroll adds somewhat to her biography, but does not challenge Braithwaite's characterization of Simmonds as being "out of the truth."

31. Braithwaite, *Beginnings*, p. 243.

32. Braithwaite, *Beginnings*, p. 254.

33. Trevett, "The Women Around James Nayler," p. 258.

34. Bonnelyn Young Kunze, "The Family, Social, And Religious Life of Margaret Fell," Ph.D. Dissertation, University of Rochester, 1986. Also see her recent book, *Margaret Fell and the Rise of Quakerism* (Stanford: Stanford University Press, 1994).

35. Kunze, "Life of Margaret Fell," p. 389.

36. Bell, Parfitt & Shepherd, *A Biographical Dictionary*, pp. 259-60. Rosemary Masek in her bibliographic essay also calls for more extensive work with women's religious texts (p. 164), and argues in favor of more research into the lives of Quaker women other than Margaret Fell in "Women in the Age of Transition: 1485-1714" in *The Women of England: From Anglo-Saxon Times to the Present,* edited by Barbara Kanner (Hamden, Connecticut: Archon Books, 1979), p. 162.

37. See, for example, David W. Maxey, "New Light on Hannah Barnard, A Quaker 'Heretic', " *Quaker History* 78 (Fall, 1989): 61-86, which suggests that her treatment by New York Yearly Meeting in the eighteenth century was based in part on her gender and not on the merits of her case; also, Trudi Abel, "Needles and Penury in 19th Century London: The Diary of a Poor Quaker Seamstress," *Quaker History* 75 (1986): 102-144, who reminds readers that "Not all Victorian Quakers were as prominent or as well-to-do as Elizabeth Fry, Elisha Bates, Joseph John Gurney or John Bright" (p. 102); Johan Winsser, in "Mary Dyer and the 'Monster' Story," *Quaker History* 79 (1990): 2-34, tells of the rumors that plagued Mary Dyer's life after the death of a deformed child; Carole D. Spencer, "Evangelism, Feminism, and Social Reform: The Quaker Woman Minister and the Holiness Revival," *Quaker History* 80 (1991): 24-48, suggests that the legacy of leadership training extended also to orthodox and evangelical Quaker women of the late nineteenth century.

38. Beatrice Carre, "Early Quaker Women in Lancaster and Lancashire," in *Early Lancaster Friends,* edited by M. Mullett (University of Lancaster Centre for North West Regional Studies, 1978), p. 45.

39. Carol Stoneburner and John Stoneburner, eds., *The Influence of Quaker Women on American History: Bibliographical Studies* (Lewiston, New York: Edward Mellen Press, 1986). Margaret Hope Bacon, ed., *Wilt Thou Go On My Errand?* (Pendle Hill Publications: Wallingford, Pennsylvania, 1994).

40. This excellent collection covers three centuries of Quaker women's writings, and includes interpretive articles which contribute to the on-going discussions about gender and religion within women's studies. See note 25.

41. Phyllis Mack, *Visionary Women: Ecstatic Prophecy in Seventeenth Century*

England (Berkeley: University of California Press, 1992), pp. 6, 9. See also Judith Scheffler, "Prison Writings of Early Quaker Women: 'We Were Stronger Afterward Than Before' " *Quaker History* 73 (1984): 25-37; and Catherine La Courreye Blecki, "Alice Hayes and Mary Penington: Personal Identity Within the Tradition of Quaker Spiritual Autobiography," *Quaker History* 65 (1976): 19-31.

42. Mack, *Visionary Women*, pp. 87, 88. Mack comments that most historians have approached the work of women of this era "from every perspective except that of religion," p. 87.

43. Brailsford, *Quaker Women*, p. vii.

44. Mack, *Visionary Women*, p. 9 .

45. The phrase, "hidden from history" was used by Sheila Rowbotham as the title for her book on women in England from Puritan times until the late 1920s and early 1930s. (*Hidden From History: 300 Years of Women's Oppression and the Fight Against It*, London: Pluto Press, 1973). Rowbotham argues that what has been "hidden" is not just the presence of women in English society, but their economic, intellectual, and emotional contributions. Her critique is echoed by other historians who have focused their research into women's lives. See Joan W. Scott's description of the development of this critique in " Women's History," in *Gender and the Politics of History* (New York: Columbia University Press, 1988), p. 202, n. 8. See also Scott's contribution to the theoretical issues involved, in "The Problem of Invisibility," in *Retrieving Women's History*, edited by S. Jay Kleinberg (Berg: UNESCO, 1988); and Joan Kelly's challenge to traditional characterizations of historical periods, "Did Women Have a Renaissance?" in *Becoming Visible*, edited by R. Bridenthal and C. Koontz (Boston: Houghton Mifflin, 1977).

46. A provisional checklist of documents written by women between 1600 and 1700 was developed by Patricia Crawford and is found in the appendix of *Women in English Society, 1500-1800*, edited by Mary Prior (London: Methuen, 1985), pp. 232-64. Mary Penington's *Some Account of the Circumstances in the Life of Mary Penington* was reprinted by the Friends Historical Society in 1992. Writings from Margaret Fell appear in Terry S. Wallace, *A Sincere and Constant Love; An Introduction to the Work of Margaret Fell* (Richmond, Indiana: Friends United Press, 1992); and a letter from Sarah Cheevers to her husband appears in *Womanhood in Radical Protestantism, 1525-1675*, edited by Joyce L. Irwin (New York: Edwin Mellen Press, 1979), pp. 235-37. Margaret Fell's *Women's Speaking Justified* was reprinted in 1980 by New England Yearly Meeting. Microfilmed versions of most of the documents are now available from University Microfilms.

47. See Phyllis Mack's excellent and thorough discussion of the Quaker understanding of gender in *Visionary Women*, especially in chapter 4 and in the Epilogue.

48. See the discussions of Quakerism and gender in "Feminist Friends: Agrarian Quakers and the Emergence of Women's Rights in America," *Feminist Studies* 12:1 (1986): 27-49, where the argument is made that the experiences of Quaker women differed from those of other women in the nineteenth century because Quakers did not separate the private and public "spheres," pp. 29-30. See also Jean Soderland in "Women's Authority in Pennsylvania and New Jersey Quaker Meetings, 1680-1760," *William and Mary Quarterly* 3:44 (1987): 722-49, where she argues that Quaker women's sense of authority came not from a sense of personal autonomy but from their sense of belonging to the whole Quaker community, pp. 722-23. H. Larry Ingle, in "A Quaker Woman on Women's Roles: Mary Penington to her Friends, 1678," (*Signs* 16(1991): 587-96), discusses the controversy surrounding the separate women's meetings. He also argues that "gender equality" did not carry the same meaning for seventeenth-century Quaker women as it does to today's feminists.   Contemporary Friends continue to struggle with these issues.

49. There are many examples of this absence of differentiation, such as William Braithwaite's chapter on "The People in White Raiment." The focus in the chapter is on the work of male leaders, and although he refers to the participation of their wives, sisters, and serving-maids, he does not mention or evaluate the particular activities of these women (*Beginnings*, p. 93). Even Hugh Barbour and Arthur Roberts' excellent collection of early Quaker writings, which refers to the "sixty-odd newly established Quaker men and women" who preached the Quaker message in the summer of 1654, comments only on the activities of Margaret Fell. Later in the same chapter they refer to the exhaustion and loss of the "original leaders," and once again name only men. (Hugh Barbour and Arthur O. Roberts, *Early Quaker Writings, 1650-1700* (Grand Rapids: Eerdmans, 1973), pp. 35, 41.)

50. Barbara Kanner, in "Old and New Women's History" (*The Women of England*) argues for studies which bring women's documents into dialogue with those written by men, with the goal of deeper and more complete understanding (p.13). Many historians have commented on the extraordinary legacy of Quaker women's leadership for subsequent generations, and we hope in this volume to suggest some of the theological roots of the leadership skills and patterns developed by Quaker women which were transferred to subsequent generations of women.

TRACTS OF PROCLAMATION AND WARNING

Sarah Jones 1650

∞

Margaret Fell 1653, 1666

∞

Sarah Blackborow 1658

∞

7000 Handmaids of the Lord 1659

∞

Esther Biddle 1662

∞

Dorothy White 1662

∞

"THEREFORE I WILL PROPHESIE"
TRACTS OF PROCLAMATION AND WARNING

by Mary Garman

Introduction

The Quaker women ministers who wrote and published tracts of warning and proclamation during the earliest decades of the movement shared
a common goal: to persuade all those who read their tracts to "overturn"
their lives and to live instead in the power of the living God. The immediacy of God's presence was central to their message, and they used
biblical phrases, stories, and poetic images to express their excitement
and their urgency. In addition to powerful emotions, modern readers
can also discover in these documents the earliest articulations of theological ideas and insights which became central for Quakers during the
later, calmer, and more reflective eras.[1]

The most common feature of all these tracts is the urgent warnings,
sometimes addressed to specific civil and ecclesiastical leaders, sometimes to particular regions or locales. The warnings urged people to recon-
sider their life circumstances, and to make decisive changes in response
to God's presence and power. Many tracts focused particularly on the
continued persecution of members of the Religious Society of Friends.
Such actions were cited as evidence of the continued faithlessness and
wickedness of both ecclesiastical and civil authorities.

Early Friends, by contrast, were frequently portrayed in these tracts
as innocent victims. As the true followers of Christ, their sufferings
were represented as horrible and undeserved, and parallels often were
drawn between their sufferings and Christ's redemptive suffering for
all of humanity.

Typically, the author of such a tract established her credentials by
claiming to be a prophet in the tradition of the ancient Hebrews. The
awful results of continued rejection of God were commonly balanced
with descriptions of the goodness of God's love, and of the power of
God to bring about the changes in people's lives. Warnings were commonly expressed in terms of judgment and dread, and contrasted with
invitations to accept God's love. Often using ecstatic language, the tracts
described the wonder, joy, and delight to be gained from living the life

of faith. Tender and loving words of encouragement, offering rest and comfort from all life's ills, often served as conclusions to the document.

Sarah Jones

Sarah Jones' early tract, *This is Light's appearance in the Truth* (1650) combined warnings and proclamations with emerging Quaker theological ideas.[2] Sarah Jones was a poor widow who lived in Bristol.[3] The name "Sarah Jones" also appears in the Yorkshire petition against tithes signed by "7,000 Handmaids" and published in 1659 (included in this volume).[4] Although on one hand it may seem surprising that a "poor widow" living in Bristol in 1650 could have signed a petition in Yorkshire nine years later, we know that many other Quaker women made longer and more dangerous journeys during the early decades of the Quaker movement. Further regional research into Sarah Jones may result in more details about her life.

In *This is Light's appearance in the Truth*, Sarah Jones declared that she "received the eternal council of the Lord, which lyes as a heavy weight upon my spirit to discharge."[5] With these words she identified herself with the biblical tradition of the prophets by claiming that she spoke because God told her to speak, and gave her the words.

The prophetic warning Sarah Jones issued to her readers in this tract was against reliance on "manifestations," which she contrasted with the "eternal." She claimed that the chief danger for her readers was "building" upon manifestations instead of "that which manifests." Jones advised her readers to "sink down into that measure of life that ye have received" and to follow that life toward the substance, the eternal, which is God. If they did not heed her warning, she predicted that God would "throw down" the idols in their hearts, and "darken the council of God" in themselves, leaving them unable to find their way back to God's presence.[6]

Sarah Jones contrasted her threats with wonderful promises which draw on biblical images taken from Paul's epistles. She spoke to her readers as "dear Lambs," and urged them to "cease thy mourning thou weeping babe," reassuring them that God would "feed thee with the Word from whence that milk proceedeth." She acknowledged that new converts might grieve for the comfort which came from their past reliances, and proclaimed that she could "testifie unto thee by experience, whosoever thou art in that state," that giving up reliance on "manifestations" would bring deeper experiences of the healing presence of God.

Sarah Jones' brief tract expressed the foundational Quaker

teaching against outward religious forms and the dangers of idolatry. Later Friends developed this idea as they began to teach that ordinary believers, if faithful, could experience God's presence directly and powerfully without clergy or sacrament or building. Throughout *This is Light's Appearance* Sarah Jones maintained that her specific word came from an eternal Word which was the source of her authority to speak as well as the source of the language she found to express herself. She called on her readers to "sink into that word for rest (p. 35)."

Jones emphasized her belief that her message, which was specific to the situation, and which she had been commanded to give, was distinct from the Word, which was pre-existent and eternal, active internally as well as externally. She believed that hearing her message would bring her readers to that eternal Word. She warned against relying on the message itself, since that could turn quickly into "building upon manifestations (p. 35)." Sarah Jones thus offered her words as a sort of theological invisible ink: once they led her readers toward the eternal Word, they would disappear, so that her readers could experience the power of God for themselves, without impediment.

Margaret Fell

The next two tracts included in this collection are addressed to particular people, but intended for a wider public in order to influence political policy. The first of two letters by Margaret Fell, published in 1653, was addressed *To Colonel West, when he was a Member of Parliament*. In 1666 Fell wrote *A Letter sent to the King* from Lancaster Prison, where she was serving a sentence after having been convicted of refusing to take an oath, and also for holding Quaker meetings in her home. Fell was finally released in 1668. Between 1653 and 1666 the political circumstances in England and the personal situation of Margaret Fell had changed radically. The Commonwealth had come to an end, and the monarchy had been restored.

In her letter to Colonel West, Margaret Fell addressed a family friend on a matter of deep concern. William West was a judge and also mayor of Lancaster and a Member of Parliament. He had shown himself simultaneously unwilling to participate in the unjust persecution of Friends.[7] Margaret Fell wrote to West on behalf of George Fox, who was being held in the prison at Carlisle. She told him the grim story of George Fox's arrest and trial, and the harsh treatment he received from the judges at the Assizes and in the jail.

While one of Fell's goals in this letter was to persuade West to help bring about Fox's release, her letter was clearly intended for a wider audience. In it she argued that the jailings of George Fox and other "Friends of the Truth" were not merely injustices against individuals, but evidence of "horrible Blaspheming of God, and Dissembling with Him." She indicted not only Fox's persecutors, but all accusers of Friends, calling them "Pretenders of Liberty of Conscience." Fell believed that the persecutions of Friends were dangerous practices that would result in calling down the wrath of God on all who persecuted the innocent. "But he is coming, who rules with a Rod of iron" she threatened, and "who may abide the Day of his Coming? or who can stand when he appears? For Terrible will he be to his Enemies."[8]

Fell portrayed the imprisoned Friends as people suffering for truth's sake, faithfully testifying "against the Abominations of the Times, and the Filthy Deceits, and the Idolatrous Worships, which is holden up, which is Abominable to the Lord."[9] She warned persecutors of Friends not to continue to "pretend to Love the Truth" while using their corrupt power to harm and to cause suffering. She called on West to do what he could to protect George Fox from banishment and from death, and assured West that "as thou act for the Truth, thou shalt be preserved by the Lord of Truth."[10]

Although the overall tone of this tract was urgent and even threatening, the harshness of Margaret Fell's warnings was balanced somewhat by her expressions of warmth toward Colonel West, to whom she sent "dear and Tender Love. . . . in the Lord Jesus" and expressed the hope that "thou abides in the Truth, and in the Love of it." She referred to West as "Dear Heart," and concluded her letter with a plea that West would remain "in the love of [God's] Truth" so that he would "escape the Plagues that will come upon [God's] enemies."[11]

Fell's second letter, addressed to King Charles II, began with a warning that "The Righteous Eye of the Almighty hath been over you, and hath seen all your Doings and Actions" since his ascension to the throne.[12] Her threats and warnings were intended for all those in authority, including "Bishops and Ministers, both Ecclesiastical and Civil,"[13] for she repeatedly held them all responsible for the suffering of Friends.

Fell portrayed herself as a prophet of God, empowered to plead for her people, and reminded the king of a former encounter when "I was sent of the Lord to you, to inform you truly of the State and Condition of our People."[14] At the center of her argument was the claim that

Quakers were being persecuted unjustly, despite the monarch's promises for protection. Quakers, she argued, had been fully open with Charles II and other authorities about their beliefs, and even supplied their persecutors with books and tracts explaining their views.

She also reminded the king that other powerful "Governors" had ignored the warnings of Quakers with disastrous results. She held him responsible for the fact that "the Lord in his Judgment hath taken many Thousands of its People away by his two Judgments, Pestilence and Sword."[15] Fell contrasted the faithlessness of the persecutors with Friends, who were likened to the earliest followers of Jesus.[16] She described her own suffering in prison, "a place not fit for People to lie in,"[17] and concluded her tract by warning the king that he, like all men, "hath but a Moment in this Life, either to Serve, Fear, and Honour the Lord, and therein to receive Mercy from him; or else to Transgress, Sin, Disobey and Dishonour him, and so to receive the Judgment of Eternal Misery."[18] She threatened the king and all other persecutors to cease their actions against the innocent, lest "the Door of Mery [sic] be shut against you."[19]

In both these letters Fell emphasized the fact that Quakers were preaching their ideas openly and innocently, for which they were being harshly and unjustly punished. She insisted that the resulting cruel treatment of Friends was an offense against truth itself, which she believed was freely available to all people, and perceived collectively by those who were faithful. Later Friends would develop more fully the theological connections between public, collective acts of resistance and private, individual faith commitments. Also in these letters Fell expressed the Quaker belief that all humans were accountable to God no matter what their social status, and that all humans would face a "day of visitation" after which they would be cut off from further choices toward God.

Sarah Blackborow

Sarah Blackborow (also spelled Blackborrow, Blackbury, Blackberry, and Blackburow) was among the earliest Quaker ministers. Living in London with her husband William, she helped to establish the Meeting at Hammersmith. Although the date of her birth is uncertain, she lived until 1665. She wrote at least two tracts.[20]

George Fox described an early encounter with her which many believe led to the founding of Women's Meetings. He wrote that Sarah

Blackborow approached him "to complain to me of the poor, and how many poor Friends was in want." Fox told her to gather "about sixty women . . . such as were sensible women of the Lord's truth and fearing God" to meet with him that very day. He concluded by praising the work done by those women over the years.[21]

Sarah Blackborow addressed her tract "Unto all you, who owns your-selves to be Ministers and Teachers of the People, Who preach for hire, and persecute, and throw into prison if you have not." She chastised those who ministered "for hire," because she considered that practice to be a violation of the true principles of Christian ministry. She called on those "hireling priests" to do "honest work" instead of "making war" on those who witnessed from their consciences. She had harsh words for those who combined the practices of "Divin(ing) for money and preach(ing) for reward;" that is, those who used their ecclesiastical po-sitions to further the persecutions of Friends. Sarah Blackborow urged her readers instead to "turn into the light, and own Gods witness." She cautioned them against participating in the persecutions of Friends, for fear of God's judgment. She identified herself as "one who in the light of the Lord stands a witnesse against the Beast and the false Prophet."[22]

In contrast with her warnings, Blackborow offered warm and loving invitations toward all who "thirst after your beloved." She invited "ev-eryone that will" to come "into Wisdom's house," urging them to "come to Christ Jesus who is the light of the world, his breathings are sweet and his shinings are pure: Oh that the Sonns and Daughters of men knew him!"[23] Throughout her tract she moves between warning and invitation, emphasizing both urgency and joy.

In *A Visit to the Spirit in Prison*, the various uses of the term "witnesse" indicated some of the ideas that Sarah Blackborow contributed to emerg-ing Quaker theology. She emphasized the understanding that God places within each human heart an ability to recognize and to do the truth, and that part of living faithfully was to heed and obey that witness, even if it meant suffering "whiping, stockings, imprisonmens [sic], scoffings."[24] Blackborow also offered some analysis of the convincement experience when she claimed that the preaching of Quakers did not bring her new ideas from outside herself, but instead "my understand-ing was opened and then I knew that that was Gods witnesse which had been working in me from my childhood, and had begotten pure breathings and desires, and thirstings after God."[25]

When Sarah Blackborow urged her readers to "come to Gods Wit-ness" she also described her concept of ministry. She did not portray herself as superior to others, since she confessed that she had felt the wrath of God herself, and "therefore am I in sorrow for all you who are laying up fuell for it."[26] Neither did she portray the life of a witness as trouble-free. Instead, she promised her readers that although they would come to "know [God's] power and its leadings" they would also discover that "if it bring you into trouble, it will bring you out again; it will pass through the fire, and through the water; though many Waters may pass over you, and Floods seek to devour you, yet shall you be preserved."[27] In publishing *A Visit to the Spirit in Prison* in 1658, she anticipated the ensuing decades of intolerance when she promised her readers preservation in the midst of persecutions.

7000 Handmaids

Equally bold in tone and content were the petitions that Quaker women sent to the Parliament in 1659 and published as *These several Papers Was sent to the Parliament. . . . Being above seven thousand of the Names of the Hand-Maids and Daughters of the Lord.*[28] These petitions were printed by Mary Westwood, who published many documents written by Quakers during the earliest years.[29] These petitions were clearly intended for general publication and circulation as part of the Quaker effort to persuade readers to change, and to explain Quaker views of the truth.[30] The introduction to the collection was addressed "TO THE READER," and included arguments against the injustices of tithes, and for the appropriateness of female participation in the public political debate. The efforts of women in this struggle were characterized as evidence that "this is the work of the Lord at this day, even by weak means to bring to pass his mighty work in the earth."[31] Drawing on a series of biblical images, the focus in the introduction was on God's power to "bring down every high thing within us and without" so that God's will might be accomplished. The author of the introduction to the collected petitions was Mary Forster (also spelled Foster), (1619-86).

These petitions included many of the same themes found in other tracts, such as pleas on behalf of those Friends who were in prison and descriptions of their faithfulness and their suffering. Invitations to repent and "live in the power of God" were also offered to all "who are in the place to do Justice, and to take off oppression which you may do while you have time."[32] These invitations were combined with warnings against those who wanted to harm Friends. Persecutors were reminded that "if any be prisoned to death, as very many have been in these

Nations, . . . that we shall be clear in the sight of God and have fore-
warned you, and let their blood be upon you."[33] The first signatures on
the petition from Lancashire were from Margaret Fell and her seven
daughters, and the first phrases reminded members of Parliament that
they were "set in place to do justice, to take off oppression, and to stop
the oppressors." The petition then demanded that Parliament recognize the oppressive nature of tithes and the injustices of punishing those
who refuse to pay them.[34]

For the Quaker women who circulated and signed these petitions,
paying tithes represented a betrayal of their newly-discovered life in
the power of Christ. In vivid terms they argued that Christ's coming
had "overturned" the old orders, and presented all people with the choice
of a new life. All vestiges of the old order, including priests, hireling
ministers, parish support, and all mandated funds for waging war, they
considered "disanulled" by the coming of Christ. The women of Essex,
Norfolk, Suffolk, Cambridge, and Huntington declared that they were
"witnesses of Christ Jesus, that he hath disannulled the
Commandment that gave Tithes, and hath ended the Priesthood that
took them,"[35] and the women of Berk-Shire, Hamp-Shire, and Wilt-
Shire declared that they refused to pay tithes because they lived "in
the power of the Lord God" which also "takes away the occasion of
War" as well as priesthood, which was "made by Colledges of men"
and not by God.[36]

Their refusal to pay tithes meant that these Quaker women condemned the social and political system in which they lived. They considered the existing system to be wicked and faithless. Drawing on the
biblical images of a just society, that would care for its most vulnerable
members, they charged that their persecutors provided "no Store-house
for Widows, for Stranger, for Fatherless" and instead were apostate and
not true Christians.[37]

The columns of names attached to each petition bear witness to the
large number of women who joined in the Quaker movement in the
earliest decades. More research into the names on each petition and the
Minutes from each area represented will no doubt reveal additional
details about the activities and relationships of these early Quaker
women.[38] The term "7,000" referred to the righteous remnant praised by
God in the Elijah story, and suggested that those who signed perceived
themselves as prophets (I Kings 19:18).

Most of the women who wrote the tracts included in this section
also signed this petition against tithes. In addition to Margaret Fell's

name on the petition from Lancashire and the name "Sarah Jones" on the petition from Yorkshire, Dorothy White's and Sarah Blackborow's names, who wrote the tracts in the final section of this chapter, appeared in the petition from London and Southwark.[39] Sarah Blackborow's *A Visit to the Spirit in Prison* (1658) addressed those who persecuted Friends. In 1662, Esther Biddle published *The Trumpet of the Lord Sounded Forth* in part to tell of her first encounters with Friends and her decision to join them.[40] In the same year, Dorothy White published her tract, *The Trumpet of the Lord of Hosts*, which includes a poetic section.

Esther Biddle

Like Sarah Blackborow, Esther Biddle was an influential minister among Friends. She was born in 1629, was raised as a member of the Church of England, and became a convinced Friend in 1654. Esther Biddle was married to Thomas Biddle, a shoemaker whose business was burned during the London Fire of 1666. Thomas Biddle had also become a Friend; he was imprisoned with Esther in 1663.[41] Of their four sons, only one, Benjamin, lived to be an adult.[42] One of her sons was born on January 1, 1661. Since Esther Biddle was in prison during December, January, and February of 1660-61, some have concluded that Daniel, who died in 1666, was born in prison.[43]

Esther Biddle is mentioned once in the *Journal* of George Fox. He recalled that a woman had come to him in 1659, during the Commonwealth, with a prophecy that Charles II would be restored to the throne. Fox realized that if Biddle made such statements in public, she would expose herself to charges of treason. He advised her to "wait upon the Lord and keep it to herself" until a later time. When she persisted in her conviction, Fox "saw her prophesy was true."[44]

Her public ministry extended from 1655, one year after her convincement, to 1694, two years before her death. Accounts of her work among Friends indicate that she travelled to Newfoundland (1656), Barbados (1657), Holland (1657-58), Ireland (1669), Scotland (1672), and France (1694).[45] Esther Biddle was imprisoned fourteen times during her ministry. In all she published eight broadsides and tracts, between 1659 and 1662.

She wrote *The Trumpet of the Lord Sounded forth into these Three Nations* from Newgate prison. In this tract she addressed the king and all other persecutors of Friends, warning them that "the anger of the Lord waxeth hot against all workers of iniquity"[46] and that even if banished,

Friends would leave behind a seed in the land "which shall witness for us when you are gone." In her challenges to those who persecuted Friends, Esther Biddle used prophetic language drawn from Amos, Micah, and Isaiah, and urged the "Rulers, Judges, and Justices, and all People high and low" to "leave off oppressing the Righteous, and set the captive free." Her tract condemned the "high and lofty ones" who "spendeth God's Creation upon your lusts, and doth not feed the hungry, nor cloath the naked, but they are ready to perish in the streets."[47]

Esther Biddle portrayed the Quakers as faithful followers of God's commands, who were being persecuted by the disobedient and corrupt civil and religious authorities. Although she condemned the rulers and leaders in her tract, warning that they would be "[b]anished from the presence of the King of Heaven for evermore, into utter darkness, where is *weeping, wailing,* and *gnashing* of Teeth," she also spoke tenderly to them, begging them to repent of their wickedness and return to God's way. To underscore her message, she used her own life as an example, telling of her baptism into the Church of England, the political unrest in her early life that added to the burdens of her heart, her years of study and prayer, and her yearning for God's presence, as "the Enemy waited to devour me." For one year "the Lord [did] take away my hearing that I was deaf as to all Teaching of Men" and during that time the "Faith which I was baptized in, did no good."[48]

In *The Trumpet of the Lord Sounded Forth* she also told of her joy when she encountered "the People called *Quakers*," in whose presence she came to know both the fullness of her sinful nature and the depth of her redemption. According to Esther Biddle, the basis of Friends' knowledge and power came from their belief that they could not "own the Teaching that is of this World," but instead must own only "that which cometh immediately from God." She offered praises to God for her conversion, claiming that "I am set at Liberty from this vain Religion." She then linked her former "captivity" as a member of the Church of England with the current captive state of Friends, and threatened those who would persecute Friends.[49] Biddle gives details of her threat in a short tract warning clergy of her concerns: *One Warning more to the Bishops, Priests, Deacons, Friers, and Jesuites,* 1662.

Dorothy White

The final document in this section was written by Dorothy White (c. 1630-85), who produced twenty known tracts during her lifetime. Although she wrote more than any other Quaker woman except Margaret Fell, few details about her life are known. Like Fell and Biddle, she wrote at least one tract from prison.[50] Before 1663, fifteen different publications are attributed to her, and in 1662 alone she published six different tracts, including *The Trumpet of the Lord of Hosts*. For the next twenty-two years no further works by Dorothy White appeared; then four more writings were published in 1684.[51]

The tract included here, *The Trumpet of the Lord of Hosts*, is addressed to "the City of London, and unto all the Inhabitants thereof." In her introduction she identified herself as one of God's prophets, proclaiming that "the Lord God hath spoken, and therefore I will prophesie" as she warned Londoners to prepare to be judged by God, as were the inhabitants of Sodom and Gomorrah.[52] Throughout the tract she continued to emphasize the impending judgment of God, reminding her readers that "the Day is coming wherin the Heavens shall be set on fire, and the Elements shall melt with fervent heat, and the Lofty in that day shall be brought low."[53]

Although she warned that God would "roar as a Lion bereaved of her young" and would send plagues on all who were corrupt, Dorothy White also promised that God could be found *within* each human. She called on her readers to "let every man come home to within" where God had "set up righteous Judgements" so that "the Inhabitants of the Earth thereby may come to learn Righteousness, and *Sion* through Judgement must be redeemed." Dorothy White's vivid language was intended to help bring about that redemption, for she beseeched her audience to see with her the possibility of turning to God. She expressed her hope that "Immortality, and Glory, and Beauty, and Holiness" would break forth in the lives of her readers, and that "Beams of [God's] Brightness shall overshadow the Mountains, and the Sun of Righteousness shall arise."[54]

Dorothy White used the prophetic term "overturn" to express her understanding of God's activities. She associated the term with the biblical concept of the Day of the Lord, and claimed that the "Decree of our God is to *Overturn, overturn, overturn,* until Righteousness rule in this Nation, until all become subject to the Authority of the Lamb." For White, the process of "overturning" within the nation would have a parallel within each heart. She invited her readers, to "overcome, overcome all your hearts, that Life may fill your vessels," and offered them the possibility that "every Soul may swim in the fulness of Love, that all may be filled with the eternal Power, that the new Wine of the

Kingdom may be poured from vessel to vessel, that all your Cups may overflow with the Consolation of God."[55]

Dorothy White appended a second tract to *The Trumpet of the Lord of Hosts*, entitled (in shortened form), *A Trumpet Sounded out of the Holy City, proclaiming Deliverance to the Captives*. In it she addressed those who "wait" for the coming of God's Kingdom. She called on them to "Arise in the Power" and challenged them to "feel this faith to work you into Love."[56]

Although in this tract White warned that the Day of the Lord will be "so dreadful, so terrible" for those who have opposed God, the predominating message is one of love, praise, and encouragement. In the middle of the tract she inserted a long series of rhymed couplets that draws on a variety of biblical texts for inspiration, reiterating many of the ideas she has already stated. White repeated the word "love" eight times in one ecstatic sentence toward the end of the tract. She appears to have been filled with a sense of love, as she claimed that her words were sent "in that eternal Love which hath no evil in it."[57]

Conclusion

The tracts of proclamation and warning reflect much of the political turmoil of the earliest decades of the movement. In these urgent warnings and forthright proclamations we can hear their exhilaration about the present and their hopes for the future. As early Quaker women sought as prophets to influence the policies and practices of the civil government, they also helped to create a distinctive Quaker theological discourse. Their writings contributed to the theological debates that would occupy Friends in the next decades and centuries.

NOTES

1. Luella Wright, in *The Literary Life of the Early Friends*, (New York: Columbia University Press, 1932), asserted that the Quaker writings published during the earliest decades have lasting significance, calling them the "groundwork out of which the later controversial and the more literary Quaker endeavors evolved" (pp. 42-43). She noted that there were thirty-three women in the group of two hundred thirty-one "Publishers of Truth" who set out to articulate the principles and practices of the Society of Friends in the early decades (p. 41), but she does not comment further on early Quaker women's tracts, nor does she quote from any of them. In their analysis of early Quaker writings, *Early Quaker Writings*,

1650-1750 (Grand Rapids, Michigan: Eerdmans, 1973), Hugh Barbour and Arthur Roberts also argue that "the earliest and the most central and authoritative form of Quaker writing was the *tract of proclamation*" (p. 27). A large number of tracts written by Quaker women survived andare pre- served in library archives at Swarthmore, Haverford, and Friends House, London.

2. In her title Jones addressed "all the precious dear Lambs of the Life;" that is, other members of her religious group. This document might have been included with the Letters and Epistles found on pp. 443-533. However, we include it here with tracts of proclamation and warning because of its early publication date and its general tone and content. The links among Friends in Bristol were only in the earliest stages in 1650, which suggests that Jones' words were meant for a wider circle of readers. Furthermore, the language of *This is Light's appearance in the Truth*, with its contrasting threats and praise, is consistent with the style of other tracts in this section.

3. Another tract, entitled *To Sion's lovers, being a golden egge, to avoid infection, or a short step into the doctrine of laying on of hands*, and attributed to a woman named Sarah Jones, was published in 1644. *To Sion's lovers* expressed views that were Congregationalists, which may mean that Sarah Jones became a Quaker sometime between 1644 and 1650, or that there were two women by that name. Bell, Parfitt & Shepherd, *A Biographical Dictionary of English Women Writers, 1580-1720* (Boston: G.K. Hall & Co., 1990), pp. 116–17. Dorothy Paula Ludlow, in *"Arise and Be Doing": English 'Preach- ing' Women, 1640-1660* (Doctoral dissertation, Indiana University, 1978) argued that there was only one "Sarah Jones," to whom she attributed two tracts published in this time frame. Ludlow also indicated that Sarah Jones was a friend of both Katherine Chidley (an Independent and early advocate of women's rights to preach) and Sara Wight (a mystic), but does not develop Jones' biography any further (See pp. 68, 80, 103n).

4. *These Several Papers was sent to the Parliament*, 1659, p. 58.

5. Jones, *This is Light's appearance*, p. 36.

6. Jones, *This is Light's appearance*, p. 36.

7. Braithwaite, *Beginnings*, pp. 107ff tells the story of West's refusal to send George Fox to jail, and his offer to put up his own property for Fox's sake. Fox's *Journal* (Cambridge University Press, 1911) tells that West, who never became a Friend, was sympathetic to their cause (pp. 136, 139ff).

8. Fell, *To Colonel West, when he was a Member of Parliament*, 1653, p. 40.

9. Fell, *To Colonel West*, p. 39.

10. Fell, *To Colonel West*, p. 40.

11. Fell, *To Colonel West*, p. 41.

12. Fell, *Letter sent to King Charles*, (1666), p. 42.

13. Fell, *Letter*, p. 43.

14. Fell, *Letter*, p. 43.

15. Fell, *Letter*, p. 43.

16. Fell, *Letter*, p. 44.

17. Fell, *Letter*, p. 44.

18. Fell, *Letter*, p. 45.

19. Fell, *Letter*, p. 46.

20. Gilbert Latey, "Brief Narrative of the Life of Gilbert Latey," in *Friends Library*, vol. 1, p. 171; Bell, Parfitt & Shepherd, *A Biographical Dictionary*, p. 27.

21. Fox, Journal 2: 342-43.

22. Sarah Blackborow, *A Visit to the Spirit in Prison: And An Invitation to all people to come to Christ the light of the World, in whom is life, and doth enlighten every one that cometh into the World. And A Warning to all people to take heed how they joine any longer with that which turns them from him*, 1658, p. 46.

23. Blackborow, *A Visit to the Spirit in Prison*, p. 50.

24. Blackborow, *A Visit to the Spirit in Prison*, p. 49.

25. Blackborow, *A Visit to the Spirit in Prison*, p. 50.

26. Blackborow, *A Visit to the Spirit in Prison*, p. 51.

27. Blackborow, *A Visit to the Spirit in Prison*, p. 53.

28. In his *Journal*, Fox described the efforts of Friends to persuade Parliament to end the tithe. He mentioned the women's efforts, saying that as Christ had sent out his messengers freely, so current disciples should not have to support priests but should minister freely (vol. 1, p. 385). In his notes Norman Penney writes that Fox suggested the action of women against tithes, since women could feel the weight of this truth just as men could (p. 468).

29. In her article, "Mary Westwood, Quaker Publisher" (*Publishing History*, vol. 23, 198, pp. 5-66), Maureen Bell explored the role of Quaker publishing within the context of both the religious and political turmoil and the publishing trade of the times. Bell also suggested that Westwood was either a committed Friend herself (her name appears on the petition against tithes, and she published numerous Quaker tracts), or a shrewd business woman who had cornered a particular market. Another possibility remains: she was both!

30. Other groups of women also petitioned Parliament during this period, and often produced impressive numbers of signatures. Bell, Parfitt & Shepherd, in their appendix on petitions, challenged suggestions that men were the authors of these petitions, arguing that the weight of the evidence is on the side of female authorship (*A Biographical Dictionary*, pp. 263-70).

31. *These several Papers Was sent to the Parliament*, 1659, p. 59; Patricia Higgins, in "The Reactions of Women, with special reference to women petitioners," (in *Politics, Religion and the English Civil War*, edited by Brian Manning, New York: St. Martin's Press, 1973, pp. 179-222), points out that it was not uncommon for women petitioners to use an "inferiority" argument as they challenged civil authorities (pp. 221-22).

32. *These several Papers*, 1659, p. 62.

33. *These several Papers*, p. 62.

34. *These several Papers*, p. 61.

35. *These several Papers*, p. 86.

36. *These several Papers*, p. 93.

37. *These several Papers*, p. 73.

38. Gilbert Cope, in 1908, arranged the names on all the petitions in alphabetical order, and commented in his introduction on some of the difficulties, such as handwriting and misspelling, that were involved in making his transcription. He suggested that perhaps the printer inflated the number of names in order to increase compensation, or that other nonconforming protestors added their names to the Quaker petitions. Curiously, Cope refers to the printer as "he" despite the fact that the title page clearly indicates the printer's name as "Mary Westwood." Cope's transcription of the petitions is in the archives at Swarthmore College.

39. Historical evidence suggests that Esther Biddle may have been in jail or in Holland when this activity was occurring.

40. Esther Biddle, *The Trumpet of the Lord Sounded forth unto these Three Nations, As a Warning from the Spirit of Truth; especially unto Thee, Oh ENGLAND, who art looked upon as the Seat of Justice, from whence righteous Laws should proceed* (London: 1662), p. 129.

41. Friends' Historical Society, *Extracts from State Papers Relating to Friends*, edited by N. Penney (London: Headley Brothers; Philadelphia: H. Newman, 1910-13), p. 159.

42. Lydia Rickman, "Esther Biddle and Her Mission to Louis XIV," *Quaker History* 47 (1955): 41.

43. Rickman, "Esther Biddle," 45n.

44. Fox, *Journal*, p. 342.

45. Fox mentions her visits to Newfoundland and Barbadoes in the *Journal* (pp. 334, 336). On her trip to Holland, see the account by William I. Hull, *The Rise of Quakerism in Amsterdam, 1655-1665*, (Swarthmore College Monographs on Quaker History, 1938), pp. 282-83. Hull claims that Esther was a "thorn in the side of the Dutch as well as the English Quak-

erism," and associates her with Ann Gargill and the excesses around James
Nayler in 1656. At this point, no corroboration of Hull's characterization
of Esther Biddle has been found, and more research into her travels and
writings is needed. Her trip to Ireland is noted in "Record of Friends Travelling in Ireland, 1656-1765," published in *Journal of the Friends Historical
Society*, vol. 10, 1913, p. 159, where she is listed as travelling with John
Wilkinson. Her visit to Scotland is found in the listing "Stranger Friends
Visiting Scotland, 1650-1797," in *Journal of the Friends Historical Society*,
vol. 12, 1915, p. 138. Only Gerardus Croese, in *The General History of the
Quakers*, pp. 268-69, speaks of her trip to France. Lydia Rickman, in her
study of this trip, also wonders if she went to the Middle East. The answer
to this question hinges on the interpretation of the word "the straites"
which appears in her letter. Rickman thinks that it means Gibralter, which
would suggest that she was on her way to the Middle East. What strengthens this claim is the fact that her letter to Fox dated 15 April 1659 lists its
location as "Cowes," which would be on the way to the Middle East. At this
point there is no corroboration of this trip.

46. Biddle, *The Trumpet*, p. 130.

47. Biddle, *The Trumpet*, p. 132.

48. Biddle, *The Trumpet*, p. 134.

49. Biddle, *The Trumpet*, pp. 131, 135, 136.

50. Bell, Parfitt & Shepherd, A *Biographical Dictionary*, p. 213.

51. An in-depth study which explores Dorothy White's life and writings and
    her role within the Religious Society of Friends is in progress. See " 'Lift
    Up Thy Voice like a Trumpet,' " unpublished paper by Janet Fiskio-Lasseter,
    Earlham School of Religion, Richmond, Indiana.

52. White, Dorothy, *The Trumpet of the Lord of Hosts Blown unto the City of
    London, and unto the Inhabitants thereof; Proclaiming the great and notable
    Day of the Lord God, which is coming swiftly on them all, as a Thief in the
    night. And this is the* CRY *of the* LORD GOD, *which is gone forth unto thy
    Inhabitants*, 1662, p. 138.

53. White, *The Trumpet*, p. 138.

54. White, *The Trumpet*, p. 139.

55. White, *The Trumpet*, p. 140.

56. White, *The Trumpet*, p. 141.

57. White, *The Trumpet*, p. 148.

(page 1) *This is Lights appearance in the Truth
to all the precious dear Lambs of the
Life, Dark vaniſhed, Light
ſhines forth: Set forth*

by Sarah Jones.

Ear Lambs, whom the Father hath visited with his eternal love, this is the Message of the Lord unto you from that word which shall endure for ever, that ye sink down into that eternal word, and rest there, and not in any manifestations, that proceeds from the word, for it is the word of the Lord once more mentioned, that shall endure forever, and those that are gathered into it; and so dear babes, this is the testimonie of the Fathers love, that ye may not rest short of himself through, one who the Lord God hath brought, and is a bringing to the loss of all things, that I may be found in him; which eternal word was before manifestations were, and this is the word that the builder refuses, which is become the head of the corner. Dear babes, read and tell me within, for those that build upon the manifestations, and not upon that that manifests, sets up an Idol in the heart, which the Lord God will shortly throw down: Dear babes, not that the manifestation from the Spirit of truth is denyed, for whatsoever is manifested or re- vealed to the Creature, it is to lead it to the substance, and so that soul and spirit that sinks down into it, it works and levens into its own crea- ture, and it will work out the nature which is contrary to divine nature; what proceeds from it is holy and pure, so let not your eyes nor minds be gathered into the manifestations, but sink down into that measure of life that ye have received, and go not out with your in-looking at what is contrary in you, for if you do you will miss of the power that should destroy it, for as ye keep in that which is pure, which is the eternal word *(page 2)* of the Lord, which is nigh in your hearts, it will work and operate so, that it will overcome what is contrary: And so, you, dear babes, that are little and weak in your own eyes, to you is this message sent, look not at your own weakness, but look at him who is calling you in his eternal love, who will make the weak strong, and will pull down the mighty from their seat. Ah my soul, canst not thou say so by experi-

(Page numbers of original document appear in text as *page __.*)

ence? yes surely; and so, dear babes, reason not with flesh and blood, nor with the voice of the Serpent, for if you do, you will darken the council of God in your selves, but in the power of the Lord shut him out, for it makes in hir [*sic*] a state of innoncence [*sic*]; had *Eve* done so, she had not been overcome, for this is meant towards ye, whom the Lord by his righteous Judgments hath made roome for a measure of his: But this is the council of the Lord to such as have been so overcome, while the trouble and conflicts are upon their spirits, through the cause before mentioned, stand still and see the salvation of God, which is in the light of his Covenant, which will stretch forth the hand of his power, as he did to *Peter* when he feared the proud waves would have prevailed over him; for I can testifie, as I have received in the eternal council of the Lord, which lyes as a heavy weight upon my spirit to be discharged, That except the Creature sink down into that that manifest and re- vealed, and so be wrought into it natures, and so all things of Gods power and authority, ye else shall fall short of that price which that soul may attain to, which daily sinks down into it: not as though I my self have altogether attained to that degree of perfection; but this I can say in the fear and truth of the Lord, that I am one that presseth hard after it, and it is the desire of my soul, that others may joyn hands with me in this work, in that measure of life that the Father hath bestowed in us: So cease thy mourning, thou weeping babe, that mourns in secret for manifestations from thy beloved, as thou hast had in dayes past; for I can testifie unto thee by experience, whosoever thou art in that state, that he is bringing thee nearer him, for that was but milk which he fed thee with whilst thou was weak, but he will feed thee with the Word from whence that milk proceedeth, if thou be willing *(page 3)* and obedi- ent to live at home with *Jacob*, which is daily to retire thy mind; though the gadding, hunting *Esau* persecutes thee for it, thou shalt receive the blessing in which all happiness and felicity doth consist for evermore. For as *Esau* went to hunt abroad, when the blessing was to be received at home, so I testifie unto thee from the Lord, whomsoever thou art, that art convinced that the Word is in thy heart, and yet goes a gadding and hunting after the manifestation that proceeds from the word in others vessels, I tell thee, in Gods eternal truth, whomsoever thou art, that thou maist receive them in a wrong ground, and that nature that is contrary to the Word of the Kingdome, may be alive in thee, and thou in it, in which thou canst not enter the Kingdome: Therefore come down, come down to the Word of his patience, which is nigh in your hearts, which if you do, he will keep you in the hour of temptation, which shall come to try all upon what foundation they are built; for saith Christ, which is the word of God, *My sheep hear my voice, and they follow me:* and I the Word will give them eternal life, and none can *pull them out of his hand,* which is that living Word, from whence this testimony of mine proceedeth. Oh how my bowels yernes in that living Word! yea, that ye may not fall short, but be crowned with Immortality and glory; for oh the glorious day of the Lord God hasteth to be revealed to those that are kept faithful in his Word.

Given forth by one whose heart the Lord hath enlarged in his own life towards ye, that I can speak it in the integrity of my soul, that if I could breath forth the measure of life that I have received, to do the least babes good, I should freely do it, who am called by the name of

S.J.

(page 40)

To Colonel Weſt, *when he was a Member of Parliament, in* Oliver's *Days, and when* George Fox *was Priſoner at* Carliſle, 1653.

Dear Friend,

My dear and tender Love unto thee in the Lord Jesus presents it self unto thee, hoping in the Lord that thou abides in the Truth, and in the Love of it, and those that are Sufferers for it, as thou hast shew'd thy self heretofore; and I am sure thou need'st not be asham'd of it, for it shall stand, when all the deceitful Devices of Man shall fall: Tho' all the Powers of the Earth combine themselves, and gather together against the Lord, and his Anointed; yet will he be glorified in his Saints, and in the Destruction of his Enemies, as they shall find, and see, when it will be too late.

(page 41) I sent thee a Paper from my dear Brother *George*, and *Robert Withers*, and likewise the Warrant, by which the Persecutors of the Truth did apprehend him, and I did expect to have heard something from thee concerning him before this: The Judges at the Assizes would not suffer him to come before them, but did Revile him, and Scoff him behind his Back, and did give what Encouragement they could to the Justices, to exercise their Cruelty upon him; he was then in the Goaler's House, but kept close up in the Assize Week, and no Friends suffer'd to go to him; both Colonel *Benson* and Justice *Pearson* were deny'd, but all Drunkards and lewd Persons were suffer'd to go in.

The next Day after the Judges went forth, there was Command given to the Goaler, that he should be put in the Common Goal, among Thieves and Murtherers, and in the most odious Place that ever Man was put into; and there he is now. *Lawson*, who is the Sheriff of the County, is his greatest Enemy, and was one of them that was the greatest Cause of his Commitment, though he had no Power to act then, he being the Sheriff of the County.

But all such unjust Actions is suffer'd, and all such Tyrants is upheld by those that are in Authority, and the Truth only suffers, and is

(Page numbers of original document appear in text as *page _.*)

imprison'd by them. Never was the like horrible Blaspheming of God, and Dissembling with Him, as in these Days, by those that profess a God in Words, and in all their Actions fight against Him, and his Truth, and the spreading abroad of it; which is Blasphemy indeed, which they so much speak of. O let all Profession, and great Words, and boasting of Light and high Forms! let them all blush and be ashamed before the Lord, who will not be mock'd with them, though they falsly pretend that they stand for Liberty of Conscience, and Propagation of the Gospel; and keeps those Men in Authority under them, who watches and lies in wait for an opportunity to destroy those, whom the Lord sends *(page 42)* forth to preach the Everlasting Gospel; and some they stone, and some they beat, and shamefully use; and ever, when they can have any colour, cast them into Prison: Most part of the Goals in the North part of *England* hath some Friends of the Truth in them, as *York*, *Carlisle*, *Appleby*, and *Lancaster*.

Now, be ye Judges your selves, ye Pretenders of Liberty of Conscience; and consider what Liberty you give to tender Consciences, which never committed any Offence to any Man, but for Conscience sake. O how dare you profess Reformation, when Cruelty and Tyranny Rules in the Land! O look back, and see, if ever there was the like, in all the Kings or Bishops time, since Queen *Mary's* Days, that slew the Martyrs, that so many Goals was furnish'd with Prisoners, only for Conscience sake! Or was there ever any that suffer'd for Conscience sake, that was put amongst Thieves and Murtherers? or scarce ever was there any, except it was Popish Priests, or Jesuits, that ever was kept in Prison; but they either spoke Treason against King, or State, or gave some other Offence, more than only Conscience; which no Man can ever justly accuse any of these with, but only they suffer for the Truth's sake; and by the Immediate Movings of the Lord, do speak against the Abominations of the Times, and the Filthy Deceits, and the Idolatrous Worships, which is holden up, which is Abominable to the Lord. But he is coming to confound, and throw down that filthy Idol, which they call their Worship, which is odious in his sight; He will destroy it by the Spirit of his Mouth, and the Brightness of his Coming: The Decree is gone out from the Lord, Destruction is coming upon it, and all the Upholders of it there; let the Powers of the Earth stand out as long as they can, the Woe and the Curse is upon them that strives with their Maker, and he will overturn them, Root and Branch; they shall not escape the Judgment of *(page 43)* God: For he is the same God that ever he was, and he will not give his Glory to another; and how his Glory suffers, by the Persecutors of the Power of Truth. But he is coming, who rules with a Rod of Iron, which shall dash to pieces all his Enemies: But who may abide the Day of his Coming? or who can stand when he appears? For Terrible will he be to his Enemies.

Dear Heart, I cannot but let thee know the Cruelty of these Tyrants: O! these Acts, and Pretences that they have to Act by, is odious to all that have but common Honesty; That the State should pretend Love to the Truth, and yet suffer such things to be of Force, that all Bloody Persecutors may have their Wills, so far as the Lord gives them Power, upon those that live in the Truth. They intend Banishment to *George*, or else to take away his Life; if it be in their power, now at their Sessions; for the Judges left him to them, to proceed against him according to the Act; and *Lawson* was in hopes to have gotten his Life taken away now at the Assizes, and gave it out, That he would come to be try'd for his Life; though they had nothing against him at all, but what they had gotten their false Witnesses to swear; and there is nothing that they swore, that is within the Act; yet they thirst so for Blood, that their Wills will be their Laws, if the Lord do not prevent them, by some Means or Instruments, that he will raise up. Do what the Lord moves thee, and what he makes way for thee: For it is no Man's Strength nor Power, that we look at, but the Lord alone; who is the same to us, that he was to *Daniel* in the Lions Den, and the Three Children in the Fiery Furnace; and the same Power do we dwell and stand in, and the same Power will deliver us out of the Hands of all Bloody Persecutors: And it is but to make up their Iniquity, and to fat them for Destruction; for that is their Portion. That, which he spoke there before them, a Thousand will witness *(page 44)* the same thing with him, and subscribe their Names, and would lay down their Lives, and are not afraid of any Man whatsoever: Everlasting Praises be to our Father for ever!

Here is some Hints of the Passages, that Justice *Pearson* and Justice *Benson* took of the Proceedings of those they call *Judges:* He that Runs may Read. Their Injustice, their Baseness was observed in all the Countries where they came; which is little Credit for them that set them to work.

Now I have let thee know how things are, I am discharged; and let my Heavenly Father work as he will, and by whom he will; and as thou acts for the Truth, thou shalt be preserved by the Lord of Truth; and if thou neglect any opportunity that is offer'd to thee, the Lord will require it at thy Hands. For he takes strict notice of you though you may take Liberty to your selves, yet never any pretended such high things for God, as you do; which is the highest Dissembling with the Lord, which he will be avenged of. Therefore let your high Formalists and great Professors consider now, who is persecuted for the Truth, and who it is that persecutes them. They have long stood in their Forms; but never was there any Perfection till now, that the Power of Truth is made manifest which will confound and break to pieces all their Forms. Now doth the Lord of Glory suffer indeed in his Saints, by those that profess him in Words, and deny his Power: But their Power is limited, and he will recover his Glory out of their Hands; which shall be to the Confusion of all his Enemies, and to the Exaltation of his great Name upon the Earth: They shall find, that the Lord of the Vineyard is coming to look for Fruits and will Reward every Man according to his Deeds for the Keeper of *Israel* neither slumbers nor sleeps but takes notice of all the Actions, Words, Thoughts and Intentions of his Enemies. So let them Act what they can, their Compass is known, their Time is but short.

(page 45) I was moved to write a Letter to thee a great while ago, and *James Taylor* wrote another the next Week after, but we never heard whether thou received'st them or not; I desire thee to let us know whether thou didst receive them, or not; if thou didst not, we shall send thee Copies of them. For though thou may'st look slightly upon them, yet will they lie upon our Consciences, till we know that thou hast received them, and then it will return to thee, and we shall be discharged. If ever thou know what the moving of the Power of the Lord is, thou wilt know the Punishment of Disobeying him: But so long as he is unknown, he is lightly look'd on. So *Fare thee well.*

And the Lord God of Power, of Heaven and Earth, direct and keep thee in his Fear, and in the Love of his Truth; and so thou shalt escape the Plagues that will come upon his Enemies.

Do not neglect in sending us word, whether thou received these Letters, or not.

Marg. Fell.

A Letter ſent to the King from M.F.

King CHARLES, *I deſire thee to Read this over,* *which may be for thy Satisfaction and Profit.*

I N the Fear of the Lord God stand still, and consider what thou and you have been doing these six Years, since the Lord brought you Peaceably into this Realm, and made you Rulers over this People. The Righteous Eye of the Almighty hath been over you, and hath seen all your Doings and Actions.

What Laws have you made or changed, save such as have laid Oppression and Bondage on the Consciences of God's People, and that of no less Penalty than *Banishment out of their Native Country?* The greatest Crime that you could find with the People of God, was, *that they obeyed and worshipped Christ Jesus:* So that the greatest Stroke that hath appeared of your Justice, hath been upon such as you counted Offenders for worshipping of God; insomuch that several of your Judges of the Land have several times said in open Court, to any that did confess that *they met to worship the Lord God,* That *that was Crime enough, whereby they could proceed to Banishment.* And when it was asked in open Court, *Whether it was now become a Transgression or a Crime in* England *to worship God?* He that was then the Chief Justice of *England* answered, *Yes, Yes.* O wonderful! Let this be Chronicled in *England* for after-Ages, that all Magistrates may dread and fear so to affront the Almighty; except they dare say, they are stronger than he.

And all this hath been without any just Cause given at any time by that People, which was the *(page 326)* Object of this Law; so that Men, that had but the least measure of Righteousness and Equity, could never have proceeded on to have inflicted such a height of Punishment, without some just ground.

And all that ever was pretended, was but Suspicion, which never can be parallel'd; to be prosecuted to such a height of Suffering without a just ground given, although Occasion hath been continually sought and watched for, but never found; but the Lord hath preserved his People innocent and harmless; and therefore is he engaged to plead their Cause, into whose Hand it is wholly given and committed.

I desire you also to consider seriously in the fear of the Lord, what Effects and Fruits these things have brought forth.

First, I believe it hath brought Hundreds of God's People to their Graves; it hath also render'd this Realm, and the Governours of it cruel, in the Eyes of all People, both within its own Body, and in other Nations; besides the guilt of innocent Blood lies upon this Kingdom.

Since which time, the Lord in his Judgment hath taken many Thousands of its People away by his two Judgments, *Pestilence* and *Sword.*

And before any of this was, when you first entred into this Kingdom, I was sent of the Lord to you, to inform you truly of the State and Condition of our People: And when I came before thee, O King, I told thee, I was come to thee in the behalf of an innocent, harmless, peaceable people; which Words I would then, and ever since, and should at this day, seal with my Blood, if I were put to it: And thy Answer was to me, *If they be peaceable, they shall be protected.*

I also wrote to thee several times concerning our Faith and Principles, how that we could not swear for Conscience sake; neither could we take up Arms, nor Plot, nor contrive to do any Man Wrong nor Injury, much less the King.

(page 327) I also told you, that we must worship God, for God required it of us.

We did likewise give you many of our Books, which contained our Faith, and Principles, and Doctrine, that thereby we might be tryed by the Scriptures of Truth (which all of you do profess) whether our Principles were erroneous or no; and to that purpose we gave our Books to the King and Parliament, and to the Bishops and Ministers, both Ecclesiastical and Civil.

Our Books were sold openly amongst all People; and our Principles declared in a Declaration, and freely holden forth to the whole World.

We also desired that we might have a Meeting of the Bishops or Ministers of the Land, and that our Friends would freely and willingly give them a Meeting, that thereby they and we might be tryed by the Scriptures, which of us was in the error; —whereupon thou wast pleased to grant us our Requests, and promised us that we should have a Meeting, which was but reasonable; but the Bishops, and those that were concerned, they turned it off, when our Friends were ready, and would not give us a Meeting;[1] this Action of theirs, did clearly manifest them to be out of the Life and Power of the Scriptures: For Christ Jesus said to those that he sent forth, that they *should not be afraid, for he would give them a Mouth and Wisdom, that all their Adversaries should not be able to gainsay nor resist;* and likewise the Apostle when he wrote to his Son Timothy, in 2 *Tim.* 2.24, 25, 26. *And the Servant of the Lord* (saith he) *must not strive, but be gentle unto all Men, apt to teach, patient, in meekness instructing those that oppose themselves, if God peradventure will give them Repentance, and come to the acknowledging of the Truth, &c.*

And they had been the Ministers of Christ, and in the Apostles Doctrine, they would have taken this way with us; they would have endeavoured to have convinced us by sound Doctrine, or at least have *(page 328)* try'd us this way, before they had agreed with the Civil Magistrates to make Laws against us; but this manifested their Spirits and Principle; for they rather chose to deliver us up to you, that had the Whip and the Scourge in your hands, and that which they could not do by sound Doctrine, they agreed with others to do it for them by Compulsion.

But the All-seeing God, hath seen all this.

And all this we did, that you should not be ignorant what we could do, and what we could not do.

I told you also, that we could give unto *Caesar* the things that are *Caesar's*, and unto God also the things that are Gods.

And this is a Witness for the Lord in this Day that he pleads with you, of which you are not ignorant.

I also write to thee to beware how thou Rulest in this Nation, for the People of this Nation was a brittle People generally; and besides them, the Lord had a People here that was dear unto him.

And I desired thee not to touch them, nor hurt them.

I also desired thee to beware of the Councel of the Bishops; for if thou hearkned to their Councel, they would be thy Ruine; for it was their Councel was the Ruine of thy Father; for their Counsel is the same as *Rehoboam's* young Men was: Read what the Lord did with that King, in 1 *Kings* 12. Thou knowest this is true, their Counsel is to make the Burthen heavier, as theirs was.

All this, with much more, I wrote to thee, and warned thee of, (I can truly say in the Fear of the Lord) in much Love and Tenderness to thee. And now I may say unto thee, For which of these things hast thou kept me in Prison three long Winters, in a place not fit for People to lie in; sometime for Wind, and Storm, and Rain, and sometime for Smoke; so that it is much that I am alive, but that the Power and Goodness of God hath been with me. I was kept a Year and Seven Months in this

Prison, *(page 329)* before I was suffered to see the House that was mine, or Children or Family, except they came to me over two dangerous Sands in the cold Winter, when they came with much danger of their Lives: But since the last Assizes I have had a little more respect from this Sheriff, than formerly from others. And in all this I am very well satisfied; and praises the Lord, who counts me worthy to suffer for his sake.

For I never did thee, nor any other Man in the Nation, any wrong; and so I may say for many more of our Friends, that have suffered even until Death; and all that we could write or speak, we were not believed, and all the Warnings that we gave of Judgments; and told you plainly we had done so with other Governors before you, and how the Lord had overthrown them; and desired you many times to beware, lest the Lord's Judgments come over you also: But all was to no purpose, for as long as there was Peace in the Land, the main Business of the Parliament was to *invent Laws to punish and persecute Quakers*; but to make Laws to punish Vice, Sin and Wickedness, and Lasciviousness, we had but a little of such Laws.

And now after all my Sufferings, in the same Love that I visited thee in the beginning, I desire thee once more to fear the Lord God, *by whom Kings rule, and Princes decree Justice; who sets up one, and pulls down another, at his pleasure.*

And let not the Guilt of the Burthen of the Breach of that Word that passed from thee at *Breda* lie upon thy Conscience, but as thou promised when thou wast in distress, and also renewed it many times since, that thou would'st give Liberty to tender Consciences: In the Fear of the Lord perform it, and purge thy Conscience of it; and hearken not to wicked Councellors, that have stopped it in thee all this time; for they will bear none of thy Burthen for thee, when the Lord pleads for Breach of Covenant with him and his People; I know it hath been *(page 330)* often in thy Heart to perform it, and thou hast seen what Fruit the want of it hath brought forth.

So if thou lovest thy Eternal Peace and Comfort with the Lord, try what the performance of it will bring forth, who wilt thereby see thou hast hearkned to wrong Councellors.

And every Mortal Man hath but a Moment in this Life, either to Serve, Fear, and Honour the Lord, and therein to receive Mercy from him; or else to Transgress, Sin, Disobey, and Dishonour him, and so receive the Judgment of Eternal Misery.

So never a one of you knows how long, or how short your Day may be; therefore *fear not Man, that can kill the Body; but fear the Lord, who, when he hath killed the Body, can cast the Soul and Body into Hell; yea, I say unto you, fear him.*

From a true Lover of your Souls, (though a Sufferer by you) and the Desire of my Heart is, that you may take these things into Consideration betime, before it be too late; and set open the Prison Doors, and let the Innocent go free, and that will take part of the Burthen and Guilt off you, lest the Door of Mery[*sic*] be shut against you.

Margaret Fell.

From my Prison at Lancaſter-*Caſtle,*
the 6th Day of the 6th Month, 1666.

---

[1] Account hereof is more fully given in a former letter of hers. (*Original printer's marginal note.*)

A

VISIT

TO THE

SPIRIT

IN

PRISON;

AND

An Invitation to all people to come

to Chriſt the light of the World, in whom is life,
and doth enlighten every one that cometh
into the World.

AND

A Warning to all people to take

heed how they joine any longer with that
which turns them from him.

By *Saraah Blackborow.*

LONDON,
Printed for *Thomas Simmons*, at the *Bull and Mouth* neer
Alderſgate, 1658.

(*Page numbers of original document appear in text as page _.*)

(page 1)   Unto all you, who own your felves to be
              MINISTERS and TEACHERS of the PEOPLE

                Who preach for hire, and perfecute, and
                    throw into prifon if you have it not:
                        this following is;

A Witnesse hath the Lord God in you, which is faithful and true,
if ever you know the day of the unstoping of your deaf eare,
and the eye which the God of this Elementary world hath made blind,
again to see; then shall you confess it had been much better for you that
you had laboured with your hands, doing the things which is honest,
then to have coveted the wages of unrighteousness, or beene fed with
the bread of deceit; how have you made your selves manifest to be of
that generation, amongst whom the horrible thing isfound, who Divine for money *(page 4[sic])* and preach for reward, and seek for your gain
from your quarters, and prepare war if they put not into your mouthes?
What a work is this you are found in, to cast the children of the Lord
into prison, because they cannot deny the witnesse of God in their
consciences, which testifies against all such cursed practises? Was ever
any of the servants of the Lord found in such a work as you are? let the
righteous witnesse of God in your consciences Judge you, that you may
be ashamed: Oh blush that ever your names should be mentioned, or
you found owning such a work as this; either deny your work, or owne
your selves, to be of that generation, who is doing the work of their
father, who abode not in the truth, who was a murderer from the beginning; and remember now you are warned to turn into the light, and
own Gods witness which would teach you to deny both your work &
your wages, & let you see that you should serve another Master; so go
learn what this meanes; the goods of the wicked is laid up for the just,
they that can receive it let them. From one who in the light of the
Lord stands a witnesse against the Beast and the false Prophet.
    And unto all you who own your selves to be Ministers and Teachers
of the people, who preach for money, and though yee have it not, yet
do for bear to cast into prison; yet it is plainly made minifest[sic], you
both are guided by one spirit, and 'tis your own, and while you are
following on in that to know, you can know nothing, and the woe is
pronounced against it; you are all bound up together in one, who is the
earthly, and his work you bring forth, and his wisdom you are in, and

it appears by your practises; for if any of the children of the Lord, be *(page 5)* moved to come into your Steeple-houses to ask you a question, or to declare what they can witnesse of that which leads to Christ? how wrathful are you and impatient, and cry to the people, carry them away or suffer the people to hail them away without reproveing them? this is far from that spirit which should be ready to give an answer to every one that asketh, or that which can bear all things, that spirit which is impatient and wrathful scatters and not gathers any to God; neither can it seek after that which is driven away and lost; the Lord is delivering his people out of your hands, that they may no longer be made a prey to the heathen, for among a poor despised people, who suffers whipings, stockings, imprisonmens [sic], scoffings, hath the Lord appeared in power and great glory, and in them hath raised up a plant of renown, and they shall no more be consumed with hunger, nor beare the shame of the heathen any more; and these are the people who some of you have been heard to call giddy-braind people; I say own it your selves, for that in your brain is what you have to boast of; be ashamed and put your mouthes in the dust, and never open them any more: From a lover of your souls, but a Witnesse against your deceits.

A Love there is which doth not cease, to the seed of God in you all; and therefore doth invite you every one Priest and people to return into it, that into Wisdoms house you may come, where there is a feast provided of things well refined, and the living bread of God is known and fed upon, and the fruit of the Vine drunk of, the unity in the Spirit witnessed, the well-beloved of the Father is here, and this is he who is the fairest of ten thousand, there is no spot nor wrinkle in him; long did my soul thirst after him; between eight and nine years of age, did Gods witnesse strive with me, and chekt me, and convincd me of sin, and sometimes gave me power over it, though I knew not what it was, nor knew not that it was given me to lead me to God, neither did I know in the least what nature it stood in; or that it was sufficient of it self without any other (page 9 [sic]) help to be my teacher, or to open the mysteries of the everlasting kingdom to me, which I now witnesse so to be, liveing praises to God the Father of mercies; notwithstanding all my profession, I never witnessed a separation between the light and the darknesse, nor never so much as heard that such a thing was to be, for when it was spoken of to me by the Servants of the living God, who declared unto me the way to life, & spake of Gods witnesse and its working in the Creature, the same in me witnessed to them, and in that I knew that their testimony and declaration was of, in, and by the life and power of God, and none shall witnesse truly to their ministery, while their minds are abroad in the visible; for this I know,

*that though there be words spoke, yet it is the testimony of Jesus, and himself
who is eternal, and therefore hath power in it to turn the mind in, out of the
visible, down to the eternall seed, & as it is reached it witnesseth to them;
and this I found the first time they spake to me, & my understanding was
opened, and then I knew that that was Gods witnesse which had been working in me from my child-hood, and had begotten pure breathings and desires,
and thirstings after God.*

Now all you who thirst after your beloved, come into Wisdoms house,
though I spake it before, its not grievous to me to speake it again: Oh
every one that will, come; all people come to my beloved; come freely,
you shall part with nothing for him that has hash [sic] either price or
value in it; therefore delay not but come to Christ Jesus who is the light
of the world, his breathings are sweet & his shinings are pure: Oh that
the Sonns [sic] and Daughters of men knew him! then would your hearts
pant after him, and your souls life breath forth it self to him;
righteousnesse is with him, and as a river it flowes forth from him;
deare and precious are his counsells: Oh that the nations could hear
him and obey him! and willingly give up, all that which hath and
yet doth blind the eye, so that they cannot see him, the everlasting
(page 7) counseller, Prince of peace, he is a broad river, his streames makes
glad the City of God; his depths none but in eternity can find, his
heights who can ascend unto? the bredth and length of his love there's
no end of it.

Having known the terrors of the Lord, and the indignation of the
Almighty against all ungodlyness, and that nature from whence it
springs; and now being made partaker of his everlasting love, in which
my bowels earnes [sic], and my heart is enlarged exceedingly in love to
you all, Neighbours, Kindreds and People; and therefore am moved to
salute and to visit the spirit in prison in you all: From a moveing of the
same love, and to warn you in plainnesse and in singlenesse to fear the
living God, and to mind his witnesse which you have long turned from,
and his spirit hath long been, and still is greived and quenched by your
ungodlynesse; Will you take Gods name in your mouthes and hate to
be reformed? Why do you talke of the fear of the Lord and depart not
from your iniquity? Will words serve you? Or are you a redeemed
people? see and consider I beseech you: Oh how my soul is greived to
see and behold your abominations! its high time for you to mind that
which calls your minds into that which strives with you, and would
give light to you, in which you might see all you have been and are a
doing, is in the ungodly nature, even your best works stands there, and

that of God in all your consciences shall witnesse to me, in the day when you shall receive condemnation for them; and then you will see that you are to be striped naked, as in the day you were born, your covering of words will be too narrow for you, and your bed of adulteries will be too short, you will then find no ease there; there are who with fear & dread cry often to the Lord for you, whose souls travels for your Salvation; they that dwell in the silent life whose eye is opened by the power of the Lord, and in the light of Jesus dwels and abides, sees even your secret workings, the ground you act in and from, bless not your selves while you are adding sin to *(page 8)* sin, and drunkennesse to thirst, living in pride in all manner of ungodlynesse, suffering every spirit which proceeds from that nature which is accursed, to act and bring forth its fruits in you, the pure spirit of the Lord which is light and life by all these lyes covered, and the seed of the kingdom buried, and the begotten of the Father of life eternall, strangled, and the Lamb of God slaying, and in some slain; and there his spirit shall no longer strive: Oh woe is me for your souls! a lamentation there is which cannot cease, what may I do that you may know your Saviour? he is neer you waiteing to be gracious to you; and this is he who under all, lyes in you all, that down all might come to him, and when that eye which the God of this world hath blinded is opened again; then shall you see and be a shamed: he lyes oppressed under that which cries peace to you, & in you it is the Hipocrite & the lyer which cries peace to you while you are unsaved from your sins, but are in the liberty in which you are acting wickednesse, of every kind, Scoffers, Mockers, heady, high minded lovers of pleasures more then God, not subject to the Government of Christs spirit, the eternall God of life bow you[sic] hearts and minds by his mighty power: Why will you strive against God? Hath any done so, and prospered, that which strives is that which rebells against his witnesse, which is faithful and true, and will not lye, and as you obey it you will come to see and know it, to be the beginning of the creation of God in you again, that which turns you from it turns you from your Saviour, and drives you from the presence of the Lord, into the earthly nature and carnall mind which is changeable, and there the enemy of your souls keeps you doing, and seeking to know God but cannot, and all its seekings actings and workings are for eternal burnings; are [——] you able to dwell with it? Oh the indignation of the Lord its hot and terrible! I have felt it; and therefore am I in sorrow for all you who are laying up fuell for it, yea verily I could be contented to be accursed again for your sakes: every one while you have *(page 7[sic])* time, prise it,

and be you warned to wait to feel the Witness which God hath placed
in your consciences to let you see what is good, and what is evil; the
careless mind shall never witness to it; Gods Witness leads to Christ
the Redeemer; but that mind which is above leads you to the destroyer,
and layes you under his Power, and here Christ reigns not, but many
Lords rules [*sic*], and a King reigns that's not the Lamb, and the body of
Christ lies dead, and death reigns over you, and all the Works that
stands there, you are to know repentance from; the resurrection of the
dead, and eternal judgement, is yet a mystery to you whose souls are
in the Grave, and feet stuck fast in the mire, and no wayes can you
be holpen out, [—] whilest you flye from that which checks and reproves you in secret, you love it not; because your deeds are evil, you
dare not bring them to the light, for that would discover them of what
sort they are; and because you love them more then that which judges
them, therefore do you turn from the one, and embrace the other:
Wisdom hath uttered forth her voice to you, but the eye and ear which
is abroad, waiting upon a sound of words without you, is that which
keeps you from your Teacher within you; & this is the reason that in all
your seekings you have found nothing; such as your seeking is, such is
your finding; if in the changeable you find that that is so, and that
perisheth with the using; if in the eternal you find that which is eternal, and that's everlasting, life and death is set before you; as you love
the one, you must hate the other; the resurrection of the life, is the
death of the death, and takes away its sting & gives victorie over the
grave; Death, Hell and the Grave must give up their dead when the
voice is heard, obeyed, and believed in which gives life; What I have
seen and known, heard and felt, that declare I unto you, and my witness is true, if I bore witness of my self, it were not true; but my Witness
stands in him, and is of him who is the light of the World: Therefore
dear hearts, you who are in the pantings and thirst, whose hearts are
breathing after the living God, in whom desires have been begotten by
the eternal spirit, and have been betrayed by entering into visibles, and
by a visible Ministrie, which hath been but as sounding brass; and as a
tincling Symbole, which hath never turned to God, nor from the powers *(page 8[sic])* of darkness, but hath begotten an imaginary in you;
likenesses of all sorts and kinds, both of things in heaven, and of things
in Earth, and under the Earth; I say, Go not forth after them; that which
carries you forth, is that which betraies your life, and leads you into the
adultery from it; there's many green Trees in Babel, worship not under
them, nor bow not down to anie likeness, but come to Gods Witness, it

will abide with you; and as you abide with it, you will know its power
and its leadings; be not afraid, but come to it, there's no other way to
life eternal; if it bring you into trouble, it will bring you out again; it
will pass through the fire, and through the water; though many Waters
may pass over you, and Floods seek to devour you, yet shall you be
preserved; it will be with you in six troubles, and also in seven, covet
nothing else, you will need no more; there's a sufficiency in it, flie not
from it, it will never leave You nor forsake You; it will lay You in the
arms of your beloved, it will lead You gently, and lay You in his bosome,
where the Well-springs of life flows forth continuallie; it will make You
inherit durable substance, and cause shadows to flie away; it will lead
you out of all that which stands in time, and its begettings: Therefore
love it, its of an eternal nature, and leads into it, out of the sorrow, out
of the curse: Therefore take heed how you deny it, it sets open the
door of the Kingdom, it separates from that which would keep You
from entering; your unclean natures offer it up to the death of the cross,
for it hath pierced your Saviour; and all that ever you have offered in
it, or by it, hath never made You perfect, as pertaining to the conscience; though You should offer Year by Year, and Daie by Daie, your
sacrifice will not avail You; the Lord is wearie of it, his soul loaths it, he
is prest under it as a Cart with sheaves; therefore cease from it, and
come out of Your manie things; there's but one thing needful, keep to
it, and wander no more as You have done, nor seek not for another, for
all the hopes that you shall have in anie other thing but this, will prove
the hope of the hypocrite, which perisheth, and will set You wandering
up and down in the Earthly, & that's in Satans path; the ginne, and the
snare, and the pit you will meet with there, it's not the equal Way, you
will lose your measure which God hath given to you *(page 9[sic])* to measure your selves withall, and then you run further and further from the
Lord, and lie liable to be deceived by *Babylons* Merchants, who will
make a prey of you, and set you seeking your Saviour upon the Mountains that's covered with darkness it matters not what Name You bear,
or what fellowship You are of while you are out of the fellowship of the
Father and the Son, and turned from that which should lead you thither
and out of the cross, which is the power of God, which would crucifie
you to the World, and the World unto you: I say, What are you more
then they who never bore any of those Names? So be not deceived, for
God will not be mocked; the light of Christ will deceive none of you,
but if you are out of it, it matters not how high your sights, your notions, your airy imaginations are, they are to little purpose, it may join

you to the more refined builders of Babel, which are talking of the Corner-stone, but reject it as well as others, and make up a building without it, a Tower which you think must reach up to Heaven, strongly fenced and Walled, but its not the Wall nor the Fence which God hath made, or ever appointed; and if ever to the light You return again, it will let you see that in that building lives the swearer, the liar, the thief, and the adulterer. Your Chamber of Imagery is there, in which all your Images are hid; your garments which you have stole in the night is laid up there; Your confused Languages, and all your stuff which proceeds out of the vessels which are dishonorable, that's your store-house, the curse is entered into the midst of it, and will consume the timber thereof, and the stones thereof, the materials; the fire must consume your fenced Wall, and your high Tower is for a throwing down; I have seen it, and therefore, in truth can witness it, the very ground it stands on must know a remove; your high things have deceived the simple, and You also; they that live in the day, see You and your building; its Babel, that's not Sion whose Walls and Bulwarks are Salvation; and this I affirm and witness, That none shall ever see the glorious City, but as they witness the Walls and Bulwarks.

Now all you who are boasting in other mens lines above the cross, you of all other people like not to stand in it, and so notwithstanding all your high words, you are out of the power, *(page 10)* in the alienation, out from the life of God, in the lying Wonders; for what some of you saw when you were waiting in the light, you are now bringing forth in your wills, and the Word of the Lord is betrayed by your subtilty & by your airie minds, which hath carryed you so far above the light, that you see not what it is that betraies you, and you are lying down at ease in a habitation which is not eternal, but are Vagrants, having no habitation in God: What's become of the righteous Seed? the blood of it cryes up in the ear of the Lord; many of you are darker then *Cain* was when he had slain his Brother; it were well if you could bow down to that which would bring you to a sence of your condition, and leave teaching of others, and looking out for a high appearance, you are deceived, and deceiving others; your expectations are all in the vanity; it's the little thing that's under all this, must restore you; so wait and watch continually to come down to that which suffers in you, and see if you can suffer with it, and wait to know whether your faces be turned toward Sion or no, and to hear the voice of the Lord calling every one in the particular, Where art thou? Alack for you! they that know the just and equal ballance, find you too light; you are to be singled out one by one to judgement, for thither must you come again if ever that be cast off which is above; you will find it hard to that mind which is so high, to bow down to it; *Moses*, and the Prophets, & *John* hath been, & is too low a thing for your eye to look after; but had you been faithful to the least of these, you had not lost your measure; the patient long suffering of God let it lead you to repentance, and so come down to the Witness, that you may see what is good, & what is evil, that you may no more be deceived nor deceive, with a seeming good, that hath a certain evil in it.

So to the light of Christ I commend you and all people upon the face of the whole Earth, that in it you may see the devourer and the murtherer, and what it is that talks of life, and yet is slaying of it: Oh! love truth and its Testimony, whether its Witness be to you, or against you, love it, that into my Mothers house you all may come, and into the Chamber of her that conceived me, where you may embrace, and be embraced of my dearly beloved one, Love is his Name, Love is his Nature, Love *(page 11)* is his life, surelie he is the dearest and the fairest; the fool hath said in his heart he is not, he can neither see him, nor know him; the wise mans Wisdom is in enmity against him; the rich are too full, there's no room for him; the Foxes have holes, and the birds of the air have Nests, but the Son of man hath not where to lay his head; the strong man offers violence against him, he is light, and in him is no darkness at all; yet will the darkness strive with him, turn from him, and stumble at him; readie are all sorts of people to receive the same of him, but few love his reprovings, turn in to him, and believe in him: Oh thou beloved of my Father, that art descended under all, that thou maist gather in all! how art thou become light in darkness, strength in and through weakness, Wisdom in and through foolishness; life in death, that through death life again may be witnessed among the sons and daughters of men: And I bring in my Testimony, *That he is the true light which lighteth every one that cometh into the world:* Love that Spirit that brings to lye at his feet, that with it you may return into his bosome, which is the desire of my heart to the mighty God of Jacob for you all.

Man looking forth after a beautiful thing which was likely to make him wise, (seemingly good for Food) thus came to lose his innocent state; Man feeding upon the forbidden food, in the day that he eat thereof, died, is now driven from the presence of the Lord, and the Tree of life he may not touch, the flaming Sword stands to cut him down which way soever he turns, and the eye being made blind which should let him see his state, he is become wholly miserable, and death reigns over him; and having lost his Guide, he is turned into a path in which he is running further and further from the Lord, into the earthlie, and there he abides captivated, and under strong bonds fettered: Yet doth the Lord so love the World, that he hath given his only begotten, that all men through him might believe: And now every one having received a measure of his life, this stands an everlasting Witness for God in man, and this God hath given him to profit withall, but the sloathful hides it in the Earth, and makes no improvement of it, and so remains ignorant of Gods *(page 12)* gift, and of the Waie that should lead him back again to God; and though the light shines in darkness, the darkness comprehends it not, and the ear remains stopped which should hear the voice that calls to him to return again, and would let him know, that as through death he went forth, so through death to that death he must return again; that which shines in darkness to him, would soon let him see his lost estate if minded; it is one thing to talk of it, and another thing to see it; death may talk of it, but it is the shining light that shows it, through which alone man must come to be convinced; and as it is loved, believed in, and obeyed, man will come to know it to be his Leader, and a Light to him, in which he may see the Seed of the Woman, and the Seed of the Serpent, and their several natures and workings, and to see what birth each of these bring forth; the Wombs they are conceived in, which it is that bears, and which it is that is barren; which it is that is to be made to bear again, and which it is that is to be made barren again; for though these two Seeds be in man, yet have they their several natures and opperations; the one brings forth to the earthly, and begets into the death, the other into the heavenly, and begets to life.

Now every one minding their measure of light, shall come to know as they are known, and to see as they are seen; and here a separation comes to be witnessed, and man begins to see what stands in death, and what in life eternal; for having a light which makes all manifest, thus man comes to see how all likenesses is come in, and now man being convinced and checked when any thing is wrought or acted in that nature wherein death reigns, then Gods Witness which stands in the divine nature, checks and reproves: And man running from this turns into the other, and so joins with the transgressor, and then will be making promises of being better, and complains that he wants power, and so tempts the Lord, this nature may bring forth a likeness of all Graces, and of all Gifts, and give up the body to be burnt, but it avails him nothing. Now every one who loves Gods Witness, and is joined to it, shall know the power of God which gives dominion over the sinful nature, and leads into a Saviour, and here man shall see *(page 13)* Christ Jesus as near him, to save him, as the Devil is near to tempt him, and shall come to know every motion and thought of his heart, from whence it springs, and to know certainly where his hope stands, and how he comes by it, and the faith of the Son of God, and when it is delivered, and how to contend for it, and to see all his Works, and where they stand, and be made able to discern of spirits, whether good or evil, and to judge of them, and so grow up in the light, unto that state which once was witnessed, and beyond it: Therefore every one prise that which leads to it.

The End.

Thefe feveral

PAPERS

Was fent to the

PARLIAMENT

The twentieth day of the fifth Moneth, 1659. Being
above feven thoufand of the Names of the

HAND-MAIDS

AND

DAUGHTERS

OF THE

LORD,

And fuch as feels the oppreffion of Tithes, in the
names of many more of the faid HANDMAIDS
and DAUGHTERS of the LORD, who witnefs
againft the oppreffion of Tithes and
other things as followeth.

LONDON,
Printed for *Mary Weftwood*, and are to be fold
at the *Black-fpread Eagle* at the Weft end
of *Pauls*, 1659.

(Page numbers of original document appear in text as *page _.*)

TO THE

READER.

FRIENDS,

IT *may seem strange to some that women should appear in so publick a manner, in a matter of so great concernment as this of* Tithes, *and that we also should bring in our testimony even as our brethren against that Anti-christian law and oppression of* Tithes, *by which many of the Servants of the Lord have suffered in filthy holes and dungeons until death; But let such know, that this is the work of the Lord at this day, even by weak means to bring to pass his mighty work in the earth, that all flesh may be silent, and the Lord alone may be exalted in them who can truly say,* Now I live, yet not I, but Christ liveth in me, and the life that I now live is by the faith of the Son of God, *which faith overcometh the world, through which faith the Saints and faithful of old* subdued Kingdoms, wrought righteousness, claimed the promises; *'Tis true, we have need of patience, that after we have done the will of God we may inherit it,* but he that shall come will come and will not tarry; *Behold our God is appearing for us, and they that be in the light may see him,* choosing the foolish things of the World to confound the wise, weak things to confound the Mighty, vile things, and things that are despised *hath God chosen, ye and* things which are not, to bring to nought things which are; *Surely the Lord is risen, he is risen indeed and hath appeared unto many, he is also ascended and is taking to himself his great power, he is owning and will own his spouse, his Church which hath long lain desolate and afflicted. But now arise and shine O daughter of* Sion, *shake thy self from thy dust, put on thy beautifull garments, for thy Maker is thy husband, the holy One of* Israel, *and he will plead thy cause, and the Mountains of the Lord shall be exalted on the tops of all Mountains; and as he is risen in us, and become our first fruits unto God, so is he also risen for us even to cast out* *all our enemies, to bring down every high thing within us and with-out, that exalteth itself against him,* and he shall ride on conquering, and to conquer till *he hath subdued all our enemies, that God alone may rule and rain, and herein lies our strength, even in the power of our God, in it we can stand still and behold the salvation that he will bring to pass* even for us, *and here shall we be hid, while all calami-ties that shall surely come upon the enemies of the truth be overpast. And while we rest under the shadow of his wings we are safe, rejoycing in his will, and in every thing giving thanks, knowing it is his will in Christ Jesus concerning us; and in this let us testifie our Saint-ship to the World, even by our obedience to his will in all things, by living in his fear and to his praise all our dayes; and herein she desires to be found, who is called,*

Mary Forſter.

(page 1)

To the Parliament of England, *who are set in place to do juſtice, to take off oppression, and to ſtop the oppreſſors.*

WE whose hands are hereunder written do testifie and declare against the oppression of Tithes, and against the injustice of them, which hath come up since the dayes of the Apostles in the Apostacy, and set up by the commands and laws of men, the author of which was the Pope; and such as were got up since the dayes of the Apostles, both out of the power of God and Christ; for the Priesthood which was made by the Law of God had a command according to the Law of God to take Tithes, and is disannulled and changed, and God never gave forth a command, after he disannulled the first, that Tithes should be taken again; these Tithes have been set up by the Papists since the Apostles, who witnessed the command of God disannulled, *Heb.* 7. and all the Scriptures proves Tithes to the Jewes, but not to the Christians, and the law-books proves tithes set up by the Pope (since the dayes of the Apostles, and not by the Christians in the Apostles times) and he was the first author of them, and so by a persecuting usuped authority were they set up since the Apostles, whereby many have *(page 2)* been prisoned till death for not paying of them, and many have had most of their goods spoiled by Priests and impropriators that have brought up in Sessions and courts for conscience sake, because they cannot pay Tithes, as knowing the command of God is disanulled, that gave tithe, and the Law is changed by which the priest-hood was made, and the Priesthood also that took them, and since that time hath the laws of men, and the commands of men been set up, by the Apostates, Papists, from the Apostles, by their law spoiled mens goods that cannot observe the Law and command that gives Tithes, of them that have taken treble Tithes, and treble; therefore these things are laid before you, that you may consider by what power you act, whether by the power that set up tithes; if so, then we can but look for oppression, prisoning till death, persecution, spoiling of mens goods, haling up and down before Courts, and still an encrease of persecution; But this we say, if you, or whosoever do come into the power of God, you will say, with us, that this commandment of men set up by them the

Apostates that be in the form of godliness and denys the power that gives Tithes, it must be disanulled. These false Christians hath set up a Law and a commandment to take Tithes of their own since the true Christians and dayes of the Apostles did witness and say the command of God was disanulled that gave Tithes, so must the commands of men be held up that gives Tithes, & the commands of God disobeyed which first gave them to the Jews, and the true Christians witnesse *(page 3)* the end of, and must not the commands of men be disanulled that takes Tithes as well as the command of God? *Heb.* 7. so who be in the Covenant of God, the Covenant of life witness the end of the command of God to the Jews that gave Tithes, and so the commands of men must be dis-annulled that take tithes, and not be obeyed by them that live in the Covenant of God? Now if you act in the same power that hath held up tithes since the Apostles days, which hath taken away many of our friends lives, that hath been Prisoned till death, in nasty holes and corners, for bearing their Testimony against that unjust oppression of tithes, and the unjust power that held them up, and Priests and impropriators, and the Law and command, and the Author of it not to be of God nor of Christ, seeing Christ disanul'd the commandment of God that give tithes, and this command hath been set up by the superstitious Papist, who was the first author of them; Therefore what havock, what spoiling of Goods, and peoples estates taken away by the Priests impropriators, worse then ever the plundering Cavilleers? and what prisoning, what haling into Courts and Sessions people all about the Nation there is, and chiefly about these Tithes? and how many of their lives have been a testimony against it, and ended their lives in nasty holes and dungeons, for their Testimony against Tithes? therefore for us to be clear of your blood, and not to be guilty of innocent blood, we lay these things upon you, that if any be prisoned to death, as very many have been in these Nations, by Priests and impropriators, that we shall be clear in the sight *(page 4)* of God and have forewarned you, and let their blood be upon you, who are in the place to do Justice, and to take off oppression which you may do while you have time, if you live in the power of God; and let not the Nation be ruined, and people prisoned to death, and the blood of the innocent be drunken, as abundance of it hath been within these few years, which lies upon the heads of some; Therefore keep it clear from off your own heads, we warn you which to you is the word of the Lord God; there are many in the Prison at this day in nasty Goals, bearing their testimony for the Lord Jesus Christ (that disanulled the command that gave Tithes) against the commands of men set up in opposition to him since the dayes of the Apostles, who witnesses the command of God disanulled that gave Tithes.

So here are our hands and Testimony to you now, not that we are weary of suffering and of Imprisonment, nor cry to you for help, but because the blood of our brethren hath been spilt, and also many thousands have had their goods spoyled and taken away, and many of the Imprisonned to death, whose blood lies upon the heads of their persecutors, but it is that you may keep your selves from blood, and stop the oppressors that causeth it, and so keep the Nation from the plagues and judgments of God, and your selves also, that you be not rooted out and cast by, by the power of the Lord God, for not doing Justice, and not relieving the oppressed, as many have been before you, and suffering his Lamb and babes and servant, their blood to be shed for bearing their Testemony [sic], *(page 5)* and suffering their goods to be spoyled, so as you are in the power of God, you will throw down the power of the Papists in these Nations, that set up tithes, and then through that power that throws them down will you come over the tyranicall oppressing power of the Papist, to live in the Power of God, which the Apostles were in before the Papist came up, and the Lawes and commandment that upholds them.

That all forced maintenance of the Priests be taken away, for while such a thing is set up, it will spoyle many idle men that will not thresh nor plant, nor dig, nor make Vineyards, and will not Plow nor Sow, that they may Reap, neither will they preach the Gospel that they may live, and these are never like to plant Vineyards, but such as are fat and lazie they will run for forced maintenance to you, and these spoyle a Nation, and keeps it from being a free Nation, and a free Ministry, and keeps the people from being a free people, and these are the filthy beasts that would have the mouth of the Lord stopped, and teaches for filthy lucre, and admires mens persons because of advantage.

And such there were in the dayes of the Apostles before these tithes came up, by the Law and commandment of men among the Papists, since the command and Law of God was denied, therefore after you have taken away tithes and forced maintenance, which is set up, and is not like the Apostles, but like such as teach for filthy lucre, you enquire what you shall do then, (well) let every one plant that they may reap, and let every one *(page 6)* sow spiritual things that they may reap carnal, and let them preach the Gospel, that they may live of it, and that is our hearts desire, and the spoyling of our goods and our brethren that hath been Prisoned to death for not paying tithes, is our Testimony to all the

world, that it is not for covetousness sake that they suffer, but for conscience, and for truth and Righteousness, and that shall be answered to
the witness of God in every one of your consciences, yea, and to the
witness of God in all our oppressors, (whether it be Priest or Impropriator,
or Lawyer, that hath bought tithes) who for conscience sake we cannot
pay them, but say his Commandment must be disanulled, that gives
them tithes, as well as the command of God which is disanulled by
Christ; and this we suffer with our lives and estates.

(page 7) We who are of the Seed of the Woman, which bruiseth the Serpents head, to which the Promise is, Christ Jesus in the Male and in the
Female, which is the Everlasting Priest, not after the Order of *Aaron*,
which took Tithes, nor of the Tribe of *Levi*, but of the Tribe of *Judah*,
and who is a Priest for ever, made by the Oath of God, after the Order
of *Melchizedech*, and remains a Priest continually; And therefore can
we set our hearts and hands against *Aarons* Order, which is disanulled,
and the Law changed, and do bear our Testimony, that Christ Jesus the
Everlasting Priest is come.

Margret Fell, senior
Margret Fell, junior
Bridget Fell
Isabel Fell
Sarah Fell
Mary Fell
Susanna Fell
Rachel Fell
Mary Askey
Ester Benson
Jane Jakes
Mabel Warner
Elizabeth Walker
Jenet Jeats
Agnus Sponder
Mary Peper
Elin Towenson
Anne Colinson
Anne Bateman
Dorothy Maskew
Margret Denison
Agnus Bank
Anne Dogson
Margret Denison

Anne Wilson
Eliz. Kitchin
Elin Newbie
Eliz. Newbie
Agnus Newbie
Elin Newbie
Jane Chester
Elin Muckelt
Margret Idle
Isabel Stephenson
Margan Shepherd
Anne Rawes
Jane Lancaster
Isabil Grave
Eliz. Sewart
Margret Thomson
Anne Brigs
Agnus Thomson
Isabel Wilson
Margret Clark
Jane Halehead
Janet Bateman
Dorothy Bateman
Mary Bateman
Dorothy Bateman

Angus Brown
Mabel Wilson
Isabel Garnet
Rebecca Storey
Jane Thomson
Agnus Wilson
Isabel Berk
Elizabeth Newbie
Dorothy Ducket
Elizabeth Simpson
Mabel Moor
Eliz. Moor
Margret Moor
Elin Rigge
Elizabeth Heline
Mabel Came
Dorothy Lorimer
Margret Wharton
Isabel Storey
Eliz. Lonsdal
Eliz. Rigg
Margret Thompson
Eling Came
Eliz. Rigge
Margret Thompson

(page 8)
Eling Came
Anne Thompson
Agnus Sill
Eliz. Hireson
Eliz. Maskel
Anne Came
Anne Heline
Eliz. Wharbrab
Dorothy Middleton
Eliz. Wison
Christobel Suttoris
Agnus Atkinson
Eliz. Maning
Eliz. Bamgrigge
Esabel Harling
Eliz. Thompson
Margret Moon
Isabel Backhouse
Margret Smith
Mary Wilson
Margret Sale
Barbrey Thompson, elder

Barbry Thompson, younger
Mary Park
Jane Johnson
Isabel Dogson
Jan Wison
Agnus Moor
Agnus Hutton
Eling Warriner
Agnus Howsman
Jenet Hinde
Mabel Mansergh
Dorothy Powe
Eling Howsman
Eliz. Howsman

Mabel Thompson
Alize Thompson
Isabel Thompson
Eliz. Cartmel
Bridget Gregge
Francis Preston
Bridget Came
Sarah Came
Margret Store
Mary Dodin
Elizabel Rigge
Eliz. Sadler
Eliz. Sewert
Eliz. Backhouse
Agnus Wharton

Alice Green
Isabel Adlington
Em. Smith
Margret Smith
Agnus Holey
Margret Cocke
Agnus Cock
Eliz. Show
Eliz. Bateman
Margret Phleming
Elin Sands
Mary Colinson
Anne Vaugh
Dorothy Vaugh
Jane Dawson

Eliz. Dawson
Eliz. Edrington
Eliz. Edrington
Dorothy Wilkinson
Dorothy Storey
Agnus Storey
Margret Beck
Agnus Whitehead
Sarah Benson
Mary Benson
Dorothy Benson
Margret Benson
Eliz. Benson
Katherine Benson

Women, Friends that have given their Testimony against the oppression of Tithes into the North part of

LANCASHIRE.

Margret Fell
Bridget Fell
Sarah Fell
Alice Corber
Mary Corber
Susanna Ormandy
Jane Wildman
Isabel Wilson
Eliz. Asburner
Margret Clayton
Rosemond Benson
Annas Fell
Alice Chambers
Eliz. Milner
Frances Hale
Dorothy Chambers
Izabel Yeates
Eliz. Kirkby

(page 9)
Jane Kirkby
Eliz. Walker
Dorothy Hutton

Jane Holme
Eliz. Park
Alice Fell
Frances Sharp
Margret Myers
Ann Harrison
Eliz. Stubbs
Ann Dixon
Jane Milner
Ann Jackes
Eliz. Bowes
Margret Kirkby
Eliz. Kirkby
Eliz. Myers
Margret Fell
Ann Ocandy
Alice Ceuper
Barba Ormondy
Jenet Fisher
Alice Curmen
Alice Goad
Izabell Birket
Mary Fell

Eliz. Saltas
Alice Milner
Eliz. Milner
Margret Cleaton
Margret Lancaster
Elizabeth Adison
Jane Symetson
Ann Rig
Margret Rig
Annas Braythwaite
Dorothy Braythwaite
Margret Braythwait
Mary Benson
Dorothy Benson
Jane Benson
Elizabeth Benson
Dorothy Brugthwait
Dorothy Saterthwait
Dorothy Braithwait
Dorothy

Saterthwait
Elin Atkinson
Elizabeth Wilson
Jane Walker
Jane Walker
Annas Penington
Annas Walker
Elizabeth Beck
Margret Walker
Barbary Benson
Dorothy Braithwait
Agnes Rig
Ann Ayray
Grace Crackenthrop
Grace Whitehead
Agnes Whinfield
Mary Ayray
Jenet Whitehead
Elizabeth Whitehead
Jenet Adkinson

Margret Bownes
Grace Barwick
Elizabeth Barwick
Ellinor Cloudsdall
Elizabeth Gibson
Ann Ayray
Kathrine Wilson
Frances Lawson
Izabell Fallowfield
Frances Steavenson
Marg. Fallowfield
Cisely Stevenson
Mary Sobinson
Frances Gilson
Jane Briham
Frances Hebson
Mary Holme
Jane Winter
Margeret Wharton
Elizabeth Holm
Jenet Smith
Margeret Smith
Sarah Smith
Izabell Holme
Annas Smith
Anas Teusdall
Margeret Smith
Annas Wilson
Mabell Bland
Mary Bland
Mabell Robinson
Barby Robinson
Jenet Denkin
Elizabeth Hebson
Elizabeth Wilson
Elizabeth Morland
Margeret Bland
Elizabeth Morland
Margeret Bland
Elizabeth Bland
Elizabeth Robinson
Annis Robinson
Jane Holme
Annas Licock
Izabell Hoglethrop
Annas Holm
Elizabeth Coupland

Elizabeth Winter
Eliz. Crackenthrop
Elizabeth Bird
Margeret Simpson

(page 10)
Eliz. Budd
Margaret Sympson
Francis Sympson
Mary Hinde
Izabel Holm
Anne Thompson
Margret Weaver
Anne Stubbs
Mary Brief
Jennet Jenkinson
Jane Dickinson
Ellin Feeler
Dorothy Bains
Margret Shearson
Eliz. Walker
Anne Holm
Anne Waling
Ellen Cunning
Eliz. Bond
Eliz. Harthwait
Eliz. Bains
Katherine Lond
Margret Wilson
Jennet Robbinson
Jane Thomson
Anne Cornbut
Margret Bond
Margret Hind
Agnus Moor
Margret Lucas
Anne Willan
Jane Hadan
Agnus Wethman
Agnus Worsley
Ellen Clarkson
Margret Turner
Isabel Turner
Isabel Kilner
Isabel Oulson
Margret Haden
Jane Huberthorn

Eliz. Robbinson
Ellen Wonn
Ester Leaper
Margret Leaper
Ellen Holm
Sarah Backhouse
Mary Beakon
Eliz. Thompson
Eliz. Thoming
Eliz. Burrough
Margret Besbrown
Mary Besbrown
Ellin Towming
Mary Cocking
Jane Corley
Math. Croft
Eliz. Hardwin
Jane Dorthwait
Eliz. Slouth
Jane Wilder
Agnus Markdal
Eliz. Fell
Mary Fleming
Margret Robbinson
Jane Wilson
Dorothy Pearson
Eliz. Pearson
Isabel Stuckled
Jennet Dickison
Alice Barrow
Ellin Park
Alice Raskel
Mary Toweson
Agnus Dibson
Kath. Clow
Eliz. Dobson
Agnus Graton
Eliz. Tomson
Ellen Thornow
Eliz. Thornol
Eliz. Bradshaw
Ellen Bark
Anne Arnan
Emery Johnson
Margret Bradshaw
Margret Puling
Jane More

Anne Park
Mary Rood
Alice Carter
Agnes Thomson
Ellin Sander
Emery Carter
Alice Archer
Margret Carter
Agnus Carter
Anne Gaunt
Margret Sonten
Jane Salthouse
Alice Singleton
Agnus Bradshaw
Ellen Park
Agnus Riskel
Mary Thompson
Agnus Dobson
Margret Dawreg
Agnus Malor
Eliz. Thompson
Ellen Thomer
Eliz. Thorner
Eliz. Bradshaw
Ellen Park
Alice Arman
Emery Jackson
Margret Bradshaw
Margret Puling

(page 11)
Jane Moor
Anne Park
Mary Rood
Alice Carter
Anna Thompson
Ellen Sander
Emery Cater
Margret Thorner
Ellen Cater
Jennet Carter
Agnus Cater
Anne Gaunt
Margret Sonton
Ellen Butler
Jane Salthouse
Alice Singleton

Agnus Breadshaw
Eliz. Tayliar
Ellen Hatton
Grace Forster
Alice Kay
Alice Smallshaw
Cicily Croper
Cicily Ascroft
Isabel Tayliar
Ellen Charles
Dorothy Wilding
Eliz. Tarlton
Edith Webster
Anne Pike
Margery Swift
Kath. Tatlock
Anne Rymmer
Dorothy
  Letherbarrow
Alice Aspinwall
Ellen White
Gennet Watson
Isabel Ambrose
Alice Ambrose
Isabel Moon
Ellin Tomlinson
Ellen Brewer
Margret
  Thompson
Eliz. Thompson
Mary Thompson
Eliz. Butler
Ellen Parkenson
Bridget Parkinson
Jennet Kirby
Marg. Eckles
Anne Smith
Ellen Tompson
J. Ashton
T. Chadock
H. Seston
E. Seston
E. Lyon
R. Wetherby
L. Hey
R. Hey
E. Bispem

R. Letherbarow
H. Letherbarow
J. Bispham
J. Lyon
R. Lyon
H. Martland
R. Webster
A. Hadock
G. Pye
J. Underwood
J. Dick
R. Johnson
J. Smalshaw
W. Longley
J. Pye
P. Westhead
A. Wetherby
P. Leadbeter
W. Bower
R. Longley
T. Fearnes
G. Barrow
G. Atherton
O. Atherton
T. Roofe
T. Atherton
H. Foster
J. Martland
R. Cubham
R. Hunter
Mary Sutton
Anne Keniby
Ellin Hodgkinson
Hannah Keniby
Margret Ashton
Mary Johnson
Deborah Lyon
Jane Letherbarow
Allis Letherbarow
Margret Lyon
Eliz. Leadebetter
Magret Pye
Margret
  Underwood
Jane Johnson
Mary Haylewood
Mary Sm[ ]ken

Elizabeth
  Gilbertson
Mary Leadbetter
Mary Underwood
Mary Lyon
Anne Bispom
Mary Foster
Jane Dicke
Jane Fearnes
Dorothy Barrow
Anne Letherbarow

(page 12)
Ann Atherton
Elizabeth Hunter
Margeret Atherton
Ellin Johnson
Edith Hilton
Ellin Smalshaw
Margeret Kendall
Mary Kendall
Mary Taylor
Elin Atherton
Allis Lyon
Sarah Lyon
R. Watmough
J. Kirkes
J. Tarlton
W. Bootle
H. Haugraice
J. Ashton
W. Harison
J. Fletcher
J. Tarlton
B. Boult
P. Leithwait
W. Hutton
G. Hindly
W. Griffith
G. Lyon
R. Litherland
Katherin Stockley
Margret Kerkes
Jane Turlton
Mary Boult
Alice Hatton
Jane Young

Margret Plumton
Alice Meddow
Grace Hindly
Margret Brindle
Margret Stretch
Rebecka Griffith
Alice Leithwaith
Alice Hide
Izabell Marrow
Mary Kenrick
Elizabeth
  Darbishire
Elin Hatton
Mary Linicar
Mary Knowles
Alice Ricroft
Elizabeth Ricroft
Ann Bootle
Ann Lyon
Elin Wessle
Margret Caldwall
Mary Souste
Alice Southworth
Mary Southworth
Margret Hallwood
Mary Millit
Katherin
  Croudson
Susana Croudson
Sara Cocker
Ann Ashton
Mary Marsh
Isabell Earle
Elin Earle
Alice Lancaster
Iane Quitquit
Ann Clear
Katherin
  Holebrook
Sarah Holobrook
Jane Benniton
Mary Cocker
Ann Mason
Margret Seddow
Mary Seddow
Jane Beniton
Margret Marsh

Ann Barnes
Mary Sharrock
Margret Barnes
Jane Earle
Mary Minchall
Elizabeth Minchall
Margret Minchall
Jane Towers
Katherin Taylor
Elin Bownes
Ann Holbrook
Ann Helwood
Susan Parker

Margret Earle
Allis Peubeth
Allis Hold
Jane Wilkinson
Elizabeth Fothergil
Ann Bowfield
Isabel Handly
Elizabeth Bowvel
Elizabeth Laidman
Elizabeth
  Creighton
Isabel Saffe
Ann Wright

Annas Crosdale
Isabel Holm
Elizabeth Crosdale
Jane Pinder
Ann Pinder
Babel Gibson
Elizabeth Fawcet
Jane Walker
Margret Pinder
Ezab. Fawcet
Annas
  Thornborough

Dorothy Knewstop
Annas Thompson
Mable Scafe

(page 13)
Eliz. Murthwaite
Mary Cleasby
Elizabeth Ayray
Jane Bouscald
Margeret Lamb
Mary Scafe

Northumberland, **and other parts,** To the Parliament
of *England, &c.*

Jane Watson
Elizabeth Watson
Mary Dawson
Elizabeth Whitfield
Iane Whitfield
Iane Younger
Alice Braidwood
Barb. Bee
Iane Davison
Elizabeth Shield
Ann Shield
Mary Shield
Margret Rowell
Anne Harbottle
Elizabeth Catsforth
Mary Spark
Anne Shield
Mary Farlam
Iane Williamston
Elizabeth
  Hutchinson
Anne Dawson
Mary Williamston
Elizabeth Neving
Margret Moor
Alice Brown

Anne Coleson
Anne Featherstone
Margret Bee
Mary Charles
Mary Boldock
Alice Burre
Susan
  Whitingstald
Dorothy Geurney
Frances Field
Anne Philip
Ursula Spencer
Elizabeth Helder
Sarah Burst
Elizabeth Robberts
Sarah Burre
Susanna Randol
Susanna Pareman
Anne Charles
Mary Charles
Cesle Hanken
Elizabeth Cook
Ellen Dunn
Elizabeth Wood
Mary North
Mary Exton

Prudence Joyce
Anne Starton
Mary Thompson
Mary Charles
Mary Godfeer
Elizabeth Mennord
Anne Stapelton
Sara Kingsley
Mary Bardwel
Anne Finch
Grace Chaklee
Margret Exton
Anne Wennuem
Jone Fisher
Anne Goodyear
Jane Jeynes
Ione Thoms
Elizabeth Thoms
Elizabeth Walker
Isabel Portor
Sara Sismore
Alice Underhil
Anna Okey
Elizabeth Haukins
Mary Fisher
Meriam Moss

Mary Ward
Hester Underhil
Iame Pullar
Anne Dobbins
Susan [ ]opcot
Alice Jefferis
Patience Alcock
Comfort Alcock
Hannah Ward
Barbara Moss
Ursulah Ward
Iane Cart
Gayes Band

(page 14)
Alice Fox
Anne Surman
Mary Surman
Elizabeth Hopcot
Elizabeth White
Margret Cook
Maxet Robeson
Jone Bene
Mary Woolman
Alice Gregry
Mary Maybifield

Alice Meral
Margret King
Alice Elise
Elin Sizmore
Rebecca Sizmore
Ann Rickels, youn.
Alies King
Anne Sanford
Hannah Levite
Priscilla Trotman
Sarah Sturmy
Sarah Hayerd
Elizabeth Joynes
Elizabeth Maies
Luce Goldson
Mary Whighthead
Elizabeth Enger

Susan Clippon
Elizabeth
  Chitcherly
Grace Burvey
Anne Burvey
Mary Baies
Jacobin Baies
Anne Folkes
Alice Offel
Elizabeth Burbey
Mercy Pedley
Anne Wilmott
Ellen Harwood
Marget Harwood
Anne Barber
Elizabeth Brett

Alice Brett
Frances Hagger
Anne Askby
Mary Hagger
Dorothy
  Thorrowgood
Ellen Rumbal
Elizabeth Westropp
Mary Stompford
Mary Asswel
Elizabeth Hughes
Sara Siser
Blanch Baggley
Prscillia Baggley
Anne Hagger
Grace Withon

Blanch Sutton
Jone Wilton
Mallun Harvy
Jone Preacher
Fastie Gibson
Annis Dennis
Anne Waler
Marget Hank
Ellen Ihand
Elizabeth Porter
Elizabeth Suttin
Jone Smith
Sarah Pattin
Elizabeth Hagger
Grace Hagger
Abarry Nodes

CUMBELAND.

ANne Fletcher
Jane Gibson
Elinor Sargin
Elizabeth Sargin
Jane Couk
Jane Sargin
Anne Pearson
Frances Palmer
Jane Hall
Anne Palmer
Elizabeth Fearron
Elizabeth Hall
Marget Ashley
Anne Dalton
Anne Mordin
Anne Fearon
Jane Huton
Dorothy Smith
Mary Smith
Anne Benson
Anne Spensor
Jane Palmer
Jane Robbinson
Anne Keay
Jane Pearson

Elizabeth Pearson
Jane Wilson
Mary Palmer
Isabel Shepherd
Marget Curwen
Anne Thumkalt
Ellin Read
Elizabeth Wilson
Ellin Bell

(page 15)
Elizabeth Ribton
Margret Threlkelt
Joyce Davis
Margret Sibsor
Mary Bowman
Jane Barker
Frances Parker
Elizabeth Coultert
Jane Dixson
Jane Whiteside
Bridget Stamper
Jane Caipe
Agnes Nickelson
Agnes Stricket

Jane Seot
Jane Relfe
Agnes Williamson
Margret Atkinson
Mary Fosken
Eliner Grainger
Mary Grainger
Margret Bewly
Jane Wilson
Mabel Fasken
Mabel Scot
Elizabeth Banks
Agnes Ritson
Margret Parker
Agnes Scot
Mabel Kingston
Jane Hodgin
Mary Sivitwaire
Jane Hasken
Jane Hasken
Isabell Scot
Katheren Ritson
Jane Relfe
Elizabeth Banks
Isabel Peacock

Agnes Fisher
Mary Fisher
Mabel Williamson
Jane Pearson
Jane Ardall
Elizabeth Slamper
Elin Plasket
Elizabeth Irton
Jane Tonter
Jane Pingry
Jane Scot
Mary Scot
Katherin Fell
Isabell Boraskil
Dorothy Simpson
Madglen Foraskill
Anne Dine
Anne Dodgin
Jane Bushby
Margret Aplbey
Elizabeth Weston
Margret Scot
Ann Person
Jane Hewetson
Frances Simpson

Isabel Buntin
Ann Carter
Isabel Suel
Jenet Watson
Isabel Fisher
Jane Fisher
Margret Grig
Jenet Johnson
Susan Sutherswait
Jenet Wilson
Mary Faucet
Isabel Nelson
Margret Fawcet
Elin Head
Frances Allinson
Jenet Allason
Jenet Allason
Jenet Allason
Elin Liteldale
Margret Jackson
Agnes Wodell
Mary Dawson
Margret Walker
Margret Mark
Jane Welling
Agnes Mark
Agnes Mark
Margret Dawson
Margret Dawson
Agnes Smith
Margret Mark
Isabel Mark
Frances Gaskath
Margret Hodgson
Jane Hodgson
Isabel Hodgson
Mabel Wharton
Mary Wharton
Elizabeth Banks
Ann Harrison
Isabell Toppin
Elizabeth Bone
Jane Stables
Agnes Pattinson
Mabel Ridgland
Agnes Nickelson
Agnes Robinson

Mary Robinson
Jane Henderson
Margret Pattinson
Jenet Blylock
Jenet Gibson
Jane Taylor

(page 16)
Elizabeth Taylor
Katherin Pearson
Jenet Godfellow
Isabel Godfellow
Margret Palmer
Agness Summers
Ayhs Summers
Elizabeth Summers
Modland Dixson
Elin Winyeat
Margret Harrison
Mary Sharp
Mary Wicklife
Agness Frear
Lucie Bell
Elin Simpson
Jenet Peel
Elin Pearson
Jane Dickinson
Ann Richinson
Isabel Maison
Mary Steele
Iasabel Fearon
Margret Willing
Agness Lowrance
Agness Allason
Margret
  Williamson
Jane Bell
Isabel Bell
Elizabeth Bell
Katherin Bell
Elizabeth Sumpton
Jane Pearson
Jenet Heston
Elizabeth Normand
Elizabeth Rodger
Jane Bank
Ann Bank

Ann Bell
Margret Fawcet
Ann Fisher
Ann Westray
Susana Bland
Elizab. Richardson
Ann Black-ston
Elizabeth Gibson
Elin Litleton
Jane Grave
Mary Bowman
Jane Basker
Frances Parker
Elizab. Conthwait
Jenet Wilson
Jenet Fearton
Jenet Willson
Isabel Robinson
Katherin Wilson
Elizabeth Rutson
Elin Bacon
Isabel Harris
Ann Harris
Isabel Harris
Mary Scraghum
Isabell Gill
Eliner Sheperd
Ann Hudson
Elizabeth Taylor
Frances Tarn
Elizabeth Dawson
Margret Collinson
Jane Readhead
Agnes Britch
Agnes Holm
Margret Sle
Isabel Sle
Agnes Sle
Mary Sle
Margret Todhunter
Mabell Peacock
Margret Grenhow
Frances Grenhow
Elizabeth Bewly
Elizabeth Mark
Jenet Mark
Elizabeth Todhunter

Agnes Cook
Agnes Sandwick
Margret Bristow
Jane Peacock
Mary Mark
Elizabeth Mark
Isabel Mark
Mabel Peacock
Agnes Peacock
Isabel Peacock
Mabel Gardhouse
Christian Watson
Barbaine Stony
Jenet Nikelson
Mary Milburn
Elizabeth Heath
Elizabeth
  Stevenson
Alice Nickelson
Dorothy Relfe
Jane Prestman
Agnes Prestman
Jane Slaughter
Margret Cook
Agnes Greenup
Mabel Fisher
Elizabeth
  Patrickson
Elizabeth Shippard
Mary Patrickson
Margret Fell
Grace Stalker
Mabel Caipe
Dorothy Bewly

(page 17)
Judeth Relf
Margret Walker
Jane Stamper
Jane Barwiss
Margret
  Richardson
Isabel Fell
Agnes Scot
Jenet Caip
Mabel Dixson
Jane Prestman

Agnes Fell
Jenet Caipe
Jane Hasken
Agnes Hasken
Jenet Scot
Jenet Disxon
Elizabeth
  Patrickson
Elizabeth Dalkon
Jane Head
Ann Maison
Jane Head
Frances Winder
Isabell Head
Magret Davis
Katherin Tolson
Ann Walker
Margret Robinson
Elizabeth Tolson
Jane Willigin
Margret Robinson
Ann Robinson
Isabell Head
Elizabeth Feron
Margret Fawcet
Margret Sergent
Elizabeth Lancaster
Ann Roger
Mary Fearon
Jenet Walker
Jenet Head
Elin Head
Elin Peile
Ann Head
Ann Dixson
Katherin Fisher
Elizabeth
  Wilkinson
Elin Whodhall
Jenet Dixson
Ann Dickinson
Ann Dixson
Elizabeth Winpeat

Ann Jackson
Margret Fletcher
Isabel Tiffin
Barbary Dawson
Jenet Fletcher
Alice Jolstock
Agnis Bowman
Margret Dickson
Eliner Freer
Isabel Heron(text
  unclear pos. "F")
Isabell Rodger
Elizabeth Rodger
Jane Jackson
Isabel Jackson
Elizabeth Harrison
Elizabeth Bowman
Eliner Dixson
Jane Dixson
Margret Robinson
Elizabeth Sturdy
Elizabeth Hodgson
Jane Reed
Ann Wilson
Agnes Harberson
Jane Ritson
Isabel Saule
Eliner Mark
Magdelen Potter
Mary Martin
Margret Martine
Dorothy Gibson
Jane Hodgson
Jane Gouldey
Agnes Robinson
Agnes Nickelson
Jane Tompson
Jane Atkinson
Mary Atkinson
Agnes Fisher
Judith Fisher
Jenet Goffray

Elizabeth Hadgan
Jane Fisher
Jenet Sherugam
Jane Saul
Elizabeth Saul
Mary Saul
Agnes Saul
Jane Hewet
Mary Messenger
Mary Laucack
Alice Lhamber
Mary Ritson
Agnes Cowen
Mary Wait
Dorothy Atkinson
Elizabeth Wait
Jane Atkinson
Jane Sp_ (text
  unclear pos. "ot")
Mary Atkinson
Elizabeth Grave
Elin Ritson
Jane Osburn
Eliza. Osmotherley
Frances
  Osmotherley
Jane Laucock
Jane Saul
Mabel Saul
Jenet Wilson

(page 18)

Elizabeth Willson
Dorothy Scragam
Mary Whinon
Elizabeth Hodgson
Elizabeth Wilson
Margret Wilson
Mary Wilson
Eliz. Baru
Mary Keedall
Mary Scrugman

Elizabeth Wilson
Frances Wilson
Mary Wilson
Margret Thrikbat
Widdow Wilson
Wid. Twentyman
Margret Wilson
Mary Coltart
Widdow Kickerby
Mabel Wilson
Agnes Him
Margret Fawcet
Mary Fearon
Dorothy Cook
Ann Beebe
Jennet Stubs
Mabell Caip
Jennet Facet
Dorothy Gill
Margret Johnson
Ann Wilson
Elizabeth Wilson
Ellin Emerson
Margret Fearon
Jennet Fearon
Jennet Salkeld
Jennet Robinson
Dorothy Salkelt
Dorothy Fisher
Katheren Peel
Elizabeth Allason
Ellen Allason
Agnes Liteldal
Iennet Marchel
Mary Christian
Elizabeth Salkeld
Margret Morgan
Win. Mordan
Isab. Young-
  husband
Agnes Thompson
Agnes Tempel

CHES-SHIRE.

To the Parliament of England, *&c. To do righteously, and to stop*
this unrighteous Ministry that makes havock, spoils mens goods,
and imprisons them, and persecutes them till death, for Tithes.

ALL Tithes since the fall that man was drove from God into
the Earth, false and true, set up by God and man; Tithes in
the War to *Melchizedeck*, the similitude like the Son of God, to which
Abraham paid the Tenths of the spoil; Tithes in the Law set up by the
Command of God for *Levi*, for Fatherless, for Widows, for strangers,
and preserved and kept in a Store-house, and Christ being come after
the Order of *Melchizedeck*, he maketh an end of all similitudes and likenesses, he ends the War and makes Peace on earth, and redeems out of
the fall and transgression, and destroyes the Devil the cause of War and
strifes, whereby he brings Peace on earth and reconciliation with God,
and all things in Heaven and things in earth, destroying the Devil the
author of transgression, that went out of truth, so leads into the Unity;
he it is, Christ, that ends the *(page 19)* Law, and ends the Priesthood
which takes away the Tithes, and the Commandment that gives them,
which is according to the Law that holds them up, and so redeems man
out of the Ninths of the earth, who ends the Priesthood, Law, Commandment and Store-house, for earthly things, that hath the Tenths,
whereby people come to know their Election before the World began,
and this we witness, drove from God, into the earth, up unto God again,
redeemed, out of the earth, up to God again, so we come out of the
Ninths and the Tenths which were offered up to God in the time of the
Law, so we come to know before the earth was, being in Christ by which
all things was made, to reign as Kings upon the earth, and Priests to
God; so man drove from God into the earth by transgression, man
brought to God out of the earth by Christ the Emanuel: a Virgin shall
have a Child, his Name shall be called Emanuel, his Interpretation is
known, which is, God with us, who hath known the time with God,
who ends the War, and ends the Law and similitudes, and figures, and
Priests, and Tithes, and Commands that gives them, and such as are
here in Christ are in the substance, and cannot hold up Tithes in the
War nor tithes in the Law, nor the Priest that takes them, nor they that
give them, but sees the end of the Law, and the Commandment by
which they are upheld, being in Christ the substance, and such holds
forth a Testimony against the contrary, that is, the Tithes in the War

and in the Law, and such knows the Election before the world began, and are out of the Ninths as well as the Tenths, and are out of the War, and knows the Kingdom that stands in Peace, and lives in the Peace, and knows the Peace on the earth, and good will towards men. So Tithes since the dayes of the Apostles in the Apostacy set up by the Pope the Papist, his Law and Command we utterly abhor, deny and detest against, which is a shame & abominable to be mentioned among them that are called Christians, and do see that they that give them, and they that take them are neither agreeable to Law nor Gospel, nor *Melchizedeck*, for the Law made provision for *Levi* and for all Strangers, Fatherless & Widows, that there need not be a begger in *Israel*; and *(page 20) Melchizedeck* took the Tenths of the spoil from *Abraham*, it is read he once did so, but you do not read that he took the Tenths of all the spoil of all the Wars of all Nations from the Souldiers, and the Gospel and they that preached it, which Christ sent forth in that time, when the Jewes Law was standing, and the Store house, and Tithes, and the Commandment; Christ did not send his Disciples with a Bagg to the Store-house, to take Tithes out of the Store-house, out of *Levies* maintenance, and Widows, Strangers and Fatherless, but sent them without a Bagg, and said, Freely ye have received, freely give; and enquire who is worthy, and what is set before you, that eat; And these that Christ sent forth, when they came back, Christ asked them, Wanted ye any thing? their answer was, they did not; so these planted Vineyards and eat the fruit, these got a Flock and eat the milk, they lived in the Gospel the power of God and preached it, and these brought people out of the Ninths, and ended the Tenths, and ended the Law, and the Commandment, and wrestled with that that caused the War, so trod out the Corn, threshed in hope, ploughed in hope, sowed spiritual things, reaped carnal things, and they that were taught in the Word communicated of those things to him that taught; so the teacher and the taught was in the Union, and they did not run unto the powers of the earth rawly for Tenths; Now Tenths are amongst them that are apostatized from the Apostles, and they have set up laws to give & take Tithes and treble dammage for Priests and Impropriators, and come with Troops of spoilers, with bills and staves, not like Preachers of the Gospel: but no Storehouse for Widows, for Strangers, for Fatherless, but all Countries and Cities are full of beggars, and streets and allies, and Steeple-house-doors, which is enough to make all them sick that fear the Lord, to see that Christianity should be worse then the Jews Law, and that they are neither agreeable to Law nor Gospel, nor Tithes in the War; So all Tithes we bear witness against, Tithes in the Law, Tithes in the War, and Tithes of Apostacy, who witness our Redemption out of the earth, and Election before the World began, and so reigns upon it afore Tithes of the War, and Law and Apostacy was, and transgression *(page 21)* both, and are redeemed out of it, who are in Covenant with God, and Peace with him.

And so we say, that all that Petition you for Tithes are Jewishly minded and Popishly affected, and are not the true Christians nor Christianly minded, and rather worse then the Jews, for they do not put the Tithes to the same use that the Jews did; and the Priests are all scandalous ministers, for they scandal their Master Christ, & their Lord, whom they pretend to serve in dishonoring him in seeking to you the Magistrates for their maintenance, as though Christ did not provide for his, and give them maintenance enough, and those Magistrates that were Jews, and since the dayse of the Apostles, the true Christians, there hath been the Popish Magistrates in the beast, false prophets, Antichristians, Dragons, false churches, dayes, since the true Church went into the Wilderness, but she is preparing her self for her Husband, and coming out in her glory, and the man-child is witnessed, the husband, and the shout of a King is amongst us, the Lord God Omnipotent, who will throw down all that is come up since the true Church went into the Wilderness; Therefore we with our names and hands do bear our Testimony against Tithes, the giver of them, the setter of them up, and the taker of them, and would that you and all People should turn to the power of God, in which ye might be in union and take off these things, which doth oppress the Nation, in which power there is no oppression.

CHES-SHIRE.

Eliz. Yardly	Juliana Painter	Fran. Yardly	*(page 22)*
Dorothy Yardly	Fran. Probbin	Dorothy Hare	Margret Lloyd
Mary Tomasin	Margret Parker	Elin Nicson	Anne Ledsome
Jane Tomlisson	Eliz. Smith	Eliz. Morrice	Kathern Andrews
Mary Pritchard	Margret Baddeley	Mary Hare	Eliz. Andrews
Susanna Maddocks	Eliz. Baddeley	Jane Hare	Jane Colley
Kathern Mills	Margret Tomlisson	Eliz. Croxton	Sarah Court
Jane Andrews	Dorothy Tomlisson	Mary Croxton	Anne Bettily
Darcas Sargeant	Jane Tomlisson	Mary Loanes	Tomasine Taylor
Hannah Sergeant	Fran. Tomlisson	Ermine Pricket	Jane Nicklas
Eliz. Ducker	Jane Nicholas	Jane Lloyd	Dorothy Llyod

Alice Johnson
Fran. Walker
Anne Read
Mary Gilbert
Eliz. Weaver
Dorothy Mear
Margret Wooly
Mary Tomlisson
Anne Johnson
Dorothy Naylor
Mary Hall
Eliz. Lewis
Mary Cawly
Margret Rowland
Mary Swan
Margret Coppock
Margret Williams
Anne Janyou
Alice Buckly
Mary Vandrey
Alice Taylor
Eliz. Moor
Alice Sanders
Kathern Shepherd
Elinor Rowlison
Sarah Mercer
Eliz. Pickring
Eliz. Swan
Kathern Crosby
Mary Jackson
Jane Hucksly
Mary Burtonwood
Anne Moreton
Eliz. Moreton
Eliz. Crosby
Hannah Crosby
Mary Bradford
Elin Crosby
Kathern Eaton
Elin Williamson
Mary Clare
Mary Williams
Kathern Anderton
Eliza. Wyrral
Jane Jackson
Eliza. Anderton
Hannah Marbury

Mary Anderton
Margret Barker
Alice Pasley
Eliz. Hutton
Jane Dunbabin
Elin Anderton
Anne Amery
Jane Shaw
Eliz. Crosby
Eliz. Yate
Margret Sanky
Margret
   Cartwright
Alice Jones
Widdow Simcock
Margret Garnet
Alice Widdens
Widdow Parcival
Mary Miller
Mary Mountford
Kathern Hill
Priscilla Hatton
Mary Browant
Margret Touchet
Alice Challiner
Eliz. Adlington
Mary Brownant
Eliz. Brownant
Mary Pickring
Elin Preston
Anne Sarrat
Anne Sharples
Mary Griffeth
Ellinor Cotgrean
Margret Higenson
Priscilla Crabb
Eliz. Sarrat
Eliz. Hall
Elin Hall
Mary Hall
Sarah Boulton
Margret Royl
Elin Boulton
Cisly Cleaton
Eliz. Asbrook
Margret Milner
Eliz. Milner

Elin Brown
Deborah Bushel
Eliz. Bushel
Eliz. Pike
Fran. Skelton
Eliz. Widart
Jone Edge
Eliz. Hatton
Eliz. Hale
Alice Hignet
Eliz. Sarret
Eliz. Bushel
Ellinor Barker
Ellin Cook
Anne Tomson
Anne Millington
Mary Bushel

(page 23)
Elin Davenport
Mary Davenport
Anne Pike
Sarah Brown
Eliz. Wood
Jone Wood
Margret Norman
Katherin Hatton
Eliz. Moberly
Mary Bradford
Eliz. Griffeth
Mary Suddern
Mary Gerrard
Elin Moberly
Eliz. Kilshaw
Martha
   Williamson
Margret Miller
Elin Hall
Elin Baxter
Alice Davenport
Eliz. Yaler
Eliz. Cowley
Alice Pickring
Margret Cordal
Margret Monk
Mary Hill
Sarah Hill

Eliz. Stringer
Ellinor Hatton
Mary Pike
Eliz. Fryer
Mary Warton
Kathern Brierwood
Mary Brierwood
Mary Key
Mary Sanderson
Alice Walley
Mary Fisher
Mary Sharples
Elin Jones
Margret Dunbabir
Lettice Perrin
Margret Wood
Grace Ellet
Margery Sharples
Eliz. Perrin
Eliz. Briggs
Susanna
   Liversticke
Cisly Whitcars
Eliz. Beeston
Jone Hill
Eliz. Husall
Anne Dicks
Jane More
Dorothy Booth
Margret Candwel
Eliz. Mear
Jone Hampton
Eliz. Green
Eliz. Hasel
Dorothy Tumkin
Cisley Pearson
Kathern Madley
Margret Hasul
Mary Hamsley
Margret Meer
Mary Endon
Margret Moreton
Anne Lounds
Anne Wardley
Margery Oakes
Isabel Thorncroft
Sarah Thorncroft

Amy Haywort
Mary Smith
Lydia Wharmbee
Kathern Walker
Margery Lownds
Alice Smith
Hester Hall
Alice Lownds
Eliz. Bradbury
Eliz. Hall
Mary Leigh
Fran Armit
Elin Steward
Hester Brumbly
Eliz. Stoniard
Eliz. Pass
Mary Morrice
Eliz. Chorley
Elin Whitakers
Margret Chorley
Jane Lownds
Kathern
  Hitchinson
Elin Antrobus
Mary Dawson
Isabel Plant
Anne Leigh
Ellin Dawson
Mary Graves
Grace Brown
Mercy Berrington
Anne Baker
Margret Picker
Dorothy Deen
Dorothy Steel
Ellin Picker
Mary Strach
Mary Bradshaw
Eliz. Bradshaw
Sarah Bradshaw
Margery Hitchin
Jane Miller
Anne Wooker
Margret Baker
Margret Baker
Hannah Baker
Eliz. Evans

Anne Frinson
Dorothy Alexander

(page 24)
Eliza. Buttely
Amy Buckly
Elizabeth Morral
Ellin Bertles
Ann Becket
Ketheren Furnisall
Elizabeth Wood
Ellin Hall
Margret Barker
Katheren
  Millington
Ann Bramal
Elizabeth Bramal
Margret Hamson
Elizabeth Sudlow
Ellin Grange
Margret Eaton
Margret Gatlist
Ann Sutton
Katheren Stockley
Mary Green
Mary Millington
Margret Midlehurst
Ann Berry
Kathren Ryther
Elizabeth Newby
Elnor Forrest
Ann Loranson
Elizabeth Robinson
Margret Bretton
Elizabeth Pickring
Alice Shak-shaff
Elin Glover
Margret Barrow
Katheren Kerkcum
Elizabeth Glover
Katheren Foxley
Margret Pickring
Margret Pickring
Margret Dewsberry
Elizabeth Gandy
Elliner Barker
Jane Deakin

Elizabeth Goulden
Margery Eaton
Ann Jamney,
  Senior
Ellin Shaw
Margret Yarwood
Mary Jamney
Mary Strettel
Alice Burges
Elizabeth Burges
Mary Smith
Ann Lamb
Elizabeth Lamb
Elizabeth Felon
Mary Jamnney
Martha Janney
Margret Burges
Ann Harrison
Margery Heath
Elizab.
  Worthington
Anna
  Worthington
Mary Worthington
Martha
  Worthington
Frances
  Worthington
Mary Worthington
Sarah Worthington
Elizabeth Burges
Joan Holm
Margret Holm
Ellin Holm
Ann Holm
Elizabeth Janney
Hester Shaw
Rebecca Shaw
Mary Shaw
Elin Stretch
Ann Milner
Mary Milner
Mary Pot
Joan Armstrong
Elizabeth Peirson
Mary Pot
Sibel Felor

Elizabeth Heeld
Ellen Alcock
Elizabeth Hobson
Margret Pownal
Sebel Hough
Margret Heeld
Mary Mallory
Ann Shield
Constant Shield
Alice Mosse
Elizabeth Ashton
Mary Bostock
Mary Brock
Mary Beely
Ann Woyd
Alice Millor
Sibel Beard
Ann Hall
Ann Boare
Alice Ridgway
Elizabeth Hoyd
Margret Harrup
Hester Arnefield
Ann Bowler
Frances Royle
Kathren Sheart
Elizabeth Hibert
Mary Hibert
Jane Burdiken
Elizabeth Sheply
Elizabeth Leech
Ann Simpson
Margret
  Broadhouse
Sibel Sikes
Ann Rowbottom
Elizabeth Bowden

(page 25)
Ellin Carrington
Mary Warrington
Margret
  Warrington
Mary Hasfort
Anne Sibert
Anne Bower
Mary Pownal

Kathern Kalshaw
Ellin Hide
Anne Oussoncroft
Anne Marsland
Ellen Hollenshed
Eliz. Astel
Anne Blemily
Jane Chanler
Mary Jamon
Anne Brown
Margret Ridgway
Margret Bealy
Ellen Bealy

Ellen Burges, elder
Ellen Burges
Margery Burges
Kathern Rylance
Eliz. Falkner
Margret Falkner
Ellen Arstenstal
Anne Cash
Mary Cash
Mary Taylor
Mary Worthington
Eliz. Kelshal

Anne Heeld
Dorothy Allen
Margret Coppock
Kathern Beck
Eliz. Morgan
Margery Owen
Ursula Hitchcock
Sarah Owen
Martha Owen
Rebecca Holm
Ellinor Dewsberry
Anne Maddock

Deborah Maddock
Elinor Underwood
Margret
  Underwood
Sarah Ghorst
Dorothy Hand
Eliz. Bristoe
Sarah Maddock
Isabel Lagh
Alice Nicholas
Hannah Watmore
Jane Gravener

YORK-SHIRE.

We whose names are here underwritten, being truly sensible of the great oppression (by reason of Tithes) in this Commonwealth of *England,* by the cruel exacting of Priests, Impropriators, Farmers and others, by imprisoning of some of our Brethren till death, others for years; and by making spoil (and waste) of others goods, to the utter undoing of them and their Families (as to the outward) we do here in the presence of the Lord God, and in the sight of men, bear our Testimony against that oppression, by setting our names to this Paper, who desire the same may be tendered to the Parliament of *England,* that that burthen may be removed.

Bridget Clark
Grace Backler
Margret Blythman
Margret Tenant
Margret Knowles
Isabel Fish
Jennet Carr
Anne Wilson
Eliz. Horseman
Jane Coates
Ellen Horseman
Isabel Horseman

Jennet Calvird
Margret Metcalf
Cicily Metcalf
Eliz. Nicolson
Isabel Lambert
Isabel Thompson
Eliz. Thompson
Margret Metcalf
Jane Richinson
Elizabeth
  Thompson
Elizabeth Rowth

Jane Metcalf
Margret
  Wethervelt
Margret Robbinson
Agnes Clough
Jennet Larock
Mary Brigg
Agnes Brigg
Mary Brigg
Anne Watson
Mary Clough
Isabel Bothamley

Anne Wood
Isabel Bothamley
Mary Smith
Anne Smith
Grace Smith
Elizabeth Smith
Susanna Smith
Mary Ambler
Elizabeth Husler
Agnes Husler
Anne Waide
Anne Waide

Barbara Clough
Eliz. Moor
Mary Taylor
Susanna
  Brookbank
Anne Watson
Grace Brigg
Anne Brigg
Ellen Smith
Martha Smith
Sarah Smith
Eliz. Rassen
Katherine Scot
Susanna Smith
Eliz. Rawson
Cicily Metcalf
Mandland
  Baraclough
Luce Smith
Susanna Warton
Mary Lawson

(page 26)
Eliz. Sampson
Priscilla Cant
Jane Chaytor
Ann Moor
Mary Jenkinson
Anne Jenkinson
Mary Hobson
Elizabeth
  Summerson
Anne Faucit
Jane Ward
Mary Brockblank
Elizabeth Robinson
Mary Brockblank
Alice Peirson
Margret Peirson
Anne Atkinson
Jane Porter
Mary Theaker
Frances Easterby
Sarah Marshal
Anne Sutton
Mary Howson
Bridget Bladworth

Jane Knowles
Agnes Wildman
June Redman
Agnes Wildman
Margret Wildman
Gennet Tennant
Elizabeth Clark
Ellen Tennant
Rebeccha Addison
Isabel Bland
Mabel Banks
Elizabeth Tennant
Dorothy Weight
Anne Watkinson
Jane Atkinson
Katherin Best
Mary Middleton
Eliz. Hogg
Jane Hinford
Katherin Hakes
Susanna
  Robbinson
Jane Kettelwol
Anne Bramley
Elizabeth Nelson
Margret Occkernly
Margret Slaughter
Mary Taytam
Margret Batty
Mary Bulcock
Agnes Horsman
Agnes Hully
Anne Dryber
Ellen Lee
Mary Whip
Elizabeth Crossdale
Anne Temple
Mary Smith
Elizabeth Tayler
Jane Oxard
Jane Wilkinson
Elizabeth Batter
Mary Tudd
Elizabeth
  Blanchard
Anne Dennison
Anne Smith

Mary Batter
Dorothy Todde
Elizabeth
  Lockwood
Anne Coocksen
Jane Cookeson
Mary Walker,
  senior
Mary Walker,
  junior
Katherin Lewis
Judeth Lewis
Margret Johnson
Elizabeth Johnson
Sythey Masterman
Mary Masterman
Elizabeth
  Middleton
Jane Woodwart
Eliz. Johnson,
  senior
Elizabeth Shepherd
Elizabeth Craik
Elizabeth Tuler
Alice Truman
Anne Dennison
Frances Crosby
Isabel Wilkinson
Anne Wilkinson
Jane Ridmond
Elizabeth Procter
Anne Procter
Frances Aeston
Elizabeth Rowth
Margret Metcalf
Elizabeth
  Thompson
Isabel Thompson
Anne Thomson
Mary Lambert
Mary Hartly
Jennet Hartly
Isabel Studderd
Anne Broun
Mary Smith
Margret Broun
Anne Pollard

Ellen Pollard
Jennet Sager
Elizabeth Bleakly
Mary Wilkinson
Jane Cleaton
Mary Bradshaw
Mary Barcroft
Alice Barcroft
Ellen Pollard
Agnes Minnis
Ellen Sager
Elizabeth Higgin
Mary Mitchel
Mary Hargreaves
Anne Knowles
Susan Heworth
Mary Heworth
Elizabeth Heworth
Susan Heworth
Mary Bertwisle
Elizabeth Bertwisle
Margret Bertwisle
Katherin Bertwisle
Katherin Doe
Agnes Robbinson
Alice Ratcliff
Mary Rosthorn
Alice Rosthorn
Alice Ashworth
Judeth Taylor
Mary Frith
Hannah Langdal
Sarah Hutton
Sarah Fawet
Sarah Fawet
Sarah Dobson
Sarah Howl
Mary Hanson
Bridget Green
Mary Godely
Anne Nubie
Anne Wilbie
Grace Midgley
Bridget Green
Mary Pellington
Sarah Denham
Elizabeth Green

Jane Leigh
Dorothy Verity
Ester Burkby
Alice Crowcher
Elizabeth Kitchin
Anne Horgreaves
Martha Boot
Ellen Jowel
Anne Swift
Martha Phillip
Sarah Bonds
Mary Fowler
Isabel Booth
Mary Fothergil
Elizabeth Sikes
Hannah Battle
Grace Marshal
Grace Croysdal
Ester Pollard
Ester Ramsden
Grace Dunster
Elizabeth Sikes
Susan Thewellis
Jone Dyson
Mary Whitly
Sarah Lees
Jane Fox
Elizabeth Ramsden
Mary Ramsden
Grace Roydes
Mary Whitly
Susan Whitly
Susan Turner
Sarah Turner
Anne Wadsworth
Mary Wadsworth
Easter Wadsworth
Elizabeth Geldart
Katherin Horner
Iddith Geldard
Mary Rider
Sarah Geldart

(page 27)
Margret Winne
Mary Robbinson
Susanna Tyreman

Isabel Fample
Barbarah Hildreth
Mary Dunning
Margret Sample
Anne Mannings
Margret Wood
Ursula Rimer
Elizabeth Johnson
Margret Parving
Katherine Rimer
Margret Pate
Rosamond
 Snowdon
Elizabeth Foster
Ellen Tyreman
Anne Smith
Elizabeth Tutin
Amey Waid
Margery
 Whitehead
Jane Robbinson
Elizabeth Bell
Margret Heddon
Mary Todd
Katherin Rimer
Mary Linsey
Ellen Rowland
Hellen Johnson
Margret Tomlinson
Rachel Garbut
Margret Simpson
Mary Mason
Isabel Orton
Isabel Ray
Susan Wim
Margery Braderig
Anne Marwood
Jane Furbank
Jane Hohn
Isabel Story
Elizabeth Tiplady
Isabel Barker
Anne Barker
Margret Stonas
Anne Graystorck
Bettrisse Tenting
Alice Nellist

Isabel Tompsoe
Margret Hodges
Margret Stonas
Jane Parrit
Elizabeth Spark
Margeret Ruddock
Margret Pursglove
Margery Coultheist
Isabel Outhwait
Elizabeth Thorp
Elizabeth Larnest
Mary Radcliff
Effam Word
Elizabeth Hodysoe
Margret Hoddysoe
Dorothy Hoddysoe
Isabel Burdstead
Anne White, senior
Anne White,
 junior
Ester Chapman
Anne Cockeril
Jane Cockeril
Magdalen
 Slightholm
Isabel Knowles
Ellen Smalwood
Margery Cockeril
Ellen Smalwood
Isabel Smalwood
Mary Pearson
Anne Pearson
Anne Greenbank
Ellis Green
Elizabeth Hart
Jane Bimstil
Ellen Hay
Katherin Stockley
Jane Rider
Susanna
 Lotherington
Jane Faston
Jane Rogers
Sarah Jones
Alice Pickering
Dorothy Smalls
Dorothy Heslam

Isabel Sulon
Margery Grange
Eliz. Pennet.
Eliz. Blenkhorn
Katherin Clark
Dorothy Rooads
Aime Freayre
Margret Leming
Dorothy Leming
Katherin Bowch
Eliz. Horsman
Jeanet Measin
Mary Hardcastle
Jane Simpson
Gennet Graing
Mary Grang
Mary Bridgwaters
Agnes Atkinson
Ester Bridgewaters
Ellen Umpelly
Eliz. Grime
Isabel Lapington
Kathe. Kirkby
Eliz. Stevenson
Eliz. Sadman
Martha Coward
Frances Beswick
Ellinor Cresby
Ellinor Hodgson
Elizabeth Star
Elizabeth Magdson
Margret Hodgson
Katherin Dickson
Alice Hopper
Eliz. Meggison
Katherin Alleson
Ellen Leak
Elizabeth
 Thomlinson
Elizabeth
 Stevenson
Frances Write
Martha
 Maincleron
Anne Caylew
Frances Kyther
Isabel Arluck

Eliz. Wats
Jane Hunter
Anne Hunter
Isabel Barker
Eliz. Pelch
Anne Northen
Barbarah Jowsey
Margret Chapman
Alice Sowly
Anne Fardin
Eliz. Jackson
Mary Mlles
Eliz. Smith
Dorothy Godd
Hellen Barwick
Mary Roundtree
Isabel Fardin
Elizabeth Jackson
Eliz. Raw
Isabel Simpson
Lucy Prat
Alice Kirton
Elizabeth Cherry
Agnes Cherry
Alice Typlady
Eliz. Cherry
Phillice Thompson
Dorothy
  Thompson
Isabel Clarkson
Agnes Langstaff
Katherin Wilson
Elizabeth Langstaff
Margret Carter
Margret Robbinson
Mary Robbinson
Eliz. Raw
Elizabeth Robbison
Eliz. Spenclay
Agnes Allenby
Eliz. Hawxwell
Isabel Clark
Agnes Langsdale

Anne Prat
Alice Waller
Alice Thompson
Eliz. Honsdail
Grace Smith
Alice Maw
Anne Parkin
Anne Dawson
Anne Taylor
Susan Mainforth
Barbarah Kirk
Barbara Tindal
Katherin Milner
Jane Goodman
Isabel Applyurd
Clare Marston
Hannah Coplaygh
Eliz. Goodbarn

(page 28)
Isabel Jordan
Grace Goobal
Eliz. Powel
Margret Lost
Eliz. Chambers
Eliz. Burland
Margret Hopwood
Anne Ably
Mary Procter
Cicily Knapton
Sarah Marshal
Anne Sutton
Mary Sutton
Anne Smith
Barbara Siddal
Jane Selly
Frances Storr
Margret Storr
Dorothy Storr
Mary Nicolson
Anne Nicolson
Jane Yeats

Elizabeth
  Whitehead
Jone Fearding
Francis Thornley
Anne Elisar
Mary Whitehead
Anne Edames
Dorothy Crontser
Frances Wright
Margret Hagget
Eliz. Turner
Jone Newby
Frances Kitching
Elizabeth Seak
Frances Sanderson
Eliz. Beck
Bridget Emerson
Alice Cass
Margret Blashel
Rebecca Sudaiber
Jezabel Huntlay
Rachel Garbur
Margret Milner
Margret Teuslay
Jane Barker
Anne Burn
Jennet Lilforth
Mary Tuinam
Susanna Plumner
Mary Barber
Jane Elliker
Mary Parkinson
Mary Smith
Eliz. Tomlinson
Mary Tomlinson
Anne Parkinson
Eliz. Brown
Mary Tomlinson
Margret
  Morehouse
Isabel Parkinson
Isabel Carr

Bennet Hill
Isabel Young
Anne Young
Anne Squire
Mary Rawson
Eliz. Weinman
Ferah Weinman
Eliz. Somerstals
Mandlin Frankland
Mary Somerstals
Mary Rowley
Jane Riply
Ann Ibbitson
Mary Ibbitson
Eliz. Ibbitson
Anne Dickinson
Eliz. Dickinson
Eliz. Watson
Margret Scot
Susanna Hill
Mary Tenant
Alice Smith
Isabel Grain
Anne Fletcheard
Martha Branne
Margret Dickinson
Anna Emerton
Isabel Dickinson
Isabel Watlingson
Mary Bollard
Eliz. Dickinson
Agnes Morhoas
Margret Hill
Alice Smith
Anne Moor
Jennet Chambers
Isabel Chapman
Margret Moor
Ellin Moor
Margret Flanklard
Anne Atkinson
Eliz. Mason
Agnes Kidar

Mary Baython
Eliz. Wilson
Ellinor Watson
Eliz. Watkinson
Ellinor Watson
Mary Robbinson
Ellen Townson
Eliz. Lucas
Margret Wildman
Jane Dickinson
Jane Totum
Martha Blahey
Eliz. Priestly
Mary Downing
Alice Shoane
Alice Jesoppe
Eliz. Couldwel
Mary Dickinson
Grace Mareden
Alice Oxley
Jane Swift
Eliz. Waterhouse
Eliz. Creswicke
Margret Dickinson
Judeth Rothwel
Katherine
  Brookbank
Sarah Woodhouse
Grace Moakeson
Anne
  Charlesworth
Mary Catlein
Anne Jessop
Dorothy Hicke
Dionice Couldwel
Anne Dison
Eliz. Crowder
Eliz. Burgess
Frances
  Hinchcliffe
Mary Morton
Martha Priest
Martha Couldwel
Grace Hurst
Margret Mourton
Eliz. Trout
Eliz. Wordsworth

Anne Wilcock
Mary Colson
Mary Cotsworth
Mary Todde
Margret Leaper
Isabel Jarret
Ellen Jarret
Alice Beeswick
Mary Story
Thomason Leaper
Jane Clough
Mary Fowler
Clare Harlas
Jane Pearson
Jane Chat
Alice Hairst
Mary Pilkington
Alice Mainprice
Anne Stringer
Anne Hedson
Dorothy Bigson
Frances Hutch
Eliz. Gilburn

Barbarah Aoklam
Betteris Stabler
Rebecca Drape
Eliz. Menson
Dirrothy Robson
Grace Barwick
Jane Drape
Jane Milner
Eliz. Botterrel
Christian Darfield
Betteris Harrison
Jane Ask
Mary Burn
Christian
  Dickinson
Mary Todde
Eliz. Farthing
Margret Mankman
Eliz. Hodgson
Isabel Jaylor
Jane Waln
Mary Clifford
Margret Smith

Martha Coats

(page 29)
Eliz. Blakey
Grace Jackson
Katherine Brown
Anne Kettlesing
Grace Swave
Grace Pawson
Helene Pape
Anne Bond
Alice Ashton
Alice Dilworth
Ellen Gardner
Dorothy
  Hodgkinson
Agnes Crossdale
Mary Crossdale
Jane Waln
Susanna Chambers
Isabel Knowles
Eliz. Bond
Alice Hairst
Margery Hairst
Ellen Walbank
Jennet Clough
Agnes Rudd
Mary Rudd
Bridget Driver
Eliz. Waddington
Jone Burrough
Ellen Cutler
Isabel Baily
Isabel Waln
Jane Killam
Margret Killam
Anne Willeston
Anne Nicolson
Jone Killam
Anne Hickson
Sarah Nicolson
Eliz. Harrison
Rebecca Hamond
Sarah Denham
Eliz. Fletcher
Alice Richardson
Anne Smith

Eliz. Bains
Anne Peck
Anne Camsal
Anne Lambart
Mary Vicars
Alice Brown
Jone Lambart
Rebecca Spavan
Mary Carrington
Martha Lambart
Trothy Young
Mary Worsely
Mary Rowbothom
Eliz. Holms
Mary Aldam
Jennet Bunting
Mary Parkin
Bridget Bladworth
Dorothy Williams
Clarah Burton
Eliz. Allisson
Jane Spencer
Anne Allisson
Alice Crabtree
Anne Scirlew
Anne Cook
Sarah Mapplebeck
Mary Howson
Jane Beamont
Mary Lavarack
Mary Law
Eliz. Iclese
Magdalen Dawny
Susanna Dawny
Mary Clarkson
Katherine
  Clarkson
Susanna Arnold
Eliz. Parker
Eliz. Clark
Katherine Knots
Anne Boulton
Mary Cook
Rebecca Cook
Katherine Cook
Jane Burnly

DURHAM.

We whose names are underwritten, seeing the unjustness and
oppression of Tithes, do in the fear of the Lord bear witness,
and give Testimony against them; And those that Receives,
and by great and cruel Oppression requires the Payment of
them by a Compulsatory Law, or condemns the refusers to
Prison for not doing it, And if the Lord suffer such a thing to
be Till by the hard-hearted Tax-masters, we are by him made
willing to give up our Bodies and Estates, for keeping our
consciences clear, rather then yield to the oppression and
unreasonableness of some men who makes shipwrack of good
Conscience, so they may have their wills of the other; And to
this is our hands put.

Margret Rayn
Eliz. Lee
Anne Bainbridge
Isabel Saire
Elenor Eyon
Kathern Shaw
Mary Richinson
Isabel Rain
Katherine Rain
Isabel Appelby
Mary Gutton
Isabel Hutton
Elenor Allinson
Mary Chapman
Elenor Pickney
Anne Tipling
Elenor Rain
Mary Morlay
Jane Walker
Barbary Eyon
Jane Bowran
Elizabeth Robinson
Elizabeth Allinson
Dorothy Heslupp

Alice Robison
Margret Bowran
Jane Wrightson
Frances Walker
Mary Appelby
Jane Barret
Mary Appelby
Anne Wrightson
Gennet Bowran

(page 30)
Mary Walker
Alice Selby
Anne Tallier
Susan Tallier
Mary Hunter
Anne Wilkinson
Eliz. Row
Eliz. Wilkinson
Mary Makepeace
Frances Vicars
Jane Whantley
Anne Whatfield
Jane Snowball

Mary Wilkinson
Mary Laborn
Anne Richardson
Eliz. Whitefield
Mary Hopper
Jane Barret
Margret Hopper
Eliz. mare
Thomleson Hunter
Eliz. mallem
Anne Sompson
Jane Hopper
Canstance Boggan
Eliz. Jackson
Jane Trotter
Alice Ireland
Eliz. Hopper
Anne Emberson
Eliz. Emberson
Jane Emberson
Margret Emberson
Mary Robinson
Isabel Henderson
Anne Henderson

Margret Ramshaw
Margret Bradley
Marg. Ramshaw
Eliz. Lidle
Mary Stevenson
Isbel Thomson
Phillis Liddle
Elliner Wardel
Jone Sanders
Sarah Horeson
Mary Chipses
Isabel Ruston
Jane Hall
Mary Heighington
Frances Hornplay
Eliz. Hoper
Anne Hall
Anne Hodshon
Allsee Adamson
Anne Guard
Suesance
  Harswhitel
Gillence
  Woodmass

Mary Richardson
Katharine Smith
Mildred Spalk
Anne Harswhitel
Anne Readhead
Margret Shaw
Ezibel Heighly
Margret Walker
Ezibel Walker
Alice Clark
Eliz. Clark
Jane Richardson
Isabel Beaton
Anne Robinson
Margret Robinsin
Mildred Foster
Frances Fall
Anne Patisson
Barbery Burdon
Ellen Rutless
Eliz. Readhead

Isabel Appelby
Alice Appelby
Anne Richardson
Anne Spark
Isabel Newby
Eliz. Brian
Anne Over
Mary worly
Kathern Smith
Mildrel Spark
Anne Haswell
Anne Readhead
Margret Shaw
Isabel Highly
Margret Walker
Isabel Walker
Alice Clark
Eliz. Brian
Jane Richardson
Isabel Reighton
Anne Robinson

Margret Lobinson
Mildrel Foster
Frances Hall
Anne Pattisun
Barbery Burdon
Ellin Rutlas
Eliz. Readhead
Alice Appelby
Anne Richardson
Anne Spark
Isabel Newby
Eliz. Brian
Grace Pearson
Anne Richmond
Margret Richmond
Ellenor Thompson
Anne Bainbridge
Barbary Emmerson
Jane Nicolson
Jane Gatley

Sarah Welberry
Margret Robinson
Katherine
 Wrightson
Johan Hodgshon
Katherine
 Dodsworth
Bridget English
Constance
 Loyselart
Anne Robinson
Jane Robinson
Anne Draper
Frances Avery
Jane Daveson
Anne Robinson
Anne Langstass
Ellinor Emerson
Eliz. Richmont
Anne Hodgson

NORTHAMPTON-SHIRE.

These are the names of the Women, who are witnesses against the oppression of the Tithes, taken at *Northampton.*

Mary Gains
Eliz. Willes
Katherine Ladd
Phi. Haddon
Frances Varney
Mary Green
Sarah Todd
Anne Hewlit
Anne Cook
Alice Ixons
Jane Hunt
Rebecca Peak
Elish. Hunt
Eliz. Hunt
Anne Richardson
Eliz. Averick

Mary Hagge
Mary Green
Anne Patteson
Katherine Gats
Abigail Lauruck

(page 31)
Anne Vincet
Anne Stanley
Ellinor Steunson
Mary Nottingham
Susanna
 Nottingham
Hannah
 Nottingham
Judeth Nottingham

Eliz. Pours
Anne Coks
Alice Juies
Dorkas Robinson
Hannah Freeman
Mary Page,
 younger
Alice Harris
Sibbil Gibs
Amey Robinson
Eliz. Roel
Sarah Palmer
Eliz. Pug
Eliz. Ellington
Eliz. Ellington
Anne Ellington

Rebecca Mekernes
Anne Witlick
Mary Bely
Hannah Day
Mary Day
Eliz. Day
Eliz. Garret
Alice Whitelock
Alice Bely
Sarah Bernes
Margret Wills
Eliz. Bely
Elen Polings
Anne Brooks
Anne Warren
Anne Wallis

Mary Young
Eliz. mekernes
Mary Kenwrden
Hester Wadsworth
Eliz. Powel
Eliz. Mekernes
Helen Garret
Eliz. Norcot
Eliz. Abbot
Mary Warren
Alice Woolston
Alice Underwood
Mary Warren

Alice Preston
Dorothy Ward
Mary Britten
Anne Key
Anne Innfield
Mary Steepens
Eling Goedbe
Margret Beeb
Eliz. Bull
Jone Goby
Anne Roberts
Anne Eare
Anne Nickols

Joice Molten
Anne Preston
Eliz. Binion
Eliz. Welles
Eliz. Weight
Mary Warren
Eliz. Knighton
Anne Ibs
Eme Durnil
Anne Mekernes
Anne Pell
Deborah Roberts
Anne Corby

Mary Tarry
Frances Houghton
Bridget Pell
Jone Wadsworth

These are the names of Friends in *Welingborough* and there-abouts.

County of NOTTINGHAM.

The names of Women Friends, who bears Testimony against the oppression of Tithes.

ANne Tomlinson
Mary Garret
Mary Sharp
Eliz. Frith
Eliz. Wood
Ellin Cook
Anne Ashwel
Susanna Touny
Anne Pattinson
Sith Green
Alice Clife
Eliz. Wood
Mary Sharp
Mary Flintham
Mary Buller
Kathern Shareman
Anne Green
Eliz. Spur
Anne Anderson
Mary Barton
Anne Dawson
Ursula Green
Anne Hazard

Anne Shaw
Mary Vicars
Margret
    Shackerdal
Eliz. Elsam
Bridget Hamman
Jone Bacon
Eliz. Barton
Alice Uston
Eliz. Kitching
Judeth Garland
Anne Bark
Isabel Cooper
Eliz. Hatfield
Eliz. Meares
Lydia Bark
Susanna Hubbard
Mary Snoden
Mary Clay
Anne Poyson
Eliz. Copla
Frances Cooper
Eliz. Cooper

Jone Hyfield
Mary Alcock
Mary Holmes
Ruth Cook
Anne Alcock
Hannah Glassop
Sarah Slater
Eliz. Gassop
Patience
    Wilkinson
Anne Need
Emet Burroughs
Mary Hand
Jone Burton
Dorothy Wyld
Mary Wightman
Rachel Slack
Jone Martine
Hannah Lister
Ellin Cooper
Mary Cooper
Mary Ledbeater
Eliz. Cockram

Mary Cockram

(page 32)
Anne Fricknal
Susanna Reynold
Eliz. Clay
Margret Whitworth
Mary Clay
Anne Langford
Sarah Clay
Sarah Brandrith
Eliz. Brandrith
Mary Blackeborn
Eliz. Brandrith
Mary Fields
Martha Grace
Anne Brandrith
Alice Woodhead
Ann Crofts
Jane Anclife
Anne Crofts
Elizabeth Rogers
Anne Noden

LINCOLNSHIRE.

We whose names are subscribed, do hereby declare that we are very sensible Tithes are a great oppression set up in the time of Popery; and we desire the removal of them.

Anne Leverton
A. Frotheringham
Eliz. Mason
Eliz. Woolsey
Susanna Holland
Jane Preston
Eliz. Brinckle
Mary Greswel
Mary Pheasant
Martha Wright
Anne Recket
Anne Northern
Sence Northern
Sarah Mosse
Eliz. Harrison
Ursula Hooton
Ursula Burroughs
Eliz. Northern
Mary Garland
Anne Pheasant
Eliz. Rogers
Anne Freestone
Prudens Fisher
Sarah Thompson
Jane Wilkinson
Mary Hudson
Jane Lightfoot
Ellen Bramby
Anne Gaunt
Anne Pheasant
Mary Northern
Eliz. Williamson
Eliz. Jackson
Ellen Gaunt
Anne Sharp
Ruth Pannel
Eliz. Harpham
Eliz. Fletcher

Martha Tess
Eliz. Jarnil
Jane Harrison
Anne Hird
Eliz. Smith
Anne Winch
Eliz. Smith, junior
Mary Smith
Susanna Cussons
Mary Maple
Mary Cussons
Ellen Smith
Katharine Makaril
Anne Thornton
Didolis Carie
Mary Oliver
Anne Beck
Alice Sharp
Anne Foster
Ester Hart
Mary Foster
Anne Cook
Eliz. Barnard
Anne Spain
Katherine Pickaver
Hannah Seaton
Mary Packins
Ellen Foster
Anne Hobson
Dorcas Mell
Dorothy Foster
Eliz. Gathorn
Dorothy Pickaver
Thomasin Norton
Eliz. Hobson
Anne Haldenby
Susanna Parrot
Mary Scot

Grace Scot
Anne Garton
Alice Beck
Margret Marston
Eliz. Marshal
Eliz. Lee
Mary Berrier
Anne Milner
Cassandra
  Chapman
Ellin Gilliot
Frances Hobson
Rachel Beck
Mary Chandler
Anne Sherman
Eliz. Robinson
Eliz. Waterfool
Eliz. Higham
Margret Darlinton
Mary Turner
Alice Tate
Mary Trevis
Susunna Torksey
Isabel Drury
Anna Brown
Sarah Otter
Eliz. Clark
Mary White
Bridget White
Mary Rosse
Alice Winsor
Ellenor Gibson
Mary Parker
Kath. Pid
Anne Pid
Eliz. Bainton
Eliz. Pid
Mary Crosby

Eliz. Gaskin
Anna Whiteworth
Susan Smith
Anne Parker
Eliz. West
Anne Bagaley
Mary Trueblood
Eliz. Parker
Anne Crosby
Susanna Billidge
Eliz. Hutchinson
Jane Sanders
Anne Berrier
Mary Thistleton
Margret Dounham
Hollen Marshall
Mary Chanler
Jone Westwood
Anne Shoreman
Grace Robinson
Anne Stoker
Bridget Turington
Sarah Classon
Sarah Kirk

(page 33)
Elizabeth Watersal
Anne Watersal
Elizabeth Haigham
Ellen Wilson
Margret Smith
Mary Wilson
Frances Seagrave
Rebecka Thornton
Mary Sowter
Dorothy Rawbuck
Elizabeth Davie
Anne Manby

Anne Havey	Margaret Ashley	Katheren Makaril	Rebecka Day
Jane Phillips	Anne Thornton	Alice Streaton	Mary Gibson
Elizabeth Mathews	Jane Hempsted	Anne Stelworth	Anne Fisher
Anne Morris	Anne Hempsted	Mary Blackney	Anne Johnson
Anne Makepeace	Mary Hempsted	Mary Lumkin	Eliz. Wray
Eliz. Boot	Dorothy Armstrong	Anne Bellamy	Anne Thomlinson
Katheren Swayer	Elizabeth Wilkinson	Anne Rose	Eliz. Kirk
Susanna Whitman	Sarah Fotherby	Anne Haris	

Essex, Norfolk, Suffolk, Cambridg, *and* Huntington.

To the Parliament of ENGLAND, *&c*

Now friends, you being first chosen by the Nation as a Parlia ment for to do the Nation the right, and to take off the Nations oppressions; are not you to search out the oppression? and are not people to lay their oppressions before you, without petitioning you to do them justice? and is not petitioning often for exalting such that will not do justice without flattering petitions, and then have but thanks, and seldom the thing done? and has not flattering petitions and addresses exalted such as God hath over-thrown, that hath not done justice, nor will not do justice to the just, when oppressions and grievances have been laid before them? the cry hath been, It hath not been a petition, it hath not been an address, because it hath not been in the Worlds method and form; therefore the oppressed shall not have justice done to them, which ought according to justice and equity, when the thing is made known unto you in the simplicity and innocency, without flattering petitions and addresses, you ought to do them justice, (for that end are you of the Nation chosen) if the grievance to you be made known, else the grievance will lie upon you; if you do approve your power and not abuse it, you will remove the grievance off you and the Nation, which if you do not, God will overturn you by it; and if you will set up a ministry, and own a ministry, let them be such as will keep the Gospel of our Lord Jesus Christ, the second Priesthood, without charge; for here are our Names who are the witnesses of Christ Jesus, that he hath dis-annulled the Commandment that gave Tithes, and hath ended the Priesthood that took them, and we are witnesses for Christ Jesus against this Popish Anti-Christian Ministry that *(page 34)* takes them, who are of the Popes tribe, got up since the Apostles, with their law and commands for Tithes (out of the power of God) which must be ended and disanulled by the power of God, which are not of the tribe of *Aaron*, nor of the tribe of *Christ*, for neither Christ nor the Apostles after they had disanulled the commandment of God, never set up a command in the World after that was disanulled, for to give the tenths to a minister; for the first command was only to the Jewes that gave Tithes, which Christ the everlasting Priest denied, whom we confess ended, in whom ye live, who is our life; and this is our Testimony given in to you, our faith stands in that power that bringeth down the mountains, and exalteth the valleys, and layeth them down with the valleys which are grown to be mountains; & thus doth God overturn by his power & arm all transgressors.

Rebecca Havens	Elizabeth Godwood	Sarah Chandler	Grace Marson
Mary Till	Sarah Reynolds	Elizabeth Green	Rebecca Hodson
Joan Johnson	Susan Swan	Alice Condel	Margret Christmas
Mary Catchpool	Mary Reeve	Susan Crumplin	Mary Dagnet
Mary Clark	Elizabeth Overel	Grace Reynolds	Anne Cookwith
Mary Ralph	Hester Potter	Alice Gorlyn	Bridget Ball
Judith Tomblin	Margret Bray	Susan Cockeril	Anne Clark
Dorothy Crisp	Elizabeth Sanders	Emlin Wyer	Anne Clark
Anna Cook	Elizabeth Selly	Mary Bliant	Sarah Clark
Elizabeth Crisp	Susan Belsher	Mary Petfeild	Mary Stampford
Anne Humphrey	Katheren Lamb	Anne Taylcot	Mary Stampford
Alice Parnel	Margret Gray	Mary Danks	Mary Boocher
Elizabeth Garlen	Sarah Osburn	Mary Grant	Eliz. Westrop
Mary Turner	Sarah Luke	Sarah Grant	Eliz. Mascal
Hannah Ham	Mary Middleton	Anne Langly	Christian Burch
Mary Love	Johannah Lamb	Jone Desborrow	Martha Went
Mary Lucas	Elizabeth Rice	Anne Stamage	Eliz. Gilman
Rebecca Lucas	Abigael Ludkin	Mary Renolds	Tomasin Warner
Elizabeth Lucas	Elizabeth Gibson	Mary Renolds	Eliz. Hospit
Lydia Chittum	Ellen Midleton	Susan Pateradg	Grace Dersly
Lydia Read	Mary Hadly	Sarah Hatcher	Judith Shortland
Mary Williams	Mary Llyod	Anne Keyes	Mary Allen
elder	Mary Ansel	Hester Haward	Mary Cream
Mary Williams	Elizabeth Langly	Hester Haward	Frances Cakebread
Mary Gibson	Anne Wethered	Eliz. Till	Elizabeth Simmons
Sarah Lonskin	Mary Steddal	Jane Banks	Margret Lenlce
Mary Cook	Margret Ball	Margret Banks	Mary Rolph
Elizabeth Rolph	Sarah Chandler,	Ellen Palmer	Dennis Miller
Sarah Banning	elder	Mary Wandewel	Ellin Hoy

Jone Barker
Jane Cakebroad
Susan Spark
Margret Web
Cordala Symonds
Margret Ludgater
Martha Bawrel
Martha Harp
Anne Green
Tasse Hulback
Mary Michel
Susan Halls
Eliz. Tober
Sarah Burch
Unes Lynly
Joan Symonds
Sarah White
Susan Upsheard

(page 35)
Faith Walker
Margret Randen
Eliz. Howlet
Jane Pledger
Eliz. Freeborn
Anne Alword
Mary Ward
Eliz. Fuller
Ellen Nicklas
Martha Pettet
Martha Baker
Frances Symonds
Eliz. Wenfel
Elizabeth
  Harrington
Judith Bretton
Mary Harrington
Elizabeth
  Harrington
Katherine
  Harrington
Dorothy Gallifants
Sarah Scot
Anne Coote
Anne Abrams
Eliz. Sparrow
Judeth Treson

Grace Morly
Eliz. Reynolds
Anne Green
Eliz. Heningham
Martha Green
Hannah Isack
Grace Christmas
Eliz. Hannick
Rebecca Savel
Anne Sach
Susan Jarvis
Eliz. Abrams
Alice Collison
Martha Sowel
Martha Beadle
Jane Pryar
Kathern Isack
Anne Morly
Eliz. Morly
Joan Barns
Eliz. Isack
Alice Norden
Sarah Norden
Margret Coppin
Dorothy Martin
Mary Hinningham
Dorothy King
Jane Walker
Margret Cant
Eliz. Jayd
Margret Bassom
Tomasin Bassom
Eliz. Bassom
Eliz. Carter
Ruth French
Margret Brag
Eliz. King
Frances Moles
Mary Maning
Katherin Stow
Margret Hat
Anne Web
Angellica
  Nicholson
Mary Nicholas
Joan Amy
Alice Bowles

Mary Carter
Mary Emery
Grace Hammant
Mathew Hudson
Rose Bridge
Rose French
Mary Ganner
Rose Mole
Eliz. Knight
Mary Hauchin
Mary Bust
Mary Colman
Eliz. Gunney
Rachel Wade
Eliz. Phillip
Martha Ellis elder
Martha Ellis
Eliz. Peter
Eliz. Kye
Grace Fluck
Grace Coote
Anne Reynolds
Joan Jarvice
Margret Clark
Mary Crow
Eliz. Body
Anne Bridg
Eliz. Bridg
Mary Bridg
Judeth Smith
Margret Bridg
Anne Hales
Mary Innevere
Mary Shepy
Jane Fann
Ellen Eve
Jane Eve
Elizabeth Perry
Margret Perry
Eliz. Elton
Frances Piggot
Mary Eve
Anne Eve
Frances Piggot
Ellen Morral
Anne Haddock
Mary Jother

Ellen Gunn
Sarah Gunn
Ellen Philbrown
Mary Coote
Mary Amie
Priscilla
  Churchman
Grace Day
Susan Adam
Margret Zuson
Elizabeth Cole
Sarah Ambros
Margret Lanworth
Jane Cakebread
Mary Allen
Margret Allen
Mercy Baker
Mary Smith
Sarah Ambros
Phillip Eve
Sarah Overal
Eliz. Guion
Eliz. Thirgood
Judeth Guyon
Mary Harvy
Mary Filbrick
Elizabeth Guyon
Ann Wright
Priscilla Ame
Eliz. Sutton
Mary Guyon
Jane Potter
Dorothy Jepps
Elizabeth Eynon
Anne Haywood
Susan Chitcock
Margret Huntsman
Sarah Drake
Barbara Coster
Sarah Guyon
Anne Cage
Mary Norton
Ellen Ambros
Anne Adams
Margret Hayard
Mary Cockerton
Mary Barker

Martha Tillingham
Eliz. Mathew
Hannah
  Hallibread
Anne Norton
Anne Blanchfeild
Susan Dynes
Martha Danbe
Mary Ludgater
Margret Gray
Susan Cooper
Eliz. Ludgater
Mary Bowman
Martha Smith
Martha Pease
Susan Sparrow
Eliz. Sparrow
Mary Winterflood
Hannah Saunders
Hannah Saunders
Sarah Cadney
Eliz. Aylet
Mary Bourn
Judith Quilter
Mary Bradey
Hannah Lake
Margret Child
Susan Chapman
Anne Islands
Jane Bigny
Hannah Ostler
Eliz. Jolly
Alice King
Eliz. Larrance

(page 36)
Rachel Mayes
Mary Lawrance
Sarah Lawrance
Anne Philbeck
Mary Lynes
Katheren Gardner
Margret Ebbs
Prudence Tuely
Mary Gilman
Mary Bennet
Anne Whitlock

Anne Read
Margret Allen
Mary Hubbert
Sarah Formon
Alice Die
Margret Took
Mary Jary
Dinah Adams
Mary Woodward
Alice Cock
Eliz. Gould
Eliz. Barton
Isbel Barnard
Eliz. Kemp
Alice Bradshaw
Kathern Bull
Eliz. Pice
Mary Priest
Eliz. Waller
Eliz. Priest
Eliz. Burton
Eliz. Carter
Mary Malton
Agnus Haselwood
Mary Whitworth
Katheren Fenn
Martha Maulton
Eliz. Good
Eliz. Hubbeard
Mary Rolph
Mary Weeks
Anne Bregster
Dorothy Ward
Frances Clements
Elizabeth Paterson
Amy Pardin
Eliza. Smith
Eliz. King
Mary Durrant
Ann Bacon
Anne Tackster
Eliz. Ransum
Eliz. Huggon
Eliz. Miller
Anne King
Eliz. Brown
Susan Brown

Frances
  Chamberlain
Anne Horn
Anne Swan
Katheren Scarling
Eliz. Cock
Susan Smith
Jone Bullin
Susan Gill
Martha Breese
Bridget Barret
Martha Barret
Amy Bonnard
Eliz. Allen
Anne Allen
Faith Wolf
Mary Couzen
Mary Moulton
Eliz. Gibson
Margret Spooner
Martha Smith
Martha Allen
Elizabeth Brody
Eliz. Roper
Alice Leada
Christian Brody
Jane Pollard
Jone Jeffery
Sarah Lawrance
Jone Salman
Martha Hawkins
Anne Hawkins
Jane Hollie
Mary Kettal
Ellen Nonne
Anne French
Hannah Ward
Eliz. Hunt
Ann Walton
Anne Potter
Joan Hawes
Frances Posford
Johannah Codlin
Sarah Hawes
Katheren Taylor
Susan Allen
Susan Lamb

Christian Pettet
Mary Jennex
Rachel Sadler
Susan Roberson
Katheren Ransom
Ellen Spark
Mary Peaches
Frances Goodwill
Frances Bond
Ann Gayford
Margret Stebbing
Rose Parker
Grace Adams
Martha Heath
Martha Gorbul
Alice Covil
Eliz. Bantock
Johanna Ridlesdale
Eliz. Kettel
Anne Brag
Margret Prick
Grace Farden
Eliz. Shipman
Anne Crosbee
Anne Cable
Alice White
Fran. Hill
Mary Boorn
Priscilla David
Margret Goddard
Mary Barnes
Mary Coote
Hester Wood
Christian Pettet
Sarah Stedman
Susan Kerrington
Katheren Baker
Martha Dikes
Mary King
Mary Peche
Sarah Norton
Mary Scot
Eliz. Stafford
Susan Driver
Alice Morphew
Susan Goldsmith
Anne Weeks

Faith Gorbul
Anne Trundle
Eliz. Bautock
Sarah Kettel elder
Eliz. Dixon
Hannah Wait
Susan Clark
Abigael Smy
Anne Bacon
Eliz. Crosbee
Eliz. Baily
Alice Talwin
Grace Bourrowgh
Anne Wateridg
Alice Wily
Anne Prentice
Barbara Gardner
Jane Nutial
Mary Yardly
Margret
  Middledich
Mary Burlingham
Susan Kerrington
Sarah Godwood
Anne Jay
Anne Root
Eliz. Pinson
Dorothy King
Bridget Driver
Eliz. Driver
Dinah Fryar
Joan Heard
Anne Warn
Eliz. Turner
Mary Turner
Christian Bundiss
Margret Bines
Sarah Kettal
Anne Ferriar
Margery Bullock
Grace Farden
Hester Farthing
Mary Phright
Eliz. Dunmore
Alice Simon
Grace Burrough

(page 37)
Anne Bourrough
Thamar Alderidg
Susan Wyly
Mary Turpen
Mary Bridges
Susan Cook
Anne Ezbel
Mary Midledick
Katherine Sadler
Eliz. Edwards
Johanna Cook
Eliz. Prick
Anne Froward
Sarah Fryar
Susan Pallen
Rose Gates
Anne Gough
Susan Rolph
Frances Gardner
Ruth Gorbul
Alice Pears
Mary Gorbul
Frances Smith
Sarah Hawes
Anne Page
Tomasin
  Bennington
Katherine Lame
Margret Shenman
Eliz. Akis
Margret Candler
Anne Dux
Katherine Sawrer
Margret Tovel
Sarah Cross
Sarah Man
Mary Vertue
Eliz. Hayle
Kinborrow Libbies
Anne Tattle
Eliz. Churchman
Eliz. Ross
Cisly Leech
Frances Ribbons
Mary Taylor
Eliz. Skinner

Jone Britewel
Abigal Camplin
Margret Cole
Margret Posford
Eliz. Akers

ESSEX

Kathern Willis
Katherine Seywell
Martha Crossier
Mary Bernerd
Rebecca Sparling
Mary Marriage
Sarah Sparkling
Sarah Bett
Sarah Bott
Sarah Belsham
Anne Barker
Martha Portway
Mary Choppin
Anne Pasival
Susanna Cutt
Darv. Bowtel
Eliz. Foster
Rebecca Davy
Frances Quilter
Mary Fordham
Mary Foster
Eliz. Crow
Jane Petchey
Rebecca Davy
Jone Skillingham
Eliz. Crow
Mary Smith
Mary Crosner
Ellinor Bugby
Hannah Scooling
Mary Bayly
Mary Evah
Mary Byat
Sarah Palmer
Alice Levite
Alice Levite
Margret Bret
Mary Special

Rebecca Emsden
Eliz. Batt
Amy Special
Mary Lark
Hannah Choppin
Priscilla Jarvis
Anne Tyler
Dianah Noakes
Katharine Jarvis
Anne Childe
Hannah Lark

CAMBRIG-SHIRE & ISLE of ELY.

Widow Matthews
Widow Prior
Widow Cole
Widow Norris
Widow Presson
Widow Ashton
Widow Purkinson
Widow Snesby
Widow Royston
Widow Pool
Widow Steevens
Widow Morlin
Widow Becton
Widow Cock
Widow Canham
Widow Bonner
Widow Lightfoot
Widow Sowrsby
Widow Sparrow
Widow Hattley
Anne Crabb
Anne Hawkes
Grace Folbig
Eliz. Asplan
Rebecca Berry
Eliz. Nunn
Eliz. Kater
Mary Place
Anne Love

Margret Hurt
Martha Dorman
Margret Payne
Sarah Drury
Anne Crabb
Susan Wilkinson
Eliz. Easy
Martha Johnson
Bridget Peachey
Margret Upin
Eliz. Ewers
Eliz. Thorrowgood
Emm Rose
Anne Watts
Bridget Blow
Anne Beech
Eliz. Blinks
Anne Forster, sen.
Anne Forster, jun.
Mary Salmon, sen.
Mary Salmon, jun.
Susan Feast
Hannah Mynit
Margret Vipence
Sarah Portis
Margret Right
Mary Vipence
Eliz. Mace
Eliz. Mills

Mary Grown
Alice Winfield
Hannah Mynit
Alice Jeffe

Parts of Huntington

Judith Kidson
Alice Ellington
Jone Aubery
Anne Ellington
Eliz. Ellington
Eliz. Goules
Sarah Goules
Rose Goodcheap
Jone Hills
Mary Jellings
Mary Nixon
Ellen Ingram
Jane Burgis
Hester Ingram
Mary Ingram
Eliz. Parnel
Eliz. Patison
Eliz. Coxon
Anne Wright
Eliz. Nursed

Anne Wooter
Alice Austler
Mary Parnel
Anne Ingram
Phebe Nicholson
Judah Thompson

(page 38)
Frances Drury
Thommison
  Bitterny
Anne Sammon
Luce Field
Anne Been
Judah Letchworth
Mary Love
Deborah Godfrey
Mary Woods
Margret Sulman
Mary Godfrey
Mary Royce
Jone Yeats
Anne Harbour
Anne Roberts
Anne Morlin
Eliz. Peace
Thommison
  Blackley
Eliz. Phiphers

Grace Cole
Anne Cole
Eliz. Berry
Anne Norris
Eliz. Norris
Mary Norris
Jane Jobson
Mary Bates
Alice Ashon
Jane Wright
Anne Seagar
Mary Marshal
Martha Pryor
Susan Tynge
Jane Smith, elder
Jane Smith, young.
Anne Ratford
Eliz. Pepper
Marget Morlin
Emm Morlin
Amy Wingfield
Anne Frizby
Clemment
  Whisson
Marget Presson
Edith Parkinson
Bridget Hilton
Ellenor Allen

BERK-SHIRE, HAMP-SHIRE, and WILT-SHIRE.

To the Parliament of England, &c. For them to do Justice, and to take off the unjust oppreſſion of Tithes that was never commanded of God.

THE Priests that sues our Friends up in Courts for Tithes, said, They could not pay the Protector his Tenths, who took the Tenths of the Tenths, except they had their Tenths, and that was their excuse; and therefore they sued us in the Protectors name, & have prisoned our Brethren to death, and drove away almost all their goods they had. The Pope took the Tenths of the Tenths, the King took the Tenths of the Tenths, the Protector took the Tenths of the Tenths, which have been overthrown before you, which hath taken the Tenths of the Tenths from the Priests, which wrestled it out of the Popes hands, which the Priests does no work for us of whom they take the Tenths, and keep us in the Ninths; and so they cannot say we are covetous, that do not pay them Tithes that do no work for us, and we never set them at work, nor hires them; Now if you take the Tenths of the Tenths, do ye walk out of the steps of the Pope, King or Protector in that? And therefore we say, all those things must be broken down by the power of the Lord, which will overturn Pope and his Tenths of Tenths, and overthrow his Ministers, and the takers of them before you: Come into a Reformed Church, as it was amongst the Apostles, ye must deny the commands of men that gave Tithes, before you come to the Church in God the pillar and ground of truth, that disannuls the Commands of God that gives Tithes: And Christ did provide another maintenance for his Ministers and Disciples then Tithes, and did not send them to the Store-house for to take the Tenths, though the Jews Law was standing, & *(page 39)* the Priests that took Tenths before Christ was offered up, and while that Law was standing, Priests was standing, and his maintenance the Tenths, and when that Law was changed, the Priesthood was changed, and the commandment disannulled that gave Tenths, and they that came into that that ended the Law, and changed the Priesthood, and disannuled the commandment, came into Christ the everlasting Priesthood and Covenant, of which we are into the Election before the World began, and here underwritten are our names that do testify against the oppression of Tithes, and they that have set them up, and held them up since the dayes of the Apostles, and that Law and Church; for the true Church suffered in the Primitive times by that Priesthood that took Tithes for bearing their Testimony against the Priesthood that took Tithes, that the commandment was disannulled, and that Law was changed by which it was made, and the Priesthood was changed also, and so he was to cease, so that Priesthood was of no force, nor Law that was made, nor commandment that gave them Tithes; And so by that Priesthood that had the form of godliness and not the power, by such the true Church and the Apostles suffered, as we now, by a false Antichristian Priesthood, and a false Law, and a Commandment set up by the false Antichristian apostatized Christians, since the dayes of the Apostles, since the true Church fled into the Wilderness, hath the false Church upon the Beast set them up, by whom the blood of the Martyrs, Prophets and Saints have been drunk, and the witnesses slain; but the true Church is coming out of the Wilderness again, and the Beast and the false prophet cast alive into the lake of fire, and the Judgment of the great Whore is come, the false church; The Lamb, the Saints shall have the victory, the Lamb, the Bride is known again, preparing for her husbands coming out of the Wilderness, and the daughters of *Abraham* are meeting of her, who gives in their Testimony against this oppressive Church, Ministry and maintenance, and their Testimony of the Lord Jesus Christ to reign, and that the everlasting Gospel is to be preached again to all Kindreds, Nations, Tongues and People, and Tithes shall be taken away and denied by them who are come into the power of God; the Gospel is the power of God which ends mens commandments that gives Tithes, as well as the Commandment of God; Tithes were thrown down by the power of God witnessed by the Apostles, though once a Command of God, and since their dayes set up by the commands of men, and must be thrown down again by the power of God *(page 40)* which never changeth, and the Christian suffered by the Jewish Priesthood that took Tithes in the dayes of the Apostles; so the Jews inward suffered by the Jews outward since the dayes of the Apostles, in the primitive times hath the true Christians suffered by the false Christians, for not paying them tithes, who have set up tithes not by the Command of God, neither is the Priesthood made by the Law of God that takes Tithes, for that Priesthood which took Tithes was made by the Law, and they were not called Ministers of the Gospel, but was made by him who ended the Law, and the Priesthood by which the Law made, and disannulled the Command that gave them, and this the Apostle witnessed the Ministers of the Gospel, and there was never no Priesthood that took Tithes who was made by the Law of God, but what was in the time of the Law, in the time of the War, which Law Christ ends, and takes away the occasion of the War; this Priesthood which takes Tithes now, made by Colledges of men, they are neither made by the Law nor Ministers of the Gospel, but by the inventions of men; So we in the power of the Lord God deny them.

Anne Curtis	Sarah Lambull	Alice East	Eliz. Bradbridge
Isabel	Mary Smith	Anne Weedon	Margret Whithart
Goddard	Anne Harrison	Tomsen Chapman	Mary Matthews
Anne Hat	Jone Wilsbee	Eliz. Bird	Mary Curtis
Eliz. Wright	Ellin Burly	Jane Hussy	Margret Mapelton
Anne Sharp	Mary Erberry	Anne Purnel	Rachel Coap
Jone Dee	Mary Emerton	Hannah Webb	Amee Bayle
Anne Creed	Mary Fellowes	Margery	Mary Stanclife
Hannah Miles	Alice Anger	Richardson	Frances Kent

Hannah Richbill
Margret Richbill
Eliz. Mideltun
Hannah Emertun
Castel Bishop
Anne Bartholm
Briget Smith
Anne Ball
Anne Wigg
Martha Hat
Anne South
Mary Dean
Grace Marlow
Mary Ren
Sarah Binfield
Grace Wix
Marth Nobes
Eliz. Dany
Anne Trew
Mary Wyron
Jane Cooper
Margret Redford
Eliz. Rason
Mary Scotton
Frances Nash
Ellin Cook
Alice Hoompheryes
Eliz. Aldridge
Frances Barret
Ursula Keand
Eliz. Webb
Mary Philpot
Jane Philpot
Jone Moth
Alice Boarnes
Mary Rickman
Jone Allud
Susanna Philpot
Eliz. Allud
Mary Allud
Jone Hancocke
Eliz. Forde
Mary Rummey
Anne Hodson
Eliz. Joyce
Anne Rawlens
Grace Beacham

Dowance Goodall
Jone Sawyer
Jone Rummey
Mary Smith
Eliz. Steel
Alice Pocock
Anne Slade
Dorothy Marks
Anne Spicer
Martha Weston
Dorothy Austel
Mary Cracy
Ellinor Hathens
Hannah Goddard
Anne Good
Anne Dod
Jone Reat
Lucy Cheaker
Katherine Sadler
Sarah Alfield
Eliz. Normanton
Eliz. Rance
Eliz. Gibbs
Jone Avenel
Sarah Osgood
Margret Hill
Judah Capon

(page 41)
Anne Champe
Ursula Clarke
Ruth Soane
Mary Oates
Mary Ozgood
Dorothy Blackberry
Susanna Hill
Elizabeth Ogborne
Emm Rance
Margaret Rotten
Jone Rotten
Sarah Harrisson
Mary Benham
Judah Hayes
Anne Holloway
Katherine Stiles
Elizabeth Morrell
Sarah Austell

Margery Rich
Elizabeth Hobbs
Anne Hinde
Anne Sheerewood
Anne Wise
Jane Kible
Sarah Rusell
Elizabeth Jarvis
Anne Lundon
Ellinor Hide
Mary Slade
Margaret Fulbrook
Anne Wix
Bridget Carve
Jane Duckeat
Agnes Slade
Elizabeth Keat
Elizabeth Smith
Elizabeth Belinger
Jane Stevens
Anne Malam
Mary Malam
Ruth Hill
Anne Hill
Sarah Malam
Ellinor Higes
Mary Tockar
Mary Slade
Mary Tocker
Ellinor Tocker
Margaret Befen
Jane Cook
Elizabeth Besen
Elizabeth Coeborne
Amy Samson
Florence Westel
Jone Mivol
Margery Ellet
Elizabeth Lamb
Anne Hall
Elizabeth Pearson
Anne Keepe
Anne Bayly
Jone Smart
Anne Fowler
Hellena Menchen
Emm Farr

Christian
  Waterhouse
Elizabeth Orchard
Joanna Waldren
Ursula Hobes
Amee Sampson
Jone Hedges
Mary Gill
Jone Stilwell
Katherine Valler
Elizabeth Valler
Mary Mills
Katherine Jessop
Jane Hunt
Tomisin Streeter
Anne Hunt
Elizabeth
  Blackman
Anne Worlidge
Frances Worlidge
Mary Worlidge,
  Sen.
Mary Worlidge,
  Jun.
Jane Streeter
Margaret Booker
Elizabeth Hewet
Elizabeth Streeter,
  Jun.
Sarah Biddle
Jone Biddle
Jone Hockley
Alice Turner
Jone Tribe
Jone Neath
Katherine Neave
Sarah Kempe
Jone Wake
Charity
  Nightingale
Joane Marshall
Mary Bayly
Mary Tukes
Mary Burges
Anne Dawes
Anne Allett
Frances Smith

Eliz. Simons
Anne March
Jone Slye
Elizabeth Gates
Jone Gates
Elizabeth Read
Anne Bullocke
Jone Carrell
Anne Bazell
Jone Wake
Jone Beacham
Sarah Murford
Parnell Cropp
Elizabeth Earle
Elizabeth Carter
Grace Senex
Anne Rainsted
Susanna Curtis
Anne Potter
Eliz. Streeter
Mary Tongs
Barbary Willis
Aune Davis
Tomisin Blinston
Jone Buckett
Jone Buckland
Ellinor Hawkins
Margery Barger
Eliz. Carter, sen.
Eliz. Carter, jun.
Honner Antram
Mary Bodicott
Magdalen Clearke
Mary Mathews
Frances Chaplin
Elizabeth Penny
Edith Tygard
Ursula Tugwell
Mary Cannons
Elizabeth Cole
Ursula Hexsent
Ellinor Embree
Susanna Hersent
Deborah Dornford
Sarah Hersent
Susanna Kiblewait
Hester Burges

Mary Hickman
Jone Whithead
Jone Manners
Rebecka Manners
Dorothy Rutter,
  Jun.
Rebecka Ennus
Avis Ford
Eliz. Chapman
Dorothy Rutter,
  Sen.
Mary Lun
Eliz. Stent
Johanna Austin
Rebecka Reeves
Sarah Jenings
Mary Marsters
Alice Munday
Eliz. Greene
Avis Cheek
Anne Whithorne
Eliz. Lun
Lettis Loes
Jone Booker
Jone Buckin
Eliz. Jenkinson
Mary Walter
Anne Reeves
Eliz. Penford
Barbery Mooren
Margery Barfoot
Eliz. Sewett
Mary White
Anne Weston
Jone Smart
Anne Cleverly
Mary Knight, sen.
Mary Knight, jun.
Anne Flood
Anne Coomes
Katherine Haines
Anne Row
Lettis Paice
Jone Wigg
Anne Wigg

(page 42)

Anne Wigg
Mary Pace
Jone Terry
Jone Appleton
Ruth Hayman
Jone Weight
Marg. Stockwell
Katherine Tees
Fran. Bidlecom
Priscilla Mosely
Winifred Newman
Grace Newman
Jane Bishop
Rebecka Hearn
Elizabeth Day
Alice Denman
Jone Barnes
Jane Newman
Anne White
Anne Read
Elizabeth Stocks
Alice Dyer, sen.
Margaret Neat
Jane Humphry
Mary Billet
Margaret West
Mary Lovegrove
Dorothy Bath
Jane Gouldney
Jone Hulbert
Sarah Bayly
Jone Haycoord
Anne Hibberd
Mary Duke
Susanna Godby
Margaret Star
Hester Bayly
Marjery Langfier
Anne Jones
Alice Dyer, junior
Margery Wastfield
Margaret Hacman
Jane Selfe
Jone Stevens
Mary Stevens
Elizabeth Phelpes
Sarah Paradice

Meliar Stavens
Anne Amor, senior
Amy Amor
Mary Whitbread
Alice Bartlet
Jane Whittacre
Margery Coole
Marg. Edwards
Mary Brice
Anne Mereweather
Kath. Mereweather
Katherine Lusse
Sarah Lusse
Jane Huddin
Anne Lyne
Mary Chivers
Ellinor Moxham
Jone Moxham
Jone Gaine
Susan Shell
Elizabeth Barloe
Elizabeth Andros
Mary Line
Frances Beacher
Ellinor Noyes
Jone Hudden
Susan Shell
Margaret Fishlake
Mary Bartlet
Mary Leonard
Sarah North
Anne Tucker
Mary Coole
Margery Coole
Margery Shell
Millicent Shell
Susan Shell, senior
Mary Wythers
Susan Wythers
Avice Andros
Mary Davye
Alice Player
Anne Merimouth
Cicily Taylor
Elizabeth Briant
Anne Tibbols
Judith Jones

Christian Tyler
Ellinor Stevens
Margery Estmeade
Deborah James
Elizabeth Tyler
Melior Rily
Elizabeth Wastfield
Margery Cawley
Jane Calle
Susan Calle
Susanna James
Jone Hale
Frances Smith
Margery Noyes
Jone Baker
Susan Cloud
Margaret Deck
Anne James
Elizabeth Bolten
Martha Leader
Mary Gale
Jone Keeping
Ellinor Bence
Susanna Mercer
Anne Bence
Jane Jennings
Elizabeth Henley
Anne Read
Elizabeth Read
Elizabeth Ethridge
Mary Hobbs
Mary Hinton
Mary Read
Anne Read
Mary Bencister
Mary Milledge
Mary Manners
Mary Crockers
Anne Harris
Elizabeth Hobbs
Deborah Daniell
Hester Matravers
Margaret Hand
Jane Potter
Jone Potter
Anne Hand
Sarah Moody

Mary Husday
Mary Matravers
Elizabeth Matravers
Dorcas Lord
Ellinor Woodam
Eliz. Wallis, junior
Sarah Hathway
Elizabeth Bridgman
Elizabeth Wallin
Susanna Paradice
Anne Bristow
Elizabeth Brown
Hester Brown
Jeames Dowse
Mary Andros
Jane Andros
Elizabeth Bond
Ursula Allins
Jean Beal, senior
Anne Matravers
Abigal Matravers
Mary Matravers
Jone Bushell
Hester Hand
Bridget Reeve
Elizabeth
  Stanmore
Sarah Stanmore
Abigal Stanmore
Sarah Clement
Jane Bollin
Susanna Bollin
Mary Paradice
Christian Aust
Alice Phelpes
Anne Phelpes
Elizabeth Phelpes
Mary Edwards
Jone Foord
Elizabeth Husdy
Margaret Barret
Elizabeth Allins
Mary Allins
Jane Beale
Sarah Beals
Sarah Edwards
Jone Woodman

Martha Edwards
Elizabeth Holbrook
Jone Mereweather
Jone Frand
Katherine Ludwell
Elizabeth Boddy
Susannah Blanford
Anne Blanford
Katherine Blanford

(page 43)
Hellen Beathop
Alice Blanford
Marg.
  Mereweather
Jane Benham
Sarah Ingram
Dorothy Davis
Bridget Fidshall
Bridget Bayly
Anne Hope
Jane May
Jone Hollaway
Anne Jacklyne
Jone Jacklyne
Elizabeth Gouldny
Margaret Uyner
Anne Swanberry
Mary Bredmer
Jane Eyre
Elizabeth Pinchen
Sarah Symson
Elizabeth Flower
Grace Flower
Edith Doddimeade
Annabel Butler
Sarah Turner
Jane Gibbes
Mary Gibbes
Susanna Butler
Elizabeth Davis
Jane Rickets
Jone White
Jane Pinchin
Margaret Greene
Anne Greene
Elizabeth Wyar

Susanna Flower
Jone White, junior
Jone Symson
Sibella Gibbons
Elizabeth West
Jane Gibbons
Elizabeth Flower
Jane Flower
Ellinor Flower
Elizabeth Salway
Margery Dobby
Elizabeth Wyar,
  jun.
Sibella Gibbons,
  jun.
Jone Foot
Cicella Little
Jane Pearce
Rebecka Little
Sibilla Foot
Jone Foot, junior
Jane West
Agnes Castle
Jane Foot
Mary Stone
Mary Foord
Jone Kelson
Mary Newman
Elizabeth Batten
Anne Batten
Edith Awdry
Sarah Batten
Millicent Castlyn
Sarah Parsens
Mary White
Jone Hatchet
Elizabeth Bull
Silvester Cave
Rebecca Phelpes
Margaret Presse
Margaret Weekes
Joanes Wythers
Perrin Selfe
Anne Walton
Margaret Rason
Anne Butler
Frances Greenhill

Jane Whatley
Kinbury Eyre
Jone Tucker
Susan Hall
Mary Adlam
Jane Hallis
Jone Adlam
Mary Adlam
Margaret Gawen
Elizabeth Swetland
Marg. Gawen,
  junior
Mary Bayly
Ellinor Widdowes
Margery Willis
Jane Wilton
Rebecca Bayly
Elizabeth Webb
Ursula Webb
Bridget Webb
Alice Webb
Anne Webb
Jane Webb
Cicilla Harris

Mary Higgins
Margaret Barnard
Jane Ryly
Alice Smith
Jane Richman
Sarah Barnes
Lucy Sheppard
Eliz. Barnes
Elizabeth Hood
Jone Angel
Sarah Gale
Margery Trewman
Margaret Hawkins
Sarah Gingell
Mary Burch
Mary Baker
Eliz. Barret
Mary Fry
Ellinor Langley
Susanna Ady
Frances Ferris

Mary Ferris
Sarah Swane
Margaret Gale
Mary Box
Mary Gale
Mary Bishop
Anne Tyler
Grace Tyler
Grace Saltar
Susanna Ferris
Genavera
  Sommers
Elizabeth Lausien
Jone Roggers
Margaret Scot
Anna Rogers
Anna Whood
Elizabeth Robers
Mary Amor
Mary Smith   ·
Jane Few
Cicilla Stevens
Jone Shelly
Margery Shelly
Marthamith
Jane Mythers
Grace Francis
Susanna Harrison
Onner Higgins
Elizabeth Eyres
Catherine Tyler
Mary Woodward
Anne Longe
Mary Parradice
Dorothy Rawlings
Alice Rawlings
Mary Nicholls
Anne Guy
Mary Lyne
Mary Hollis
Mary Bradman
Margaret Summers
Jone Sloper
Mary Swayne
Susannah Dyer
Margery Webb

Jane Pearce
Jone Webb
Anne Mundy
Jane Beazer
Bridget Hitchcock
Lucy Laurence
Hannah Williams
Abigal Smith
Mary Laurence
Margaret
  Greenaway
Martha Laurence
Margery Clark
Anne Kingsman
Sarah Crabb
Mary Bunn
Alice Kinsman
Anne Kinsman
Jone Hancock
Mary Sterry
Martha Scealy
Elizabeth Mundy
Mary Hathaway
Jane Barret
Lucy Lambe
Jone Sealey
Jane Smith

(page 44)
Mary Hadnam
Rebeccah Lambe
Anne Mabbet
Faith Boxe
Mary Boxe
Eliz. Smith
Kearsey Sparrow
Ruth Kington
Mary Deeke
Katherine
  Hathway
Alice Pallet
Mary Gale
Sarah Player
Abigall Barrett
Jone Smart
Mary Hutchins

Grace Huckins
Hester Browne
Joice Jaques
Elizabeth Holbrow
Jone Packer
Katherine Atkins
Mary Winckworth
Anne Atkins
Jone Huckins
Deborah Hort
Elizabeth Pointer
Jone Hort
Mary Punter
Mary Edwards
Grace Hort
Mary Power
Mary Shingells
Prudence Punter
Jone Beake
Margaret Sparrow
Margery Miles
Sarah Bond
Jane Whiteing
Anne Sergeant
Deborah Stevens
Sarah Stammon
Margaret Wimbler
Margaret Gardner
Jone Warman
Rose Warman
Jone Hicks
Dorothy Burg
Dorothy Woulton
Eliz. Sanders
Jone Wimblet
Mary Morse
Jone Morse, jun.
Mary Morse
Alice Woodward
Anne Oately
Anne Waulton
Alice Gutterige
Jone Bath
Jone Morse, wid.
Anne Sanders

SUMMERSET-SHIRE

We whose Names are here under-written, being by the Light of Christ
entered into the New Covenant, and seeing the Unjustnesse of
Tythes do witnesse, and testifie against them, and the great
Oppression by them; having hereunto subscribed our Names.

Elizabeth Addams	Mary Browning	Susan Budd	Mary Thacher
Margaret Ley	Dorothy Clace	Elizabeth Hart	Mary Stevens
Jone Rodgers	Jone Hopkins	Jone Hutchens	Elizabeth Oldales
Mary Lang	Elizabeth Munden	Jane Hutchens	Lucie Travers
Hanna Guire	Mary Hide	Margaret Willet	Mary Langdon,
Anne Colburne	Mary Hide, junior	Margaret Jacob	jun.
Jane Smith	Dorothy Brook	Alice Turner	Debora Higdon
Ellinor Dean	Anne Swetman	Ursula Kelloway	Sarah Janes
Anne King	Dorothy Parsons	Elizabeth Thecher	Sarah Bart
Frances Leveret	Tomison Parsons	Jone Hart	Edith Bart
Alice Chessicke	Jone Hart	Anne Hart	Agnis Tylor
Jone Day	Jone Thecher		Anna Tylor
Mary Coggen	Elizabeth Sampson	*(page 45)*	Mary Tylor
Agnes Bennet	Hester Long	Jone Olice	Anne Gundry
Bazell Wilmunton	Elizabeth Mores	Elizabeth Swetman	Elizabeth Wats
Mary Wornell	Jone Allen	Julian Coggen	Jone Wats
Anne Thecher	Ellinor Pranket	Mary Wilmington	Hanna Porch
Elizabeth Hodges	Avis Stage	Alice Wilmington	Mary Gundry
Sarah King	Alice Quantick	Sarah Starr	Margaret Gundry
Mary Wilmunton	Elizabeth Humphry	Grace Beaton	Lydia Gundry
Frances Bishop	Anne Pittard	Dorothy Chivers	Agness Hillier
Jone Wilmington	Rose Pittard	Grace Pidle	Agness Barrat
Mary Starr	Christian Lace	Anne Swetman,	Jone Pitman
Hester George	Maudlen Hart	jun.	Elizabeth Masters
Sarah Goodson	Bridget Bishop	Frances Estmont	Mary Lyde
Jone Loscome	Philip Rittard	Edeth Corpe	Jone Bacon
Rachell Phillips	Dorothy Fevor	Jone Bull	Elizabeth Mallet
Hanna Savage	Mary Addams	Frances Andrews	Agnis Jones
Christian	Dorothy Bicknell	Susan Leveret	Agnis Day
Waterman	Frances Addams	Thomaze Bennet	Mary Waliss
Mary Hurford	Frances Lockier	Anne Beaton	Jone Letsham
Sarah Marten	Mary Winsor	Margaret Downe	Anne Nicholas
Alice Beare	Jone Winsor	Mary Creese	Mary Taylor
Jone Browning	Winifred Winsor	Mary Longe	Julian Shepherd
Margaret Browning	Susan Wardfield	Emm Roman	Elizabeth Shepherd

Jone Metford
Jone Mabson
Abigal Martyn
Joyce Mabson
Precilla Gapper
Margaret Pille
Mary Moore
Dorothy Moore
Mary Piper
Judeth Wottis
Mary Lambert
Anne Boord
Mary Boord
Hanna Boord
Alice Oram
Jone Pavior
Mary Pinkerd
Jone Cook
Mary Cook
Alice Cook
Anne Sampson
Ellinor Pomury
Anne Huchens
Edeth Huchens
Agath Huchens
Martha Gibbs
Jone Cole
Ellinor Gane
Amee Sage
Agnus Sage
Elizabeth Day
Elizabeth
  Wickham
Bridget Nash
Mary Sanborne
Anne Melles
Sara Greene
Jone Allen
Ales Gane
Waborogh Short
Garteret Gane
Christian Frances

Jone Frances
Charity Hill
Elizabeth Veal
Anne Hill
Anne Chilson
Susanna Clement
Margaret Boulter
Sarah Boulter
Anne Minchen
Anne Jones
Jone Mawsell
Susannah Goslet
Susannah Poope
Elizabeth Poope
Alice Hiscox
Anne Nash
Abigall Nash
Jane Pinker
Judeth Daniell
Jone Daniell
Jone Pearce
Sarah Pearce
Anne Gottell
Susannah Pearce
Jone Small
Margery Radford
Ellinor Dogget
Elizabeth Sturedge
Mary Cammons
Mary Lusbury
Jone Douting
Sarah Ledhat
Elinor Biggs
Susannah Jones
Susannah
  Landsdon
Jone Doggett
Alice Skidmore
Anne Collins
Sarah Sargant
Rebecca Scrime
Jane Morle

Elizabeth
  Stockman
Mary Emsbury
Sarah Morley
Jane Murford
Elizabeth Evins
Hanna Collins
Alice Collins
Mary Downe
Sarah Reede
Anne Candell
Elizabeth
  Browning
Joice Cowling
Rebecca Cowling
Precilla Rowlings
Precilla Allin
Alice Bennat
Martha Warden
Eliz. Daniell
Anne Brock
Mary Hasell
Eliz. Barson
Elizabeth Price
Frances Barson
Mary Jones
Ruth Brock
Margaret Baugh
Eliz. Milkens
Mabell Wastfild
Mary Hicks
Anne Gillet
Jane Bayle
Abigal Selwood
Susanna Barnes
Ellinor Daniell
Rachell Jobbins
Alice Withey
Kather. Withey
Anne Lock, sen.
Elizabeth Lock

Anne Lock, jun.
Anne Lambert
Anne Lewes
Mary Mapson
Elice Hull
Mary Bryan
Ustul Plumly
Anne Feare
Hannah Blemman
Gartery Clothier
Anne Preston
Sibbil Stroad
Mary White
Rebeckah Gibbs
Jone Bryan
Esbell Stroad
Dorothy Scot
Dorothy Waters
Mary Weeb
Anne Rucke

(page 46)
Mary Cosens
Eliz. Davis
Mary Horwood
Luce Rocke
Eliz. Wethyman
Eliz. Stacy
Alice Vinson
Eliz. Tucker
Anne Marshall
Anne Wilmote
Eliz. Atkins
Mary Pitts
Anne Giles
Mary Giles
Grace Giles
Jone Giles
Jone Salsbury
Jone Stent
Elizabeth Key

OXFORD.

We whofe Names are under-written, do here fet our Hands againft the Injuftice of Tythes, and long Oppreffion of them, which hath been upheld contrary to Chrift Jesus, the everlasting High Prieft, who is after the Order of *Melchizedeck* and not after the Order of *Aaron*, &c.

Jane Bettris	Alice Stephens	Christian Martin	Anne Sessions
Anne Taylor	Susan Taylor	Jone Gilpin	Elizabeth Hawkins
Eliz. White	Eliz. Digby	Hester Good	Eddy Cripes
Eliz. Constable	Mary Busby	Margaret Westly	Jone Seacole
Eliz. Francklin	Anne Carter	Jane Wittney	Anne Adams
Anna Squier	Anne Stoe	Hester Good	Hester Harris
Ellen Seale	Joyce Bucher	Alice Reade	Anne Nutt
Jone Hayward	Eliz. Watson	Margaret Hichman	Maude Writon
Anne Lankett	Mary Busby, jun	Emm Emett	Grace Busby
Ann Lanket, jun	Eliz. Bulle	Frances Lavell	Elizabeth Watts
Hester Mansill	Mary Hedges	Elizabeth Beast	Anne Barnes
Elinor King	Margery Hedges	Mary Francklin	Lettice Wrighton
Hanna Pickering	Eliz. Coutes	Elizabeth Shadd	Isabell Nicholls
Mary Loe	Anne Marchell	Alice West	Anne Trepass
Elizabeth Loe	Isabel Stapell	Elizabeth Larner	Ellinor Elsritt
Anne Boxe	Anne Cunington	Anne Brinckfeild	Dians Min
Martha Patrick	Eliz. Bager	Elizabeth Cole	Susanna Bruse
Ann Williard	Eliz. Buttler	Katherine Strenth	Bridgett Merry
Mary Williard	Eliz. Cruch	Elizabeth Baker	Elizabeth Cheires
Eliz. Daken	Mary Harden	Margaret Baliss	Anne Upstone
Anna Bettris	Kath. Hichman	Dorothy Bennet	Ellinor Flecher
Jone Lankett	Ursula Hall	Margaret Castle	Mary Barrett
Rebecca Lanket	Dyna Leaver	Anne Harris	Mary Flecher
Mary Harris	Jone Prier	Liddia Bayliss	Ellen Flecher
Ellen Huggins	Bridget Coles	Frances Quatterman	Mary Haughten
Jone Attley	Kath Tarrent	Jone Shepheard	Anne Haughten
Anne Ryland	Jone Small	Josion Shepheard	Alice Horne
Kath. Wheeler	Anne Cater	Eliz. Sesheons	Alice Coulling

(page 47) BUCKINGHAM.

A remnant of the Lords hand-maids in *Buckingham-ſhire* : Truly wee cannot, whoſe hearts are upright to the Lord, but joyn our teſtimony with our Bretheren, againſt the unjuſt Oppreſſion of Tythes; and have with one conſent our Hands ſet, in the Power of God, to ſtand in the time of Tryal, witneſſes for the Lord againſt the ſame.

Anne Sherwood
Mary Britnall
Martha Brown
Constance Dearson
Hester Nicholas
Alice King
Jane Saverson
Margaret Knight
Susan Fanimore
Mary Chalman
Eliz. Goodman
Elizabeth Glidwell
Alice Hall
Mary King
Eliz. Balding
Susan Cleark
Mary Busby
Eliz. Thornton
Eliz. Cuningham
Sarah Ansell
Alice Milling
Mary Groome
Elizabeth Glidwell
Susan Mouse
Mary Steele
Jane Marke
Martha Mably
Anne Buttifant
Mary Breirly
Anne Hunt
Christian Bedford
Margaret Marshall
Susan Hollis
Hannah Glidwell
Jone Vaugh
Dorothy Robinson
Anne Hicks
Elizabeth Vessey
Martha Ansely
Jane Woolrich
Jane Dyons
Elizabeth Taylor
Anne Arnot
Elinor Dearson
Elizabeth King
Mary Glidwell
Mary Kaindkin

Katherine Steevens
Rebecca Deaverick
Anne King
Dorothy King
Hester Barridge
Elizabeth Starling
Mary White
Elizabeth Swelson
Alice Hutton
Rebecca Courston
Constance Dearson
Mary Arnot
Ruth Pingham
Elizabeth Medien
Mary Burkett
Anne Parfert
Jane Randel
Mary Reading
Guielmamaria
   Springet
Martha Giger
Mary Pennington
Priscilla Hatborn
Anne Sweame
Mane Pensen
Anne Hersent
Frances Mead
Martha Spot
Jone Dant
Anne Gibbions
Elizabeth Cragg
Mary Burket
Rebecca Spott
Anne Higgens
Sarah Body
Elizabeth Alderige
Mary Aldrige
Martha Spot
Ann Alding
Dorothy Morete
Elizabeth Peck
Sary Russel
Mary Garret
Sarah Russel
Bridget Kibble
Dorothy Moorer
Judith Alderidge

Elizabeth Betton
Martha Bluck
Katherine Saxton
Faith Jusley
Mary Swayn
Margaret Hatborn
Jane Puffy
Ruth Harwood
Ellen Cane
Anne Corke
Emery Streemen
Alice Clarke
Ellin Clark
Jemine Brickwel
Mary Rowell
Susan Wheeler
Hary Batas
Isable Feild
Elizabeth Alford
Katherine Kingham
Sarah Fripe
Mary Winckolls
Johanna Cock
Johanna Redman
Anne Morley
Annas Elliat
Elizabeth Sanders
Elizabeth Rumsey
Anne Ayre
Jone Pously
Hannah Gay
Sarah Shrimpton
Frances Rame
Elizabeth Spyar
Jane Turner
Elizabeth Judensden
Anne Steevens
Anne Spyer
Martha Johens
Sarah Fenner
Jone Borrowes
Phillichriste Noy
Dorothy Lucas
Judith Goodwin
Elizabeth Symcock
Elizabeth
   Hampshire

Mary Goodwin

(page 49 [sic])
Mary Goodwin
Eliz. Littleboy
Eliz. Stryar
Eliz. Stryar
Anne Hampshire
Eliz. Shempton
Eliz. Shempton
Mary Knight
Eliz. Shrimpton
Alice Turner
Alice Belshker
Anne Cooper
Jone Rosse
Anne Bennet
Ruth Ayres
Sarah Smyth
Susan Gallant
Jone Jorden
Anne Dorell
Dorothy Rosse
Winifret Cledon
Sarah Lamborn
Dorothy Douden
Mary Weaver
Katherine White
Mary Besson
Sarah Cosford
Judith Belson
Mary Hutchinson
Alice Sliven
Anne Baker
Mary Crancknel
Hannah Skidmore
Susan Child
Elinor Noy
Mary Goodwin
Anne Sherwood
Anne Harvy
Eliz. Kellow
Eliz. Austin
Margaret Sterton
Susan Smith
Jone Page
Jone Underwood

Mary Cooper
Jone Cook
Sarah Sutton
Anne Sutton
Alice Brinckler
Jane Cook
Margaret Cook
Susan Kendall
Elizabeth Border
Mary Burdes
Alice Wheeler
Jone Larrith
Eliz. Glidewell
Susan Newman
Eliz. Black
Margery Biggs
Jane Brown
Sarah Lamborn
Martha Deacon
Hester Weedon
Judith Johnson
Ellinor Hawkes
Eliz. Davies
Sarah Mortiner
Jane Jones
Mary Dean
Eliz. Kingham
Anne Sear
Amey Streattin
Katherine Venner
Sarah Batt
Elizabeth Grace
Susan Tombes
Joyce Prentice
Mary Pearce
Mary Lucas
Mary Lucas
Alice Greeing
Susan Bedal
Sarah Mortimur
Alice Axtel
Rachel Puatt
Jone Davison
Mary Hoar
Jone Ward
Ellinor Dearbuck
Eliz. Lockfeild

Susan Todd
Eliz. Pewiruce
Sarah Brown
Martha Cruch
Anne Trayer
Martha Treacher
Jone Abey
Elizabeth Science
Margaret Aldy
Eliz. Winter
Susan Witney
Mary Witney
Hannah Halsy
Susan Dover
Joyce Gardener
Anne Winch
Elizabeth Gray
Eliz. Hickman
Sarah Foar
Deborah Wilkins
Mary Brewer
Jane Craften
Mary Baker
Elizabeth Parret
Mary Parret
Mary Prat
Anne Nash
Susan Childe
Mary Nickson
Eliz Hooper
Hannah Norwood
Margaret Pewsey
Sarah Gardner
Sarah Tench
Martha Winter
Sarah Bayly
Alice young
Ellinor Pleasants
Sarah Harden
Anne Honer
Anne Tranmore
Anne Ashburn
Sarah Nash
Susanna Emerton
Widow Salter
Hannah Hastings
Constance Winge

Mary Dingly
Hannah Alcocke
Mary Steward
Mary Wagstaffe
Michell Blabe
Anne Weston
Anne Hill
Mary Hill
Jone Goode
Mary Smith
Anne Smith
Mary Lampery
Hannah Thorpe
Mary Ladbrooke
Mary Vivers
Margaret Parker
Anne Mercer
Anne Baylis
Joyce Arts
Anne Kindall
Mary Wright
Anne Greene
Sarah Butcher
Anne Cole
Eliz. Kecke
Hannah Wing
Eliz. Morley
Mary West
Eliz. Alcocke
Eliz. Smith
Eliz. Hawkins
Ellinor Shelswell
Em Taylor
Katherine Taylor
Frances Toard
Mortha Bloxham
Sarah Hucks
Eliz. Greene
Mary Masson
Deborah Greene
Jone Ward,
   Widdow
Mary Haynes
Ursula Ward
Sarah Bloxham
Sarah Jakeman
Philip Lord

Ksander Hawten
Sarah Hiron
Ursula Gunn
Anne Pargeter
Anne Gunn
Mary Tomson
Eliz. Ball
Penellope Tustian
Eliz. Fardon
Eliz. Knoles
Anne Penn
Elizabeth Penn
(page 49)
Mary Howkings
Margery Hawtin
Anne Hawtin
Elenor Alcock
Jone Hiron
Eliz. Bradley
Alice Mathias
Eliz. Robbins
Dorothy Claredge
Christian Tims
Sarah Tims
Anne Tims
Eliz. Tims
Isabel Camden
Eliz. Poynter
Mary Gilks
   widdow
Alice Huckel
Anne Eales
Mary Lovedreme
Anne Persons
Eliz. Bennet
Ithamer Taylor
Eliz. Ason
Luce Peek
Luce Hall
Mary Batman
Eliz. Plumer
Eliz. Hudson
Anne Ionson
Dorcas White
Mary Berry
Alice Taylor
   widdow

Eliz. Belcher
Anne Hastings, wid.
Susannah
  Woodfeild
Eliz. Butcher
Philip Sandige
Sarah Tomkins
Susannah East
Mary Knight
Hannah Strength
Eliz. Hickman
Eliz. Buckingham
Anne Tustian
Sarah Browne
Sarah Williams
Anne Draper
Avis Fifeild
Mary Coates
Hannah Edwards
Eliz. Grant
Bathiah
  Hazelwood
Jane Batchelor
Mary Mansel
Martha Goodbee
Sarah Shepard
Jone Mansell
Grace Claredge
Mary Borton
Eliz. Mason jun.
Jone Haselwood
Alice Fletcher
Eliz. Mason sen.
Anne Stanton
Jane Claredge
Alice Hitchman
Susanah Rush
Anne Doyly
Jane Gilkeson
Margret Parker
Anne Mercer
Anne Coleing
Eliz. Gullipher
Eliz. Good
Anne Smith jun.
Eliz. Shelswell
Mary Crasse

Sarah Wailes
Susannah Wats

Warwickshire

Anne Tims
Mary Times
Alice Emes
Mary Times
Eliz. Gibbins
Jone Parker
Hannah Rose
Rebeckah Rose
Hannah
  Whitehead
Dorothy Brary
Margery Wilcocks
Yeedah Ropin
Yeedah Simpson
Eliz. Young
Mary Whittring
Mary Southum
Isabel Edes
Margret Tustien
Margret Rose
Jane Smalewood
Jone Smalwood
Jane Eedes wid.
Dorothy Corbit
Mary Corbit
Bridget Wyat
Mary Wyat
Alce Burrough
Eliz. Knib
Susannah Knib
Mary Nichols
Frances Jarvisse
  wid.
Jone Abrey
Anne Tenent
Dorothy Fapsen
Dorothy Williams
Sarah Archer
Anne Ward
Elner Wrench
Anne Banner

Anne Sabel
Mary Veares
Katherin Clarke
  wid.
Anna Mardock
Eliz. Astbury
Eliz. Estwick sen.
Eliz. Estwick jun.
Prudence Gamball
Sarah Streeter
Jone Berry
Eliz. Hanx
Ellen Sanders
Alice Nubard
Milbrow Davis
Sarah Rogers
Eliz. Clive
Mary Written
Mary Hands
Mary Lord
Mary Reading
Anne Reading
Mary Meedes
Mary Headen
Patience Hankock
Anne Moore
Elizabeth Eares
Mary Burton
Anne Hands
Margery Beesly
Alice Knibb
Percy Veares
Prudence Thomas
Anne Duttridge
Mary Beesly
Eliz. Whitehouse
Sarah Whitehouse
Sarah Hibel
Jane Carter
Mary Murthal
Alice Hadaway
Mary Reading
Eliz. Hall
Mary Stover
Mary Harris
Margaret Swinsen
Anne Walker

Temperence
  Meeke
Ellen Jackson
Sarah Swinson
Margret Bickly
Margery Bickly
Phillip Barefoot
Mary Meeke
Eliz. Read
Hannah Read
Eliz. Healy
Frances Bridges
Ann Kiff
Pearcere Bearfoot
Mary Ludford
Hannah Barfoot
Jone Weate
Ellen Jaxon the
  elder
Mary Allen you.
Jone Gest
Margret Swensen
the younger
Sarah Harris
Mary Baylies
Dorothy Burton
Sarah Renolds
Eliz. Edwards
Eliz. Heath
Mary Heath
Olive Badgley

(page 50)
Anne Baker
Eliz. Hale
Sarah Farmer
Anne Maxfield
Eliz. Aldrig
Alice Hall
Grace Hall
Alice Wriit
Mary Pease
Mary Croxel
Mary Sanders
Mary Burton
Sarah Standly
Jone Burton

Jane Byech
Hana Hopkines
Mary Food
Mary Nims
Anne Phillips
Elizabeth Batchilor
Sarah Parke
Mary Carter
Susan Smart
Mary Weare
Alice Toucy
Elizabeth Gibbon
Anna Hollister
Kathrine Phillips
Mary Chambers
Jone Weals
Jone Holister
Jane Web
Magdalen Bradford
Sarah Swead
Anne King
Anne Long
Elizabeth Wilkison
Mary Willis
Elinor Lewis
Joyce Ayres
Elizabeth Abbat
Jone Howell
Martha Swade
Anne Joanes
Jone Hosier
Ellinor Allen
Anne Snelgrove
Anne Davis
Mary Hampton
Alis Loyd
Elizabeth Loyd
Anne Warren the
    eld.
Anne Davis the eld.
Sarah Smyton
Anne Purdy
Jone Day
Margret Reves
Joyce Reves
Margret Walker
Mary Stemason

Hannah Neves
Anne Sowle
Margret Bickhead
Alice Nurdan
Mary Hilly
Sarah Smith
Mary Leath
Eliz. Gibbons the el.
Anne Long the
    elder
Elizabeth Brown
Margret Taylor
Margret Wilkee
Francis Holdstone
Elizabeth Maynard
Sarah Wilkison
Susana Freeman
Jone Northal
Jone Seager
Anne Cooper
Mary Fry
Mary Cole
Philice Cole
Jone Coale
Margret Crome
Jone Hilsly
Sarah Coale
Anne Ames
Mary Burgis
Eliz. More the eld.
Anne Chaffie
Jane Batho
Mary Belcher
Elizabeth Eagles
Mary Burleigh
Rebeckah Howel
Katherine Hughes
Katherine
    Hammond
Rebeckah Watkins
Margret Thomas yo.
Elizabeth Williams
Mary Goldney
Anne Jordan
Jone Hilley
Anne Burden
Mary Cook

Deborah Dyer
Garterit Poil
Anne Brinkworth
Rachel Jarret
Margery Cook
Bridget Templeman
Elizabeth Parmiter
Judeth Byfeild
Mary Byfeild the
    eld.
Mary Byfeild the yo.
Briget Horseman
Anne Gannocliff
Mary Leveret
Dorcas Ball
Elizabeth Seward
Margret Prince
Mary Croker
Martha Croker
Sarah Croker
Margret Piskin
Mary Prince the
    eld.
Mary North
Margret Arnold
Mary Evans
Elizabeth Woory
Katherine Smith
Christian Jayne
Jone Potterfeild
Sarah Bennet
Joyce Warren
Elizabeth Ford
Elizabeth Milner
Sarah Bourne
Francis Price
Jone Dapwel
Catherine Clarke
Ruth Davis
Sarah Davis
Jone Farmer
Alice Hignil
Margret Lovel
Martha Jenkins
Margret Turner
Ellinor Sorrow
Jane Bricksworth

Eliz. Merrick
Judith Batten
Rachel Mogridge
Alice Hall
Margery Wall
Sarah Mynor
Eliz. Harris
Judith Comly
Anne Jellet
Mary Roberts
Eliz. Dowell
Anne Daniel
Margret Thomas
    eld.
Mary Ford wid.
Jennet Williams
Mary Lovel
Eliz. Hubbert
Martha Choik
Anne Speed
Margret Yeamens
Eliz. Oliver
Bridget Hollister
Eliz. Pyott
Deborah Pyat
Anne Day
Mary Wastfield
Katherine Millerd
Mary Blagdon
Eliz. Yeamans
Mary Linday
Mary Huntington
Mary Noake
Lydia Toney
Martha Mason
Barbara Blagdon
Elinor Jones
Jane Weale
Margret Taylor
Sarah Price
Margret Price
Katherine Oatley
Hester Francklin
Jane Dowle
Jane Farmer
Alice Moore
Sarah Peake

	Mary Marks	Briget Winfeild	Mary Bird
(page 51)	Sarah Allyes	Eliz. Cannings	Margret Phelps
Sarah Prince	Eliz. Faint	Sarah Staturne	Ilith Bowes
Jane Lord	Margret Griffin	Anne Warran	Mary Haggat
Bethsua Speed	Mary Stanford	Britewood Jeffryes	Eliz. Dolphin, eld.
Jane Burrough	Margret Gallay	Margery Warren	Grace Bullock
Dorothy Hulet	Eliz. Gottey	Jane Warren	Mary Perry
Sarah Grave	Eliz. Balromb	Jane Mabb	Anne Bateman
Sarah Granger	Hannah Loxtone	Eliz. Sanders	Anne Wathen
Alice Philips	Mary Copeman	Anne Ling	Eliz. Morris
Sarah Champnies	Eliz. Driver	Katherine Davis	Deborah Stiles
Alex. Parkins	Blanch Phillips	Anne Redwood	Anne Ford
Grace Priver	Margaret Hall	Jone Tippet	Margret Hunt
Margery Claxan	Frances Handiman	Eliz. Martyn	Sarah White
Anne Mayes	Margret Nuton	Jone Dixon	Anne Hall
Hannah Parker	Margret Farnal	Eliz. Neale	Alice Droyton
Mary Didicot	Eliz. Child	Sarah Baugh	Anne Iff
Judith Weeks	Eliz. Morgan	Mary Sanders	Eliz. Bowen yo.
Judith Rac	Anne Long eld.	Jone Shepman	Eliz. Hunt
Alce Slauter	Elizabeth Parke	Mary Wathen	Eliz. Gibbins yo.

GLOCESTER—SHIRE.

To the Parliament of *England*, &c.

*To do equity, to take off this unequal maintenance of the Teachers, which do
take of people whom they do no work for, who swallowes down the needy
for a thing of nought; and the Judges of their Courts have been like raven-
ing Wolves, prisoning such unequally on the Priests behalfe, whom they
do no work for, and will not give them maintenance; Therefore if you
equally do weigh and consider things to bring the Nation into peace, it
must be in equity, for if you do but consider these Priests which are the
bringers of the Nations into troubles, setting them one against another
(which was not the way of the Ministers of Christ, whose) throates are as
open Sepulchres, who drinks up iniquity, and who swollowes down all;
(mark) the fatherlesse part, the widdowes part, and the strangers part,
and so are worse then the Jews.*

HOW do you who are the heads of the Nation expect we should
pay your taxes, when you suffer the Priests to take away our
goods, that do no worke for us, and they come and claim through the
pretence Tythe from you, of us for their preaching, that to us does not
preach, and will not suffer us to try their doctrine, but we must receive

all whether bad or good; and if we do question it, six moneths in the house of correction, or five pounds fine: And if the Priest come and pretend 15 l. Tythes they will take a hundred pounds; You grant them fifteen pound of us whom they do not work for, and they will take a hundred *(page 52)* pounds, & drive away our horses and oxen, and plough geer, and take ten times as much as the value, as they have done, which is upon record, whether this be the way to ruin a Nation, or to preserve it, judge in your selves, and how in this case we are like to pay taxes; this is not the way to bring the creation into liberty, which would be at liberty, but to keep it in bondage, and it is an unrighteous thing to force people to maintain a Minister that they know in their consciences they are contrary to God; & then again it is an unrighteous thing that they should not have their liberty to question and try their doctrine without imprisonment; and friends, yet this unrighteous Ministry shall have their liberty, and be tollerated by the power of the Nation to spoil the goods, to summon to Courts, to prison to death, to take treble and treble more then themselves demand, and to drive away the goods, Catele and Oxen of them they work not for; judg in your selves concerning these things, here are our names against it.

Perses Warner	Hannah Dorney	Mary Tovey	Alice Small
Anne Prigg	Eliz. Long	Anne Champneis	Eliz. Smith
Susanna Fryer	Mary Jeffery	Agnes Feild	Mary Smith
Rebecca Cooke	Hester Geffery	Bridget Taylor	Margret Pullen
Edeth Scarlet	Eliz. Mousell	Lydia Roberts	Alice Baker
Cicilly Turner	Edith Bingham	Lucy Waite	Jane Campneis
Hester Doding	Eliz. Dando	Susan Andrews	Jane White
Mary Cox	Mary Jefferies	Eliz. Taylor	Jane Parker
Alice Barkely	Abigal Bousball	Mary Walker	Eliz. Smith
Sarah Howel	Anne Milledge	Edith Dando	Alice Wilson
Sarah Hampton	Mary Stinchcome	Elia. Picke	Mary Wilson
Florence Long	Meriam Weare	Eliz. Noote	Mary Sommers
Mary Mills	Mary Munday	Jane Lippiatt	Elliner Thuruston
Anne Mills	Sarah Power	Agnes Edmonds	Alice Haynes
Sarah Venn	Clara Robbins	Silvester Baker	Eliz. Haucock
Jane Hathway	Hester Boy	Iane Whiting	Eliz. Edwards
Eliz. Pouting	Jane Collings	Briget Thurston	Eliz. March
Susana Champnes	Mry Howborow	Sarah Champneis	Eliz. Field
Briget Ames	Jane Clarke	Mary Walker	Anne Stoner
Anne Silcocke	Mary Howborow	Sarah Budding	Jane Smith
Katherine Dorney	jun.	Alice Hollester	Jane Smith
Susan Venn	Eliz. Parsons	Ellioner Holder	Katherine Smith
Hester Ashford	Margret Hollester	Jane Sturges	Mary Hall

Mary Hall
Eliz. Budden
Rachel Trueman
Anne James
Anne Joanes
Frances Cole
Eliz. Atwood
Edith Tipper
Rebecca Scuse
Mary Marshal
Katherine Graves
Elioner Weston
Margery Stambag
Anne Warner
Anne Williams
Anne Thornedel
Frances Brodeford
Christian Kite
Venice Russel
Hannah Evans
Anne Norris
Hester Walker
Katherine Eastburg
Jane Pirrine
Eliz. Green
Sarah Russel
Mary Durey
Alice Butcher
Anne Keite

(page 53)
Sarah Bramsgrove
Mary Mosely
Elioner Walker
Jane Fowler

Jane Wiggen
Jane Harwood
Christian Reite
Anne Pettifer
Mary Pettifer
Jane Pettifer
Sarah Pettifer
Sarah Meaks
Ursula Upton
Diana Meaks
Sarah Woolley
Eliz. Tomlinson
Bridget Ball
Mary Woolley
Susannah Roach
Rachel Cabbel
Hester Alesop
Alice Sifford
Martha Hathway
Sarah Long
Margret Cabbel
Anne Symons
Anne Jeffery
Martha Jeffery
Sarah Abbot
Sarah Somers
Edith Mills
Eliz. White
Marg. Graves
Jane Beese
Anne Cox
Sarah Hollester
Anne Hill
Anne Deeks
Hester Davis

Anne Dickson
Eliz. Wickham
Mary Merrick
Eliz. Cox
Mary Tiler
Ruth Ogborn
Lidda Thurston
Mary Davis
Anne Atwood
Alice Sellman
Maudline Jackson
Jone Swine
Susanna Deveres
Sarah Curtis
Sarah Meal
Priscilla Prigg
Rebecca Wodham
Mary Flower
Anne Wickham
Elioner Wodham
Mary Brittian
Eliz. Wodham
Mary Bullock
Eliz. Mowsel
Mary Edwards
Mary Clement
Mary Smith
Eliz. Smith
Anne Bampton
Widow Cad
Jone Freeman
Mary Surman
Joice Surman
Margery Surman
Anne Surman

Jone Surman
Sarah Surman
Mary Beale
Alice Beale
Mary Jones
Jone Wall
Jone Simmens
Abigal Silly
Margret Smith
Felice Carter
Ruth Currier
Anne Rykets
Margret Duke
Alice Merrel
Eliz. Hapward
Margret Griving
Margret Heaps
Anne Heaps
Anne Rickets
Eliz. Joyes
Jane Irey
Mary Webb
Comfort Michal
Ellinor Hatcher
Anne Holland
Anne Winyeat
Anne Wasfield
Eliz. Orkey
Eliz. Smith
Eliz. Ready
Anne White
Mary Long
Jone Moor
Anne Edmonds
Margret Lambert.

LONDON and SOUTHWARK.

To the Parliament of England, *&c.*

TO you which should do Justice, we who are of the female kind, whose names are underwritten, do bear our Testimony against Priests and Tithes, who have spoiled our Friends goods, and prisoned many of them to death, and hath many of them in prison, because they cannot put into their mouths that doth no work for us and them, which is an unreasonable thing, and they that be so much crying up Tithes for maintenance for their Ministry, are such as are covetous and great men, whose fruits declares which is manifest that they have not so much love to their Ministers as to maintain them themselves, but would have others to maintain them with Tithes, them that own not their Ministry, and is not of their *(page 54)* Church, and this is their end, we see their crying up their Ministry is not to maintain them themselves, but that others should maintain them for them, whom they do no work for, and this is their covetous end; so this is to save themselves, and not so much that they care for their Ministry, if they did, they would maintain them themselves, and would not seek to others to maintain them.

1. Let no man be prisoned for observing the Order of the Church of God and Doctrine of the Apostles, that is, if anything be revealed to him that sits by, the other is to hold his peace, that all may learn and be comforted, least you be the men that quench the Spirit, and limits the holy One, and dispiseth prophecies, comforting and edification.

2. Let none be prisoned for not paying Clerks wages, for saying Amen, turning the hour-glass, and such like services.

3. Let none have their goods spoiled or be imprisoned, because they would not come to the old Mass-house, which is called the Steeple-house; for we are prisoned and fined for not going to the Steeple-house, & we are prisoned & fined for going to the Steeple-house, and asking the Priest a Question, and yet our goods are strained and spoiled, and we are prisoned because we cannot mend the Steeple-house, and yet will not suffer us to come there; and in some places will hardly let us stay from it without fines, and we are prisoned and our goods strained for not giving the Priests Tithes, who will not answer us a Question, and they hale us out if we come but into the Steeple-house; and there never was in the world such an untoward and unreasonable generation, Edification, Comforting, Learning and Prophecying is destroyed in your Church, 1 *Cor.* 14. 13.

4. Let none have their goods taken away for not paying for the Priests bread and wine, their Communion, those they do not eat withal nor hath not for these many years, yet the Church-Wardens, so called, strains the goods of our Friends, to make them pay for their bread and wine, and Communion which they eat and drink.

5. Let the Creation have its liberty; how do you who are the Heads of the Nation expect that we should pay taxes when that the Priests takes our Friends goods, and plunders them whom he doth no work for? and some of our friends who have been for the Parliament ever since

the beginning of the late Wars, have suffered more by these plundering Priests, then by the plundering Caveliers, and *(page 55)* you have sadned the hearts of them that are your Friends, by setting up Tithes, and tollerating of them, then all that have gone before you, who have pretended to take them away.

MAry Elsan
Mary Foster
Anne Sampson
nne Robbinson
Amey Matthews
Mary Lonejoy, sen.
Mary Lonejoy, jun.
Margret Hutle
Alice Richinson
Dorothy Taylor
Mary Bassenden
Mary Johnson
Frances Transom
Eliz. Hutle
Mary Wilkinson
Grace Parly
Anne Ostinge
Agnes Pool
Agatha
  Netherwood
Martha Watson
Ursula Garret
Mary Westwood
Ruth Brown
Eliz. Peacocke
Anne Jempel
Margret Mekins
Frances Standis
Priscilla Eccleston
Authry Carpenter
Sarah Yeats
Sarah Sager
Anne Merricke
Alice Stodart
Sarah Blackborrow
Barbarah Jarman
Jone Crane
Ursula Ford
Anne Cart

Anne Cart
Margery Clipsham
Susanna Tysoe
Ruth Brown, jun.
Mary Goodman
Sarah Giles
Sarah Knowles
Eliz. Perkinson
Magdalen Person
Eliz. Harris
Katharine Askew
Sarah Ataway
Jane Long
Isabel Emms
Ester Baldwin
Mary Hall
Anne Vose
Mary Fox
Mary Basely
Eliz. Fordham
Rebecca Ward
Anne Gilman
Sarah Ward
Margret Holms
Eliz. Lock
Jone Hill
Mary Sanders
Amme Brampton
Margret Jeanaws
Margret Page
Eliz. Hautilane,
  sen.
Eliz. Hautilane,
  jun.
Cibel Carter
Liddia Oades
Jane More
Eliz. Drew
Sarah Knowles

Sarah Pool
Mary Harris
Margret Sharle
Rachel Giles
Hannah Thorndal
Mary Vouse
Mary Shoutwell
Alice Thompson
Margret Orinel
Anne Lee
Eliz. Pool
Mary Corford
Anne Austin
Margery Hope
Mary Mackeral
Sarah Coppock
Rebecca Pool
Dorothy Billing
Frances Hudson
Eliz. Worlidge, sen.
Eliz. Worlidge, jun.
Eliz. Tibbots
Anne Hemes
Eliz. Palmer
Anne Alice
Ellinor Chicket
Eliz. Whilwright
Jane Laurance
Eliz. Matthew
Jona Clapton
Margret Stevens
Grace Roberts
Eliz. Robison
Beatrix Oziar
Alice Evance
Margret Freebody
Mary Smith
Martha Wooden
Rose Hamm

Ellinor Roman
Jane Whitleg
Anne Hawood
Annis Gaunt
Anne Holland
Aquila Gifford
Ellen Barnet
Anne Goodaker
Katherine Charles
Susanna Laurance
Margret Bickner
Ely Hutchins
Liddia Farmer
Mary Jenkes
Frances Bourn
Mary Laurance
Margret Kirton
Dorothy Bergot
Ester Matson
Margret Syrah
Mary Neave
Ruth Powel
Clare Smith
Sarah Bates
Anne Thompson
Sarah Martin
Susanna Bond
Anne Wallis
Margret Stamper
Rebecca Trevise
Eliz. Stoddart
Jane Nicolson
Mary Vaughan
Constance
  Cushman
Alice Stoddart
Jane Raynor
Ester Shearwood
Katharine Bently

Bridget West
Frances Loda
Eliz. Emmut
Mary Ellet
Katharine Prestho
Anne Applin
Anne Coniers
Eliz. Proody
Eliz. Farewel
Jane Terkeridge
Eliz. Rogers
Mary Powel
Mary Peirce
Eliz. Dalton
Ursula Walkin
Anne Langston
Jone Parre
Jane Parre
Susanna Young
Thomason
  Matthew
Jane Hall
Luce Wilkinson
Eliz. Shaw
Mary Deveruck
Martha Pickot
Eliz. Whiteman
Jane Botterfield
Mary Cox

(page 56)
Judeth Fordham
Mary Loyd
Frances Facley
Margret Facley
Eliz. Pane
Margret Welsby
Prudence Pink
Judeth Mullen
Elinor Brook
Eliz. Bristow
Sarah Wetherly
Margret Hall
Jane Hunter
Anne Moor
Eliz. Wilkinson
Alice Lake

Jane Dadford
Isabel Mattain
Philip Wescote
Eliz. Smith
Jane Nicolson
Magdalen Peirson
Annis Gregory
Eliz. Ratclief
Eliz. Sawon
Julian Barret
Anne Stanford
Rebecca Painter
Eliz. Oliver
Rachel Green
Eliz. Baily
Abigal Darceg
Rachel Alford
Mary Draper
Anne Cully
Susan Jefferies
Mary Pye
Jone Mickel
Christian Jones
Eliz. Hart
Margret Cumens
Eliz. Upcut
Margret Bateman
Susannah Bateman
Susannah mansel
Grace Randolph
Sarah Noras
Alice Whitpain
Eliz. Cox
Margret Woodward
Phillipy Croutch
Mary Woodward
Eliz. Woodward
Martha Woodward
Grace Reeve
Anne Gardner
Anne Hart
Sarah Plumley
Eliz. Munden
Eliz. Hall
Anne Ingram
Eliz. Burg
Anne Gardner

Mary Fowler
Anne Boucher
Jane Pattison
Anne Flagden
Margret Shargen
Dorothy
  Champion
Mary Holcraft
Anne Winch
Mary Goodal
Ester Swift
Rebecca Haywood
Sarah Hinson
Anne Swift
Eliz. Fallow
Jane Scot
Isabel Dickinson
Anne Bibby
Mary Hackleton
Beatrix Berthes
Ellen Paddley
Grace Michel
Eliz. Green
Eliz. Webster
Frances Hull
Sarah Weight
Sarah Bird
Katherin West
Jone Bery
Anne Tyler
Lucretia Speed
Judeth Davis
Anne Hudson
Mary Booth
Katherine Catin
Mary Beet
Rose Hull
Eliz. Nicols
Susannah Keet
Nevel Simmons
Sarah Allen
Frances Pointer
Amy Ketten
Eliz. Morsel
Susan Kilby
Margret Davis
Tacy Davis

Susannah Harris
Bridget Fraily
Katherine
  Maderkel
Margret Rogdon
Jone Stark
Alice Lawson
Frances Meek
Deborah Flavel
Mary Strut
Eliz. Newman
Eliz. Sweet
Jone Wingreen
Dorothy Cooper
Anne Richardson
Margret Bradish
Barbarah Pick
Rachel Philpot
Martha Houghton
Eliz. Taylor
Frances North
Alice Clark
Alice Boolman
Mary Grey
Mary Hinkins
Barbarah Handy
Jone Raurha
Jone Coll
Lydia Newman
Eliz.Slater
Anne Smith
Jone Mabson
Margret Brook
Deborah
  Coachman
Anne Waker
Barbarah Adle
Joanna Lovelesse
Willnint Benson
Anne Grassingham
Eliz. Davis
Ames Stanton
Mary Oker
An. James
Margret Poulson
Katherine Foukes
Anne Grascock

Margaret Kirton
Anne Eyre
Eliz. Terrel
Eliz. Smither
Alice Pickering
Ellen Edmonds
Elizabeth Good
Ellinor Belton
Mary Bagnald
Isabel Selbe
Lydia Saunders
Susanna Goodal
Eliz. Thorrowgood
Katherine Marman
Jane Lockley
Mary Marden
Anne Write
Mary Taylor
Eliz. Sansom
Susanna Fry
Sarah Alexander
Isabel Lounes
Katherine Price
Elizabeth Hall
Sarah Pickering
Mary Laiton
Alice Davis
Dorothy Stacy
Katherine Duplier
Isabel Bartlet
Mary Kirkman
Grace Hall
Rachel Steward
Mercy Wally
Jone Noble
Ellen Colly
Eliz. Dorwood
Jone Lewis
Ellen Jones
Ellen Taylor
Eliz. Bouner
Eliz. Hurlstone

(page 57)
Margret Westcot
Anne Sodley
Anne Cox

Rebecca Every
Mary Carter
Sarah Millman
Alice Harne
Eliz. Milner
Mary Yeare
Katherine Fisher
Jone Cooke
Anne Clifford
Abigaill Warne
Faith Warden
Mary Lee
Thomason Dicker
Dorothy White
Katherine Blann
Kath. Atkins
Susan Adkins
Alice Nicolas
Ellinor Bellamy
Eliz. Broughton
Anne Coapeland
Isabel Wats
Anne Hart
Anne Gardner
Ellen Burgess
Margery Parker
Dorothy Doore
Ellen Bigrave
Margery Allen
Ann Lam
Eliz. Stone
Susannah Cock
Katherine
  Hutchinson
Margret Wintrey
Phillip Friend
Bridget Brand
Crysable Triming
Jane Bellamy
Mary Hall
Margret Davis
Katherine Marcross
Mary Burrage
Sarah Nut
Mary Holford
Grace Hudson
Eliz. Keeine

Doras Erbery
Mary Priest
Olive Chayre
Eliz. Parker
Christian Bryan
Frances Hawkins
Loveday Killow
Judith Linsoe
Duglas Temple
Anne Winchester
Katherine
  Winchester
Mary White
Mary Boucher
Mary Mease
Idith Beomon
Maudlin Carter
Joane Shink feild
Rebecca Mullens
Katherine
  Baranton
Mary Phillips
Alice Foun
Jone Bigs
Agnes Dolman
Chischan Saunders
Mary Saunders
Sarah Low
Mary Saunders
Anne Knolman
Priscilla Stoite
Mary Lenthal
Mary Doves
Anne Astin
Bridget Hawine
Margret Peterson
Jone Gosse
Sarah Hutchens
Sarah Smethet
Susanna Wright
Eliz. Lane
Eliz. Boylor
Martha Perkins
Hannah Corlimore
Ruth Sevel
Mary Smart
Dorothy Brend

Sarah Stent
Eliz. Craft
Lewis Saule
Anne Lowbridge
Susanna Robson
Eliz. Mitton
Eliz. Pottery
Mary Cooke
Alice Parsons
Sarah Parsons
Hannah parsons
Anne Lucy
Mary Heckers
Jane Cooke
Susanna
  Clemments
Sarah Watson
Eliz. Cowes
Charity Robbinson
Anne Jeuner
Jone Trevant
Alice Tuckinson
Eliz. Damson
Rachel Seany
Abigal Craft
Rebecca Newham
Anne Durly
Mary Ruberbon
Liddia Jesset
Ellen Brown
Mary Chaplin
Sarah Mane
Marg. Kitcher
Anne Samson
Grace Tanner
Eliz. Grove
Katherine Cashby
Margret Beanes
Sarah Hall
Christian Carrier
Anne Yarrington
Eliz. Basel
Eliz. Cole
Mary Border
Mary Heirs
Sarah Carter
Barbarah Partridge

Rebec. Everet
Barba. Marshal
Eliz. Bedwal
Bridget Sly
Eliz. Baker
Sarah Poael
Mary Baptester
Eliz. Bird
Mary Fuller
Dorothy Annis
Ester Cale
Susanna Gammon
Judeth Everton
Eliz. James
Alice Watten
Sarah Milet
Anne Peterson
Rose Gobsel
Jone Boyce
Jone Woles
Margret Nargrave
Mary Downes
Jane Busy
Margret Webb
Dorothy Price
Eliz. Williams
Sarah Mayham
Christian Webb
Agnes Cock
Eliz. Roberts
Eliz. Pate
Susanna Child
Eliz. Conway
Anne Bennit
Eliz. Marle
Ester Edwards
Mary Russel
Katherine Russel
Frances Broakbanck
Eliz. Dix
Eliz. Lambel
Eliz. Newman
Eliz. Russel

Eliz. Baker
Jane Wanesly
Jane Watters
Mary Roulse
Mary Yease
Mary Stanton
Magdalene Fuller
Tabitha Dwan
Margret Watling
Margret Warden
Jane Cock
Isabel Parlour
Deborah Medo

(page 58)
Hannah Downes
Hannah Chrisle
Ellen Hartly
Martha Simonds
Mary Datteon
Eliz. Frelman
Sarah Brariar
Eliz. Darby
Eliz. Croude
Liddia Edper
Eliz. Oliver
Margret Allen
Frances Seale
Aven Dance
Jane Holden
Margret Butler
Mary Patty
Mary Gallog
Sarah Swen
Glare Goldesmith
Mary Joanes
Ellinor Ebells
Mary Carver
Alice Harrison
Jone Bennet
Alice Heart
Margret Green
Venus Cabet

Jone Green
Rebecca Glangre
Anne Rollnes
Eliz. Young
Anne Mouses
Eliz. Bacon
Mary Webb
Mary Foster
Judeth Smith
Eliz. Leanerd
Ellen Web
Jone Holland
Sarah Prask
Sarah Collie
Mary Tye
Anne Wardal
Margret Collins
Mary Falls
Eliz. Strickland
Jane Fauks
Eliz. Perkins
Eliz. Martel
Susanna Perkins
Mary Foukes
Sarah Gyles
Hannah Wise
Eliz. Watson
Alice Thoston
Anne Hoope
Eliz. Larwood
Eliz. Luar
Eliz. Pukes
Susanna Morris
Abigal Pittin
Jone Carter
Mary Copper
Mary Foster
Sarah Bristow
Eliz. Jalafe
Katherine Germyn
Margret Fouler
Mary Bedford

Susanna Parkes
Ellen Bartles
Eliz. Catter
Jone Losmore
Bennet Nokes
Ursula Harwood
Mary Bradshaw
Mary Pettifer
Ruth Feild
Mary Darnel
Mary Horne
Elizabeth Brown
Mary Browne
Lucretia Crispe
Alice Stampe
Jone Harwood
Eliz. Stevens
Dorothy Kent
Mary Roberts
Jane Bullock
Mary Boreman
Deborah Favel
Sarah Luke
Arebella Wison
Abigal Goden
Anne Bibel
Mathew Bidel
Eli. Buck
Anne Allen
Margret Uster
Mary Crakford
Eliz. Mills
Anne Johnson
Sarah Godfry
Eliz. Root
Lones Powel
Judith Patchine
Tebytha Harris
Martha Vincent
Sarah Harloc
Dorothy Tompson
Margret Greenway

To the P A R L I A M E N T of E N G L A N D.

We would have you to read these things, and do justly as it speaks.

Et the Impropriators who bought or rents their Tithes of the
Colledges, turn them up to the Colledges again, or unto whomsoever they bought them of, and demand their money again; and let the
Colledges be taken away that makes Ministers, and do not let them
stand up in the Lords place, nor you neither; for God is able to make
and send forth Ministers into his own vine-yards; and do not take the
authority from Christ, unto whom all power in heaven and earth is
given; and cannot *(page 59)* he make Ministers without Schollars or
Colledges? And doth not *John* a Minister, say, as many as receive him,
to them he gives power; And so whom he sends forth are content with
his wages; receive freely, give freely, and that is set before them, that
they must eate; they must not go trouble Magistrates, the powers of the
earth, which Christ bids go into all nations to preach the power of
God, which is the Gospel; but Ministers of men, not by the will of God,
whom men sends forth, that makes not vineyards, that plowes not, nor
threshes not, such as they seek to men for Tenths, and keeps people in
the ninths, that hath set up tenths by a Law, that sends labourers into
the World, such as are made by natural tongues, which be natural men;
And those are them that have persecuted us for maintenance, and hales
us up to their Courts for their Tenths; which hath made the Gospel
burthensome, and have been the stirrers up of Magistrates, who gives
them the tenths for persecuting of such whom the Lord sends into his
vineyard, and these have made the tumults in the Nations amongst
people, about outward things, which is their maintenance, not for
preaching the Gospel, but about outward things; do ye think people do
not see these things?

And you may sell all the Gleab-lands, and Abby Lands, and Monasteries, and the Nunneries, and Kings Rents, and his houses, and the
bells to pay the Impropriators, who have bought the Tythes of Kings,
let their rents and parks be sold to pay them again, and let the Earth be
restored again to its place, and they that have bought them of Colledges,
let the Gleab-lands be sold to pay them, andso let the Earth be
redeemed.

Dorothy Gotherson	Emery Beenne	Eliz. Dofes	Jone Hart
Judith King	Jone Nichles	Rebecca Peece	Emlem Turnbridge
	Gilliam Grimes	Jone Clowes	Eliz. Lucks

Mary Greenland
Eliz. Prichares
Eliz. Hoper
Rebecca Elkinton
Jone Gilman
Jane Clemans
Mary Standen
Mary Rinnington
Alice Birckham
Anne Spice
Mary Hoult
Mary Bartlet
Mary Methus
Anne Hoult
Eliz. Hills
Mary Chambers
Jane Gore
Eliz. Kite
Margret Grinstead
Martha Deplock
Win Reeve
Eliz. Everndeme
Eliz. Housegoe, jun.
Eliz. Housegoe
Mary Turner
Frances Martar
Jone Hart
Lidia Mormere
Mary Cumber
Eliz. Philpot
Abieazer Boykin
Jane Hopper
Mathew Helly
Jone Mowlen
Anne Thrum
Anne Picker
Mary Gomber
Alice Noakes
Mary Noakes
Mary Forman
Eliz. Denn
Mary Hills
Anne Howard
Eliz. More
Alice Spurgen
Eliz. Richeson
Mary Blake

Eliz. Dingle
Avery Kingsfoot
Susan Cook
Anne Gower
Mary Joans
P. Harris
Ellinor Bredgate
Eliz. Fox
Thomazin Hogben

(page 60)
Eliz Toos
Alice Goodwin
Mary Howson
Eliz. Cock
Eliz. Pollard
Susan Wats
Mary Goldherts
Alice More
Mary Gener
Anne Foule
Mary Catchford
Martha Bishop
Rebecca Parthon
Mary Foul
Margret Couchman
Jane Elmenston
Susan Wills
Anne Dorly
Eliz. Fowle
Elinor Olid
Mary Campine
Alice Newman
Sara Rite
Martha Standly
Martha Copper
Kath. Darley
Eliz. Couchman, sen.
Eliz. Couchman, jun.
Mary James
Margret Holland
Eliz. Highway
Eliz. Rolan
Eliz. Becraft
Mary Correr

Judith Dirrum
Jone Stamer
Mary Day
Susan Brooks
Anne Godfrey
Ellen Fowler
Eliz. Coee
Anne Barker
Mary Roe
Eliz. Stroud
Thamar Pike
Eliz. Barwell
Ruth King
Mary King
Alice Clapson
Cameler Peces
Isabel Iserd
Jone Humfrey
Dennis Brand
Eliz. Reeves
Katherine Edwards
Alice Waltham
Anne Farmer
Anne Newman
Mary Bly
Mary Windbanck
Judeth Warren
Eliz. Crow
Rebecca Burch
Susanna Hackna
Grace Roberts
Mary Apthorp
Mathew French
Jane Astwood
Anne Tilly
Eliz. Burt
Katherine Ballwith
Anne Scot
Jane Collisor
Cisil Gilbart
Hannah Allen
Ursula Bond
Em. Hamman
Tomazin West
Beatrice Dawson
Mary Sanders
Jane Albright

Eliz. Albright
Sarah Coleman
Eliz. White.
Eliz. Smith
Anne Smith
Mary Lawrance
Frances Ireland
Eliz. Coleman
Mary Sheineld
Sarah Baker
Annis Ketle
Hannah Wilson
Eliz. Ketle
Alice Lycot
Jane Taylor
Mary Wilson
Eliz. Chester
Rebecca Elingham
Sarah Tayler
Milbrew Smith
Eliz. Rolan
Eliz. Highway
Margret Holland
Eliz. Becraft
Mary Coxer
Judith Dyrum
Jone Stamer
Mary Day
Susan Brooke
Anne Godfrey
Anne Taylor
Eliz. Taylor
Mary Chandler
Katherine Miller
Cleare Smith
Susannah West
Frances Reeve
Sarah Gray
Anne Osburn
Susanna Arnot
Anne Burgis
Anne Heath
Alice Walker
Anne Scot
Isabell Allen
Margret Hannersly
Margret Briston

Eliz. Green	Dorothy Alcock	Sarah Sleigh	Sarah Jordan
Ellen Johnson	Susannah Taylor	Eliz. Stonier	Jone Jordan
Anne Fisher	Margret Eurenal	Eliz. Ford	Eliz. Breeland
Ellin Joanes	Jane Lownes	Margret Woolrich	Margret Babb
Jane Sligh	Anne Machin	Jane Allen	Eliz. Gent
Ellin Mason	Sarah Clowes	Sarah Rowley	Jone Brandly
Margret Hall	Anne Feirnhough	Anne Rowley	Alice Dale
Anne Titterton	Hester Dale	Rachel Rode	Margret Clowes
Anne Johnson	Hester Brinly	Mary Woolrich	Jane Waywood
Anne Hall	Martha Sleigh	Sicily Jordan	Judith Cowley

To the Parliament of England who ought to free the Nation from oppreſſion and oppreſſors.

FRiends, a Compelling Worshipper hath a Compelling Ministry; a compelling worship and a compelling maintenance; so this is *(page 61)* the false Churches way, got up since the dayes of the Apostles, which is not by the constraining of Love; so we with our hands and names, lives and estates go against it, now in the day in which the Lamb and the Bride his Wife is coming out of the Wilderness.

ELiz. Alye	Alice Dane	Mary Partridge	Jane Carter
Eliz. Smith	Mary Hacket	Susannah Cole	Anne Bagley
Given Owen	Elner Price	Bettredge Roberts	Mary Caddick
Sarah Dren	Jone Price	Elner Brace	Margret Geffres
Mary Hacket, young.	Aperlin Letsom	Mary Bell	Mary Bilingham
	Anne Walker	Sarah Reynolds	Eliz. Crumpe
Eliz. Carelesse	Katherine Jones	Anne Holiack	Alice Lacy
Mary Amphlet	Joyce Jones	Anne Asson	Margret Roberts
Katherine Pooly	Anne Griffin	Jane Newey	Hester Allen
Isab. Amphlet	Alice Parker	Anne Newey	Allnor Smart
Mary Amplet, young.	Sarah Floyd	Isabel Newey	Mary Meek
	Margret Knight	Mary Huniat	Eliz. Kinward
Susan Pierson, young.	Eliz. Fido	Eliz. Baylis	Sarah Bryenton
	Elner Frankomb	Hannah Chandler	Margery Higgins
Lydia Clark	Frances Walton	Eliz. Booker	Susannah Dukes
Margery Walker	Mary Townsend	Mary Tilsly	Anne Abere
Frances Ball	Eliz. Dane	Anne Ardin	Katherine Goseline
Isab. Walker	Ursula Hill	Jane Heckes	Eliz. Reed
Anne Skiller	Mary Hill	Anne Hodges	Eliz. Phillips
Edbrough Bearcraft	Eliz. Hanns	Margret Lacy	Jane Abra
Margret Stevens	Jone Chandler	Mary Croly	Jone Neckols

Susanna Jones
Sibel Sagave
Susanna Pierson
Eliz. Wright
Anne Skiller,
  young.
Dorothy Martin
Joice Darling
Jone Stollerd
Eliz. Rawson
Margery Callath
Mary Bradly
Sarah Butter
Eliz. Parish
Margret Harves
Mary Hay
Mary Hoday
Mary Hunt
Dorothy Hunt
Frances Palmer
Sarah Carwright
Susannah Guen
Bridget Smith
Sarah Glifear
Margery Cotton
Mary Harris
Eliz. Lea
Mary Woodward
Susanna White
Deborah King
Anne Meadwell
Joyce Evens
Eliz. Pitway
Deborah Blick
Anne Harris
Alice Welch
Jone Woodward
Alice Davis
Eliz, Hardman
Rebecca Welch
Sarah Freasam
Eliz. Shartharle
Marg. Robins
Hannah Ball
Mary Woorly

Fra. Pitway
Margret Taudy
Martha Woorly
Sarah Walker
Barbarah Walker
Eliz. Tombos
Hannah Radge
Jane Walker
Eliz. Allifear
Mary Hardman
Mary Godfree
Kath. Allinton
Mary Turner
Jone Rudge
Mary Langston
Sarah Walker,
  youn.
Kath. Knight
Mary Beard
Jone Hulland
Eliz. Walker
Kath. Hay
Mary Izard
Eliz. Haines
Jane Taudy
Anne Welch
Rebecca Bennit
Alice Bennit
Sarah Bennit
Anne Brautby
Eliz. Clemmens
Mary Dolbins
Hannah Williams
Sarah Kators
Alice Jarkith
Anne Tayler
Anne Fowler
Isabel Plasterer
Mary Roberts
Sarah Box
Eliz. Baines
Cicilla Pitway
Isabel Dove
Eliz. Emes
Jane Keatler

Mary Treadwel
Eliz. Walker
Frances Smith
Kath. Cartwright

(page 62)
Anne Yeeds
Anne Godfree
Elizabeth Harton
Anne Rock
Anne Cartwright
Frances Guese
Anne Whittle
Eliz. Bennit
Mary Ballard
Isabel Banner
Mary Banner
Anne Sheakle
Eliz. Shekle
Mary Sheakle
Eliz. Kinril
Jane Harris
Alice Riland
Mary Riland
Anne Baylis
Eliz. Clark
Mary Pregin
Alice Booker
Jane Booker
Mary Dudsil
Mary Hitchins
Mary Cleavens
Joyce Washborn
Eliz. Wheeler
Kath. Smith
Kath. Smith
Mary Judg
Priscilla Salsbery
Alice Turner
Jane Goastly
Elinor Hay
Alice Harris
Mary Walker
Alice Woodward
Elizabeth Ems

Elizabeth Andrews
Sarah Phelps
Mary Smith
Grace Peakock
Mary Doom
Mary Brooks
Mary Bag
Mary Box
Eliz. Wheeler
Jane Goastly
Alice Abery
Mary Edwards
Jane Strain
Mary Strain
Mary Kirman
Mary Trudy
Christian Boom
Alice Maundor
Kath. Given
Jone Given
Jone Walker
Sarah Maunder
Eliz. Give
Elizabeth Willis
Eliz. Taylor
Marian Musbin
Mary Hind
Jone Fox
Sarah Richarson
Homer Richarson
Rebecca Richarson
Ester Harris
Mary Pare
Anne Tompkins
Anne Cook
Alice Given
Anne Wilkinson
Jone Crosse
Mary Bomdbery
Susan Simmonds
Susan Brinckly
Mary Carnake
Sarah Bortwight
Mary Blemint

Part of WALES and HEREFORD-Shire.
To the PARLIAMENT *of* ENGLAND, *&C.*

FRIENDS,

YOU have thrown your selves away out of the affections of the sober people in setting up Tithes, notwithstanding the many Petitions and addresses unto you against them up and down the Nation from the sober people therein, and the well wishes of the choicest of the Nation towards you; Now the contrary part in whose hands you fall, and to whom you joyn and yeeld to, will not stand you in stead in the time of your Tryal; and how should they but fear you, and stand in question of you that have not taken off the Tithes, the oppression? and by which the cause not taken away the Priests and the Parishes be on heaps, and persecuting their hearers, and oppressing of them with treble and treble damage; and therefore the sober people of the Nation would have had you to have taken away Tithes that caused the difference in the Nation, and to bring peace in the Nation, which if you do not, the Lord by his *(page 63)* power will remove you as unfit for his use, and break you to pieces, if that you do not dwell in his power that doth break to pieces; and fear the Lord God and dwell in it, the power of God, and his wisdom, that thereby you may know the supreme power over all the world, and transgressors in it, in that line. You have hindred your selves from the love of the sober people of the Nation, and if you do not take off oppression, how should the Lord stand by you, or the people of the Lord either.

Therefore consider these things, and the Lord give you understanding, for all eyes are upon you, good and bad, and wait to look what fruits you bring forth. Therefore it is the Word of the Lord to you, joyn to no wicked thing set up by the Papists, to no accursed thing, to no abominable thing, for if you do, the Lord will throw you out and overturn you; Therefore joyne to that which is good, if you do intend to have his blessing.

If you querie how you should do with Impropriators; Sell all the Gleab Lands, and the Bells, except one in a Town, or two in a city, to give notice of fire, and all the late Kings Parks and his Rents, that had Tenths, and sold the Tithes, to make up these, to give to the Impropriators that have bought Tithes, and the Abbies and the Monasteries, which much of the Tithes were given to, if you do intend to satisfie the Nation, and deny your selves of his Parks, houses and Rents;

So let them be sold, and the Colledges sold, and all the Tithes that belong to them thrown down, and then if you will have Schools to teach boyes Natural Languages and several Tongues to make Merchants of them, let every one that sends his Son pay him his wages; and if any neighbours be moved to help them, let them help them, that none be compelled by a Law to maintain anothers Ministry, but what is done, let it be in love; So let Christ send forth his Ministers and Labourers into his Vineyard, and so cumber not your selves about the Ministry of the Gospel and its maintenance, and let no man be persecuted about Worship, Church, Ministry, Priests maintenance; but if any man hath received freely, let him give freely, so let the Nation be brought to a free Nation, and the People to a free people; for we declare with our hands, and with our lives and estates against the Ministry that takes Tithes, and the setters of them, and the first Author of them up, and the Law that upholds them, which have been set up since the dayes of the Apostles; but keep the peace, and give them what you will give of your own Freely, and do not compel people to maintain a Minister *(page 64)* which they know to be false, and to be in errour, and a Persecutor and a Minister of unrighteousness. Trust not in the arm of flesh, for the arm of the Lord which is the power, is able to overturn all, and which will wither all flesh, and the reasonings of flesh, and all who trust in any carnal thing, or strength, or weapons, but onely the power of the Lord God, his strength and hopes will fail him, and the power of the Lord God will go over him, which hath no end; Therefore trust in the power of the Lord God, which comprehends the whole world which hath no end.

Eliz. Jenkins, sen.	Cicil Hanbury, sen.	Lucy Hix	Mary Hughes
Eliz. Jenkins, jun.	Jane Thomas	Jone Edy	Mary Bowen
Ruth Evans	Margret Hanbury	Eliz. Holms	Ellen John
Rose Taylor	Cicil Hanbury	Isabel Hopkin	Jone John
Alice Price	Anne Edward	Eliz. Hix	Eliz. Thomas
Mary Phillip	Anne Ellis	Anne Hubbert	Margret Williams
Katherine Morgan	Margret Thomas	Anne Thayer	Eliz. Harry
Gwenllian Jenkins	Jane Dawson	Kath. Cox	Kath. Thomas
Rebec. Price	Blanch Lewis	Hannah Cox	Jone Hopkin
Mary Price	Ellinor Barber	Alice Grindal	Mary Prichard
Eliz. Morris	Dasy Rosser	Jane Cox	Mary Collenbeach
Barbary Hoskins	Jennet David	Mary Merrick	Kath. David
Eliz. Morgan	Kath. Benowe	Sarah Hughes	Jone Thomas
Ursula Williams	Anne Morgan	Jone Hibbs	Malte Williams
Anne Rice	Jane Curtis	Kath. Foord	Jennet John

Eliz. David
Gwellen Williams
Anne Hannon
Eliz. Hannon
Margret Hopkin
Ruth Granford
Jane Daniel
Kath. Morgan
Hannah Riderth
Margret Wybern
Eliz. Morgan
Jone Jones
Margret Baret
Mary Barrow
Alice Selman
Mary Williams
Eliz. Griffeth
Mary Protherough
Eliz. Therburn
Sarah Bateman
Jennet Jones
Rebecca Howel
Jone Spark
Eliz. Relly
Jane Watkin
Eliz. Thomas
Anna Freeman,
  wid.
Mary Jones
Mary Roberts
Mary Powel, wid.
Eliz. Reed, wid
Hannah Grimer
Margret Matthews
Jone Mars
Ellinor William
Mary Preece
Mary Sarch
Mary Grimer
Mary Rogers
Kath. William
Mary Robert
Anne Roberts
Mary William
Sibel Thomas
Eliz. Thomas
Eliz. Lewis

Mary Evan
Anne Beevan
Mary Beevan
Ursula Hodg
Eliz. Richards, wid.
Margret Gibbon
Eliz. Gibbon
Eliz. David
Mary Ingram
Mary England
Anne Evan
Wellthian Thomas
Eliz. Vaughan
Jone Gawler
Mary Jenkin
Mary Robert
David Jones
Mary Plant
Mary Pain
Margret Pain
Eliz. Cowles
Eliz. Cater
Margery Ingram
Eliz. Cater, jun.
Hannah Ashmead
Eliz. Mind
Mary Pain
Alice Fareal
Mary Freeman
Mary Grime
Eliz. Grime
Margret Alcop
Eliz. Ekelee
Jone Jones
Eliz. Barber
Eliz. Prichard
Katherine Prichard
Mary Carners
Frances Gawler
Ellinor Hodges
Joyce Beaven
Mary Rosse
Elenor Beavan

(page 65)
Frances Young

Eliz. Ekley
Joyce Bibb
Eliz. Gwilliams
Isabel Caldwal
Margery Powle
Bridget Davies
Mary Hoult
Anne Powel
Frances Jones
Elinor Gwyn
Lucia Powel
Anne Powel
Anne Baker
Alice Williams
Eliz. Smith
Gladis David
Tanglust Thomas
Maud Iohn
Eliz. Thomas
Jenis Vaughard
Jane Hanard
Ivan Iohn
Eliz. Thomas
Mary Lawrence
Mary Watkin
Jane Holdinge
Mary Williams
Joyce Steven
Sarah Philips
Winniffred Williams
Owen Price
Jane Edwards
Margret Umphery
Dorothy Lewis
Dorothy Mores
Elinor Price
Kathrine Parkers
Katherine Guyn
Jane Jones
Katherine Prees
Margret Jones
Katherine Edward
Elinor Lloyd
Margret Lewis
Margret Ewards
Katherine Jones
Margret James

Maud Thomas
Given Powel
Markred Iohnes
Jonet Oliver
Katherine Morise
Eliz. Morise
Mary Danis
Anne Hughs
Jane Cleden
Margret Price
Margret Watson
Anne Watson
Anne Bage
Margret Cleaton
Anne Cleaton
Anne Jones
Jone Perkes
Mary Moor
Katherine Oliver
Margret Oliver
Katherine Price
Mary Houd
Jane Oliver
Jone David
Eliz. David
Mary Moore
Bridget Watson
Jone Rees
Elinor Jones
Sarah Thomas
Elinor David
Jone Mills
Anne Meridith
Jane Moris
Anne Griffith
Gwen Morgan
Gwen Evens
Margret Moris
Margret Rees
Katherine Powel
Anne David
Margret Crowder
Jane Crowder
Anne Owens
Katherine Meredith
Elinor Meredith
Jone Jones

To the Parliament *of* England, &c.

1. YOu who are the Parliament of this Nation, you should have thrown down tythes, which is the cause of so great troubles in the nation at Courts, Assizes & sessions; and many families in the Nations their goods spoiled, and their estates ruined, many prisoned to death by Priests and Impropriators, which abundance of the sober people of the Nation hath petitioned you, and sent to you by addresses, to have them taken away; which your voting them, up have voted your selves out of the sober peoples affection of the Nation, among the bruits; and such as be brutish will not stand by them in the day of your tryal.

2. If you querie, how shall the Impropriators be satisfied, who bought the tythes of the King, have you not his parks and his rents? have you not his houses to sell and make up their mony, and give them again? or will you set down in his houses and take the possession? hath not God thrown out such before you? will you be like them that kils and takes possession? will ye stain your selves? have you not houses of your own to sit in? this is a warning to you lest you dishonour your selves and your names.

3. You should have sold all the Gleab-lands, and sold all the Bells, saving one only in a Town, and Colledges and their Lands, and given them to all the poor of the Nation; that there need not have been this lamentable cry for bread and cloathes among the poor in the Nation; and have paid the Impropriators with the overplus.

4. All that would have a Minister, let them maintain him.

5. All that would have meeting houses, let them maintain them; and all that would have Clerks to turne the houre glasse, and say amen; and hang the pulpit-cloath, let them maintaine them, and not suffer others to be cast into prison because they would not maintain such, and hold up such, and maintain such things for others who have not the use of them.

(page 66[sic]) 6. And all such as have bread and wine for their communion, not let others to be forced to pay for it, that eates nor drinks not with them, neither hath any communion with them, not suffer them to be compelled to pay for it, which neither eats nor drinks, for that is a beggerly communion; but they that will have a communion let them pay for it.

7. Let none be fined and imprisoned for not doffing their hats, and let none be persecuted for saying thee, and thou, thee to a particular, and you to many, and give over setting up of images, in your steeple-houses,

and daubing them over with gold, as at *Tantlins* steeple-house in *London*; let the money that you bestow on such vain things be given to buy the poor cloathes and bread, and that wholsome places may be provided for them, as Nurseries, that none may be starved or perish for hunger.

8. Let no one be fined or imprisoned, or compelled, or forced to go to the steeple-houses, and that no one should be whipped for vagabonds or rogues which speak the word of the Lord, as they have been , which are worth 40. or 60 pounds by the year; and that none should strike or fight, or that none be banished about Religion or worship, seeing Christ said love your enemies, and the Apostles said, we wrestle not with flesh and blood and how have you obeyed Christ and fulfilled his will, when there hath been so much whipping and blood-shed, and wrestling with flesh and blood, by Church and ministry for maintenance in this Nation; let none goe under the name of a Minister of Christ that will have any persecuted for speaking to him, or persecute any because they will not give him maintenance, imprisoneth, or hales before magistrates and Courts, let not these go under the name, of threshers, or plowers in hope, such as serves not the Lord Jesus Christ, but their own bellies; let all such as these which are called ministers, be looked upon as popish, and not according to the Apostles, that the Tythes, Easter reckonings, Gleab-lands, mortuaries, ten groats a grave, 10 or 20 shilling for a sermon over the dead; Church women for money, sprinkle infants for money, and are made ministers of men, and by men, just like the Heathen as they make their Powoughs, which priests are not made by the Law, these that profess themselves to be ministers of the Gospel are not made by the will of God, nor by the revelation of Jesus Christ, for revelation they deny & so are made manifest to be the false Church, and not the true Church, which Christ is the head of, in whom he is in the midst, prophet and King, who doth reveal himself to his Church and people, to all these which Christ and God hath not sent into the vineyard, but which are made by the will of men, and are sent but from men, these have been traytors to Christs doctrine, and to Christ their King, who saith love your enemies, but these persecute their chief friends, which are friends to their soules, for their maintenance, and so are out of the Apostles doctrine, which saith, wrestle not with flesh and blood, which never prisoned any for their benefits, nor haled before Magistrates, as this popish tribe hath done since the daies of the Apostles; so the Lord give you and all people an understanding to consider of these things, and what hath been lost since the dayes of the Apostles, and what now hath been come in again.

Rachel Hatcher
Eliz. Jackson
Alice Life
Mary Life
Katherine Plat
Anne Hatcher
Amie Titchbourn
Anne Donefeild
Sarah Growner
Anne Bonick
June Gray
Anne Fielder
Elles Lewen
Mary Burket
Margret Millit
Ruth White
Eliz. Hubbard
Bridget Pitts
Ellin Birkhead
Anne Garrat
Jone Horly
Anne Horly
Mary Becket
Sarah Lather

(page 67)
Anne Edlin
Grace Edlin
Ursly Abroc
Jane Amery
Rose Biddel
Eliz. Amery
Sarah Everard
Jone Cleere
Sibel Lisnee
Margret Morris
Eliz. Cowles
Anne Slade
Eliz. Andras
Jane Ruming
Rachel Carter
Dorothy Hollis
Catron Person
Jane Rance
Eliz. Smalepeede
Jane Siggings
Jone Horsley

Mary Simons
Anne Goage
Mary Manhood
Dorothy Rusel
Frances Ribman
Frances Chandler
Mary Cooke
Eliz. Pensold
Sarah Marner
Mary West
Sarah Hayle
Eliz. Blacksun
Anne Barnard
Jane Marnar
Mary Barber
Mary Brian
Eden Murnar
Eliz. Brocket
Mary Sleet
Mary Sleet
Sarah Brocket
Mary Parkar
Mary Femmand
Judith Shaw
Anne Voytch
Margery Colstock
Anne Batter
Agnes Soole
Mary Jounner
Mary Flete
Sarah Houlden
Anne Odden
Margret Pettel
Eliz. Shaw
Jone Eakman
Anne Tompson
Susan Knowles
Anne Femand
Anne Killingbanck
Margret Knowles
Anne Smight
Anne Chuse
Mary Sayers
Eliz. Willperfors
Jane Cleare
Frances Mathew
Jone Mills

Margret Crattenden
Eliz. Crattenden
Eliz. Elles
Mary Dobson
Anne Dobson
Eliz. Brickstocks
Grace Reding
Judith Buckman
Mary Allder
Margret Wilkinson
Margery Wilkinson
Ellen Willey
Katherine Bowen
Jane Kemsull
Mary Markwick
Susan Copper
Eliz. Adams
Anne Heuryote
Jone Stowan
Anne Dapson
Mary Danes
Sarah Weler
Eliz. Burnden
Elenar Danes
Mary Copper
Eliz. Ashfoold
Eliz. Ludford
Mary Houlden
Eliz. Killingbanck
Mary Grover
Mary Bynnes
Anne Steeve
Ellinor Tugwel
Martha Wilbersofe
Anne Linvell
Jone Luggins
Eliz. Michael
Dorothy Pearce
Alice Banckes
Mary French
Mary Haines
Mary Addams
Susana Beard
Eliz. Cottingham
Margret Smith
Eliz. Wilbore
Dinnis Hyland

Jone Tappen
Anne Baylie
Jone Wenham
Eliz. Gallaway
Eliz. Hilton
Susan Hilton
Eliz. Gould
Grace Percey
Anne Franke
Mary Akeburst
Anne Beard
Sarah Cottingham
Mary Cottingham
Sarah Beard
Jane Roots
Eliz. Averidge
Kath. Boyse
Mary Hollman
Anne Lee
Mary Well
Susan May
Jone Wheeler
Kath. Hoy
Lucretia Hakins
Eliz. Pashing
Eliz. Walker
Anne Lee
Anne Lockfold
Jone Clarke
Mary Loyas
Margret Palmer
Jone Patching
Eliz. Woods
Jone Hampshire
Martha Silling
Dorothy Woodger
Jane Dawson
Mary Hoggesflesh
Rebecca Patching
Sarah Deane
Susan Dean
Mary Wheatly
Jone Hoggsflesh
Anne Dawson
Anne Jesay
Mary Killingberk
Lidia Brommell

Margret Capenter	Mary Swan, Wid.	Jone Wheeler	Jone Stockdale
Mary Hollman	Anne Boy	Mary Langburst	Alice Poterten
Eliz. Scalle	Sarah Wanham	Eliz. Blace	Jone Stone
Katherine Seaman	Margret Wounch	Eliz. Batchelor	Eliz. Kneling
Eliz. Chelsam	Jone Pilfold	Anne Batchelor	Jone Haman
Bridget Seaman	Eliz. Higsome	Sarah Seman	Ione Woodward
Rose Peter	Susan Slening	Susan Watford	Eliz. Lee
Frances Boughton	Sarah Batchellor	Dorothy Stedman	Anne Mildred
Susan Burtenshaw	Jane Yates	Katherine Patten	Jude King
Jone Peeter	Mary Woollard	Jone Clarke	Eliz. Protsone
Jone Heethe	Mary Comber		Ione Pitson
Mary Boorn	Jone Chaismore	*(page 68)*	Mary Braborn

DORCET-SHIRE.

1. Friends, It is manifest that those called Priests and Teachers of the World, are them that serve not the Lord Jesus, but their own bellies, and the Priests and Teachers of the World seeks ours and not us, it is now made manifest.

2. The Priests and Ministers of the World, are such as loves enemies, and persecutes their friends.

3. And they are not such as wrestle not with flesh and blood, but with flesh and blood; nor such as wrestle with the powers of darkness, and brings the Creatures in the Liberty of the Sons of God.

And the Priest cry to You the Magistrates for Tithes, the Popes Almes, and this they lye begging with their Petitions, and lye ready at your doors; and we would have you to maintain these begging Priests some other way then by the Popes Almes, and not suffer them to go plundring up and down the Countrey; and this is our desire.

Now whether the people of God hath not suffered more in your dayes concerning Worship, Church, Priests and Maintenance, Clerks and Tithes, and in Courts, and spoiling their goods, and death, imprisoned, and whipping (for speaking the truth) as Rogues and Vagabonds, those that be worth three or four score pounds a year and in the Counties where they dwel; and some for not doffing their hats, and for speaking the word thou to one, and you to many (singular and plural) then the Puritans did in the Bishops time?

And are not you worse then the Ecclesiastical Courts, who held up their Tithes, Priests, Steeple-houses, Clerks, Vicars, Curates, their maintenance by a Law, but you have none, and yet profess Liberty of Conscience.

And Friends, as long as any of you have any Interest in Tithe, or any thing else which doth oppress the Nation and the people, it must be a greater power then self that must bring you to deny your selves, and to work the Nations Redemption, and to bring it into Liberty from under that which doth oppress it; and so let that man *(page 69)* appear, which in this day of the Lamb without Augmentations, Stipends, Easter-reckonings, Midsummer-dues, Glebe-lands, Mortuaries, men seeking gain from their quarter, divining for money, & for filthy lucre, and not minds earthly things; and that is the man we own, and except you take Councel at the Just, you shall not sit.

MAry Williams
Anne Ellet
Jone Lane
Mary Hazard
Lydia Lugge
Lore Bagg
Mary Bagg
Sarah Bagg
Abigal Bagg
Jone Stone
Rose Oakes
Eliz. Orsborn
Anne Orsborn
Mary Meltedg
Edith Barlet
Mary White
Katherine Hutchens
Grace Brown
Hannah Partridge
Eliz. Curtis
Anne King
Mary White
Mary Mash
Jone Brown
Eliz. Partridge
Susanna Hutchens
Mary Willington, eld.
Mary Willington, yo.
Annis Willington
Jane Willington
Edith Harris

Dorothy Harris
Eliz. Harris
Sarah Ring
Agnes Ring
Mary Masters
Eliz. Willming
Mary Ring
Martha Ring
Dorothy Ring
Eliz. White
Jone Sommers
Jone Brake
Mary Hodges
Melliar Hodges
Ruth Stickland
Eve Dumbarfield
Mary Coward
Alice Stevens
Eliz. Sommers
Anne Coward
Dorothy Coward
Ellinor Tribbuck
Eliz. Hodges
Mary Maber
Mary Griffin
Mary Maber
Dorothy Fook
Mary Whiffen
Eliz. Whiffen
Katherine Whiffen
Mary Share
Jone Critchell
Mellis Masters
Jone Ashbey

Agnes Wats
Sarah Wats
Edith Miller
Hester Maber
Hester Hodges
Dorothy Sherrin
Winfrute Winsor
Jone Winsor
Mary Hide
Jone Martine
Susanna Vincen
Ruth Phillips
Grace Ferris
Eliz. Douch
Jane Kenway
Margret Smith
Sarah Deming
Anne Coleburn
Dorothy Sanders
Priscilla Dove
Frances Dove
Eliz. Randle
Mary Roberts
Barbary Clark
Sarah Brimstone
Rebecca Senior
Sarah Reap
Dorothy White
Susanna Wayman
Sarah Beer
Hannah Senior
Susannah Senior
Sarah Pit
Eduth Pit

Thomson Tucker
Martha Maber
Eduth Bagge
Mary Knight
Sarah Harvey
Clare Williams
Katherine Wall
Elinor Sadler
Katherine Barker
Sarah Waldron
Alice Roberts
Jone Beer
Barbary Collens
Annis Cribb
Anne Anner
Annis Sanders
Sarah Brimmstone, eld.
Edith Pith, elder
Sarah Wilson
Jane Hammon
Christian Bridges
Sarah Tizer
Loveday Hambly
Jen. Grewdon
Anna Upcot
Loveday Killew
Sarah Hancock
Jone Hancock
Jane Hodg
Blanch Hodg
Grace Billing
Hannah Bevel
Tomazin Trevaness

Jone Beard
Jane Cardew
Grace Dening
Margret Russel
Alice Dening
Sarah Dening
Tabitha Rush
Rebecca Steevens
Margret Crouly
Alice Acock
Eliz. Lockey
Hannah Hydutch
Prudence Lockey
Phill. Saunders
Anne Hacknes
Dorothy Godman
Susanna Witfield
Eliz. King
Mary Williamson
Constance King
Susannah Whorrel
Mary Bullard
Mary Crouch
Martha Whorrel
Margret Bolock
Anne Welford
Eliz. Welford
Mary Ashbolt
Anne Mouse
Katherine Johnson
Anne Webb
Anne Haukins
Mary Wadope
Anne Hells
Ruth Allen
Rose Scarborough
Alice Eden
Frances Andras
Anne Baber
Eliz. Barber
Eliz. Emes

(page 70)
Jone Grant
Anne Ganble
Anne Broker
Grace Richardson

Sarah Bishop
Anne Impy
Anne Sam
Martha Sam
Mary Sam
Jane Sam
Eliz. Alborn
Margret Lamens
Hannah
    Nightingal
Dorothy Neel
Eliz. White
Eliz. Cox
Sarah Cripcy
Anne Sam
Mary Sam
Mary Emees
Mary Tatnaum
Jone Wood
Eliz. Wood
Jone Leverit
Anne Leverit
Sarah Leverit
Jone Beale
Anne Wells
Deborah Bilcock
Susanna Norris
Cattorn Linly
Eliz. Brace
Mary Farnly
Mary Huckel
Eliz. Huckel
Margret Fisher
Anne Squire
Mary Squire
Eliz. Squire
Christian Squire
Ruth Squire
Mary Parles
Sarah Winch
Sarah Cripey
Eliz. Dix.
Mary Cune
Rachel Beadles
Hannah Crouch
Eliz. Wernar
Mary Prior

Mary Inroad
Eliz. Andrews
Dorothy Smith
Martha Worsman
Doglass Jorden

Hertford-shire.

Eliz. Robins
Hester Ringsal
Eliz. Ringsal
Anne Goodman
Grace Briddon
Mary Dearmer
Eliz. Wight
Jone Parrot
Eliz. Weelles
Anne Wight
Mary Evastafe
Mary Goodale
Mary Danestafe
Anne Stevens
Anne Karnes
Mary Keyes
Margret Ridge
Barbary
    Granborrough
Eliz. Kinner
Susanna Certain
Susanna Sergeant
Jone Harris
Ursula Terred
Alice Bland
Patience Robinson
Hannah Nenhal
Susanna Biges
Eliz. King, elder
Eliz. King, young.
Eliz. Ironmonger
Alice Steel
Eliz. Stout
Jone Lewis
Judeth Almond
Magdalene Marshal
Martha Tayler
Margret Barnraft

Alice Pander
Mary Ragdal
Mary Harris
Eliz. Turner
Jone Brocksop
Susanna Frith
Jane Brilsford
Alice Pinder
Margret
    Waterhouse
Eliz. Shingleton
Isabel Hynam
Anne Holmworth
Eliz. Berrie
Mary Bunting
Eliz. Foulds
Anne Holms
Alice Hill
Mary Fauk
Helen Wheatly
Anne Hall
Jane Stones
Frances Farnsworth
Eliz. Toundrow
Eliz. Wosnam
Helen Fletcher
Alice Hunt
Katherine Fletcher
Grace Fletcher
Margret Tomson
Mary Stones
Margret Grinder
Hester Bunting
Eliz. Buxton
Cleer Brouckhouse
Eliz. Brouckhouse
Alice Jolly
Jane Yeats
Eliz. Yeats
Eliz. Foulds
Anne Wilson
Eliz. Caulton
Frances Bunten
Anne East
Eliz. Wosnam
Elen Dranfield
Eliz. Neuton

Eliz. Beard	Eliz. Hevek	Anne Mellor	Frances Pym
Eliz. Kirk	Eliz. Hartly	Eliz. Smith	Katherine Miles
Eliz. Right	Eliz. Harton	Constance Pym	Bennit Parsons
Elen Kirk	Jone Hatton	Anne Coundall	Mary Rose
Alice Woodhead	Anne Stancer	Eliz. Smith	Eliz. Horms
Anne Brilsford	Elen Fretwell	Anne Drapper	Mary Fretwek
Anne Waterhouse	Mary Kirk		

W AS it not a great crime in the dayes of the Jews, and Temple, and Tithes, and offering, the command of God, for the Apostles to deny the Temple, and Tithes, and offerings? were they not looked upon as men disturbing the Common-Wealth, and sowers of sedition, & makers of Sects, who witnessed Christ, by whom the world *(page 71)*was made, the end of Tithes, and temple, Priests and offerings? and was not this to be preached in all Nations? did not this disquiet Kings and setled worship, and setled teachers in all Nations, the Jews in their Temple, and the Heathen in their invented temple, and their Priests, to bring people off from them to Christ, the everlasting Priesthood, to the Temple of God? Now is it a greater thing to cry against your Tithes, and Priests made at Schools and Colledges, and to cry against the Steeple-house, made east and west, as you have invented since the days of the Apostles, as makers of Sects, and tumults, destroyers of Government, that which is set up by a Government, as not subject to the higher power? Was not the Apostle subject to the higher power, that denied the Jewes Temple, tithes and offerings held up by the Law, and Priests made by the Law? was not Christ, the power of God, come which ended the Law whom God was in? was not the Apostles subject to the higher power when they went among the Heathen Priests, and brought them off from their Dianish worship, and brought them off their Priests, which were set up by Laws and Government? therefore were not they subject to the higher power, that separated people from them to God? are their souls subject to the higher, yea or nay? are their souls subject to the higher Power that denies the Tithes, the Papist, invented since the days of the Apostles, and the Colledges they made their Priests at, Easter reckonings Midsommer-dues, Gleab-lands, which are got up since the days of the Apostles? can they deny these things without denying the higher Power? Was not the Popes power the first that set them up? or do not all they deny the higher Power that holds up all these things; which higher power is ordained of God, to which the soul must be subject to, which Power goes over the Dragon, Beast, False Church, and Devil, out of Truth, and was before the Devil was? and is not that the higher Power that makes him worship and bends him under, which destroyes him and all his works, to which the soul must be subject to? and are not all they that hold up Tithes, Temple, Offerings, Heathens, Jews or Christians in the Dragons power, and outward set will-worships, invented Temples, invented Schooles for men to serve prentiships, to be made Ministers, and limited to hour-glasses, and persecute, and prison such as be moved of the Lord God to speak to them? are not all these set up by the Dragons power, and held up by the Dragons power, the devourer, the destroyer, (and not in the power of God) that destroyes Creatures, and wrestles with flesh and blood? is not this the power of the Devil? and is not that the power of God, the higher power *(page 72)* to which the soul must be subject to, that wrestles with powers of darkness and spiritual wickedness in high places, and wrestles not with flesh and blood, but saves mens lives and not destroyes them, and brings the creatures into the liberty of the Sons of God? and is not this the higher power, and the power which God hath ordained to which the soul must be subject? and is not this power known wherever it be in the hand of a supream or King if he be in it? and is not the great cry against them that say, God is not worshipped in these old Mass-houses set by Papist, which you call Synagogue or Temple? and was it not the great cry among the Jews that God was no where worshipped, but in the Temple at *Jerusalem*, and thither all Nations should come to worship, and he that would not come, his cattle should die, and his eyes should eat out of his head, as in *Zacharia* the Prophet; yet when Christ came, he told them not at *Jerusalem*, not at *Samaria*, neither at the Mountain, but they which worships the Father, must worship him in spirit, mark, in the spirit, and in the truth; and would not the *Jews* say that Christ denyed the higher power, and the Prophets, which said all Nations must come to worship at *Jerusalem*? and doth not the Sects and opinions that differ one from another hold up his worship by his authority, and compel all to come to his worship by his compelling power? see heres the worship, see heres the worship at this place, or at that place; so run all from the spirit in them, and from the truth in which they should worship the Father, and they that will not go to worship with them, fine them and imprison them, these disquiet authority, these are not subject to the higher power, compel all small and great, and if they will not, they are not fit for the Common-Wealth, and all is in the errour or blasphemy that will not come to worship at this or the other great house, or at this or the other place; this is not like *Jerusalem* or *Samaria*, or the mountains? Did *Jerusalem* or *Samaria* kill so many about Religion, as they have done since the days of the Apostles? come let us reckon with you outward worshippers, and come, must not all the *Jews*, Papists, Professors upon the earth be called to account for the blood that you have shed upon the earth, with *Cains* weapons and hung out *Cains* flag of defiance against the truth in this great City, all you outward worshippers not in spirit and truth; if not in the truth, mark, that which the destroyer and murderer is out of, if truth, that which saves mens lives, and destroyes the powers of darkness, and spiritual wickedness, that wrestles with flesh and blood and destroyes mens lives about their sacrifice, Church, Ministry & maintenance, which is the Dragons power, not the true power.

THE END.

(Editors' note: In the 1659 document the pages 64-69 are numbered correctly but they were out of sequence. Dortha Meredith corrected this error.)

THE

TRUMPET

Of the Lord Sounded forth unto thefe

THREE NATIONS,

As a WARNING from the Spirit of Truth; efpecially
unto Thee, Oh *ENGLAND*, who art looked
upon as the Seat of Juftice, from whence
righteous Laws fhould proceed.

Likewise, unto Thee, thou great and famous City of
London, doth the Lord God of Vengeance sound one
W A R N I N G more into thine Ear, that (if poffible)
haply thou mayeft hearken unto him, and amend
thy life before it be too late.

With a Word of wholfome *Counfel* and *Advice* unto thy
King, Rulers, Judges, Bifhops and *Priefts*, that they may
prize the Day of their Vifitation, before it pafs away:
As alfo, a Word of *Prophefie* of the fore Deftruction
that is coming upon them if they Repent not.

Together with a few Words unto the *Royal Seed*, which
is chofen of God, and feparated from the World, to
do his Will for ever.

By one who is a Sufferer for the Teftimony of Jefus, in Newgate,
ESTHER BIDDLE.

L O N D O N, Printed in the Year, *1662*.

(Page numbers of original document appear in text as *page _.*)

(page 9)

The Trumpet *of the Lord sounded forth*
unto England, Scotland, *and* Ireland; *with a Word*
of wholfome Advice *and* Counsel *to the*
King, Rulers, *and* Judges *thereof.*

OH *King!* this is my Counsel unto thee, and thy Rulers and Judges; Oh! hearken unto the Light of Christ in your Consciences, that it may bear rule in your hearts, that you may Judge for the Lord, and oppression may be expel'd in your Dominions! Oh! that you would *do Justice, and love Mercy, and walk humbly with the God of heaven,* then would the Lord give you length of dayes, and a long life, Peace and Plenty shall be in your Dominions, every one shall sit under his own Vine and Fig-tree, and none shall make them afraid, joy and tranquility *(page 10)* shall be in your Palaces; this shall you see and know to be accomplished, if you will leave off oppressing the Righteous, and set the Captive free.

Oh ye *Rulers, Judges, and Justices,* and all People high and low! be it known unto you from the mighty Judge of Powerful Majesty, that he is risen, who will scatter Rulers in his anger, and will pluck down Kings in his Wrath. Oh! the anger of the Lord waxeth hot against all workers of iniquity, and he will set his oppressed seed free, which cryeth unto him for deliverance; and know this, what cruelty soever be in your hearts against us, the Lord will confound it and bring it to nothing; for the Lord is on our side, and we fear not *Imprisonment, Banishment, Fire* or *Tortures,* or whatever the wrath of man can inflict upon us; for our hearts are firmly fixed upon the Lord, and we are freely given up in Body, Soul, and Spirit to suffer for God's Cause: Oh you Rulers! if the Lord suffereth you to Banish us, I know that the Lord will go along with us, as he did with *Abraham* in a strange Land, but know this, we shall leave a seed behind us, which shall be your tormentor, and shall witness for us when you are gone.

Oh Lord! I commit our case unto thee, who art faithful, and keepeth Covenant forever, and I know thou wilt fight our Battel, and plead our cause with the mighty on earth, who would destroy us from being a People if thy Power did not preserve us; Glory and Honour be given unto thee, who hath compassed us about with songs of everlasting praises; and we may blesse the hour and time that thou raised up a People in the North, even a dreadful and terrible Army, who Marched swiftly in thy Power through the Nations, and by them we were convinced, and turned towards the Lord, and they shall be the dread of all Nations, and God hath crowned them with an everlasting Crown, which neither Men nor Devils shall be able to take from them.

Oh you *Rulers* and *Judges* of these Nations! do you think to overcome us or make us yeeld by keeping them in Prison, which you think are our Teachers, and Ring-leaders? nay, Christ is our Teacher, and he cannot be removed into a corner, who is the Antient of Dayes, and will cause us to increase dayly; and *(page 11)* to grow as Calves in the stall; we are not like the World, who must have a Priest to Interpret the Scriptures to them, and when he is removed, they are scattered and knows not what to do; but my friends, we witness the Scriptures fulfil'd, who hath said in the latter dayes, *He would pour out his Spirit upon Sons and Daughters, and they should Prophesie; and they shall all be taught of me, and great shall be their peace, and in righteousness shall they be established:* So the Lord doth not speak unto us in an unknown Tongue, but in our own Language do we hear him perfectly, whose voice is better than life; and for this cause doth the unlearned hate us, and the uncircumcised revile us, because we cannot own the Teaching that is of this World, but that which cometh immediately from God, and that is pure and refresheth the Soul, and holdeth up the head in the day of Battel, and it causeth us to meet together, to worship the Lord as we ought to do; and Oh you Rulers, and People! it is in vain for you to strive against us, for the God of heaven is with us.

Oh *England, Scotland* and *Ireland!* but more especially thou O *England,* that art the most fruitful and famous Land, in which the Lord hath been pleased to make manifest his Life and Power, Beauty and Glory, more than in any Nation under the Heavens; in so much, that he hath raised his sons and daughters from death to life, and hath made them bold and valiant Souldiers for his Testimony, which he hath given them to bear forth unto all Nations; and by the Glorious and Powerful Word of Life, which hath proceeded out of their mouthes, hath thy *Judges* and *Rulers* been convinced of the evil of their way, and have been made to confess to the Truth, both Priests and People, both High and Low, Rich and Poor, hath the Lord visited in this day of great Salvation, and everlasting love; so that none could plead ignorance, but many like *Demas* hath denyed the Truth, and Imbraced this present evil World: And now Oh *England!* will the Lord try and prove all thy Inhabitants, from the King that sitteth upon his Throne, unto the Beggar that sitteth upon the dunghill, even all sorts of professors and prophane; Oh! the Fire is kindled, and the Furnace is even hot, in which your works and worships, Faith and Religion *(page 12)* must be tryed, and that which will not remain in the Furnace, must be consumed by the Fire of the Lord; for the most high and Glorious King is a trying and purifying his Children in the Furnace, as *Jerusalem*, that they may come forth as pollished Silver, and well refined Gold; and he hath brought many through the Furnace, and hath set them as Pillars in his house, to bear forth a Valiant and Noble Testimony of what they have seen, tasted and handled of the Word of Life, unto thy inhabitants, and unto the whole World, that they may fear that dreadful God, who made Heaven and Earth, in whose sight the whole World is but as the drop of a Bucket, and at whose presence the heavens shall wax old as a garment that moths have eat, and the Elements shall passe away with a great noise, the Earth shall be dissolved, and all things therein shall mourn, and the souls shall fail before him which he hath made.

Oh! let your *King and Queen, Dukes* and *Earls, Lords* and *Ladies, Judges* and *Rulers,* and all *Bishops, Deacons, Priests* and *People* in these three Nations, and all the World, consider their wayes, worships, and religions, and fear and tremble before the mighty God, who hath the hearts of Kings and Rulers in his hand; times, and seasons are with him, the Dominions of the World are at his disposing, who is the high and lofty One, and doth Inhabit Eternity; what is the *Pope* or the *Kings* of the Earth, will he not bring them to judgement, and turn them to dust again from whence they came?

Oh you high and lofty ones! who spendeth God's Creation upon your lusts, and doth not feed the hungry, nor cloath the naked, but they are ready to perish in the streets; both old and young, lame and blind lyeth in your streets, and at your Masse-house doors, crying for bread, which even melteth my heart, and maketh the soul of the righteous to mourn; did not the Lord make all men and women upon the earth of one mould, why then should there be so much honour and respect unto some men and women, and not unto others, but they are almost naked for want of Cloathing; and almost starved for want of Bread? and are you not all brethren, and all under the Government of one King? Oh repent! least the Lord consume you, and be ashamed, and cloath the naked, and feed the hungry, and set the oppressed free.

(page 13) Oh *King!* thou art as head under God over these three Nations, & the Lord hath set thee as overseer, to see Justice and true Judgement Executed in thy Dominions; Oh! let all unjust Lawes and unrighteous Decrees make in thy dayes, and before thy dayes, be all disanul'd and made of none effect, and henceforth let there be good

and wholsom Lawes Established, that all the honest-hearted in thy Dominions may worship the God of their Life, without any molestation; and if thou decreest any thing, let it not grieve theLord, for the Lord God of *Israel* looketh for better fruit at thy hands than he did of all that are gone before thee; *for in the time of Ignorance God winked, but now is the glorious Light of the Morning risen, and God calleth all men everywhere to Repentance.*

Oh you *Rulers, Priests,* and *People* of these three Lands! I most humbly intreat you to learn Wisdom before it be too late, and prudence before it be hid from your eyes. Oh! leave off your old wayes andWorships, and observing *Dayes, Times* and *Seasons,* and learn the *new* and *living way,* which is the way in the Wilderness, though a *wasering man or a fool shall not err therein;* this calls for *Holiness* and *Purity,* without which you *cannot see the Lord;* therefore consider you are but Men, and made of the dust of the Earth, and you know not how soon you may return to your long homes; and shall be seen no more; have you the length of your life, or the number of your dayes in your own hands? have you the command of Death, or can you stay its stroke? nay, you are but as potsheards broken by the hand of the Potter, you are here to day and gone to morrow, *your Beauty is as the grass, and your glory as the Flower thereof,* cut down by the hand of the Mower; your Crown is mortal, and will fade away; Ah, poor dust and ashes, why do you persecute us even to Death, for no other cause but for worshipping the God of Heaven? Oh! do you think that the Lord is such a one as your selves? or are you so vain to believe, that he winks or joyns with you in Persecuting, Knocking down, and spilling our blood in your Streets, and Murdering of us in your Prisons? nay, nay although he hath suffered such things to be done, for the Tryal of our Faith, and the filling up of the measure of your Iniquity, which is near full; Now will I *arise,* saith the dreadful and terrible *(page 14)* God, who am cloathed with *Vengeance* as with a *Robe,* and with *Zeal* as with a *Garment,* and I will tear and devour, and for *Sions* sake I will not be quiet, and for my beloved *Jerusalem* I will not be silent, but I will roar and thunder forth my voice out of my Holy Mountain, and the Beasts shall tremble, the Earth shall be as a smoke, the tall Cedars shall fall, and the sturdy Oakes shall be plucked up by the Roots, and all things of this World shall be afraid; the Bats shall go into their Holes, and the Lyons into their Dens, when the Lord appeareth in his Beauty, to make Inquisition for blood, then shall your hearts fail you for fear of those things that are coming upon you; in that Terrible Day, all your lovers will do you no good, and your familiars will stand afar off;

then must you be left to the Judge of Judges, where you shall see the
Book of Conscience opened, where your Indictments will be read at
large, and he will Judge you according as your deeds shall be. Oh then!
if you have not done Justice, nor loved mercy, or did the thing that was
Just in the sight of the Lord, then shall you be Banished from the presence of the King of Heaven for evermore, into utter darkness, where is
weeping, wailing, and *gnashing* of Teeth, and you shall be a stink to Ages
to come.

Oh! blessed and happy will it be for those *Judges*, and *Rulers*, and
Poople [sic], who hath clean hands, and pure hearts, and have not joyned
with the wicked in persecuting the Innocent; surely there reward will
be great in Heaven.

My Friends, I was once of this Religion which is now in Power, I was
signed with the sign of the Cross, & baptized into the Faith; my *Godfa-
thers and Godmothers Promised and Vowed,* that *I should forsake the Devil
and all his works, the Pomps and Vanities of this wicked World, and all the
sinful lusts of the Flesh,* and that I should *keep God's Holy Will and Commandments all the dayes of my life;* and when I was young, my Father had
me *Bishop'd,* thinking thereby to gain a blessing for me: I spent many
years in *Oxford,* where the carriages of the Schollars, did trouble me in
that day, they were so wilde; after the best sort of Religion and custom
of the Nation, was I brought up; then the Lord drew me to this City,
where I applyed my heart both Evening and Morning, and at noon day,
unto reading and hearing the *Common-Prayer; (page 15)* when there was
but one place of Worship left in this City, I went to it, and when there
Books were burned, I stood for them, for my heart was wholly joyned
unto them; and when the King's head was taken off, my heart and Soul
was burdened, that I was even weary of my Life, and the Enemy waited
to devour me; then did the Lord take away my hearing that I was deaf
as to all Teachings of Men for a year; then that Faith which I was baptized in, did no good, for all that the Man and Women had promised,
and vowed, I should do, I could not forsake the Pomps and Vanities,
and sinful lusts of the Flesh I run into; and they stood alwayes before
my eyes, my cry was continually unto the Lord, that I might put off that
body of death, which hindred me from his presence; then did the Lord
carry me to a Meeting of the People called *Quakers,* where I was filled
with the dread and Power of the Lord, and it raised my Soul to bear
Testimony to the Truth, and after a little season the Lord set my sins in
order before me, and every idle word which I had spoken was brought
to my remembrance, where I received a just reward from the Lord, and

so came to have Peace of Conscience with my Saviour, which I never could obtain whilst I walked with those People.

Oh my Friends! I can truly say, ever since I was a Child, the witness of God pursued me, and what ever I did, I had no Peace in this worship, or Service, which is now in being; it tired and vexed my tender Soul, to see what a sad estate I was in; but now Glory be to the Lord, I am set at Liberty from this vain Religion, which never profited me at all; and would you have me to conform to this Religion, which keepeth the Soul in the grave? nay I shall never conform unto this worship whilst I have breath, but shall bear my Testimony against it, for I know the powerful God is risen to throw it down, and wo be to all that uphold it.

Oh your Rulers! be it known unto you, if you will not do Justice and ease the oppressed, and set the Captives free, the Lord will overturn you, and destroy you from being a People, as he hath done in years past; for his sword is in his hand, and it will cut you down, unless you do repent, ye shall likewise perish.

(page 16)

One WARNING more to the Biſhops, Prieſts, Deacons, Friers, and Jeſuites.

OH! Woe be unto you *Bishops, Priests, Deacons, Friers,* and *Jesuits,* and all other Officers under you, for the Lord is risen in Power, yea, he is risen in dreadful and terrible Wrath; Oh! I have seen, I have seen this Night, the dreadful Flames which the Lord God will cast you into; Oh! your *Communion-Tables* which you sacrifice upon unto Devils, and not unto the living God, your *Altars* which you bow down unto, and make an Image of, will the dreadful Lord of Vengeance overthrow in his fiery Indignation; your *Surplices* and *Tippets* and all your loathsome *Robes,* which you dress your selves withall, which are like unto a menstrous Cloth before the Eye of the pure *Jehovah,* he will rent them all off, who is the Bishop of our Souls: Oh you *Bishops, Priests, Deacons, Friers* and *Jesuites!* once more will the Judge of Heaven and Earth plead with you, because you are a blood-thirsty Generation, you are a building of *Zion* with Blood, and *Jerusalem* with Iniquity, as your Forefathers did in the dayes of old: Therefore will the Lord of the Harvest cast you heaps upon heaps, as stones in the street, and as mire in the high-way; the Lord of Heaven and Earth loaths your *Worships*, your *Singing*, and the Noise of your *Organs* doth the Lord abhor; and instead of your Instruments of Musick, will the Lord make you howl and lament bitterly, inso much that the Earth shall be astonished, and your Downfal shall be so great, that Nations shall fear and tremble before our God; your *Communion* and *Union* is with Devils and unclean Spirits, and not with the powerful God, which creats a new Heaven, and a new Earth; and this shall you see fulfilled in its time and season; for the Lord hath determined your utter Destruction, both *Pope* and *Bishops*, both root and branch, from off the face of the Earth: Oh it hastens, it hastens, and Wrath will not stay.

(page 17)

> In this glorious day, in which Zion is rayed in beauty bright,
>
> To stand in her strength against this dark Night;
>
> Whose Clouds are so many, and Skie so dim,
>
> That *Zions* Beauty can hardly be seen;
>
> But the Lord is risen in this his glorious Day,
>
> To sweep *Bishops*, *Prelates*, and Clouds away.

> *Babylons* Destruction is very near,
>
> let all the World fear for evermore.

A
TRUMPET

OF THE

Lord of Hoſts,

Blown unto the

CITY of LONDON,

And unto the *Inhabitants* thereof; Proclaiming the great
and notable Day of the Lord God, which is coming ſwiftly
on them all, as a Thief in the night. And this is the
CRY of the Lord God, which is gone forth
unto thy Inhabitants.

AS ALSO, A

TRUMPET

Sounded out of the HOLY CITY, proclaiming Deliverance
to the Captives, Sounding forth the Redemption of *SION,*
which hasſteneth. And this is ſent unto all her bleſſed
Children, who wait for her Advancement; this
Meſſage of glad Tydings from GOD
the Father of our Lord *JESUS,*
is sent unto you all.

Publiſhed by me, D. White

Printed in the Year, 1662.

(Page numbers of original document appear in text as *page _.*)

O LONDON! hasten, hasten, prepare; prepare, to meet the Lord God, who is riding swiftly to the Battel; whose day of Vengeance is coming upon all flesh, which hath corrupted its way; yea, and the Lord God is risen to be avenged on thy Inhabitants. O *London*, thy Streets are risen like *Sodom* whom the Lord God destroyed, and thy Inhabitants abound in iniquity like unto *Gomorrah*; the blood of the Righteous cryeth in thy Streets, whose cry is ascended up on high, and is entred into the ears of the Lord God, who is risen in jealousie, to plead by the Sword of Justice, and for the sake of the Oppressed the Lord God will roar upon the Mountains, and the Earth shall tremble before him, and great astonishment of heart shall come upon all flesh; Yea, the day is at hand, it is at hand, from the Lord God I do declare it, who is bringing of a flood of destruction upon thy Inhabitants, O City of *London*, which stands ready, and is even at the door of the wicked; yea, the Lord God hath spoken, and therefore I will prophesie; and thus saith the Lord of Hosts, the mighty and terrible God, I will arise, I will arise, I will roar as a *(page 4)* Lion bereaved of her young, I will tear through the darkness, I will rend the Mountains down, I will throw the Hills into the Valleys; I will exalt my own Name in the Earth, I will set my King upon my holy Hill of *Zion*, and this is the Prince of the Scepter of *Judah*, which shall sway the Nations; and this is the day of the mighty God, wherein he is coming in Eternal Beauty, in Holiness he is shining forth, and in Everlasting Glory hath the King of Saints appeared unto the sons of men, and before him goeth a consuming fire, to burn up and to destroy all that would not that he should reign whose right it is; yea, I do proclaim the day of Vengeance upon all flesh that liveth in corruption; yea, the plagues of the Lord God must suddenly come upon the unclean, the proud and ambitious; the Lord God who made the Heavens and the Earth by the Word of his mouth, hath now spoken, and terrible is the Word of the Lord unto all flesh; and all must come to feel the Sword of the Justice of God to plead his righteous Cause in them; all must come to feel the fire of God's Consumption to burn as an Oven; and who live in Lust, Pride, and Envy, must know the Wrath of God poured forth: for the Day is coming wherein the Heavens shall be set on fire, and the Elements shall melt with fervent heat, and the lofty in that day shall be brought low; and now is the day of the Lord God sounding once more in your ears, that you may all know it is near you, that so you may escape it by repentance; so that all such that have not wholly quenched the motion of the holy Spirit of God, may now return to reproof thereof, whilst it is striving with you, imbrace it as your choicest treasure, and let every man come home to *within*, and search his own house, that he may find that precious Pearl which hath been lost, even that *true Light* which leadeth unto Eternal Life; so that every man may come to know his Leader the *Lord of Hosts:* For all that are saved, must be led by the saving Power which redeems and brings up the soul of man out of death, and out of captivity. O that I could cry aloud, and so loud that the sons of men may hear the sound of the Glory of the Day of God which is now revealing. O that every soul had a deep sense of the Word of the Eternal Power engraved in his *(page 5)* heart by the finger of the Lord God! and unto the Nations that it shall hear, I do proclaim the Day of Free-love, even the Day of Everlasting Mercy from the God of *Abraham*, who is faithful, just and true, who hath a Remnant yet to gather of the Seed of *Abraham* the Just, which Seed shall inherit all things; for with it God hath made an Everlasting Covenant: Therefore be ye awakened unto Righteousness, O ye Inhabitants of the Earth; for the Day is come wherein the Lord God is come to Judgment, and all must know the righteous Judgements of the Lord God to be set up *within*, that the Inhabitants of the Earth thereby may come to learn Righteousness and *Sion* through Judgment must be redeemed, and her Converts by Righteousness must be set free for Freedom; in the Name of the Lord God, and in his Authority I do proclaim *Liberty* and *Freedom* to the Captives, that the Seed of the house of *Jacob* may arise unto the Resurrection of Life, and Immortality, and Glory, and Beauty, and Holiness is broken forth, and the Glory of the Day of the Lord God is shining forth, which will cover the whole Earth, and the Beams of his Brightness shall overshadow the Mountains, and the Sun of Righteousness shall arise in his healing vertue, to heal the Nations that have been long wounded; yea, the Prisoners of hope shall come forth rejoycing in the God of the Tribes of *Israel*, who sitteth on the Throne of true Judgment. And now is the last Trumpet sounded, and an Alarm is given from the Lord God Almighty, proclaiming the Day of Restoration and of mighty Salvation, and of glad-tydings unto the poor and meek of the Earth. I will blow the Trumpet of the Lord God Almighty over all Mountains; O let the Heavens rejoyce and sing, for He is come who doth glad-tydings bring, whose Glory is broken forth, and the Heavens cannot contain it, but the Earth must hear the sound of the holy Day, and the dawning thereof expelleth the mist of the cloudy night which hath been over the Nations, and the Lord is rending the Vail of the Temple in sunder from the top to the bottom, and he is rouling away the Stone from the door of the Sepulchre where the Lord *JESUS* hath been laid;

for all *(page 6)* Nations must see him with *open face, and they shall mourn over him whom they have pierced*, who is now risen and arising in his Glory over all, to reign in his Majesty and in his Brightness, as he did before the Fall; and a Reign of the Lamb is come, and Him God is exalting on the Throne of Everlasting Glory; and he is assembling the Nations and gathering unto him, and this day he is lifting up Him himself on the tops of the Mountains; as *Moses* lifted up the Serpent in the Wilderness, even so is the Son of Glory lifting up himself, and he shall draw all men after him; and this is the Top-stone, the *Elect and Precious*, which shall grind all to pouder: Therefore, hearken O Heavens, and hear O Earth, for the mighty Day of the Lord is come and coming upon all flesh, wherein the Mighty shall bow before Him, and the stout-hearted shall be broken in pieces; for the day of Vengeance and the year of Recompence is coming unto the Rebellious and hard-hearted, and the uncircumcised, and the Lord is risen to plead with the pot-sherds of the Earth, whom he will dash one against another, and the Decree of our God is to *Overturn, overturn, overturn*, until Righteousness rule in this Nation, until all become subject to the Authority of the Lamb, whose Government is righteous, whose Dominion is eternal and everlasting; and this is the Supream Power that all souls must be made subject to; and all that will not that our King should reign, must be by the Sword of his Power slain: Therefore prepare to the Battel, for the mighty JEHOVAH is coming in Power, and the slain of the Lord shall be many.

You Branches of the true Vine, you Spouses of the Beloved, you Daughters of *Sion* and Sons of *Jacob*, rejoyce and sing you Virgins and Followers of the Lamb; yea, let the tribulated rejoyce and sing, let the poor in spirit be glad; let them that dwell in the Valleys rejoyce, who drink of the Springs of the Fountain of Love; where Peace and Joy encreaseth, where Love to the Brethren is multiplied; *And by this shall all men know that we are of God, because we love the Brethren;* For our God is *Love*, and we must be made like unto him in all things. O little Love, overcome, overcome *(page 7)* all your hearts, that Life may fill your vessels, that bowels of compassion and tenderness may flow one into another, that every Soul may swim in the fulness of Love, that all may be filled with the eternal Power, that the new Wine of the Kingdom may be poured from vessel to vessel, that all your Cups may over-flow with the Consolation of God. And this is the breath of my Life in the Love of my eternal Father, sending Greetings of Peace unto the flock of the Faithful, the Seed of the Covenant who are Heirs of the Promise of Life and Salvation; yours is the Kingdom of Glory, who keep your Habitations; for you are the Crowns of Diadems prepared and laid up in the Heavenly places, in the Kings Paradise, in the Palace of the Lord God: Oh! Rejoyce for ever, and sing *Hallalujahs* and Praises unto the God of Power, from whom this is sent and Published; and in his Dominion and Authority I do send it forth, being faithful unto what the Lord hath instructed me with; I do not with-hold but I freely let it go: So in the Spirit of Life, and Love, and Eternal Peace, I salute all the Faithful in Heart, and in the Union of the holy Life,

I bid you all Farwel.

D.W.

(page 8)

A TRUMPET

Sounded out of the HOLY CITY, proclaiming Deliverance
to the Captives, Sounding forth the Redemption of SION,
which hafteneth; and this is fent unto all her bleffed
Children, who wait for her Advancement: This
Meffage of glad Tydings from GOD
the Father of our Lord *JESUS*,
is fent unto you all

Arise O Seed of *Sion*, arise in thy Beauty, in the Glory, in the Brightness, in the Majesty of the most High; I say, Arise in the Power, and in the Authority of the King of Glory, whose day is come wherein you the Children and Seed of *Abraham* shall shine forth, in the beauty, in the excellency of the *Most High;* You that are of the Faith of your Father *Abraham*, which Faith standeth in *God's* Covenant, that giveth Dominion over all the World, You all are to feel this faith to work you into Love, and therein is the victory known, as there is a dwelling and abiding in the Faith of the Covenant, in which the Promise of the Father is fulfilled: So all are to wait, to know the Promise of the Father fulfilled in them; and all are to wait, to know the Spirit of Life poured forth upon them, even that holy Anointing which the holy Prophets came unto, from which they speak as the Spirit gave them utterance, and from the Anointing of the holy Power which they received from on High. And *this* is the Glorious Day of the Lord God, wherein he hath appeared in great power, for the gathering of the Sons of Men from far, and the bringing of his Daughters from the ends of the Earth: So all must be gathered into the Fold, all must know an entering into the Rest, all must know a gathering into the Life, and into the Power, which maketh all things new; and all must know the powerful work of the Lord God wrought in them, so the *(page 9)* working down of the high Mountains, for the laying low of the high Places of the Earth, and for the breaking down of the strongholds of Sin: And all must feel the overturning of the Mountains which have stood in opposition against the Appearance of the Lord of Glory, who is risen in his beautiful brightness, before whom the Clouds flye, and the Hills melt; So dreadful, so terrible is the coming of the Lord God, before whom nothing can stand but that which is like unto him: And now is the Day of the Redemption of *Sion* proclaimed unto all her Children who wait for her Advancement; her Glory shall shine unto the Nations, her Beauty shall over-spread the Earth, and within her Gates shall Praises be sounded forth by the Redeemed, who are entered again into Paradise; These shall sing the new Songs who follow the Lamb through the Tribulation, who come through the washing of Regeneration. These shall be Crowned with everlasting Salvation. These shall sing the Heavenly Harmonies; These shall play on the Harp of *David* before the Throne of the King of *Israel*, the renown of whose Name shall sound to the ends of the Earth; and this is the work of the Lord God, yea, and it is marvelous in our eyes, who see his Wonders wrought in the deep: and behold, his path is in the great Waters; and his footsteps are not known by suchwho have not learned of the Lamb.

> Who leadeth in the narrow way,
> Who bringeth out o'th darkness unto the perfect day;
> Where the light in fulness springeth up,
> Where Salvation also fills the Cup
> Of all the faithful, who upon the Lord do wait;
> Their Consolation alwayes doth abound,
> And Praises with rejoycing unto God they sound:
> With Praises sweet they sing to God on high,
> Who fills the Earth with's glorious Majesty.
> Oh! therefore shout, and with Praises sing,
> Rejoyce ye holy Hosts, give glory to your King.

(page 10) Yea, let the Heavens shout, and sing for joy,
And all who're come to th' glory of the day,
For much life and vertue all must feel,
To burn in love with pure holy Zeal;
And so this love will carry thorow all,
Through death, if God unto it call.
Therefore, Arise, thou blessed Noble Seed,
With bread from Heaven God will thee alwayes feed,
So thou shalt not need hunger any more,
The fulness of all Treasure is laid up in store;
And thou shalt drink Wine of his most holy pleasure,
And likewise feed on choicest of all treasure;
On hidden Manna which cometh from above,
And on the life which is sollac'd in love;
And so with love all must be overcome,
Even with the brightest beams of th' glorious Sun,
Which shall shine clear, as at noon-day,
And cover all, who walk i' th' narrow way:
Such as from his Command do not back-slide,
Of him, before his Father, shall not be denied,
Who follow him to death, and do him not forsake,
Such of the Crown of Glory for ever shall partake;
But such as for him will not now stand,
Them God will sweep out of his holy Land.
Rejoyce ye God's redeemed, and Praises sing,
This day to you will God glad tydings bring;
Stand fast, rejoycing over all,
Stick fast in him who keepeth from the fall;
His power alwayes on you will attend,
And his Glory from Heaven on you will descend.
And then your enemies before your face shall fall,
And you, the Seed of *Abraham*, shall be renown'd o're all,
In this the day, God's glory shall so shine,
Which open shall the eyes that are yet blind,
That your beauty shall all Nations come to see,
And glorifie your Father in this his holy day;
Who hath appeared in his Eternal power,
Who is shining forth in this his glorious hour;
(page 11) So that the Heavens shout and eke rejoyce,

And all that hear the Bridegroom's pleasant voice;
Who maketh Valleys with Ecchoes for to ring,
And makes the mourners to rejoyce and sing;
Therefore abide in this Eternal love,
From which you Death nor Hell can move;
As you in it abide, and eke do dwell,
You'l feel God's virtue flow from *Jacob's* Well.
O *Sion! Sion*, thy beauty hath now fill'd me,
And eke thy Glory mine eye is come to see;
And all the World to be ev'n as a bubble,
With all her treasure too, as Hay and Stubble:
For in this day, God's glory doth abound,
And where it doth appear, the World's not to be found;
So blessed are all they that keep their habitation,
Such shall not come more into condemnation:
But such as watch upon their Tower,
Do then escape the evil hour;
An evil hour is coming unto all,
But they that watch, are kept out of the fall:
The Devil fear they not, nor all his power,
But know the God of Hosts, is their strong Tower;
And all who dwelleth in the light,
They dwell in that which Devil hath no right.
Which sure preserveth from all sinning,
And restores again as in beginning:
And in that life which raigneth over Death,
Which stand, i' th' Seed, born of the Royal birth.
Arise all ye, rejoyce and sing,
For he is come who doth glad tydings bring;
And he's rising in's Glory over all,
And by him, God from death doth call
All, who his Counsel will receive,
Who in the light his Love believe,
Whose Grace is known, doth freely save,
Whose love redeems, and bringeth from the grave:
(page 12) And greater loves there is not known,
Than God the Father sendeth to his own;
And now this love is in the Babes begotten,
Which far excels before the love of Women:
Which Love extends so freely unto all,

Yea, unto those which remains yet in the fall.
This is the day of Love and Consolation,
The day of everlasting free Salvatian;
Which publish'd is so freely unto all,
For *Abraham's* Seed God now is come to call;
Yea, yea, the bands he's come to break
Death nor Hell the Seed no more shall keep
Under in Captivity:
For God's exalting it
I'th Heavens high,
And he is setting it again on *David's* Throne,
To Reign in the Earth as King alone;
And now in his most holy Majesty,
He Ruleth on his Mountain high:
His Saints, who do in his Power dwell,
They know that Life which reigneth over Hell,
Which doth the Devil bind and chain,
Ore whom the victory they have got again.
Therefore Arise, Triumph and Sing,
For all Power stands alone in him,
Who is our Life, and is become our Head,
Who in his Glory is risen from the dead;
Who is riding swiftly to the battel,
And 'gainst the wicked he'l make his Thunders rattle;
As Lightning from the sky,
So swiftly shall his Thunders fly,
Which shall the World affright and maze,
And all shall know that God all Power has,
Both to cut off and to destroy,
All that oppose him in the way
And all must know this work begun within,
For to destroy wholly the man of Sin.
(page 13) This must first rooted be out of the heart,
Before to God can be a true Convert;
And all must know the Sword placed within,
Before to Paradise they enter in:
And in a way that's yet unknown,
Deliverance God will bring his own;
Therefore let the Seed arise and sing,
For over all shall reign our King;

Tracts of Proclamation and Warning

For on his Mountain shall stand his holy Throne,
And in this day, God will renown his own,
Which alwayes trusteth in his holy Name,
The fame spread forth, and sound out glorious Fame:
Men shall be gathered into his holy Mountain,
And drink the Waters shall from the pure Fountain;
Such shall be filled with the newest Wine,
Who are ingrafted into th' holy Vine,
Whose Fame this day shall over-spread,
Likewise whose Life hath now appear'd, and is become their
     Head:
Who is the end and all, of all Profession;
And bless'd are all who have him in possession;
Such in the Storm will never fly,
Nor in the Winter cannot him deny;
Who are joyned unto the God of Love,
From whose Foundation Death nor Hell can move;
Such are come to the Everlasting day,
Who leads i' th' light, leads to the narrow way,
Such do live in the living power;
They know the God of Hosts the strong Tower,
In the ore-whelming Floud which pursueth all,
Who upon the God of *Abraham* cry and call;
But all that are builded on the Foundation,
Shall sure be kept in th' hour of temptation,
Which now is come to try all on the Earth,
And also them that are redeem'd from death;
So in that Word which was in the beginning,
Which lead all out of the race of sinning:
As all do dwell, and do the same obey,
Are led to Life, who tread the narrow way;
(page 14) Whose path is strait, and leadeth to the Crown,
All, who upon God wait, do in his Rest lye down;
They see his saving health and great Salvation,
Which is at the end o' th' race through tribulation.
Let the Wilderness sing and eke rejoyce,
For in the Wood is heard the Turtle's voice,
Sounding forth most pleasant melody,
Giving Glory and Praise unto his Majesty,
Whose Glory is now shining exceeding clear,

Whose glorious Voice the Earth is come to hear;
By which all cometh to rejoyce,
At the sound of the Bridegroom's pleasant voice;
By which the Dead are rais'd again to Life,
This is the Day wherein the Lamb is married to his Wife:
And all must now be retired in,
To th' Paradise of the glorious King,
Where he sitteth, and shall for ever Reign,
And by his Power, his Enemies shall be slain.
Therefore rejoyce O Heavens, and be glad O Earth,
For the Life is come, which Reigneth over Death.

And now is the Glory of all Nations come, and the Bridegroom's Voice is heard in the Land of the Redeemed, who are come again out of *Egypt*, who are become the first Fruits unto God, and to the Lamb; These shall arise in the glorious power; These shall mount upward, as upon Eagles wings; These shall sit on Thrones, judging the twelve Tribes of *Israel;* These who are come unto the everlasting day of God the Sabbath, the Rest which God hath blessed for ever; These shall come unto the holy Mountain, where the Feast of Fat things is prepared; These, I say, shall come up upon Mount *Sion*, where the Song of *Moses* and the *Lamb* is sounded before his Throne, who hath now appeared in his Eternal Glory; therefore blessed are all who keep the Word of Faith, who dwell in the Patience of Jesus, such shall inherit the Promise of Life, which is to him that overcometh, for whom the Crown is laid up; And so blessed are all whose Feet are upon the Rock, the *(page 15)* Foundation of God which standeth sure. I will make my people as Mount *Sion*, saith the Lord of holiness; and as the Walls are about *Jerusalem*, even so is the Lord God round about his People; and blessed are they that dwell in the defence of the most High, they shall abide under the over-shaddowing of the Almighty in the Day of Tryal that is coming on all flesh; for God is coming to try all Foundations of the Sons of Men and tried stones are fit for the building of the House of the most High, living stones, elect and precious; These must be tryed through the fire, for there is a fire in *Sion* for the purging and purifying of the Daughter of *Jerusalem*, and she shall come forth shining in the Glory of the Lord God, whose day of rejoycing is come unto such who have followed the Lamb through the washing of Regeneration, who have been led through the great Tribulation; such are come unto the day of rejoycing, who are learning the Songs of the Redeemed, which none can learn but they that come through the Fire and through the Floods, and through the Wilderness, and through the Red Sea where the Son of Perdition is drowned; and now rejoyce thou barren Womb, which hath brought forth the first Begotten of God, for more shall be thy Children than of her that was the married Wife, for the Vine shall yield its increase, and the blessing of the Lord shall multiply upon the works of his hands, his new Creation; and the former Heavens are passing away, and the new Heavens are created again, wherein the Son of Righteousness shineth in his beauty, where the Glory of the Lord filleth the Earth: And all must feel the overcoming Life of Love to overcome; that is that which must remain Love to the Brethren; and this must convince the World that we are of God, because we love the Brethren; and he that is born of Love, overcometh the World, and so in the Faith that worketh by Love, the Victory is known; so by Love we overcome, as we know it to overcome in our own hearts: and greater Love hath no man received, than that Love which God first manifested in the Light of his Son, who was and is the Foundation which must abide forever. So in that eternal Love which hath no evil in it, is this gracious Salutation sent, with *(page 16)* the voice of glad tydings unto the poor in Spirit, unto whom the day of Deliverance is proclaimed. And this was upon me from God, to publish in this the Day of his Reign. So the Grace of God, the Father of our Lord Jesus, rest and remain upon you all who fear him.

Dorothy White.

THE END

Journals, Autobiographies, and Travel Narratives

Katharine Evans & Sarah Chevers 1662

❦

Mary Penington 1668–1672

❦

Margaret Fell 1690

❦

Joan Vokins 1691

❦

Barbara Blaugdone 1691

❦

S. B. (Susannah Blandford) 1698, 1700

❦

"TO LISTEN, TO STRUGGLE, AND TO OBEY"
JOURNALS, AUTOBIOGRAPHIES, AND TRAVEL NARRATIVES

by Judith Applegate

Introduction

Quakers were not the first religious group in the seventeenth century to publish spiritual narratives.[1] However, published Quaker narratives represent vivid and powerful testimonies to both the vitality and the struggle of early Friends. In addition, the stories left by Quaker women add insights into their prophetic ministry, the ideal of equality for female and male leadership, and the struggle to maintain that equality in the early movement. The publication of narratives by Quaker women testified to their role as "exemplars" of the religious experience of Friends.[2]

The writings included in this section represent a variety of narrative genres written at different times and for different purposes during the seventeenth century: a prison narrative, a death-bed account written to children, a spiritual autobiography, two autobiographical journals, and two accounts of various aspects of ministry. These journals all reinforce common Quaker values. Some would see these various forms as steps on the evolutionary path culminating in the "full story of outward life, sufferings and travels and of the inner experience," specifically the *Journal* of George Fox.[3] Viewing Fox's book-length journal, however, as the end result of nascent attempts to tell one's spiritual story may devalue the power and function of other narrative forms. Such a perspective fails to account for shorter seventeenth-century Quaker journals which contain the basic "ingredients" of Fox's journal.[4] In this sense the "full journal" can be viewed simply as an expanded version of an earlier, more concise, but fully developed narrative genre.

Katharine Evans and Sarah Chevers

The first and earliest of the texts included in this section, *This is a short Relation of Some of the Cruel Sufferings* is a travel narrative written jointly by Katharine Evans and Sarah Chevers who travelled together in the ministry.[5] Evans and Chevers had been among the earliest Quaker missionaries to Scotland (1653) and had suffered many persecutions.[6] In 1655 Evans was banished from the Isle of Wight after she "suffered many abuses from the rude people there."[7] That same year she was imprisoned as a vagrant along with eight other female Friends and thirteen male Friends (including James Nayler) for visiting Friends in prison. During this imprisonment (in Cornwall) the women "were lodged among Felons, and lay only upon straw in such filth that Jane Ingram died."[8] In 1656 Katharine was taken from her bed by night and banished from the Isle of Man.[9] Evans also suffered imprisonment in Exeter in 1656, and both were humiliated in Salisbury in 1657 by being stripped and whipped.[10] Unfortunately, Evans and Chevers did not leave a full account of their conversion, lives, and ministry.

Instead of a complete biographical account, they left the document included here which tells of one particular imprisonment on the Island of Malta that lasted three years. This narrative relates the sufferings they endured together at the hands of the Spanish Inquisition, thereby exposing the horrible treatment received by those who professed to be Christians. It also provides a vivid description of the calling, courage, dedication, and fortitude of these two Quaker ministers. It includes not only glimpses of their daily sufferings, but also lengthy scriptural debates that they had with their captors. These debates demonstrate how adept these women were at defending the faith of Friends.

In 1658 Evans and Chevers undertook a sea voyage from England to Alexandria.[11] When the captain of the ship docked in Malta, the women went first into a "nunnery" and then into the streets to preach and distribute Quaker books in Spanish to passers-by.[12] It is not surprising that these Quaker missionaries were arrested and held by the Inquisitors; what is surprising is that they were not executed as heretics. Instead, their lengthy imprisonment on Malta allowed them to express the calling that they had intended for Alexandria. They defined that calling as bearing the name of the Lord God; witnessing forth God's truth; fighting the Lord's battle with spiritual weapons before high and mighty men on earth; and breaking down the strongholds, high lofty looks, vain imaginations, and spiritual wickedness in high places.[13] This calling took Evans and Chevers away from family and friends in England and into imprisonment in an unfamiliar land.

Katharine had joined Sarah as "a beloved yoak-mate in the work of the Lord,"[14] and left behind husband, John (also a minister), and their daughters.[15] It seems that this did not mean, for her, however, a break in the marriage and family relationships.

Instead, Evans' letter to her husband and children from prison in 1661 calls him "Most dear and faithful Husband, Friend and Brother."[16] It says that she had "unity and fellowship" with him "day and night." The same letter relates that she prayed for her "precious" daughters, whom she calls "wise virgins," that they "might be kept pure and single in the sight of our God." This letter, full of emotion, assured her family of her love and her confidence that they were in the care and direction of God and of other Friends. She prayed only that they continue to be purified and strengthened. Few of her sufferings were mentioned in the letter, and then only in the context of testimony to God's love. Even though Katharine wrote that she looked "for every breath to be the last," she and Chevers were both released in 1662.

The condition for Evans' and Chevers' release was that they would return to England. The reunion with Evans' family must have brought great joy at the end of this long imprisonment. But it did not mean the end of her or her husband's ministry, or their testimony of faith. Her husband, John, died in prison on November 20 of 1662, with Katharine at his side. The two had been taken together from their own house along with another couple to be imprisoned for refusing the oath of allegiance. Katharine and the others remained in the prison for some time.[17]

Earlier, Katharine's "yokemate" in the Malta prison, Sarah Chevers, had also left her family behind to follow her call to Alexandria. However, in 1661, a letter to Sarah's husband, Henry, and her children from her imprisonment on Malta suggests that her family, unlike Katharine's, was not converted.[18] In the opening of Chevers' letter, while she calls her husband "my love," she explains to him that "my life is given up to serve the living God." Later she tells the family twice that she "breathes" to God "night and day" that they be "joined to the Light of the Lord." She prays that her family might "find your Savior to purge and cleanse you from your sins, and to reconcile you to his Father." She prays for these things, not only for the sake of their souls, but also that she might "enjoy unity with you in the Spirit," and "in the Eternal." The letter creates a sense of pathos as Sarah shares with her family only a hint of her prison sufferings. She, like Katharine, believes she will "remain all the days of my life" in prison.

In fact, however, Sarah died two years later, in 1663, shortly after returning from another missionary trip to Ireland with Katharine.[19] Both of these women expressed deep love and respect for their spouses and their children. However, that love did not constrain them to remain home and provide nurture for their loved ones. They both obeyed their calls to travel in the ministry.

After the deaths of Evans' husband and Sarah, her beloved travelling companion, Katharine continued to travel in the ministry and suffered for doing so. In 1666 she was imprisoned at Welchpool in Montgomeryshire and in 1681 in Newgate prison in Bristol. Later, she visited prisoners at the prison in Ivelchester (1683). According to John Whiting, "She lived to a great age, notwithstanding all her great travels and sufferings; and at last died in peace about the fourthe month, 1692."[20]

Mary Penington

Unlike Evans and Chevers, Mary Penington did not travel in ministry. But she did suffer the social ostracism and the financial loss common to landed aristocracy who converted to Quakerism. She apparently never received a call to travel in the ministry and spent her life with her family. Her spiritual autobiography, *A brief account of some of my exercises from childhood*, is included next in this section.[21] The first part of this autobiography, written in 1668, includes her childhood and adult search for authentic prayer and relationship with God. She wrote the second part in 1682, shortly before her death, and described a dream she had in 1676 as well as the material loss that she and her husband suffered in 1681.

Born in 1616,[22] and orphaned at age three, Mary Proude lived then with an Anglican family whose religion she rejected. Her search for true prayer led her to the Puritan practice of giving up such "vain pleasures" as card-playing, dancing, singing, parties, and drinking. She refused to wear a wedding ring or to practice formulated songs and prayers, sacraments, and infant baptism. Refusing to marry the man chosen by her adoptive family, she later married William Springett (1642), who agreed with her religious leanings. This marriage lasted for only two and a half years before his death. Her later marriage to Isaac Penington brought her firmly into the Quaker fold.

Her journal relates a dream that provided a foreknowledge of Quakerism before she married Isaac Penington and, later, joined Friends. In this remarkably gender-balanced dream, she saw Christ and the Lamb's wife as brother and sister in "plain" Quaker gray with just and sweet spirits.[23] Penington's inclusion of this and another dream in her autobiography illustrates an unusual belief in gender balance, both in the godhead and among Friends. Her

inclusion of these dreams in her narrative works as a possible justification for her decision to join Friends, since this section emphasizes
that she had never heard of Quakers before the first dream. It also illustrates her belief in a prophetic mysticism.

After the description of the Peningtons' conversion and her second
dream, the remainder of Mary's journal relates the details of her material suffering, Mary's attempts to provide a home in which she and Isaac
might live (near Amersham), and her concern to provide financial security for her children before her death. This portion of her journal
provides an interesting juxtaposition between her financial leadership
and her deferential stance toward her husband concerning financial
matters. While she began building their home only after he released
her to carry on according to her "own mind,"[24] she clearly took charge
of this project and all the financial arrangements that it required. It
also gives a glimpse of the great financial loss suffered by land-owning
Quakers in the seventeenth century. While Penington left money in
her will to establish the Chalfont Friends Meeting, only one reference
in her autobiography suggests that she and Isaac were active in the
ministry of spreading the gospel.[25]

Margaret Fell / Fox

Margaret Fell (1614-1702) was another seventeenth-century Quaker
woman who struggled to secure property for her own family residence
and a meeting place for Friends. Like Evans and Chevers, Margaret Fell
was moved by God to speak truth to power and she suffered imprisonment for the actions that testified to her beliefs. Like Mary Penington,
she suffered financial loss, and also provided a place for Friends to worship. We include two of her many writings, both autobiographical, in this section: *The Testimony of Margaret Fell concerning her
late Husband George Fox: together with a brief Account of some of
his Travels, Sufferings, and Hardships endured for the Truth's Sake*[26]
and *A Relation of Margaret Fell, Her Birth, Life, Testimony, and
Sufferings for the Lord's Everlasting Truth in her Generation.*[27] While
the two documents relate events from the same period, each provides important data not found in the other.

Fell's *A Relation* begins with a list of her aristocratic credentials.
Margaret Askew came from a respected, ancient, and land-own-
ing family. She married her first husband, Thomas Fell, at age 17.
He was sixteen years older than she.[28] Thomas was a barrister at

the time of their marriage, but advanced to Justice, member of Parliament, Chancellor, and Judge in the north part of England. The Fells lived together for twenty-six years and had nine children before Judge Fell died in 1658.

In 1652, George Fox visited the Fell home, which was regularly open to travelling ministers and religious people, during a time when Judge Fell happened to be away.[29] After receiving hospitality for the night, Fox preached the next day at Ulverston "steeple-house." During this sermon, Margaret Fell was dramatically moved and soon became a Friend. Later, with permission from Judge Fell, the Fell home became the headquarters for Quakerism in the North of England. Quakers continued to meet at Swarthmoor Hall for thirty-eight years. While Judge Fell never joined their ranks, Quakers found a good friend and protector in him.[30]

But it was Margaret's convincement and protective efforts that had a greater influence on the safety of Friends and the development of Quakerism. By the mid-1660s she had organized the Kendal fund which gave financial aid to travelling and imprisoned Friends and their families.[31] For twenty-five years after her husband's death, Margaret Fell took on the responsibility of defending Fox and other Friends in prison. But even before his death she began publishing Quaker tracts. In 1652-53 she asked her husband to publish some Quaker documents and to distribute them while he was in London.[32] She also maintained correspondence and wrote other tracts and epistles: twenty-one were published in the 1650s and eighteen tracts published by 1668.[33] After Judge Fell's death in 1658, Margaret, whose Quaker activities had previously been restricted to the Swarthmoor residence, was free to travel in the ministry as well.

The first of her ten trips to London in the service of Friends occurred in June of 1660, one month after George Fox had been arrested at Swarthmoor and imprisoned in Lancaster Castle. She travelled to London with her oldest daughter, Margaret, leaving twenty-six-year-old Bridgett in charge of the large Fell estate and the four youngest daughters. By appealing to the king and other powerful members of the aristocracy, Margaret Fell was able to secure Fox's release by September. In October George Fox returned to London. After his arrival, Margaret stayed on in London even though Bridgett wrote often expressing loneliness and longing for her mother. Fell says, "And then would I gladly have come home to my great Family; but was bound in my Spirit, and could not have Freedom to get away for a whole year."[34]

In January of 1661 the uprising of the millenarian Fifth Monarchy Men caused nationwide persecution and imprisonment of Quakers. Margaret, still in London, stayed to work for the release of Friends from prison. Her influence and efforts must have been remarkable because she secured their release before she returned home to Swarthmoor in September of 1661. While the fifteen-month separation from her home had been difficult for the family, Fell's journals emphatically express her sense of calling to stay in London for those months.[35] She seemed to have complete confidence in her children to oversee the Swarthmoor estate without her.

This confidence testifies to the fact that Margaret Fell had trained her daughters to have a sense of autonomy uncommon to British women in the seventeenth century. Each had her own bank account, most married late (Susannah, age 41 and Sarah, 39), and each chose her own husband. Even before the death of Judge Fell, Margaret allowed them to choose mates not according to social class but according to shared religious values.[36] All Margaret Fell's children married Friends and supported the Quaker movement except her son, George, who had moved to London to study law shortly after the family was converted.

After Margaret married George Fox, Margaret's son and daughter-in-law fought bitterly for control of the Fell estate. In 1670 George Fell even initiated his mother's second imprisonment in Lancaster jail to acquire what he believed to be his. But he died suddenly in October of that year. Although he had bequeathed Swarthmoor to his wife and son, Margaret Fell persuaded the court to award it to George's sisters Susan and Rachel Fell, thereby preserving it for use by Friends.[37]

The incident with Margaret Fell's son suggests that she was financially and politically shrewd, even with members of her own family. On the other hand, Friends often referred to Margaret as the "nursing mother" of Quakerism. This terminology, applied by early Friends to both men ("nursing fathers") and women, suggested that Margaret was considered a tender and warmhearted source of support.[38] While at Swarthmoor, she supported Friends far and wide through hospitality, visitation, financial contributions and correspondence, encouraging the faithful and rebuking the errant. Travelling ministers who received her patronage were naturally grateful for her care and easily thought of her as a nurturing mother figure. But it would be a mistake to conclude that such activities were her only or her most important contributions to the Religious Society of Friends.

Her early activities of tract writing and lobbying on behalf of Friends probably contributed as much to the early formation of Quakers as her openhearted support did. Bonnelyn Young Kunze proposes, in fact, that Margaret Fell greatly influenced George Fox and other early Quaker leaders in the organization of the Religious Society of Friends and the articulation of its doctrine. She promoted social and gender equality, but did not forsake her own class standing. Like William Penn, Margaret did not hesitate to use her social privilege to promote the causes in which she had particular interest. Thus, Margaret Fell should be remembered as a supportive, wise, and shrewd lobbyist, minister, author, and administrator among early Friends.

Joan Vokins

Like Margaret Fell, Joan Vokins was called to move back and forth between the responsibilities of rearing a large family (she had seven children) and travelling in the ministry. Friends and family also called her a "nursing mother."[39] Memorial testimonies from her children affirm that she had "a great care in her family of us her children, that we might be *nurtur'd and brought up in the Fear of the Lord.*"[40] Indeed, while Joan was the first in her family to be convinced, her father, husband, and children all eventually followed her into Quakerism. Her longtime friend Theophila Townsend attributed their joining Friends to Vokins' "Christian Motherly care" and "good example."[41] The genuineness of the family's conversion is demonstrated by the fact that her husband and son were both incarcerated in the Reading jail for refusing to pay tithes at the time of her death (1690). But her "nurturing" instincts extended beyond her local family to the weak, with a special concern for the "younger generation" of convinced Friends. She exhorted "them to be inwardly staid in their Minds, that they might grow in the Love and Life of Truth . . . that they might come up to serve the Lord and succeed their Heavenly minded Parents."[42]

Her autobiographical writings, entitled *God's Mighty Power Magnified*, penned aboard ship in 1691 during her travels in the "new world," seem to have been written with an eye to that younger generation, to provide an example. In these documents Vokins also addressed her opponents and defended her travelling ministry.[43] The first half of her journal-like narrative entails a disconnected but thorough account of her spiritual conversion.

In it she mentions early searchings for truth; her salvation from the evils of youth; the inadequacy of priests and professors to answer her questions; her conversion through the Spirit and later confirmation by Quaker messengers; her struggle against and protection from the enemy (others backslid, she did not); her labor to convert her husband and children; an internal fight against self-righteousness; and her eventual submission to God's call to travel in the ministry. One would expect to find all of these elements in a full, self-conscious autobiography written in the later seventeenth and early eighteenth centuries. Such "full" autobiographies generally include an account of the author's spiritual searchings, which culminate in God's call to ministry.[44]

Vokins' call took her to New England, New York, Rhode Island, Antigua, St. Nevis, and Barbados. She then returned to England to fight for the women's meetings, and went on to Sandwich, Kent, and Ireland. Though she earned high respect among many Friends in the latter part of her life, her narrative shows a defensiveness about her decision to travel. Such an attitude may suggest that she had encountered criticism about leaving her family (her youngest daughter was age 9) to travel in the the ministry. In relating her struggle for freedom to follow God's call, Vokins justaposed the deep care she felt for her family with her belief that those who ignore God will have no excuse in the "Day of Account."[45] She argued for a redefinition of all household and familial relations, because she believed that husbands, wives, parents, children, and servants are all individually accountable to God, rather than to any human authority.[46] Vokins never mentions the need to appeal to the Friends Meeting for affirmation of her call. This strong belief in an unavoidable accounting led Vokins not only to be faithful to her own call, but also prompted her to defend the ministry of women both in preaching and in the women's meetings.[47] Indeed, she interrupted her ministry in New England to return to Berk County, England to "labour for the Settlement of our Womens Meetings."[48] So serious was the threat to these meetings, that she calls this labor, "no small Cross to take up." But she attributes the salvation of the women's meetings to the fact that "our good Shepherd did visit his Handmaids, and . . . filled us with his overcoming Power, when the Mothers in Israel were so dismayed as were likely to have lost our Womens Meeting."[49]

In this short section Vokins mentions God's power no less than six times: encouraging Power, overcoming Power, Almighty Power, excellent Power, preserving Power, secret arm of his Power. God provided this power to the women, considered "weak" and "contemptible vessels," to help them resist those interested in giving "Honour to Man," and preferring "Man's Wisdom" to God's. These were the motives that Vokins attributes to attempts to destroy "our women's meetings," which she believed were owned by the Lord.

This theme of God's various provisions of power infuses Vokins' account of her battle for the women's meetings and is found throughout the travel narrative. She said this power preserved her from danger at sea, "comforted her poor soul," made her willing to go where she didn't want to, supported her, and conducted her to each place.[50] She spoke often of the refreshment that God's power provided for both herself and the people she met. Through this power Vokins was also enabled to fulfill her calling in spite of illness.[51] Finally, God's "Providential Power" provided female travelling companions, even though none of her own friends or any designated Friend from her home meeting was provided as companion for her.[52] Vokins referred to these women by name or as "Maiden Friends" or "Women Friends." They appeared as if out of nowhere, one after the other, to accompany her throughout her travels. These "providential" companions must have been a great help to the physically weak Vokins during her many journeys. In her narration, however, she never uses the "yokemate" language of Evans and Chevers, and continually focusses on her private callings to travel from place to place, leaving one companion behind to be joined by another at the next stop.

Barbara Blaugdone

Unlike Vokins or Evans and Chevers, Barbara Blaugdone of Bristol seems to have travelled in the ministry unaccompanied by either yokemate or serial companions, nor did she leave a family behind. Blaugdone, born in 1606 and a tutor of children, was convinced and joined Friends in 1654. One of the earliest Quaker missionaries to Ireland, she lived to the remarkable age of ninety-five. Her narrative, published in 1691 as *An Account of the Travels, Sufferings and Persecutions of Barbara Blaugdone*, has been called "racy" or "hysterical" by some contemporary Quaker historians.[53] Blaugdone, like Vokins, intended her writing to stand as a "testimony to the Lords power, and for the encouragement of Friends."[54]

Unlike Vokins' account, Blaugdone's includes only brief references to her early search for God. And yet she did mention youthful tenderness to the Lord, fear of offending him, zeal in her profession, and earnest seeking for the Lord. She explained that she did not know where to find the Lord until John Audland and John Camm came and directed her to wait on the light of Christ.[55] Through this waiting, she related her conversion as a private process in which she was convinced to take up her "cross to obedience," which meant adopting the Quaker "plain Speech and Habit." She seems to have modelled the story of her missionary journeys after Paul in the New Testament book of Acts. She linked her ministry of travelling from place to place, speaking in "Publick Places and Steeple houses," with the same inevitable social ostracism and brutal treatment at the hands of local authorities faced by the apostle Paul.

Originally, Blaugdone had so dreaded the call to go forth that she delayed her travels in the ministry until after she had fasted from meat, wine, and beer for one year. In its emphasis on the waiting and fasting, her narrative invites comparison with biblical accounts (cf. Jesus fasts in the wilderness forty days before beginning his public ministry, Luke 4:1-30) and thus assures the reader that God was with her. The narrative can seem humble, even apologetic as it emphasizes her care in exercising public gifts of ministry. It includes the words, "The Power and Spirit of the Lord was so strong in me, that it set me upon my Feet, and constrained me to speak the words; for I was never hasty or forward" as a disclaimer before the description of her missionary travels.[56]

Blaugdone related the sufferings along with the successes that this powerful speaking provoked. The first of these was the loss of both her students and her aristocratic friends.[57] Even so, Blaugdone, who called herself a prophetess, emphasized that she paid her own way in all of her travels.[58] Because of her public speaking she was physically attacked and imprisoned. She continued to compare her responses to imprisonment to those of Paul. In three different prison terms she told of fasting: first for six weeks, then for six and finally fourteen days and nights. [59] She also suffered imprisonment in Devonshire, Molton, Bastable, and Bediford, probably "a quarter of a year at a time."[60] In Bath she gave credit to God when she was rescued from a vicious dog sent to attack her in the backyard of a Countess whom she had tried to convince.

She related being miraculously preserved through sea storms and shipwrecks during her two trips to Ireland and in her return to England.[61] In Ireland, she was accused of witchcraft (Cork), imprisoned (Dublin and Limerick), and finally banished in 1664 along with other Friends. Both in England and in Ireland she worked for the release of imprisoned

Friends, complaining to Henry Cromwell in Ireland about the unjust treatment Friends were receiving.

Above all, while her account reads as an action-packed adventure, what stands out is Blaugdone's sense of God's guiding and powerful presence in all that she did. Unlike the other narratives by women, but similar to that of George Fox's *Journal*, Blaugdone's story is full of the miraculous in physical manifestation. Rather than relying on her own strength, she testified that God repeatedly "opened" her mouth to preach in public places, gave her special knowledge about the inner dealings of various strangers, protected her life and that of the crew and ship from all damage after six days and nights of stormy weather, struck people dead after she "cleared her conscience" with them, and enabled her to argue victoriously against both priests and professors. In all of this she saw herself as an "instrument in the hand of the Lord." She claims to have been, "faithful and obedient unto his Power," and to have grown and prospered through her sufferings, and through her experience of his love and power.[62] And while at the end of her narrative she cites Elizabeth Gardiner, Rebecca Rich, and Samuel Clarges' wife as references, she describes her work and ministry with a minimum of self-defensiveness or apology. Apparently without the benefit of the financial or emotional support of a home meeting, Barbara Blaugdone went forth sustained by the strength of her own internal convictions that God had called her and travelled with her.

Susannah Blandford

The last documents included in this section were written by a woman who found sustenance not only in her own strong convictions, but also from the company of those Friends who called themselves "Christian Quakers."[63] While early Quakerism is often idealized as a uniquely and fully egalitarian movement,[64] from the beginning the leadership of women found resistance among some who called themselves Quaker.[65] The texts by Susannah Blandford are included to call attention to this opposition to women's full and equal status as ministers and leaders.[66]

While Blandford's is not strictly a narrative text, *A Small Account Given Forth* provides some biographical data. It describes Blandford's early struggle to find a genuine relationship with God. Raised in the Church of England, her convincement of God's love and truth came three years before she had seen or heard any Quakers. She received an "Account" of Quaker principles and as a result experienced a sense of "power" that delivered her from her "dark thoughts," and enabled her to understand the Scriptures.

While Blandford, like Penington, emphasizes the fact that she was initially afraid of Quakers and that she was converted before she ever met any, she also claims to be a true Quaker. Her association with "Christian Quakers" has caused her to be labelled a "dissenting Quaker," which she finds troubling and denies fervently. In her mind, she has remained faithful, a "true Traveller," while others have fallen into heresy.

She describes one form of heresy as the spirit of Martha. Her opposition to those with "Martha's Spirit" is likely a criticism directed at the institution of separate women's meetings and at the public speaking of women ministers. Blandford claims that those with Martha's spirit "runs, and serves, and cumbers themselves with striving to utter Words."[67] Such "Marthas" encourage others like herself to do likewise and thus become stumbling blocks. Blandford thanks God that she has been preserved from this temptation and deceit. She feels that she has been "kept low" rather than being exalted "by Visions, Sights, nor Revelations."[68]

Blandford's lowliness is illustrated by the fact that she never spoke in a "Publick Assembly." She agrees with the apostle Paul that women should be silent in the church.[69] In her opinion, women should limit their ministry to being good examples in their families. They must preach only in private to children, friends, neighbors, and servants.[70]

Such an attitude stands as a criticism of the many Quaker women who travelled in the ministry and organized an effective relief effort for the poor and imprisoned. While Blandford's "Account" was not published until the end of the seventeenth century, the ideas that it represents existed as challenges to "mainstream" Quakerism from the very beginning. The strong leadership and powerful ministry of women among early Friends did not exist without opposition from within the ranks.

Conclusion

All the Quaker women whose writings are included in this narrative section functioned as exemplars of Quaker faith. Even Susannah Blandford, who opposed women's public speaking, defied social norms by writing and publishing her own faith story and theological understandings. These narrative texts continue to challenge men and women of all ages to be faithful to God's callings, even in the face of social ostracism, rejection, opposition by friends and enemies, and through sufferings of all kinds.

NOTES

1. See Hugh Barbour and Arthur O. Roberts, "Journals of Lives Led by the
    Light," in *Early Quaker Writings, 1650-1700* (Grand Rapids: Eerdmans,
    1973), pp. 149-242 and the citations in n. 1, p. 151. Also, Luella M.
    Wright, *The Literary Life of the Early Friends, 1650-1725* (New York:
    Columbia University Press, 1932), pp. 155-97 and Judith Scheffler, "Prison
    Writings of Early Quaker Women," *Quaker History* 74:2 (Fall, 1984), pp.
    23-37. Carol Edkins ("Quest for Community: Spiritual Autobiographies
    of Eighteenth-Century Quaker and Puritan Women in America," in
    Women's Autobiography: Essays in Criticism, Estelle C. Jelinek, ed.
    [Bloomington: Indiana University Press, 1980], pp. 39-52) also considers
    women's narratives, but from the early eighteenth century.

2. Edkins, "Quest for Community," p. 40.

3. Barbour and Roberts (pp. 152-53) treat four Puritan types of narrative as
    early ingredients which merged into the Quaker journals published toward
    the end of the seventeenth century. These "ingredients" include: narrative
    material found in letters of counsel; spiritual obituaries or memorials; the
    introduction to proclamation tracts which often mention the leading of
    the proclaimer to write and the call to address a particular group; and
    collections of healing accounts, deliverances from danger, disasters to
    persecutors, and accounts of missionary journeys. Wright in *The Literary
    Life*, pp. 155-97, suggests that the genre of Quaker journals was set between
    the years of 1689 and 1694 during which time journals by William Caton,
    John Burnyeat, Stephen Crisp, and George Fox were published. She does
    not mention Barbara Blaugdone's 1691 journal. On the other hand, she
    reminds us that Friends seemed to have experienced an early "need" for
    self-expression and such needs produced a variety of narrative forms long
    before 1694.

4. Both Barbara Blaugdone and Joan Vokins published texts in 1691, three
    years before Fox's *Journal* appeared in print. While Barbour and Roberts
    list Joan Vokins' narrative among those called "intermediate forms," they
    mention neither Blaugdone's more complete account nor any of the other
    autobiographical writings included in this section.

5. *This is a short Relation of some of the Cruel Sufferings
    (For the Truths sake) of Katharine Evans & Sarah Chevers, In the Inquisition
    in the Isle of Malta* (London: Printed for Robert Wilson, 1662). The origi-
    nal includes a lengthy narrative introduction (of which we have included
    only a small portion) and letters by Daniel Baker, the man who labored
    for their release and who was able, by tricking the Inquisitor, to make

copies of the letters and papers that Evans and Chevers wrote during their imprisonment. While Baker's introduction is not included here, a letter from each of these women to her family appears after her narrative.

6. Joseph Besse, *A Collection of the sufferings of the people called Quakers* (London: L. Hinde, 1753) 2:495.

7. Besse, *Sufferings*, 1:229.

8. Besse, *Sufferings*, 1:149.

9. Besse, *Sufferings*, 1:269.

10. Maureen Bell, George Parfitt & Simon Shepherd, *A Biographical Dictionary of English Women Writers, 1580-1720* (Boston: G.K. Hall & Co., 1990), p. 75.

11. See pp. 171-72 of *Relation* where Daniel Baker, Evans, and Chevers name Alexandria as their final destination, and also p. 173 where Evans emphasizes that she intended to go to Alexandria not Jerusalem. While John Whiting, in *Persecution Exposed in Some Memoirs Relating to the Sufferings* (London: James Phillips, 1791), p. 471, also claims that they left for Alexandria in 1659, more recent sources claim that they left in 1658 for Jerusalem (Cf. Bell, Parfitt & Shepherd, eds., *A Biographical Dictionary*, p. 75.) The Bell work, however, also has an apparent error in citing 1664 as the date of their release. It was actually 1662. (This temporal inconsistency may possibly be the result of the change of calendar.)

12. Evans, *Relation*, pp. 172-73.

13. Evans, *Relation*, p. 172.

14. See *Katharine Evans to her Husband and Children*, p. 205.

15. Apparently, while some women travelled alone and found female travelling companions along their way (see Joan Vokins below), it was uncommon for married Quaker couples to travel together in the ministry.

16. See *Katharine Evans to her Husband and Children*, pp. 203-5.

17. Besse claims that they were in prison for five years (*Sufferings*, 1:749), but also places Katharine Evans and Sarah Chevers returning from a trip to Ireland and arrested from a Friends meeting in Wivelscombe in 1664. Shortly after the imprisonment that followed, Sarah Chevers died (*Sufferings*, 1:596).

18. See *Sarah Chevers to Her Husband and Children*, pp. 206-7.

19. Besse, *Sufferings*, 1:596.

20. Whiting, *Persecution Exposed*, p. 476.

21. Neither "A letter from Mary Penington, to her Grandson, Springett Penn," (1680) nor other extant letters are included in this collection. While *A brief Account* was written between 1668-72 and published first in 1797, the version provided here is that which was published in 1821 by Harvey & Darton (Grace church street, London). This publication was entitled, "Some account of the circumstances in the Life of Mary Pennington, from her Manuscript, Left for her Family." It included both of the above documents.

22. Though the *Dictionary of British and American Women Writers* (Totowa, New Jersey: Rowman & Allanheld, 1988, p. 244), *A Biographical Dictionary of English Women Writers* (p. 153), and Gil Skidmore's "Preface" to the 1992 Friends Historical Society's reprint (p. x) of Penington's autobiographical material all claim she was born in 1625, the preface to the 1821 edition of this material and Besse's *Catalogue of Friends' Books* (p. 361) cite the year of her birth as 1616.

23. Penington, *Account*, p. 225.

24. Penington, *Account*, p. 228.

25. Penington, *Account*, p. 226. She speaks about feeling sad about leaving a people "whom we had been instrumental in gathering to the truth . . . " to settle elsewhere.

26. This version, first printed for Thomas Northcott in George-Yard in Lombard Street 1694, was taken from the first edition of George Fox's *Journal*.

27. Written in 1690, when Margaret Fox was 76 and found in *A Brief Collection of Remarkable Passages and Occurrences Relating to Margaret Fell, Fox* (London: J. Sowle, 1710), pp. 1-13.

28. Fell, *A Relation*, p. 245.

29. Fell, *A Relation*, p. 245, *Testimony*, p. 235.

30. Judge Fell died in 1658 (*Testimony*, p. 239).

31. Bonnelyn Young Kunze, "The Family, Social and Religious Life of Margaret Fell" (Ph.D. dissertation, University of Rochester, 1987):184. See also *Margaret Fell and the Life of Quakerism* (Stanford: Stanford University Press, 1994).

32. According to Kunze ("Life of Margaret Fell," pp. 35-37), there is evidence that in 1657 some tension had developed between Judge Fell and Margaret Fell about her Quaker activities. In that year she tried to go behind his back to publish a tract in Holland through a London publisher. Since the tract was not published, it is supposed that the Judge had intervened.

33. Kunze, "Life of Margaret Fell," p. 186.

34. Fell, *Testimony*, p. 246.

35. Fell, *Testimony*, p. 246. While Fell only relates her sense of spiritual obliga-tion to stay in London, Kunze proposes that Margaret might also have enjoyed the political excitement of that city, her son's proximity, and her new freedom as a widow (Kunze, "Life of Margaret Fell," p. 52). It *is* hard to explain her remaining in London from October 1660 to January 1661. Her specific goal of securing Fox's release had been accomplished, and the "Great and General Imprisonment of Friends" to which she refers did not occur until some three months later. It is likely she welcomed this oppor-tunity to spend time with George Fox, as well.

36. Kunze, "Life of Margaret Fell," pp. 26, 39, 58. Mary was the youngest to marry, at age twenty-one, and George married at twenty-two. All the oth-ers were between the ages of twenty-seven and forty-one.

37. While most Quaker scholars harshly judge George Fell's "betrayal" of his mother, Kunze concludes that George, as natural heir to the Fell fortunes, was displaced by a shrewd mother who wanted to retain Swarthmoor Hall for personal and religious reasons, and who out-maneuvered him for the spoils. See Kunze's fascinating discussion of this controversy on pp. 70-74.

38. The Fell family referred to George Fox as a "nursing father" in a very early letter sent to convince him to return to Swarthmoor to speak to Judge Fell. The same letter says, "Take pity on us, whom you have nursed up with the breasts of consolation." References such as this signify the word "nursing" has a connotation of spiritual parent and mentor, rather than of a passive, supporting presence. For the full text of this letter, see Terry S. Wallace, *A Sincere and Constant Love: an introduction to the work of Margaret Fell* (Rich-mond, Indiana: Friends United Press, 1992), pp. 102-3.

39. *An Account and Testimony concerning Joan Vokins, from the Quarterly Meet-ing for Berkshire*, and *A Testimony concerning Joan Vokins, by Theophila Townsend*, both included in Thomas Northcott's 1691 publication of Vokins' narrative *God's Mighty Power Magnified; as manifested and revealed in his faithful handmaid, Joan Vokins.* (London, printed for Thomas Northcott, in George-Yard in Lombard Street, 1691).

40. *God's Power*, and *Concerning our Dear and Tender Mother, Joan Vokins, who departed this Life the 22d of the 5th Month, 1690.*

41. *God's Power*, and *A Testimony . . . by Theophila Townsend.* This and sev-eral other letters are included with Vokins' narrative in the original pub-lication. Their pages are not numbered.

42. *God's Power*, and *Mary Drewet's Testimony Concerning Joan Vokins.* Theophila Townsend's letter also referred to Vokins' concern for young people by calling her "a Nursing Mother over the Young convinced."

43. Vokins says, "This I do write, that no one should murmur, and say, *No Exercise is like mine*," (*Power*, p. 264) and Townsend mentions that "her greatest grief and heaviest Burden, and most grievous to be born, was her suffering by false Brethren and Apostates, who under the form and profession of Truth, did make War, and kick against the Life and Power of it." Townsend suggests that this opposition continued throughout Vokins' life: "the Lord bore up her head and supported her at all times and brought her through it all, and now hath taken her to himself out of all their reach, where she rests from her labours, and her works do follow her."

44. Howard Brinton, ed., *Children of the Light*, (New York, 1938) pp. 388-406, and Edkins,"Quest," p. 45, list a basic framework of spiritual development that became common in journals by the eighteenth century. While Brinton's was developed by focussing primarily on male journals, Edkins' focusses more on the writings of women. Both concentrate heavily on journals from the eighteeenth century. Edkins' list includes the following six "uniform series of experiences:" 1) religious questioning and seeking at an early age, 2) an attempt to discern an adequate basis for religious life from prevailing teachings, 3) a record of the first knowledge of Quakerism, 4) a struggle in the soul against surrender to God and the Quaker community, 5) submission, 6) entry into the activity and defenses of the Society of Friends. Brinton lists eight elements that form a pattern of religious development: 1) a childhood with the knowledge of God's grace and strict parents who did not appreciate it, 2) intervals of wild oats, 3) periods of legalistic righteousness, 4) full conversion experience, 5) later finding it inadequate or slipping back, 6) hypocrisy of so-called Christians, 7) emptiness of mere doctrines even about Christ, 8) own hypocrisy in accepting forgiveness while still sinning. The elements that are omitted in Edkins' account are those of the back-sliding and inner hypocrisy, while pre-Quaker backsliding could certainly be seen as an element in Mary Penington's journal. Perhaps because many of the narratives by women seek, in part, to justify their ministries, these elements are not as prominent in women's journals as they are in the stories told by men.

45. Vokins, *Power*, p. 260.

46. Vokins, *Power*. She emphasizes that in marriage, "Man and Wife should be helpful one to another in Righteousness, yet too many there are, since the fall, that hinder and hurt each other for which an account must be given avoidable," p. 260.

47. Vokins, *Power*, pp. 263, 267.

48. Vokins, *Power*, p. 263.

49. Vokins, *Power*, p. 263.

50. See Vokins, *Power*, pp. 265-70 for these adventures. God's power carried

her safely to Barbados and Nevice where she was called to go, against the will of the captain of the ship on which she sailed. Because the captain refuses to cooperate with her, she "clears her conscience" to him, warning him about disobeying the Lord. Later "his Vessel was split on a Rock" (p. 269).

51. Her physical problems are mentioned repeatedly by Vokins and by each of those who wrote memorial epistles at her death. God's power enabled her to attend a Quaker Meeting on Long Island, though she was so ill that her companions thought she would die. Two women Friends helped Vokins get to the Meeting place where God enabled her to stand and speak so powerfully that "*Friends* were very much comforted and refreshed, and the Power of Darkness so chained, that the opposing *Ranters* and *Apostates* could not shew their antick tricks, nor oppress Friends" (p. 265).

52. While she refers to some of these simply as "Women Friends" or "Maiden Friends," she names Sarah Yoklet, Lydia Wright, Elizabeth Dean, Mary Humphrey, and Margaret Kerby, pp. 267, 269, 272.

53. *An Account of the Travels, Sufferings and Persecutions of Barbara Blaugdone given forth as a Testimony to the Lord's Power, and for the Encouragement of Friends* (Printed and Sold by T. S. at the Crooked-Billet in Holywell-Lane, Shoreditch, 1691), pp. 274-284.

54. This phrase is from the subtitle of her narrative. See page 274.

55. Mabel Richmond Brailsford (*Quaker Women, 1650-1690* [London: Duckworth, 1915]) claims that Blaugdone was converted in 1651 at age forty-six and surmises that she had probably been widowed at a fairly early age. She also assumes that Blaugdone had a "slender fortune," since she did not depend on financial assistance from Friends for her missionary travels (pp. 158-76).

56. Blaugdone, *Account*, p. 276.

57. Besse, *Sufferings*, 2:459.

58. She refers to herself as a prophetess on p. 283, and gives an example of prophetic knowledge earlier (p. 280). In her prophetic message she refers to Acts 5:34-39 where Gamaliel warns the Jewish leaders not to persecute the Christian apostles. For examples of Paul's prophetic visions and messages from the Lord, see Acts 16:6-10, 18:9-11, 22:17-21, 23:11.

59. Blaugdone, *Account*, pp. 276-77. She was stabbed in Bristol, imprisoned for six weeks in Marlborough, and whipped and imprisoned in Exeter. In Marlborough prison she speaks of fasting for six days and nights from both bread and water. In Exeter prison she fasted from food and drink fourteen days and nights, and like Paul in Acts 16:25, she sang aloud while she was being whipped until blood ran down her back.

60. Blaugdone, _Account_, p. 275.

61. Blaugdone, _Account_, pp. 279, 281, 283. See Acts 27:13-44 for an account of Paul's shipwreck.

62. Blaugdone, _Account_, p. 283.

63. While Blandford is judged by T.C. (Thomas Curtis?) because she criticises George Keith for his ruthless slander of many Quakers, she refers to herself and her supporters as "Christian Friends," a group associated with the Wilkinson-Story and William Rogers splinter. George Keith, full of criticism of Quakers, returned to England from Pennsylvania in 1694 after being disowned there. Blandford wants nothing to do with his kind of slander and grieves over the backsliding and divisions that she sees among Friends.

64. William C. Braithwaite (_The Second Period of Quakerism_ [London: Macmillan, 1919]) says, "The equality of men and women in spiritual privilege and responsiblility has always been one of the glories of Quakerism" (p. 270).

65. Such opposition was focussed not simply on the role of women, but against the general organization of Friends encouraged by George Fox from 1667 on. The establishment of monthly meetings among Friends formalized procedures for disciplining members who failed to live up to Quaker ideals. Such Friends were considered "delinquent as true Friends" and disowned from the Society. A contingent of Friends, so disciplined, protested against Fox's organizational imperatives. Part of their protest was against the setting up of women's meetings. For a good summary of these controversies, see Braithwaite, _Second Period of Quakerism_, chapters 8-11.

66. We have included _A Small Account Given Forth by one that hath been a Traveller for these 40 Years in the Good Old Way_ printed in 1698. Blandford also published _A Small Treatise Writ by one of the True Christian Faith' who Believes in God and in his Son Jesus Christ_ in 1700. See pp. 285-306.

67. Blandford, _Account_, p. 289.

68. Blandford, _Account_, p. 290. It is interesting that in Blandford's later publication, _Testimony_, she relates a dream illustrating the fall of many of her Christian Friends. She did not totally oppose "Visions, Sights and Revelations," but cautioned against being overly influenced or exalted by them (_Account_, p. 301).

69. Blandford, _Account_, p. 294.

70. Blandford, _Account_, p. 294.

(*Excerpt*)

This is a fhort

RELATION

Of fome of the

Cruel Sufferings

(For the Truths fake) of

KATHARINE EVANS & SARAH CHEVERS,

In the Inquifition in the

ISLE of MALTA,

Who have suffered there above three years, by the Pope's Authority, there to be deteined till they dye. Which Relation of their fufferings is come from their own hands and mouths, as doth appear by the following Treatife. These two Daughters of *Abraham* were passing to *Alexandria*, and to *Cilicia*, And thus may that part of Chriftendom fee their fruits, together with the Pope's, and of what birth they are; and that thofe that are called Chriftians are worfe than Heathens: For they falling into their hands, fhould have been refrefhed by them with neceffary things; but the provifion which the Inhabitants and Knights of *Malta*, (called *Chriftians*) provided for them, is the Inquisition. Now it was not fo when *Paul* fuffered shipwrack there among the barbarous people; which is a manifeft token they are not in the love of God, whose fruits fhew they are not in the true Spirit.

And this is to all fellow-brethren that are partakers with them in the Power of God and have a feeling and fellowship with them in their sufferings, that they might see and know how it is with them and what unkindness they find abroad among them that profess themselves Christians.

LONDON, Printed for *Robert Wilfon, 1662.*

(Page numbers of original document appear in text as *page _.*)

(page 1) O Yee Eternal and Blessed ones, whose dwelling is on high, in the fulness of all Beauty and Brightness, Glory and everlasting Joy, Happiness and Peace for evermore; We who are poor sufferers for the Seed of God, in the Covenant of Light, Life, and Truth, do dearly salute and imbrace you all, according to our measures, Blessing and honour and Glory be given to our Lord God for ever, of all who know him, who hath counted us worthy, and hath chosen us among his faithfull ones, to bear his name and to witness forth his truth, before the high and mighty men of the earth, and to fight the Lords battle with his spirituall weapons, to the breaking down of strong holds, high lofty looks and vain imaginations, and spirituall wickedness in high places.

The Lord did give us a prosperous journey hither, and when we came to *Legorne,* we were refreshed with friends [who were there before us] and they did get a passage for us (and lodging) but as soon as we heard of the Vessel, we did feel our service. So went into the City in the living *(page 2)* power of the Lord, and there were many tender hearts did visit us, to their comfort, and our joy: The little time we staid there we gave some of our Books, and one Paper: so journying towards *Alexandria,* the Captain told us that *Malta* was in the way, and he must put in there a small time. But before we came there, our burthen was so heavy, that I was made to cry out (saying,) Oh we have a dreadfull cup to drink at that place ! Oh how am I straitned till it be Accomplished!

And when we came there, the walls of the City were full of people; some stood on the top of the walls, as if something had troubled them: before we came there we stood upon the deck of the ship, and I looked upon them, & said in my heart, Shall yee destroy us? *If we give up to the Lord, then he is sufficient to deliver us out of their hands; but if we disobey our God, all those could not deliver us out of his hand:* So all fear of man was taken from us. The English Consul came abord the ship (as the Captain said) but we did not see him, and invited us to his House, it was the seventh or last day of the week: The next morning being moved of the Lord we went a-shore, and the Consul met us, and we gave him a paper, who sent us to his House, with his Servant; and when we came there at the present we well were entertained (like Princes) their *Neighbours* and *Kinsfolk* came in, and some *Jesuits,* and we gave them Books, they read a little, and laid them down, they were too hot; we declared our message to them in the Name of the Lord, and we gave some Books in the Street, so they were all set on work: Away went the Friers to the King (or Supreme in the Island) and he would not meddle with us, but said, we were honest women, we might go about our business, and that night we went a-bord the Ship again, the Consul was troubled, for their snare was laid, and we felt it; being moved of the Lord we went in again the next day, and the Consul having a sister in the Nunnery, desired us to go there, that she might see us; and we went to them, and gave them a book, then to the Consuls we returned again, and sitting to wait to know the mind of the Lord, what he would have us to do, he said we must give in the great Paper; and if we would go to save our life, we should lose it.

(page 3) Here followeth a Copy of some more words which they had written before the former was given forth.

A True Declaration concerning the Lord's love to us in all our Voyage: We were at Sea, betwen *London* and *Plymouth*, many Weeks, and one day we had some trials; and between *Plymouth* and *Legorn* we were 31 days, and we had many trials and storms within and without; but the Lord did deliver us out of all: And when we came to *Legorn*, with the rest of our friends, we went into the Town after we had product, and staid there many dayes, where we had service every day; for all sorts of people came unto us, but no man did offer to hurt us, yet we gave them Books and having got passage in a Dutch ship we sayled towards *Cyprus*, intending to goe to *Alexandria,* but the Lord had appointed somthing [*sic*] for us to do by the way, as he did make it manifest to us, as I did speak, for the Master of the ship had no business in the place; but being in company with another ship which had some business at the City of *Malta,* (in the Island of *Malta* where *Paul* suffered shipwrack) and being in the Harbour, on the first day of the Week, we being moved of the Lord, went into the Town, and the *English* Consul met us on the shore, and asked us concerning our coming, and we told him truth, and gave him some Books, and a Paper, and he told us there was an Inquisition, and he kindly entreated us to go to his house, and said all that he had was at our service while we were there. And in the fear and dread of the Lord we went, and there came many to see us, and we call'd them to repentance, and many of them were tender; but the whole City is given to Idolatry. And we went a ship-board that night; and the next day we being moved to go into the City again, dared not to flie the cross, but in obedience went, desiring the will of God to be done. And when we came to the Governor, he told us that he had a Sister in the Nunnary did desire to see us if we were free; and in the fear of God we went, and talked with them, and gave them a Book, and one of their Priests was with us (at the Nunnery) and had us into their place of Worship, and some would have us bow to the high Altar, which we did deny; and having a great burthen, we *(page 4)* went to the Consul again, and were waiting upon the Lord what to do, that we might know.

And the Inquisitors sent for us, and when we came before them, they asked our Names, and the Names of our Husbands, and the Names of our Fathers and Mothers, and how many children we had; and they asked us, *Wherefore we came into that Countrey?* And we told them, We were the Servants of the living God, and were moved to come and call them to repentance; and many other questions, and they went away, but commanded that we should be staid there. And the next day they came again, and called for us, and we came, but they would examine us apart, and called *Sarah*, and they asked, *Whether she was a true Catholick?* She said, that she was a true Christian that worshippeth God in spirit and in truth; and they proffered her the Crucifix, and would have had her sware that she would speak the truth; and she said, *she should speak the truth*, but she would not swear, for Christ commanded her *not to swear*, saying, *Swear not at all:* And the *English* Consul perswaded her with much entreating to swear, saying, *None should do her any harm:* But she denied; and they took some Books from her, and would have had her swear by them, but she would not: And they asked, *Wherefore she brought the Books?* And she said, Because we could not speak their Language, and they might know wherefore we came; and they asked of her, *what* George Fox *was;* and she said, he was a Minister. And they asked, *wherefore she came thither?* She said, To do the Will of God, as she was moved of the Lord. And they asked, *how the Lord did appear unto her?* And she said, by his Spirit. And they asked, *where she was when the Lord appeared unto her?* and she said, upon the way. And they asked, *whether she did see his Presence; and hear his Voice?* And she said, she did hear his Voice, and saw his Presence, and they asked, *What he said to her?* and she said, the Lord told her, she must go over the Seas to do his Will; and then they asked, *how she knew it was the Lord?* and she said, he bid her go, and his living presence should go with her, and he was faithful that had promised, for she did feel his living presence; and so they went away.

Two dayes after they came again, and called for me, and offered me the Crucifix, and told me *the Magistrate commanded me to (page 5) swear that I would speak the truth.* And I told them that I should speak the truth, for I was a Witness for God; but I should not swear; for a greater than the Magistrate, saith, *Swear not at all, but let your yea be yea, and your nay be nay, for whatsoever is more, cometh of evil.* But said they, *You must obey the Justice, and he commands you to swear.* I said, *I should obey*

Justice, but if I should swear, I should do an *unjust thing*; for (the just) Christ said, *Swear not at all*. And they asked me, *Whether I did own that Christ which dyed at Jerusalem?* I answered, We owned the same Christ, and no other, he is the same yesterday, to-day and for ever.

And they asked me, *What I would do at Jerusalem?* I said I did not know that I should go there, but I should go to *Alexandria;* and they said, *What to do?* and I said, to do the Will of God; and if the Lord did open my mouth, I should call them to repentance, and declare to them the day of the Lord, and direct their minds from darkness to Light. Then they asked me, *Whether I did tremble when I did preach?* and I told them, I did tremble when the power of the Lord was upon me. And they asked, *Whether I did see the Lord with my eyes?* I said, God was a Spirit, and he was spiritually discerned.

That day that we were had from the *English* Consuls to the Inquisition, the Consul's Wife brought us meat to eat, and as she past by me, I was smote with an Arrow to the heart, and I heard a voice, saying, *It is finished, she hath obtained her purpose*. I did not taste of her meat, but went aside, and wept bitterly. The Consul did affirm to us the night before, that there was no such thing (as to ensnare us) intended; but it was in us as fire, and our souls were heavy even unto death; for many dayes before we saw in a Vision of our going there, (to prison) and we said *Pilate* would do the *Jews* a pleasure, and wash his hands in innocency. He required *a sign of me if we were the Messengers of God;* and the Lord gave me a sign for him, that stuck by him while he lived. The same day it was, he called me, and told me the Inquisition had sent for us, and they had Papers from *Rome*, and he did hope we should be set free; which was a lye: For he knew there was a room prepared for us. And there came a man with a black Rod, and the Chancellor, and the Consul, and had us before their *Lord Inquisitor*, and he asked us, *Whether we had changed our minds yet?* We *(page 6)* said, Nay, we should not change from the truth. He asked, *What new Light we talkt of?* We said, no new Light, but the same the *Prophets* and *Apostles* bare testimony to. Then he said, *How came this Light to be lost ever since the primitive times?* We said, it was not lost, men had it still (in them) but they did not know it, by reason that the night of Apostacy had, and hath overspread the Nations. Then he said, *If we would change our minds, and do as they would have us to do, we should say so, or else they would use us as they pleased*. We said, The Will of the Lord be done. And he arose up, and went his way with the Consul, and left us there. And the man with the black Rod, and the Keeper, took us, and put us into an inner Room in the Inquisition, which had but two little holes in it for light or air; but the glory of the Lord did shine round about us.

After the *Consul* came with tears in his eyes, and said he was as *sorry as for his own flesh; but there was some hopes in time;* and so he went away, but never had peace while he lived. He would have given up the thirty pieces of silver again, but it would not be received; the Witness was risen much in him, but slavish fear possest him. This was upon the sixt day of the Week, and our stomacks were taken away from all meat.

The next second day came a *Magistrate,* two *Fryars,* and the man with the *black Rod,* and a *Scribe,* and the *Keeper,* to the *Inquisition,* to sit upon Judgement, and examined us apart concerning our faith in Christ. The Magistrate would have had us to *swear,* and we answered, No; Christ said, *Swear not at all;* and so said *James* the Apostle. He asked, *if we would speak truth?* We said, yea. He asked, *Whether we did believe the Creed?* We said, We did believe in God, and in Jesus Christ, which was born of the Virgin *Mary,* and suffered at *Jerusalem* under *Pilate,* and arose again from the dead the third day, and ascended to his Father, and shall come to judgement, to judge both quick and dead. He asked, *How we did believe the Resurrection?* We answered, We did believe that the just and the unjust should arise, according to the Scriptures. He said, *Do you believe in the Saints, and pray to them?* We said, We did believe the Communion of Saints; but we did not pray to them, but to God onely, in the Name of Jesus Christ. He asked, *Whether we did believe in the Catholick Church?* We said, We did *(page 7)* believe the true Church of Christ; but the Word *Catholick* we have not read in Scripture. He asked, *if we believed a Purgatory?* We said, No; but a Heaven and a Hell. The Fryar said, *We were commanded to pray for the dead; for those that were in Heaven had no need; and they that were in Hell there is no redemption; therefore there must be a Purgatory.* He asked, *if we believed their holy Sacrament?* We said, We never read (the Word) *Sacrament* in Scripture. The Fryar replied, *Where we did read in our Bibles* Sanctification, *it was* Sacrament *in theirs.* He said, *Their holy Sacrament was Bread and Wine, which they converted into the Flesh and Blood of Christ by the virtue of Christ.* We said, they did work Miracles then, for Christ's virtue is the same as it was when he turned Water into Wine at the Marriage in *Cana.* He said, *If we did not eat the flesh, and drink the blood of the Son of God, we had no life in us.* We said, the Flesh and Blood of Christ is spiritual, and we do feed upon it daily; for that which is begotten of God in us, can no more live without spiritual food, than our temporal bodies can without temporal food. He said, that *we did never hear Masse.*

We said, We did hear the voice of Christ, he onely had the words of eternal life, and that was sufficient for us. He said, *We were Hereticks and Heathens*. We said, they were Hereticks that lived in sin and wickedness, and such were Heathens that knew not God. He asked *about our Meetings in England?* And we told them the truth to their amazement. And they asked, *Who was the Head of our Church?* We said, Christ. And they asked, *What George Fox is.* And we said, He is a Minister of Christ. They asked, *Whether he sent us?* We said, No, the Lord did move us to come. The Fryar said *We were deceived, and had not the faith; but we had all virtues.* We said, that faith was the ground from whence virtues do proceed. They said, *If we would take their holy Sacrament, we might have our liberty, or else the Pope would not leave us for millions of Gold, but we should lose our souls and our bodies too.* We said, the Lord had provided for our souls, and our bodies were freely given up to serve the Lord. They askt us, *if we did not believe Marriage was a Sacrament?* We said, it was an Ordinance of God. They ask't us, *if we did believe men could forgive sins?* We said None could forgive sins but God onely. They brought us that Scripture, *Whose sins ye remit in earth, shall be remitted in heaven.* We said, All Power was God's and he *(page 8)* could give it to whom he would (that were born of the Eternal Spirit, and guided by the same; such have power to do the Fathers Will, as I answered a Fryar also in the City of *Naples*) and they were silent, the Power greatly working. We asked them wherein we had wronged them, that we should be kept Prisoners all dayes of our lives, and said, Our innocent blood would be required at their hands.

The Fryar said, *He would take our blood upon him, and our Journey into Turky too.* We told him, the time would come he would find he had enough upon him without it. They said, *The Popes was Christ's Vicar, and we were of his Church, and what he did, was for the good of our souls.* We answered, The Lord had not committed the charge of our souls to the Pope, nor to them; for he had taken them into his own possession, glory was to his Name for ever. They said, *We must be obedient.* We said, We were (obedient) to the Government of Christ's Spirit. The Fryar said, *None had the true Light but the Catholicks; the Light that we had, was the Spirit of the Devil.* We said, Wo to him that calleth Jesus accursed: Can the Devil give power over sin and iniquity? then he would destroy his own Kingdom. He said, *We were laught at, and mockt at of every one.* We said, What did become of the mockers? It was no matter. He said, *We did run about to preach, and had not the true Faith.* We said, the true Faith is held in a pure Conscience void of offence towards God and man; and we had the true Faith. And he said, *There was but one Faith, either theirs or ours;* and askt us *which it was?* We said, Every one had the true Faith, that did believe in God, and in Jesus whom he had sent but they that say they do believe, and do not keep his commandments, are lyars, and the truth is not in them. He said *it was true;* but he did thirst daily for our blood, because we would not turn, and urged us much about our Faith and Sacrament, to bring us under their Law; but the Lord preserved us.

They said, *It was impossible we could live long in that hot room.* So the next Week-day they sate in Council; but oh how the swelling Sea did rage, and the proud waves did foam even unto the clouds of Heaven, and Proclamation was made at the Prison-Gate, we did not know the words, but the fire of the Lord flamed against it, [K.] my life was smitten, and I was in a very great agony, so that *(page 9)* sweat was as drops of blood, and the righteous one was laid into a Sepulcher, and a great stone was roll'd to the door; but the Prophesie was, that he should arise again the third day, which was fulfilled. But the next day they came to sit upon Judgement again, [but I say, in the true Judgement they sate not, but upon it they got up unjustly above the righteous, and upon the same they sate; a child of Wisdom may understand] and they brought many Propositions written in a paper, but the Fryar would suffer the Magistrate to propound but few to us, for fear the Light would break forth; but they askt *how many friends of ours were gone forth in the Ministry, and into what parts.* We told them what we did know. They said, *all that came where the Pope had any thing to do, should never go back again.* We said, the Lord was as sufficient for us, as he was for the children in the fiery Furnace, and our trust was in God. They said, *we were but few, and had been but a little while, and they were many Countreys, and had stood many hundred years, and wrought many Miracles, and we had none.* We said, we had thousands at our Meetings, but none (of us) dare speak a word, but as they are eternally moved of the Lord; and we had Miracles, the Blind receive their sight, the Deaf do hear, and the Dumb do speak, the Poor do receive the Gospel, the Lame do walk, and the Dead are raised. He asked, *Why I lookt so, whether my Spirit was weak?* I said, Nay, my body was weak, because I eat no meat, [it was in their *Lent*] *He offered me a License to eat flesh.* I said I could not eat any thing at all. The terrors of death were strongly upon me; but three nights after, the Lord said unto me, about the 11*th.* hour, Arise, and put on your Clothes; I said, *When wilt thou come Lord?* He said, Whether at midnight, or at Cock-crow, do thou watch. My Friend and I arose, and the Lord said,

Go stand at the Door. And we stood at the door in the power of the
Lord, I did scarce know whether I was in the body, or out of the body;
and about the 12*th.* hour there came many to the Prison-Gate; We
heard the Keys, and looked when they would come in: They ran to and
fro till the 4*th.* hour; the Lord said, he had smote them with blindness,
they could not find the way. And we went to bed, there I lay night and
day for 12. days together, fasting and sweating, that my bed was wet,
and great was our affliction.

   (page 10) The tenth day of my fast there came *two Fryars,* the *Chancellor,*
the man with the *Black Rod,* and a *Physician,* and the *Keepers;* and the
Fryar commanded my dear Friend to go out of the room, and he came
and pull'd my hand out of the bed, and said, *Is the Devil so great in you,*
that you cannot speak? I said, Depart from me thou worker of iniquity, I
know thee not; the Power of the Lord is upon me, and thou call'st him
Devil. He took his Crucifix to strike me in the mouth; and I said, Look
here! and I asked him, Whether it were that Cross which crucified *Paul*
to the World, and the World unto him? And he said, *it was.* I denied him,
and said, the Lord had made me a Witness for himself against all workers of
iniquity. *He bid me be obedient,* and went to strike me: I said, Wilt thou
strike me? He said, *he would.* I said, Thou art out of the Apostles Doctrine,
they were no strikers; I deny thee to be any of them who went in the
Name of the Lord. He said, *he had brought me a Physician in charity.* I
said, the Lord was my Physician, and my saving-health. He said *I should*
be whipt and quartered, and burnt that night in Malta, and my Mate too:
wherefore did we come to teach them? I told him I did not fear, the Lord
was on our side, and he had no power but what he had received; and if
he did not use it to the same end the Lord gave it to him, the Lord would
judge him. And they were all smitten as dead men, and went away.

   And as soon as they were gone, the Lord said unto me, The last
Enemy that shall be destroyed is Death; and the Life arose over Death,
and I glorified God. The Fryar went to my friend, and told her, *I called*
him worker of iniquity. Did she, said *Sarah? Art thou without sin?* He said
he was; Then she hath wronged thee. [But I say, the wise Reader may
judge:] For between the eighth and ninth hour in the evening, he sent
a Drum to proclaim at the Prison-Gate; We know not what it was, but
the fire of the Lord consumed it. And about the fourth hour in the
morning they were coming with a Drum and Guns; and the Lord said
unto me, Arise out of thy Grave-Clothes: And we arose, and they came
up to the Gate to devour us in a moment. But the Lord lifted up his
Standard with his own Spirit (of Might) and made them to retreat, and

they fled as dust before the Wind praises and honour be given to our God for ever. I went to bed again, *(page 11)* and the Lord said unto me, Herod will seek the young childes life to destroy it yet again; and great was my affliction; so that my dear fellow and labourer in the Work of God, did look every hour when I should depart of body for many days together, and we did look every hour when we should be brought to the stake day and night, for several weeks, and *Isaac* was freely offered up. But the Lord said, he had provided a Ram in the Bush. Afterwards the Fryer came again with his Physician; I told him, that I could not take any thing, unless I was moved of the Lord. He said, *we must never come forth of that Room while we lived, and we might thank God and him it was no worse, for it was like to be worse.* We said, if we had died, we had died as innocent as ever did servants of the Lord. He said, it was well we were innocent. They did (also) look still when I would dye.

The Fryer bid my friend *take notice what torment I would be in at the houre of Death, thousands of Devils (he said) would fetch my soule to Hell.* She said, she did not fear any such thing.

And he asked *if I did not think it expedient for the Elders of the Church to pray over the sick?* I said, yea, such as were eternally moved of the Spirit of the Lord. He fell down of [sic] his knees and did howle, and with bitter wishes upon himself if he had not the true faith; but we denied him. The Physitian was in a great rage at *Sarah,* because she could not bow to him, but to God onely.

The last day of my fast I began to be a hungry, but was afraid to eat, the enemy was so strong; but the Lord said unto me, If thine enemy hunger, feed him; if he thirst, give him drink, in so doing thou shalt heap coales of fire upon his head; be not overcome of evil, but over-come evil with good. I did eat, and was refreshed, and glorified God; and in the midst of our extremity the Lord sent his holy Angels to comfort us, so that we rejoiced and magnified God; and in the time of our great trial, the Sun and Earth did mourn visibly three dayes, and the horror of death and pains of Hell was upon me: the Sun was darkned, the Moon was turned into Blood, and the Stars did fall from heaven and there was great tribulation ten dayes, such as never was from the beginning of the world; *(page 12)* and then did I see the Son of man com-ing in the Clouds, with power and great glory, triumphing over his en-emies; the Heavens were on fire, and the Elements did melt with fervent heat, and the Trumpet sounded out of *Sion,* and an Allarum was struck up in *Jerusalem,* and all the Enemies of God were called to the great day of Battle of the Lord, And I saw a great wonder in Heaven, the Woman cloathed with the Sun, and had the Moon under her feet, and a Crown of 12 Stars upon her head, and she travelled in pain ready to be delivered of a Man-child, and there was a great Dragon stood ready to devour the Man-child as soon as it was born; and there was given to the Woman two Wings of a great Eagle to carry her into the desert, where she should be nourished for a time, times, and half a time; and the Dragon cast a Flood out of his mouth, &c. And I saw War in Heaven, *Michael* and his Angels against the Dragon and his Angels, and the Lamb and his army did overcome them; and there was a Trumpet sounded in Heaven, and I heard a voice saying to me, The City is divided into three parts; and I heard another Trumpet sounding, and I looked and saw an Angel go down into a great pool of water, and I heard a voice saying unto me, Whosoever goeth down next after the troubling of the Waters, shall be healed of whatsoever Disease he hath. And I heard another Trumpet sounding, and I heard a voice saying, Babylon is fallen, is fallen, Babylon the great is fallen. And I looked, and saw the smoke of her torment, how it did ascend; and I heard another Trumpet sounding, and I heard a voice saying, Rejoice and be exceeding glad, for great is your reward in heaven; for he that is mighty hath magnified you, and holy is his Name; and from henceforth all generations shall call you blessed: And I heard another trumpet sounding in Heaven, and I heard a voice saying unto me, Behold! and I looked, and I saw *Pharoah* and his Host pursuing the Children of *Israel*, and he and his Host were drowned in the Sea.

Dear Friends and People, whatsoever I have written, it's not because it is recorded in the Scripture, or that I have heard of such things; but in obedience to the Lord I have written the things which I did hear, see, tasted and handled of the good *(page 13)* Word of God, to the praise of his Name for ever.

And all this time my dear Sister in Christ Jesus was in as great affliction as I (in a manner) to see my strong travel night and day; yet she was kept in the patience, and would willingly have given me up to death, that I might have been at rest; yet she would have been left in as great danger, wo and misery, as ever was any poor captive for the Lord's truth; for they did work night and day with their divinations, inchantments and temptations, thinking thereby to bring us under their power; but the Lord prevented them every way, so that great was their rage, and they came often with their Physician, and said it was in charity; I askt them whether they did keep us in that hot room to kill us, and bring us a Physician to make us alive.

The Fryar said, *the Inquisitor would lose his head if he should take us thence; and it was better to keep us there, than to kill us.* The Room was so hot and so close, that we were fain to rise often out of our bed, and lie down at a chink of their door for air to fetch breath; and with the fire within, and the heat without, our skin was like sheeps Leather, and the hair did fall off our heads, and we did fail often; our afflictions and burthens were so great, that when it was day we wished for night; and when it was night we wished for day; we sought death, but could not find it; We desired to die, but death fled from us; We did eat our bread weeping, and mingled our drink with our tears. We did write to the Inquisitor, and laid before him our innocency, and our faithfulness, in giving our testimony for the Lord amongst them; and I told him, if it were our blood they did thirst after, they might take it any other way, as well as to smother us up in that hot room. So he sent the Fryar, and he took away our *Inkhorns,* (they had our *Bibles* before) We asked why they took away our goods? They said, *it was all theirs, and our lives too, if they would.* We asked, how we had forfeited our lives unto them; they said, *For bringing Books and Papers.* We said, if there were any thing in them that was not true, they might write against it. They said, *they did scorn to write to fools and asses that did not know true Latine.* And they told us, *the Inquisitor would have us separated, because I was weak, and I should go into a cooler room;* but *Sarah* should abide there. I took her by the arm, and said, *The Lord hath joined us (page 14) together, and wo be to them that should part us.* I said, I rather chuse to dye there with my friend, than to part from her. He was smitten, and went away, and came no more in five weeks, and the door was not opened in that time. Then they came again to part us; but I was sick, and broken out from head to foot. They sent for a Doctor, and he said, *We must have air, or else we must dye.* So the Lord compelled them to go to the Inquisitor, & he gave order *for the door to be set open six hours in a day;* they did not part us till ten Weeks after: But oh the dark clouds and the sharp showers the Lord did carry us through! Death it self had been better than to have parted in that place. They said, *we corrupted each other, and that they thought when we were parted, we would have bowed to them.* But they found we were more stronger aftewards than we were before; the Lord our God did fit us for every condition. They came and brought a Scourge of small Hemp, and asked us, *if we would have any of it.* They said, *they did whip themselves till the blood did come.* We said, that could not reach the Devil, he sate upon the heart. They said, *All the men and women of Malta were for us, if we would be Catholicks, for there would be none like unto us.* We said, the Lord had changed us into that which changed not. They said, *all their holy women did pray for us, and we should be honored of all the world if we would turn.* We said, we were of God, and the whole world did lye in wickedness; and we denied the honor of the World, and the glory too. They said, *We should be honored of God too, but now we were hated of all.* We said, it is an evident token whose servants we are; the servant is not greater than the Lord, and that Scripture was fulfilled which saith, *All this will I give thee, if thou wilt fall down and worship me.*

Upon the first day of the Week, we were fasting and waiting upon the Lord till the second hour (after mid-day) and the Fryars came and commanded us in *the Name of the Lord to kneel down with them to prayer.* We said, we could not pray but as we were moved of the Lord. They commanded us the second time. Then they kneeled down by our bed side, and prayed, and when they had done, they said, *they had tryed our spirits, now they knew what spirit we were of.* We told them, they could not know our spirit, unless their minds were turned to the Light of the Lord Jesus in their Consciences. The English Fryar was wrath, and shewed *(page 15)* us his *Crucifix,* and bid us *loook* [sic] *there.* We said, The Lord saith, *Thou shalt not make to thy self the likeness of any thing that is in heaven above, or in the earth beneath, nor in the water under the earth; thou shalt not bow to them nor worship them, but I the Lord thy God only.* He was so mad, he called for the irons to chain *Sarah,* because she spake so boldly to him: She bowed her head, and said to him, *Not onely my feet, but my hands and my neck also for the Testimony of Jesus.* His wrath was soon appeased, and he said, *He would do us any good he could; he did see what we did was not in malice,* the power had broken him down for that present; they came to us often, saying, *If you would do but a little, you should be set at liberty; but you will do nothing at all, but are against every thing.* We said, We are against nothing that is of God, but would do any thing that might make for God's glory.

Many did think we should not have been heard nor seen after we were in the Inquisition but the Lord did work wonderfully for us and his Truth: For they new built the *Inquisition,* and there were many *Labourers* for a year and a half, and the great men came to see the building; and we were carried forth with great power to declare in the Name of the Lord Jesus, not fearing the face of man; the Lord was our strength. But behold they threatned us with *Irons* and *Halters,* for preaching the Light so boldly, and they said, *None ought to preach but Prelates to a Bishop,* (as they use to say in *England.*) Now their *Lord*

Inquisitor (so called) and the *Magistrates* were kept moderate towards us, and gave order, *we should have Ink and Paper to write to England*. But we were hindered still; and we do believe they would have set us at liberty, had it not been for the Fryars; it was they that wrought against us still to the *Pope* and to the *Inquisitors*; and we told them so. They sought three quarters of a year to part us, before they could bring it to pass; and when they did part us, they prepared a bed for *Sarah,* and their own *Catholicks* lay upon the boards, that had not beds of their own. When we were parted, the Lord would not suffer me to keep any money, I knew not the mind of God in it. Their Fryars came and said, *We should never see one anothers faces again, but the Inquisitor should send me my food*. But the Lord would not suffer him to send it. *Sarah* did send me such as she could get neare three Weeks: then the Fryar came and askt me, *what I did want?* I said, one to wash my *(page 16)* Linnen, and something hot to eat: I was weak. He sent to *Sarah* to know *if she would do it for me*. She said she would. And by that means we did hear of each other every day. The Fryar said, *You may free your self of misery when you will; you may make your self a Catholick, and have your freedom to go where you will*. I told him, I might make my self a Catholick, and have a name that I did live, when I was dead, and said, he had Catholicks enough already; he should bring some of them to the Light in their Consciences, that they might stand in awe, and sin not. He said, *He would lose one of his fingers if we would be Catholicks*. I said, it was *Babylon* that was built with *blood*, Sion was redeemed through Judgement. They would have me to a Picture set at my beds head for a representation. I askt them if they did think I did lack a Calf to worship? And whether they did not walk by the Rule of Scripture? The Fryar said, *They did, but they had traditions too*. I said, if their traditions did derogate or discent from the fundamentals of Christ's Doctrine, the Prophets and Apostles, I denied them in the Name of the Lord. He said, *they did not*. I askt him where they had their Rule to burn them that could not join with them for Conscience? He said, *St. Paul did worse, he gave them to the Devil, and that they did judge all damned that were not of their Faith*. And he askt whether we did judge them so? I said, No, We had otherwise learned Christ. I askt him why they did bind that which the Lord did not bind? and set tyes, chains and limits, where the Lord did not? as in *meals* and *drinks*, or in respect of *dayes* or *times*, which the Apostle called *beggarly Elements,* and *rudiments of the world,* and *forbidding to marry,* (a Doctrine of Devils said *I*.) He could not tell what to say, but told me, *That Saint Peter was the Pope of Rome, and did build an Altar there; and the Pope was his Successor, and he could do what he would.* I denied that, and said, We never read any such thing in Scripture; for *Peter* Christ's Apostle had no money to build Altars, he himself did offer Sacrifice upon the Altars made without hands. And he said, *We were but a few, and risen up but late, and they were many, and had stood fourteen hundred years, and God was a lyar if they had not the true faith; for he had confirmed it to them by a thousand miracles.* I said, the few number, and the little Flock is Christ's Flock. He askt if we were then all the World, said he. I said, our faith *(page 17)* was from the beginning. *Abel* was of our Church; and *the world by wisdom did not know God.* He went to *Sarah* with the same temptation, and she told him also, that *Abel* was of our Church. He said *Abel was a Catholick, and* Cain *and* Judas *were so.* She said, Then the Devil was a *Catholick,* and she would not be one. He threatned her, and told her *how many they were.*

She said, *Daniel* was but *one;* and if there were *no more* but *she* her self, she would not turn; but took her fingers and shewed them, if they would tear her joint-meal, she did believe the Lord would enable her to endure it for the Truth.

So they went from one to another thinking to entangle us in our talk; but we were guided by one Spirit, and spake one and the same thing in effect, so that they had not a jot nor tittle against us, but for righteousness sake: Our God did keep us by his own Power and Holiness out of their hands; honor and praises be given to his powerful Name for ever.

He (the said Fryar) came to me another time like a Bear robbed of her Whelps, and told me, *if I would be a Catholick, I should say so; otherwise they would use me badly, and I should never see the face of* Sarah *again, but should dye by my self, and a thousand Devils should carry my soul to Hell.* I asked him if he were the Messenger of God to me. He said he was. I said, What is my sin? or wherein have I provoked the Lord, that he doth send me such a strait Message? He said, *Because I would not be a Catholick.* I said, I deny thee and thy Message too, and the Spirit which spake in thee; the Lord never spake it. He said, that *he would lay me in a whole Pile of Chains, where I should see neither Sun nor Moon.* I said, he could not separate me from the love of God in Christ Jesus, lay me where he would. He said, *He would give me to the Devil.* I said, I did not fear all the Devils in Hell, the Lord was my Keeper; Though he had the Inquisition, with all the Countreys round about, on his side, and was alone by my self, I did not fear them; if there were thousands more, the Lord was on my right hand, and the worst they could do, was but to kill the body, they could not touch my life no more than the Devil could *Job's*. He said, that *I should never go out of the Room alive*. I said, the Lord was sufficient to deliver me: But whether he would or would not, I would not forsake a living Fountain to drink at a broken *(page 18)* Cistern: And they had no Law to keep us there, but such a Law as *Ahab* had for *Naboth's* Vinyard, He curd [*sic*] himself, and call'd upon his gods and went forth, and as he was making fast the door, he put in his hand at the hole of the door, and said, *Abide there Member of the Devil*. I said, The Devil's Members did the Devil's Work; the Woes and Plagues of the Lord would be upon them for it. He went and told the Inquisitor of it, and he laught at him: I saw it, and felt it in that which is Eternal. I was moved out of that Room before he came again; and when he came, he brought one of the Inquisitors men with him, and two very good Hens, and said, *the Lord Inquisitor has sent them in love to me*. I said, his love I did receive, but I could not take his Hens, for it was not the practice of the Servant of the Lord to be chargeable to any while they have of their own. He said, *We must not count anything our own; for in the primitive times they did sell their possessions, and laid them down at the Apostles feet*. He said, *We should not want any thing if they did spend a thousand Crowns*. I believe he would have had us lay down our money at his feet. He said, *I was proud, because I would not take the Inquisitors Hens when he sent them me in Charity*. I asked whether he kept me in Prison, and sent me his Charity. He said, *it was for the good of our souls he kept us in prison*. I told him, Our souls were out of the Inquisitors reach or his either, he told me before, *if we had not been going to preach, we might have gone where we would*. I askt him, What should our souls have done then? and why their love should extend more to us, than to their own family? They could not charge us with sin: and they did commit all manner of sin; they might put them into the inquisition and bid turn. He said again *We had not the true Faith*, and shew'd me his Crucifix, and askt me *if I thought he did worship that?* I askt him what he did do with it? he said *it was a Representation*. I said, it did not represent Christ, for he was the express image of his Father's glory, which is Light and Life. I said, if he could put any life in any of his images, he might bring them to me. And I askt him what *Representation Daniel* had in the *Lyons Den;* or *Jonas* in the *Whales belly*, they cryed unto the Lord, and he dilivered them. He said, *I talkt like a mad woman, I talkt so much against their idols*. He was in a rage, and said, *He would give me to the Devil*. I bid him give his own, I am the Lords. *He* stood up, and *(page 19)* said *He would do by me as the Apostles did by* Ananias *and* Saphira. He stood up and opened his mouth; and I stood up to him and denied him in the

Name of the Lord, the living God, and said he had no power over me. And away he went to *Sarah* with the Hen, and told her *that I was sick, and the Lord Inquisitor had sent two Hens, and I would be glad to eat a piece of one if she should dress one of them presently, and the other tomorrow,* [Mark, this Deceiver! this Lyar!] But she standing in the Counsel of the Lord answered him accordingly as I did, and he carried them away again. We did not dare to take them, the Lord did forbid us. He said, *You would fain be burned, because you would make the World believe you did love God so well as to suffer in that kind.* I said I did not desire to be burnt but if the Lord did call me to it I did believe he would give me power to undergo it for his truth and if every hair of my head was a body, I could offer them up all for the Testimony of Jesus. He came twice *to know whether I had not been inspired of the Holy Ghost to be a Catholick since I came into the Inquisition.* I said, No; he said, *we were,* he said, *We called the Spirit of the Holy Ghost the Sipirit* [sic] *of the Devil.* We said, the Spirit of the Holy Ghost in us will resist the Devil. We told him the inspiration of the Holy Ghost was never wrought in the Will of man, nor in man's time, but in the Will of God, and in God's time. He asked, *How we did know a clean from an unclean Spirit?* We said, an unclean spirit did burden the Seed of God, and dam up the Springs of Life; and a clean spirit would open the Springs of Life, and refresh the Seed, it was a Riddle to him, but he said it was true: He would assent to pure truth sometimes.

We asked him Whether every man and woman did not stand guilty before God of all the sins they ever committed before Regeneration? He said, *Yea.* And he did confess all their Learning and Languages (in their places) was but to serve the Lord. We told him, all their Praying, Preaching and _rouding [sic], was no more accepted than *Cain's* Sacrifice, unless they were moved of the Eternal Spirit of the Lord. We askt him, if he that was in them, was greater than he that was in us; and why they had not overcome us all that time? We were very sensible of their workings day and night. He said, *Because we resisted still.* We askt him for our Bibles? He said, *We should never see them again, they were false.* *(page 20)* We said, if they were conjuring Books, they had no warrant from the Lord to take them from us.

They always came two Fryars at a time, and they would fall down and howl, and with bitter wishes upon themselves if they were not in the truth. We would deny them, and preach truth to them, the Light of the Lord Jesus in the Consciences of every one to lead them to a pure life, and did ask them where the pure and holy life was, and what all of them did do, that the people did live in sin and all manner of wickedness? And whether words and forms would serve without life and power? He was as bloody a fiery Serpent, as ever was born of a Woman, and did strike as hard at our lives, & would hold up his hand often to strike us, but had never the power, he would quickly be cut down, that he would say, *we were good women, and he would do us any good.* He was compell'd to work for us sometimes, and would say it was for God's sake, and would have us thank him for it. We would tell him, those that did any thing for God, did not look for a reward from man. He said, *We were the worst of all creatures, and we should be used worse than any; the Turks, Arminians, Protestants and Lutherans should be used better than we.* We said, the pure Life was ever counted the worst, and we must suffer; we were the Lords, and could trust him; let him do what he would with us, we did not fear any evil tydings, we were setled and grounded in the truth; and the more they did persecute us, the more stronger we did grow; We were bold and valiant for God's Truth, that whatsoever we did suffer, we could not fear. We were separated two years; I had neither fire nor candle in that time above two hours, none did bring me any, nor I had not freedom to call for any.

The Fryars went to *Sarah*, and told her, *if she would, she should go forth of the Prison, and say nothing, nor do nothing.* She said, she would upon that account. He said, they would come in the morning, and so they did; but the Lord saw their deceit, and forewarned *Sarah*, and bid her mind *Esau, who sold his Birthright for a morsel of meat; and* Judas, *that betrayed his Master for thirty pieces of Silver:* That when they came, she (was strengthened against them, and) said, she stood in the Counsel of God, and could take up nothing in her own will; they had not power to have her forth. They said the Inquisitor said, if we did want Linnen, Woolen, *(page 21)* Stockins, Shooes or Money, we should have it.

But there was a poor *English* man heard that *Sarah* was in a room with a Window next to the Street, it was high; he got up, and spake a few words to her; and they came violently & hall'd him down, and cast him into prison upon life and death: And the Fryars came to know of us whether he had brought any Letters. We said no; I did not see him: They said, they did think he would be hang'd for it. He was one that they had taken from the *Turks*, and made a Catholick of him. *Sarah* wrote a few lines to me of it, and said she did think the English Fryars were the chief actors of it, (we had a private way to send to each other.) I wrote to her again, and after my Salutation, I said; Whereas she said the Fryars were the chief actors, she might be sure of that, for they did hasten to fill up their measures, but I believe the Lord wil preserve the poor man for his love: I am made to seek the Lord for him with tears: And I desired she would send him something once a day, if the Keeper would carry it; and I told her of the glorious manifestations of God to my soul, for her comfort, so that I was ravished with love, and my Beloved was the chiefest of ten thousands; and how I did not fear the face of any man, though I did feel their arrows, for my Physician is nigh me; and how I was waiting upon the Lord, and saw our safe return into *England*, and I was talking with G.F. to my great refreshment: The Name of G.F. did prick them to the heart. I said, it was much they did not tempt us with money, I bid her take heed, the Light would discover it, and many more things, let it come under what cover it would.

And this Paper came to the Fryar's hands, by what means we could never tell, but as the Light did shew us; the Lord would have it so; it smote the Fryar, that he was tormented many days, and he translated it into *Italian*, and laid it before their Lord Inquisitor, and got the Inquisitor's Lievtenant, and came to me with both the Papers in his hand, and askt me *If I could read it?* I said, *Yea,* I writ it. *O! did you indeed!* (said he) And *what is it you say of me here?* That which is truth, said I. Then he said, *Where is the Paper* Sarah *sent? bring it, or else I will search the Trunk, and every where else.* I bid him search where he would. He said, *I must tell what man it was that brought me the Ink, or else I should be tyed (page 22) with Chains presently.* I told him I had done nothing but what was just and right in the sight of God, and what I did suffer would be for Truth's sake; and I did not care. I would not meddle nor make with the poor Workmen. He said, *For God's sake tell me what* Sarah *did write?* I told him a few words, and said it was truth. Said he, *You say it is much we do not tempt you with money.* And in few hours they came and tempted us with money often. So the Lieutenant took my ink and threw it away: and they were smitten as if they would have fallen to the ground, and went their way. I saw them no more in three Weeks; but the poor man was set free the next morning.

They went to *Sarah*, and told her *that I had honestly confest all, and that she was best to confess too, and threatned her with a Halter, and to take away a Bed and Trunk, and her Money, to have half of it for me.* She answered, she might not send to me any more. She askt him, Whether he was a Minister of Christ, or a Magistrate? If he were a Magistrate, he might take her money, but she would not give it him: And they that were with him, said, *No, he should not meddle with any thing.* He was a bitter wicked man. He told her, *She was possest.* She answered and said, she was with the power of an endless life.

The Lord was not wanting to us at any time, for Power nor Words to stop the mouths of gainsayers of his Truth, neither in Revelations nor Visions; Praises be to his Name for ever. He kept us in our weakest condition, bold for his Truth, declaring against all sin and wickedness, so that many were convinced, but did not dare to own it, for fear of *Faggot* and *Fire*. There were none that had any thing to say against what we spake, but the Fryers. but would have us to join with them. There were none did come into the inquisition but the judgements of the Lord would be upon them, so that they would cry and foam, and send for a Physician many of them. The unclean spirits would cry out as much as ever they did against Jesus and would gnash with their teeth when we were at prayer; there was a Fryer and other great men, the Fryer would run as if he had been at his Wits end, and call to the Keeper, and he would run for the *English* Fryer, and he would get the Inquisitor for counsel, and sometime they would send them word they should have a remedy, I should be sent to *(page 23) Rome;* and sometimes the Fryers would come, but had not power to say any thing to me of it) The Lord did say to us, Lift up your Voice like the noise of a Trumpet, and sound forth my Truth like the shout of a King. There was one that life was arisen in him but they were upon him as Eagles til they had destroy'd him; he did undergo terrible Judgements all the time he was in the Inquisition.

Our money served us a year and seven Weeks; and when it was almost gone, the Fryars brought the *Inquisitor's Chamberlain* to buy our Hats. We said, we came not there to sel our clothes, nor any thing we had. Then the Fryar did commend us for that, and told us *we might have kept our money to serve us otherwise*. We said, No, we could not keep any money, and be chargeable to any; We could trust God. He said, *He did see we could,* but *they* should have maintained us while they kept us Prisoners.

And then the Lord did take away our stomacks; we did eat but little for three or four Weeks; and then the Lord called us to fasting for eleven dayes together, but it was so little, that the Fryars came and said, that *it was impossible that Creatures could live with so little meat,* as they did see we did for so long time together; and asked *what we would do?* And said their *Lord Inquisitor said, We might have any thing we would.* We said, We must wait to know the mind of God, what he would have us to do. We did not fast in our own Wills but in obedience to the Lord. They were much troubled, and sent us meat, and said *the English Consul sent it.* We could not take any thing till the Lord's time was come. We were weak, so that *Sarah* did dress her head as she would lye in her Grave. (poor Lamb) I lay looking for the Lord to put an end to the sad trial which way it seemed good in his sight. Then I heard a voice, saying, Ye shall not dye. I believed the Lord, and his glory did appear much in our fast; he was very gracious to us, and did refresh us with his living presence continually; and we did behold his beauty to our great joy and comfort, and he was large to us in his promises, so that we were kept quiet and still, (the sting of Death being taken away) our souls, hearts and minds were at peace with the Lord, so that they could not tell whether we were dead or alive but as they did call to us once a day, till the time the Lord had appointed we should eat; and they were made to *(page 24)* bring *many good things*, and laid them down by us; so that Scripture we wit-nessed fulfilled, *Our Enemies treated us kindly in a strange Land, said I.* But we were afraid to eat, and cryed to the Lord, and said, We had rather dye, than eat any thing that is polluted and unclean. The Lord said unto me, *Thou mayest as freely eat, as if thou hadst wrought for it with thy hands; I will sanctifie it to thee* through the Cross. And he said to *Sarah, Thou shalt eat the fruit of thy hands, and be blessed.* We did eat and were refreshed, to the praise and glory of our God for ever. We did eat but little in two Months; and they did bring us what ever we did speak for, for 8 or 10 dayes; and afterward we were so straitned for want of food, it did us more hurt than our Fast. Yet the Lord did work as great a Miracle by our preservation, as he did by raising *Lazarus* out of the Grave. The Fryars did say, *the Lord did keep us alive by his mighty power, because we should be Catholicks.* We said, the Lord would make it manifest to us then; they should know the Lord had another end in it one day.

But still they said, *There was no Redemption for us.* We said, with the Lord there was mercy and plenteous Redemption. We bid them, take heed ye be not found fighters against God. They said, *We were foolish women.* We said we were the Lord's fools, and the Lord's Fools were right dear, and precious in his sight, and wo to them that do offend them. He said, *they were the Lord's fools*, and shewed us their deceitful Gowns, and their shaven Crowns, and said, *they did wear it for God's sake, to be laught at of the world.* We said, they did not wear it for God's sake, unless they were moved of the holy Spirit of God to wear it. He said, *it was no matter, they did wear it because of their Superiors.* [mark, and before it was for God's sake, as he said] He thought to bring us under him for our food, and did make us suffer a while, though the Inquisitor and the Magistrates had taken a course we should want for nothing. But the Lord did torment him and all the rest, till they did bring us such things as were fitting. Then he did work all that he could to send me to *Rome*, and was coming two or three times (for what I know) to fetch me forth, but the Lord would not suffer them; and when they saw they could not prevaile that way, they said we should go both; but the Fryar should go first, because he was not well; he got leave to go, he was so weary *(page 25)* of coming to us, that he did beseech the Lord Inquisitor he might come no more to us. He told *Sarah, I was a Witch*, and *that I knew what was done at London*, and he would come to me no more, he said, Because when he did tell me a company of lyes, I said, *I had a witness for God in me, which was faithful and true, and I did believe God's witness.*

The Diviners did wax mad, and did run as at their wits end, from Mountain to Hill, and from Hill to Mountain, to cover them: They ran to the Inquisitor, and writ to the Pope, and went to him; their King did not hide them at all; some of them did gnash with their teeth, and even gnaw their tongues for pain: Yet the rest would not repent of their blasphemy, sorcery, nor inchantments [sic], but do post on to fill up their measures; Oh! the Lord reward them according to their works. A little before the Fryar went to *Rome*, he came to the Inquisition Chamber with a Scribe, to write concerning us, to carry it with him; I saw him, as God would have it; the Lord said, *There is thy deadly foe.* They were writing part of three dayes; and when they had ended it, the Lord would not let me eat till the Scribe did come where I was, that I might pronounce wo against it, and defie it, which I did do in the Name of the Lord, and it did wither with all the rest: After it was gone, the *English Consul* came to us with a Scribe, and he brought us a doller from a Master of a Ship that came from *Plymouth;* I told him, I did receive my Countrey [sic] man's Love, but could not receive his Money. He askt me, *What I would do if I would take no money?* I said, the Lord was my portion, and I could not lack any good thing. I said to him, We were in thy House near 15. Weeks, didst thou see any cause of Death or Bonds in us? He said, *No.* I askt him, how he would dispence with his Conscience for telling us, *He would have us before the Inquisitor,* and thon [sic] didst know that Room was provided for us; and had not we been kept alive by the mighty Power of God, we might have been dead long since. He said, *How could I help it!* I said, We are the Servants of the living God, and were brought here by permission, and in the Spirit of Meekness gave in our Testimony for the Lord in faithfulness, and told you the truth as it is in Jesus, and called you all to repentance, and fore-warned you in love to your souls, of the evil the Lord is bringing upon you, if you do not *(page 26)* repent. He said, *However it be, it will go well with you.* [Mark that.] I told him, he required a sign of me when we were at his house, if we were the servants of the Lord God; I gave him a sign from the living God, and my friend gave him another from the Lord, to his shame and destruction for ever. I askt him, Whether it were not true we spake to him, he said it was, *but how should he help it?* I said, Thou art a condemned person, and stands guilty before God; yet nevertheless repent, if thou canst find a place. He smil'd upon the Scribe in deceit, but his lips did quiver, and his belly trembled, and he could scarce stand upon his legs. He was as proper a man as most was in the City, and full, and in his prime age. O! he was consumed as a Snail in a shell, which was a sufficient sign for the whole City, if their hearts were not harder than Adamants. He said, *How should he help it?* He might have helpt it, but he was as willing to prove us, as any of them all. He was sworn upon his Oath to protect the *English;* and their Ruler bid him let us go about our business, and said, *We were honest women;* and then he might have let us go before we were under the black Rod.

Then he went to *Sarah* with the Doller; she told him she could not take the Money; but if he had a Letter for us, she should be free to receive that. He said, *he had not any.* He askt her *what she did want?* She said, the Lord was her Shepherd, she could not want any good thing; but she did long for her Freedom. He said, *That you may have in time.* He told us, *we should have ink and paper to write:* But when he was gone, they would not let us. The next time we heard of him, he was dead. We could have rejoiced if he had dyed for righteousness sake; for the Lord delighteth not in the death of a sinner.

The Fryar was gone to *Rome,* and they said, *he must stay there till we came.* There was great working to send us there, but the Lord did prevent them, that they could not send us there. Then the Lord did work to bring us together again after so long time we had been parted. There were five doors between us with Locks and Bolts, but the Keeper had not power to make them fast, but as *Sarah* could undo them to come where I could see her, but could not speak to her; for there were them that did watch us night and day; yet she being moved of the Lord, did come to *(page 27)* my door by night; she must come by the *Fryars* door, he and the Doctor of Law were together, and they did set a trap to take her in, and many did watch about the Prison, and would complain. Then she was lockt up again; but they had no peace in that, till the doors were open again; then we did sit in the sight of each other, to wait upon the Lord, so that our voices were heard far; the Magistrates would hear and bow to it sometime; then the complainers were weary, and did work to have us brought together; and we did wait and pray, and the Magistrates would come in and look upon us many times, but would say nothing to us: There were of divers Nations brought into the Inquisition Prisoners, and the Fryars, and the rest that were great, would go in their way to make Christians of them; and we were made to stand up against them and their ways, and deny them in the Name of the Lord, and declare the truth to the simple-hearted continually, if we did suffer death for it; We could not endure to hear the Name of the Lord blasphemed, nor his pure Way of Truth perverted, nor the ignorant deceived. They did write all they understood of what we spake, and sent it to the Court-Chamber before the Inquisitor and Magistrates, but the Lord did blast it with the Mildews of his wrathful indignation, and burnt it up with the brightness of his Son, and we rejoiced in our God; but still our burdens continued very heavy, and our righteous souls were vexed with the filthy Conversation of the Wicked, and the pure Seed of God was prest from day to day, that our spirits did mourn, and our hearts were grieved because of the hardness of their hearts, and their Rebellion against their Maker, who was so gracious to them, to suffer them so long in all their abominations, and waited to be gracious to them, and knock at the Door of their hearts, calling for *Justice*, *Mercy* and *Humility*; but behold *Oppression*, *Cruelty*, and *Self-Exaltation*, notwithstanding the Lord did strive so much with them, and sent so many undeniable truths, and infallible testimonies of the coming of his Son to Judgement, and so clear a manifestation of the way to eternal Salvation, given forth of his own mouth, by his eternal Spirit, and having us for an example who were kept by his Power and Holiness; they had not a jot nor tittle against us, but for righteousness sake, though they had winnowed and fanned us so long: *(page 28)* Glory, honor and praises be given to our God for ever. O they would not let us know of any *English* Ship that came into the Harbour, as near as they could, but the Lord would make it manifest to us; We had a great working and striving in our bodies, but we knew not what it meant; the arrows of the Wicked did flye, so that my soul was plunged and overwhelmed from head to feet, and the terrors of the unrighteous had taken hold of us, and the flames of Hell compassed us about; then the Lord appeared unto me in a dream, and said, *There were two English Friends in the City which did plead for our liberty in our behalf, and he had taken all fear away from them, and made them bold.* And in a little while after the Magistrates sent for us forth, and askt us, *whether we were sick*, or *whether we did want any thing*; and were very tender to us, and said *we should write to England*, and bid the Scribe *give us Ink and Paper;* he said he would; but he was so wicked he did not. They did not tell us of any *English* that were there; but there was one *Francis Steward* of *London*, a Captain of a Ship, and a Fryar of *Ireland*, which came to the City together (for what we know) and they did take great pains for us, and went to their Ruler, and the Inquisitor, and to several Magistrates and Fryars, and the new English Consul with them, and wrought much amongst them that all were willing to let us go, save the Inquisitor; they said; and he said, *He could not free us without an Order from the Pope*. But we had many heavy Enemies besides, which would not be seen; but they obtained the favour to come and speak with us, which was a great thing in such a place.

They sent for us to the Court-Chamber, and the *English* Consul askt us, *if we were willing to go back to* England? We said, if it were the Will of God we might. The Captain spake to us with tears in his eyes, and told us what they had done for us, but could not prevail; It is this Inquisitor (said he) the rest were made free; you have preached among these people he said. We told him, we were called upon the Testimony of our Conscience, and the truth that we have witnessed forth among them, we should stand to maintain with our blood. He said, *if they could get us off, he would freely give us our passage, and provide for us*, and the Vessel was his own. We told him, his love was as well accepted of the Lord, as if he did carry us. He offered us money; he saw the Lord would *(page 29)* not suffer us to take any. He took our Names. We told them they took us out of our way, and put us into the Inquisition, and bid us change our minds; and we could not, the Lord had changed us into that which changed not, if they would burn us to ashes, or chop us as Herbs to the Pot. The Fryar said, *We did not work;* which was false; we had Work of our own, and did work as we were able. We told him, our Work and Maintenance was in *England*. And they said, *it was true*. He said, *We would not accept of the Inquisitors Dyet*. We did not know who did prepare for us, we did receive our meat as we had freedom in the Lord. Then he said, *We had suffered long enough, and too long, but we should have our freedom in a few days, and that they would send to the Pope for an Order*. And there were many English ships that way; but the Captain saw it was a very hard thing; so that it grieved him to the heart: He prayed God to comfort us, and he went away; and we do beseech God to bless and preserve him unto everlasting life, and never to let him nor his go without a blessing from him, for his love: he did venture himself exceedingly in that place. But after he was gone, they arose up against us with one accord; the Inquisitor came up into a Tower, and lookt down upon us as if he would have eaten us, and they did try us for our lives again, and did shut up our doors many Weeks; we could not tell for what; at length the Inquisitor came into the Tower again, and *Sarah* was moved to call to him, to have the door opened for us to go down into the Court to wash our clothes. Then he gave command for the door to be opened once a Week; and in a little while 'twas open every day. But great was our affliction indeed; and she told him, if we were the Popes Prisoners, we would appeal to the Pope, and he should send us to him. But them in the prison with us, especially the Fryar, were mortal Enemies to us, but yet they would have fed us with the choicest of their meat, and would gladly give us whole Bottles of Wine, if we would receive it, and were greatly troubled because we did refuse to eat and drink with them, and did persecute us exceedingly; but the Lord did visit them with his dreadful Judgements, the Fryar was tormented night and day, his body did perish, the Doctors and Chyrurgions did follow him a long time.

(page 30) And there were two or three *English* Ships there, came into harbour, and *Sarah* saw the coming of them in a Vision of the night, and there was great pleading for us, that we saw; but she heard a Voice, saying, *We could not go now.* So we were made willing to wait the Lords time.

Then they sent for us forth when the Ships were gone, and askt us *if we would be Catholicks:* And we said, we were true Christians, and had received the Spirit of Christ, and he that had not the Spirit of Christ, was none of his. The *English* Consul told us of the Ships, and said, *they would not let us go unless we would be Catholicks; and that we must suffer more imprisonment yet;* and said, *he did what he could for us.* One of the Magistrates shewed us the Cross; We told them, and said, We did take up the Cross of Christ daily, which is the great Power of God to crucifie sin and iniquity. So we told them that one of their *Fathers* did promise us our liberty. We did think that Fryar was too tender hearted to stay among them; he did take a great deal of pains for us (the Captain said) we told him, he would never have cause to repent it; the blessing of God would be upon him for any thing he should do for us; for we were the Servants of the living God, and he promised us our freedoms in a little time.

A VISION.

IN a Vision of the night I saw in the Firmament six Suns, one at a distance from the rest, that did appear to be but half an hour high; the other five stood four-square, one in the middle; and they did cross over each other; the highest did not seem to be above an hour high. And when I did awake, I was troubled in my spirit to know the Vision; and I waited upon the Lord, and he signified to me in the Light, The six Suns were six Nations, whose Lights were near out; and the five which crossed each other, signified to me some rising amongst them.

And the Fryar came to me and said, *It was God's will we should be kept there, or else they could not keep us.* I told him, the Lord did suffer wicked men to do wickedly, but did not will them to do it. He did suffer *Herod* to take off *John Baptist's* head, but he did not will him to do it; and did suffer *Stephen* to be stoned, and *Judas* to *(page 34)* betray Christ, but he did not will them to do it; for if he had, he would not have condemned them for it. He said, *Then we are wicked men:* I said, They are wicked men that work wickedness. The Fryar would say still, *We had not the true Faith.* We said, By Faith we stand, and by the Power of God we are upholden; dost thou think it is by our own power and holiness we are kept from a vain conversation, from sin and wickedness? He said, *That was our pride.* We said. No, We could glory in the Lord, we were children of wrath once as well as others; But the Lord hath quickned us that were dead, by the living Word of his Grace, and hath washed cleansed and sanctified us through soul and spirit, in part, according to our measures, and we do press forward towards that which is perfect. He then did say, *We were good Women, but yet there was no redemption for us except we would be Catholicks.*

Now the Lord said, *Fear not Daughters of Sion, I will carry you forth as Gold tryed out of the fire.* And many precious promises did the Lord refresh us with, in our greatest extremity, and would appear in his glory, that our souls would be ravished in his presence; I had the Spirit of Prayer upon me, and I was afraid to speak to the Lord, for fear I should speak one word that would not please him. And the Lord said, *Fear not Daughter of Sion, ask what thou wilt, and I will grant it thee, whatsoever thy heart can wish.* I desired nothing of the Lord but what would make for his glory, whether it were my liberty or bondage, life or death, wherein I was highly accepted of the Lord.

The Room wherein I was separated, was near the Chancery, where all the Bishops Courtiers did resort, and would come into the Inquisition Courts, and I had Work amongst them daily; they would come on purpose to their condemnation: some would be smitten, and run as if they hunted; and some would be set on fire, and cry, *Caldere, caldere,* and *fuoco, fuoco,* and many would pitty us because we were not Catholicks; the Fryars would say, *We might be Catholicks, and keep our own Religion too; and we should not be known we were Catholicks, except we were brought before a Justice of Peace.* We askt if we should profess a Christ we should be asham'd of?

But as for the poor Workmen, they were willing to do any thing for us, and were diligent to hear us, the Witness of God in *(page 35)* them did answer to the truth; there were many eyes over them; had it not been for the great opposition, there were hundreds would have flown to the truth.

And because I said I did talk with G.F. he (the Fryar) asked, *Whether G.F. did bring me money to maintain me in prison.* I said no, but though I was absent in body, yet I was present in spirit, and was refreshed in him, and in hundreds more besides. They said, *I had seen Revelations, and had talkt with G.F. and he was God's Revelation.* Sarah said, Christ was God's Revelation; he said, *she came under the Halter for saying Christ was God's Revelation.* She answered, St. *Paul* said, *As soon as it pleased God to re-veal his Son in me, I did not consult with flesh and blood, but immediately I went and preacht him;* and is not Christ God's Revelation then? He said, *Who denied that?*

What they would have done to *Sarah* if they had taken her forth, we know not; but the Lord did work so wonderfully that night for the pres-ervation of her poor soul out of their net, that he is worthy to be glori-fied for ever.

The next time he came to me, he came in sheeps clothing, but he had a Woolf under his Gown; he gave me words as soft as Butter, and as smooth as Oyl, when he had a Sword in his heart, and a Spear in his hand, when they speak most fairest, then beware of them.

He desired us *we would not think so hardly of him, as if he were the Author of all our wrongs and troubles; he was not* (he said) *but would do any good he could for us, were it with his blood.* But we thought he had been the chiefest that cast the poor man in prison, but he was the man that hope [*sic*] him out without any punishment at all, though the In-quisitor did say he should be severely punished. I told him he did well, he would have peace in it, and would never have cause to repent it. He

did entreat us, *he might not bear all the burthen.* We told him of many
wicked things he did act against us, and of his lying and cruel words. He
bid us *take no notice what he did speak.* But we did feel his spirit, that
what he spake, he would do, if he had not been chained. I did use to tell
him, My Conscience was not seared with a hot iron. I was not past
feeling. At last he was so weary of coming to us, he did entreat the
Inquisitor he might not come to us any more; the Judgements of the
Lord did *(page 36)* follow him so, it was like to kill him.

When we were parted, the Lord did work mightily for us, and we
were kept by the Power of the Lord over our Enemies, and were bold for
God's Truth, and did make war with them in righteousness, so that they
could not gain-say us in the truth: So that Scripture was fulfilled, *The
wicked mouths must be stopped;* and they were put to silence, praises be
to our God, and were made to confess or say, *Of a truth God was in us;*
our God was a consuming fire to them, they were not able to stand in
his presence, but they would howl and make a noise like Dogs, and cry,
Jesu, Maria, and flye as people driven by a mighty rushing Wind; the
Power of the Lord did pursue after them like a Sword; that Scripture
was fulfilled, which saith, *Christ came not to send peace on earth, but a
sword,* to cut down his Enemies; the Lord was on our side, and did take
our part, and did fight for us, and did tread down our Enemies under our
feet, that they could not hurt us. Mighty was the Work of God daily,
our tongues cannot express it; they did work day and night with their
Inchantments and Divinations, Sorceries, unclean Spirits crying and
foaming; insomuch we could take little rest day or night sometimes;
but the Lord was with us, and did work mightily by his power, and kept
us over them in the life of the Son of God. My Prison was nigh to the
Pallace, and to their Worship, that I could be heard of both; and it was
laid upon me of the Lord to call them to repentance, and to turn to the
Light wherewith they were enlightned, which would lead them out of
their wicked Ways, Works and Worships, to serve the true and living
God in spirit and in truth; the Power did raise the Witness in many,
and troubled them; they did sigh and groan; and some did stay to hear
me, so long as they durst; for there were many did watch; and it was
upon pain of death, or at least to be imprisoned: As was the poor *English* man that did come and speak to me, whom they hall'd down violently, and put him in prison; but the Lord delivered him for his love.

And we were parted near a year, but great was the Work of the Lord,
and great was the Power to carry it on. He was not wanting to us, glory
be to his Name; but did give us Words and Wisdom according to our

Work: So that Scripture was fulfilled which saith on this wise, Ye need not premeditate afore-hand what *(page 37)* to speak, or what to say; for it shall be given you of my Heavenly Father what ye ought to speak, that the Enemies shall not gain say; they were so tormented, that they did run to the Hills and to the Mountains to cover them from the presence of the Lord, and from the Wrath of the Lamb which sits upon the Throne to judg them righteously, and to condemn them of all their wicked deeds; which they so ungodlily had committed against him.

Oh! the goodness of the Lord, and his long-suffering and forbearance which would lead them to repentance, but they would not hearken to his counsel, but turned his laws behind their backs, and hated to be instructed by them; therefore the Lord did laugh at their destruction, and did mock when their fear came: Their wickedness was so great, and my burthens so heavy to bear it that I cryed to the Lord, and said, It is better for me to dye, than to live; and would gladly have given up my life in testimony against them all; I was (as't were) compell'd to declare against all their ways, works and worships, insomuch that they ran to the Inquisitor to have me chained, or punished some other way; but the Power of the Lord chained them, that they could not diminish a hair of my head, the Lord was my safety, praises be to his Name for ever.

Now some as they passed to their Worship Houses, would sigh; and some pray, and some did throw stones at my Window, they did work night and day about the Prison, as though they would have broke through to slay me; but the Lord was with me, and did fight for me, and did scatter his Enemies as the dust before the Wind: Glory be to his Name for evermore.

I cannot expresse the large love of our God, how he did preserve us from so many deaths and threatnings, as they did come to me with falling down upon their knees, saying Miss [sic], and would have me to say after them; but in the Name of the Lord I denied them. They would howle like Dogs, because they could not beguile the innocent, and slay my righteous life; but praises be to the Lord our God, who did preserve me from the Woolf and the Devourers, denying them and their Sacrifices.

And when they saw they could not prevail to betray us from the truth, then they said, they would give us to the Devil to be tormented, and deliver us over to their bad Catholicks, to do by us as they (page 38) pleased; for they would use us badly, and so they did seek to do: Oh the cursed noises and cryes the *Sodomites* did make, crying, *Quake, Quake,* running about the Prison raging, and some singing and crouding round the Prison night and day, as if they would have broke through to slay me; and the sons of *Belial* did run to bear false witness, so that I looked every hour when they would fetch me out, and slay me. The Enemy did so work to perswade, that they had pelt [*sic*] my dear yoke-fellow with stones, which was a great trouble to me, because I could not suffer death with her; I did yeild she had been slain: And afterwards this great tribulation being ended, then they said my (dear and faithful) yoke-fellow should be sent to *Rome*, and I should tarry at *Malta*, which did so encrease my sorrow, and wrought upon my spirit to try and examine wherefore the Lord should deal so hardly with me, as to leave me behind; or whether he did not count me worthy to go and give in my testimony with her to *Rome*, and offer up my life for the Testimony of Jesus, than to have my liberty to return to *England* with her, and I cryed day and night to the Lord, and would not give my soul rest, nor my eyes sleep, till the Lord did answer me; glory and praises be to his Name for ever. But we saw *Jacob* must part with all, *Benjamin* must go too. So we were willing to give up in obedience to the Lord; our trials were unspeakable. Oh the unclean spirits! they would speak to us at noon-day; but the Lord did give us power over them, that we did not fear the wild Bores out of the Wood, nor the wild Beasts out of the Field.

Then there was one came and said, that *Catherine and I must be sent both to Rome;* Which did rejoice my soul, and renewed my strength, because the Lord did count me Worthy to go and give in my Testimony for his Truth, the Word of his Prophesie, before the great and mighty ones of the Earth. The Lord said, *I should not be afraid;* and he shewed me in the Light how he had bowed them down before us, and saw them in the Light of Christ, how the Pope, the Fryars and Sorcerers stood in ranks, bowing down before us. So we saw our Dominion in Spirit: They did work to send us to *Rome*, but the Lord did blast it, and sought against them that they could not send us.

(page 39) Now our Testimony was as largely given in at *Rome*, as at *Malta:* The Fryars came to me, and shewed me *Mary* and her Babe pictured against the Wall, and would have me look upon it. I stampt with my foot and said, Cursed be all Images and Image-makers, and all that fall down to worship them, Christ Jesus is the express Image of his Fathers brightness, which is Light and Life, who doth reveal the mysterie of iniquity, the cunning working of Satan, to draw out the mind to follow him, from the pure life, and to veil over the Just One from beholding the Presence of the Lord. But glory be to the Lord, who hath made him manifest in thousands of his, in this Day of his Power, When we were separated, we spake one and the same thing, being guided by one Spirit.

They would go from me to *Catherine*, they would bid her *speak as Sarah did;* and so she did to their condemnation: Praises to the Lord, *Amen.*

(page 41) The Fryar then came to me, and askt me, *why I did not work?* I said unto him, What Work dost thou do? He said *he did write.* I told him I would write too, if he would bring me a Pen, Ink and Paper; and I would write truth. He said, *He would not that we should write; for St. Paul did work at* Rome, *and we might get nine or ten grains a day, if we would knit, that is three half pence.* I told him, if we could have that priviledge amongst them, that *St. Paul* had at *Rome,* under *Cæsar,* which was a Heathenish King, we would have wrought, and not have been chargeable to any. St. *Paul* lived in his own hired House two years, with a Souldier to look to him, and had friends of the same Occupation to work with him, and could send where he would, and whosoever would come to him, might, and he taught them in the Name of the Lord Jesus, and no man forbad him. So I askt him, Whether he knew the holy War of God, yea or nay? if he did, I told him he then did know we could not be without exercise day nor night. Then his mouth *(page 42)* was stopped, and he spake no more to me of work: But though our affliction of body was great, and our travel of soul was greater, yet we did knit Stockins, and gave to them that were made serviceable to u.,xZZ[*sic*] and did make Garments for the poor prisoners, and mended their Clothes which had need, and were made helpful to them all, to their condemnation, that did persecute us. But we could not work at the Fryar's Will, nor any man's else, but as we had freedom in the Lord.

As I was weak in my bed, the Fryar came to me, and said, *We did deny the Scriptures:* I told him, they did deny them, we did own them, and hold them forth, thou dost know it: He was in a rage because I said, they denyed the Scriptures, bid me *eat my words again, and threatned death upon me.* I said, Christ Jesus was the Light of the World, and had lighted every one that cometh into the World, which Light is our salvation that do receive it, and the same Light is the World's condemnation that do not believe in it. Then he said, *He would lay me in Chains, where I should neither see Sun nor Moon.* They say, *The* Father *hath almost killed you,* said he, *but I will kill you quite, before I have done.* He had a Book in his hand, and he did study in it; I told him he did comprehend the Words in his carnal mind; and he was wrath, and said *he would give me to the Devils to be tormented.* I said, I deny the Devil and all his Works and Workers.

Some would come unto the Prison upon their Saints days, and ask us *what day it was?* We did answer, We did not know, neither did we observe dayes nor times, months nor years. Then answer would be made, *It was St. Joseph's day*, or some other Saint; *and St. Joseph should punish us that night, because we did not observe his day*. We answered, We did know the Saints to be at peace with us, and we did not fear them. We further said, St. *Paul* did call it beggarly Elements and Rudiments of the World, to observe days, times, months and years; and their mouths would be stopt for a time. Then came the Fryar another time, and told me, *it was seventeen dayes to their Christmas;* and said, *the Virgin Mary conceived with child that day*, being the same day he spake to me on; as if she did go with Child but seventeen dayes. And he said, *the next day as Lady Ann's day, the Virgin Mary's Mother, a Saint.*

(page 43) Then as I was crying to the Lord in Prayer because of our long-suffering, & our strong travel & labour, & no fruit (as did appear) the Lord said unto me, *Be not grieved, though* Israel *be not gathered; the seed of* Malta *shall be as the stars of the skie for multitude: That which ye have sown, shall not dye, but live: Glory be to the Name of the Lord for ever.*

(page 53)

Katharine Evans *to her Husband and Children.*

For the hand of *JOHN EVANS*, my right dear and precious Husband, with my tender-hearted Children, who are more dear and precious unto me, than the apple of mine eye.

*M*Ost dear and faithful Husband, Friend and Brother, begotten of my Eternal Father, of the immortal Seed of the Covenant of Light, Life and Blessednesse, I have unity and fellowship with thee day and night, to my great refreshment and continual comfort, praises, praises be given to our God for evermore, who hath joined us together in that which neither Sea nor Land can separate or divide.

My dear heart, my soul doth dearly salute thee, with my dear and precious Children, which are dear and precious in the Light of the Lord, to thy endless joy, and my everlasting comfort; glory be to our Lord God eternally, who hath called you with a holy Calling, and hath caused his Beauty to shine upon you in this the day of his Power, wherein he is making up of his jewels, and binding up of his faithful ones in the Bond of everlasting Love and Salvation, among whom he hath numbred you of his own free Grace; in which I beseech you (dear hearts) in the fear of the Lord to abide in your measures, according to the manifestation of the Revelation of the Son of God in you; keep a dili-

gent watch over every thought, word and action, and let your minds be staid continually in the Light, where you will find out the snares and baits of Satan, and be preserved, out of his Traps, Nets and Pits, that you may not be captivated by him at his will. Oh my dear Husband and Children, how often have I poured out my soul to our everlasting Father for you, with Rivers of tears, night and day, that you might be kept pure and single in the sight of our God, improving your Talents as wise Virgins, having Oyl in your Vessels, and your Lamps burning, and cloathed with the long white Robes of Righteousness, ready to enter the Bed-Chamber, and to sup with the (page 54) Lamb, and to feed at the Feast of fat things, where your souls may be nourished, refreshed, comforted, and satisfied, never to hunger again.

My dear hearts, you do not want teaching, you are in a Land of Blessedness, which floweth with Milk and Honey, among the faithful Stewards, whose mouths are opened wide in righteousness, to declare the Eternal Mysteries of the everlasting Kingdom, of the endless joys and eternal glory, whereunto all the willing and obedient shall enter, and be blessed for ever.

My dear hearts, the promises of the Lord are large, and are all Yea and Amen to those that fear his Name; he will comfort the Mourners in Sion, and will cause the heavy-hearted in Jerusalem to rejoice, because of the glad tydings; they that do bear the Cross with patience, shall wear the Crown with joy; for it is through the long-suffering and patient waitings, the Crown of Life and Immortality comes to be obtained; the Lord hath exercised my patience, and tryed me to the uttermost, to his praise and my eternal comfort, who hath not been wanting to us in anything in his own due time; We are Witnesses he can provide a Table in the Wilderness both spiritual and temporal. Oh the endless love of our God, who is an everlasting Fountain of all living refreshment; whose Chrystal streams never cease running to every thirsty soul, that breatheth after the springs of Life and Salvation.

In our deepest affliction, when I looked for every breath to be the last, I could not wish I had not come over Seas, because I knew it was my Eternal Father's Will to prove me, with my dear and faithful Friend; in all afflictions and miseries, the Lord remembred mercy, and did not leave nor forsake us, nor suffer his faithfulness to fail us, but caused the sweet drops of his mercy to distil upon us, and the brightness of his glorious countenance to shine into our hearts, and was never wanting to us in Revelations nor Visions. Oh how may I do to set forth the fulness of God's Love to our souls! No tongue can express it, no heart can conceive it, nor mind can comprehend it Oh the ravishments, the raptures, the glorious bright-shining countenance of our Lord God, who is our fulness in emptiness our strength in weakness, our health in sickness, our life in death, our joy in sorrow, our peace in disquietness, our praise in heaviness, our power in all needs or necessities; He alone is a full God unto us, and to all that can trust him; he hath emptied us of our selves, and hath unbottomed us of our selves, and hath wholly built us upon the sure Foundation *(page 55)* the Rock of Ages, Christ Jesus the Light of the world, where the swelling Seas, nor raging, foaming Waves, nor stormy winds, though they beat vehemently, cannot be able to remove us; Glory, honor and praises is to our God for ever, who out of his everlasting Treasures doth fill us with his Eternal Riches day by day; he did nourish our souls with the choicest of his mercies, and doth feed our bodies with his good Creatures, and relieve all our necessities in a full measure, praises, praises be to him alone, who is our everlasting portion, our confidence, and our rejoicing, whom we serve acceptably with reverence and God-like fear; for our God is a consuming fire.

Oh my dear Husband and precious Children, you may feel the issues of Love and Life which stream forth as a River to every soul of you, from a heart that is wholly joined to the Fountain; my prayers are for you day and night without ceasing, beseeching the Lord God of Power to pour down his tender mercies upon you, and to keep you in his pure fear, and to encrease your faith, to confirm you in all righteousness, and strengthen you in believing in the Name of the Lord God Almighty, that you may be established as Mount Sion, that can never be moved. Keep your souls unspotted of the world, and love one another with a pure heart, fervently serve one another in love; build up one another in the Eternal, and bear one anothers burdens for the Seeds sake, and so fulfil the Law of God. This is the Word of the Lord unto you, my dearly beloved.

Dear hearts, I do commit you into the hands of the Almighty, who dwelleth on high, and to the Word of his Grace in you, who is able to build you up to everlasting life, and eternal salvation. By me who am thy dear and precious Wife, and Spouse, in the Marriage of the Lamb, in the bed undefiled.

K.E.

My dearly beloved Yoak-mate in the Work of our God, doth dearly salute you; Salute us dearly to our precious Friends in all places. I do believe we shall see your faces again with joy. Dearly salute us to T.H. R.S. and his sister, S.B. and his daughter, N.M. and his dear Wife, with all the rest of our dear Friends in Bristol. T.C. and his dear Wife and Daughter, and all Friends in Bristol or else-where. J.G. and his precious Wife, Children and Servants, with all Friends. Our dear love to E.H. with her Husband and Children at Alderberry.

The original of this was written in the Inquisition in *Malta*, in the 11*th* Month of the year 1661.

Sarah Chevers to her Husband and Children.

MY Dear Husband, my love, my life is given up to serve the living God, and to obey his pure Call in the measure of the manifestation of his Love, Light, Life and Spirit of Christ Jesus, his onely begotten Son, whom he hath manifested in me and thousands, by the brightness of his appearing, to put an end to sin and Satan, and bring to light Immortality through the preaching of the everlasting Gospel by the Spirit of Prophesie, which is poured out upon the sons and daughters of the living God, according to his purpose, whereof he hath chosen me, who am the least of all; but God who is rich in mercy, for his own Name sake hath passed by mine offences, and hath counted me worthy to bear testimony to his holy Name before the mighty men of the Earth. Oh the love of the Lord to my soul! my tongue cannot express, neither hath it entered into the heart of man to conceive of the things that God hath laid up for them that fear him.

Therefore doth my soul breath to my God for thee and my Children, night and day, that your minds may be joined to the Light of the Lord Jesus, to lead you out of Satans Kingdom, into the Kingdom of God, where we may enjoy one another in the Life Eternal, where neither Sea nor Land can separate; in which Light and Life do I salute thee my dear Husband, with my Children, wishing you to embrace Gods love in making his Truth so clearly manifest amongst you, whereof I am a Witness even of the everlasting Fountain that hath been opened by the Messengers of Christ, who preach to you the Word of God in season, and out of season, directing you where you may find your Saviour to purge and cleanse you from your sins, and to reconcile you to his Father, and to have unity with him and all the Saints, in the Light, that ye may be fellow-Citizens in the Kingdom of Glory, Rest and Peace, which Christ hath purchased for them that love him, and obey him: What profit is there for to gain the whole world and lose your own souls? Seek first the Kingdom (page 57) of God, and the Righteousness thereof, and all other things shall be added to you; Godliness is great gain, having the promise of this life that now is, and that which is to come; which is fulfilled to me, who have tasted of the Lords endlesse love and mercies to my soul, & from a moving of the same love and life do I breath to thee my dear Husband, with my Children; my dear love salutes you all; my Prayers to my God are for you all, that your minds may be joined to the Light wherewith you are lightened, that I may enjoy you in that which is Eternal, and have community with you in the Spirit: *He that is joined to the Lord, is one Spirit, one heart, one mind, one soul, to serve the Lord with one consent. I cannot by Pen or Paper set forth the large love of God in fulfilling his gracious promises to me in the Wilderness, being put into prison for God's Truth, there to remain all days of my life, being searched, tryed, examined upon pain of death among the Enemies of God and his Truth; standing in jeopardy for my life, until the Lord had subdued and brought them under his mighty Power, and made them to feed us, and would have given us money or clothes; but the Lord did deck our Table richly in the Wilderness; the day of the Lord is appearing, wherein he will discover every deed of darkness, let it be done never so secret; the light of Christ Jesus will make it manifest in every Conscience; the Lord will rip up all coverings that is not of his own Spirit. The God of Peace be with you all.* Amen.

> Written in the Inquisition-Prison by the hand
> of *Sarah Chevers*, for the hand of *Henry Chevers*
> my dear Husband; give this, fail not.

(page 60)

Another from *K.E.* to her Husband and Children, with somewhat from both the Lords Prisoners, to Friends, the which was taken with the rest of the Letters, in the Inquisition, and copied out for their Lord Inquisitor.

DEar Husband, with my dear Children, I beseech you together, to wait in the patience, having your minds always staid upon the Lord: Keep out of incumbrances, for that is the Enemies opportunity to step in, when the mind is gone forth, and to vail the pure, and darken the understanding, and so hinder you of the pure enjoyment of the beholding the glory of God in the face of Jesus Christ.

Take no more upon you then you are able to perform in the Spirit of moderation and meekness, for that is in the sight of God of of [sic] great prize: See the Lord going before you in all your occasions, that you may be prosperous in all your undertakings, wait diligently upon the Lord, to be seasoned with his Grace, that you may come to a pure understanding of the motions *(page 61)* of his Eternal Spirit, and to a true knowledge of the operation of his hands; So you will be able with all Saints, to comprehend what is the heigth, and the depth, and the length, and the breadth of the riches of his Grace and Love towards mankind in Christ Jesus our Lord; *Amen*, saith my spirit: This is the counsel of the Lord unto you.

I do often remember M.H. I do desire she may be brought up in the fear of God, and want for nothing that is convenient for her; salute me to her dearly. I have been very sensible, dear Husband, of thine, and our Children, and many dear friends more, of your sorrowful souls, mourning hearts, grieved spirits, troubled minds for us, as being Members of one body, Christ Jesus being our Head, we must needs suffer together, that we may rejoice together; a true sorrow begets a true joy; a true Cross a true Crown. We do believe it is our heavenly Fathers will and purpose to bring us back as safe to *England*, as ever he brought us thence, for his own glory, though we are some of the least of Christ's Flock, yet we do belong to the true Fold, and our Shepherd hath had as great a care of us, as he could have for any of his Lambs; and hath brought us through great affliction, praises be given to his glorious Name, of us, and you, and all that know him, for ever. Though we are absent in body in the Will of God, from you, yet we are present in spirit in the Will of God, with you, and do receive the benefit of all your prayers daily, and do feel the Springs of Life that do stream from all the faithful hearted, to our great refreshment and strengthening.

After our money was gone, the Lord Inquisitor, with the rest in Authority, put a great allowance in one of their servants hands for our maintenance, because we could take no money our selves; the Lord of Heaven did forbid us to meddle with any; and he did send to know whether we did want any clothes, he would send it to the Prison to us: This was the large love of our God to us, and we were made contented with that we had, till the Lord God (who is rich in mercy, and full of all Grace, and is never unmindful of any which trust in his Name) of his everlasting love did send his faithful Messenger, whose feet are beautiful, and face is comely, cloathed with a bright shining Garment from the Crown of the head, to the sole of the foot, and came in great power and *(page 62)* strength indeed, armed with the whole Armour of Light, and drest in the Majesty of the Most High, and being commissioned of the Higher Power, went to the *Lord Inquisitor* to demand our lawful liberty, which would not be granted, except we could get some *English* Merchants of *Legorn* or *Messana* to engage four thousands Dollers that we should never come into those parts again; the Lord (who alone is our Life and Redeemer) moved our dear Brother to offer his own body to redeem ours, but it would not be received; then he offered to lay down his own dear and precious life for our liberty: Greater love can no man have, than to lay down his life for his Friend; the Lord will restore it into his bosom double; his service can never be blotted out; his Name is called *Daniel Baker;* his outward being is near *London,* a right dear and precious heart he is: The blessing, strength, and power of the Almighty be upon him and his, and overshadow them for ever, *Amen.* Greater comfort could never be administred to us in our conditions; Glory, honor and praise to our God for evermore, *Amen.*

This is a dear and sweet Salutation in that which never changeth, fadeth away, nor waxeth old, from us whom the Lord hath counted worthy to bear his Name, and to suffer for his sake, to all our Christian Friends, Fathers and Elders, Pillars of Gods spiritual House, Brethren and Sisters in the Lord Jesus Christ.

Oh my dear Husband, with our dear and precious Children, Lambs of God, and Babes of Christ, begotten of the Immortal Seed of Light, Life and Truth, with us, and all the whole Family of everlasting blessedness.

Pray for us believingly; all things are possible with our God. So my Dearlings, in the arms of everlasting love do I take my leave of you; the blessing and peace of the Most High be upon you ever, *Amen, Amen.*

Oh my dear Husband! praise the Lord that ever thou hadst a Wife that was found worthy to suffer for the Name of the Lord. Inasmuch as I can understand the moving of the Spirit of God: My dear and faithful Yoke-fellow, Sister and Friend, is worthy *(page 63)* to be embraced of all friends for ever; the deeper the sorrow, the greater the joy; the heavier the Cross, the weightier the Crown. This was written in the Inquisition at *Malta,* of us

Malta the 11*th.* Month
   of the year 1661.

Katharine Evans
Sarah Chevers.

SOME

ACCOUNT

OF

CIRCUMSTANCES

IN THE

LIFE OF MARY PENNINGTON,

FROM HER

𝕸𝖆𝖓𝖚𝖘𝖈𝖗𝖎𝖕𝖙,

LEFT FOR HER FAMILY.

𝕷𝖔𝖓𝖉𝖔𝖓 :

PRINTED FOR HARVEY AND DARTON,
GRACECHURCH-STREET

1821.

(Page numbers of original document appear in text as *page _.*)

(page 1) ACCOUNT, &c.

A brief account of some of my exercises, from my childhood, left with my dear daughter, Gulielma Maria Penn.

Mary Pennington.

The first scripture I remember to have taken notice of was, "Blessed are they that hunger and thirst after righteousness, for they shall be filled." This I heard taken for a text when I was about eight years of age, and under the care of people who were a kind of loose Protestants, that minded no more about religion than to go to their worship-house on first days, to hear a canonical priest preach in the morning, and read common prayers in the afternoon. *(page 2)* They used common prayers in the family, and observed superstitious customs and times, days of feasting and fasting, Christmas, (so called,) Good Friday, Lent, &c. About this time I was afraid, in the night, of such things as run in my mind by day, of spirits, thieves, &c. When alone in the fields, and possessed with fears, I accounted prayers my help and safety; so would often say (as I had been taught) the Lord's Prayer, hoping thereby to be delivered from the things I feared.

After some time I went to live with some that appeared to be more religious. They would not admit of sports on first days, calling first day the sabbath. They went to hear two sermons a-day, from a priest that was not loose in his conversation: he used a form of prayer before his sermon, and read the common prayer after it. I was now about ten or eleven years of age. A maid-servant that waited on me and the rest of the children, was very zealous in their way: she used to read Smith's and Preston's sermons on first days, between *(page 3)* the sermon times. I diligently heard her read, and at length liked not to use the Lord's Prayer alone, but got a prayer-book, and read prayers mornings and evenings; and that scripture of "howling on their beds," was much on my mind: by it I was checked from saying prayers in my bed.

About this time I began to be very serious about religion. One day, after we came from the place of public worship, the maid before mentioned read one of Preston's sermons, the text was: "Pray continually." In this sermon much was said respecting prayer: amongst other things, of the excellency of prayer, that it distinguished a saint from a sinner;

that in many things the hypocrite could imitate the saint, but in this he could not. This thing wrought much on my mind. I found that I knew not what true prayer was; for what I used for prayer, an ungodly person could use as well as I, which was to read one out of a book; and this could not be the *(page 4)* prayer he meant, which distinguished a saint from a wicked one. My mind was deeply exercised about this thing. When she had done reading, and all were gone out of the chamber, I shut the door, and in great distress I flung myself on the bed, and oppressedly cried out: "Lord, what is prayer!"

This exercise continued so on my mind, that at night, when I used to read a prayer out of a book, I could only weep, and remain in trouble. At this time I had never heard of any people that prayed any other way than by reading prayers out of a book, or composing themselves. I remember one morning it came into my mind that I would write a prayer of my own composing, and use it in the morning as soon as I was out of bed; which I did, though I could then scarcely join my letters, I had learnt so little a time to write. The prayer I wrote was something after this manner: "Lord, thou commandest the Israelites to offer a morning sacrifice, so I offer up the sacrifice of prayer, and *(page 5)* desire to be preserved this day." The use of this prayer for a little while gave me some ease. I soon quite left my prayer-books, and used to write prayers according to my several occasions. The second that I wrote was for the assurance of the pardon of my sins. I had heard one preach, "that God of his free grace pardoned David's sins." I was much affected by it, and, as I came from the worship place, I thought it would be a happy thing to be assured that one's past sins were pardoned. I wrote a pretty long prayer on that subject, and felt, that as pardon came through grace, I might receive it, though very unworthy of it. In said prayer I used many earnest expressions.

A little time after this, several persons spoke to me about the greatness of my memory, and praised me for it. I felt a fear of being puffed up, and wrote a prayer of thanks for that gift, and desired to be enabled to use it for the Lord, and that it might be sanctified to me.

These three prayers I used with some *(page 6)* ease of mind, but not long, for I began again to question whether I prayed aright or not. I was much troubled about it, not knowing that any did pray extempore; but it sprung up in my mind, that to use words descriptive of the state I was in, was prayer, which I attempted to do, but could not. Sometimes I kneeled down a long time, and had not a word to say, which wrought great trouble in me. I had none to reveal my distress unto, or advise with; so, secretly bore a great burden a long time.

One day as I was sitting at work in the parlour, one called a gentleman (who was against the superstitions of the times) came in, and looking sadly, said "it was a sad day: that Prynne, Bastwick, and Burton, were sentenced to have their ears cut, and to be banished." This news sunk deep into my mind, and strong cries were raised in me for them, and the rest of the innocent people in the nation. I was unable to sit at my work, but was strongly inclined to go into a private room, which I *(page 7)* did, and shutting the door, kneeled down and poured out my soul to the Lord in a very vehement manner. I was wonderfully melted and eased, and felt peace and acceptance with the Lord; and that this was true prayer, which I had never before been acquainted with.

Not long after this an account was brought to the house, that a neighbouring minister, who had been suspended by the bishops for not being subject to their canons, was returned to his flock again, and that he was to preach at the place where he did three years before, (being suspended so long.) I expressed a desire to go thither, but was reproved by those that had the care of my education, they saying that it was not fit to leave my parish church. I could not be easy without going, so I went. When I came there, he prayed fervently (he was one called a Puritan) and with great power. Then I felt that was true prayer, and what my mind pressed after, but could not come at in my own will, and had but just tasted *(page 8)* of it the time before mentioned. And now I knew that this alone was prayer, I mourned solely because I kneeled down morning after morning, and night after night, and had not a word to say. My distress was so great, that I feared I should perish in the night, because I had not prayed; and I thought that by day my food would not nourish me, because I could not pray.

I was thus exercised a great while, and could not join in the common prayer that was read in the family every night; neither could I kneel down when I came to the worship-house, as I had been taught to do; and this scripture was much in my mind: "Be more ready to hear, than to offer the sacrifice of fools." I could only read the Bible, or some other book, whilst the priest read the common prayer. At last I could neither kneel nor stand up to join with the priest in his prayer before the sermon; neither did I care to hear him preach, my mind being after the Nonconformist, the Puritan already mentioned.

(page 9) By constraint I went with the family in the morning, but could not be kept from the Puritan preacher in the afternoon. I went through much suffering on this account, being forced to go on foot between two and three miles, and no one permitted to go with me; except some-

times a servant, out of compassion, would run after me, lest I should be frightened going alone. Though I was very young, I was so zealous that all the tried reasonings and threatenings could not keep me back. In a short time I refused to hear the priest of our parish at all, but went constantly, all weathers, to the other place. In the family I used to hear the Scripture read; but if I happened to go in before they had done their prayers, I would sit down though they were kneeling.

These things wrought me much trouble in the family, and there was none to take my part; yet at length two of the maid-servants were inclined to mind what I said against their prayers, and so refused to *(page 10)* join them, at which the governors of the family were much disturbed, and made me the subject of their discourse in company, saying that I would pray with the spirit, and rejected godly men's prayers; that I was proud and schismatic; and that I went to those places to meet young men, and such like. At this time I suffered, not only from those persons to whose care I was committed by my parents, (who both died when I was not above three years of age,) but also from my companions and kindred; yet, notwithstanding, in this zeal I grew much, and sequestered myself from my former vain company, and refused playing at cards, &c. I zealously kept the sabbath, not daring to eat or be clothed with such things as occasioned much trouble, or took up much time on that day, which I believed ought to be devoted to hearing, reading, and praying. I disregarded those matches proposed to me by vain persons, having desired of the Lord, that if I married at all, it might be a man that feared him. I had a belief, that *(page 11)* though I then knew of none of my outward rank that was such a one, yet that the Lord would provide such a one for me.

Possessed of this belief, I regarded not their reproaches, that would say to me, that no gentleman was of this way, and that I should marry some mean person or other. But they were disappointed, for the Lord touched the heart of him that was afterwards my husband, and my heart cleaved to him for the Lord's sake. He was of a good understanding, and had cast off those dead superstitions; which, that they were dead, was more clearly made manifest to him in that day, than any other person that I knew of, of his rank and years. He was but young, compared to the knowledge he had attained in the things of God. He was about twenty years old. We pressed much after the knowledge of the Lord, and walked in his fear; and though both very young, were joined together in the Lord; refusing the use of a ring, and such like things then *(page 12)* used, and not denied by any that we knew of.

We lived together about two years and a month. We were zealously affected, and daily exercised in what we believed to be the service and worship of God. We scrupled many things then in use amongst those accounted honest people, viz. singing David's Psalms in metre. We tore out of our Bibles the common prayer, the form of prayer, and also the singing psalms, as being the inventions of vain poets, not being written for that use. We found that songs of praise must spring from the same source as prayers did; so we could not use any one's songs or prayers. We were also brought off from the use of bread and wine, and water baptism. We looked into the Independent way, but saw death there, and that there was not the thing our souls sought after.

In this state my dear husband died, hoping in the promises afar off, not seeing or knowing him that is invisible to be so near him; and that it was he that showed *(page 13)* unto him his thoughts, and made manifest the good and the evil. When he was taken from me I was with child of my dear daughter Gulielma Maria Springett. It was often with me that I should not be able to consent to the thing being done to my child, which I saw no fruit of, and knew to be but a custom which men were engaged in by tradition, not having the true knowledge of that scripture in the last of the Galatians, of circumcision or uncircumcision availing nothing, but a new creature. This was often in my mind, and I resolved that it should not be done to my child. When I was delivered of her, I refused to have her sprinkled, which brought great reproach upon me; so I became a by-word and a hissing among the people of my own rank in the world; and a strange thing it was thought to be, among my relations and acquaintance. Such as were esteemed able ministers, (and I formerly delighted to hear,) were sent to persuade me; but I could not consent and be *(page 14)* clear. My answer to them was: "He that doubteth is damned."

After some time I waded through this difficulty, but soon after I unhappily went from the simplicity into notions, and changed my ways often, and ran from one notion into another, not finding satisfaction nor assurance that I should obtain what my soul desired, in the several ways and notions which I sought satisfaction in. I was weary of prayers, and such like exercises, finding no peace therefrom; nor could I lift up my hands without doubting, nor call God father. In this state, and for this cause, I gave over all manner of religious exercises in my family and in private, with much grief, for my delight was in being exercised about religion. I left not those things in a loose mind, as some judged that kept in them; for had I found I performed thereby what the Lord required of me, and was well pleased with, I could gladly have continued in the practice of them; I being zealously affected about the several things that were *(page 15)* accounted duties; a zealous sabbath-keeper, and fasting often; praying in private, rarely less than three times a day, many times oftener; a hearer of sermons on all occasions, both lectures, fasts, and thanksgiving. Most of the day was used to be spent in reading the scriptures or praying, or such like. I dared not to go to bed till I had prayed, nor pray till I had read scripture, and felt my heart warmed thereby, or by meditation. I had so great a zeal and delight in the exercise of religious duties, that when I questioned not but it was right, I have often in the day sought remote places to pray in, such as the fields, gardens, or out-houses, when I could not be private in the house. I was so vehement in prayer, that I thought no place too private to pray in, for I could not but be loud in the earnest pouring out of my soul. Oh! this was not parted with but because I found it polluted, and my rest must not be there.

I now had my conversation among a people that had no religion, being ashamed *(page 16)* to be thought religious, or do any thing that was called so, not finding my heart with the appearance. And now I loathed whatever profession any one made, and thought the professors of every sort worse than the profane, they boasted so much of what I knew they had not attained to; I having been zealous in all things which they pretended to, and could not find the purging of the heart, or answer of acceptation from the Lord.

In this restless state I entertained every sort of notion that arose in that day, and for a time applied myself to get out of them whatever I could; but still sorrow and trouble was the end of all, and I began to conclude that the Lord and his truth was, but that it was not made known to any upon earth; and I determined no more to enquire after Him or it, for it was in vain to seek Him, being not to be found. For some time, pursuant to my resolution, I thought nothing about religion, but minded recreations as they are called, and ran into many excesses and vanities; as foolish *(page 17)* mirth, carding, dancing, singing, and frequenting of music meetings; and made many vain visits at jovial eatings and drinkings, to satisfy the extravagant appetite, and please the vain mind with curiosities; gratifying the lust of the eye, the lust of the flesh, and the pride of life. I also frequented other places of pleasure, where vain people resorted to show themselves, and to see others in the like excess of folly in apparel; riding about from place to place, in the airy mind. But in the midst of all this my heart was con-

stantly sad, and pained beyond expression; and after a pretty long in-
dulgence in such follies, I retired for several days, and was in great trouble
and anguish.

To all this excess and folly I was not hurried by being captivated
with such things, but sought in them relief from the discontent of my
mind; not having found what I sought after, and longed for, in the practice of religious duties. I would often say to myself, What is all this to
me? I could easily leave it all, for my heart is not *(page 18)* satisfied therewith. I do these things because I am weary, and know not what else to
do: it is not my delight, it hath not power over me. I had rather serve
the Lord, if I knew how acceptably.

In this restless, distressed state, I often retired into the country, without any company but my daughter and her maid; and there I spent
many hours each day in bemoaning myself, and desiring the knowledge
of the truth; but was still deceived, and fell in with some delusive notions or other, that wounded me, and left me without any clearness or
certainty. One night, in this retired place, I went to bed very disconso-
lately and sad, through the great and afflicting exercise of my mind. I
dreamed that night that I saw a book of hieroglyphics of religion, of
things to come in the church, or a religious state. I thought I took no
delight in them, nor felt any closing in my mind with them, though
magnified by those that showed them. I turned from them greatly oppressed, and it being evening, went out from the company *(page 19)* into
a field, sorrowing, and lifting up my eyes to heaven, cried: "Lord, suffer
me no more to fall in with any wrong way, but show me the truth."
Immediately I thought the sky opened, and a bright light, like fire, fell
upon my hand, which so frightened me that I awoke, and cried out so
that my daughter's servant, who was in the room, not gone to bed,
came to my bed-side to know what was the matter with me. I trembled
a long while after, yet knew not what to turn to; or rather believing
there was nothing manifest since the apostles' days, that was true religion; for I knew nothing to be so certainly of God, that I could shed my
blood in the defence of it.

One day, as I was going through London, from a country-house, I
could not pass through the crowd, it being the day the Lord Mayor was
sworn: I was obliged to go into a house till it was over. I, being burdened with the vanity of their show, said to a professor that stood by
me: "What benefit have we from all this bloodshed, *(page 20)* and Charles
being kept out of the nation, seeing all these follies are again allowed?"
He answered: "None, that he knew of, except the enjoyment of true

religion." I replied, "that it is a benefit to you that have a religion to be protected in the exercise of, but it is none to me."

But here I must mention a state that I then knew, notwithstanding all my darkness and distress about religion, which was in nothing to be careful, but in all cases to let my requests be known to the Lord in sighs and groans; and help he was graciously pleased to afford me in the most confused disquieted estate I ever knew; even in that day when I had no religion I could call true. Wonderful is the remembrance of his kindness! If I wanted to hire a servant, or remove to any place, or do any other thing that concerned my condition in this world, I always retired and waited upon the Lord, to see what the day would bring forth; and as things presented to me I would embrace them, without making much enquiry after accommodations *(page 21)* of that kind; but was in all things else in a dissatisfied, hurried condition; for I thought the beloved of my soul was neither night nor day with me. Yet in the anguish of my soul I would cry to Him, and beseech that if I might not come to Him as a child, not having the spirit of sonship, yet, as he was my Creator, I might approach him as the beasts that have their food from him: "For, Lord, thou knowest I cannot move or breathe as thy creature, without thee: help is only in thee. If thou art inaccessible in thy own glory, yet I can only have help where it is to be had, and thou only hast power to help me."

O, the distress I felt at this time! Having never dared to kneel down to pray for years, because I could not in truth call God father, and dared not mock or be formal in the thing. Sometimes I should be melted into tears, and feel inexpressible tenderness; and then, not knowing from whence it proceeded, and being ready to judge all religion, I thought it was some *(page 22)* influence from the planets that governed the body, and so accounted for my being sometimes hard, and sometimes tender, as being under such or such a planet; but dared not to own any thing in me to be of God, or that I felt any influence of his good spirit upon my heart; but I was like the parched heath, and the hunted hart for water, so great was my thirst after that which I did not believe was near me.

My mind being thus almost continually exercised, I dreamed that I was sitting alone, retired and sad; and as I was sitting, I heard a very loud, confused noise: some shrieking, yelling, and roaring in a piteous, doleful manner; others casting up their caps, and hallooing in a way of triumph and joy. I listening to find out what the matter was, it was manifested to me that Christ was come; and the different noises I heard were expressive of the different states the people were in at his coming—some in joy, some in extreme sorrow and amazement. I waited in much dread to see the issue; at length I found *(page 23)* that neither the joying nor sorrowing part of the multitude were they that truly knew of his coming, but were agitated by a false rumour. So I abode still in the room solitary, and found I was not to join with either party, but to be still, and not affected with the thing at all, nor go forth to enquire about it. Sitting thus a while, all was silent. Remaining still in the same place, cool and low in my mind, all this distracted noise being over, one came in, and speaking in a low voice said: "Christ is come indeed, and is in the next room; and with him is the bride, the Lamb's wife." At this my heart secretly leaped within me, and I was ready to get up to go and express my love to him, and joy at his coming; but something within me stopped me, and bade me not to be hasty, but patiently, coolly, softly, and soberly go into the next room, which I did, and stood just within the entrance of a spacious hall, trembling and rejoicing, but dared not to go near to him, for it was said unto me: "Stay and see whether he will own thee, *(page 24)* or take thee to be such an one as thou lookest upon thyself to be." So I stood still at a great distance, at the lower end of the hall, and Christ was at the upper end, whose appearance was that of a fresh, lovely youth, clad in gray cloth, very plain and neat, (at this time I had never heard of the Quakers or their habit,) of a sweet, affable, and courteous carriage. I saw him embrace several poor, old, simple people, whose appearance was very contemptible and mean, without wisdom or beauty. I seeing this, concluded within myself, that though he appeared young, his discretion and wisdom were great; for he must behold some hidden worth in these people, who to me seem so mean, so unlovely and simple. At last he beckoned to me to come near him, of which I was very glad. I went tremblingly and lowly; not lifted up, but in great weightiness and dread.

After a little while it was said: "The Lamb's wife is also come;" at which I beheld a beautiful young woman, slender, modest, and grave, in plain garments, becoming *(page 25)* and graceful. Her image was fully answering his, as a brother and sister. After I had beheld all this, and joyed in it, I spoke to Thomas Zachary, (whom I then knew to be a seeker after the Lord, though tossed, like myself, in the many ways, yet pressing after life,) saying: "Seeing Christ is come indeed, and few know it; and those that in the confusion mourned or rejoiced, know it not, but Christ is hid from them; let us take the king's house at Greenwich, and let us dwell with and enjoy him there, from those that look for him and cannot find him." Without receiving any reply, I awoke.

Several years after this, I had another dream about Friends in their present state, which I shall relate in the close.

In the situation I mentioned, of being wearied in seeking and not finding, I married my dear husband, Isaac Pennington [*sic*]. My love was drawn towards him, because I found he saw the deceit of all *(page 26)* nations, and lay as one that refused to be comforted by any appearance of religion, until he came to His temple, "who is truth and no lie." All things that appeared to be religion and were not so, were very manifest to him; so that, till then, he was sick and weary of all appearances. My heart became united to him, and I desired to be made serviceable to him in his disconsolate condition; for he was as one alone and miserable in this world. I gave up much to be a companion to him in his suffering state. And oh! the groans and cries in secret that were raised in me, that I might be visited of the Lord, and come to the knowledge of his way; and that my feet might be turned into that way, before I went hence, if I never walked one step in it, to my joy or peace; yet that I might know myself in it, or turned to it, though all my time were spent in sorrow and exercise.

I resolved never to go back to those things I had left, having discovered death and darkness to be in them; but would *(page 27)* rather be without a religion, until the Lord taught me one. Many times, when alone, did I reason thus: "Why should I not know the way of life? For if the Lord would give me all in this world, it would not satisfy me." Nay, I would cry out: "I care not for a portion in this life: give it to those who care for it. I am miserable with it: it is acceptance with thee I desire, and that alone can satisfy me."

Whilst I was in this state I heard of a new people, called Quakers. I resolved not to enquire after them, nor what principles they held. For a year or more after I heard of them in the north, I heard nothing of their way, except that they used *thee* and *thou*; and I saw a book written in the plain language, by George Fox. I remember that I thought it very ridiculous, so minded neither the people nor the book, except that it was to scoff at them and it. Though I thus despised this people, I had sometimes a desire to *(page 28)* go to one of their meetings, if I could, unknown, and to hear them pray, for I was quite weary of doctrines; but I believed if I was with them when they prayed, I should be able to feel whether they were of the Lord or not. I endeavoured to stifle this desire, not knowing how to get to one of their meetings unknown; and if it should be known, I thought it would be reported that I was one of them.

One day, as my husband and I were walking in a park, a man, that for a little time had frequented the quakers' meetings, saw us as he rode by, in our gay, vain apparel. He cried out to us against our pride, &c. at which I scoffed, and said he was a public preacher indeed, who preached in the highways. He turned back again, saying he had a love for my husband, seeing grace in his looks. He drew nigh to the pales, and spoke of the light and grace which had appeared to all men. My husband and he engaged in discourse. The man of the house coming up, invited the stranger in: he was but *(page 29)* young, and my husband too hard for him in the fleshly wisdom. He told my husband he would bring a man to him the next day, that should answer all his questions, or objec- tions, who, as I afterwards understood, was George Fox. He came again the next day, and left word that the friend he intended to bring could not well come; but some others, he believed, would be with us about the second hour; at which time came Thomas Curtis and William Simpson.

My mind was somewhat affected by the man who had discoursed with us the night before; and though I thought him weak in managing the arguments he endeavoured to support, yet many scriptures which he mentioned stuck with me very weightily: they were such as showed to me the vanity of many practices I was in; which made me very seri- ous, and soberly inclined to hear what these men had to say. Their solid and weighty carriage struck a dread over me. I now knew that they came in the power and authority of the Lord, to *(page 30)* visit us, and that the Lord was with them. All in the room were sensible of the Lord's power manifest in them. Thomas Curtis repeated this scripture: "He that will know my doctrine, must do my commands." Immediately it arose in my mind, that if I would know whether that was truth they had spoken or not, I must do what I knew to be the Lord's will. What was contrary to it was now set before me, as to be removed; and I must come into a state of entire obedience, before I could be in a capacity to perceive or discover what it was which they laid down for their prin- ciples. This wrought mightily in me. Things which I had slighted much, now seemed to have power over me. Terrible was the Lord against the vain and evil inclinations in me, which made me, night and day, to cry out; and if I did but cease a little, then I grieved for fear I should again be reconciled to the things which I felt under judgment, and had a just detestation of. Oh! how I did beg not to be left secure or quiet till the *(page 31)* evil was done away. How often did this run through my mind: "Ye will not come to me, that ye may have life." "It is true I am undone if I come not to thee, but I cannot come, unless I leave that which cleaveth close unto me, and I cannot part with it."

I saw the Lord would be just in casting me off, and not giving me life; for I would not come from my beloved lusts, to him, for life. Oh! the pain I felt still. The wrath of God was more than I could bear. Oh! in what bitterness and distress was I involved! A little time after the friends' visit before mentioned, one night on my bed it was said unto me: "Be not hasty to join these people called Quakers." I never had peace or quiet from a sore exercise for many months, till I was, by the stroke of judgment, brought off from all those things, which I found the light made manifest to be deceit, bondage, and vanity, the spirit of the world, &c. and I given up to be a fool and a reproach, and to take up the cross to my honour and reputation in *(page 32)* the world. The contemplation of those things cost me many tears, doleful nights and days; not now disputing against the doctrine preached by the Friends, but exercised against taking up the cross to the language, fashions, customs, titles, honour, and esteem in the world.

My relations made this cross very heavy; but as at length I happily gave up, divested of reasonings, not consulting how to provide for the flesh, I received strength to attend the meetings of these despised people, which I never intended to meddle with, but found truly of the Lord, and my heart owned them. I longed to be one of them, and minded not the cost or pain; but judged it would be well worth my utmost cost and pain to witness such a change as I saw in them—such power over their corruptions. I had heard objected against them, that they wrought not miracles; but I said that they did great miracles, in that they turned them that were in the world and the fellowship of it, from all such things. Thus, by taking up the cross, I received strength *(page 33)* against many things which I had thought impossible to deny; but many tears did I shed, and bitterness of soul did I experience, before I came thither; and often cried out: "I shall one day fall by the overpowering of the enemy." But oh! the joy that filled my soul in the first meeting ever held in our house at Chalfont. To this day I have a fresh remembrance of it. It was then the Lord enabled me to worship him in that which was undoubtedly his own, and give up my whole strength, yea, to swim in the life which overcame me that day. Oh! long had I desired to worship him with acceptation, and lift up my hands without doubting, which I witnessed that day in that assembly. I acknowledged his great mercy and wonderful kindness; for I could say, "This is it which I have longed and waited for, and feared I never should have experienced."

Many trials have I been exercised with since, but they were all from the Lord, who strengthened my life in them. Yet, *(page 34)* after all this, I suffered my mind to run out into prejudice against some particular Friends. This was a sore hurt unto me: but after a time of deep, secret sorrow, the Lord removed the wrong thing from me, blessing me with a large portion of his light, and the love and acceptance of his beloved ones. And he hath many times refreshed my soul in his presence, and given me assurance that I knew that estate in which he will never leave me, nor suffer me to be drawn from all which he has graciously fulfilled; for though various infirmities and temptations beset me, yet my heart cleaveth unto the Lord, in the everlasting bonds that can never be broken. In his light do I see those temptations and infirmities: there do I bemoan myself unto him, and feel faith and strength, which give the victory. Though it keeps me low in the sense of my own weakness, yet it quickens in me a lively hope of seeing Satan trodden down under foot by his all-sufficient grace. I feel and know when I have slipped in word, deed, or thought; *(page 35)* and also know where my help lieth, who is my advocate, and have recourse to him who pardons and heals, and gives me to overcome, setting me on my watch-tower: and though the enemy is suffered to prove me, in order more and more to wean me from any dependance but upon the mighty, Jehovah, I believe he will never be able to prevail against me. Oh! that I may keep on my watch continually: knowing, the Lord only can make war with this dragon. Oh! that I may, by discovering my own weakness, ever be tender of the tempted; watching and praying, lest I also be tempted. Sweet is this state, though low; for in it I receive my daily bread, and enjoy that which he handeth forth continually; and live not, but as he breatheth the breath of life upon me every moment.

POSTSCRIPT.

After I had written the foregoing, it lay by me a considerable time. One day it came into my mind to leave it with Elizabeth Walmsby, to keep till after my decease, and desire her then to show *(page 36)* it to such as had a love for me. So one day I desired her to meet me at John Mannock's, at Giles-Chalfont. There I spoke to her about it, read it to her, and desired she would write it out, (intending to leave it with her,) but it afterwards went out of mind. It was in the year 1668 that I made this proposal; it is now almost 1672, when I found it among some other writings, and reading it over, found it was a true, though brief account, of many passages from my childhood to the time it was written. I am now willing to have it written over fair, for the use of my children, and some few particular friends who know and feel me in that which hungereth and thirsteth after righteousness, and many times being livingly satisfied in God my life.

MARY PENNINGTON.

I now come to relate a dream that I had at Worminghurst, between twenty and thirty years after the foregoing, mentioned *(page 37)* in page the 25th. I insert it here, because, at the close, I dreamed that I related a part of the foregoing one.

Being at Worminghurst, at my son Penn's, 30th of the 7th Month, 1676, at night, in bed and asleep, I dreamed I was with two other persons in an upper room; (who the persons were I do not perfectly remember;) I looking out of the window, saw the sky very black and dismal, yea, the appearance of it to me, and the rest that beheld it, was very dreadful; but keeping cool and low in our spirits, to see what would follow, at length the sky grew thinner, and began to clear; not by the descending of rain, in the usual way, but by one great vent of water, issuing out of the midst of these thick clouds, which seemed quite driven away, divided into heaps, and a great clearness left in the midst; out of which clearness appeared a very bright head, breast, and arms, the complete upper part of a man, very beautiful, (like pictures I have seen to represent an angel form,) holding in his hand a long, *(page 38)* green bough; not so green as a laurel, but of a sea, or willow-green colour, resembling a palm. This palm or bough he held over his head, which to us was such a signification of *good*, that both by voice and action we made acclamations of joy; uttering forth, through fulness of joy and sense, indistinct sounds, expressive of being overcome with the greatness of our sense, which we could not set forth in words: sounds something like, oh! oh! ah! ah! in an astonished manner; spreading our hands, and running swiftly about the room, with constant acclamations of admiration and joy, signifying, by our manner, a being likely to burst with astonishment and joy, and our tongues or voice unable to deliver us of what we were so big with. After a little while there appeared lower in the element, nearer the earth, in an oval, transparent glass, a man and a woman, (not in resemblance, but real persons;) the man wore a greater majesty and sweetness than I ever saw with mortal: his hair was brown, his eyes black and sparkling, his *(page 39)* complexion ruddy; piercing dominion in his countenance, blendid with affability, great gentleness, and kindness. The woman resembled him in features and complexion; but appeared tender and bashful, yet quick-sighted.

After having beheld these heavenly forms awhile, we, in a sense of their majesty and dominion, did reverence to them, falling on our faces in a solemn, not in a disturbed, confused manner, crying glory! glory! glory! glory! glory! at which the man ascended, but the woman came down to us, and spoke to us with great gravity and sweetness; the words I have forgotten, but the purport of them was, that we should not be formal, nor fall out. Then she disappeared, and we looked one at another, after a melted, serious manner; and I said to them: "This is a vision, to signify to us some great matter and glorious appearance; more glorious than the Quakers at their first coming forth. I added, that I had a distinct vision and sight of such state in a dream, before ever I heard of a *(page 40)* Quaker, but it was in a more simple, plain manner than this. For I then saw Christ like a fresh, sweet, innocent youth, clad in light gray, neat, but plain; and so, likewise, was the bride, the Lamb's wife, in the same manner: but under this plain appearance, there was deep wisdom and discernment; for I saw him own and embrace, such as I could not see any acceptable thing in; such as I thought Christ would not own, being old, poor, and contemptible women. But now," said I, "his countenance and garb are altered: in the former was united to sweetness, majesty; in the latter, to plainness and neatness is joined resplendence." Without any further conversation I awoke.

I shall now proceed to make an addition to the foregoing narrative. After my dear husband and I had received the truth of God's faithful servants, to the light and grace in the heart, we became obedient to the heavenly voice, receiving the truth in the love of it, and took up the cross to the *(page 41)* customs, language, friendships, titles, and honours of this world; and endured, patiently, despisings, reproaches, cruel mockings, and scornings, from relations, acquaintances, and neighbours; those of our own rank, and those below us, nay, even our own servants. To every class we were a by-word: they would wag the head at us, accounting us fools, mad, and bewitched. As such, they stoned, abused, and imprisoned us, at several towns and meetings where we went. This not being enough to prove us, and work for us a far more exceeding weight of glory, it pleased the Lord to try us by the loss of our estate, which was wrongfully withheld from us, by our relations sueing us unrighteously. Our own tenants withheld what the law gave, and put us into the Court of Chancery, because we could not swear. Our relations also taking that advantage, we were put out of our dwelling-house, in an injurious, unrighteous manner. Thus we were stripped of my husband's estate, and a great part of mine.

(page 42) After this, we were tossed up and down from place to place, to our great weariness and charge. We had no place to abide in, near our former habitation at Chalfont, where our meetings used to be held; yet were we pressed in our spirits to stay amongst the gathered flock, if a place could be found any way convenient, though but ordinarily decent. We sought within the compass of four or five miles, but could find none; yet we had such a sense that was our proper place, that we had not freedom to settle any where else. So we boarded at Waltham Abbey, for the sake of having our children accommodated at a school there, and desired our friends to enquire after, or provide a place for us, at a Friend's house, to winter in, hoping to be provided with a house against the ensuing summer.

All the time we were seeking for a place, we never entertained a thought of buying one to settle ourselves in; not choosing to be cumbered with either house or land by purchase, as we both desired a disentangled *(page 43)* state. I, seeing no provision likely to be made for us in this country, near Friends, told my husband, that, if we must leave them, I should choose to go to my own estate in Kent; which proposal he did not approve of, objecting against the badness of the air, and dirtiness of the place.

I was now greatly perplexed about what to do: my husband's objections, together with my own extreme unwillingness to leave those people whom we had been instrumental in gathering to the truth, and who had known our unjust sufferings respecting our estate, and many others of our trials, and had compassionated us: (we had suffered together, and had been comforted together:) I say, these considerations, and to be obliged to go, and not to go to my own estate, was cause of sore exercise to me. How irksome was it to think of going among strangers! The people in our neighbourhood knew of our former affluence, and now pitied us for being so stripped; and did not expect *(page 44)* great things of us, suitable to our rank in the world; but wondered how it was that we could still support a degree of decency in our way of living, and were able to pay every one their own. We contentedly submitted to mean things, and so remained honourable before them.

Whilst I was thus distressed, and we had nearly concluded on going to Waltham Abbey, R.T. came to see us, and much bewailed our going out of the country, and having no place near them to return to. At length he asked why we did not buy some little place near them? I replied, that our circumstances would not admit of it; for we had not one hundred pounds, beside rents becoming due; and, that to do that, we must sell some of my estate. He said he had an uncle, that had a little place that he would sell for about thirty pounds a year, that stood about a mile from the meeting-house, in a healthy situation; that there was a house on it, which might be trimmed up, and made habitable for a little expense. My husband was not there *(page 45)* when mention was made of this place. Soon after T.B. came in: I told him of the proposal made by R.T. He encouraged the thing, saying, he had heard there were some rooms in the house that might serve. That night Thomas Elwood came out of Kent, and told me he had much to do to come back without selling my farm at Westbeer.

I laid all these things together, and said: "I think our best way is to sell Westbeer, and purchase this place which R.T. has mentioned; and, with the overplus of the money, put the house in a condition to receive us." For now I saw no other method for our remaining in the country. Next day I took Anne Bull with me, and went on foot to Woodside, to John Humphrey's house, to view it and its situation. We came in by Hill's Lane, through the orchard. The house appeared in such a ruinous condition, so unlikely to be fitted up, that I did not go into it; and we gave over all thoughts about it, till we were disappointed of a house at Beacon's *(page 46)* field, which my husband was in a treaty about. Upon this we were pressed to go and see the house, which T.E. H.B. and I did. Whilst I went about the house, they viewed the grounds. In less than half an hour I had the whole thing clearly in my mind, what to pull down, and what to add; and thought it might be done with the overplus money of the sale of Westbeer, that being valued at fifty pounds a year, and this at thirty. I was quite reconciled to the thing, and willing to treat about it. The day we went to see it, we walked to Chalfont, and took my son Penn's coach thither, desiring him to make enquiry respecting the title, &c. and let us know at Waltham; which he did, and sent us word that the title was clear, but that it was judged fifty pounds too dear.

After reading this information, my mind was much retired to the Lord, desiring that if this was the place we ought to settle in, he would be pleased to order it for us. Seeing we had now lost all but my estate, and had no other provision for ourselves or *(page 47)* children, and were so tossed about, without having any dwelling-place, I requested my husband to give me leave to engage for it; for my mind was quite easy so

to do. I told him he should not be troubled about the building; that
should be my care, (he being very averse to building.) At length he,
considering that the estate was mine, that he had lost all his own, and
had been the innocent cause of bringing great sufferings upon me, he
willingly consented that I should use my own mind about it; adding,
that it was, and ever should be his delight, to gratify me in every respect. So I sent to desire my friends to conclude for it; saying, I did not
mind fifty pounds, if they thought it would answer for us in other re-
spects. The bargain was concluded. I often prayed, with tears, that I
might be kept free from entanglements and cumber, and that it might
prove such a habitation as would manifest that the Lord was again restoring us, and had regard unto us. I went cheerfully and industriously
about the business of making *(page 48)* alterations, entreating the Lord
that I might go through it in his fear, keeping my mind from cumber or
darkness. Every difficulty seemed to vanish, and I went on to plant,
and make provision for the building; but I was put out of my own way
by surveyors, who were for raising from the ground a new part. My husband falling in with it, I would not contend about it; though it brought
great trouble upon me, for I could not see my way about the business
as before; nor could I see the end of it, it being far beyond my own
proposal; and I thought I could not compass it, on account of the great
charge. I took no pleasure in doing any thing about it: I fell ill, and
could not look after it. Great was my exercise: one while fearing the
Lord did not approve of our undertaking, and another while that I
did wrong in consenting to it. I would often say: "Lord, thou knowest I
did not seek great things for myself: I desired not a fine habitation."
As I intended doing it, it would have been very ordinary. When I first
(page 49) consented to the addition, the very great expense was not
discerned by me. The Lord knew my earnest prayers, close exercise,
and honest intent.

  After a while I felt freedom to go on, and was freed from care or
disquiet. The building was wholly managed by me, with great ease and
cheerfulness. Part of the old house undesignedly fell down. I was most
remarkably preserved from being hurt thereby, yet the loss was a little trial
to me; but after that all things went on well, and whenever I had occasion to pay money, I never wanted it. Having contracted our family greatly;
the rents coming in; and having sold some old houses, bark, and several
other things, instead of pain, I had now pleasure in laying out my money.
Indeed, my mind was so daily to the Lord in this affair, and I was so
constantly provided with money, that I often thought, and sometimes

said, that if I had lived when building houses for the service of the Lord was accepted and *(page 50)* blessed, I could not have had a sweeter, stiller, and pleasanter time. I set all things in order in the morning, before I want to meeting, and so left them till my return; rarely finding them rise up in my mind when going to, coming from, or whilst sitting in meeting: so my mind was mercifully kept in a sweet, savoury frame.

My chief care about my business in hand, was, by my own eye, to prevent any waste; which was done without any disquiet, fretting, or anger. I lay down sweetly, and rested pleasantly, and awoke under a grateful sense of the Lord's goodness to me. The labour of my body kept it healthy, and my mind was easy. In less than four years the building was completed, except the wash-house part. I could have compassed it in much less time, but then I should have been straitened for money: my doing it by degrees, made it steal on undiscerned, in point of expense; the whole of which amounted, in planting, building, &c. to but about one hundred pounds. During this expensive time, we *(page 51)* did not omit being helpful, by giving or lending to such as were in distress.

And now the Lord has seen good to make me a widow, and leave me in a desolate condition, by depriving me of my dear companion; yet, through his mercy, I am quite disentangled, and in a very easy state as to outward things. I have often desired the Lord to make way so for me, as that I might continually wait upon him, without distraction or the cumber of outward things. I most thankfully, and gratefully, and humbly, under a deep sense of the Lord's kind and gracious dealing with me, receive the disposal of my lands from his hands. Through his kindness I have cleared off great part of the mortgage that was upon them, and paid most of my bond debts; and can now very easily manage the land in my hands. And in this 4th month, 1680, I have made my will, and disposed of my estate, which is clear of any considerable debt. I have left a handsome provision for T.P. *(page 52)* M.P. and enough for my younger children, to put them out to trades or decent callings; and also provision for the payment of my legacies and debts. I call my children's a handsome provision, considering it is all out of my own inheritance, having nothing of their father's to provide for them with.

And now I am mourning for the loss of my dear, worthy companion, and exercised with the great sickness and weakness of my children; but my outward situation and habitation is to my heart's content. I have no great family to cumber me, am private, and have leisure to apply my heart unto wisdom, in the numbering of my days to be but few; holding myself in readiness to bid farewell to all transitory things. In reference to my outward affairs, having set my house in order, I am waiting, sensible of the approach of death; having no desire after life, enjoying the satisfaction that I shall leave my children in an orderly way, and having less need of me, than when things were less contracted and *(page 53)* settled. I feel that death is a king of terrors, and know that my strength to triumph over him, must be given me by the Lord, at the very season when the trying time cometh. My sight to-day of things beyond the grave, will be insufficient in that hour, to keep me from the sting of death when he comes. It is the Lord alone will then be able to stand by me, and help me to resist the evil one, who is very busy when the tabernacle is dissolving: his work being at an end "when the earthen vessel is broken." O, Lord, what quiet, safety, or ease is there in any state but that wherein we feel thy living power. All desirable things are in this; and nothing but sorrow, amazement, anguish, distress, grief, perplexity, woe, and misery, and what not, out of it. O let me by helped by thy power, and in it walk with thee, in thy pure fear; and then I matter not how low, how unseen I am in this world, nor how little friendship, or any pleasant thing I have in it. I have found thy power to be sufficient for every *(page 54)* good word and work, when stripped of every pleasant picture, or acceptable, or other helpful things. O Lord, thou knowest what I have yet to go through in this world; but my hope is in thy mercy, to guide and support. Aided by thee, I need not be doubtful or concerned about what is to come upon me.

Thus far I wrote before I went to Edmonton, which was in the sixth Month, 1680. It appeared as if I was to go thither, on purpose to put all the foregoing things in practice, and to be proved by the Lord according to what I have before written; and to be exercised by him in all the things that were in my view when I set my house in order, and that I was to return no more. In about a week after my arrival, it pleased the Lord to visit me with a violent burning fever. It was the sorest bodily affliction I had ever experienced since I was born: indeed, it was very tedious and trying to me, insomuch that I made my moan in these doleful words: "distress! distress!" finding these *(page 55)* words comprehended all my feelings, which were sickness, uneasiness, want of rest, lowness of spirits, &c. besides ill accommodations in the house, it being at a school. I was greatly disturbed, and but a little attendance was to be had.

All these things made it very heavy upon me; far from my own house, where I might have needed nothing. All this was attended with many aggravations. My two youngest children lay sick in the same room, one of them in the same bed with me; my elder children many miles from

me, ignorant of my melancholy situation, now most desperate; my physician and others about me believing I could never recover. In all this
illness I had scarcely one quarter of an hour wherein I should have been
able to do any thing about my outward affairs, if I had then had it to do;
but such was the eminent kindness and mercy of the Lord to me, that
he put it into my heart to consider that it may be, I might never return
home again, as he did into the heart of my dear *(page 56)* husband. So I
had nothing to do in this sickness, but to suffer patiently, waiting upon
the Lord; and, if it had been his will, to lie down this body without
distraction about outward concerns.

These memorable, merciful dealings of the Lord with me, I now re-
count, the 3d day of the 9th Mo. 1681, in an humble sense of his mercy,
being still in bed, unrecovered of the forementioned illness, it being
eight months since. And now it is in my heart, in the holy fear of the
most High, to declare to you, my dear children, of what great service it
was to me in my illness, to have nothing to do but to die, if it had been
his holy will: for the Lord was pleased to assure me of his favour, and
that I should not go down to the pit with the wicked, but should have
a mansion, according to his good pleasure, in his holy habitation. This
assurance left me in a quiet state, out of the feelings of the sting of
death, not having the least desire to live. Though I did not witness any
great measure of triumph or joy, yet I could say: *(page 57)* "Lord, it is
enough: I am quiet and still, and have not a thought about any thing
that is to be done in preparation for my going hence. Though thou
afflictest, thou makest me content both night and day."

In about fourteen days my fever was abated, and in about a month I
came from Edmonton to London, favoured with some degree of strength.
After having been absent about seven weeks, the Lord brought me home
again to my own house. That very night I was smitten with a distemper,
from which I remain weak and low in body to this day; on which morning, it springs in my mind to express something of the dealings of the
Lord with me in my present sickness and exercises.

On the 27th of the 4th Mo. in the morning, as I was waiting upon
the Lord with some of my family, I found an inclination to mention the
continuation of my illness to this day, which, from the time of my being
visited, is near a year; in all which time, such was the goodness of the
Lord to me, that as it was said of Job *(page 58)* "In all this he sinned not,
nor charged God foolishly," so I may say, (through the power of his
might,) in all this time I have been a stranger to a murmuring, complaining mind; but this hath been my constant language: "It is well I

have no very grievous thing to undergo," except some severe fits of the stone, which have been full of anguish and misery. And the Lord hath graciously stopped my desires after every pleasant thing, that I have not been at all uneasy at my long confinement, for the most part to my bed; and to this present day to my chamber, where I have very little comfort from sleep, or pleasantness from food, or any thing of that kind. Yet I have not found in my heart to ask of the Lord to be restored to my former health and strength, that I might have the pleasure of natural sleep, and eating my food with acceptation to my palate, or be able to attend to my outward affairs, or go abroad in the air to view the beautiful creation; but all I have desired respecting my house of clay is, that *(page 59)* the Lord would be mercifully pleased to make my future fits of my distemper less severe that the former ones were; in which I have cried earnestly to the Lord for help, or that he would be pleased to direct me to some outward means that would lessen my anguish. Except in these violent fits, I have not asked any thing of the lord concerning life or health, but here rather felt pleasantness from being debarred from those things which are acceptable to the senses; because thereby I have been drawn nearer to the Lord, and have waited upon him with much less distraction than when in my health. I have many times said, within myself: "Oh! this is sweet and easy. He makes my bed in my sickness, and withholds my eyes from sleeping, to converse with him."

Death hath many times been presented to me, which I have rather embraced than shrunk from; for the most part finding a kind of yielding up in my spirit to die, like as it is said: "He yielded up the ghost." Even before I came to be settled in the *(page 60)* truth, I entertained an awful sense of death, and was in subjection to the fear of it. But now that fear of death, and the state of death is removed; but there remaineth still a deep sense of the passage from time to eternity, how strait, hard, and difficult it is; and even many times to those on whom the second death hath no power, yet subjected to such feelings as were our dear Lord's and Saviour's, when in agony he cried out: "My God! my God! why hast thou forsaken me!"

Another striking instance is that of my certainly blessed husband, whose mind was constantly with the Lord in his last illness; yet, when the last breath was breathing out, his groans were dreadful. I may call them roarings, as it seemed to be, through the disquiet of his soul at that moment. Indeed, this hard passage of his hath so deeply affected me, that I have often since said: "If it be thus with the green tree, how will it be with me, who am to him but as a dry tree."

A

JOURNAL

or

HISTORICAL ACCOUNT

of

the Life, Travels, Sufferings, Christian
Experiences & Labour of Love in the Work
of the Ministry of That Ancient, Eminent
and Faithful Servant of Jesus Christ,

George Fox

Who departed this Life in great Peace with the
Lord the 13th of the 11th Month, 1690

The First Volume.

London.

Printed for Thomas Northcott in George-Yard,
in Lombard Street

MDCXCIV

(Page numbers of original document appear in text as *page _*.)

(page i)

The Testimony of Margaret Fox Concerning her Late Husband GEORGE FOX: *together with a brief Account of some of his Travels, Sufferings, and Hardships endured for the Truth's Sake.*

It having pleased Almighty God to take away my *Dear Husband* out of this *Evil, Troublesome World,* who *was not a Man thereof;* being Chosen out of it, and had his *Life* and *Being* in *another Region,* and his *Testimony* was against the *World,* that the *Deeds* thereof were *evil,* and therefore the *World hated* him: So I am now to give in my Account and *Testimony* for my *Dear Husband,* whom the *Lord* hath taken unto his blessed *Kingdom* and *Glory.* And it is before me from the *Lord,* and in my *View,* to give a *Relation,* and leave upon Record the *Dealings* of the *Lord* with us from the Beginning.

He was the *Instrument* in the *Hand* of the *Lord* in this present *Age,* which he made use of to send forth into the *World,* to preach the *Everlasting Gospel,* which had been hid from many *Ages* and *Generations;* the *Lord* Revealed it unto him, and made him *open* that *New* and *Living Way,* that Leads to *Life Eternal,* when he was but a *Youth,* and a *Stripling.* And when he Declared it in his own Country of *Leicestershire,* and in *Darbyshire, Nottinghamshire* and *Warwickshire,* and his Declaration being against the *Hireling Priests* and their Practices, it raised a Great Fury and Opposition amongst the *Priests* and *People* against him: yet there was always *some,* that owned him in several places; but very few, that stood firm to him, when *Persecution* came on him. There was *he* and *one other* put in *Prison* at *Darby,* but the other *declined,* and left him in *Prison* there; where he continued almost a *whole Year,* and then he was *Released* out of *Prison:* And went on with his *Testimony* abroad, and was put in *Prison* again at *Nottingham;* and there he continued awhile, and after was *Released* again.

(page ii) And then he Travelled on into *Yorkshire,* and passed up and down that Great *County,* and several received him; as *William Dewsbury, Richard Farnsworth, Thomas Aldam,* and others, who all came to be faithful *Ministers* of the *Spirit* of the *Lord.* And he continued in that Country; and Travelled thorow *Holderness* and the *Wowlds,* and abundance were *Convinced;* and several were brought to *Prison* at *York* for their *Testimony* to the *Truth,* both *Men* and *Women:* So that we heard of *such* a *People* that were *Risen,* and we did very much *inquire* after them. And

after awhile he Travelled up farther towards the *Dales* in *Yorkshire*, as *Wensdale* and *Sedbur*; and amongst the *Hills*, *Dales* and *Mountains* he came on, and *Convinced* many of the Eternal *Truth*.

And in the year 1652. it pleased the *Lord* to draw him towards us; so he came on from *Sedbur*, and so to *Westmore-land*, as *Firbank-Chappel*, where *John Blaykling* came with him: and so on to *Preston*, and to *Grarig*, and *Kendal*, and *Under-barrow*, and *Poobank*, and *Cartmel*, and *Staveley*; and so on to *Swarthmore*, my Dwelling-House, whither he brought the blessed Tidings of the Everlasting *Gospel*, which I, and many *Hundreds* in these parts, have cause to praise the *Lord* for. My then Husband, *Thomas Fell*, was not at home at that time, but gone the *Welsh Circuit*, being one of the *Judges* of *Assize*: And our House being a Place open to entertain *Ministers* and Religious People at, one of *George Fox* his Friends brought him hither; where he stayed all Night. And the next day, being a *Lecture* or a *Fast-day*, he went to *Ulverston Steeple-house*, but came not in, till *People* were *gathered*; I and my *Children* had been a long time there before. And when they were *singing* before the *Sermon*, he came in; and when they had done *singing*, he stood up upon a Seat or Form, and desired, *that he might have liberty to speak:* And he that was in the *Pulpit*, said *he might.* And the first words that he spoke were as followeth: *He is Not a* Jew *that is one outward, neither is that* Circumcision *which is outward: But he is a* Jew *that is one inward, and that is* Circumcision *which is of the heart.* And so he went on and said How *that Christ was the* Light *of the* World, *and lighteth every Man that cometh into the World; and that by this* Light *they might be gathered to God*, &c. And I stood up in my *Pew*, and wondered at his *Doctrine*; for I had never heard such before. And then he went on, and opened the *Scriptures* and said, *The Scriptures were the* Prophets' *words, and* Christ's *and the* Apostles' *words, and what, as they spoke, they enjoyed and possessed, and had it from the Lord:* And said, *Then what had any to do with the* Scriptures, *but as they came to the* Spirit *that gave them forth.* *You will say,* Christ *saith this, and the* Apostles *say this; but what canst thou say? Art thou a Child of* Light, *and hast walked in the* Light, *and what thou speakest, is it inwardly from God?* &c. This opened me so, that it *cut* me to the *Heart*; and then I saw clearly, we were all wrong. So I sat down in my *Pew* again, and *cried bitterly*: And I cried in my *Spirit* to the *Lord, We are all Thieves, we are all Thieves; we have taken the (page iii)* Scriptures *in* Words, *and know nothing of them in our selves.* So that served me, that I cannot well tell what he spoke afterwards; but he went on in declaring against the *false Prophets*, and *Priests*, and *Deceivers* of the *People*. And there was one *John Sawrey*, a

Justice of *Peace*, and a *Professor*, that bid the Churchwarden, *Take him away:* And he laid his hands on him several times, and took them off again, and let him alone; and then after a while he gave over, and came to our House again that night. And he spoke in the *Family* amongst the *Servants*, and they were all generally *Convinced*; as *William Caton*, *Thomas Salthouse*, *Mary Askew*, *Anne Clayton*, and several other Servants. And I was stricken into such a sadness, I knew not what to do; my *Husband* being from home. I saw it was the *Truth*, and I could not deny it; and I did, as the *Apostle* saith, I *received the truth in the love of it*: and it was opened to me so clear, that I had never a Tittle in my Heart against it; but I desired the *Lord*, that I might be kept in it, and then I desired no greater *Portion*.

And then he went on to *Dalton*, *Aldingham*, *Dendrum* and *Ramsyde-Chappels* and *Steeple-houses*, and several places up and down, and the *People* followed him mightily; and abundance were *Convinced*, and saw, that which he spoke, was *Truth*: But the *Priests* were all in a Rage. And about *two Weeks* after *James Naylor* and *Richard Farnsworth* followed him, and enquired him out, till they came to *Swarthmore*, and there stayed a while with me at our House, and did me much *Good*; for I was under *great Heaviness* and *Judgment*. But the *Power* of the *Lord* entred upon me, within about *two Weeks*, that he came; and about *three Weeks*-end my *Husband* came home: And many were in a mighty Rage. And a deal of the *Captains* and Great Ones of the Country went to *meet* my then *Husband*, as he was coming home, and informed him, *That a Great Disaster was befallen amongst his* Family, *and that they were* Witches; *and that they had taken us out of our* Religion; *and that he might either set them away, or all the* Country *would be undone*. But no *Weapons* formed against the *Lord*, shall prosper; as you may see hereafter.

So my *Husband* came home greatly offended: And any may think what a Condition I was like to be in, that either I might displease my *Husband*, or offend God; for he was very much troubled with us all in the *House* and *Family*, they had so prepossessed him against *us*. But *James Naylor* and *Richard Farnsworth* were both then at our *House*, and I desired them to come and speak to him; and so they did very *moderately* and *wisely*: But he was at first displeased with them, till they told him *They came in Love and good Will to his house*. And after that he had heard them speak awhile he was better satisfied, and they offered as if they would go away: but I *desired them* to stay and *not to go away yet, for* George Fox *will come this Evening*. And I would have had my *Husband* to have heard them all, and satisfied himself farther *(page iv)* about them;

because they had so prepossest him against them of such *dangerous fearful things* in his coming first home. And then was he pretty *moderate* and *quiet,* and his Dinner being ready, he went to it; and I went in, and sate me down by him. And whilst I was sitting the *Power* of the *Lord* seized upon me, and he was stricken with *Amazement,* and knew not what to think; but was quiet and still. And the *Children* were all quiet and still, and grown Sober, and could not *play* on their *Musick* that they were learning; and all these things made him quiet and still.

And then at Night *George Fox* came: and after *Supper* my *Husband* was sitting in the *Parlour,* and I asked him, *If* George Fox *might come in?* and he said, *Yes.* So *George* came in without any Complement, and walked into the Room, and began to speak presently; and the Family, and *James Naylor,* and *Richard Farnsworth* came all in: and he spoke very excellently, as ever I heard him; and opened *Christ* and the *Apostles Practices,* which they were in, in their Day. And he opened the *Night* of *Apostacy* since the *Apostles Days,* and laid open the *Priests* and their Practices in the *Apostacy;* that if all in *England* had been there, I thought, they could not have denied the *Truth* of those things. And so my *Husband* came to see clearly the *Truth,* of what he spoke, and was very quiet that Night, and said no more, and went to Bed. And next Morning came *Lampit, Priest* of *Ulverston,* and got my *Husband* into the *Garden;* and spake much to him there: But my *Husband* had seen so much the Night before, that the *Priest* got little Entrance upon him. And when the Priest, *Lampit,* was come into the House, *George* spoke sharply to him, and asked him; *When God spoke to him, and called him to go and preach to the people?* But after a while the Priest went away: This was on a *Sixthday* of the *Week* about the *Fifth Month,* 1652. And at our House divers *Friends* were speaking one to another, how there were several *Convinced* here-aways; and we could not tell, where to get a *Meeting:* My *Husband* also being present, he over-heard, and said of his own Accord; *You may Meet here if you will:* And that was the *First Meeting* we had, that he offered of his own *Accord.* And then Notice was given that *Day* and the *next* to *Friends;* and there was a good large *Meeting* the *First-day,* which was the *First Meeting,* that was at *Swarthmore:* and so continued there a *Meeting* from 1652, till 1690. And my *Husband* went that Day to the *Steeple-house,* and none with him but his *Clerk* and his *Groom* that rid with him; and the *Priest* and *People* were all fearfully *troubled:* but praised be the *Lord,* they never got their *Wills* upon us to this day.

And then after a few *Weeks George* went to *Ulverston Steeple-house* again, and the said Justice *Sawrey,* with others, set the *Rude Rabble* upon him, and they beat him so that he fell down as in a *Swoon*, and was sore *bruised* and *black'ned* in his *Body*, and on his *Head* and *Arms*. Then my Husband was not at home: but when he came home, he was displeased that they should do so; *(page v)* and spoke to Justice *Sawrey*, and said, *It was against* Law *to make Riots*. And after that he was sore beat and stoned at *Walney*, till he fell down: And also at *Dalton* was he sore *beat* and abused; so that he had very hard Usage in divers places in these parts. And then when a *Meeting* was settled here, he went again into *Westmoreland*, and settled *Meetings* there; and there was a great *Convincement*, abundance of brave *Ministers* came out there-aways; as *John Camm, John Audland, Francis Howgil, Edward Burrough, Miles Halhead*, and *John Blaykling*, with divers others. He also went over Sands to *Lancaster*, and *Yelland*, and *Kellet*, where *Robert Widders, Richard Hubberthorn*, and *John Lawson*, with many others, were *Convinced*. And about that time he was in those parts, many *Priests* and *Professors* rose up, and falsely accused him for *Blasphemy*, and did endeavour to *take away* his *Life*, and got People to *swear* at a *Sessions* at *Lancaster* that he had spoken *Blasphemy*. But my then *Husband* and Colonel *West*, having had some *Sight* and *Knowledge* of the *Truth*, withstood the *two* Persecuting Justices, *John Sawrey* and *Thompson*; and brought him off, and cleared him: for indeed he was *Innocent*. And after the *Sessions* there was a great *Meeting* in the Town of *Lancaster*; and many of the *Towns People* came in, and many were *Convinced*. And thus he was up and down about *Lancaster, Yelland, Westmoreland*, and some parts of *Yorkshire*, and our parts above one *Year*; in which time there was above *Twenty* and *four Ministers* brought forth, that were ready to go with their *Testimony* of the *Eternal Truth* unto the *World*: And soon after *Francis Howgil* and *John Camm* went to speak to *Oliver Cromwel*.

In the Year 1653. *George's* drawings was into *Cumberland* by *Milholm, Lampley, Embleton* and *Brigham, Pardsey* and *Cockermouth*, where at or near *Embleton* he had a *Dispute* with some *Priests*, as *Larkham* and *Benson*, but chiefly with *John Wilkinson*, a *Preacher* at *Embleton* and *Brigham*; who after was *Convinced*, and owned the *Truth*, and was a serviceable *Minister* both in *England, Ireland*, and *Scotland*. And then he went to *Coldbeck* and several places, till he came to *Carlisle*, and went to their *Steeple-house*: And they *beat* and *abused* him, and had him before the *Magistrates*; who Examined him, and put him in Prison there in the *Common-Gaol* among the Thieves. And at the *Assizes* one *Anthony Pearson*, who had been a *Justice* of *Peace*, and was Convinced at *Appleby* (when he was upon the Bench) by *James Naylor* and *Francis Howgil*, who were then *Prisoners* there, and brought before him; so *Anthony Pearson* spake to the Justices at *Carlisle*, he being acquainted with them, having married his *Wife* out of *Cumberland;* and after awhile they *Released* him. And after he went into several other parts of *Cumberland*, and many were *Convinced*, and owned the *Truth:* and he gathered and settled *Meetings* there amongst them, and up and down in several *Parts* there in the *North*.

(page vi) And in the Year 1654. he went *Southward* to his own Country of *Leicestershire*, visiting *Friends*. And then Colonel *Hacker* sent him to *Oliver Cromwel:* and after his being kept *Prisoner* awhile, he was brought before *Oliver*, and was *Released*. And then he stayed awhile, visiting *Friends* in *London*, and the *Meetings* therein; and so passed Westward to *Bristol*, and visited *Friends* there: and after went into *Cornwal*, where they put him in *Prison* at *Launceston*, and one *Edward Pyot* with him; where he had a bad, long *Imprisonment*. And when he was *Released*, he passed into many parts in that County of *Cornwal*, and settled *Meetings* there. And then he Travelled thorow many *Counties*, visiting *Friends* and settling *Meetings* all along; and so came into the *North*, and to *Swarthmore*, and to *Cumberland*.

And so for *Scotland* he passed in the Year 1657. and there went with him *Robert Widders, James Lancaster, John Grave*, and others. And he Travelled thorow many places in that Nation, as *Douglas, Heads, Hamilton, Glascow*, and to *Edenborough*, where they took him, and carried him before General *Monk*, and the *Council*, and Examined him, and asked him his *Business* into that *Nation:* who Answered; *He came to visit the Seed of God*. And after they had threatened him, and charged him to depart their *Nation* of *Scotland*, they let him go. And then he went to *Linlithgow*, and *Stirling*, and *Johnstons* and many places, visiting the *People;* and several were *Convinced*. And after he had stayed a pretty while, and settled some *Meetings*, he returned into *Northumberland*, and into the *Bishoprick* of *Durham*, visiting *Friends* and settling *Meetings*, as he went; and them returned back again to *Swarthmore*, and stayed amongst *Friends* awhile, and so returned *South* again. And in 1658. Judge *Fell* died.

And in 1660. he came out of the *South* into the *North*, and had a great *General Meeting* about *Balby* in *Yorkshire;* and so came on visiting *Friends* in many places, till he came to *Swarthmore* again. And *King Charles* being then come in, the *Justices* sent out *Warrants*, and took him at *Swarthmore*, charging him in their *Warrants, That he drew away* the King's *Liege People, to the endangering the embruing the Nation in Blood*, and sent him *Prisoner* to *Lancaster-Castle*. And I having a Great *Family*, and he being taken in my House, I was moved of the *Lord* to go to the *King* at *Whitehall*; and took with me a *Declaration*, and an *Information* of our *Principles*; And a long time, and much ado I had, to get to him. But at last, when I got to him, I told him; *If he was Guilty of those things, I was Guilty, for he was taken in my House*: And I gave him the *Paper* of our *principles* and desired *that he would set him at Liberty, as he had promised That none should suffer for tender Consciences, and we were of tender Consciences, and desired nothing but the Liberty of our Consciences.* And then with much ado, after he had been kept *Prisoner* near *half a Year* at *Lancaster*, we got a *Habeas Corpus*, and *Removed* him to the *King's Bench*, where he was *Released.* And then would I gladly have come home to my great *Family*; but was bound in my *Spirit*, and could not have Freedom to get away for a whole *(page vii)* Year. And the *King* had promised me several times, that we would have our *Liberty*: And then the *Monarchy-Men* rose; and then came the *Great* and *General Imprisonment* of *Friends* the Nation thorow: And so could I not have Freedom nor Liberty to come home, till we had got a *General Proclamation* for all our *Friends Liberty*; and then I had *Freedom* and *Peace* to come home.

And in 1663. he came *North* again, and to *Swarthmore*: And then they sent out *Warrants*, and took him again, and had him to *Holcros* before the *Justices*, and tendered him the *Oath of Allegiance*; and sent him *Prisoner* to *Lancaster-Castle.* And about a *Month* after, the *Justices* sent for me also out of my *House*, and tendered me the *Oath*; and sent me *Prisoner* to *Lancaster.* And the next *Assizes* they tendered the *Oath* of *Allegiance* and *Supremacy* to us again *both*, and *Premunired* me: But they had missed the *Date*, and other things in his *Indictment*, and so it was quasht; but they tendered him the *Oath* again, and kept him *Prisoner* a *Year* and an *half* at *Lancaster-Castle.* And then they sent him to *Scarborough-Castle* in *Yorkshire*, where they kept him *Prisoner* close under the *Soldiers* much of a *Year* and an *half*; so that a *Friend* could scarcely have spoken to him: yet after that it pleased the *Lord.* that he was *Released.* But I continued in *Prison*, and a *Prisoner four years* at that time: And an *Order* was procured from the *Council*, whereby I was set at *Liberty.* And in that time I went down into *Cornwall* with my *Son* and *Daughter Lower*, and came back by *London* to the *Yearly Meeting*; and there I met with him again: And then he told me, *The time was drawing on towards our Marriage; but he might first go into* Ireland. And a little before this time was he *Prisoner* in his own Country at *Leicester* for a while; and then *Released.* And so into *Ireland* he went: and I went into *Kent* and *Sussex*; and came back to *London* again: And afterward I went to the *West*, towards *Bristol*, in 1669. and there I stay'd, till he came over from *Ireland*. And then it was *Eleven years* after my former *Husband's Decease*. And in *Ireland* he had had a great *Service* for the *Lord* and his Eternal *Truth* amongst *Friends* and many *People* there, but escaped many *Dangers*, and *Times* of being taken *Prisoner*; they having lain in *Wait* afore-hand for him in many places. And then being return'd, at *Bristol*, he declared his *Intentions* of *Marriage* and there also was our *Marriage* solemnized. And then within *ten Days* after I came homewards; and my *Husband* stayed up and down in the *Countries* amongst *Friends*, visiting them.

And soon after I came home, there came another *Order* from the *Council* to cast me into *Prison* again; and the *Sheriff* of *Lancashire* sent his *Bailiff*, and pulled me out of my own House, and had me *Prisoner* to *Lancaster-Castle* (upon the Old *Premunire*;) where I continued a *whole Year*: And most part of all that time I was *sick* and *weakly*; and also my *Husband* was *weak* and *sickly* at that time. And then after a while he *Recovered*, and went about to get me out of *Prison*; and a *Discharge* at last was got *(page viii)* under the *Great Seal*: and so I was set at *Liberty*. And then I was to go up to *London* again, for my Husband was intending for *America*: And he was full *two years* away, before he came back again to *England*; and then he arrived at *Bristol*, and then came to *London*: and he intended to have come to the *middle* of the *Nation* with me. But when we came into some parts of *Worcestershire*, they got there Information of him; and one Justice *Parker* by his *Warrant* sent him and my Son *Lower* to *Worcester-Gaol*: and the *Justices* there tendered him the *Oath*, and *Premunired* him, but *Released* my Son *Lower*; who stayed with him most of the time he was *Prisoner* there.

And after some time he fell *sick* in a *long, lingering Sickness*, and many times was very ill: so they writ to me from *London*, That *if I would see him alive, I might go to him*; which accordingly I did. And after I had tarried *Seventeen Weeks* with him at *Worcester*, and no *Discharge* like to be obtained for him, I went up to *London*, and writ to the King an *Account* of his *long Imprisonment, and that he was taken in his Travel homewards; and how he was sick and weak, and not like to live, if they kept him long there*. And I went with it to *Whitehall* my self; and I met with the King, and gave him the *Paper*: And he said, I must go to the *Chancellour*, he *could do nothing in it*. Then I writ also to the *Lord Chancellor*, and went to his *House*, and gave him my *Paper*, and spoke to him, *That the King had left it wholly to him; and if he did not take pity, and Release him out of that Prison, I feared he would end his days there*. And the Lord Chancellor *Finch* was a very *tender Man*, and spoke to the *Judge*; who gave out an

Habeas Corpus presently. And when we got it, we sent it down to *Worcester*; and they would not part with him at first, but said, he was *Premunired, and was not to go out on that manner*. And then we were forced to go to Judge *North*, and to the *Attorney General*, and we got another *Order*, and sent down from them; and with much ado, and great Labour and Industry of *William Mead*, and other *Friends*, we got him up to *London*, where he *Appeared* at *Westminster-Hall* at the *King's Bench*, before Judge *Hales*, who was a very honest, tender Man; and he knew they had *Imprisoned* him but in *Envy*. So that, which they had against him, was *Read*; and our *Counsel* pleaded, *That he was taken up in his Travel and Journey*: And there was but little said till he was *quitted*. And this was the *Last Prison*, that he was in, being freed by the *Court* of *King's Bench*.

And when he was at Liberty, he *Recovered* again: And then I was very desirous to go home with him, which we did. And this was the *first time* that he came to *Swarthmore* after we were *Married*; and so he stayed here much of *two years*. And then went to *London* again to the *Yearly Meeting*; and after awhile went into *Holland*, and some parts of *Germany*, where he stayed a pretty while: and then Returned to *London* again at the next *Yearly Meeting*. And after he had stayed a while in and about *London*, he came into the *North* to *Swarthmore* again, and stayed *(page ix)* that time nigh *two years*: And then he grew *weakly*, being troubled with *Pains* and *Aches*, having had many *sore* and *long Travels, Beatings*, and *hard Imprisonments*. But after some time he rid to *York*: and so passed on thorow *Nottinghamshire* and several *Counties*, visiting *Friends*; till he came to *London* to the *Yearly-Meeting*, and stayed there, and there-aways till he *finished* his *Course*, and laid down his *Head* in *Peace*.

And though the *Lord* had provided an outward *Habitation* for him, yet he was not willing to stay at it, because it was so *remote* and *far* from *London*, where his *Service* most lay. And my *Concern* for God and his holy, Eternal *Truth* was then in the *North*, where *God* had placed and set me; and likewise for the *Ordering* and *Governing* of my *Children* and *Family*: so that we were willing *both* of us, to live *a-part* some years upon *God's Account*, and his *Truth's Service*, and to deny our selves of that *Comfort*, which we might have had in being together, for the sake and *Service* of the *Lord*, and his *Truth*. And if any took Occasion, or Judged hard of us because of that, the *Lord* will *Judge* them; for we were *Innocent*. And for my own part, I was willing to make many *long Journies*, for taking away all *Occasion* of *evil Thoughts*: And though I lived *Two hundred Miles* from *London*, yet have I been *Nine times* there, upon the *Lord*, and his *Truth's Account*; and of all the times that I was at *London*, this *last time* was most *Comfortable*, that the *Lord* was pleased to give me *Strength* and *Ability*, to travel that *great Journey*, being *Seventy six years of Age*, to see my *Dear Husband*, who was better in his *Health* and *Strength* than many times I had seen him before. I look upon that, that the *Lord's special Hand* was in it, that I should go then; for he lived but about *half a Year* after I left him: Which makes me admire the *Wisdom* and *Goodness* of *God* in Ordering my *Journey* at that time.

And now he hath *finished* his *Course*, and his *Testimony*, and is entered into his Eternal *Rest* and *Felicity*. I trust in the same *powerful God*, that his *holy Arm* and *Power* will carry me thorow, whatever he hath yet for me to do; and that he will be my *Strength* and *Support*, and the *Bearer* up of my *Head* unto the *End*, and in the *End*. For I know his *Faithfulness* and *Goodness*, and I have *Experience* of his *Love*; To whom be *Glory* and *Powerful Dominion* for ever. *Amen*.

M.F.

(page 1)

A
RELATION
OF
Margaret Fell,

Her Birth, Life, Teſtimony, and Sufferings
for the Lord's Everlaſting Truth in her
Generation

Given forth by her Self, as followeth, *Viz.*

I Was Born in the Year 1614. at *Marsh-Grange*, in the Parish of
Dalton, in *Fournis* in *Lancashire*, of good and honest Parents,
and of Honourable Repute in their Country. My Father's Name
was *John Askew*, he was of an Ancient Family, of those esteem'd and
call'd Gentlemen, who left a considerable Estate, which had been in
his Name and Family for several Generations. He was a Pious Chari-
table Man, much valu'd in his Country for his Moderation, and Patience,
and was Bred after the best way and manner of Persons of his Rank in
his Day. I was brought up and liv'd with my Father, until I was between
Seventeen and Eighteen Years of Age, and then I was Married unto
Thomas Fell of *Swarthmore*, who was a Barrister-at-Law of *Grays-Inn;* who
afterwards was a Justice of the *Quorum* in his Country, a Member of
Parliament, in several Parliaments; Vice-Chancellor of the County Pa-
latine of *Lancaster*, Chancellor of the Dutchy-Court at *Westminster,* and
one of the Judges that went the Circuit of *West-Chester,* and North-*Wales.*

(page 2) He was much esteem'd in his Country, and valu'd and honour'd
in his Day by all sorts of People, for his Justice, Wisdom, Moderation
and Mercy; being a Terror to Evil-doers, and an Encourager of such as
did well, and his many and great Services made his Death much la-

(Page numbers of original document appear in text as *page __.*)

mented. We liv'd together twenty six Years, in which time, we had nine Children. He was a tender loving Husband to me, and a tender Father to his Children, and one that sought after God in the best way that was made known to him. I was about sixteen Years younger than he, and was one that sought after the best Things, being desirous to serve God, so as I might be accepted of him; and was Inquiring after the way of the Lord, and went often to hear the best Ministers that came into our Parts, whom we frequently entertain'd at our House; many of those that were accounted the most Serious and Godly Men, some of which, were then call'd *Lecturing-Ministers*, and had often Prayers and Religious Exercises in our Family. This I hop'd I did well in, but often fear'd I was short of the right way: And after this manner I was inquiring and seeking about twenty Years.

Then in the Year 1652. it pleas'd the Lord in his Infinite Mercy and Goodness to send *George Fox* into our Country, who declar'd unto us the Eternal Truth, as it is in Jesus; and by the Word and Power of the Eternal God, turn'd many from Darkness unto Light, and from the Power of Satan unto God. And when I and my Children, and a great part of our Servants were so convinc'd and converted unto God at which time my Husband was not at Home, being gone to *London*. When he came Home, and found us the most part of the Family chang'd from our former Principle and Perswasion which he left us in, when he went from Home, he was much surpriz'd at our suddain change: For some envious People of our Neighbours, went and met him upon the Sands, as he was coming Home, and Inform'd *(page 3)* him, that we had entertain'd such Men as had taken us off from going to Church, which he was very much concern'd at; so that when he came Home, he seem'd much troubled. And it so happen'd, that *Richard Farnsworth*, and some other Friends (that came into our Parts a little time after G. *Fox*) were then at our House when my Husband came Home; and they Discours'd with him, and did perswade him to be still, and weigh things, before he did any thing hastily, and his Spirit was something calmed.

At Night G. *Fox* spoke so powerfully and convincingly, that the witness of God in his Conscience answer'd that he spake Truth; and he was then so far convinc'd in his Mind that it was Truth, that he willingly let us have a Meeting in his House the next first Day after, which was the first Publick Meeting that was at *Swarthmore*; but he and his Men went to the Steeple-House (our Meetings being kept at *Swarthmore* about 38 Years, until a new Meeting-House was built by G. *Fox's* Order and Cost near *Swarthmore-Hall*,) and so through the good power and word of God, the Truth encreas'd in the Countries all about us, and many came in, and were convinc'd, and we kept our Meetings peaceably every first Day at *Swarthmore-Hall*, the residue of the time of his Life. And he became a kind Friend to Friends, and to the practicers of Truth upon every occasion, as he had opportunity. For he being a Magistrate, was Instrumental to keep off much Persecution in this Country, and in other Places where he had any Power.

He Liv'd about six Years after I was convinc'd; in which time it pleas'd the Lord to visit him with Sickness, wherein he became more than usually loving and kind to our Friends call'd *Quakers*, having been a merciful Man to the Lord's People. I, and many other Friends were well satisfy'd the Lord in mercy receiv'd him to himself. It was in the beginning of the 8th Month, 1658. that he *(page 4)* died, being about sixty Years of Age: He left one Son, and seven Daughters, all unpreferr'd; but left a good and competent Estate for them.

And in the Year 1660. King *Charles* the Second came into *England*, and within two Weeks after, I was mov'd of the Lord to go to *London*, to speak to the King concerning the Truth, and the Sufferers for it, for there was then many hundreds of our Friends in Prison in the three Nations, of *England, Scotland,* and *Ireland,* which were put in by the former Powers. And I spake often with the King, and writ many Letters and Papers unto him, and many Books were given by our Friends to the Parliament, and great Service was done at that time.—And they were fully inform'd of our peaceable Principles and Practices. I staid at *London* at this time one Year and three Months, doing Service for the Lord, in visiting Friends Meetings, and giving Papers and Letters to the King and Council whenever there was occasion. And I writ and gave Papers and Letters to every one of the Family several times, *viz.* To the King, to the Duke of *York*, to the Duke of *Gloucester*, and to the Queen Mother, to the Princess of *Orange*, and to the Queen of *Bohemia*. I was mov'd of the Lord to visit them all, and to write unto them, and to lay the Truth before them, and did give them many Books and Papers, and did lay our Principles and Doctrines before them, and desired that they would let us have Discourse with their Priests, Preachers, and Teachers, and if they could prove us Erroneous, then let them manifest it: But if our Principles and Doctrines be found according to the Doctrine of Christ, and the Apostles and Saints in the Primitive Times, then let us have our Liberty. But we could never get a Meeting of any sort of them to meet with our Friends—Nevertheless they were very quiet, and we had great Liberty, and had our Meetings very peaceably for the first half

Year after the King came in, until the Fifth-Monarchy-Men raised an Insurrection and Tumult *(page 5)* in the City of *London*, and then all our Meetings were disturb'd, and Friends taken up; which if that had not been, we were inform'd the King had intended to have given us Liberty. For at that very time, there was an Order Sign'd by the King and Council for the Quaker's Liberty, and just when it should have gone to the Press, the Fifth-Monarchy-Men rose, and then our Friends were very hardly used, and taken up at their Meetings generally, even until many Prisons throughout the Nation was filled with them. And many a time did I go to the King about them; who promis'd me always they should be set at Liberty; and we had several in the Council were Friendly to us, and we gave many Papers to them; and with much adoe, and attendance in that time, about a quarter of a year after their first taking Friends to Prison, a General Proclamation from the King and Council was granted, for setting the Quakers at Liberty, that were taken up at that time; and in some time after the Proclamation came forth, and Friends were set at Liberty. Then I had freedom in Spirit to return Home to visit my Children and Family, which I had been from fifteen Months. And I staid at Home about nine Months, and then was moved of the Lord to go to London again, not knowing what might be the Matter or Business that I should go for. And when I came to Warrington, in my way to London, I met with an Act of Parliament, made against the Quakers for refusing Oaths. And when I came to *London*, I heard the King was gone to meet the Queen, and to be Married to her at *Hampton-Court*. At this time Friends Meetings at *London* were much troubled with Soldiers, pulling Friends out of their Meetings, and beating them with their Muskets and Swords; insomuch that several were wounded and bruised by them; many were cast into Prison, through which, many lost their Lives; and all this being done to a peaceable People, only for Worshipping God, as *(page 6)* they in Conscience were perswaded. Then I went to the King, and Duke of *York* at *Hampton-Court*, and I wrote several Letters to them, and therein gave them to understand what desperate and dangerous work there was at *London*; and how the Soldiers came in with lighted Matches, and drawn Swords amongst Friends, when they were met together in the fear and dread of the Lord to worship him; and if they would not stop that cruel Persecution, it was very like that more Innocent Blood would be shed, and that would witness against their Actions, and lie upon them, and the Nation. And within some certain days after, they beat some Friends so cruelly at the *Bull-and-Mouth*, that two died thereof.

The King told me when I spake to him, and writ to him, that his Soldiers did not trouble us, nor should they, and said the City Soldiers were not his, and they would do as they pleas'd with them; but after a little time they were more Moderate, and the King promis'd me that he would set those at Liberty that were in Prison; and when he brought his Queen to *London*, he set them at Liberty. And then I came Home again, when I had staid about four Months in and about *London*. And in the 3d Month, 1663. I was mov'd of the Lord again to Travel into the Countries to visit Friends; and I Travel'd through the Countries visiting Friends, till we came to *Bristol*, where we staid two Weeks, I, and some other Friends that were with me, and then we went into *Somersetshire*, *Devonshire*, and *Dorsetshire*, visiting Friends, and then came back to *Bristol*: From whence, we passed through the Nation into *Yorkshire*, to *York*, and into *Bishoprick* and *Northumberland*, visiting Meetings all along amongst Friends, and then went into *Westmoreland*, and so Home to *Swarthmore*.

This Journey, that I then went, and one of my Daughters and some others that were with me, it was thought we Travelled about a Thousand Miles *(page 7)* and in our Journey we met with G. *Fox*, who came to *Swarthmore* with us, and stay'd about two Weeks; and then the Magistrates began to threaten: For G.F. went into *Westmoreland*, and *Cumberland*, and had some Meetings amongst Friends, and came again to *Swarthmore*; and they sent out Warrants for him, and took him, and committed him to *Lancaster*-Castle. About a Month after, the same Justices sent for me at *Alverstone*, where they were sitting, at a private Sessions; and when I came there, they asked me several Questions, and seem'd to be offended at me, for keeping a Meeting at my House, and said, They would tender me the Oath of Allegiance. I answer'd, They knew I could not Swear, and why should they send for me from my own House, where I was about my lawful Occasions, to ensnare me? What had I done? They said, If I would not keep a Meeting at my House, they would not tender me the Oath. I told them, I should not deny my Faith and Principles, for any thing they could do against me; and while it pleased the Lord to let me have a House, I should endeavour to worship him in it. So they caus'd the Oath to be read, and tender'd it unto me; and when I refused it, telling them, I could not take any Oath for Conscience sake, Christ Jesus having forbid it. Then they made a *Mittimus*, and committed me Prisoner to *Lancaster*-Castle, and there G. *Fox* and I remained in Prison until the next Assizes; and then they Indicted us upon the Statute for denying the Oath of Allegiance: For they tender'd it us both again at the Assizes; but they said to me, if I would not keep a Meeting at my House, I should be set at Liberty. But I answer'd the Judge, That I rather choose a Prison for obeying of God, than my Liberty for obeying of Men, contrary to my Conscience. So we were called several times before them at the Assizes, and the Indictments were found against us. The next Assizes we came to Tryal, and G. *Fox's* Indictment was found to be dated wrong, both in the *(page 8)* Day of the Month, and in the Year of the King's Reign, so that his Indictment was quash'd; but mine they would not allow the Errors that were found in it, to make it void, altho' there were several; so they passed Sentence of *Præmunire* upon me, which was, That I should be out of the King's Protection, and forfeit all my Estate, Real and Personal, to the King, and Imprisonment during Life. But the great God of Heaven and Earth supported my Spirit under this severe Sentence, that I was not terrified; but gave this Answer to Judge *Turner,* who gave the Sentence, *Although I am out of the King's Protection, yet I am not out of the Protection of the Almighty God;* so there I remained in Prison Twenty Months, before I could get so much Favour of the Sheriff, as to go to my own House; which then I did for a little time, and returned to Prison again. And when I had been a Prisoner about Four Years, I was set at Liberty by an Order from the King and Council in 1668.

And then I was moved of the Lord again, to go and visit Friends; and the first that I went to visit were Friends in Prison; and I visited the most part of the Friends that were Prisoners in the *North* and *West* of *England,* and those in my way to *Bristol;* after I had stay'd two Weeks there, I visited Friends in *Cornwall, Devonshire,* and *Somersetshire;* and then through all the Western Counties to *London.* And I stay'd in and about *London* about three Months, and then I went and visited Friends throughout all *Kent, Sussex,* and some part of *Surrey;* and then to *London* again, where I stay'd above two Months; and then I returned through the Countries, visiting Friends, until I came to *Bristol,* in 1669.

And then it was Eleven Years after my former Husband's Decease; and G. *Fox* being then returned from visiting Friends in *Ireland.* At *Bristol* he declared his Intentions of Marriage with me; and there was also our Marriage solemnized, in a publick Meeting of many Friends, who were our Witnesses.

(page 9) And in some time after, I came homewards, and my Husband stay'd in the Countries visiting Friends. And soon after I came home, there came another Order to cast me into Prison again; and the Sheriff of *Lancashire* sent his Bailiff, and pulled me out of my own House, and

had me to Prison to *Lancaster*-Castle, where I continued a whole Year; and most part of that time I was sick and weakly. And after some time, my Husband endeavoured to get me out of Prison; and a Discharge at last was got, under the great Seal, and so I was set at Liberty.

And then I was to go up to *London* again; for my Husband was intending for *America*, and he was full two Years away, before he came back into *England*; and then he arrived in *Bristol*, where I went to meet him; and we stay'd sometime in the Countries thereabout, and then came to *London*, and stay'd there several Months. And I was intending to return home into the North, and he came with me as far as the middle of the Nation. But before we parted, we went to a Meeting in *Worcestershire*; and after the Meeting was ended, and Friends mostly gone, he was taken Prisoner, together with my Son-in-Law *Thomas Lower*, by one *Parker*, Justice a so called, and sent to *Worcester*-Jayl; the Account whereof is set forth in his Journal. And when I came home, with my Daughter *Rachel*, leaving him confin'd in Prison, where he became much weaken'd in Body, and his Health impair'd, by his long Confinement. Howbeit, after much endeavours used, he was Legally Discharged, and set at Liberty. We got him home to *Swarthmore*, where he had a long time of Weakness, before he Recovered. And when he had stay'd there about One and Twenty Months, he began his Journey towards *London* again, in 1677. although he was but weakly, and unable to ride well, but the Lord supported him. And when he had stay'd some time in *London*, then he went over into *Holland*, and travelled to *Hamburgh*, and into some part of *Germany*, and to several places *(page 10)* in those Countries, and then returned to *London*; and then went to *Bristol* to visit Friends, and back again to *London*: And then, after a little time, came to *Swarthmore*, where he continu'd again above a Year. And then he began his Journey, and travelled through several Counties, visiting Friends, until he came to *London*.

And when my Husband was at *London*, it being a time of great Perse-cution by Informers, the Justices in our Country were very severe, and much bent against me, because I kept a Meeting at my House, at *Swarthmore*-Hall: So they did not Fine the House as his, he being ab-sent, but fined it as mine, as being the Widow of Judge *Fell*; and fined me 20 *l.* for the House and 20 *l.* for speaking in the Meeting; and then fined me the second time 40 *l.* for speaking; and also fined some other Friends for speaking, 20 *l.* for the first time, and 40 *l.* for the second time; and those that were not able, they fined others for them, and made great Spoil amongst Friends, by distraining and selling their Goods, sometimes for less than half the Value; they took Thirty Head of Cattle from me: Their Intentions were to ruine us, and to weary us out, and to enrich themselves; but the Lord prevented them.

So I was moved of the Lord to go to *London*, in the 70th Year of my Age; and the Word was in me, *That as I had gone to King* Charles, *when he first came into* England; *so I should go, and bear to him my last Testimony, and let him know, how they did abuse us, to enrich themselves.* And so I went up to *London*, and a Paper was drawn up, to give a true and certain Account, how they dealt with me, and other Friends. And it was upon my Mind, to go first to the Duke of *York*; and I writ a short Paper to him, to acquaint him, That as he had sometimes formerly spoke in my behalf to the King, my Request was, that he would now do the like for me; or Words to that effect. And I went with this Paper to *James's* House; and after long waiting, I got to speak to *(page 11)* him. But some who were with him, let him know, that it was I that had been with him and his Brother, soon after they came into *England*. So I gave him my little Paper, and asked him, If he did remember me? He said, *I do remember you*. So then I desired him to speak to the King for us, for we were under great Sufferings, and our Persecutors were so severe upon us, that it look'd as if they intended to make a Prey upon us: And he said, He could not help us, but he would speak to the King. And the next Day, with much ado, I got to the King, and had my great Paper, which was the Relation of our Sufferings, to present to him; but he was so Rough and Angry, that he would not take my Paper; but I gave several Copies of it to his Nobles about him. And afterwards I went to Judge *Jefferies*, and told him of our Sufferings: For he had been in the North-Country with us, but a little before, and he told me we might speak to the King. I answer'd, it was very hard to get to the King; he said, give me a Paper, and I will speak to him; but said, Your Papers are too long, give me a short Paper, and I will speak to him. So I writ a little Paper from my self to him, to this effect;

King Charles, *Thou and thy Magistrates puts very great and cruel Sufferings upon us: But this I must say unto thee, If you make our Sufferings to Death it self, we shall not, nor dare not but confess Christ Jesus before Men, lest he should deny us before his Father which is in Heaven.*

There were some more Words in it, but this was the Substance. So *Jefferies* read it, and said, He would give it him; and we gave Papers to several of those that waited on him, and they gave us some Encouragement, that we should be helped: So we expected and waited for it. And about a Week or two after, in the beginning of the 12th Month, *Geo.*

Whitehead and I were going to one of the Lords, who promised *George* before, that he would speak to the King for us: We went to his Lodgings *(page 12)* early in the Morning, thinking to speak with him, before he went out; but his Servants told us, he was not within, being gone to the King, who was not well. Then we came forth into *White-Hall-Court* again; but all the Gates were shut, that we could not get forth. So we waited and walked up and down, and several came down from the King, and said, *He could not stand;* others said, *He could not speak.* Then, after some Hours waiting, we got through *Scotland-Yard*, and came away; and the King continued Sick and Ill until the Sixth Day after, and then he died. So this confirmed that Word, which God put into my Heart, That *I was sent to bear my last Testimony to the King.*

Then *James* Duke of *York* was proclaimed King; and about two Weeks after, I went to him, and gave him a Paper, wherein was writ to this effect:

King James, *I have waited here some Months, until this Change is come, and now I would return Home. But I cannot live peaceably there, except I have a Word from thee, to give a Check to my Persecutors.*

I spoke to him to the same purpose, that I had writ in my Paper So after a few Weeks I went home.

And a little time after, *William Kerby*, a Justice, one of our greatest Persecutors, met with my Son-in-Law, *Daniel Abraham*, upon the Road, and said to him, Tell your Mother, that now the Government will be settled again, and if you keep Meetings, you must expect the same again. My Son answered him, We must keep Meetings, unless you take our Lives. Then *William Kerby* said, We will not take your Lives, but whilst you have any thing, we will take it. So I writ a Letter to King *James*, in which I said, *Thou bid'st me come home, and so I am; but as I said to thee, I could not live peaceably, so it is like to be:* And then I hinted in my Letter, *W. Kirby's* Discourse with my Son. And I desired of the King, *to let me have something from him, that I might live peaceably at my House.*

(page 13) This Letter was deliver'd to him, and, as I heard, he carried it to the Council, and it was read; and that some of the Council said, She desires a Protection, that she may live Peaceably at her own House; and that some made answer, They could give no Protection to a particular—. However (I do suppose) they gave our Persecutors a private Caution, for they troubled us no more; but, if that had not been, it's likely they had a mind to begin a new upon us. For, a little before the time of the Informers, they brought that Law upon us, concerning Twelve Pence a *Sunday*, so call'd; and they carry'd me, and my Son and Daughter

Abraham, to *Lancaster*-Prison, and kept us there about three Weeks. And when they consider'd, that they could not Fine me, nor my House, when I was in Prison, then they let us go home; and soon after, they did fine us both for the House, and for Speaking, as is before hinted.

And thus have they troubled and persecuted us divers ways: But the Lord God Almighty hath preserved me, and us, till this Day; Glorious Praises be given to him for evermore.

And the Lord hath given me Strength and Ability, that I have been at *London* to see my dear Husband and Children, and Relations and Friends there, in 1690. being the Seventy Sixth Year of my Age: And I was very well Satisfied, Refreshed, and Comforted in my Journey, and found Friends in much Love; Praises be returned to the Unchangeable Lord God for ever. This being Nine times that I have been at *London*, upon the Lord's and his Truth's Account.

And after I returned Home, I writ this short *Epistle* following, to the Women's Meeting in *London*.

Dear Friends and Sisters,

IN the Eternal Blessed Truth, into which we are begotten, and in which we stand, and are preserved, as we keep in it, and are guided by it: In this is my dear and unchangeable Love remember'd *(page 14)* unto you all; acknowledging your dear, tender, and kind Love, when I was with you; in which my Heart was rejoyced, to feel the Ancient Love and Unity of the Eternal Spirit amongst you: And my Soul was, and is refreshed in my Journey, in visiting of my dear Husband and Children, and you my dear Friends. And now I am returned to my own House and Family, where I find all well: Praised and Honoured be my Heavenly Father.

And, dear Friends, our Engagements are great unto the Lord, and he is Dear and Faithful unto us: And Blessed and Happy are all they, that are Dear and Faithful unto him. And those who keeps single and chaste unto him, they need not fear Evil Tidings, nor what Man can do: For he that hath all Power in Heaven and Earth in his Hand, he will surely keep his own Church and Family, those that worshippeth him, within the Measuring Line, that measures the Temple, and the Altar, and those that worships therein, they are kept safe, as in the Hallow of his Hand.

And so, dear Friends, my Heart and Soul was so much Comforted and Refreshed amongst you, that I could not but signifie the Remembrance of my dear Love unto you: And also my Acknowledgment of your dear Love and Tenderness to my dear Husband; for which, I doubt not, but the Lord doth and will Reward you: Into whose Hand, and Arm, and Power, I commit you.

M. Fox.

Swarthmore, *the 10th of the 5th Month, 1690.*

God's Mighty Power Magnified:

As MANIFESTED AND REVEALED

IN HIS Faithful Handmaid

JOAN VOKINS,

WHO Departed this Life the 22nd of the 5th Month, 1690, Having finiſhed her Courſe, and kept the Faith.

Also some **Account** of her Exercises, Works of Faith, Labour of Love, and great Travels in the Work of the Miniſtry, for the good of Souls.

2 COR. 4.7. *But we have this Treaſure in Earthen Veſſels, that the Excellency of the Power may be of God, and not of us.*

2. COR. 12.9. *And he ſaid, my Grace is sufficient for thee for my ſtrength if made perfeƈt in Weaƙneſs.*

London, Printed for Thomas Northcott, in *George-Yard* in *Lombard Street,* 1691

(Page numbers of original document appear in text as *page _.*)

(page 15)

Some account given forth by **Joan Vokins** *of the great Goodneſs and Mercy of the Lord towards her, and of the wonderful Works that he hath done for her; conducing to his Glory and her great Joy and Comfort: Written with her own Hand (a few Months before her deceaſe) as followeth.*

S Omething of the tender dealing of the Lord with me ever since my Childhood, for (blessed be his Name) he preserved me from many Evils that Youth is often ensnared with; and by his Light (that I then had no acquaintance with) shewed me the vanity and *(page 16)* vain Customs of the World when I was very young, and all along my youth his Good Spirit did still strive with me to preserve me from Sin and Evil: And if I had at any time, through persuasion of others, gone to that they called Recreation, I should be so condemned for passing away my precious time, that I could have no peace, so that I could take no delight in their Pastime, but was still condemned. And many times I cried to the Righteous God to reveal his way unto me; and I promised to walk therein whatever I endured. For the snares of the World, the Lord was pleased to discover, and in some measure to make known the Cross of Jesus that Crucifies unto the World; and as I enclined to take it up and follow Jesus through the many Tribulations, he endowed me with his Almighty Power, wherein hath been my help, blessed be his Worthy Name for ever: for his Loving-Kindness never fails, but his Mercies endure for ever: and his great Compassion and tender Dealing towards my Soul, when in Darkness and under the Region of the Shadow of Death, is never to be forgotten; for it hath been largely extended unto me, when in deep distress.

When my cry is often, Lord reveal thy Way unto me, that I may walk therein, whatever I undergo. But when I found the way so strait and narrow, I could very willingly have turned aside for ease; for Flesh and *(page 17)* Blood could not bear that which I had then to undergo; but blessed and renowned be the Spirit of Truth, my Comforter, which leads into all Truth; for when I was in a dejected condition about *Reprobation* and *Election,* neither *Priest* nor *Professor* could open the Mystery of *Election* and *Reprobation;* but the Spirit of Light and Life (which is the Spirit of Jesus) opened my Understanding, and revealed the Mystery of the two Seeds, how that the one is for ever blessed, and the other cursed:

And also what Happiness might be received by taking heed to the Light that shined in my Heart, which makes manifest, that the way to the Crown of Glory is through the daily cross to my own Will, and to take Christ's Yoke upon that Nature that would not be subject. Oh how precious is the Counsel of him who said, *Take my yoke upon you, and learn of me; for my yoke is easie, and my burden is light, and ye shall find rest for your souls:* And that Rest I sorely wanted, until I learned of Jesus to be meek and low in Heart, and to suffer for well-doing; and then (glory unto his Holy Name for ever) his blessed Reward my Soul was daily made a partaker of; though hated by evil doers, yet loved by the Lord, and that engaged me to give up to his dispose, and to answer his requirings, not accounting my self, nor any thing he hath give me, too much to part with, that the Truth may be propagated, and my tender God honored: For (blessed be his Worthy Name) he *(page 18)* hath filled my Cup, with the sweet Salvation of his Son Christ Jesus, the Light and Saviour of his poor and helpless Ones, who have no other to depend upon for Help at all times, but wait daily to be furnished upon every occasion to serve him in all Faithfulness; for he is Worthy, my Soul can truly say, for he gave me of his good Spirit, and it was with me (yet unknown) when I rebelled against it, and was not willing to be subject to its Leadings, nor observing of its Dictates as I ought to have been: Oh then, did I want power (as many do now), not knowing the sufficiency of the engrafted Word of God's Grace that is able to save: But when I followed its counsel, I found it sufficient to bring good to me, out of great afflictions, beyond my expectation; and then could I plead no excuse, knowing that unto the Lord Jesus (who had brought great things to pass) I must give my account: for he hath manifested his Power, and I have cause to believe it will never fail towards his People, if we fail not to obey the manifestation of it; but Faithfulness is required to the Talent received, for which we must give an account; and then what can stand us in stead, if we have not an increase? This was my concern for many Years, and I could not take comfort in Husband or Children, House, or Land, or any visibles, for want of the Marriage Union with the Lamb of God, that takes away the sins of *(page 19)* the Souls of those that cannot be satisfied in them; but are weary of the burden of them, as I was; and God by his Spirit shewed me, he abhorred my self-righteousness; and let me see that in him was Righteousness, Life and Power; and then I was sensible that he is the Light of the World, that enlightens every one that comes into the World; and that it was striving with me from my Youth, which was before ever I heard

the name *Quaker*; and then I did believe that there was a People or
Church over whom Christ Jesus was Head, though I could yet not find
them, nor be a Member of them; yet long sought after it sorrowfully,
with many strong and fervent cries and desires: But the Lord in his own
due time answered my weary Soul, and made known more and more of
the way of his Truth and People, and at length sent some of his
Messengers, as Instruments in his Hand, for my Encouragement and
Confirmation: Then was I, and many desolate Ones, right glad (whose
Souls had long languished) for the glad Tidings that they brought with
them, how that we might inherit Substance which we had long sought
and been searching for, both in the Scriptures, and amongst Professors
of many sorts of Profession; for we would fain have filled our Souls with
the Husks, but that could not satisfie, we knew not the saving Health
of him who said, *I wisdom lead in the midst of the Paths of Judgment, to
teach (page 20) them that love, and follow me to inherit Substance:* Oh this is
that which did at first convince us, and tendered our Hearts in the
beginning: Then what was too near or dear for us to part with in the
Day of our deep Distress, when none could cure our wounded Souls?
Oh how precious was the Heart-searching Light when we first knew it
to shine upon our Tabernacles, to guide us in the narrow Way wherein
is Life, and perfect Peace for those whose Minds are staied on the Lord!
And when I have read, that he would keep them in perfect Peace whose
Minds are staied on him, what would not I have done, that it might
have been my condition? But then I could not watch nor wait, but was
as a Ship without an Anchor among the merciless Waves; but Praises
unto the Lord for ever, he caused the Living Hope to spring that
anchored in trying Times. And I was, even as *Israel* at the *red Sea*,
compassed all round on every Hand; great was the strait that I was then
in, much hardship; the Sea before, and the Enemy presenting so much
impossibility, that his proud Waves of Temptations, Buffetings, and false
Accusations had almost sunk me under: Oh then did I cry unto the
God of Mercy and tender Compassion, that I might but stand still and
behold his Salvation; and he did arise and rebuke the Enemy, and made
way for me to travel on in my Heavenly Progress, and overturned the
Mountains that were on each *(page 21)* hand, and dismaied *Pharaoh* and
his Host (which I may compare my Relations and the Professors unto,)
for they pursued me and made my Suffering great, till they had wearied
themselves; and their Oppression was so sore, that I sometimes was
ready to faint, and even to say, Surely, I shall one Day fall; but Living
Praises unto the Almighty, he hath made me a partaker of the sure

Mercies of *David*, and hath subdued Truth's Enemies before him, and
kept and preserved me faithful, till several of my Relations were
convinced, that God's Power was with me; and now when my Husband,
and Children, and Relations are with me in a good Meeting, and the
Powerful Presence of the Lord is amongst us; it is a blessed Reward for
all, for one Soul is more worth than all the World, as saith the Scripture:
Therefore Faithfulness is very needful, for it doth produce a good effect,
whatever we may endure; for the momentary Affliction that we meet
with here, doth produce a further weight of Glory hereafter; and in the
sense of the same my Head was born up to endure hardships, when I
could willingly have hid or gotten ease; but I considered that I could
not hide from the Lord, who brought to my remembrance my Promise
that I made before his Way was revealed to me; and if I broke Covenant
with the Lord, I should never enter into his Rest: Oh then a suffering in
the Flesh, and a ceasing from Sin, was the *(page 22)* delight of my Soul;
although the Enemy ceased not, but Night and Day, as a roaring Lyon,
and a cunning Hunter, seeking for the precious Life, and chased my
poor Soul as a Partridge on the Mountains; but my God had shewed me
that the way to Rest was through many Troubles, and that he would be
at hand to Deliver out of them all by his Almighty Power: (but I could
hardly trust it then,) but yet, turning to it, I found Preservation by it,
when the backsliding of some had like to have caused me to stumble;
but the unerring Spirit of Jesus showed me that if thousands fall on the
one hand, and tens of thousands on the other, that should not defile
me; and if all the rest were Righteous, that should not justifie me, if I
did not obey the Truth, now he had made known his Covenant of Life,
which I so deeply engaged to be faithful unto; and then I turned my
back on the World, and all the friendship and glory of it, that I might
obtain the favour of Jesus, who condemned me for my Self-righteousness,
as for my known Sins, for I was cautious of Sinning against the Lord
ever since my Youth, and desired after the best Religion and Company;
and when I was very young in years, I greatly delighted to go to *Professors*
Meetings, and could bring home the Text, and repeat much of their
Sermons, but yet that brought no benefit to my poor hungry Soul; and
when I was in secret, before the all-seeing *(page 23)* Eye of the Lord, he
administred Condemnation upon it all, and I had no Peace inwardly;
although none could condemn me for any misdemeanor, as outwardly;
but when my own Righteousness became loathsome to me, then I was
made willing to part with all that had been near and dear unto me, that
I might feel and witness the Robe of Christ's Righteousness revealed,

and be cloathed therewith. And as for my Husband and Children, my true and tender Love was so great, that I could have done or suffered much for them: But if I had disobeyed the Lord, to please them, I might have provoked him to have withholden his Mercies from us all, and to bring his Judgments upon us; And then who shall excuse in the Day of Account? Then if a Man (as the Scriptures says) should give the Fruit of his Body for the Sin of his Soul, it will not be accepted. Then Husbands, and Wives, and Parents, and Children, and Servants, shall all receive according to their doings; and none that disobeys the Lord will [*sic*] be excused, no more than *Adam* was, when he said, That the Woman gave him the forbidden Fruit, and he did eat, and so provoked the Lord, that the Curse came upon himself and could not be excused. And although Man and Wife should be helpful one to another in Righteousness, yet too many there are, since the fall, that hinder and hurt each other for which an account must be given unavoidably: *(page 24)* And this did I consider many a time, and earnestly endeavour to avoid; notwithstanding the false Aspersions that might arise, yet I still endeavoured to keep my Conscience clear in the sight of my tender God; and none can lay any thing to my Charge, except it be for serving the Living and True God, though in that way that many may call *Heresie*, yet I do worship him in Spirit and in Truth. For as Christ Jesus hath said, it is come to pass, that our Heavenly Father seeketh such, and always sought such to worship him, in his own Spiritual way of Worship; which shall stand, when all Idolatry and invented Worships shall fall.

The 1ft month, Written aboard the first Ship as I went to New-England,
1680. when none that saw me, expected my life; but the Lord was with me, and relieved me, and his blessed Power raised me, as at many other times.

And I arrived at *New York* the 4th day of the 3d Month, 80, and a Maiden Friend, whose Name was *Sarah Yoklet* went with me from *England*, and travelled with me until I came to *Oyster-Bay* in *Long-Island;* and the Lord so ordered it, that when she left me, another Woman- *(page 36)* Friend, that had a Testimony, was my Companion several Months, whose name was *Lydia Wright.*

Oh matchless Mercies of the Lord, who can rightly consider them as they have been *(page 25)* manifested, and not be tendered, as I am! Oh how long did his tender Spirit strive with me before I gave up to go to Sea? How did his long Patience wait and suffer? Surely it's worthy to be

remembred; for he might have cut me off in a disobedient Condition:
But blessed and magnified be his Heart-tendering Power; it bowed me
from Year to Year, and brought me into Subjection, when in a low Condition I could not help my self, nor had no other to help me: O then did
it support me in Exercises, sore both in Body and Spirit; when my Mind
hath been so dejected, that my Faith almost failed, then did my tender
Father, through the Son of his Love, Christ Jesus, yield me sweet relief,
though in a weary Land, and sweetly encouraged me to travel on; and
many sweet Promises, which before he gave me, as I stood singly re-
signed to obey his Commands, and be at his dispose, he was never wanting to fulfil; but by Sea and Land hath multiplied his Mercies, *and
renewing a right Spirit in me*, to the resolving of Doubts, and casting out
of false Fears (everlasting Praises to his most holy Name); for often did
that cause Torment, when the dark Reasoner was very busie: Then did
I cry unto the Lord, and say, Surely thou knowest all, and I have none
but thee to help, and many Eyes are over me, and great Difficulties
surround me on every hand, and I am the poorest and weakest that I do
know; and if *(page 26)* I should fail by the way, how would the Enemy
rejoice, and the Truth be reproached? And much buffeting did I undergo in my long and sore Exercises; but as I cast my Care upon him, he
hath cared for me; and blessed be his Name, he hath helped in my
greatest straits, and hath made hard things easie, and what he shewed
me by his pure Spirit of Light for my encouragement, before I came
forth, he hath brought to pass: Glory to his Name forever, may all those
say with my Soul that love the Leadings of the Light of Jesus; for though
it leads through Tribulation, yet it brings the Soul sweet Consolation,
and therefore worthy to be followed through the Self-denial; for it's
through the daily Cross to obtain the Reward of the Crown; and precious is the feeling of the life of Jesus to the awakened and illuminated
Soul, and that made the roaring Sea, and dry Land, and lonesome Wilderness all one to me by Night and by Day; and great was my encouragement to commit all that my Heavenly Father had given me, to his
keeping, and to follow him, and in taking up the daily Cross, I found
Power to preserve me from looking out at my affliction of Body, when
sorely exercised in Mind, ready to sink under the oppression of it; had
not the Spirit of Truth, the Comforter, helped my Infirmities, and taught
me, I had never known how to pray as I ought, but I often read, That
the Prayers of the Lord's *(page 27)* Children avail much with him, and in
these latter Days, according to his Promise, his are taught by him, and
in Righteousness they shall be established, and great shall be their Peace:

and this is the Effect of our Heavenly Father's great unspeakable Love to those that watch unto Prayer, and continue in the same; for I know not how any can expect a Child's Portion, that breaks his Father's Commands, and does not repent; and who is it but knows that watching and waiting is generally commanded? Surely it is a Duty that ought to be performed by every one that is come to an understanding; and by believing in Jesus, the Light and Power of God, all may receive strength to perform it; and for want of Understanding how nigh he was to me in Years that are past, I was long in a desolate Condition, and could not be satisfied without acquaintance with the Teachings of his Spirit, which is light: But I was then in darkness, and under the shadow of Death, longing after the countenance of the Lord to shine upon my Tabernacle; for if it should be dissolved, I was not sensible of a better Building eternal in the Heavens; though I read of them that had, yet I knew not their Foundation; and whatsoever I builded, it came to loss, till I knew Christ Jesus, the Rock and sure Foundation of the Heavenly Building: And blessed be his Name, the Inspiration of his Spirit is very precious, without which none can have a *(page 28)* right Understanding; and I could not find peace with God while I did err for want of this good Understanding. And my Cry was often to the Lord, to give me an understanding Heart, that I might discern between things that differ; for the crooked Serpent, who is very subtle in his Workings, endeavours by Flattery and Threatenings, Temptations, Buffetings, and false Accusations, to darken the Heart, and enfeeble the Mind; and if he cannot prevail so, he can transform himself into the likeness of an Angel of Light, to hinder the travelling ones, whose Understandings begin to be opened, yet watching in the Light, they come to see his Snares; then he bestirs him, as a strong Man armed indeed, as by Experience much might be spoken, since I was first exercised about going this Voyage; but I shall omit as much as I can, having nothing in my View but Truth's Prosperity, and preferring it above all, because it's better to me than all; I can do no less than bare my Testimony unto all People, That it's Excellency far exceeds the choicest Gold, and the precious Pearls; and the Spirit of Truth comforts the comfortless, and strengthens the weak, and relieves the needy: Oh what can be compared to its Power! for it works a change of the heart, and preserves from sinning against the Lord, all those that follow the Leadings of the Light thereof unto amendment of Life, and honours the Lord by ordering *(page 29)* their Conversation aright, according to the Dictates of his Spirit. Oh, I had rather mourn away all my Days than grieve it or walk contrary to it, whatever

Reproach I suffer; for I have had a blessed Reward when I have observed it, and obeyed it; and I hope I shall never forget how the Power
of it brought me into Subjection, and made me willing to be disposed of
by it; and when it had wrought me into a single Resignment, then was
my weighty Concern (touching my Journey to *New-England*) taken off,
and a Service laid upon me to go back, and labour for the Settlement of
our Womens Meetings in our County of *Berks*, which has no small Cross
to take up: But as I daily followed Jesus, (honoured be his worthy Name)
he endowed me with his eternal encouraging Power, and also
strengthned the weak and hindermost of the Flock; though *Amalck* lay
in way by the way and the opposite Spirit did strongly strive, yet our
good Shepherd did visit his Handmaids, and (blessed be his Name)
filled us with his overcoming Power, when the Mothers in *Israel* were
so dismayed, as we were likely to have lost our Womens Meeting; but
Praises, Honour, and Renown, be ascribed unto that Almighty Power
that hath set up and setled his Womens Meeting, saith my Soul; for it
hath been a good Reward to me, and fitly furnished me for the Service
that was required, and wonderfully upheld me therein *(page 30)* unto admiration; and I can truly say, my Reward is sufficient, and can give in a
true Testimony, that the Lord owns our Womens Meetings, and hath
manifested and magnified his excellent Power therein, to the gladding
of our Hearts, and the refreshing of our Souls wherever came. Glory to
his Name, and magnified be his preserving Power for ever: He is a God
of Wisdom unto the Foolish, and Strength unto the Weak, and honours
his Power in contemptible Vessels, that it may have its due; for all
Honour belongs thereunto: But those that are in the Wisdom of the
World, which comes from beneath, and have many Arts and Parts, and
mind not the Wisdom that comes from above, they take that to themselves which belongs to God, and that provokes him to Wrath, and he
is angry with such as seek Honour one of another, and do not seek his
Honour more than their own Interest, and Honour to Man; for that
hath been the overthrow of many; for God is jealous of his Glory; *he
will not give it to another, nor his praise to graven images;* but the secret
Arm of his Power is stretched out to overturn them, and he is on his
way, and it's in vain for *Flesh to strive against him, before whom all Nations
are but as the drop of a Bucket: for out of the Mouths of Babes and Sucklings
he will perfect his praise,* both in Males and Females that give up to serve
him; and he brings great things to pass, contrary to Man's Wisdom or
(page 31) Expectation, *that no Flesh might glory in his Presence.*

For when I was exercised about setling the Womens Meeting, I little thought to be concerned again with going for *New-England*; but after a short time it was more weighty than ever, and my Exercises more than before; and this I do write, that no one should murmur, and say, *No Exercise is like mine*; and this followed me until the Hand of the All-wise God was so heavy upon me, that I could no longer stay at home, although both sick and lame, and much to undergo both inwardly and outwardly, yet did not dare to plead with the Lord any longer, or to make any Excuse, but truly gave up all, both Life and all that he had given me, when he required it; and he brought me to be *as Clay in the hand of the Potter.* He filled my Vessel with his Heavenly Treasure, and fulfilled that Scripture that testifies that he hath said, *I honour them that honour me*; and blessed be the Lord, such Honour have the Earthen Vessels of a Remnant, and the Excellency of the Power is his, and the Glory of all; for he is worthy of it; for he is no hard Master, but a sure Rewarder of his faithful Servants, and he endues them with Power that delights in his Law, and inclines to keep his Commands, and unto such they are not grievous, but joyous; but looking out hinders; and therefore let none look at their own Weakness; let my *(page 32)* Harms make others beware, and let's be depending on our good Physician; for he hath the Balm of *Gilead* that cures both Soul and Body, which makes the weak strong, with the sweet Cordials of his Life, that relieves the faint hearted and feeble minded, and through tender Mercy I have found it very needful, and very useful at all times in all Conditions; else what could I have done when in such a weak Condition, so many Thousands of Miles from my Habitation? but blessed be the Lord and magnified be his preserving Power; as Tryals did abound, Patience did superabound, and that brought me to a good Experience of that which sweetned my bitter Cups, and that caused the living Hope to spring, that anchors in stormy times; and then did the Light of my Soul's Beloved shine upon me, and he shewed me what great deliverances he had wrought for me, and what great cause I had to trust in his Name, that had been a comfortable Refuge unto me at home and abroad, and also shewed me, that his *Rod and Staff had comforted me*; and he was always with me, and in the Enjoyment of his Presence did my Soul rejoice in the midst of great Tryals, and then was my cry, *Lord, give me and mine the comfortable enjoyment of thy presence for ever, and then try us as thou pleasest: Thy preserving Power is all that I desire of thee, and unto it I commit all, and with thee I leave all; for thou aretworthy to dispose of all; and then would Life flow in as a River, to the comforting (page 33) and strengthening of Soul and*

Body. Everlasting Praises, and holy Thanksgivings be returned to Christ Jesus; for he is worthy, my Soul can truly say; for I have experienced his dealings, and seen his mighty works that he hath done, even marvelously for his tender Seed, with which my Soul hath travelled, and is often concerned; for they have much to bear wherever I have been. The Lord my God relieve them more and more, and work their deliverance for thy own Glory, and the comfort of thy true travelling ones for evermore.

Written aboard the Ship in the 3rd Month, ANNO 1681.

A further Testimony for the magnifying of that Power that supported my weak Body, and comforted my poor Soul in my Travels in America: *I feel my self concerned to give a Relation of some particular Places and Service.*

First I came to *New York*, and there had been hurt done by some, that Friends had lost their 5th Day Meeting, and I laboured to settle it again, and God's Eternal Power wrought wonderfully in me several Meetings with his people, and we were well refreshed: And when the Meeting aforesaid was setled again, it was with me to go to *Long Island*, and *(page 34)* there the *Ranters* oppressed *Friends*, but the Lord had a tender People there, and his Power was amongst them, and we were sweetly refreshed together; for God's *Almighty Power was over all*, in all Meetings wherever I came, to the subduing of the dark Power that raged in the *Ranters*, and the relieving of the tender hearted: Honour and Praises be ascribed unto it for ever; for it made me sensible of the oppression of the tender Seed, and for its sake my Soul was in deep travel; and the Night before the general Meeting, I was near unto death, and many *Friends* were with me, who did not expect my Life, and I was so weak when I came there, that two *Women-Friends* led me into the Meeting, and there was a great Meeting of several sorts of people, and in a little time the God of Wisdom, Life and Power, filled me with the Word of his Power, and I stood up in the strength thereof, and it was so prevailing over the Meeting, that *Friends* were very much comforted and refreshed, and the Power of Darkness so chained, that the opposing *Ranters* and *Apostates* could not shew their antick tricks, nor oppress *Friends*, as they did use to do; for they were very abusive in those remote Islands, and commonly did much Mischief in *Friends* Meetings: And they that had been convinced, and were *turned again with the Dog to its Vomit*, as saith the Scripture, with the *Sow that was washed, to wallow again in the mire, and had made Shipwreck of Faith and a good Conscience*, they were most wicked; and preached Scripture, *(page 35)* and had Truth's Words, and grieved Truth's Spirit, and burdened *Friends* exceedingly, and honest *Friends* could hardly be clear, that had a Testimony, except they spake while they were speaking: But when God's Power did arise over them; it many times put them to silence, even to admiration; and altho *Friends* Exercise was great, especially them that declared, yet the blessed Effect of the Almighty Power was, and is a precious Recompence, and a good Reward.

And when my Service was over in *Long Island*, it was in my Heart to go to *Road Island*, to the General Meeting that approached soon after I arrived there; yet we had a quick passage; through Providence; and when I came to the General Meeting of *Friends*, there was that abominable Crew, and *Tho. Case*, the grand *Ranter*, was bawling very loud; and I had been there but a very little time, but God's living Power did arise most wonderfully, and I declared in the demonstration thereof, and soon put him to silence; and he went forth, and the powerful Presence of the Lord was amongst his People; and this General Meeting in *Road Island* lasted Four Days together, and I had good Service there, and God's Eternal Heart-tendering Power was over all, Glory and Living Praises be unto it for evermore.

And still it was upon me to go to *Boston*; for that was with me before I came from home; and I hastened to take a passage in a Sloop, and went with some *Friends*, and one was a *Maiden-Friend*, that had a few Words sometimes in Meetings, who had been there once before, and she and another *Friend* suffered much there, both Imprisonment and other Cruelty, for Conscience-sake: But blessed be the God of all our Mercies, we had peaceable Meetings there, and his excellent Power was so, that it tendered the people, and there was hardly any that I saw, but shed tears; there was a *Lawyer* that had a hand in the suffering of our *Friends* that were put to Death, and he was very solid all the while. And after this I travelled by Sea and Land in the strength of the supporting Power to many places, whithersoever the Lord ordered me; and as I followed the Line of his Divine Light, he failed not to endow me with the renewing of his precious Power, and my Soul hath cause to magnifie it, because it enabled me to answer what the Lord required of me, and fitted me, who was most unfit, and the poorest and most helpless that ever I did see concerned in such a Service: But it was the more to the Honour of the Power of my God that so wonderfully wrought in my poor weak and helpless Vessel; and many *Friends* were tendered thereby (in many places in the sense of my Weakness). Honoured and Renowned be it for ever, saith my Soul; for its Manifestation made the Hearts of his People glad, and we were well refreshed together in all the Meetings that I was at in *New England.* And from thence I returned back to *Road Island* and *Long Island* ; and when I was clear thereabout I *(page 37)* took Shipping for *East Jersey*, and the Power of God was greatly manifested, and through his special Providence we were preserved, being in great peril and danger of being cast away when we were in sight of Land; for the Winds being boisterous, and the foaming Sea in so great a Rage, that we could not cast Anchor to stay the Vessel, being near the Shoals; but the Lord who hath all Power in his hands, delivered us (Praises to his holy Name), and we safely landed at *Shrewsbury* (and *Elizabeth Dean*, that then travelled with me, was very sick); and we had very good Meetings in *East Jersey*, where I met with the Lord among his people, as at other times, blessed be his Name; and after some time spent amongst them, and that we had been well refreshed with God's holy precious living Power, it carried me from thence to *West Jersey*, and into some part of *Pensilvania*, (but it had not that Name then) and in the sense of God's great Love to his tender Seed, I encouraged his Children to suffer, and to be careful that they did not cause Truth to suffer for if they tendered it in their own Bosoms, and travell'd with it, the Lord would bring it all over its Enemies, and it shall reign over all in his due time; and blessed be his most worthy Name, he soon after brought it to pass by his delivering Power; and when I had laboured that the Gospel-Life might be lived in, and the Gospel-Order established amongst them, there remained the heavenly power among the tender ones. And the Lord heard the cry of the poor, *(page 38)* and granted the desire of the needy, and visited them with the Gospel-Power; for a little time after I came home, I had an account, that they had Mens Meetings and Womens Meetings in the Gospel-Light, Life and Power, and were establishing in the Blessed Order that was testified of, when I was there with them.

And when I was clear of *West Jersey*, and those parts, I returned to *New-York*, in order to take my passage for *England*; but before I came there, the Living God (whom I served with all my Heart) further tryed me, and laid it weightily upon me to go to *Barbadoes*, which was no little cross to my Mind; but the over coming Power of the true and living God wrought so strongly with me, that I was made willing to take up the *Cross, and follow Jesus*, through many Tribulations, and he (magnified be his Power) most wonderfully supported and conducted me all along: For I took Shipping at *New York*, and as the Lord put it into my Heart to visit *Friends* in the *Leeward Islands*, so he carried the Vessel, let them that fail'd do what they could; and they could not steer their Course *Barbadoes-Road* , altho they endeavoured it with all their might; and I had good Service amongst them in the Vessel; and they were made to confess to the Almighty Power that I testified of; and we laid by *Antego* a Week before the Owner would let me go a-shore: But an All-wise God ordered it so, that the Vessel could not go away till I had been there, and performed what Service he had appointed for *(page 39)* me; and blessed be his Name, his Reward was precious; for we came a-shore on a First Day, and I hastened to a *Friends* Meeting; and when I came in, I found the Lord's Power was amongst his People, and I had a precious time with them: There was a little handful of plain hearted *Friends*, and our Hearts were tendered, and our Souls comforted, and we rejoiced that the Lord Jesus had visited us, and caused us in his Love to visit each other.

So when I returned to the Sea again, it came into my Heart to visit *Friends* at *Nevice*; and when I had taken leave of *Friends* of *Antego* that came aboard with me, and God's Heavenly Power was with us, and sweetly refreshed our Souls, as we were aboard the Vessel, and remained with us; and we were concerned one for another, not knowing that we should ever see each others Faces more: But see how the Lord ordered it; as we were sailing on the Sea, it opened in my Heart to Visit *Friends* at *Nevice*; but the Owner of the Vessel being a hypocritical Professer, caused my Exercise to be the more; but the Power of the Lord was manifest; and *the Winds and Sea obeyed*, that we were carried to *Nevice* against his will; but he would not let me go a-shore; for he had heard, *That those should pay a great Fine that carried any Friend thither*; and hoysted Sail again for *Barbadoes*, and said, he would weather the Point of *Cordilopa*; and he laboured Three Weeks, but could not do it: for the Hand of the Lord was against him; else he might have done it, in a few Days, *(page 40)* but he provoked the Lord, and trusted in his Vessel, and in his own Skill; and he locked up the Bread, and dealt hardly with his Passengers when he saw he should be longer at Sea than at first he did expect; and he knew that for Three Weeks there was stinking Water, and we were close by a *French* Island, and they said, the *French* would not let us have any, if we starved: They were *Papists*, and said, *If we came for water, they would take our Ship for a Prey, and us for Captives:* And yet this Owner of the Vessel would not go to any other Island, until the *Merchants* that were aboard threatned him very sorely; and then he put in at a mountainous place, called *Mount Serat;* and they went all away from me as soon as they were landed; for I was very weakly, being aboard the Vessel so long, with such bad Accommodation: I went aboard with my Clothes, so wet, that I could wring Water out of them, and so dried them upon my weakly Body, which cast me into such a Feverish condition, that I was very dry, and I sate down on the Shoar, and a Girl came to fetch fresh Water near where I sate, and I drank till I sweat, and then I swooned, and lay some time; but the arising of the Life of Jesus set me on my Feet again, and in the strength and relief thereof I went to enquire for a passage for *Barbadoes*, and heard of none; but I was not clear of *Nevice*, but hearing of a leaking Vessel to go to *Antego*, took my passage in that, hoping that way might be made from thence to go to *Nevice* , and then having got a passage, it being *(page 41)* Night and rainy, I tried to get me a Lodging on the Land, and the People were generally *Irish* Papists, but the Lord did so order it, that I met with an *English* Woman, and she treated me kindly, but she had neither Bread nor Drink, but Wine and Sugar; and I desired half a Pint of *Madary* Wine to be boiled, and that served me Night and Morning, and the Lord blessed it to me, and his Holy Power accompanied me; and, while I staid for the Vessel, I had good service there, though there was no Friend in all the Island; they had banished a Friend out of it, as I heard, but a little before, and the People told me they did not dare to have a Meeting, yet I published Truth in the Streets, and they confessed to it; and so I left Truth honorably amongst them, and then came aboard the Vessel, where I last took my Passage, and sailed to the other Vessel, that I had suffered in, and called for the Owner and cleared my Conscience to him, and told him the Hand of the Lord was against him, and warned him to Repent, else he should suddenly feel the stroak of it to be heavy upon him; and inasmuch as his Herat [*sic*] had been too much set on that Bark, he should shortly see that the Lord would destroy it, and accordingly his Vessel was split on a Rock in a little time after. So when I, through tender Mercy, came to *Antego* again, the Friends told me how they had been concerned for me, and so had *Nevice* Friends, and there was a Passage ready for *Nevice*, and an honest Woman-Friend, whose *(page 42)* name was *Mary Humphrey*, was very ready to go with me, and Friends there were very joyful of my coming, and we had many good and powerful Meetings in that Island; and there was a Judge and his Wife came to Meeting, and People of several sorts, and we had some Meetings at the Houses of them that were no Friends, and Friends were well satisfied and comforted, and the mighty Power of God was with us: Glory unto it, for it is worthy over all, and in us all: Oh that we may have an Eye to its Glory in our whole Lives and Conversations; for it is by it we live, move, and have our Being; and its dealing with us, and working for us in that place is worthy to be remembred; for this was the place that the Owner of the Vessel afore-mentioned was afraid to carry me to; but the Lord was on my side, and prevented much Evil when it was intended; and the Governor of that Place was so kind that he gave us his Letter of Recommendation to carry with us; and so I came back with M. *Humphery* to *Antego* and to *Five Islands*, and there we and some Friends that went with us visited a poor People that complained of their Priest, and said he came to them but once a Year, and then it was to take that which they had from them; and we had a precious opportunity to manifest the Truth, and they were very kind to us, and seem'd to be well satisfied and affected.

And then I being clear, and a passage presented for *Barbadoes*, as soon as I was *(page 43)* ready I went aboard, and was there sooner than could have been expected: And when I arrived, I met with many Friends at *Brid-Town*, and there took an account of the Monthly Meetings, and went to them and other Meetings as brief as I could; and most Days I had two or three Meetings of a Day, both among the Blacks, and also among the White People: And the Power of the Lord Jesus was mightily manifested, so that my Soul was, often melted therewith, even in the Meetings of the *Negro's* or *Blacks*, as well as among Friends. And when I had gone through the Island, and was clear, having been well refreshed with Friends, in the feeling of the Heavenly Power; and in the strength of the same I came aboard the Ship of my Native Land again.

Written a board the Ship coming from Barbadoes, *in the 3d Month*, 1681.

Before I went to Sea I was two Weeks in the service of Truth in *Kent*, and then it was shewed me, being at *Sandwich*, that I should bear my Testimony for God, and his Divine Spiritual Worship, in a *Steeple-House* there; and coming home, the Heavenly Power wrought mightily in my Heart. And when I was clear of those Countreys, I was better in Health than I had been for many Years. And, as the Light of Jesus shewed me before, I left *England (page 44)* as is afore hinted; so the Power thereof ordered me when I came back, & it was so weightily on me before I came ashore, that I thought it long ere I came to *Kent* to clear my Conscience, and the God of Sea and Land brought me safely thither, and I hastened to *Sandwich*, on a *First-day*, being the 5th of the 4th Month, 1681, I went to the *Steeple-House*, as it was before me, and had been of a long time, and in the strength of the Almighty Power I delivered that Message which I received of the Lord Jesus, saying, *The Day is come, spoken of and foretold by the Prophet, of the pouring forth of God's Spirit upon all Flesh, Sons and Daughters, &c.* And I exhorted them, both Priest and People, to take heed to a Measure or Manifestation thereof in their own Hearts, (and leave off their Idolatry) and come to be true Spiritual Worshippers; and I laid before them the danger of the one, and the benefit of the other; till the Priest caused me to be haled out; and when I came forth many of his Hearers followed me, and I had a good opportunity with them, and clear'd my self to them, and left them. And as I was going away, I felt the arising of that Power that is worthy to be obeyed, and it was with me to go to them again; and when they came from their worship I met them, first the Mayor and his Company, then the Lawyer and his, and after that the Priest, with many more; and I invited all to come to our Spiritual Worship, and I would engage that if any of them, young or old, *(page 45)* male or female, had a Message from the Lord to deliver there, that they should have liberty, and not be abused, as the Priest caused me to be; for the Man that haled me out hurt my Arm, so that it was swelled some time after, and I told the Priest that he was not of the Primitive Faith and Church of Christ, testified of in Scripture, for there, if any thing was revealed to the Standers by or Hearers they might speak one by one; the first holding his peace; and he was silent before I spoke, and he said I should not have spoken in the Church: and I asked him what Church that was? for I had spoken in the true Church many times amongst God's People, and they did not hinder me; and he said *Paul* spoke against a Womans speaking in the Church: I asked him what Woman that was, and what Church that was that she should not speak in? and he did not answer me, but went away; and a Woman Friend that was with me took hold of him, and said, My Friend, answer the Womans question, (and the *Dutch* People were coming from their worship the while,) but the Priest put off his Hat to us and busled away, and afterwards endeavoured to send me to Prison; but the God of Power (who preserved me when much Evil hath been intended) prevented him, that he could not prevail with the Mayor, but he endeavoured to harm the Friends of that place after that I was gone: And after the *first Day* Meeting was over, I went the beginning of the Week to some other Meetings, and *(page 46)* came again a *fourth Day*, and God's Power was over all, and Friends had no harm; and we had another Heavenly Meeting, and so I came away and left Friends peaceable, and all was well, blessed be the Lord, and magnified be his preserving Power, over all, for evermore. *Amen. saith my Soul.*

J.V.

I was informed that the Priest above specified, did do his endeavour to stir up Persecution against Friends, and put the Mayor to some trouble, for not punishing me; but therein he did, nor could do, no more than manifest his own Malice, and what Birth he was of: The Lord had set his Bounds.

J.V.

In all this long Journey, this I can say, (to the Honour and Glory of my tender God, and, to the Praise of his Providential Power,) and be it known to all, That altho' I had none to accompany me of my own or Friends providing, yet the Lord so ordered it, that I had still some honest Woman, or Maiden Friend, both by Sea & Land. In the first Vessel thatever I was in, I had an honest ancient maiden Friend, namely *Sarah Yoaklet*, who was my Companion from *London* until I came to *Long-Island*: And then in *New-England*, one *Lydia Wright*, another faithful Friend, was willing to travel with me and did accompany me a considerable time and still the Lord so ordered it, that when ever one left me, that another was ready to take her place to be my Companion. And when I returned home, there came with me an ancient *(page 47)* Maiden Friend, who had been out in those Countries in the service of Truth six Years, whose name was *Margaret Kerby*; and on the 3d of the 4th Month, 1681, I arrived safely at *Dover* in the County of *Kent*, where I was three Weeks in the service of Truth: And after that (blessed and renowned be the Holy Name of Jesus) I came to *London*, and after a little time spent in visiting Friends at *London*, I came safe

home: And as I pondered weightily, and beheld the Preservation of me
and mine, and the manifold Mercies that we received when so far remote
one from another, my Heart, was truly tendered in the sense of my
Heavenly Father's Love, and my Soul magnified, the Preserving and
Delivering Power, and the cry run through me, *Lord God of my Life, let
me and mine never forget thy Goodness, for it is wonderfully to be admired;
and thy unexpressible Love to be considered, by all those unto whom it hath
been so largely extended. And as I consider our nothingness, and thy tenderness
towards us, I cannot but abhor self, and breath, unto thee that I and mine
may for ever hold self in no reputation, and follow Jesus through the daily
cross; wherein I (through tender Mercy) have found power, when of my self
I could do nothing whereby to fulfil what was required of me, but self was
very ready to hinder me, as the self-seeking Spirit is always those that are not
aware of it: And therefore I desire above all things, that I and mine, whom
the Lord hath been so good unto, may be watchful; and, in order thereunto,
I commit all (page 48) unto that God of Power that hath preserved hitherto,
and is able to keep and preserve unto the end: To whom be all Glory and
Praise for evermore. Amen.*

J. V.

An Account

OF THE

TRAVELS,

Sufferings & Perſecutions

OF

Barbara Blaugdone.

Given forth as a Teſtimony to
the Lord's Power, and for
the Encouragement of
Friends.

Printed, and Sold by *T. S.* at the *Crooked-
Billet* in *Holywell-Lane, Shoreditch, 1691.*

(Page numbers of original document appear in text as *page _.*)

(page 5)

An Account of the Travels, Sufferings and Persecutions of B.B., &c.

In my Youth and Tender Years, I feared the Lord, and was afraid to offend him; and was zealous and diligent in the Profession I was in, and sought the Lord earnestly, although I knew not where to find him, until I was directed by Friends that came from the North, *John Audland* and *John Camm* by Name, whose Behaviour and Deportments were such, that it preached before ever they opened their Mouths; and *(page 6)* it was then revealed to me, That they had the Everlasting Gospel to Preach in this City: And when they did open their Mouths, I was made to bless God that I had lived to hear the everlasting Gospel preached; and they directed my Mind unto the Light of Christ, therein to wait, which I was diligent to do, and found the Vertue of it; and as the Evil was made manifest, I departed from it, and willingly took up the Cross, and yielded Obedience unto it, in plainness of Speech and in my Habit: & the People were so offended with it, when I went into their Publick Places and Steeple-houses to speak, that they took away their Children from me, so that I lost almost all my Imployment; and they kept me in Prison a quarter of a Year at a time: And great was my Sufferings in that Day, but the Lord so filled me with his *(page 7)* Power, that I was preserved through it all: And the Diligent and Faithful did prosper then, and so they do now.

And therefore my Counsel to *Friends*, is, that they keep in God's Power; for there is no other way to be preserved, nor to receive Life and Salvation; its my Testimony for God: For whosoever shuns the Cross, and goes out of the Power, they lose their way, and dishonour God; but whosoever keep in the Faith, and abide in the Power, they are in Safety: I have had living Experience of it, therefore I mention it, and it has been with me a pretty while to publish it, for the benefit of those that are passing through, and are yet to pass through the Sufferings, and therefore I do declare my Experience.

(page 8) And so, *dear Friends*, the Cross is the Way to the Crown of Life, and to the Crown of Glory; and they that continue Faithful and Obedient, they obtain the Eternal Crown, which they that are disobedient, lose. I speak my Experience of the Dealings of the Lord with me, in my Travels and passings through my Spiritual Journey, for the benefit of those that Travel rightly after. And I can speak it to the glory of

God, he never moved me to any thing, but that he gave me Power to perform it, and made it effectual, although I past through much Exercise in the performance of it. And the Power of God wrought in me long before I knew what it was; and when Friends came, that my understanding was opened, I soon took up the Cross and came into the Obedience, and the Lord cleansed me by his *(page 9)* Power, and made me a fit Vessel for his Use.

And when I had laboured pretty much at home, he called me forth to labour abroad, and I stood so in the dread, awe and fear of the Lord, that his Spirit strove much with me, before I could open my Mouth; and the Word of the Lord came unto me in a Meeting, *That the Lord would have War with* Amalek *from Generation to Generation:* And the Power and Spirit of the Lord was so strong in me, that it set me upon my Feet, and constrained me to speak the words; for I was never hasty nor forward.

And then the Lord caused me to abstain from all Flesh, Wine and Beer whatsoever, and I drank only Water for the space of a whole Year; and in that time the Lord caused me to grow and to prosper in the Truth: And then *(page 10)* I was made to go and to call the People forth from among the dumb Idols, and suffered much Imprisonment for it; but yet I was made to go till the Lord gave me dominion, so that I could go into their Places, and say what I had to say, and come forth again quietly. And as *Mary Prince* and I was coming Arm in Arm from a Meeting, that was at *George Bishop's* House, there was a Rude Man came and abused us, and struck off *Mary Prince* her Hat, and run some sharp Knife or Instrument through all my Clothes, into the side of my Belly, which if it had gone a little farther, it might have killed me; but my Soul was so in love with the Truth, that I could have given up my Life for it at that day.

And then I was moved to go to *Marlborough,* to the *(page 11)* Marketplace and Steeple-house, where I had pretty much Service, where they put me in Prison for six Weeks, where I Fasted six Days and six Nights, and neither eat Bread nor drank Water, nor no earthly thing; then I came to a feeding upon the Word, and had experience that man doth not live by Bread alone, but by every Word that proceedeth out of the Mouth of the Lord. And when I was released, I went to *Isaac Burges,* the man that committed me, and discoursed with him; and he was really Convinced of the Truth, but could not take up the Cross; but was afterwards very loving to Friends, and stood by them upon all occasions, and never Persecuted a Friend any more: and when he came unto this City, he came unto my House to see me, and confest, That he could not take *(page 12)* up the Cross, although he knew it was the Truth. And a while after I was made to go into *Devonshire*, to *Molton*, and *Bastable*, and *Bediford*, where I had a Prison in all those Places: and I went to the *Earl* of *Bathes*, where I had formerly spent much time in Vanity, to call unto them to come out of their Vanity; and I asked to speak with the *Countess*, and they refused to let me in, but one of the Servants that knew me, bid me go to the Back-Door, and their Lady would come forth that way to go into the Garden; and they sent forth a great Wolf-Dog upon me, which came fiercely at me to devour me, and just as he came unto me, the Power of the Lord smote the Dog, so that he whined, and ran in crying, and very Lame; so that I saw clearly the Hand of the Lord in it for my *(page 13)* preservation, blessed be his Name: and then the Lady came forth, and stood still and heard me all that I had to say unto her; and when I had done she gave me Thanks, but never asked me to go into her House, although I had eat and drank at her Table and lodged there many a time.

And then I was moved to go to *Great-Torrington* in *Devonshire*, unto the Steeple-house there, where was a very bad Priest indeed, though I had little to him, but to the People; and when I had spoken in the Morning, I went to my Lodging, and what I had not room to clear my self of, I went to Writing, and the Constables came and took away my Writing, and commanded me to go along with them to their Worship; and I answered them, That they would not suffer me to speak there, and that I knew *(page 14)* no Law would compel me to go twice in a day, and they all knew that I was there in the Morning; and so I would not go. So the next day the Mayor sent for me, and when I came the Priest was there, and the Mayor was moderate, and loath to send me to Prison, but the Priest was very eager, and said, *I ought to be Whipt for a Vaga-bond*. And I bid him prove where ever I askt any one for a bit of Bread; but he said, *I had broken the Law by speaking in their Church*. So he was so eager with the Mayor, that he made him make a *Mittimus*, and send me to *Exeter*-Prison, which was Twenty Miles distant, where I remained for some time, and was commanded of the Lord to Fast fourteen Days and fourteen Nights, without tasting Bread or Water, or any earthly thing, which I performed for a *(page 15)* Witness against that dark professing People; and there I was until the Assizes, and was not called forth to a Tryal: but after the Assizes was over, a petty Fellow sent for me forth, and read a Law, which was quite wrong, and did not belong to me at all, and put me to lodge one Night among a great company of *Gypsies* that were then in the Prison; and the next day the Sheriff came with a Beadle, and had me into a Room, and Whipt me till the Blood ran down my Back, and I never startled at a blow; but the Lord made me to rejoyce, that I was counted Worthy to Suffer for his Name's sake, and I Sung aloud; and the Beadle said, *Do ye Sing; I shall make ye Cry by and by*: and with that he laid more Stripes, and laid them on very hard. I shall never forget the large Experience of the Love and Power *(page 16)* of God which I had in my Travels, and therefore I can speak to his Praise, and glorifie his Name: for if he had Whipt me to Death in that state which then I was in, I should not have been terrified and dismayed at it; Ann *Speed* was an Eye Witness of it, and she stood and lookt in at the Window, and wept bitterly. And then the Sheriff, when he saw that the envy of the man could not move me, he bid him *forbear, for he had gone beyond his Orders already*. So when he had left me, Ann *Speed* came in and drest my Wounds; and the next day they turned me out with all the *Gypsies*, and the Beadle followed us two Miles out of the City; and as soon as he left us, I returned back again, and went up into the Prison to see my Friends that were Prisoners there at the same time: So I took my *(page 17)* leave of them, and went to *Topsom*, where there was a fine Meeting of Friends, among whom I was sweetly refreshed, and staid there one Night, and then I came home to *Bristoll*; and in my Travels I went several Miles upon long Downs, and knew nothing of the way, but as the Lord was with me, and did direct me; and in all this I have experience of the Love and Power of the Lord to me wards, blessed be his Name for ever: I cannot forget his Loving-kindness to me in my Distress.

And in my Travels near *Bridgewater*, I went to speak to a Priest that I had formerly known, one *Edward Piggot*; and when I came back to the Inn, where I had bespoke my Lodging, they would not let me come in; so I lookt about for shelter to keep me from the fierceness of the Frost, and *(page 18)* I found the Pig-stye swept very clean, and the Trough turned up and never a Pig in it, and I sate me down on the Trough, and that was my Lodging all that Night: and the next Night I could get no lodging, but was fain to lodge in a Barn: and in all this the Lord exercised me in the Patience.

Then I went to *Bediford*, and there I was put into the Town-Hall, and they searched me to see whether I had Knife or Scissers about me; and the next day they brought me before the Mayor for speaking in a private Meeting, and he discoursed much with me, and had a sence of what I said unto him, and received it; and at last he set open two Doors, one right against the other, and said, *He would give me my choice which I would go forth at? whether I would go to Prison again, (page 19) or go home?* And I told him that I should choose Liberty rather than Bonds: So I went homeward, and then he took his Horse and came and followed me, for there was some tenderness in him; and he would have had me Rid [*sic*] behind him, but I found that when any Body which he knew did meet us, then he would draw back and lag behind, and as soon as they were gone, he would come up to me again; so therefore I would not ride behind him, but he rode three or four Miles with me, and discoursed me all the way; and when we parted, I was made to kneel down and pray for him, in which time he was very serious; and afterwards he grew very solid and sober, and in a little time he dyed, but I writ to him once before he dyed, a little after I came home.

(page 20) And then I was moved of the Lord to go to *Bazing-stoke*, to endeavour the Liberty of two Friends, (*viz.*) *Thomas Robison* and *Ambrose Riggs*, which were taken up at the first Meeting that Friends had there; and when I came, they would not let me come in to them; and I having a Letter from *John Camm* unto them, put it in at a Chink of the Door to them; and then I went to the Mayor to desire their Liberty, and he told me, *That if he should see the Letter which I brought them, they should have their Liberty;* and I told him he should, so I went and fetcht it to him, and he read it, and could see no hurt in it: So he told me, *I should have my Brethren out but he would not let them out presently.* Nevertheless we had a fine Meeting the next day, being First Day, and coming from the *(page 21)* Meeting, I met with the Priest, and told him his portion, and in a few days the Friends had their Liberty: and thus the Lord made my Journey prosperous.

And then the Lord moved me to go for *Ireland*, and I went in a Vessel bound for *Corke*, and the Lord so ordered it, that the Ship was carried about to *Dublin*, and we had much foul Weather, so that the Sea-men said, That I was the cause of it, because I was a *Quaker*; and they conspired to fling me over-board; but it being made known to me, I went to the Master and told him what his Men had designed to do, and told him, that if he did suffer them to do it, my Blood would be required at his Hands. So he charged them not to meddle with me: And afterwards we were in a Storm upon a First Day, *(page 22)* and I was moved to go upon Deck, and speak among them, and Pray for them; and they were all made very quiet, and said, *They were more beholding to me then they were to their Priest, because I did Pray for them, and he could not open his Mouth to say any thing amongst them.* We were six Days and six Nights at Sea, and the Master himself did not know where he was,

nor which way he was going, until we were put into the Harbour at
Dublin; and although we had abundance of very Stormy Weather, yet
we sustained no manner of loss nor dammage; so that the Master said,
He could never say before that he was in so much foul Weather, and
received no hurt: And we were put into *Dublin* the very same day that
Francis Howgill and *Edward Burrough* were Banisht from thence. And
then I saw my *(page 23)* Service there, and was moved to go to the Deputy,
and when I came there, the People said, their was no speaking with
him for me; for did I not know that he had Banisht two of our Friends
out of the Nation but yesterday. But in the Faith I went, and the Power
of the Lord had great weight upon me, and I met with the Secretary,
and I desired him to help me to the Speech of the Deputy. And he
answered me, *That he did think he could not.* And I told him, if he would
be so civil, as to go up and tell the Deputy, that there was a Woman
below that would speak with him; and then if he refused, I was answered. So he went up, and their came a Man to fetch me up into the
with-drawing Room; and after I had been there a while, their came a
Man out of the Deputy's Chamber and they all stood bare-headed *(page
24)* before him, because they knew I never saw the Deputy; but I had a
sence it was a Priest; and there was almost a whole Room full of People,
and they askt me, *Why did not I do my Message to their Lord.* And I
answered, When I do see your Lord, then I shall do my Message to him.
So in a little while he came forth, and sate down on a Couch, and I
stood up and spake to him that which the Lord did give me to speak,
and bid him beware, that he was not found fighting against God, in
opposing the Truth, and Persecuting the Innocent, but be like Wise
Gamaliel, To let it alone, and if it be of God, it will stand; but if it be of
Man, it will fall; and the Enmity did not lie so much in himself, as he
was stirred up to it by Evil Magistrates and bad Priests; and that God's
People are as dear to him now as *(page 25)* ever, and they that toucht
them, toucht the Apple of his Eye. But in his Name, and by his Power
their was much hurt done to the People of God all the Nation over, and
it would lie heavy upon him at the last; and that the Teachers of the
People did cause them to Err, and he knew the Priests portion; and
when I toucht upon that, he would say, *There's for you Mr. Harrison,* to
the Priest that stood there. And the Power and Presence of the Lord
was so with me, that it made the Man to be much concerned. And
when I had done, he asked the Priest, *What he had to say to that which I
spake:* And the Priest said, *It was all very true and very good, and he had
nothing to say against it, if he did speak as we meant.* Then I told the

Priest, that the Spirit of God was true, and did speak as it meant, and meant as it spoke; *(page 26)* but men of Corrupt Minds did pervert the Scriptures, by putting their own Imaginations, and Conceivings, and Apprehensions upon it, and so did deceive the People: but holy men of God spake the Scriptures, and gave them forth as they were Inspired by the Holy Ghost, and they are of no private Interpretation; but none understood them, but those that read them by the same Spirit that gave them forth. So I returned to my Lodging, which was at one Captain *Rich* his House, and he came home, and said, *That the Deputy was so Sad and Melancholy, after I had beed with him, that he would not come forth to Bowls nor no Pastime at all.*

This my Service for God was great, and he made it to prosper; And then I went to *Corke*, where my Motion was at first, and great *(page 27)* were my Sufferings there, for I had a Prison almost where-ever I came; and I was made to call to my Relations and Acquaintance, by the Word of the Lord, and was made to follow them into several Steeple-houses; and great were my Sufferings amongst them, but where-ever the Lord opened my Mouth, there were some that received me, and would plead my Cause against my Persecutors; and I was in Jeopardy of my Life several times, but the Lord prevented it. And I was made to speak in a Market-place, and there was a Butcher swore he would cleave my Head in twain; and had his Cleaver up ready to do it, but their came a Woman behind him and caught back his Arms, and staid them till the Souldiers came and rescued me. And those that were my former Acquaintance, with whom I had formerly been very *(page 28)* conversant, and spent much time, and lodged at their Houses several times, even those now were afraid of me, and would not come near me, but the dread of God was upon me, and it made some of them to Tremble; and some said, I was a Witch: and when I would go to their Houses to reprove them, they were so mad that they would run away, and then their Servants would come and hale me out; and when I would go to sit down, they would drag me along upon the Stones, and hale me out and shut the Doors: So I came to witness that a Prophet is not without Honour, save in his own Country. So when I found my self pretty clear there, I returned home to *Bristoll*.

And in a while after I was moved to go for *Ireland* again, and then I was in great Perils by Sea, where I saw the Wonders of the *(page 29)* Lord in the Deep; and there was one man Friend, and one woman Friend then in the Ship besides me, and the Ship was broken near *Dungarvan*, and it foundred in the Sea, something near the Shore, and we were all like to be cast away; and I was ordered of the Lord to stay in the Ship, until they were all gone out of her, and the Master and the Passengers got into the Boat, (all save one Man and one Woman, which were cast away) and they got to Shore, and stood there to see what would become of me, who was still in the Cabbin, and the Waves beat in upon me in abundance, almost ready to stifle me: And so when I found freedom I went and stood upon a piece of the Deck that was left, and then the Master of the Vessel & the Man Friend called to me, and told me, *If I would venture to leap down, they would venture to come (page 30) into the Water to save me:* So they came into the Water up so far as their Necks, and I leaped down to them, and they caught hold of me, but I being intangled in the Ropes in leaping down, was drawn from them again; but as the Lord ordered it, a Wave came and beat the Ship out, where as if it had beat in, it would have killed us all three, but beating out, they recovered me again and drew me to Shore: So the Lord's Power and Mercy was wonderfully shown at that time for my preservation; I cannot but bless his Name for it.

So then I went to *Dublin*, where I spake in the High-Court of Justice amongst the Judges; and then they put me in Prison, where I lay upon Straw, on the Ground and when it Rained, the Water and Filth of the House-of-Office ran in under my Back: And they *(page 31)* Arraigned me at the Bar, and bid me plead Guilty, or Not Guilty: And I answered, that there was no guilt upon any ones Conscience for what they did in Obedience unto the Lord God: And the Judge could not speak to me, but spoke to another Man that stood by him, to speak to me. So I could not say as they bid me, and they returned me to Prison again, where I had very hard Exercise. And there was a Man that could not injoy some Land, except he could prove that his Brother was dead; and he brought a Man into Prison, that said, *he would prove that he was killed at such and Inn, and buried under a Wall.* He accused the Inn-keeper and his Wife, and their Man, and Maid, and a Smith, to be guilty of this Murther. So I went to him and sate down by him, and spake a few Words to him, and askt him, *(page 32)* how he could conceal this Murther so long, when he was as guilty of it as either of them, if it were true. He trembled, and shook exceedingly, and his Knees smote one against another, and he confest, That *he never saw the People with his Eyes, nor never was at the place in his Life, nor knew nothing of it, but only he was drawn in by the Man that was to have the Land, and was perswaded to Witness it.* And the Prisoners heard this his Confession to me; so I sent to the Deputy, to send down his Priest, that he might hear his Confession: So he came, and he confest the same to him as he had done to me: and the five Persons which he accused was then in Prison, but only the Maid in the Prison with me; and the Man confest the same once before the Judge: But the Man that brought him in, *(page 33)* came to him every day, and filled his Head with Drink, and caused the Goaler to lock him up, that I might not come at him: So I writ to the Inn-keeper and his Wife, and the Coach-man; and I writ to the Judge also, and told him the Day of his Death did draw nigh, wherein he must give an Account of his Actions; and bid him take heed how he did condemn so many Innocent People, having but one Witness, in whose Mouth their were so many Lyes found; (and they all said they were Innocent.) They called him Judge *Pepes* who Condemned them all. Then a Priest came to speak with the Maid that was Condemned, which was with me in the Prison; but she would not see him, but said, *Nay, he can do me no good; I have done with Man for ever. (page 34) But God, thou knowest that I am Innocent of what they lay to my Charge.* So they were all Hanged, and the Man that accused them was hanged up first, for fear he should confess when he saw the rest hanged: And a heavy day it was, and I bore and suffered much that day. Then there were some Friends of mine, namely *Sr. William King,* Colonel *Fare,* and the Lady *Browne,* these hearing I was in Prison, came to see me, and they would needs go to this Judge, to get me released; so when they came, he told them, that *he was afraid of his Life.* And they laughed, and told him, *they (page 35) had known me from a Child, and there was no harm in me at all.* And they were all very earnest to get my Liberty, and at last they did obtain it. And then I was moved to go to the Steeple-house, where this Judge was, and the Lord was with me, and I Cleared my self of him; and he went to Bed and Died that Night: And one of the Prisoners had writ the Letter which I sent to him, and when they heard he was dead, they all said, *That I was a true Prophetess unto him.*

And thus as an Instrument in the Hand of the Lord, to do his Work, I was faithful and obedient unto his Power, *(page 36)* and he caused me to grow and prosper through my great Sufferings; blessed be his Name for ever, that I had great experience of his love and power. *Elizabeth Gardiner,* and *Rebecca Rich,* and *Samuel Clareges* Wife knew all this to be true.

And then I went to *Limrick,* where I had some Service, and they put me in Prison. So in a while I was released, and then I took Shipping for *England* again, and then there was a great Storm took us at Sea, and the Lord moved me to go to Prayer; and I went to Prayer, and in a little time the Storm ceased, and we *(page 37)* were preserved; And coming towards *Mineyard*, we met a Pirate, which had abundance of men on board, and I began to consider, whether there was any Service for me to do among those Rude People, but I found little to them: so they came on Board us, and took away all that I had, and one of my Coats from off my Back; but they were not suffered to do me any further harm. So they took away the Master with them, until he should pay them a sum of Money for the Ship and Goods. And so we came home to *England*.

(page 38) But in all my Travels, I Travelled still on my own Purse, and was never chargeable to any, but paid for what I had. And much more could I declare of my Sufferings which I passed through, which I forbear to mention, being not willing to be over-tedious.

And I have written these Things that Friends may be encouraged, and go on in the Faith, in the Work of the Lord: For many have been the Tryals, Tribulations and Afflictions the which I have passed through, but the Lord hath delivered me out of them all; Glory be given to him, and blessed be his Name for ever, and evermore.

Barbara Blaugdone

THE END.

A Small

ACCOUNT

GIVEN FORTH

By one that hath been a

Traveller

For thefe 40 Years in the Good

O L D   W A Y.

And as an Incouragement to the
Weary to go forward; I by Experience
have found there if a Reft remains for
all they that truly trufts in the Lord.

PSALMS 31.14. *I trufted in thee, O Lord, and faid, thou art
my God.*
24.2 *All ye that truft in the Lord, be ftrong, he fhall eftablifh
your Heartf.*

S. B.

Printed in the Year, 1698.

(Page numbers of original document appear in text as *page _.*)

A S God by his Grace having inclined my Heart to be Merciful, and I have had the Comfort of doing Good, whilst I had an opportunity, in the things as he in this Life is pleased to commit to my Care: I have, as in his sight, walked in the uprightness of my Heart, and as in those things partaining to this Life, I have endeavoured to keep a good Conscience. So in Love to all that may have the Reading of this small Book, I am willing to give them an understanding, as I have found where it is to be attained; as Christ said, *There is but one good, and that is God;* and as we come to be guided by his good Spirit, it will lead us into all things that are good; without which we cannot inherit *Eternal Life.* And whatever any may think of me, who look with an evil Eye, yet to my *Friends* that looks with an Impartial Eye, it will be received, as it is intended good will to all; and to those remain a Friend.

S. B.

(page 3)

The Fear of the Lord is the beginning of Wisdom. A good understanding have all those that keep his Law.

A ND as a *Traveler* to the good Land, of *Rest* and *Peace,* and having in measure attain'd thereunto, by that *Heavenly* Guide *Christ Jesus* the true *Light,* that hath been my Instructor and Helper, without which I am nothing, nor can do any thing as I ought to do; I am made free to relate something of my attainment thereunto. I was Born of Good Parents, Educated according to the *Church of England;* and tho' Young, Zealous, therein; yet could not my Immortal Soul be therewith satisfied, but a desire was begotten in me, to know the true God, the which to attain I endeavoured the best way I could, by Prayer and Fasting in secret, not to be seen of any: But God, whose Eye saw me, and my true desire therein; knowing herein I was not safe, tried me, and by one thought which arose in my Heart concerning God, which I could not help, dashed all in my Building to pieces *(page 4)* and I thought my self the worst Creature living; thus night and day I had great trouble within, but resolv'd in the midst of all, and made it my resolution to follow the thing that is good, and that God that saw me, thought I saw not him; I was by this often comforted, and it became my Song, *Great are the Troubles of the Righteous,* but *the Lord delivers out of them all:* and sometimes betwixt Hope and Fear, I travelled from Twelve Years of Age to Eighteen; about which time, by Providence I was led into the *North,* at

which time, by wonderful changes wrought in them (by which they
had the name given them) called *Quakers*, a People so contrary to my
Education; and the many strange Reports, that were raised of them,
was rather frightful, than desireable to me; but that God, that saw the
great desire I had to know him, the only true *God*, and *Jesus Christ* his
Son, led the blind by a way I knew not, and by one not called a *Quaker*,
but one true to the *Church* of *England*, and a sufferer for King *Charles*
the first.

I received a true *Account* of the Principles and good Lives of these
People, which in Simplicity of Heart was related *(page 5)* to me, of which
I was made seriously to consider; and in a short time, felt a Power arise
in my Heart, and I said this is it I have waited for, and with great Power
it rent the Vail, chased away my dark thoughts, gave me some understanding of the Scriptures, and I could say, *I have heard of thee, and have
read of the Wonders thou didst for the Children of Men;* but that was not
mine, but now by thy great Power and Change thou hast wrought in
me, I came to know thee O God, and by this, and in no other way can
I be satisfied, and that thou the Immortal God, may'st have the Glory
of thy own *good Work*, which I never received of Man, neither did I
ever see or hear any of them called *Quakers*, till three Years after or
more, but returned into my own Country (*North-Hamptonshire*) to my
Relations, and not long after came to *London*, and made it my business,
and went secretly amongst all persuasions (except *Papists* and *Ranters*)
to see if I could find any, that had the sence to know God, and his Son
Jesus Christ within them.

But, I could find no outward thing could give my Soul satisfaction,
neither *(page 6)* then, nor now, and in that State I walked alone three
Years, but being at a Meeting in great *Allhallows*; one *Edw. Burroughs*
came in, and stood up, and spoke; at which I with others was amazed,
having never seen nor heard any of them before; but was resolved to
hear him again, I was afraid, but by the many strange reports raised of
them, but I Prayed to the Lord my God in whom I trusted, that I might
not be deceived, for he knew I had nothing in my Eye, but to have a
further manifestation of *Him, whom to know is Life Eternal,* of the which
he resolved me, and with Signs and Tokens of his *Love*, confirmed me,
and I could and can say it was, and is of God, and is the *Truth*, and
proceeds from the same *Rock*, from which all the *Patriarchs, Prophets,*
and *Apostles,* had their teaching, *Christ Jesus* the *Rock*, the *Mystery hid
from Ages and Generations, is made known unto us,* of which Knowledge
I have learn'd, as they did, who said, what is to be known of God, *is*

manifest in them, which is the *Key* of *David,* which opens and shuts, and gives the true Understanding of the Mystery of the Kingdom of Heaven, and the true knowledge to all those *(page 7)* who have in true Obedience submitted to his Yoke, and their Wills subjected to his Will; these shall find his saving Virtue of Life, which Life being received, and joyned too with all the Heart, it will endow them with the Heavenly Virtue, in *Christ Jesus* our *High Priest,* and Captain of our Salvation: And with Righteousness, Peace and Joy, in the Holy Spirit of God, and those that willingly give up all they have unto him, shall find in it more than they can believe, or the Carnal Mind can apprehend, for they knew what they said, that the Carnal Mind knows not the things of God, for they are Spiritually discerned, and to be carnally minded is Death, but to be spiritually minded is Life and Peace, which is a certain Truth, and according to the Holy *Scriptures,* from which I desire neither from Them, nor my Neighbour to borrow Words, or a Profession; but to have a right to them, and be made one with them, by the same Spirit of *Jesus Christ,* the Lord of all our Mercies; and as in him they lived, moved, and had their being, who gave them forth, he is so to the faithful this day, and what I have heard and seen, I declare, that he is the true God, *and (page 8) the Poor in Spirit receive the Kingdom of Heaven,* and see a nothingness and emptiness in themselves, without a dayly supply from him, and they are led and made to understand the Mystery of *Election* and *Reprobation,* as in the two Seeds and Births, the one *elect* and *blessed* of God before the World was; if the mind of Man joyns to *Christ,* who is God's Elect, *Isa. 42.* they are saved by him, and *Works out their Salvation with Fear and Trembling;* and this is the *Elect* and *Corner-Stone, Christ Jesus,* whom soever Builds thereon, *The Gates of Hell shall not prevail,* and will over turn overturn [sic] till *he come whose right is to Reign;* and as unto this *Elect* and *Precious Seed* we Unite, we are therein and thereby blessed of God: this is not of our selves, but the free Gift given of God, by which we make our *Calling and Election sure,* and in this we have learn'd to know the Reprobated, and the *Enemy* of all Mankind, that leads the mind from God, into the *Lust of the Eye,* the *lust of the Flesh,* and the *Pride of Life,* and all other Evils, which if joined unto the Evil conceived in the mind brings Death, and separates Man from God his Maker, and here the strong Man keeps the *House,* and by his Temptations therein, prevails on Man to eat the forbidden *Fruit,* by which he breaks the Law of God, and falls under Condemnation, from which State there is no coming; nor the *Fig-leaf* Garment, nor nothing without will cover, but a turning to the blessed Appearance and Gift of God in the Soul, and there find the Mystery, *Christ within, the Hope of Glory*, who hath many Names, and his Kingdom is compared to a *little Leaven*, the *Lost Groat*, a *grain of Mustard Seed*, and many other Parables, and it is vailed from Man, who is in the first nature of the Earth, Earthly, but revealed in the second Man, who is the Lord from *Heaven*, which gives us to know the first Man *Adam* a living Soul, and the last Man, quickning Spirit, by which, unless we be Born again of the true incorruptible Seed, which enlightens us, we cannot see the Kingdom of *Heaven*, nor the Glory thereof, which Man in the first Nature have strove to know; but we must receive that knowledge by the ingrafted Word of God, not in our will and time, these things God gives us to know, but being ac-quainted *(page 10)* with his Mercies, and the Temptation of the evil *One*, as we may read and learn of *Christ*, who left us an example as all true Travellers shall find in themselves, him near in their best performances; as I have seen, and do see his approach, and when I have heard, or seen any on the high Mountains, in their Imaginations, who pretend they see all the World, and their selves in conceit above all, for which I have been grieved, as well-knowing the danger of that State, and willing I was to have advised them, but knowing they was so highly set up in themselves, my voice could not reach them, calling that God which is not God, taking the Name of the Lord God in Vain, for which he will not hold them guiltless, some of them having blown a loud Trumpet, *Jehu* like, saying, *Come and see my Zeal for the lord of Hosts*, which I have been grieved to see in some, both Men and Women, and have lived to see divers fall, which I well knew as they stood could not hold out to the end, and many of *Martha's* Spirit I have seen, and now do, which runs, and serves, and cumbers themselves with striving to utter Words, and have got *(page 10 [sic])* the true Notion in their Heads, but the true Seed hath not taken root down-wards; and those are they which are stumbling-Blocks, who have been by some encouraged, as I might have been, but the Lord my God kept me out of that Temptation, and many others not loving Hyprocricy, nor a feigned imitation whereby I might deceive others, in what I was not truly to God, who called me to take up the Cross, to that which my Heart loved, whether they were Idols of Silver, or Gold, or other things tho' useful, yet if over-valued, they fill the Heart, of which there must be an emptying, to make room for the Heavenly *Jesus*, under whose Reign, *Israel* shall falsely possess their Souls in Peace, and have the new Name given them, and the *White Stone* which none knows, nor can believe, but those that have it, and those are they that are come through great Tribulations, and are washed with the Blood of the

Lamb: and all those of this Faith, I dearly salute, as being Children of one Father, whose *Voice* I know from the Voice of a *Stranger*, and I thank God, who hath raised up the Poor in Spirit, all that are therein gathered, will out-last all other *(page 12)* Notions, and the Lord give Wisdom to them, that have not as yet thereto attained, to know the true Ministration and the right Season, when they should, and when they should not, which in some hath been lacking; which causes the weak to stumble, and keeps out more than it brings in.

Thus have I given a short but true Account as I have passed through the Wilderness of this World, and have seen many fall on the Right Hand, and on the Left, where also I might but have had for my preservation, the cloud over me by day to keep me low, that I might not be exalted, neither by Visions, Sights, nor Revelations; many have been hurt thereby, and cast that on others, which concerned themselves: And as the cloud stood over me, it kept me low from self-exaltation, to know my self nothing, but what I received from the God of all my Mercies: and as I see the *Cloud by day*, I also see the *Pillar of Fire by Night*, which caused me to stand still, and see the Salvation of God, and the bright appearance of his Glory. I am sorry for some that are backslidden, and may say to them, what have you or your Fathers found in *(page 13)* the God of *Jacob*, that you should depart from him? But let all the strong will'd, know little *David*, who trusts not in Bow nor Sword, but in the living God; he by his Sling and smooth *Stone*, shall hit the Head of those that defies the Armies of *Israels* God.

And to all you workers of Iniquity, who have charged us that we deny *Christ Jesus* come in the *Flesh*, the Holy *Scriptures* and the *Resurrection*, and say we are *Heathens*, and *Hereticks*, all which we know to be false, and can appeal to God in the integrity of our Hearts therein, and with him we can with Joy leave our Cause, as well-knowing he is able in his time to plead it, tho' there may be evil doers amongst us. If *Christ* had one in twelve, that was not enough for the Jews and some that followed him, to say he was not in the Truth, because *Judas* betrayed him, and *Peter* deny'd him, and he in that Agony bearing our griefs, *Isa.* 53. to cry out, *My God my God why hast thou forsaken me*, all this must needs stumble the Eye that looked out, but they remembred his promise, and waited at *Jerusalem* for the fulfilling of it, who said, he would come, and he did come, which *(page 14)* confirmed them, and so it hath done us.

And now something to you my dear Children, whom I never deck'd in the extreams of formality, to make my self, or you seem what you were not; but this was, and is my desire for you, seek first the Kingdom of Heaven, and the Righteousness thereof, and all other things shall be added unto you, be sure to *Remember your Creator in the days of your Youth,* and you shall find the Comfort of it in your Old Age, or at your Death, when all the Glory of this World will stand you in no stead: And though some of you have met with some Disappointments, yet you shall find (as I have done) all things work together for good, and bring you nearer to God, which I have ever desired for you, more than for Silver or Gold, tho' therein some of you have had a blessing beyond my desire, and my comfort is, you all set your Faces *Sion-ward,* and to your Parents have been Dutiful, Loving and Obedient, for which God will bless you, as you continue in his Grace.

This is written by one that hath been called a *Dissenting Quaker,* which I desire not to be from faithful Friends, for *(page 15)* I never knowingly *(page torn)*
Truth, but loved it,
things was not satisfi
as I could in Word a
one, but endeavoured
Conscience towards
Which I have found
and the blessing to my
have a true Love to
Heart, by what name
And as through Disp
ministrations and Gifts, (
the same Spirit) God is pleased to
further manifestation of Himself, who is a Spirit, in that way shews Himself to Man as he can receive him, which was, and is his great Love, knowing how happy he is made by it, and unhappy without it, and God's great Condescension therein, who seeks Man, before Man seeks Him, because he is good, and would have Us be like unto Him, and take delight in Us, and we in Him: and in this way he led all his faithful People, before the *Law* and after, which *Law* was given by *Moses* by Divine Inspiration, many Years after some of those things were done, which all had their signification, and pointed at *Christ Jesus* coming in the *(page 16)* Flesh,
(page torn)   come, said, *before A-*
                   and they in the Wil-
                   e same Spiritual *Rock,*

(page torn) ist, and Messinger of
Covenant, the Law
rt, unto Him must all
ly know the Interpre-
ontained in both Old
ent, which was decla-
spirit and Power of God
, and that were left to be
e, especially to the Man of God,
through *Faith* in Christ Jesus, by which we may see (as our Minds are
turned to God) the Examples of those that followed the Lord their
God, and there make a true spiritual Application, and see how far we
are come; into the good work of God, in the proving of our Hearts; as
Abraham Offered up *Isaac,* so must every one offer up what God requires, to manifest our love to God; and for all such who by Faith walk
God will provide himself a Sacrifice; and so *Jacob* the wrestler with
God, sent from his Father's House to go into a strange Land, and have
no dependency on any outward or visible thing in this his Journey, yet
Travels on, and the Sun sets, night comes on, on this Stone *(page 17)* lays
his head, and thus rests on the faithfulness of God to him in all conditions and then is the ladder of true experience seen, where the *Angels*
of God ascend, and descend, at the foot abode, and you will say God
was here and I knew it not; and here *Jacob* received his blessing, to
whom Children was given, and there was a striving, as by the best Mind
and Spirit you shall find the Eldest by Nature will seek to rule, and
strive against the beloved of the Father: And *Joseph* the true born Son
sold into *Egypt,* to provide Corn for *Jacob* and his Sons, but they must
go down to fetch it; and this is to be known in its time and season, and
the Scripture fulfilled, and the spiritual meaning therein known: As
Saul the first King over *Israel* for stature and appearance Beautiful,
anointed of the Prophet to be King; but God saw beyond outward appearances into the Heart, and they that go out from God their strength,
their defence is gone, and they shall become weak as *Saul* did, and their
Enemies prevail; then contemptible *David,* who by his Brethren was
dispised, him God saw, and by the Arm of God's strength had killed the
Lyon and the *Bear,* and in that Power by which he *(page 18)* overcame the
Latter, by believing in the same Power he overcame the greatest of his
Enemies, and this made him King in *Saul's* stead, though with him he
had long Wars to Fight the Lord's Battle: but *Solomon* by the true Wis-
dom of God must Build the House, in whose Reign there is Peace and

Safety, and he shall Judge and give true Judgment betwixt the Mother and the Child; and *Christ's* Kingdom (Typified in *Solomon's*) consists of Righteousness, Peace and Joy, which is very delightful and desirous, because, the satisfaction the Soul receives thereby, and hath a true sight of the Love of God in all he doth, is but to make his Creature Man happy, which Love is so great it cannot be expressed, for the which, all those that have received it praise God, and all that have not come out of themselves, and seek the Kingdom of Christ not in words, but in Truth, that they may partake with thy Saints in Glory, and thereby see the Emptiness and Vanity of this World, whether it be Profession, Pleasure, Riches, Honour; the Excellency of this Excels them all.

And to all you sincere hearted, as *Cornelius* was, to whom *Peter* was sent, who *(page 19)* said, *I see of a Truth, God is no respecter of Persons*; but amongst all that truly fears God, and works Righteousness, are therein accepted, yet God was pleased by *Peter*, to Preach and Testifie unto Jesus Christ as his anointed, who was crucified, and to his Resurrection from the Dead; *Acts* 10. that in and through him they might believe, and receive the Gift of the *Holy Ghost* and of Power, and thereby the inward cleansing from Sin and Pollution, and by the Power and Work of *Christ*, to become the Sons of God, which no outward thing can do; but whoso therein believes, shall find Power in that Gift which God hath given, which is a true discerner of the thoughts and intents of the Heart, to which, I would persuade all that are weary and heavy laden to come unto, and they shall assuredly find Rest to their Souls, by Christ Jesus the Substance, unto which all Men must bow in the inwardness of their Hearts, for the day of his bright Appearance is at hand; and *Behold he comes with Clouds, Rev.* 1.7. yet they that are gazing abroad, cannot see him, being veil'd from that Eye and Mind, as he was unknown to the *Jews* formerly, *(page 20)* who had a great expectation of the coming of the *Messiah*, who came in the will of God at the appointed time; yet he not coming in that Glory, and great Appearances they expected him, they could not believe nor think that it was he, and now there is great expectation in some of his second appearance, some saying, *Lo here*, and some *Lo there*, and yet still are disappointed, and strangers to his appearance in Spirit: but to them who truly look for him, he shall appear the second time without Sin, unto *Salvation*, and there the true inward Christians shall see him in his Glory, and enter into his Kingdom, which exceeds all the glory of this World, neither can the wise imaginary part in Man give a true description thereof, but as God's Wisdom rises up into the Throne, and hath the Government of the

Mind, they shall know the depth of these things from him that gives it; and give him the Praise, who hath brought them into so happy estate, who desires well for every Creature, both Man and Beast, who groans for deliverance: And as a Man comes to be gathered into the light, and changed into the Nature of Jesus Christ, the whole Creation will reap *(page 21)* great benefit thereby, and as many as have seen the beginning of the good Work of God in what he did, *He divided the Light from the Darkness*, and *saw the Light*, and *it was Good*; and so he went on in every day's Work, till the whole Creation was finished; and as we read in the Old, we must find it in the New, for he saith, *I will make a new Heaven, and a new Earth, wherein shall dwell Righteousness.* And as in the first, he went on in order in his Work, so you shall find him now; and though by him called into the Vine-yard to work, it shall find in many a high and strong will, which would obstruct the good Work of God, and that *Hammon*-like, strives to get upon the Kings *Horse*, but he's not *Mordica*, that sits low in sackcloth at the gate, and where this is, in what pretence so ever, in whom Pride rises and prevails, it will (if suffered) destroy the Seed of the *Jews;* but he that sees in secret will reveal the matter, and that Spirit shall be brought down, let its cloathing be never so glorious: God hath decreed to exalt *Mordicai*, who is of the true Seed, he is found worthy, and the Lord lives; he shall Reign whose Right it is, though the *Heathen* rage, and the People imagine a vain thing, *(page 22)* yet will he set his Son upon the holy hill of *Sion.*

I could not well omit one thing more, to give satisfaction to some, who may think, I am one that goes under the name that ministers to the People, but I am not; but this I give as my experience, to all that are traveling to find rest with God in his *Kingdom of Peace;* but to appear in a *Publick Assembly*, there to speak, I never did; and I am of the *Apostle's* mind, *Let such Women (as want Instruction, or would usurpe Authority over the Man) keep Silence in the Church, and give place to Man, to whom God hath given Preheminency, and made fit for that great Work;* in which *Work*, had not I satisfaction in my self, and been strengthened by those worthy good *Ministers*, through the weakness of some others who thereto pretend, and, as I well know, run when they are not sent, I might have stumbled; but I saw, how ever Justified by others, divers of them were not, nor are not upon the right Ground, and some of them have been blown away like Chaff with the Wind, not but that I know there is many Good and Vertuous *Women*, who are appointed for good Examples in their *(page 23)* Families, who in *Modesty, Sobriety, Charity*, and *good Works*, a *good Life*, and *Conversation*; with these I joyn, and in that Life

I desire to Preach to my Children, Friends, Neighbours and Servants; and they that in this rightness of Heart Live, shall deceive none, but gain to themselves a lasting Establishment, which shall be of good Savour, never to be repented of; and as in this I desire to do unto all as I would be done unto, and that in Truth and Sincerity I have here writ, may be for the good of all; to help the Feeble, and strengthen the Weak, and that from the ground of Integrity, and in Good Will to all Men; and it being received in the good Mind, will cover any Weakness herein contained, and make that use of it as it is intended, *Good Will to all, and Glory to God.* Yet as there was formerly, so there is now *he that is born after the Flesh, Persecutes him that is born after the Spirit,* whose Censures I expect not to escape, it being so natural to the Litteral *Jews,* when they could find nothing to accuse Christ of, whilst upon the Earth, sought what they could to intrap him in his Words; but God gave him that Wisdom to see in them, and cautioned his *(page 24)* Disciples, *not to give the Childrens Bread to Dogs, not Pearls to Swine, least they trample them under Foot, and turn again and Rent you*; under Christ's Protection I leave my self.

This writ by one that hath waited by *Wisdom's Gate* for Instruction, who hath given me an entrance to know as I have here declared, and all that would go higher to see the Bride, the Lambs Wife, must be guided thereto by the Meek and Humble Spirit of *Jesus,* without which there is no Safety, though they may understand all Mysteries, and give much to the Poor, and have all those Gifts the Apostle mentions (in the 13 of the 1. Epistle to the *Corinthians*) and yet if the most excelent gift of Charity be wanting that thinks no Evil, which boasteth not, &c. but Suffereth, Believeth, Hopeth, and Endureth all Things, and rejoyceth in God alone, he that is here will out-last all other let their pretences be what it will, and they that come not here let them change their Habits, their Customs, and as some call it the *Worlds Fashions,* yet if they come not to see the *World's Covetousness* (unto which the Heart of Man is naturally inclined) rooted out, the Earth will open *(page 25)* and swallow up that Mind, and the Heart will be dead to God, and they will loose their part in the blessed Inheritance.

Some on the other hand notwithstanding they may have seen the good way, set forward therein, but soon forgot what the Lord did for them, who brought them out of the *Land of Darkness,* from under their hard *Taskmasters,* who put them to make *Brick* without *Straw*; their Hearts not being throughly Converted, they lusted for the *Garlick* and *Onions* again, their old Diet; and though they had past the *Sea,* many dyed in the *Wilderness*, and all them that delighted in the Sins of *Sodom*, and make a mock at the good *Angel*, that God hath sent to pull just *Lot* out of *Sodom*, they shall be struck Blind, and the Fire of God's Wrath shall destroy all such that come not in at the right Door of him who said, *I am the Way, the Truth, the Life, and the Light*; who ever striveth by any other way will be found Thieves and Robbers, and deprive the Soul of its Inheritance with God.

This by one who for many Years hath been counted a *Dissenter*, being never forward to intrude into those things I had not seen nor adhered to, what I had not a *(page 26)* clear sight as my duty to God, and there I stand still waiting on God to reveal to me; yet that God that sees the inside, the Heart, hath rewarded me according to the sincerity thereof; and I have found his Love so great and unexpressible, which hath made up all again more than I have lost by any Man, and hath safely preserved where Man could not see me, whose Eye is abroad and looks at the outside appearance; but as God's Eye, who beholds both Evil and Good, so have I seen in both Parties things acted and done, which my Soul had no Pleasure not Unity with, but was willing the Lord should bring me off from those from whom he was departed, and that the sincere hearted of both sides might be Reconciled, for the accomplishing of which I have used my best Endeavours, desiring there may not be a looking at what is past, but an endeavouring for the good of all, as I have really done, as may be seen in this following *Letter* which I writ in answer to a Friend, who was and is dissatisfied with some for appearing therein; but let them be what they please, I am well satisfied in this good Work.

(page 27) But I have seen the new Wine put into the old Bottle, it not being well seasoned there becomes a Sowerness, and the good Relish thereby seems to be lost, that is in it self good; in which state there is many that keeps to the old Leaven of the *Pharisees*; Christ gives this Mark by which they should be known, *They love the uppermost Places, and to be Master, make long Prayers, and to preach in their own Wills, different in their Robes, makes a fair show in the Flesh, that they may appear well unto Men*; this hath been and is a great grief to the Just, but I am comforted in this, I see many right-hearted and Good Christians, who speaks from the Truth the anointed of God, those God will bless, and he will appear in them who reigns in Righteousness, and all such shall reign with him for ever and ever; and as I have seen this Good, I have also seen this Evil, which Man is prone to, and apt to set a great value upon themselves, and they not see it, and let the Truth be never so

plainly discovered, and from the Spirit of the Living God dictated; yet if it comes not in their way, and after their manner, as they have set it up in themselves, there is no room for any thing to *(page 28)* enter, though never so good; of this have made to my self a good Caution and said, O Lord, *if this Iniquity remains in me, search it out; for I see it looks ill in others, and so it will in me if I am found therein.*

S. B.

How mean soever I may appear to Man,
A Witness in my Soul there lives that can,
Bear Record to the Father *this, that I*
Seek not Mortals praise, but Immortality;
That Crown of Rest and Peace I may receive,
Which Mortals have not in their Power to give,
Which he must do who sets me free from Sin,
And being clean in Peace there Rules that King.
Who will not joyn unto Iniquity,
But love's Uprightness and Integrity.
Thinks Human Wisdom, *I can easily see,*
The Scripture *can this thing declare to me;*
But 'tis not known by Pleasure, Ease *or* Sleep,
Who find this Pearl, *thou must dig low and deep;*
And whoso finds before it be his own,
They must sell all to purchase that alone,
And cast-up all his Stock and look within,
Before to Build his House he doth begin,
(page 29) And learn by true experience rightly for to know,
The thing that's realy good from what's but good in show.
Remember Babel, *do not build too High,*
Nor make a Tower to reach unto the Skie,
Nor look thou out, but turn thy Eye within,
See Christ there laid, then build thy House on him.
Who build not on that Rock *shall surely fall,*
For he is that Corner Stone *uniteth all.*
Cease then a while you Humane Learned Men,
That know your Wisdom cannot find out him.
Thou Willing and Obedient, know it's thee,
Whose Vale is rent to see this Mistery,
It's not the prudent learned Wit that shall
Him comprehend who is the Light of all,

The Lamb of God, who comes in love to gain
And bring lost Man (stray'd from God) back again;
And make Man happy, the greatest good that can
Befall to Mortals, or the Sons of Men;
Which if not rightly known, what E're we do
Wants the good Oil, and God's acceptance too.
He sees the Heart and what rules there full well,
Whether it be Pride or Passion, Husk, Fame or Shell;
Of all that cumber we must come to see,
Man strip'd of all and Christ alone to be
The true conducter, from the ways wherein
(page 30) He'll not appear, because they lead from him;
And all that goes in this true blessed way,
Shall by his Light be sav'd both Night and Day
And as I have walk'd unseen and all alone,
In secret to my God I made my moan.
Its restless eye that makes complaint to none,
But unto thee from whom relief must come;
Out of my Troubles, many Doubts and Fears,
Hath send the Harvest which was sown in Tears;
Tho' sorrow may indure for a Night,
Thy morning Presence brings my Soul delight;
Thou art a God of Truth, in all things Just,
And those that know thy Name will in thee Trust.

An Answer to a Letter from a Friend.

THine I received, and have considered thereof, and could have been more large in my own, and my Friends Vindication therein concern'd; but am gathered into that, not to strive, but to commit my Cause to God in well-doing; having in my self, and many others, seen *Pride* to beget *Passion*, and *Passion Prejudice*, by which the *Eye* of the right *(page 31)* understanding is made Blind. As for rehearsal of all those former failings therein contained, if they were true, yet rightly considered, and impartially weighed; may say, since those Divisions, a great manifestation there hath been of such Spirits, to whom those names may deservedly be attributed; tho' for many Years I have been counted a *Dissenter*. Yet I, nor many more, never took pleasure to lay the Nakedness of any open, but rather to cover for his Names sake, who hath kept us in his Truth, by which we have been preserved.

I have seen, I have seen, [*sic*] an *Enemy* enter the House, and hath
not been discover'd till they come into the Cool, out of the Hurry and
Noise, and hear the call of the *still Voice*; and herein my Soul, with
many other of my Christian Friends, have been Blessed; and by this we
are led to Unite, and to be truly reconciled in that *Spirit*, by that Heavenly *Jesus*, that true *Reconciler* of Man to his *Maker*.

And of this, from thy true Friend, be assured, it was not from the
Spirit of *Hypocrisie*, *Policy*, or any *carnal* or *selfish End*, no, no, our House
is not Built on that *Sandy Foundation*, but on *Christ Jesus*, *(page 32)* that
Rock of Ages, which leads his in the way of Everlasting *Peace*, which
Peace cannot be declared, but as it is felt, of which *Peace* hath my Soul
tasted largely, and can say truly, since into this happy state the Lord
hath brought me, I have experienced more of that *Heavenly Joy*, and
Everlasting Peace, than ever I knew before, but I thank the Lord who
gave me a share thereof, under every dispensation he hath led me
through, and can say, they were all good in their time, but this excelleth
them all, well knowing the Administration of *John* to be Glorious in its
Time, yet, *He that is least in the Kingdome of Heaven is greater than he*;
into which *Kingdom*, that thou may'st have an entrance after all thy
Travels, and come into this *Sabbath* and *Rest* with God, will be a true
Joy to thy Friend, of which I can say, with many more of my dear Friends
whom I know not, but as I feel them in this Spirit, *It is the Way and there
is not another*: And for all those that are otherwise-minded, the Lord
sned [*sic*] a Famine to come on the outward *Knowledge*, that they may
know to be led to the Spiritual *Joseph*; whoever comes unto him, he
upbraideth no one with what is past, *(page 33)* but he receives them with
his Love, and embraceth them, and they partake with him of the Fat-
ness of the good *Land*. Of this I am a witness, and remain

Thy True Friend,

S.B.

Postscript.

I Did not intend to have Printed this *Letter* I sent to a *Friend*, but
finding he hath Printed the *Letter* he sent to me, as an Answer to
W. R's Book I sent him, which Book I had good Unity with, and with
all that are of a reconciling Spirit, which to my Comfort, I find many
sincere hearted therein, and as the vail of Prejudice *(page 34)* comes to be
taken of the Heart, we shall see one another as God seeth us, to whom
I approve my Heart, let Men Judge of me as they please; it is not from

any Evil or Insinuating self-end, I can truly say for my self, and many more true *Christian Friends*, whose Hearts in this matter of Reconciliation is not to gain Praise of Men, God is our witness; but we are led to Unite by that blessed Spirit, who hath shewed us of what and in what the *Kingdom of Heaven* consists, of which is true Righteousness, Joy and Peace in the holy Spirit, which I with many more have tasted, and could be glad all that oppose would come and taste and see how good the Lord is, and with what the *Immortal Soul* is Refreshed.

I could never find satisfaction in any visible thing, till I received the *Word* of God, in which *Word* I find the *Key* of *David, Which opens and none can shut, and shuts and none can open*; and that is that, that opens the *Mystery of the Kingdom of God*, in which the *Father, Son* and *Spirit* is to be koown [*sic*]; which *Word of Faith*, gave the true understanding to the *Prophets* and *Apostles*, and to all the *Faithful* of God to this day: *And in that way (page 35) which some call Heresie, Worship I the God of my Fathers, believing all the Law and the Prophets, and in Jesus Christ, who is the Author and Finisher of our Faith.*

S. B.

O Lord! Out of the deep I cried unto thee, and thou pluckedst my feet out of the Mire and Clay, and hast set them in the right way: And being converted, strengthen my Brethren. Unto which I have this further to add, when I first heard the confused noise, made by G. K. and T. B. which appearance was, and is to me like the *Golden Calf*; and beholding many I knew, which I thought had been more grafted in the *Word of Life*, than to go after it, for which I was greatly troubled, but the heavenly *still Voice* gave me this Satisfaction, fret not thy self, be still, it is a Cloud I suffer, the Wind thereof shall blow away the Chaff, but I will gather my Wheat thereby nearer together; and this I know to be a certain Truth, by which my Heart hath been often refreshed, for which my Soul, Praise thou the Lord.

S. B.

(page 36) And unto all those who have raked up the miscarriages and evils, and printed it, and given it abroad to defame the People called Quakers, whose Principles shall out-last their Malice; and was some of us of their Spirit, to render evil for evil, revileing for revileing, might say that of some of them that would cause shame, who covered their foolish actions with the name of the Lord, but it was, and is such a

Lord, of which there is many, but not the true God as some can witness, but cover'd it from Men, hopeing time might work them to see their weakness, and know the true Lord over-ruling all their false Imaginations, who may be truly compared to *Saul*, when gone from the true *God*, he goes to the *Witch* of *Endor*, and she raised up what he would see, but not what he should see; so he was never the better for it, but his Enemies prevailed, and he fell by his own Sword; so shall envy slay the wicked Man; and they in darkness shall grove for the door, but shall not find it: All this is true, and I own before all Men the Principle of the *Quakers*. And have this to say for my self, and many more I well know, however our Enemies may render *(page 37)* us; we know this by our selves, and our Consciences bears us witness, we have in good Conversation walked before God and Men, which will speak for us in the gates of our Enemies; and we find the answer of a good Conscience a continual Feast, who have not received the Truth by observation, but by the true administration, by which we have learn'd what lets into the Kingdom of our God, and what keeps out, let Mens pretences be what they will; they that makes lies there refuge, and takes away Mens good names, shall be found workers of Iniquity.

I having in this small account hinted of many States, and several ways of the Lord's working in man, that he may come to know him, and on him rely in all estates. I have one thing further to add; I have lately seen an exercise at hand, but when or in what I know not, but leave it to God and his appointed time, let it be in Mercy or in Judgment, I believe all is for good, as I have ever found all his dealings to me, it was unpleasant to the fleshly part, but I turn'd in, and saw God's preservation near to all that truly on him relies; and in nothing else was there safety, and therefore I desire all *(page 38)* to draw their minds from Vanity and consider their latter end, that I may go well with them, what change so ever comes; for the glory of this World passes away, therefore *Work while the Day lasts, for the Night cometh wherein no Man can Work:* I have also by my experience learned that in Sights and Visions, without watchfulness, there is a Temptation near, there being a readiness in Man to cast that on others, which God intends for our selves, if we could patiently wait till the Vision speaks; for want of that many have run fiercely into things without, and have fail'd, and have brought Reproach on themselves, and God not glorified thereby: this I have also seen, and is often before me, and as there is no outward thing I more truly rejoyced in than to hear the Faithful Ministers of Jesus Christ, in the which I am Comforted, that *God* hath given such a manifestation of his Heavenly good Spirit to instruct his People in the Right and everlasting Way, which *God* will Establish in the Earth; though I could be glad for the sake of many who take offence and are kept back, because it is very discernable, *Martha's* Spirit speaks when they had better be Silent, *(page 39)* goes hastily forward, but would find a greater gain in themselves, if they learn'd to obey, and stand still and see the *Salvation of God;* such may be angry that others rise not up and serve after their manner, but *Jesus* that rightly knows the Spirits of all, saw *Mary* sit at his Feet, low in her self, she chose the better Part, which shall never be taken away, and the Seed sown in that good Ground shall bring forth Fruit to the *Lord of the Harvest;* but there is several sorts of Ground in which the good Seed is sown, and there are many Obstructions in the Ground which hinder the Prosperity of *Gods* holy and good Seed; but the *Harvest* will come, and the good *Husband-man* will discern the *Tares* from the *Wheat,* which none else can do, there being such a likeness; the Administration of *John* was Glorious, in its time, but he said, *Behold the Lamb of God, that takes away the Sins of the World,* shall be preferr'd before and above all appearances, be they what they will, here *many that are Last shall be First, and the First Last:* these are *Christ's* own Words, and are certainly true, and beleived [sic] by one who wishes well to all.

S. B.

(page 40) I being incouraged by the *Immortal God* to Print this, and the matter contained therein, and gave it to several *Friends;* and it coming into the hand of T.C. he came to me, and asked me, Whether I meant *George Keith?* To whom I replied, *I did* who made this Application, because he Preached up the Man *Christ Jesus;* therefore he said, I made him the *Golden Calf;* and so he reported it: And to all that shall hear this Report, I have this to say, and take Almighty *God* to be my Witness, I do believe *Jesus of Nazareth,* Born at *Bethlehem,* according to *God's* Divine Appointment, to be the *Eternal Son of God,* and all those things to be true, as the Scriptures declare of him, and have received so great a benefit by him, as my Tongue cannot express; and for this false Aspersion and wrong interpretation of T.C. I leave *God* to plead my Cause, whom I know is able, and in his time will do it; but must say, as I have once before, *He that is born after the Flesh Persecutes Him that is born after the Spirit.*

FINIS

A SMALL

TREATISE

Writ by one of the

True Chriſtian FAITH;

WHO

Believes in G O D and in his Son
JESUS CHRIST.

Aɛts. 24.14. *After the way which Men Call Hereſie, ſo worſhip I the God of my Fathers, Belieҍing all things which are writ in the Law and the Prophets.*——

Pſalm. 78.1. *What I haҍe heard and known, and our Fathers haҍe declared we will not hide from our Children, but to the Generation to come we will ſhew forth the Praiſe of the Lord; his Power alſo; and his wonderful Works that he hath done, and declare it to our Children, that they may ſet their hope in God; and forget not the Works of God, but keep his Commandments.*

By S. B.

London, Printed in the Year, 1700.

(Page numbers of original document appear in text as *page _.*)

(page A2)

THis small Treatise is given forth by one who hath not
designedly insinuated into any Man's favour, nor wittingly
to offend, but desires to follow Peace with all Men; having in the
sight of the All-seeing God declared what I have seen, and what I have
heard and received by the Word of Life; not boastingly, but in simplicity
of Heart; and whoever sows in that Ground, shall find encrease: They
that sow in the Hypocritical ground, to be seen of Men, shall in the
Harvest reap a poor and barren Crop; but those that have in sincerity
followed the Lord their God, and have gon on weeping, bearing Precious Seed, shall come again rejoyceing, bringing their Sheavs with them,
with such I have mourned, and with such I now rejoyce, and have not
consulted with Flesh and Blood nor earthly advantage, but with many
of my dear Friends have wrestled with the good Angel until the day
dawn, and the Day-Star arise in our Hearts, and hath not let him go
until he hath blessed us; and of that Stone have made a Pillar, and he
was there though we knew it not, and have not received these things by
Tradition, though born of good Parents (though of another perswasion)
yet could not my Heart be satisfied but thirsted, to know the True and
Living God, who hath fully satisfied me, of whom I asked the true Bread,
and he hath not deceived me, nor given me a Serpent instead of a Fish,
but like a good Father hath given me that Bread which daily nourisheth
my Soul; Blessed are all those that have a part in the first Resurrection,
on such the second Death shall have no power.

---

*It is not to the Rich nor the full, but to those that are asking the way to Sion
with their Faces thitherward, to whom I thus write.*

THE Lord having given to Man a Measure of his Spirit to
profit withal, hath by his Son the Light of the World
knocked at the Door of our Hearts, to whom we opened, and
let him in, and he is become our Salvation; and all those that fight
against this his Blessed Appearance, and will not that he should rule
over them, he will come in an hour that they look not for him, and
give them their portion with Hypocrites and Unbelievers.

Having beheld many good Men casting their gift into the Treasury, I of my little cast in my Mite, which I would not through negligence omit any thing wherein I might serve the Lord, his Truth and People; believing it my Duty, having found that satisfaction and rest to my travelling Soul, that I could not find by all my undertakings, though I sought them sincerely in visible things; until I turned into the Word of God in the Heart, and by the light thereof saw to sweep my own House, wherein I found the lost Piece, *Luke* 15.9. the Pearl of great Price, the little Leaven hid in three measures of Meal, and the Parable therin truely opened, and thereby have learned to know the true God, and Jesus Christ whom he hath sent; which to know is Life Eternal, which leads into the Kingdom of Rest and Peace; and am so well satisfied with the truth thereof, that I may say with *Paul*, if an Angel from Heaven should Preach any other Doctrin, I could not receive it: Though I have met with many Tryals and Temptations in the way, yet none so great as to cause me to question the truth thereof, when I have beheld many to fall on the Right Hand, and on the left, and many go back again, I was preserved, and firmly fixed, and grounded on the Rock, which Rock is Christ, and he is my King, Priest, and Prophet and hath led me through dispensations, and administrations, and hath brought me to praise his Name in the Land of the Living, and in this we rejoyce, notwithstanding the fury of Men, well knowing from what Spirit it comes, even the same that called the Son of God a Devil, a Blasphemer, a Friend to Publicans, and Sinners, a breaker of the Law, and his Apostles, turners of the World upside down, *Acts* 17.6. and as he was then, so are we, accounted by some as deceivers, yet true, though called *Hereticks*, Worshiping the God of our Fathers, Believing the Law and the Prophets, and in Jesus Christ the Son of God, and in the Anointing, which he promised to send, and he hath sent, and we have received it, and the sufficiency whereof we have experienced, and is become our Teacher sufficient to guide into all Truth: This is the Day he Promised, which many desired to see, but saw it not; and many might have seen, but have rejected the Lord of Life; and like the Dog returned to the Vomit, and as the Sow washed, to the wallowing in the Mire; and think to cover themselves by laying open what they judge the weakness, or infirmities of others, and make Men offenders for words, and make their own perverse Constructions thereof, and not what they intended that writ or spake them; but if some were so weak as they have Represented them, should not every one Answer for himself? But the Innocent, and many who were not then Born, must be Charged therewith. O ye workers of Iniquity, your strength in the Arm of Flesh shall not secure you; for he against whom you are risen is too mighty for you, to whom all must bow; though he is great in Mercy, yet just in Judgment, and will judge the Secrets of all Hearts, by Jesus Christ our Lord and Saviour, who with his Spiritual Eyes sees through all carnal imaginations of Mens Traditions and Imitations, and will get himself a Name above all, Lord of Lords, who in the time of Ignorance winked at these things; but now he looks that all should come to the knowledge of his Son, who gives unto his Children to know the God of *Abraham* and his Seed; that he will bring them to the Land of Promise; who raised up his Servant *Moses* to go before *Israel,* and delivered them (out of the Hand of *Pharaoh* and his *Task-Masters*) who passed through the Sea, and came into the Wilderness, and there wandred, and murmured, as some have done in our day, and have gon round until they came near the Place where they came in, some went forward toward the good Land, and brought an evil Report thereof, but praised be God who hath raised up a Spirit of Courage, as was in *Josuah* and *Caleb,* and they press forwards toward the good Land, and have entred the Border thereof, and found it as God Promised, a Land following with all good things; of which whoever have tasted, it is beyond all carnal apprehensions or Imaginations, which if the Heart be filed therewith, it must be emptied. All that would know the True God, in the Heavenly still Voice, and the Prophet, of which *Moses* said the Lord your God shall raise up, him shall you hear, and him we do hear, and have Learned subjection to his Will thereby, as well knowing, all things work together for good: And have this to say to all true Christian Friends, be of good Courage, fear not the Reproach of Men, there is nothing come to pass but what was for a Tryal for us, and what I said once I may say again, it is a Cloud God suffereth to rise, and the Wind shall blow away the Chaff, but he will gather the Wheat thereby nearer together; this I know to be a certain truth, by which my heart hath been strengthned, and so I have by this Prophetical Dream, which I had many years ago, when I had no thought or suspicion of what is since come to pass. Which was as followeth,

I was with some of my Christian Friends, was fallen into their Hands who had been of the same Profession, but they were changed into so cruel a Nature, as I thought I never saw the like; for, for my Friends I was grieved more than for my self, but they were taken out of my sight, and I

(Last page missing)

Theological Works

Rebecca Travers 1669

&

Elizabeth Bathurst 1695 (1679) & 1695 (1683)

&

"SPELLING THE WORD WITHOUT KILLING THE SPIRIT" THEOLOGICAL WORKS

by Margaret Benefiel

Introduction

Early Friends emphasized experiential forms of religious expression. They had had powerful experiences of Christ's presence, and they wrote tracts, letters, and narratives to relate their experience and to invite others into that presence. They criticized systematic theology as "empty notions," as "soaring airy head-knowledge,"[1] which distracted people from true faith. Despite Friends' suspicion of intellectual speculation, however, persecution forced them to clarify their beliefs and to move toward a systematic statement of them. George Fox's trial for blasphemy in 1650 started this process. By the late 1670s, when Robert Barclay and Elizabeth Bathurst published the first Quaker systematic theologies, this move toward articulation of Friends' beliefs in a systematic way was mature.

Between the time of Fox's trial and the publication of Barclay's and Bathurst's works, increasingly systematic forms of expression were produced, one of which was the debate tract. Since the mid-1640s, when government censorship temporarily lifted, various religious groups in England had been publishing their views and debating with one another. In a debate tract, one side would list its opponents' theological arguments and then refute them point by point. Though not confined to Friends, the debate tract came to full fruition in the debates between Friends and other religious groups. Debate tracts constitute more than half of seventeenth-century published Quaker writings.[2]

Rebecca Travers

Rebecca Travers wrote the debate tract included here in 1669. A *Testimony for God's Everlasting Truth* rebutted Robert Cobbit's anti-Quaker tract, *God's Truth Attested according to Scripture*. Travers grew up in a time and place where public theological disputation was common. Perhaps her skill as a polemicist and concern for conversion came from this environment which nurtured her. Born in 1609, she grew up in a Baptist family and enthusiastically embraced her family's faith. In 1654, she heard James Nayler dispute the Baptists. Surprised that a rude country-man could defeat the learned Baptists, she kept returning to listen to him, claiming that if she had lived in the apostles' day she "could not have heard truth . . . in greater power and demonstration of the spirit."[3] Convinced by Nayler, she soon moved into leadership among Friends. In 1659 she felt led to go to St. John Evangelist's, a church she had attended for many years, and publicly ask the minister a question after his sermon. As a result the congregation rejected and beat her. She then wrote them a letter, pleading with them to hear her experience of God, maintaining that, although she had been reading the Scriptures since she was six years old, she now "saw things unutterable" as she "came to learn of that spirit which gave them forth."[4] A powerful preacher, Travers frequently questioned and confounded ministers publicly. Because of her public preaching she was imprisoned five times: three times in 1664, again in 1670, and again in 1686. In addition to her preaching, she helped establish women's meetings and visited many Friends in prison.

In her debate with Cobbit, Travers raised several major issues which recur in all the Quaker theological works of the period. Cobbit had claimed that Friends denied the humanity of Christ, that Friends preached a false doctrine of Christ being the Light in the conscience, that Friends denied Christ's ascension, that Friends made Christ all Spirit and no body, that the foundation of Quaker faith and practice was natural, not supernatural. Travers answered each of these charges, as well as other related ones. The Light in the conscience was an important issue for Travers, one to which she kept returning (partly because Cobbit did). Travers argued from Scripture that Christ was the light manifested in all people's consciences and that, by attending to that light, one could know and follow Christ. According to Travers, it was not enough to give intellectual assent to beliefs about Christ's historical life, death, and resurrection; one needed also to listen and respond to Christ's present reality in daily life. Those who focussed merely on the historical issues were missing the most important part of Christ's message. Teachers (like Cobbit) who focussed merely on the historical issues were leading innocent sheep astray.

In her debate tract, Travers demonstrated masterfully her grasp of this form of argumentation. Though somewhat tedious to the modern reader, *A Testimony for God's Everlasting Truth* exhibits all the signs of a good debate tract: a careful listing of the opponent's arguments, a precise response to each point, a further expansion of one's own theology, an effort to get behind the opponent's argument to his or her motivations.

Through her deft use of argumentation, Travers cleared away misunderstandings and then called readers into an encounter with God. For example, she did this with Cobbit himself. She thoughtfully and clearly dismantled his arguments and then turned many of them on their head, demonstrating how he was doing the very thing of which he accused Friends. She then exhorted him to face the living God and allow himself to be transformed. Her thorough argumentation, addressing each of Cobbit's points and leaving no stone unturned, stands as a tribute to her skill.

Travers took care as a writer not to make her skill an idol. In *A Testimony*, she contrasted trying to "know and comprehend the incomprehensible God in your minds" with "know[ing] the will of God to do it."[5] Her aim was to bring Cobbit and those who had read him to an understanding of God's truth that they might respond to it with their whole beings and live in faithfulness to it.

In addition to *A Testimony for God's Everlasting Truth*, Travers wrote at least eight other tracts, as well as prefaces to Nayler's books. Much of her writing focused on clarifying and defending Friends' beliefs, and exhorting people to turn to the Light of Christ. When she wrote to Friends, she emphasized their original experience of Christ and urged them to live in that power and Light daily, not allowing themselves to be sidetracked by specious arguments and false teaching.

Elizabeth Bathurst

While Travers chose to use the debate tract to express her theological views, Elizabeth Bathurst (1655-85) in 1679 chose a more systematic expression for her thoughts.[6] A year after her convincement, Bathurst wrote *Truth's Vindication*, a systematic theology of Friends' beliefs, included in full in this section. Because it is such a careful and well-articulated treatise, some doubted that a woman could have written it.[7] George Whitehead, a leading Friend, dispelled this rumor by affirming that Bathurst had shown him the book while she was working on it, in her own handwriting, and that he was certain that it was her work. Like Travers, Bathurst wanted to clarify Friends' beliefs against their detractors. She, like her detractors, had once believed the misconceptions about Friends that she set out now to refute. She addressed her book to those of her former friends and acquaintances who had rejected her when she became a Friend, as well as to all others who misunderstood and classified as heretical Friends' beliefs and practices. Eager to clear away misunderstandings and invite people into an encounter with the living God, she skillfully answered many objections to Friends' beliefs. Her work is organized into three parts: the first is a list of controversial points; the second is the "Principle of Truth" which Friends believed; and the last is a defense of Quaker methods of disseminating their beliefs.

Most Protestant systematic theologies of the period were modeled after Calvin's *Institutes*. Four years prior to Bathurst's *Truth's Vindication*, Barclay had written his *Apology*, the first Quaker systematic theology, in Latin. He rewrote it in English one year before Bathurst wrote her systematic theology. Barclay followed the structure of the *Institutes*, modifying it only when he wanted to accentuate a difference between Quaker beliefs and Calvinist theology. Although Bathurst's structure is not dissimilar to Barclay's, it is not clear whether Bathurst had read Calvin's *Institutes* or Barclay's *Apology*, or simply reinvented what Barclay and Calvin had already discovered.

Many of the themes from Travers' work reoccur in *Truth's Vindication*, where Bathurst explored them in greater detail, composed variations on them, and embellished them. In addition, Bathurst developed related themes not found in Travers. In Part I, Bathurst focussed on Friends' view of Scripture, the humanity of Christ, original sin, the sacraments, free will, and related issues, in a clearly organized and readable way. Part II is an extended discussion of the "Principle of divine Light and Life of Christ Jesus placed in the Conscience,"[8] carefully organized to delineate and dismiss misunderstandings, to provide a clear and thorough exposition of Friends' beliefs, and to invite people to attend to that light within themselves.

Also published with *Truth's Vindication* was a collection of testimonies about Bathurst. In them, Elizabeth Bathurst was portrayed as a weak, sickly, and very intelligent child. She was recalled as a voracious reader, spiritually inclined, and one who spent much of her childhood alone reading the Bible and other "pious books." She was known to be zealous for God's truth, and, although she adopted her parents' Presbyterianism, she hungered for something that would be more deeply satisfying spiritually for her. When she was twenty-three years old, she, her parents, and her brother and sister embraced Quakerism, when some Friends visited their home:

> And sitting with them and their children, the presence of the
> Lord was manifested among them, and a visitation of his living

power was extended to them; the word of life was opened, the ancient path of the just.[9]

In the same month, she went (accompanied by her sister, Ann) to Samuel Ansley's Presbyterian congregation, where she was a member, to preach against predestination and for universal redemption. Just as Travers' Baptist congregation rejected her, Bathurst's Presbyterian church reacted violently to her ministry, "haling [her and her sister] out from amongst [them]."[10] Soon thereafter she wrote "An Expostulatory Appeal to the Professors of Christianity, Joyned in Community with Samuel Ansley" to them, exhorting them to listen to her message in writing, since they were unwilling to listen to it in person.

In addition to writing, Bathurst travelled in the ministry to Bristol during the time of the most intense persecutions of Friends there, and was imprisoned in Marshalsea soon thereafter. In both cases she was amazed at how she experienced the presence of God and at how God sustained her, despite her weak body and poor health. She died at thirty years of age, just seven years after her convincement, having left, in the words of her mother,

> something for the vindication of [God's] blessed truth, which she had received a measure of, to her great satisfaction, and to the satisfaction and comfort of us that were related to her, and to many of the Lord's people that were refreshed in the feeling of the streams of life that filled and ran through her earthly tabernacle.[11]

Besides *Truth's Vindication* and *An Expostulatory Appeal,* Bathurst wrote *The Sayings of Women* in 1683, a collection of biblical passages designed to show how God had spoken through women. In all her writings, Bathurst demonstrated a sharp intellect, compassion for opponents as well as Friends, and a deep faith.

Conclusion

Rebecca Travers and Elizabeth Bathurst, through their experience of God's power and their deep convictions resulting from that experience, spoke out in ways which broke down the gender barriers and expectations of their time and culture. Our own time has different but no fewer barriers and expectations. These two Quaker women serve as models of conscientious intellectual and spiritual leadership for persons stifled by gender, class, race, or other expectations to emulate.

NOTES

1. See, for example, William Penn, *A Key, Opening the Way to every Capacity how to Distinguish the Religion Professed by the People Called Quakers, from the Perversions and Misrepresentations of their Adversaries*, in *The Select Works of William Penn* (London: Phillips, 1825), vol. 1, p. 125 and vol. 3, pp. 272, 276, 440-41; Samuel Fisher, *Rusticus ad Academicos, the Rustick's Alarm to the Rabbies or The Country Correcting the University and Clergy, and Contesting for the Truth* (London: Robert Wilson, 1660); George Fox, *Journal*, ed. John L. Nickalls (Philadelphia: Religious Society of Friends, 1985), p. 36; Robert Barclay, *Apology for the True Christian Divinity* (Philadelphia: Friends' Book Association, n. d.), pp. 30, 34, 296.

2. Hugh Barbour and Arthur Roberts, *Early Quaker Writings* (Grand Rapids, Michigan: Eerdmans, 1973), p. 262. Also, Barbour writes that debate tracts were "8% of the women's titles against 21% for the men's." See "Quaker Prophetesses and Mothers in Israel," in *Seeking the Light: Essays in Quaker History*, ed. J. W. Frost and J. M. Moore (Wallingford and Haverford, Pennsylvania: Pendle Hill and Friends Historical Association, 1986), p. 46.

3. John Whiting, *Persecution Exposed in Some Memoirs Relating to the Sufferings of John Whiting and Many Others of the People Called Quakers for Conscience Sake, in the West of England* (London: Phillips, 1791), p. 374.

4. Whiting, *Persecution Exposed*, pp. 375-76.

5. Rebecca Travers, *A Testimony for God's Everlasting Truth* (n. p.: 1669), p. 46.

6. *Truth's Vindication* was first published in 1679. Because of the inaccessibility of that edition, we have included the 1695 edition here from her collected works, *Truth Vindicated*.

7. Such doubts are suggested by George Whitehead's preface to the work.

8. Elizabeth Bathurst, *Truth Vindicated* (London: Sowle, 1695), pp. 381-414.

9. Whiting, *Persecution Exposed*, p. 327.

10. Elizabeth Bathurst, "An Expostulatory Appeal to the Professors of Christianity" (n.p., n.d.), p. 4.

11. Bathurst, *Truth Vindicated*, prefatory material.

A
TESTIMONY
for God's
Everlaſting Truth,
As it hath been learned of and in
JESUS;

Teſtifying againſt ſuch as through unbelief have
departed from, or been diſobedient to the Spirit that
convinces the World of Sin:

Among whom *R.C.* hath appeared with his many things,
to oppoſe and withſtand the one thing, the Spirit of Life, that ſets free
from Sin and Death, which is the Truth which the Peo-
ple called *Quakers* have and do teſtifie to and of.

R. T.

They went out from us, but they were not of us; for if they had been of us, they would
no doubt have continued with us; but they went out, that they might be made
manifeſt, that they were not of us, I Joh. 2.19.
But ye have an Unɛtion from the holy One, and ye know all things, V.20.
This then is the meſſage which we have heard of him, and declare unto you, that
God is Light, and in him is no Darkneſs at all, I Joh. 1.5.
Beloved, when I gave all diligence to write unto you of the common Salvation, it was
needfull for me to write unto you, and exhort you, that ye ſhould earneſtly contend
for the faith which was once delivered to the Saints, Jude ver. 3.

Printed in the Year, 1669.

(Page numbers of original document appear in text as *page _.*)

(page 3) These following Lines are to such as have, or may meet with R.C's Writing, Entitled, God's Truth attested according to Scripture; *and I reading it over, and finding it not only contrary to Scripture, but in darkness opposing and contradicting the Light and Spirit that gave forth the Scriptures; exalted and exalting his own image over and against the express Image of the Everlasting God, I could not but in answer thereto give unto you what I have received of the Fountain of Life; which all that make opposition against the Light and Spirit which is Everlasting, are out from, and know neither the Soul that God takes pleasure in, nor the Salvation thereof, but remains in darkness, and under the power of Death, not knowing the Gift of God which is Eternal Life; but to so many as believe in him* [the Light of the World] *he giveth power to be the Sons of God, Heirs with him, yea Co-heirs of the Inheritance of Light and Glory.*

So to all mankind, I and all that partake of the common salvation (that hath appeared unto all, for deliverance from death, and Deaths power, again to recover into the good state that was before transgression entred, or the Night of Apostacy overspread the Earth; for Light was in the beginning, and indeed the beginning of all, and shall abide when all imaginations shall cease;) and by Faith therein have obtained Life, have good will unto every one, travelling therein to bring others thereto, and to preserve out of the many snares which the evil One hath and doth lay to deceive; but the increase of Light, and the dominion thereof must never have end, and the enlargement and growth hereof hath and doth inrage the whole World that love Darkness better then Light; so they have bent their Bowes, and prepared their Arrows, and their tongues are become as a two-edged Sword, to wound the Innocent for the poyson of Asps is under that which speaks dispitefully against the Spirit of Grace; for no other have the Children of Light testified of, or believed in, but the Spirit of Jesus; which they that do and have erred from are devising against,(page 4) and so cry up the greatness of their own Diana, to turn aside or draw out of the way of peace; but he has & will rebuke them; yea in his hot displeasure, who either rage or imagine vain things against his Christ, which he will exalt above all the Mountains: and such is my love, and the love of all that in the love of the Father live, that we desire none might perish, but have Life Everlasting, which the Father giveth freely unto all, without respect of persons, that in his Light believe and walk, to receive Salvation thereby; and so this is testified of, and spoke to in all, that all that come to the Faith of it, may with us witness it saves from sin; and his Name was and is called Jesus, but all out of the Faith discern it not; how should they, being carnally minded? though it sometimes prick them, they kick against it, and so pervert from it lay stumblings in the way, and bring forth their carnal imagination of God and Christ, and of his Person and Flesh, which was never learned, but in that they resist, for darkness cannot comprehend Light but in the Light is Life and Salvation; and this they have, and do bear testimony of who have learned the Truth, as it is in Christ Jesus; and for the Truth sake which must prevail over all the Opposers thereof, and for your Souls sake this is written, that no simple ones may be turned out of the way, nor stumble or fall, but come to believe in the Light, and the redemption thereof they will come to be partakers of and there is no other that can work the work of God, to free from evil and error, but the Christ of God, the express Image of the Father, only learned in the Spirit and Light that cometh or proceeds from the Father & Son, and the obedient and faithful thereto have been, and are led out of the World where Sin and Error are, to the victory over it, and such will not believe only from what we declare of it, though it be true, but finding this heavenly Treasure in themselves, and the freedom thereby attained, shall confess this is the Son of God that maketh free indeed; and I know they who are not captivated under the power of Sin and Darkness, nor Lovers of themselves more then of God, will feel that in the Love of the Father to the Souls of all this is written.

R. T.

(page 5)

A T E S T I M O N Y for *God's Ever-lasting* TRUTH, &c

THe Light which I with many thousands have believed in, and found, saves from sin, and none in the Faith of God, are at a question what it is, but know it is of the Father, bringing to the Life, *Christ Jesus*, whose first appearance was and ever is to *condemn sin* in the flesh; and being believed in, quickneth in Spirit, by which only the Son of God was & is revealed; and all that have gone another way to know the Father or the Son, but in the Spirit of Jesus, are vain Image-makers, Robbers and Theeves, leaving the Door, to clime another way; So *none cometh unto me but whom the Father draws*, and by the Spirit only is the drawing, saith *Christ*, which is Life and Salvation, witnessed by all that have Faith therein, and this is that which, according to his faithfulness that hath promised, is and must be exalted over all, that in darkness have and do invent against the Light; amongst which R.C. will be found a worker, to whom I have this to say, that if they were and are accursed that come not forth to help the Lord against the mighty; What shall become of thee, and such as have helped the mighty in force and falshood against the Lord? who will bring to pass (as he hath spoken) Light and Salvation to the ends of the Earth; and

all that contend against it shall fall before it, and thou as one strong to
deceive; and therefore wouldst colour thy work with that which testifies against thee; Saying, in thy title, *thou wilt attest according to Scripture*, and so beginst with a lye, for thou detests both Scripture and the
words of Christ therein; for thou deniest his Doctrine, and callest it a
new opinion to preach the Light up *for Christ*; though Christ saith, *I
am the Light of the World*; how hath Satan deceived thee, that thou
shouldst think any should receive thy *fallasies*, that callst the Doctrine
which Christ & the Apostles taught *fallasies*? shalt thou or the Apostle
John be *(page 6)* believed? he saith, *In the beginning was the Word, and the
Word was God, and by him ‖all things were made,*

‖But he in his Queries
denies Christ to make all
things; some marvel not
that he should deny
our Doctrine, that denies
Christ and his Apostles.

*and in him was Life, and the Life were the Light of
men, and this is the true Light that enlighteneth every man, and* thou lightly and slightly sayeth;
this of the first of John *is their ground*, and so resists the Scripture, and yet saith thou wilt attest
according to Scripture, and then speaks of the
Humanity in conjunction with the Deity; so far art thou from attesting
according to Scripture, that the words thou usest I never read in Scripture, but know, they with other words used by thee, have not a ground
from the Scriptures, (as thou confessest the Preachers of the Light have)
but from the Antichristian Spirit, that having despised the Light, and
offered despight unto the Spirit of Grace, cannot express their matters
and inventions in the Language of the Spirit, by which the Scriptures
were given forth, except they steal them where they are already written; and so have joyned words in the dark, where all images are framed;
and amongst these thou hast got som [sic] to strengthen thee against
the Light, and to lay falsehood on the obeyers thereof, in saying, *they
deny the bodily Humanity of our Lord;* who is thy lord, indeed is to be
denied; but *the Lord from Heaven by whom all things were made, thou
never heardst any to deny, that have faith in the Light; or any of those names
which the Scripture gives, as the man Christ Jesus, as he that became flesh
and lived amongst us,* and that was, and is a great Mystery, *God manifested in flesh, the Christ indeed*, appointed of God, to be both Priest and
King, and for thy attesting according to Scripture, is only a relating
what thou hast read; which Pope and Prelate as well as thee can talk of
the Virgins conceiving, bringing forth, and of Christs Suffering, Death,
& Resurrection and Ascension, & none of those things there written
didst thou ever hear denied by any of the Children of Light: But the
imaginations of others, and thee thereon, were and are to be testified

against; for it was vain imaginations that the Lord did and doth complain on and however thou camest to be in Prison, and elsewhere with
the people of the Lord; yet it was then seen and in that which discerns,
that the chamber of imagery was never destroyed in thee, nor the old
bottle broken, but the ground standing in thee that brings forth Briers
and Thorns, and is neer unto *(page 7)* cursing and the fruits thereof thou
hast brought forth, in perverting some, and laying stumblings in the
way of the simple; thou wert a climer at the first, and got some words of
the same of Life, but was and art in Death, and to this day bringest forth
therein; and so being in blindness thy self, thinkest others cannot see;
and so after thy relating part of what is written, concerning Christ Jesus,
we see, sayest thou, *what Testimony the Scriptures gives of the Lord's Christ,
that he is not the Light in any mans Conscience, nor the Principle of Light:*
art thou not ashamed to call to see that which cannot be seen? for doth
the Scriptures any where say Christ is not the Light in the Conscience,
nor the Principle of Light? so, see thy work is to deceive, and make
people believe lies; whose work art thou a doing, that art drawing from
believing in the Light, to believe a lye? doth not the Scriptures by the
mouth of Christ say, believe in the Light? and do the Scriptures hold
out any Faith, or any to believe in, but Christ? and is not the cause and
being of all things Christ? and yet thou deniest him to be the principle
of Light? what would thy dark minde make the principle of Light, that
denies the Lord Christ, that saith, *I am the Light of the World?* thou
shewest thy ignorance of the mystery of Faith which in the pure Conscience is hid; but whose Conscience is defiled, and feared, hath no
feeling of Light nor Faith, and so would blind the eyes of others, to lead
captive as the Divil [sic] doth all that disobey the Light; for it is an
everlasting Truth, *who resist the Light, that gave forth the Scriptures, doth
pervert the Scriptures to their own destruction,* not knowing the Interpreter
of a Thousand, for in the motion of Light and Spirit were the Scriptures given forth, and by the same only is the   *Holy men gave them forth*
true understanding thereof, and those that   *as they were moved of the*
have, and do bring forth, without being   *Holy Ghost, 2 Pet. 1. 21.*
learned of the Light, have filled the World
with Errors and Falshoods; *Babel* indeed, and thou a chief Builder
therein, ignorant *of the Covenant of Light, Christ the Covenant to Gods
people,* and a *Light unto the Gentiles to the ends*
of the Earth; thus saith the Scripture, with   *As the Prophet* Isaiah *and*
much more in Testimony to and for the Truth,   *old* Simeon *declared*
he is the Light. of the World; and so all that have an eye to see may see,

that thou *(page 8)* goest about to attest a Lye, and the Scriptures testifie against thee, and are contrary to thy Doctrine, that denyest the Christ of God; who art framing an Image, but thy Snare is broken, and all that love and obey the Light, have and shall escape, and thy own work shall turn upon thee; *for he that commanded Light to shine out of Darkness, hath shined into our hearts, to give us the knowledg of himself, in the face of Jesus Christ; but who resists the shining in their own hearts, wax worse and worse until they come to war against that, to which those sent of God turned men to, from Darkness to Light, from the Power of Satan unto the Power of God;* but who sent thee, that turns from the Power of Light, to believe thy dark Imaginations, of a *creaturely Soul?* and instead of bringing Scripture for thy Proof, thou bringest a Proof from *Beamond,* or thy own Imaginations, that we *should have found our souls creaturely from the flames of the Righteous burning of God's Wrath in our souls for sin;* Oh, thick Darkness! is this thy Argument to prove the Soul creaturely, that it can live with everlasting burnings; the least child of Light could give thee a clearer knowledg of the Soul, then thee, or thy Teacher J.B. ever attained to; but who hates the Light is, and must be bound in Chains of Darkness for evermore, and there I leave thee, in that matter as concerning the Soul, and return to thy opinion of the Light; thou sayest in thy fourth page, *Christ is not the Principle of Light,* and in the sixth page thou sayest, *the Light in the Conscience which these new Preachers cry up for Christ, is but the Principle of Christ, which is his own Habitation:* This is such Logick as the Framers of *Babel* use to Build with; vain Phylosophy indeed, from which all that believe in the Light know redemption; how different is thy Way and Doctrine from the Way of the Lord, where the wafering man, though a fool, errs not; wherein the simple may walk & be safe; but what profit is there of thy winding and turning Christ not the principle of Light, yet Light the principle of Christ? what serves thy opinion and Doctrine for but to lay stumblings in the way of the simple, and instead of appearing wiser then others, thou hast bewrayed [sic] ignorance in this thy work, and former practices, in perverting from the good Way of the Lord, not knowing what thou sayest nor whereof thou affirmest; hast thou not yet learned what the word Principle is? is it not the *beginning?* is not Christ the *(page 9)* beginning of all things?

‖ *Thou in thy Queries sayest, all was not made by Christ, contrary to Light or to Scripture.*

‖by him, and for him was all made, and yet wilt thou deny him to be the beginning, or Principle of Light, as in thy fourth page, and in thy sixth page thou sayest, Light is but the Principle of Christ, so whilst in thy Dark

minde, thou wouldst debase the Light in the conscience, see how thou
hast lifted it up; for instead of saying the Light comes from Christ, thou
holdest out the Light to be the beginning of Christ; for doth not every
rational Creature know the principle of any thing is before that which
comes of it? *the Principle of Christ* sayest thou? *which is his own Habitation:* so thou confessest the Light in the Conscience to be the dwelling
place of God, and yet would cry out against such as preach the Light in
the conscience; thou dost indeed darken knowledg by words without
understanding; for never any that despised the Light knew him that is
the Light of the World, or his Dwelling place: thou hast devised against
that which is too hard for thee; may all the Enemies of the Light be
covered with confusion, as thou art; then thou goest on (in the same
page 6.) again to make a relation of his Death, Resurection [*sic*] and
Ascension, and so saying no more, nor so much in that matter then
formerly I have taught a Child or Children of 7 years old to say; and
here sayest thou, *that Opinion is condemned by the Scriptures that denies
the Ascension of the Lords Person;* who they be that deny the ascension
of the Lords Christ I know not, for all that have Faith in the Light bare
testimony thereto; but for the word person, it is any where written in
Scripture his Person Ascended? how darest thou add to the words? and
thou farther sayest, that *our Foundation is built upon the ground of Nature:* if thou hadst said our Foundation is the ground, or cause, or being
of all natural things, thou hadst spoke true, though thou knowest it
not, for by him that is our Foundation *all things were made;* and *without
it was nothing made that was made,* John 1.2. *and this is the true Light that
enlightens every man that comes into the World;* and the Children of Light
never denied his Person, that took upon him the Seed of *Abraham,*
became flesh, and lived amongst us: so instead of proving the Children
of Light in error, thou hast proved thy self an Accuser, and the Scripture hath and doth testifie against thee, for us, that have not, nor do
not declare of any other Christ, but he of *(page 10)* whom the Scriptures
declare to be the Light of the World: and so thou goest on to repeat
many good words in the relation of some thing written in the Scriptures, and adds thy own words, that *the everlasting Gospel is his Death,
Burial and Resurrection, as the Scriptures declare,* (sayest thou) and notes
a Scripture to prove it, that is not to be found in all the Bible I *Cor.* 25.1.
is this to attest by Scripture to direct to that which was never there? but
the Apostle *Paul* saith, *the Gospel is the Power of God unto Salvation,* and
that the *Word in the heart, and in the mouth,* was the Gospel he preached,
and the everlasting Gospel proclaimed by an Angel through Heaven

was, *fear God and give Glory to him, for the hour of his Righteous Judgments is come;* these did not say Christ's Death and Burial were the Gospel, but who are Witnesses of his Resurrection do know the Gospel; but the Opposers of the Light in Conscience see it not. But to take farther notice of thy unlearned words, the rest of thy 7th page is filled with such words as thou hast either borrow'd or rather stolen because thou namest not the Author, from *Beamon*, or it may be some of *John Jacksons*, for he once brought out such a work of Darkness as thine is, and thou hast the same words, so the answer given him may come over this part of thy work, for Truth must forever be over the head of Falshood: and thou that sayest thou wouldst *attest thy truth according to Scripture*, thou drawest a conclusion from thy own, and thy borrowed words, without any Scripture; and now, sayest thou, that *it is manifest from hence that this Light that doth condemn the Heathen's, is not the Lord Christ that doth justifie;* but shews neither good reason nor Scripture for it; but makes mention of *Paul* to the *Romans*, which words being taken as they were given forth by the Apostle proves thy affirmation false, for the Apostles words are these, speaking to the Romans or *Heathens*, Rom. 1.19. *The wrath of God is revealed from Heaven against all ungodliness and unrighteousness of men, who hold the Truth in unrighteousness, because that which may be known of God is manifest in them; for God hath shewed it unto them:* now without R.C. can make any so blind as himself, will *Pauls* words here, or any where, prove that he which Condemns is not Christ that Justifies? and farther, would not these words prove against thee that brings the proof that the Truth is held in unrighteousness by the *Heathens?* for is not Christ the Truth? but who knows not Christ to be the Light, knows him not to be the Truth, *(page 11)* and so builds on a lye, and makes lyes the defence thereof; but who have faith in the Light, by which the Scriptures were given forth, believe them, and to them they witness, that into Christ's Hands all Judgment is given, and he was made manifest *to destroy the works of the Devil;* doth not he Condemn that which he Destroys? and hast thou not read that his first Appearance was and is to Condemn sin in the flesh? thus say the Scriptures; but thou sayest *he is not the Justifier that condemns;* so the Scriptures say, Christ condemns, and whom he justifies none can condemn; but thou wouldst have another to justifie then the Christ of God, into whose hands God hath committed all Judgment; but, sayest thou, the *Romans had this Light, though they were Heathens;* yea, they had, and didst thou know and believe the Scriptures, wouldst thou thus write, and say, thou wouldst attest by Scripture, and write contrary to it? Is not the Promise

and Covenant of the Father, Christ? and did not Prophets and Apostles
testifie of him? and say not the Scriptures, *I will give him for a Covenant
to my People, and a Light unto the Gentiles?* the same that was the Covenant to them that believe the same, was a Light to the *Heathens*, as say
the Prophets; not two, but one: and as saith Christ, *The Comforter shall
come, and this shall condemn the World of sin:* And so, is it not plain that
he that condemns the Sinner comforts the Saints? and that is the
Justifier; him that Christ saith *should convince and reprove the World of
Sin, of Righteousness, and of Judgment,* was and is Comforter and Justifier,
For we are justified in Spirit, as saith the Apostle, and by this only come
to know the Father and Son in the Spirit and Light, and desire no more
to know him after the Flesh, as saith the Apostle; but thou bringest a
Doctrine contrary to Christ, Prophets, and Apostles: for, sayest thou,
*the Apostles came not to turn them to that Light that accuses or excuses
them, as their Saviour; but preached Christ Jesus at Jerusalem:* be ashamed
to affirm falshood; did not the Apostle say, *he was sent to turn from Darkness to Light?* and did they ever preach two Lights, as thou wouldst do?
but gave all to understand, that that which did accuse was that which
did excuse, *and that the Grace which brought Salvation had appeared unto
all men, and taught them that believed therein, to deny all ungodliness,* and
to this *he committed all, to the Word of Grace, that was able to save their
Souls;* telling them, he was an able Minister of the Spirit, and not of the
(page 12) Letter; and did not run over the History of Christ's Conception,
Birth, Death and Resurrection in words, as thou dost, but turned them
to that Light and Spirit whereby they had learned him; though his outward appearance at *Jerusalem* he never saw, nor desired any more to
know after the Flesh; but pressed all to obedience of that Grace and
Light that he had found the sufficiency of; declaring the Son of God
was revealed in him; and *his travel was, that Christ might be formed in
them,* to whom he was sent preaching to them, *That a measure of the
Spirit was given to every one to profit withal:* so let all that have an eye see
whether the Scriptures of Truth give testimony to thy Doctrine, that
would prove them in Error that cry up the Light for Salvation; or thy
Doctrine, that says, *Christ is not the Light in every mans Conscience, nor
yet the Principle of Light;* the wise in heart can judge: And then goest on,
and sayest, *The Light in the Conscience is but the Law:* it is the *Law* indeed, that if thou hadst not thrown behind thy back, thou mightst have
come to have known the new Covenant [*Christ*] which God promised
in the last dayes *to write in the heart;* and this did and doth make perfect,
teaching, and bringing, or binding to God, that they shall not depart

from him: and he that abideth with him, not departing from him, is perfect in him, and by him in the *Law of the Spirit of Grace, that sets free from Sin and Death*. But of this Law thou art not learned, nor of him that was made under the Law, that art using the Apostles words spoken of the Law in the Letter, to oppose the Law of the Spirit: but who are come to the Law of the Spirit, know freedom, and that he is Christ that sets free; and such thou shalt never turn backward, who by believing in the Light have found Salvation, and know, *that he which saves is Jesus*, and by his Power hath freedom in Righteousness from all that has or would oppress the holy Seed: and this is the Son that hath set free, even the Christ of God. And thy tongue confess, that the Believers in the Light, and they only have attained freedom indeed, and cannot be entangled with the cunning deceits of men. And for these thy following words (page 8.) now that Christ is *Light, who is he that denies; but that Christ is the Light of Conscience, who is he that will not deny,* (sayest thou.) Indeed R. thou dost in this manifest what thou art a battering & breaking, thy own works, for Truth is out of thy reach: for didst thou ever all thy time thou *(page 13)* wert in Prison, or elsewhere with us, ever hear any preach up, (or write) the Light of Conscience? It seems thou are both deaf and blind, and so art to remain till by obedience to the Light (thou invents against) thou comest to be for the Light that we believe, testifie of, and call to, is Everlasting, and none in thy comprehending nature knows the power and glory thereof: and so such as thou hast thou bringst forth; and having a Lump of thy own framing, a *formed light, created light,* or *light of Conscience* that may be defiled, and sets this up, wouldst make people believe thy Image were our God: and so falls a beating thy own image, crying, who will not deny. I answer, all who believe in that true Light deny all and every of thy imaginations, to be Christ; and from the knowledg of the true Christ, are all Image-makers shut out.

Yet another Christ then he that dyed at *Jerusalem* didst thou never hear the Children of Light declare, or testifie of or to, and he is not divided, he and his Light is one: and thou confessest he is a Light, and yet not in the Conscience.

But Darkness cannot comprehend Light; and as for the remainer of thy eighth page, and the greatest part of thy nineth page, being but a repetition of some of J. B's dark sayings, or writings of that History of Scripture, formerly being taken notice of; with some like Logick, as thou hast before mentioned I shall pass; but in the latter end of thy 9th page, thou thus concluds; *now having this Demonstration from Scripture of the ascension of the body of our Lord Jesus; and this* (thou sayest) *may judg them that would have Christ all Spirit and no Body;* To this I cannot but answer, who they are that deny Christ's Body or Ascension, (as in Scripture it is declared) I know not; for all that confess to the Light in Conscience testifie thereto; but thou mayst well mistake others Doctrine that so forgets thy own! as to say, now having this demonstrated from Scripture of the Ascension of the Body of our Lord, when there is not a word brought by thee (in a page or two before) of Scripture to prove it; but that he Ascended into Glory, and we in the Faith know it; but for thy so stoutly affirming by Scriptures, that thou hast no Scripture for, it will appear unto all that have an eye to see but as Sorcery; even as *Jannes and Jambres withstood Moses, so thou withstands the Truth:* and those who through negligence to attend, or disobedience to the Light have been overtaken with *(page 14)* the Night, have or may stumble at thy work of Darkness: yet who have learned of the Light, the Truth, as it is in Jesus, thou canst not turn aside: For what manner of blind stuff doest thou bring forth, as though thou wouldst make people believe thou hast Scripture, against those that confess to the Light in Conscience, but canst bring none against them, and so brings for them; and confesses the *birth of their opinion is from the first of* John: so thou confessest they to whom thou opposest have Scripture to prove; but thou art so far from having any to prove thy words and imaginations, that thou wouldst if thou knew it now deny the Scripture, that thou mightest hide Light and Truth, by thy imaginations, thou sets up a fiction, and accuses us of it; for sayest thou, where is it said of Christ, not of Light of Conscience: I would thou wert so honest as to speak true words, and then thou wouldst confess, that though for years thou hast watched for evil against us, thou never heardst any amongst the Children of Light, but declare, what is spoken in the first of *John* was spoke of Christ, and that by his own Light and Spirit was he to be learned, he says the Scripture, *A man sent of God to bear Testimony to the Light;* did he bear Testimony to an other then Christ? no, all that have been, or are sent of him testifie of the Light; but they that run and are not sent, strive against it, as thou doest and bring the Scripture that sayes, the *Life of Christ is the Light of men, and he it is that inlightneth every man that comes into the World; and that the Scriptures are true, none contends with us about that; but that we understand not our own Doctrine, and thence set up a fiction of our own invention:* doest thou think thy denying to contend with us about the Scriptures, when all that can see do see thou doest contend, will make any believe thy accusation that we do not understand our own Doctrine, and so set up a fiction? why hast not thou with thy great understanding, that seems so wise in thy own eyes, as to gainsay the Truth that is received and believed by thousands, come forth, and tell where this Light testified of by the Apostle is, if not in the Conscience? for thy fancy is contrary to the Apostle, *that appealed to that of God in every mans Conscience; and to that was manifest:* but where the conscience is feared, they see not, nor feel not, and being out of the Truth, which is no where to be found, but where God requires it, in *the inner parts;* and who are gone out to seek it abroad, whatever they may think of *(page 15)* their own Doctrines, know nothing of the Truth; but are found contenders against it, and against the Scriptures; which testifie of him that is the Christ of God, *to be in the Heart and in the Mouth; that he dwels in Light;* and thou hast confessed in thy words, though in darkness, not knowing what thou sayest: *that in Conscience is Gods Habitation;* yet art contending that any should preach Christ the Light in the Conscience; is he not in his dwelling place, does not the Scripture say, *God dwels in Light, and that God is in Christ,* and that *he will gather all things unto him? and is not Christ the Rest, into which all that the Father hath given him must be gathered into him and be in him?* as saith Christ, *I in them, and thou in me:* So thou hast proved Christ the Light in the Conscience, when thou goest about to disprove it, confessing the Light in the Conscience the Principle of Christ, and his own Habitation, and they his whom the Father gives him: and Christ said, I in them, so the Scriptures prove, that according to Scripture thou attest not, but contrary thereto, that sayest, *God hath made a formed Light for a Habitation of mans Rest,* Page 7. What new opinion art thou a crying up, that art setting up another rest for Gods people then Christ? what wouldst thou have them rest in? *a formed Light (sayest thou)* God is Light saith the Scripture, but no where that he was formed that gave form and being to all: and another Light then that which gives Salvation did not the people of God ever seek, or find to be a Rest, but he that saves from sin, and *his Name is Jesus,* and in him thousands are come to know sure Salvation by the Light made manifest in Conscience, and are kept thereby, that they could no more believe thy *formed light,* nor Doctrine thereof, then in the Papists Eucharist, which indeed are both Idols, formed in one ground, and the Scripture plentifully testifies against you both; yet the Papist in their carnal understanding have a Scripture for their Idols; but where canst thou get any word to make a cover for thy Image; that sayest, *I give you to know, that the Light in Conscience is but the Spirit of the humane Soul, and is creaturely?* what

Scripture hast thou for the ground of thy Opinion? So all that love the
Light see thy ground is not from Scripture; there not being a word from
the first of *Genesis*, to the last of the *Revelation* for this thy new Doctrines, for a *formed light, made into a habitation for mans Rest, and the
Light of the Conscience, but the (page 16) Spirit of the humane nature:* And so
thou that in thy Title sayest, *thou wouldst attest by Scripture*, art teaching new Doctrine, that thou hast no word in the Scripture for.

But to proceed, in page 10. thou sayest, our Doctrine is this, *That
which makes manifest is Light, and the Light is Christ:* and hast not thou in
these words manifested thy self to be a Contender against Scripture, as
well as against us that in the Spirit that gave forth the Scripture witness; and therefore to us doth it witness: for are not those very words
(as thou sayest we say) the words of the Apostle, *that it is Light that
manifests?* so saith Christ, *I am the Light:* so thou contends with the
People of the Lord, for saying as the Apostle and Christ says. Then
thou goest on to ask three Questions: First, *Was the Light in mans Conscience that personal appearance that* John *bore witness to.* (Second, *Was
the Light in mans Conscience that word of God that was God, by which all
things were made that were made.*) Third, *Was the Light in Conscience
personally, to be seen by the firmental eye, to be felt with the outward hand.*
And from these thy own words, thou drawest a conclusion, *that if the
Light of Conscience be not to be understood in these capacities, our Doctrine
is false:* Though thou hast brought no more reason to prove it, then if
thou hadst said, *I would have it so;* for as to the Apostles words we testifie,
and have learned in that Spirit, which the carnal man could never
discern, nor the things thereof; but the Apostle answers himself, and
hath declared, of whom he testified, by whom all things were made; *and
that this was the true Light, that enlightneth every man that cometh into the
World;* and it was the Christ of God which he bore Testimony to; so
instead of proving us in error that confess Christ the Light in every
Conscience, thou bringst thy self under the Plagues threatned for adding to the Scriptures: For where did ever the Apostle, in that place, or
any other, speak of *personal and firmental*, as thou dost, and conclude all
false that are not of thy mind? And to answer thee further, the Apostle
did preach and testifie of Christ, and as he taught him, so is he learned
in Light or Spirit; is not this in the Conscience? How wouldst thou
have *Christ seen, felt and handled? how is Christ with his people to the end of
the World*, according to his Promise? and *how is he in them that was with
them?* Is it to be seen *firmental*, as thou callest? though no other did the
Apostle testifie of, then he that became flesh, and *(page 17)* dwelt amongst

us: *Yet no more did they know him after the Flesh, but after the Spirit:* but thou, and such as thou, who in your carnal minds would comprehend spiritual things, bring forth your carnal apprehensions, and having no knowledg but what you have sensually, know neither Christ's Flesh nor glorious Body, but that which could be pierced, wounded and crucified, all Image-makers are still oppressing; for he is still slayn in spiritual *Egypt* where thou art: and though thou knowest, we, that thou seemest to strike at, did and do confess to him, and no other, that made a good confession before *Pilate*, of whom *John* bear witness to be *the Light of the World*; and this is true, and they are found Liars before God, that would set up any thing to be believed in, be he that in Spirit is revealed; for thousands of those that saw his personal appearance at *Jerusalem* knew him not to be the Christ; nay, by Spirit then was he to be learned, as thou may read, where *Peter* confesseth him; and Christ saith, *Flesh and Blood hath not revealed this to thee, but the Spirit of my Father,* and against this art thou fighting, and those that are lead thereby; for by Light and Spirit have we learned Christ, and so teach him; and this is he which is testified of, that is the Eternal Gift of God, and he that is sent of God, *whom to know is Eternal Life*; but of this are they all ignorant that call the Light in Conscience a *formed thing, and the Spirit of the humane earthly Soul*; but their ignorance of the great Power of God is not to be marvelled at, that says, *The Light and Spirit is of the humane earthly soul*; and so would make all believe, that the souls of men and women were no other then the Dogs, or Cats, and Beasts that must perish, for what is of the Earth must to the Earth: hast thou not read, *God breathed into man, and he became a living Soul?* and thou callest this *Human or Earthly*; needs then must they stumble and fall, that walk in the dark, as thou, and all do that would comprehend the Light to dispute against; but over thee, and all vain Image-makers it shall rise, that with your dark Images and inventions have filled the World with Idolatry, Profainness and Athism; and what doctrine more then thine doth it? that preachest the Soul *Human and Creaturely and the Light formed of it*; so neither Soul nor Light Immortal & Eternal, but of the Earth; a beastly doctrine, which hath manifested the Teacher to know nothing but what he knows sensually: yet thou goest on repeating what Christ did and suffered, *(page 18)* when manifest at *Jerusalem*, and then sayest, *this manifests Christ is Formative, and not a Defusive Principle*; this, like thy former stuff, which thou hast got in thy dark mind, & so in dark words expressest it; what manner of Christ thou wouldst have people believe in, all in the Light see; but the Christ of God is he that filleth all things, as the Scriptures testifie: And then thou goest on to confess, *that the Light of conscience was in the Apostles, and by this Peter confessed Christ to be the Son of God*: How hath Satan blinded thee, that loves darkness better then Light! that thou shouldst bring this Scripture, that callest the Light *the Spirit of the human Soul;* and Christ saith *the Spirit of the Father revealed it in* Peter: and was not, and is not Christ in the Father? so whatever thou hast denied, thou hast now proved Father, Spirit and Son the Light in the Conscience; for they were never divided: or else thou must hold after thy former dark doctrine, the Father and the Spirit are *but the Spirit of the human Soul:* thus shall all they be snared that invent against the Truth, which is the same yesterday to day and for ever; and let them all be so confounded, as thou art, that devise against the Light, saith my soul; for thou sayest, *Peter by his Light in Conscience bares witness to Christ the Son of God;* and Christ saith, not *Flesh and blood, but the Spirit of my Father revealed it;* and knowest thou not that God is one, not divided? *I in the Father, and the Father in me,* saith Christ; and *none ascends to Heaven, but he that comes down from Heaven, the Son of man in Heaven;* but this thou, nor any that saith *the Light is the Spirit of the humane soul,* could ever see; but who in the Light and Spirit learn him, know he filleth all things, even the same to whom Peter confessed blest for ever; as saith the Apostle, *One God and Father of all, who is above all, and thorow all, and in you all,* Ephes. 4.6. and this is he we testifie of, that dwells in the Light in Conscience, where thou confessest the Son of God is revealed; and yet sayest the Light in Conscience is not Christ; for he saith, he *is ascended far above all Heavens, that he may fill all things;* and then goest on, saying, *Now, O man, open thy eyes, and see how dangerously thou standest, that denies the Body of our Lord Jesus Christ in his Person.* And to this I answer, none that discerns it can or doth deny it, and *their eyes are open* to see thy confusion, that wouldst prove that the Light in Conscience is not Christ, by bringing this proof that he ascended that he might fill all things: O gross *(page 19)* darkness! Doth he fill all things, yet not the Conscience? or hast thou so long strove against the Light in Conscience, that thou accountest Conscience nothing? for if any thing, then thou provest he is in it; for he fills all things: and doth he fill with darkness or with Light? for thy following words in the latter end of thy 11th page, are a false Accusation, in saying, We *make that Body that did the Fathers Will, by whom we are saved, to be extinguished, and as to any Substance vanished away as smoke.* To this I answer, I never knew any that had faith in the Light (against which thou hast been devising) deny Christ's Body, but all such know it is a glorious

Body: and so there needs not much be said to a Lye, but the Truth will
come over it; for no Lye is of the Truth: and thou boasts of a better
Foundation then those thou accusest, yet all in the Light know the
Devil is the Foundation and Author of every lye; but who are in the
Light, and build upon the Light, are come to him that is the true Foundation of Generations too, and of which Prophets and Apostles bare
testimony, and is now testified, that *God was Light, and in him was no
darkness at all,* so Life and Truth is over Darkness and falshood; this is
our Foundation that have not cryed up any Light, but Christ that Corner-Stone that grinds to powder all that it falls upon: and in page 11.
thou goest on to speak of Christ's Church, we having said it was his
body, as though thou wouldst contradict that Truth as well as others,
sayst it is *but his members for whom he layed down his Life; but this heady
notion being altogether,* (sayest thou) *condemned by Scripture, I cease putting pen to paper in this matter:* what thou meanest by the heady notion,
I well know not that, except thy own Accusation that thou speakest
before; but if thou didst apply it to thy precedent words, in saying, the
Saints were but Members, in contradiction to those that in truth say,
his Church is his Body; for thou art the first that wouldst make difference between the Members and the Body of Christ, that I have heard
of; but some as blind as thy self have gone about to make him two
bodies; but Members without a Body, as thou mak'st, *(with a but)* I never
heard of before: but his fulness, that filleth all in all, is known to them,
and them only that discern his Body spiritual indeed, and seen only
with the spiritual eye, which being blinded in thy self, thou wouldst
darken in others: And so thou goest on repeating some Scriptures; and
then calling *(page 20)* after thy wonted manner to see, that thou canst
not show; and then again thou beginst, and sayest, thou givest us to
know, *that the Body of our Lord was humane;* and when thou hast gone
on as well as thou canst to prove the first *Adam* and Christ one; then
thou goest to make a difference, *for this man, of whom we speak, is not
the made Image of God, as was* Adam, *sayest thou, but the express Image of
the Fathers Person:* so having spoken of things thou understands not;
thou brings a Scripture that thou imaginest would prove it, by which
thou provest thy own ignorance, both of the day, and the Scripture,
that thou art my beloved Son this day I have begotten thee, which was (sayest
thou) *when the holy Ghost overshadowed* Mary: All that believe in the
Light know the day of his begetting, *Abraham* saw it, and was glad,
David saw it, and testified of it hundreds of years before the Virgins
Conception at *Jerusalem*: So thou that wouldst not have the Son of

God begotten, till he was conceived of Mary, who art not only out of the Faith of *Abraham* and *David*, but blinder then the Priests of the World; for they have and do preach, for ought I know, that he was begot and begetting from all Eternity, and that the day of his Resurection was prophesied of by these words, This day have I begotten thee; so thou hast so much pored on the humane body (as thou callest it) that thou must bring forth a birth like thy conception in the dark; but I think, there is but few that will bow to thy image, for thou canst not give it a seeming life neither from Scripture nor Reason.

And thou goest on, and sayest, *He calleth not God Father*, as we; but how wilt thou prove it? no more then thy other imaginations: for Christ saith, My Father, and your Father, without making a difference, but thou differs and denies it: But thou deniest Christ, Prophets and Apostles words, if they will not sute thy imaginations, and bringest forth thy blasphemous thoughts: for the Son, sayest thou, *was from the Substance of the Father, which was not the Diety that was begotten:* so by thy words, wouldst thou make it appear, that the substance of God is not *Diety nor Divine:* O stop thy mouth thou imaginary man, that in confusion and darkness wouldst speak of that which thou art shut out of! for the key of *David* thou hast not, and so canst not know the womb that bare him which was pure, nor the seed he took upon him, nor his begetting; for he, the Christ, was not conceived in sin, as thou wert, nor as *(page 21)* thou imaginest; so thou wert better be silent, then exercise thy self in things to high for thee; for all that strive against the Light must be shut up in darkness, as thou art: and so goest on in thy (twelf page) saying, *God was in Christ reconciling;* here thou hast brought a Scripture to overthrow all thy former Doctrine, for then it is not the *humane that reconciles,* but God; and then thou goest on to repeat what Christ saith, *had I not come into the World, you had had no sin, but now your sins remain, because ye believe not on him whom God hath sent; for I come a Light into the World:* and this his coming thou wouldst have only at that time at *Jerusalem,* as if he had not come before, or since. I would enquire of thee, Was there no sin, nor sins till Christ was manifest at *Jerusalem?* for *had I not come into the world, you had had no sin:* for the cause of all sin was and is the not coming to him which saves from sin, who was, and is, and is to come: and so he that was the Light saith, *I am come a Light into the World,* and the condemnation of the World was, and is, *that men love darkness better then Light;* because they come not to the Light, their sins remain; and who refuses the Light *come not to him that they may have life,* but in darkness and death read and talk of the Scriptures, as thou doest, that brings this Scripture, that sath, *God was in Christ reconciling the World to himself, and that Christ saith, I am come a Light into the World*; seeming thereby to prove, that Christ was begotten that day the holy Ghost overshadowed *Mary*, and that *in humanity or earthly, and not by Deity*, as thou called it; and all this thou sayest, to prove Christ is not the Light in the Conscience, and then brings a Scripture where Christ saith, *I am come a Light, and that if he had not come, they had had no sin*: so instead of proving thy humane earthly Doctrine, the Scripture proves, that the cause and ground of all sin, from the entrance of transgression to this day, is the not coming to, or believing in the Light; for here Christ condemns of Sin, and convinceth of Sin, because of unbelief in that which condemned them, which was the Spirit or Light: So thou hast brought Scriptures, that Christ saith, he is come a Light, to prove thy Humane against the Light; and it proves against thee, and for us that testifie of the Light.

But thou sayest in another place, Christ is not defusive, that is I confess, a word that is neither Scripture, nor the Spirits Language: but if thou meanest, he is not within his people, how doth this Scripture *(page 22)* overthrow thee in this error, as in others? for the Light searcheth into the inner-parts, as thou confessest; and *I am come a Light*, saith Christ: so thou seest the Scripture manifests thy darkness and error: so thou wouldst have been more covered if thou hadst brought no Scripture, but hadst delivered thy Doctrine against Christ a Light in the Conscience, and hadst brought thy Teacher J.B. to have proved it: for so contrary to Scripture art thou, that in thy very following words, page 12. where Christ saith, I am come a Light, thou sayest, *You have it clear, and out of doubt, who it is that is the Saviour, and the Lord Christ, not the Light in Conscience, but he that died and rose again*, & this thou wouldst seem to prove by the former words, where Christ saith, *I am come a Light into the World, and if I had not come you had not had sin*: so that all whose eyes are not dark see thy weakness, and that the Scriptures are for us that love the Lord Christ, of whom the Scriptures declare, that say, he is a Light, and this has enlightened every man; and yet thou art offended at those that say he is in the Conscience, though thou sayest Gods Habitation is there: but the Light, against which thou strivest, will wear out and destroy all thy vain imaginations, for it is everlasting, and from Heaven, and must prevail over thy *humane earthly Image*; yet that man Christ Jesus, all that learn of the Light in the Conscience know and confess unto; and his Flesh is Meat indeed, and his Blood is Drink indeed; and the World one day shall be judged by him: but this

thou, nor none that are in the Night, striving against the Light, know
or believe: so as a Thief in the night will he come on all such. But thou
goest on with the repetition of a Scripture out of the *Hebrews, of a high
Priest after the order of* Melchisedeck, *to make intercession for us;* but how
contrary to thy purpose of proving thy *humane Christ not to be begotten,
till conceived at* Jerusalem, *to be the high Priest that makes intercession for
all:* the wise in heart can see, who have learned in the the [sic] Light
that hath visited us from above, what the order of *Melchisedeck* is, *no
father, no mother, no beginning of dayes, nor end of Life, who lives forever to
make intercession for all that comes to God by him:* and this is the Christ of
God, that thou, and all the Despisers and Resisters of the Light are
ignorant of, and so come not to God by him that is without beginning
of dayes or end of life; but in the carnal comprehension would measure
Heavenly things, and so brings *(page 23)* forth earthly imaginations, and
by this would come to God, by your own devisings, as *Babels* Builders of
old; Theeves, and Robbers, that leave the Door, and for such he
enterceeds not; but for all that comes by him that is without beginning
of dayes or end of life, he lives to make intercession, even for all that in
Truth and Spirit Worship, and by the Spirit of Truth are lead into all
Truth; such that have abiding in, and testifie of that, are come to the
mystery of Faith held in the pure Conscience: but this the Image-makers are ignorant of, as thou that wouldst set up *an invented Light of the
humane Soul, for a Habitation of Rest for God, and those that God hath
given to Christ;* in which thou hast bewrayed thy own ignorance of the
Rest of God, and his people, which the obedient and profiting servants
enter into, even the joy of the Master, even the Glory of the Father,
which was before the world was; & this is not from the Earth, nor of the
Earth, but before the Earth was: and so *the Light & Spirit of the human
Soul that thou settest up, as created to be a Habitation for God, and those
that God will give to Christ,* will be thine, & thy disciples burthens, in
the day that you will most stand in need of Rest: but to proceed, thou
goest on with thy own words, and some Scriptures that may easily, by
all that can see, come over thy darkness, and is as though thy self hadst
had a glimring of thy own darkness, and wert afraid of the blowes or
smitings due to thee, and so to save thy head, goest on in words, as if
thou meanest to undo all thou hadst done; saying, *thou must not be
traduced by those that trade in corrupted mens words, to the hindring of the
passage of the Truth:* but before I take notice of thy following words, I
have something to say to these: who thou mean'st by traders in corrupted mens words, I know not; but some have bin constrained, as I at

this time, not to hinder the passage of Truth, but for Truths sake; to bring forth the Truth over such like corrupt words and writings as thine are; that the Truth may stand upon the head of deceit, that turnes every way to save it self, as thou doest in thy following words, when after thou hast brought forth so many accusations against those that cry up the Light, and borrow'd so many Scriptures with thy own private inter-pretations, to make truth thy seeming falshood, and to set up thy own imaginary light: After all and much more to this purpose, as if thou means thy self, (like the foolish woman) to pull down thy own house, thou beginnest to preach in words, the same that in words and *(page 24)* writings thou publickly hast so appeared against; saying, *This writing is not to draw the mind forth from waiting within it self, for the manifestation of God in it self, for that which is to be known of God is to be revealed in man:* I answer, if that which is to be known of God be manifest in man, is it not in the conscience? and is not that Light, that manifests? and doth not Christ say he is the Light? and doth any bring to the Father but Christ? and is any appointed to be hearkened unto for Life and Salva-tion, but Christ? and thou confessest, in the Apostles words, that *what is to be known of God is manifest in man;* and can any reveal the Father but the Son? which, thou sayest, *thou wouldst not have any drawn forth from hearkning to that which manifests:* which is that, and that only that the worshipers of the true God testifie of and to; and if this thou wouldst not have any drawn forth from, what meanest thy invented story, of a created Habitation within, and the Light of a human Soul? so thou must confess thou hast been setting up other lords to attend to, then the Lords Christ, or else with us in Truth, that Christ only gives the knowledg of God in man, but thy windings to and fro manifests what root bares thee: so I not meaning to say any thing farther to thy twelf page, who ends it with few of thy own words, or thy Teacher *Beamon,* I shall go on to thy 13th page, where thou sayest, *that the promise is to the inward man of the heart, being quickned by the holy Ghost:* to this I answer, God is not divided, whereever the Spirit is, Christ is, and of him have and do the Witnesses of the Light testifie the same yesterday to day and forever, the gift of the Father, that was never known nor learned, but in the measure of his own Spirit, as any may read, when Christ was visible amongst them at *Jerusalem,* and discoursed with the woman of Samaria, he did not call her so much to the beholding of his visible Appearance or Person, as to know the gift of God, whereby she could only have the knowledg who he was; and though he was present, he doth not say, believe in this Person at any time; but *believe in the Light, that you may be Children of the Light:* and when he came (that thou readest of) that said, *Good master, what shall I do that I may inherit eternal Life?* he doth not say come, handle and feel this Person; but, saith he, *why callest thou me good? there is none good but God;* for Christ knew then and now, none could sell all for him, but who in Spirit *(page 25)* learned him to be God blessed forever; and therefore he knew his going from them was expedient, that the promise of the Father's Spirit of Life might be more fully poured out upon them, in which he promised *to be with them to the end of the world;* and all that have Faith in the Gift of God, which is Eternal Life, free unto every creature, are witnesses thereof, and the Resurrection of this Light and Truth hath and doth torment the whole World of Idolaters, that have or are hunting in the many ways, from the one thing needful, the Kingdom, Power and Spirit in them: yea, in the *Heathen*, at which the professing Idolaters rage, though the Scriptures in which they trust, testifie of it, that the very Crucifiers of Jesus had the *Kingdom in them;* and so from they [sic] 12fth page to thy 15th, I have little to meddle with of thy stolen words, *of an in-eye and internal root, and of the stirring of the center,* which all that have read *Jacob Beamon's* mysterious mist of imaginations, knows where thou hadst them: though thou wouldst make people believe they were thy own, and so namest not thy Arthours, as honest Writers use to do: but letting all that pass, and thy so often repeating, as formerly, *the Light of Conscience is not the Christ:* I answer, I never knew any but thee say it was; so it seems thou hast been a confuting thy self, hoping thereby to confound others; but the Light only shews that in us, is not of us; but to the blind all is alike, else surely thou wouldst not after all thy Arguments and framed Reasons to draw the mind from the Light within, to eye the Person without, to confound and destroy thy own Doctrine, by saying *my intent in this writing is not to draw the mind forth from waiting within it self, for the manifestation of God in it self; for that which is to be known of God is to be revealed in man:* what, will the Scriptures (think'st thou by thy winding, adding and diminishing) serve thee to prove or disprove as thou wouldst have it? sure all that have an eye see thee, that hast deny'd *the Light within to be either God, Christ, or his Principle, and yet would have them wait within for it:* what then wouldst thou have them wait on? thou talkest indeed of a Sword *that God had set in the human Soul, to keep the way of the Tree of Life;* then *Robert* is the Tree of Life, where the human Soul is; and yet neither Christ nor his Principle: and in the sixth page thou sayest, *there is a Light in man that is the Habitation of God;* and in thy fourteenth page, *that God hath chosen the heart of man*

for his Habitable Place; so it seems *(page 26)* the Light thou speakest of,
and mans heart in thy sence are one; and *wouldst thou have man wait*
within his own heart, from whence proceed all manner of evil; for thou
concludest it *is mans duty to wait in his heart for the promise of the Father,*
and yet neither Christ nor his Principle there, as thou saist; and so if thou
know'st another thing to be waited on, or to open the heart then Christ,
thou shouldst have declared it; for the internal Root, what is it? or that
which can bring into the heavenly *Canaan,* if not Christ? then thou
hast another root to be brought to or wait on, then the Christ of God;
or to lead then he; it is an Idol: So thou that hast been so long crying
against them that preach up the Light within the way to God, *cryes up*
an internal root, an in-man of the heart, and what not, so thou mayst keep
from *the one thing needful,* in the many things: Oh how vain is man in
his imaginations, and that continually! witness this precedent relation
of R.C. that would set up any thing of his own or others inventions, to
draw from the one safe, sure, and unalterable Way of Life; and which
all that are come to, and have life in, cannot but testifie that it is almighty, and in the strength thereof, as we receive, must testifie against
all and every one that would deceive, or draw aside by subtil divising
and craftiness of men, to blind the eye of the mind, presents *that there is*
other wayes and means to be looked to, and to be waited on, then the only
begotten of God, which alone hath been testified of, and witnessed to by
us that have learned of the Light, and therin received the earnest and
assurance of a Kingdom that cannot be shaken: the sure rock against
which Hells strength shall never prevail: And so knowing assuredly
that he is in us that saves from sin, and his name is *Jesus,* cannot but
testifie against all Images, and their makers; for unto him alone is our
eye, that is from everlasting to everlasting, that in the fulness of time
took flesh upon him, and dwelt amongst us, and this is our Light, our
Life, our Root, Spirit and Power; and shall wear out all created lights,
imagined internal roots, and natures light, with all R.C.'s and others
imaginations, who not being able to get from under the Righteous Judgments of God, goes about to speak evil of the things he knoweth not;
and so the natural light, and the spirit of a man & the light of Conscience, or what the carnal man can see and know, being his own, he
brings forth, and saith, these are our opinions; so in the Truth must all
lyes and falshood be turned on the head of the lyar, from whence they
come, and *(page 72[sic])* in Truth are we established more and more, having no God but one, and he everlasting and almighty; *who commanded*
Light to shine out of darkness, and hath shined in our hearts to give us the

Light of the knowledg of the Glory of himself in the face of Jesus Christ, and this is that I had of the Lord to give forth as a testimony against R.C. his paper, entituled *God's Truth attested according to Scripture*, about 8. months since, and about that time was it written; but having the knowledg that a brother (whom in the Lord I honour for his faithful continued service in and for God's Truth's sake) was answering of it, I laid these my papers aside not knowing a use for them, not looking on them, as I know, for seven months time; but about three weeks since, or thereabouts, looking among my writings, I lighted on them, and had something, as I was reading them, in my heart that it must be published.

But not at that instant giving up clearly to it, the next night, or the next after, the Lord visited me with a sore and dangerous Distemper of body, and I being an ancient woman, that have and do wait for my change, received it as a Messenger for my removal out of this Tabernacle of clay; and not at all grievous unto me, having by obedience to, and by Faith in the Light obtained redemption out of that which must come to an end, and an entrance into the Life and Kingdom that shall never have end: so waiting quietly on my weak bed for the revelation of his will whom I serve in my spirit day and night, what his will and pleasure was to do with me, for I have learned that its better to live to God, then to have a life in this World: and whilst I thus waited, my sleep being short, I had in them several sights of something I was to suffer and do in this present World, among which a sight of a late work of R.C. in which he would bespatter the servant or servants of the Lord; and the morning after this Vision, one came in and related to me, that R.C. had sent his Queries out to G.F. and his ministers, but G.F's life is where the evil one, nor any of his ministers can come; sent of God, Blest and a Blessing to the Generation of the Righteous: Then the Lord clear'd it to me, that what I had writ, or should farther be given in unto me, as to or of R.C. to give forth, and then an assurance I had of being healed of my weakness, and declared it to one Friend, that the Lord had somthing more for me to do ere I went hence, & if but this, in bearing testimony against this Instrument of the evil one, *(page 28)* I shall lye down in peace, for I speak the truth, I lye not, the Lord in a Vision by night, afore ever I saw R.C. in the outward, shewed me him, and his dwelling and family, in the night season, and that he should be a Troubler of the House of God and cause his people to suffer; and I have seen and traced him in his work, and am well acquainted with his outside love & feigning whereby he hath deceived some simple in his pretended singularity and elocution of his own doctrine & way: and though he long

walked with us, yet never came to the knowledg of the Truth; and the
old bottle being unbroken, such as he had, & hath, he brings forth of it,
and has by cunning led some silly ones captive by perverting the good
way of God; yea, so prosperous has he been in his cursed practice among
those that were willing again to imbrace this present world, that he has
perverted whole families, that were called with the high and heavenly
Call, but never come to the election; and so have been deceived, and
are found such as have taken the name of God in vain, and are not, nor
shall not be held guiltless; and though they have or may make merry
over the slain, perverters and perverted from the good way of the Lord,
yet their Condemnation slumbers not, and the Lord hath and doth
behold their wicked works, that having betrayed the Truth in themselves, would tempt others to believe a lye, as if we were like unto
themselvs, & looked for Salvation by another way, then by Christ Jesus
the Son of God: so that none may believe a lye is this sent abroad, that
he, and he *only* of whom the Scriptures declare is our Salvation, and
there is not another way to God; and what is recorded of him, and by
him in the Scriptures of Truth, from the first of *Genesis* to the last of the
Revelation, knowing that they were given forth as holy men were moved
of the holy Ghost, & not of a private interpretation for the unlearned
of this Spirit, have and do interpret to their own destruction; for none
have seen God at any time but the only begotten, and they to whom he
reveals him, and by spirit only was and is made manifest, and that a
measure of this is given to every one to profit withal, the Scriptures
bear witness; and this, and no other is their Principle that are called
Quakers, and by Faith we have profited, dwelling in this Light and Spirit,
know the blood of Jesus which clenseth from all sin, and gives us fellowship with the Father and Son, in the measure of this Spirit that
hath filled our hearts with love and good will unto all; and so with the
hazard of all this World hath, *(page 29)* through sufferings, accusations
and bad reports we pass, sounding forth the good-will of God unto every one, that he hath given a measure of his own Spirit to profit withal;
and they that will not hearken unto it, will not believe though one
from the dead should be sent unto them; & this is that which was given
unto me to be sent forth as an answer, and to come over the imagined
doctrines of R.C. in his first paper, that is called *the Truth attested according to Scripture*, but is found contrary to Scripture and Truth, and by
us testified against, that have cryed up no light but that which he that
was sent of God bears witness to, Christ Jesus.

Truth Vindicated

By the Faithful

TESTIMONY

AND

𝕎ritings

Of the Innocent Servant and
Hand-Maid of the Lord,

Elizabeth Bathurst,

DECEASED.

Hos. 6.3. *Then ſhall we know, if we follow on to
know the Lord, his going forth is prepared as the
Morning; and he will come unto us as the Rain, as
the latter and former Rain unto the Earth.*

Job. 8.7. *Though thy beginning was ſmall, yet thy
latter-end ſhall greatly encreaſe.*

LONDON.
Printed, and Sold by T. Sowle near the Meeting-Houſe
in *White Hart-Court* in *Gracions Street* 1695

[Page numbers of original document appear in text as *(page __).*]

Truth's Vindication,

OR,

A gentle Stroke to wipe off the Foul Afpertions,
falfe Accufations, and Mifreprefentations,
caft upon the People of God call'd

QUAKERS,

Both with refpect to their Principle, and their
way of profeliting People over to them

PROV. 4.18,19. *The Path of the juft is as the fhining
Light, that fhineth more and more unto the perfect
day: The way of the Wicked is as Darknefs; they
know not what they ftumble.*

ISA. 51.7.& 41.14. *hearken unto me, ye that know Righteoufnefs,
the People in whofe heart is my Law; fear ye not the
Reproach of Men, neither be ye afraid of their Revilings:
Fear not thou Worm Jacob, and ye men of Ifrael; I will
help thee, faith the Lord and thy Redeemer, the holy
one of Ifrael.*

Alfo, an EPISTLE to fuch of the
Friends of Chrift, that hath lately been
Convinced of the Truth as it is in JESUS.

Hosea 6.3. *Then fhall we know, if we follow on to know the
Lord, his going forth is prepared as the Morning; and he
will come unto us as the Rain, as the latter and former
Rain unto the Earth.*

JOB 8.7. *Though thy beginning was fmall, yet thy latter end
fhall greatly encreafe.*

London, Printed and Sold by *T. Sowle*,
near the Meeting-houfe in *White
Hart-Court* in *Gracons ftreet*.

A N

EPISTLE

T O

You five in particular, *viz.*
A.W. E.T. M.J. B.P. & E.F.
unto whom this is more efpecially
intended to be Delivered.

FRIENDS,

N OT *in Affectation to be Popular (for that I do not desire) but
in Obedience to Christ Jesus, my Lord and Master, have I pen'd
this matter; that so the Innocency of his Truth and People may more con-
spicuously appear.*

*Neither have I fondly desired to get my Name in Print; for 'tis not Inky
Character can make a Saint: Such must be sanctified and cleansed in Body,
Soul and Spirit; through which they come to be prepared, God's Kingdom to
inherit.*

*Wherefore I write unto you, my Friends, that you may not content your
selves barely in an out-ward Separation, whilst not wholy separated from that
within which is the cause of Transgression, to wit, that Adulterate Spirit of
the Man of Sin, that's got not only into the Pontifical Chair at* Rome(*whence
so many corrupt Customs, both in Worship and Practice are come abroad
into the World) but doth also sit on the Throne in the Hearts of many People,
even in this our Native Land: And this Spirit hath led man into many false
Ways and Forms in his fallen Condition, whereby he hath strayed from the
right Way of Restoration; which way being made known to a Remnant, whose
Minds are turned to Christ's Light within (God's saving Power) these cannot
but call to their Friends and Acquaintance to turn in hither; and therefore
have I been made to send this* Friendly Invitation *abroad in the World,*
That People may be invited to that Feast of fat things, which the Lord
hath prepared for them that turn in unto him: *But more especially doth it
lie upon me for you* Five *to whom I write this* Epistle Dedicatory, *to let you*

know, his Oxen and his Fatlings are ready, only come away, do not tarry; for I well know, this is the time of the Lords Love towards you, because of the sounding of his Bowels, which I have heard within me, I know they are not restrained from you, because of the constraint that he hath laid upon me, which have been so powerful, that my Heart hath been pained in me, and my Soul hath been distressed for you, and often have I been bowed down in Spirit, yea, till I could hardly stand upon my Feet, until the Lord who bowed me down raised me up, and set before me a door of Hope, whereat his Pris-oner in you may be brought forth, which is that for which God's Seed in me hath travailed through many Tribulations; and now having deliver'd me from that cruel Bondage of corruption which once I groaned under, this makes me restless in my Spirit, that others may believe in that inward Power that's able to rescue from the fury of their Souls Oppressor: Yet I write not this by way of Complaint, as though I thought it a weariness to serve the Lord, in answering his requirings; no, that I cannot think; for I must acknowledge, so gracious is he in his Condescension, that he hath made this my Exercise become also my Divertion; yea, though I was his Prisoner by Indisposition of Body occa-sioned through the Pressure of my Mind whilst the weight of this Matter lay upon me, yea, I wished for no walks of Pleasure, nor was I weary of my Pain, the Reward given into my Bosom, in returns of Peace and sweet Secu-rity, that my Soul enjoys amidst the disturbing Fears and Perplexities that are abroad, is sufficient Recompence for all these light Afflictions.

What the subject matter hereof is, read and you will find; wherein I have first endeavour'd to remove the Stumbling blocks from before you, and then to cast up the way of Truth for you, and that by Scripture Road, as you may read in those cited Texts, which here have been brought unto my hands with-out the help of humane Concordance.

Read in Charity, *what I have written in* Humility: *knowing you are my Elders in Years, I would address my self unto you in all* Christian Manners; *but I dare not Flatter you, nor can I complementally crave Excuses of you:* Accept it therefore from me, who can truly say, For some time I have not been mine own, the Lord having made me your Servant in this thing; *but now the Truth hath (in measure) set me Free, which also made me will-ing to serve you, as it gave me Ability; that God might have the Glory, and ye the Profit of these my Spiritual Labours;*

Who am Your

Faithful Friend

Elizabeth Bathurſt.

An *Introduction,* by way of *Preface,* to the enſuing Treatiſe.

M Y former Friends and Acquaintance, for whose sakes this is written; it is to rectifie your Mistakes about, and to inform you in that which some stick not to call A *New Religion:* But though the old Enemy of all Righteousness has found this new opprobrious Term to asperse and undermine the Truth with, blessed be the Captain of our Salvation, he hath defeated him of his design, and out of the Mouths of Babes and Sucklings hath ordained Praise to his own Name, for, let me tell you, my Friends, True Religion is of great Antiquity; 'tis as old as *Abel, who by Faith offered up a more excellent Sacrifice than* Cain, *by which he obtained Witness, That he was Righteous,* God testifying of his Gift; and by it *he being dead, yet speaketh,* as you may read, *Heb. 11.4.* And now I appeal to you, What Faith was this by which *Abel* pleased God? Was it not a living Faith, which God had wrought in him, and not a dead Faith, received by Tradition, of Man's teaching? Yet such was the nature and kind of it, that he did not only believe in the true God his Creator, but also in Jesus Christ his Redeemer, although he was not come in the Flesh then; yet doubtless *Abel,* as well as *Abraham,* saw Christ's day to come, notwithstanding neither of them had any Scrip-ture-Revelation of him: For *Abraham* saw Christ's day afar off, and rejoyced, many Ages before the Scriptures were recorded; and by the same faith, no doubt, *Abel* looked beyond the Firstlings of his own Flock, to Christ the First-born of God, who was to be made an Offering for Sin, as the Anti-type, which these typified, otherwise his Sacrifice had not obtained acceptance with the Lord; for he is the Propitiation for our Sin, and through Faith in his Blood we come to know Remission; which agrees to that of the Apostle, *Rom. 3.25.*

    Again, I appeal unto you; What Witness was it that *Abel* obtained of his being Righteous: or how did God testifie of his Gift: since *Moses,* who writes the story in *Gen. 4.4, 5.* (to whom the author to the *Hebrews* refers) gives us no farther account but
only this, *The Lord had respect to* Abel, *and to his Offer-*   Chap. II. v.4
ing; but to Cain, *and to his Offering, he had no respect.*
Now I ask, How was this Manifested, or how came they to know it? How should *Abel* know that his Offering was accepted, since *Cain* was as forward, yea, beforehand with His Brother in offering) had

not God signified it to them by the manifestation of his Spirit in them, even that same Spirit by which they came to know it to be their Duty to offer Sacrifice unto him: But *Cain* sticking in the Form, and not flying on the Wing of Faith to Christ, the one Offering, mist the mark that should have been aimed at by him, and for this cause God rejected both him and his Offering, as you may read in the following Verses of this 4th Chapter of *Genesis;* where the Lord expostulates the case with *Cain,* saying, *Why art thou Wrath, and why is thy Countenance fallen? if thou dost well, shalt thou not be accepted? but if thou dost not well, Sin lieth at thy door.* So that it was for Evil-doing *Cain* lost the Acceptance of his Offering: Which seems clear to me, that God had no Respect to *Abel* personally, more then he had to *Cain,* but as he had an Eye to the promised Seed to be accepted in, even Christ Jesus, the Eternal Son of God, in whom alone the Father is well pleased. And it is also as clear to me (through the openings of the same Spirit) That by the Spirit of his Son in their Hearts, he gave Testimony of their Gifts, to *Abel,* that his was accepted; and to *Cain,* that his was rejected; for *Cain* must needs have a Manifestation of the Spirit; otherwise how should he know it to be his Duty to offer Sacrifice, as you may see he did? for we read not of any outward precept that either of them had to enjoyn it. Now then, if it was a living in-wrought Faith, whereby *Abel* obtained Acceptance of his Offering; & if it was by an inward Manifestation of the Spirit, by which God gave testimony thereof unto him; if this be granted, I hope the way of Truth will no longer be evil spoken of, which is the same now that it was in the beginning. And this brings me to that which I chiefly intend, which is, as I said, to rectifie your mistakes concerning, and to inform you in, that which (I hope) you will see not to be a New, but the old true Religion; which is the way of this People, amongst whom I now walk, and desire to walk, notwithstanding they are accounted a Sect everywhere spoken against: I marvel not that the World hates them, since it hated him (to wit, Christ Jesus) whom they have believed in, because he testified thereof, *That the Works of it were evil; see John* 7.7. And truly, my Friends, this is the Testimony this People bears this day against the corrupt Ways and Practices of the World, both among Professors and Profane, telling of them plainly, *That all Unrighteousness is Sin;* and for this cause, I know, were Power given into mens hands, they should quickly be rooted out from amongst them; but though they put no trust in an Arm of Flesh, yet they have a strong Tower of Defence, (even the Name of the Lord) which they run into, and are safe: This is their Munition of Rocks, where unto their Adver-

saries cannot climb up; and though they do what in them lie to pull
them out from thence, yet their Arm is too short to reach them, their
Strength to weak to hurt them, their Power of no force against them,
whilst they abide in this safe place, notwithstanding, great is the wrath
of the Enemy, who intends them Mischief, so that what he cannot do
by Power, he will seek to do by Policy, insinuating into the Minds of
People, *That though 'tis the Spirit of Truth which they pretend unto, yet 'tis
a Spirit of Error that they are led by:* Which Suggestion of Satan has
taken place in the Hearts of so many, that were not the God of Truth
engaged on their side, to persuade People from this false Opinion concerning them, it would seem an utter impossibility: But knowing and
being well assured of this, (*viz.*) That the Lords strength is made perfect
in this Peoples weakness; I, as one of the least of the Thousands of
Israel, have undertaken in his Name, to go forth against those who
have risen up against them; though I know many are the cruel Mockings
and hard Usings from Prophane on the one hand, with evil Surmisings
and severe Censurings from Professors on the other, that hath been the
Lot of this People to bear; some of which from the latter of these (to
whom I chiefly write) I hope has not been so much out of disaffection
to the Truth, as Misapprehension about the Principle of it; as believing
that this People, (In whose behalf I am now constrained to write) preach
damnable Doctrine, the which I have heard reported of them, some
saying, *They deny the Scriptures;* others saying, *They deny the Man Christ
Jesus, with all the Benefits that by his Active and Passive Obedience, as also
by his offering up of himself a Sacrifice to God for us, do thereby accrew to
us, together with Justification by Faith which is in him, and the Imputation of
his Righteousness to Man;* others somewhat more moderate, yet have
affirmed, *That whatever they may own, as to the Death of Christ, yet they
deny the Resurrection of his Body, and of the Bodies of Believers;* so that they
have said, *Tho' they dare not charge them with damnable doctrine, yet certainly they are of very dangerous Opinions as concerning Original Sin, and
the Institution of the Sacrament, and in Point of Free-will and Inherent Righteousness, and in holding a possibility of a total Fall from true Grace; and yet
they plead perfection, and reckon themselves Infallible* (say they) *for all this;*
and herein they liken them to the *Papists.* These are some of the foul
Aspersions, false Accusations and Misrepresentations that have been
cast upon this People, which I my self have been an Ear witness of, and
must needs confess, through the Respect I had to the splendid Profession of those that did help forward (at least) the Report thereof, *I have
given too much Credence to some of them;* so that though I can truly say,

I have no guilt to charge my self with, as to spreading these false Reports, yet my keeping too much silent heretofore, when I was convinced in my Conscience I ought to have spoke, in answer to those whom I might have contradicted in many of these false Accusations, obliges me now to put forth this Vindication.

And now my Friends, if I can demonstrate to you how falsly this People have been accused, which I doubt not to receive Power from on high to enable me in, I hope to be believed when I come to speak (according to the measure of the Grace of God, which I have received) concerning that Principle of true Religion, which through this People is promulgated.

Willing I am to give you satisfaction in matters whereon so great *concerns* are depending, and that the more, because many of these things are *points* wherein I my self lately doubted; concerning which, when I came to a Solution of in my own Mind, I can truly say, I then was made willing to answer the Lords requirings, in taking up the daily Cross, which Jesus Christ hath said every one must take up that will be his Disciple; and so I hope may may [*sic*] some of you, as the Lord shall make way for his Truth's taking Impression upon your Minds, in this the day of your Visitation.

So ſhall the Deſire of her Soul be anſwered, whoſe Spirit was exceedingly preſſed to write this Matter.

(page C)

THE

C O N T E N T S.

READER;

I t is some time since I set about this Treatise, which makes me now think, that the latter part hereof may seem to some to be unseasonable; for as it swelled beyond my Intention, and took up more time in writing than I thought it would; so also hath it occasionally been hindred from the Press since it hath been wrote; in which time those former Discourses, which were the occasion of the Subject, may possibly be forgotten by those which spoke them; but as they were afresh brought into my Memory by the Remembrancer, the holy Ghost, by which I was pressed in Spirit to give Answer thereunto, and vindicate Truth therein (that so I might ease the *Pressure* of my *oppressed Spirit*) I have in some sort stated, and I hope, satisfactorily answered the same: In which, 'tis like, I may be thought prolix; but I knew not how to comprize the matter shorter; for the truth is, though I at first thought to have filled but one Sheet of Paper, when I set about it, I saw a Field before me, which cost me some spiritual Travel before I got thorow. And now, lest any should think the Trace too long to follow, I have taken pains to prefix and page Contents to every material Point, that so they may readily turn to that which they are most desirous to be at.

The Book being divided into Three Parts, The *First* is in answer to some controverted Points, ranked under Ten Heads: The *Second* points to the Principle of Truth, what it is, from whence it comes, and whereto it leads: The *Third* is a Confutation of People's false Opinions, concerning the manner how we have been convinced of the Principle of true Religion.

The C O N T E N T S.

PART I.

PART II.

A general description of Truth's Principle.

PART III.

(page 1)

Truth's Vindication, &c.

CHAPTER I.

Concerning the Scriptures.

In the first place I shall begin with the *holy Scriptures,* which hath
been said by some, *This People called* Quakers *do not own.*

Answer; That is a great Slander, their many Writings and Declarations make manifestly appear, in which their Testimonies are also
consonant, and agreeable to the Records of Scripture, that I never
met with the like amongst any other: And besides this, I am well
assured of it, not only from their own Witness of themselves, but from
the *(page 2)* Witness of God in my own Breast, *they do believe all things
that are written in the Law and the Prophets;* so that those which do so
clamorously charge them, cannot prove the things whereof they so much
accuse them.

But then it hath been replyed, viz. *They own the Scriptures indeed, but
'tis in their own Way; they believe them as they do a moral History; just*

barely giving credit to them, owning that they are Truth; but they do not believe they are the Word of God and the Rule of Faith and Life.

As to this, *I Answer*; They do believe the Scriptures, so far as Scripture it self requires Faith in it self; that is, that they are able to make wise unto Salvation, through Faith, which is in Christ Jesus, being given by Inspiration of God, according to that of the Apostle, 2 *Tim*.3.15,16. And they do also believe, that this same Jesus here spoken of, who is said to be the Messenger of the Covenant, *Mal.* 3.1. The same and not another, did Inspire his Prophets and Apostles, in writing of the Scriptures: But still, he is the Word, as well as the Wisdom of the Father; and I ask, Where do the *(page 3)* Scriptures themselves declare any other? Where do they say they are the *Word of God?* or the *Rule of Faith* and Life? Though I have heard it said, that *The Prophets*, Isaiah, Jeremiah, Ezekiel, &c. *often call their Prophecies by the Name of the Word of the Lord, which*, say some, *is all one if we say the Word of God.* Now such I would advice to take a second view of the Text, and then they may find that the Prophets did not call the Prophecies and Writings *The Word of the Lord* (for they were the Lord's Words) he being *The Word of the Lord*, who revealed their Prophecies unto them: As for instance, *Ezek. 29.1*, says the Prophet there, *In the tenth Year, in the tenth Month, in the twelfth day of the Month, came the Word of the Lord unto me, saying,* &c. So then it was the Word of the Lord that came and said unto him: The Prophecy was that which he said. So in *Jeremiah*, (Chap. 7. ver. 1. &c. old Translation) 'tis said, *The words that came to* Jeremiah *from the Lord, saying, Stand in the Gate of the Lord's House, and proclaim there this Word; and say, Hear the Word of the Lord all ye of* Judah. [Mark] the Prophet was to make *(page 4)* Proclamation of the Word of the Lord, that the Men of *Judah* might hear what he saith; as it followeth, *Thus saith the Lord, Amend your Wayes and your Doings, and I will cause you to dwell in this place, &c.* And this was he, as I said before, who is the Messenger of the Covenant, appointed by the Father, to reveal his Secrets, unto his Servants, the Prophets, who came to *Jeremiah* with this prophecy, so that it was not what he said, but he himself, whose Name is called, *The Word of God*, Rev. 19.13. And this is that Word which came unto *Abraham* in a Vision, *Gen.* 15.1. saying *Fear not* Abraham; *I am thy Shield, and thy exceeding great Reward:*

Unto whom, in the very next verse, *Abraham* gives the Titles of *Lord* and *God*; which proves the Word to be Eternal and Divine; but so are not the Scriptures Eternal; for we know they had their Beginning in time: And though they are Words and Declarations of divine Things, yet must we distinguish between the Declaration, and that which is

Declared of, so as not to call them both by one Name. Those written words (for Scriptures signifies a *(page 5)* *Writing*) they are Publications in Testimony of that Creating Word of Power, by which the Worlds were framed; see *Heb.* 11.3. yet they do not declare, that the World was made by them; but by that eternal Word which was in the beginning, as its recorded, *John* 1.1. the same is that which liveth and abideth for ever, 1 *Pet.* 1.23. which Word is quick and powerful, and sharper than any two edged Sword, Piercing, even to the dividing assunder of the Soul and Spirit and of the Joynts and Marrow; and is a discerner of the thoughts and intents of the heart; neither is there any Creature that is not manifest in his Sight, but all things are naked and open unto the *eyes* of him with whom we have to do, even as 'tis written, *Heb.* 4.11.13. This is that *Word* to whom the Scriptures directs us, *as a Light unto our feet, and a Lanthorn unto our Paths, to guide our feet in to the way of peace; the very entrance of which giveth Light; yea, it giveth Understanding to the simple.* So that the Scriptures themselves, say not of themselve [*sic*], that they are the *Word of God*, but that they bear witness *(page 6)* of him. And this is he, who said to those great *Scripturians* (namely, the *Jews* of old) who so greatly exalted the Scriptures, but had not the living Word abiding in them; *Search the Scriptures, for in them ye think ye have eternal Life; and they are they which testifie of me*, saith Christ, *but ye will not come to me that ye might have Life*, John 5.38, 39, 40. So here it may be seen, there is good reason to distinguish between the *written Words*, the *Writing* or *Letter*, and the *living Word*, which is a *quickening Spirit*.

Luke 1.79. Psalm 119. 130.

But now; as to the other part of the Charge, which is *That this People* (of whom I am now writing) *do not own the Scriptures to be the Rule of Faith and Life.*

In their behalf I *Answer:* They do own the Scriptures to be a Rule, and they direct unto him (to wit, Christ) who is the Object of our Faith, and Lord of Light and Life: They do also believe that the Scriptures are profitable, for Doctrine, for Reproof, for Correction, for Instruction in Righteousness, that the Man of God may be thoroughly furnished unto every good Work, as saith the Apostle, *2 Tim.* 3.16,17. *(page 7)* But yet still it is in Christ Jesus, whom his People do believe; and he is the Rule by which they Live, according to the Example of the Apostle, who saith, *The Life that I now Live in the Flesh, I live by the Faith of the Son of God*, Gal. 2.20. He must needs be his Peoples Rule; for *he is the Way, the Truth and the Life; no man cometh to the Father but by him*, John, 14.6. And 'tis *his Spirit that leads into all Truth*, John, 16.13. even that Spirit which *searcheth all things, yea, the deep things of God*, as saith the Apostle, *1 Cor. 2.10.* which Spirit *teacheth them of all things, and bringeth all things to their Remembrance*, according to Christ's Promise, *John 14.26.* Therefore the Spirit of Christ is the Rule of his Peoples Faith, and the Guide of their life; yet doth not this detract from the Scriptures, nor the Estimation of this People (called *Quakers*) concerning them; for I know they do believe, that *whatsoever things were written aforetime, were written for our Learning, that we through Patience and Comfort of the Scriptures might have Hope*, as 'tis recorded, *Rom. 15.4.* So that it appears, the Scriptures are owned of *(page 8)* them, and are believed by them, and are Practiced amongst them, but they dare not ascribe them that Glory which is due to God, nor exalt them above his Son Christ Jesus, nor prefer them in his Spirit's stead; neither yet is it any Derogation from the Scriptures, to exalt Christ and his Spirit more than they; for Scriptures themselves exalt Christ and the Spirit above themselves: So that it is not in any slight or disrespect they have to those holy Writings, wherefore they do not call them the *Word*, and the *Rule* of *Faith* and *Life*; but as they have declared, 'tis from that reverend regard they owe and ought to bear to Christ Jesus, the great and eminent *Word of God*, to whose *Spirit*, all Scripture directions, in matters of Salvation, refer us, as to an Infallible Rule and Guide, direct us thereunto, that we may not live in them, but in him, who is the Author and Dispenser of them. Thus, though the Scriptures are granted to be a Righteous Rule, and of Divine Dispensation (*for the Prophecy came not in old time by the will of Man, but holy men of God spoke as they were moved by the holy Ghost*, even as the Apostle testified, *(page 9)* 2 Pet. 1.21. And my Soul praises the Lord, that he hath preserved the Records of so many Prophecies and Testimonies of his primitive Servants, through so many Contingencies, unto this present age; yet can I not think, that the God of infinite Wisdom and Grace, whose Mercy is over all his works, would leave Mankind in so great a Concern, whereon their Eternal Salvation is depending, to such a Rule alone for *guidance* therein, as is subject to Concealing, Mis-translation, Mis-interpretation, False-Application, as we find the Scriptures have been by Corrupters of them: Much less can I believe that he would suffer the greatest part of the World to live without them (as they do) were there no other means appointed for their Salvation; Yea, moreover, I am very sensible, that where the Scriptures are, many occurrences may fall out in the course of our Lives, about which the Scripture gives no particular Advice; and yet it is necessary we should have a guide near in all our affairs: But I well know, many Cases there are, where Scripture is altogether silent in the matter. Admit then *(page or [sic])* here, that the Creature, in such a strait, not knowing what to do, betake it self to inquire of the Lord by Prayer; alas! what will that avail, unless it receive an Answer? which is already granted not to be found in Scripture, neither can it now be had by the meer Litteral Priesthood, nor by their pretended *V-rim* and *Thummim*; and say they (who cry up solely Scripture to be the Rule of Faith and Life) *Neither must we expect Answer by Dream, nor yet by Vision, no, nor by Revelation nor Inspiration; for these* (they say) *are ceast many Ages past*. Whom I ask, What way then can the Creature come by Advice? which till they can resolve me in, I shall still retain my Opinion, viz. *That that inward Oracle* (which is a Measure of God's Spirit, whereby we obtain access to him, with Answer and Direction from him in all our Concerns, about which we enquire of him) *undeniably is of greater Authority, both to beget living Faith, and order us therein; and a more perfect Rule to guide our lives, than the outward Writings of the Scriptures, which in many things leave us without either counsel or instruction*. And here I shall leave this *(page 11)* point, which is in Answer to an Accusation, which is, *That we deny the Scriptures*; A thing often charged upon, but never proved against the People called *Quakers*.

CHAP. II.

Concerning the Humanity of Chriſt, &c.

A Second Charge which I have heard brought in against the Quakers, is *That they deny the Humanity of Christ Jesus, and the obedience that he yielded in the days of his flesh, by his Sufferings, Death, Burial, Resurrection from the dead, together with all the Benefits that thereby accrue unto Believers, as also Justification by faith, and the imputed Righteousness of Christ*. Now that this hath been as falsly charged upon them as the former, I shall undertake to prove by Scripture: But first let me mind the Reader; this I have observed, *viz.* That there are many that have Born false witness *(page 12)* against them, yet they do not seem to accord in their witness; for first comes out a Learn'd Doctor and he declares publickly (tho' somewhat ambiguously)   Doctor *Owen*, that this People deny that Christ which died at   Independant *Jerusalem*, to be God equal with the Father. But when

this was refuted so as not to be believed, then comes out another and he
would give the World to know, as if they *only* deny the Son
John Faldo   of God to have assumed Humane (or Man's) Nature: Thus
their Accusers contradict one another, (for both seem to
grant we own a Christ) which well they may do, since they differ in
Principles amongst themselves; however they agree thus far, like *Herod*
and *Pilate*, to unite against Jesus, so have they against his Followers; but
I need not enlarge upon Particulars, since rather than they will want a
Host to go out against the *Quakers*, look but into the Master, and thou
mayst see *One and Twenty Divines* (as they give themselves the Style)
enter the List together, of whom I shall say no more here, lest *(page 13)* it
should be taken for a Digression from the Answer.

1*st*. Therefore to clear Truth from Slander, both on the one hand
and the other; I do in the first place affirm, and that upon certain
Grounds, *viz.* That all who may be rightly denominated *Quakers* (such
as Tremble at the Word of God) they are of the Faith of one Substance,
which the Ancient *Christians* so earnestly contended for, and suffered
such hard things in maintaining, to wit, that Christ the Blessed Son of
God (as to his Divinity) was of the same Eternal Substance with the
Father, as may be read at large in *George Bishop's* Looking-glass for the
Times, Page 85. 86.

2*dly*. I affirm, they faithfully own the Scriptures: And therefore what
John the Divine saw in his *Revelations* concerning him, as 'tis Recorded,
Chap 13.8. *That he* (to wit, Christ) *was the Lamb slain from the Foundation of the World.* And what the Apostle said of him, *Phil.* 2.6. *Who
being in the Form of God, thought it no Robbery to be equal with God.*
Likewise *John* the Evangelist in *(page 14)* his first Chapter 1,2,3. saith
concerning Christ. *In the Beginning was the Word, and the Word was with
God, and the Word was God, the same was in the Beginning with God; all
things were made by him, and without him was not any thing made that was
made; for by him were all things created that are in Heaven, and that are in
Earth, Visible and Invisible, whether they be Thrones or Dominions, Principalities or Powers; all things were created by him, and for him, who is over all,
God blessed for ever, Amen,* Col. 1.16. Rom. 9.5. These, together with
the Testimonies Jesus gave of himself, *John* 8. 58. *Verily, verily, I say
unto you, before Abraham was I am.* John 10.30 *I and my Father are one.*
John 15.5. there he prays, *And now, O Father, glorifie thou me with thine
own self, and with the Glory which I had with thee before the World was.*

In like manner he speaks of his own Eternity, *Proverbs* Chap 8. from
the 23rd to the end, to which agrees that application given to him, of

wonderful Counsellor, the mighty God, the everlasting Father, the Prince of Peace. Isa. 9.6. These things, I say, the *Quakers* believing according as they are written, *(page 15)* and having an experience of in themselves, by the effectual working of the mighty *Power of Christ Jesus* in their Hearts, are sufficient proofs to them of his Divine Substance; and also to make them see what is the Fellowship of the Mystery, which from the beginning of the World hath been hid in God, who Created all things by Jesus Christ, as 'tis written, *Ephes. 3.9.* Wherefore they know the Son to be one, and equal in Power with the Father.

Now if any shall Object that Scripture, where Christ saith, My *Father is greater than I.*

Answer: That must needs be understood only as he assumed the Name of Man; not at all relating to the fulness of the God-head that dwelleth bodily in him; as 'tis written, *Col. 2.9.* So likewise the Author to the *Hebrews* describes him, Chap. 1. 2, 3, Verses, *To be the brightness of the Father's Glory, and the express Image or Character of his Substance* (for so the word *Person* ought to be rendered) *by whom also he made the World.* And therefore I believe (and so do *(page 16)* they, in whose behalf I write) that Jesus Christ is very God.

3dly. I affirm, they do believe that this Jesus, or this God, was manifest in the Flesh, as saith the Apostle, 1 *Tim.* 3.16. And *John* the Evangelist, Chap. 1.14. *The Word was made Flesh, and dwelt amongst us, (and we beheld his Glory, the Glory as of the only begotten of the Father) full of Grace and Truth.* And *Paul* to the *Hebrews*, Chap. 2.16. speaking of Christ, saith, *For verily he took not on him the nature of Angels, but he took on him the Seed of* Abraham.

4thly. Therefore in the fourth place I affirm, The *Quakers* do faithfully own this Jesus to be the Mediator, according to the Testimony of the Apostle, *I Tim.* 2.5, 6. *For there is one God, and one Mediator between God and Man, the Man Christ Jesus, who gave himself a Ransom for all, to be testified in due time.*

5thly. I affirm they own his Obedience also; for I know they do believe, that Christ Jesus in the Days of his Flesh was obedient to God, as becometh a Son unto a Father in all things: For he came not to do his own Will, but the Will of him that sent him; *(page 17)* wherefore we find him praying to his Father, *Not my Will, but thine be done.* Yea, moreover 'tis written of him, *Heb. 5.8. Though he were a Son, yet learned he Obedience by the things which he suffered:* For he was a Man of Sorrows, and acquainted with Grief; he was wounded for our Transgressions; he was bruised for our Iniquities: The Chastizements of our Peace was upon him, and with

his Stripes we are healed, as saith the Prophet *Isaiah,* Chap. 53.3,5. Therefore these do confess to his Sufferings, according to the
Scriptures; for Christ also hath once suffered for Sin, the Just for the
Unjust, that he might bring us to God, being put to Death in the Flesh,
but quickened by the Spirit; see I *Pet. 3.18.* Likewise they own his
Death, as an acceptable and most satisfactory Sacrifice to God for the
Sins of all, and is of blessed advantage to all that shall receive Faith in
his Blood, which agrees to *Rom. 3.25. Ephes. 5.2. Whom God hath set
forth to be a Propitiation through Faith in his Blood, to declare his Righteousness for the Remission of Sins that are past, through the forbearance of God:
And he hath given himself for us an Offering, (page 18) and a Sacrifice to God
for a sweet smelling savour.* Also they believe, that as Christ died for our
Sins, so he was buried likewise, and rose again, according to the Scriptures, I *Cor. 15.3,4.* Again, Verse 20,21. 'tis said, *But now is Christ risen
from the dead, and become the First-fruits of them that sleep: For since by
Man came Death, by Man came also the Resurrection of the Dead.* So in
Acts 17.31. the Apostle mentions this as the Assurance which God
gave to Men, of his Judging the World at the Great Day, by his Son
Christ Jesus, namely, his having raised him from the Dead.

Now 6*thly* and *lastly,* I affirm, they do believe, That from Christ Jesus
these and such like Benefits extend to true Believers.

1. *Election in him,* according as God hath chosen us in him before the
Foundation of the World, that we should be holy and without blame
before him in Love, as 'tis Recorded in *Ephes.* 1.4. [Mark] 'Tis *in him* we
are elected; not in ourselves, as though personally some were chosen,
and others past by: But in the Seed Christ, the Elect of *(page 19)* God, the
Object of the Father's Love, all who are gathered into him are made a
Chosen Generation, an Elect People by the Lord.

2. *Vocation;* this also they own to be a Benefit bestowed on them by
the Father, in the Son; for that they who were by Nature Children of
Wrath as well as others, have been called of God in Christ, with an
High and Holy Calling, to obtain Mercy from him, even to become
Saints, that so they should shew forth the Vertues of him who hath
called them out of Darkness into his Marvellous Light.

3. *Reconciliation to God;* as saith the Apostle, 2 *Cor. 5.18, 19. All
things are of God, who hath reconciled us to himself by Jesus Christ, and
hath given to us the Ministry of Reconciliation, to wit, that God was in
Christ reconciling the World unto himself.* So *Col. 1,20,21,22.* it's said,
*And having made Peace through the Blood of his Cross, by him to reconcile
all things unto himself, by him, I say, whether they be things in Earth, or*

Elizabeth Bathurst 1695 (1679)

things in Heaven; *and you, who were sometimes alienated, and Enemies in your Minds by wicked Works yet now hath he reconciled, in the Body of (page 20) his Flesh through Death, to present you Holy, Unblameable, Unreproveable in his sight.*

4. *Sanctification* and *Justification*; put both these together, because, though I do grant they may be distinguished, yet I cannot see how they can be divided, being so near of kin, that if one languish, t'other cannot but greatly mourn: Besides, the Apostle is my Precedent in coupling of them, speaking to the *Corinthians* in his first Epistle, Chap. 6.11. saith, *But ye are Washed, but ye are Sanctified, but ye are Justified in the Name of our Lord Jesus, and by the Spirit of our God.* But more of this in another place.

5. *Adoption*; as 'tis written, *Ephes. 1.5. Having predestinated us unto the Adoption of Children by Jesus Christ to himself, according to the good Pleasure of his Will:* To the like purpose is that in *Rom. 8.29. For, whom he did fore know, he also did predestinated* [sic] *to be conformed to the Image of his Son, that he might be the First-born among many Brethren:* To which accords *John 1.12. To as many as received him, to them gave he Power to become the Sons of God, even to as many as believe in his Name.*

(page 21) 6. A sixth Benefit is, *Forgiveness of and Redemption from all Sin;* as saith the Scripture, *Ephes. 1.7. In whom we have Redemption through his blood, the Forgiveness of Sins, according to the Riches of his Grace:* So *Titus 2.13,14. Looking for that blessed Hope, and Glorious Appearing of the great God, and our Saviour Jesus Christ, who gave himself for us, that he might redeem us from all Iniquity, and purifie unto himself a peculiar People, zealous of Good Works:* And 1 *John 3.8.5.* 'tis said, *For this purpose the Son of God was manifested, that he might destroy the Works of the Devil: and ye know that he was manifested to take away our Sin.*

7. *Victory over Satan; Forasmuch as the Children are Partakers of the Flesh and Blood, he also took part of the same, that through Death, he might destroy him that had the power of Death, that is, the Devil;* see *Heb. 7.14.* So that his strength being broken, and his power destroyed by the Captain of our Salvation, if we resist him steadfast in the Faith, he will flee from us, as 'tis written, *James 4.7.*

8. Another Benefit is *Access to God by Faith;* as saith the Apostle, *Ephes. 3.12. (page 22) In whom we have Boldness and Access with Confidence by the Faith of him:* And as we have Access to God by him, so likewise we find Acceptance with God in and through him.

9. Through him we receive *A sure Hope of Eternal Life;* as 'tis recorded, *Hebr. 9.15. And for this Cause he is the Mediator of the New Tes-*

tament, that by means of Death for the Redemption of the Transgressions that were under the first Testament, they which are called might receive the Promise of the Eternal Inheritance.

Thus 'tis confest, that in Christ Jesus we are Elected, Called Reconciled to God, Sanctified, Justified, Adopted; by him we obtain Pardon and Redemption from all Sin; through Faith in his Name we find Access to God, and Acceptance with him; in him we are made Victors over Satan and Heirs of Life Eternal.

Now, *Reader*, thou may'st see how falsly the *Quakers* have been accused, in laying to their Charge, *They deny that Christ which came in the Flesh, with the Obedience he therein performed by his Sufferings, Death, Resurrection from the Dead, &c.* As also the benefits that thereby are obtained; which things never were by them denied; *(page 23)* for they know, that the Son of God is come, and hath given them an Understanding, that they know him that is true, and they are in him that is true, even in his Son Jesus Christ; this is the true God and Eternal Life; see 1 *John* 5.20. But for further satisfaction concerning their Faith herein (if any do desire it) they may see a Book put forth by *George Whitehead*, intitled *The Divinity of Christ, and Unity of the Three that bear Record in Heaven, with the Blessed End and Effects of Christ, Appearance in the Flesh, Suffering and Sacrifice for Sinners, Confessed and Vindicated.*

Now concerning *Justification by* Faith in Jesus Christ, and the Imputation of his Righteousness to believers: Here also it may be seen how grossly this People have been abused, and how greatly their Principle hath been misrepresented: for Justification by Faith they own (as hath publickly been confessed by them) according to these Scriptures; *By the deed of the Law shall no Flesh be justified in his sight; wherefore the*

Rom. 3.20
Gal. 3.14.
Rom. 3.26.
Ephes. 2.8,
9, 10. Tit.
3. 5, 6, 7.

Law was our School-Master to bring us unto Christ, that we might be justified (page 24) by Faith: To declare, I say, at this time his Righteousness, that he might be just, and the justifier of him which believeth in Jesus: For by Grace are ye saved through Faith, and that not of our selves, it is the Gift of God; not of Works, lest any man should boast: for we are his Workmanship, created in Christ Jesus unto good Works: Not by Works of Righteousness which we have done, but according to his Mercy he saved us, by the washing of Regeneration, and Renewing of the holy Ghost, which he shed on us abundantly, through Jesus Christ our Saviour, that being justified by Grace, we should be made Heirs according to the hope of Eternal Life. But then it must be a living Faith, according to the definition of the Apostle *James* in the second Chapter of his Epistle, *And it must be*

such a faith as purifies the Heart, and is held in a pure Conscience,
and is manifest in the Life by Works of Love, and gives Victory   Acts 15.9.
over the World. For in Christ Jesus neither Circumcision availeth
anything, nor Uncircumcision, which worketh by Love, saith Paul,   1 Tim. 1. 5.
Gal. 5. 6. *And this is the Victory whereby we overcome the World,*
even our Faith, (page 25) saith *John,* I John 5.4. Therefore, say I, without this
real Faith, 'tis impossible we should please God, or be justified in his
sight. Yet now because these my Friends have distinguished between
Faith and Fancy, therefore they have been calumniated, and their Principle traduced by many. So likewise as to the imputed Righteousness of
Jesus Christ, this they own according to the Scriptures, even as *David*
described the blessedness of the man whose Transgression is forgiven,
and whose sin is covered, saying, *Blessed is the man unto whom the Lord*
imputeth not Iniquity, and in whose Spirit there is no Guile, Psal. 32.1,2.
And *Abraham* being justified by Faith, 'tis said, he received the sign of
Circumcision, a Seal of the Righteousness of the Faith which he had,
yet being Uncircumcised, that he might be the Father of all them that
believe, though they be not Circumcised, that Righteousness might be
imputed to them also, *Rom.* 4.11. Wherefore this People believe acceptance with the Father, is only in Christ, and by his Righteousness made
ours, or imputed unto us, by the inward Work and applicatory *(page 26)* Act
of God's Gift of Grace whereby he is made unto the Soul, Wisdom, Righteousness, Sanctification and Redemption: But because they deny the
Righteousness of Christ to be imputed, where it is not imparted, and
distinguished between Imagination and Imputation; between reckoning or imputing that is real, and reckoning or imputation that is not
real, but a fancy, and dare not own the point in the Latitude of that Sin-
pleasing Principle, to which it is stretched, as if men might be imputatively Holy, though not inwardly Holy, and imputatively Righteous,
though not really Righteous; therefore they are clamoured upon, as if
they denied the Imputation of Christ's Righteousness, when it is only
to those who are not made Righteous by it, to walk as he walked: For
the Scripture doth not say, That he that saith he is Righteous by the imputation of Christ's Righteousness, but *he that doth Righteousness is Righ-*
teous, even as he is Righteous, 1 John 3.7. What then? shall we Sin? (and yet
think to be saved by the imputed Righteousness of Christ because we are
not under the Law, but *(page 27)* under Grace) *God Forbid that we should Sin,*
(*in this state of Grace*) saith the Apostle, *Rom.* 6.15. Indeed the whole
Chapter speaks the same sense (*viz.*) that it is not our Imputation or
reckoning of Christ's Righteousness to our selves will justifie us; but he

imparting and imputing it to us: And this shall suffice in Answer to the second general Charge against this People; in every particular of which it may be seen, what gross abuses have been cast upon them, whereby the envious and ill affected have sought to cover their Principles wih [*sic*] their own Perversions, and so to make Truth it self become rejected. But I shall in the next place speak to those I take to be more moderate, and such whom I have found sometime myself much swayed by: But since I find it was more by Education and Tradition, then any certain evidence I could have of the Truth of that Religion, I find my self obliged to detect those Errors in publick, which I have heard divers of them cast upon the People called *Quakers* in private, charitably judging they speak not so much against them out of ill will, as ignorance of, and unacquaintance with *(page 28)* their blameless Principle; though this is bad enough for People to speak Evil of things they know not; and for such as are divided amongst themselves, to joyn together against others (as some have confessed to me, that though they differ in many par-ticulars, yet they all agree in this, to set their Seal against the *Quakers*) but who they were, I have and shall at present conceal, desiring not to expose them, but to inform them, that so setting before them their Errors and Mistakes, some of them, at least, may see and Repent them, wherein they have spoken and done amiss.

(page 29)

CHAP. III.

Touching the Resurrection of the Body of Christ, and of the Saints.

AS concerning the Resurrection of the Body of our blessed Lord Jesus, and also the Bodies of Believers; this I have been born down in, that the *Quakers* do not own.

In answer to which, though I had something to reply in their behalf at that season, yet I must confess, the respect I had to my Friend who affirm'd the same, made me a little incline to that persuasion of them; but now being better acquainted with their Principle, I must needs add that this Report is an utter Falshood; for they do believe as 'tis recorded in the Scriptures, that Christ Jesus, who descended into the lower parts of the Earth, the same ascended up far above all Heavens, that he might fill all things and sits now at the Right hand of God in his glorious *(page 30)* Body, and therefore shall the low estates and humbled Body of Believers be made like unto his glorious Body, through the working of his mighty Power, whereby he is able to subdue all things unto himself; and then shall this *Corruptible put on Incorruption, and this Mortality put on Immortality, and Death it self shall be swallowed up of Victory.* So here likewise it may be noted, how their Adversaries have been disappointed; for first, it was the design of some, to have made Saducees of them, by giving out, *That they deny the Resurrection;* as it was said of them, *Acts. 23.8.* For *the Saducees say, There is no Resurrection, neither Angel nor Spirit.* Thus some have sought to render these, as if at death they believed Soul and Body were both to be annihilated: But when this would not take, then they reported, *That the Body only was that which the* Quakers *held should never rise again.*

Ephes. 4. 10.
1 Pet. 3. 22.
Phil. 3. 21.
1 Cor. 15.
53, 54

Here, *Reader,* thou mayst see how they have been slandered both ways; for they do believe the *Resurrection of the just and of the unjust,* the one to *Salvation,* the other to *Condemnation, (page 31)* according to the judgment of the great day, *and then shall every Seed have its own Body,* saith the Scriptures, *Acts 24.15., John 5.29., I Cor. 15.38.* But because they dare not be so foolishly inquisitive as to ask, nor so arrogant in their minds as to determine *with what bodies they shall rise;* therefore do some say *They deny the Resurrection of the Body of Christ, and of all that are or shall be dead:* But this is most falsly charged upon them; for they do believe the Resurrection of the dead; *for if the dead rise not they are of all men most miserable.* But what can be a ballance of an equal Poiz with the Tryals, Exorcised of Afflictions and Persecutions, that are their lot and portion in this life, short of an eternal Inheritance, and a Crown of Glory that fadeth not away? Therefore they also believe, *That every man shall be raised in his own order; Christ the first Fruits,* afterwards they that are Christ's at his coming; yea, they do believe, *That the dead shall be raised incorruptible, and that God giveth a body as it pleaseth him, and to every Seed his own Body; there is a natural Body and a Spiritual; there are Bodies Terrestrial, and Bodies Celestial,* wherein *(page 32)* they agree with the testimony of the Apostle, *I Cor. 15.23,43,44.* which I think is sufficient to give all sober Inquiries full, satisfaction herein: For, as to my own particular, I freely do confess it suffices me that God will give unto my Spirit such a Body as it pleases him.

CHAP. IV.

Concerning Original Sin.

A S to *Original Sin*, in which the *Quakers* are judged to be of so dangerous an Opinion, without shewing to me what that Opinion was,

I Answer; Though the word *Original* be not found in Scripture, yet if any mean hereby the *inward Corruption* and *Seed of Sin,* which Satan hath sown in us, and wherewith we are defiled in our first and fallen Nature, I am sure this will not be denied by any true *Quaker;* for they know and believe, that in the *first Adam* all are sinners, but in *(page 33)* the *second Adam,* which is the Lord from Heaven, we are made righteous; for *as in* Adam *all die, even so in* Christ *shall all be made alive,* as 'tis written, *1 Cor. 15.22.* But though it be granted, that by one Man sin entred into the World, and Death by sin; and so Death passed upon all Men, for all have sinned, even over them that had not sinned after the similitude of *Adam's* Transgression, who is the figure of him that was to come, *Rom. 5.12,14.* yet this doth not prove the Lord to be so partial in his Love towards his Creatures, as to chuse some, but leave the greatest part of Mankind in the fallen state, without affording them any benefit by Christ, or a measure of his Grace and Spirit; for want of which, and being so past by of God (as some have asserted) they become under a necessity of sinning, and a necessity of dying: Oh, harsh Doctrine! and so I must confess, I often thought it, whilst I was industriously striving to work my self into a belief of it: But now, from a certain experimental Knowledge, and in full Assurance of Faith, can I testifie for God, *he is no Respecter of Persons, (page 34) but in every Nation he that feareth God, and worketh Righteousness is accepted of him:* For though all have sinned, and come short of the Glory of God, wherefore *he hath concluded all under sin,* ('tis) that he might have Mercy upon all, not willing that any should perish in sin, but that all might come to Repentance: Moreover than this, the Scriptures do abundantly speak forth the extent and benefit of Christ's Death for all Mankind, upon condition of *Faith* and *Repentance,* join'd with new and continued *Obedience,* which are the Gospel Terms, on which he is offered to them: For Christ Jesus *gave himself a Ransom for all; he tasted Death for every man;* so saith the Apostle, *1 Tim. 2.5. Heb. 2.9.* So that it is a certain truth, all that are, or shall be saved, are elected only in Christ Jesus, that whosoever believeth in him *should not perish*, but have Everlasting Life. There is no *Pre-exception*, or *absolute Fore-appointment*, as partially designed in relation to Persons, but upon Man's disobedience; wherefore *it shall not be said, The Fathers have eaten sour Grapes, and the Children's Teeth are set on edge; but he (page 35) that eateth the sour Grapes, his Teeth shall be set on edge: for all Souls are the Lord's as the Soul of the Father, so also the Soul of the Son is his;* and he hath said, *The Soul that sinneth it shall die, Ezek. 18.2,4.* Yet hath the Lord *no pleasure in the death of the Wicked, but that the Wicked turn from his way and live:* (*Ezek.* 33.11.) Wherefore, he hath given the Beloved of his Soul out of his Bosom, to come into the World to save Men from their sins, that they might be made accepted in him: Therefore as by the Offence of one, Judgment came upon all Men to Condemnation; even so by the Righteousness of one, the Free Gift came upon all Men unto Justification of Life; read *Rom.* 5.18. which makes it clear to me, the Lord will not condemn any for *Adam's* sin, who have not demerited his Wrath by Actual Transgression.

(page 36)

CHAP. V.

Concerning the Sacraments.

AS touching the Institution of the *Sacraments* (so called) by which is meant *Water-baptism*, and the outward *Supper;* here also is another great Charge brought in against the *Quakers*, unto which I cannot but be very tender in the Answer; for I must confess, I myself did once think them very chargeable in this matter. Now that *Baptism*, even the Outward and Typical Baptism was an Ordinance, (that is to say, a thing ordained by one that hath power to ordain) as *John Baptist* had command from God to Baptize; this I do believe and own: But then the Lord himself hath ordained a higher *Baptism*, whereby he saveth, which surely is not the outward; no, that's not of efficacy to obtain or effect such an end, which is Salvation (as that I think our Enemies themselves will grant; and then, *(page 37)* why are they so angry with us, that we do not own it in their Outward Form? But the *One Baptism*, necessary to Salvation, I do believe, is *inward* and *spiritual*, being that of the Holy Ghost, foretold by *John* the *Baptist, Mat.* 3.11. *I indeed bap-*

tize you with Water, unto Repentance; (saith he) *but he that cometh after me is mightier than I, whose shoes I am not worthy to bear, he shall baptize you with the Holy Ghost, and with Fire.* This is the *Baptism* which Christ Commanded his Disciples, that they would wait for, (and therefore I call it an Ordinance, because ordained by Christ) as you may read, *Acts* 1.45. *And being assembled together with them, he commanded them, that they should not depart from* Jerusalem, *but wait for the Promise of the Father, which,* saith he, *ye have heard of me; for* John *truly baptized with Water, but ye shall be baptized with the Holy Ghost not many days hence.* The same did *Peter* witness, *Acts* 11.15,16. *And as I began to speak,* (saith he) *the Holy Ghost fell on them, as on us in the beginning; then remembred I the words of the Lord, how he said,* John *indeed baptized with Water, but ye shall be baptized with the Holy Ghost.* Now if *(page 38)* any shall oppose these Scriptures, to prove *Outward* and Water-Baptism now in force, *Mat.* 28.19. *Go teach all nations, baptizing them in the Name of the Father, &c.* John 3.5. *Except a man be born of Water, and of the Spirit, he cannot enter into the Kingdom of God.* I *Pet.* 3.21. *The like figure, whereunto even Baptism doth now save us, not the putting away the filth of the flesh, but the answer of a good Conscience towards God, by the Resurrection of Jesus Christ from the dead.*

Something I shall write by way of Answer to them, these being the chief Texts that ever I heard brought to prove the same: As to the first, I say, that must needs mean the Baptism of which I am now speaking, (*viz.*) Spiritual Baptism; for Christ's bidding of them *Go,* denotes their being impowred from him, to Baptize in, or rather [*into*] his own and his Father's Name; which is the true *Spiritual Baptism:* Besides, here is no *Water* made mention of, whence we may infer the Apostles Ministry was to be the Laver in which they were to be Baptized: See here their Mission, Christ bids them, *Go Teach, Baptizing; Baptizing* is in the *present (page 39) Tense,* whilst they were teaching; and as it was then, so it is now, the spiritual and inward Baptism goes along with the preaching of the Word of Life. To the second Scripture I answer; If our Opponents will have that mean *material Water,* may not we then as well conclude, that *John Baptist* meant, Christ would Baptize them with *material Fire?* But if we understand the *power* of the Holy Ghost to burn up the stubble (that naturally grows in us) by the latter, then must we also understand the same Power to cleanse us from our natural filth by the former: But I know it will be expected I should prove this by Scripture; for which see *Tit.* 3.5. *Not by works of Righteousness, which we have done,* (saith the Apostle) *but according to his Mercy he saved us, by the Washing of*

Regeneration, and renewing of the Holy Ghost. Here is the Washing of
Regeneration to parallel being Born again of Water, and the renewing
of the Holy Ghost, to answer being Born again of the Spirit; for the
washing of Regeneration, or renewing of the Holy Ghost, and being Born
again of Water, or being Born again of the Spirit, *(page 40)* are Terms
Synonimous, or Expressions of to the same purpose, all pointing at that
One Baptism of the Spirit, so faithfully believed, and experimentally witnessed by the *Quakers,* who are said to deny *Baptism* to be an *Ordinance:*
But how is it they deny it? Let their Cause be examined, or there can no
true Judgment be given, whether they ought to be acquitted or condemned. *Infant Baptism* or *Sprinkling of Infants,* this they utterly deny, as
a thing by Men imposed, and never by God or Christ instituted; neither is there any Scripture Precept or President for it: Indeed how should
there, since it was not taken up, nor innovated for above 200 years after
Christ died; and then it was first brought in by
one *Fidus* a *Roman* Priest, in the Year 248 which   Read *Thomas Lawson's*
was assented to by *Cyprian,* Bishop of *Carthage,*   Treatise concerning
and first preach't up by *Augustine;* then decreed   Baptism, page 53, 55.
by the *Melivitan* Council; last of all ratified and confirmed by Pope *Innocent* the Third, which was not done till the Year 402. yet we grant the
Baptism of *(page 41)* those that were adult, or come to Age, and had Faith
to entitle them unto it; this was the *Baptism* of *John;* who was a fore-
runner of Jesus Christ; but this was not permanent and continuing, but
to pass away, that Christ's might take place; *for he must increase, but I
must decrease,* saith *John* himself, *Joh. 3.30.* For *John's Baptism* was but a
Figure of *Christ's Baptism, but that he should be made manifest to* Israel,
therefore am I come baptizing with Water, saith *John,* Chap. 1.31. However, where any now have believed it simply their Duty to be Baptized,
as thinking it, either for the furtherance of the Gospel, or Trial of their
Faith, the *Quakers* are tender of judging them in that Case; but if they
stick in the Shadow, and reject the higher Ministration, then they are
more reproveable. But there is a third Scripture I am yet to speak to,
and that has reference to *Noah's* Ark, which was a Figure (I have heard
some of your selves say) of our Ark Christ, *The like Figure, whereunto*
(saith the Text) *even Baptism doth now save us,* (it must be a Baptizing
into Christ then) for the Apostle saith, *'Tis not the putting away the filth
(page 42) of the flesh;* so then 'tis not *Water-baptism,* for that can but purifie
the outward Man; that that is external cannot cleanse the Spirit that is
internal, and give the answer of a good Conscience towards God, as it
followeth in the next words; wherefore saith *Beza,* (a Man whose Memory

ye pretend to honour) *The Baptism which answereth to* Noah's *Ark, was not material Waters, but the Power of Christ within, which preserves us cleansed, and enables us to call on God with a good Conscience:* But then the last Clause of the Verse ought to be considered, which having Co-herence with the foregoing words, saith, *by the Resurrection of Jesus Christ.* Lo here is the true Baptism indeed, the which I am now pleading for; and of which the Apostle speaks, *Col. 2.12. Buried with him in Baptism, wherein also ye are risen with him, through the faith of the Operation of God who hath raised him from the dead.* And now, Reader, since there is but *one Lord, one Faith, one Baptism,* as saith the Apostle, *Eph. 4.5.* whether this *Baptism* be the *Sprinkling of Infants,* or outward *Washing of grown Persons,* or the *inward Cleansing by the Holy Ghost,* I'll *(page 43)* leave the Witness of God in thy own Conscience to judge; and then to deter-mine whether the *Quakers* are not greatly wronged in being charg'd with denying Baptism. Now I come to speak concerning the *Sacrament* (so called) so the *Lord's Supper:* In answer to which in the first place, I must needs say I find not the word *Sacrament* in all the Scripture, but if by Sacrament, ye mean a Sign then can it not be of necessity to continue longer then till the thing signified is come, and clearly dis-covered: so that granting it to be a Practice enjoyned, it was to last but its Day and Time, that was till Christ, who is the *Bread* of God that cometh down from Heaven (which Bread is his Flesh, that he gave for the Life of the World) should come according to his own Intention; see John *6.33,35.* Indeed the whole Chapter speaks of Christs being the true Bread wherewith the Saints are nourished; &. that *he would come again after his Departure;* see his Promise to his Disciples, *John 14.18. I will not leave you Comfortless, I will come to you;* and, that he meant an inward coming, see Verse 20. of the same chapter; *At that Day ye shall know that (page 44) I am in my Father, and ye in me, and I in you,* saith Christ. And therefore saith the Apostle, *I speak as to wise men, judge ye what I say, the Cup of Blessing which we bless, is it not the Com-munion of the Body of Christ, &c? for we being many, are One Bread, and One Body; for we all are Partakers of that One Bread,* 1 Cor. *10.15,16,17.* And indeed, I do believe, that herein is the Communion of Saints (namely) in eating of the Flesh and drinking of the Blood of Jesus Christ; not carnally, as the Jews thought when they murmured at him, saying, *How can this man give us his flesh to eat?* John *6.52.* but spiritually, wherein conflicts the true Brotherhood and Fellowship of that Church which is in God, as with one another, so with the Father and the Son, by the holy Spirit, at the Spiritual Table of the Lord.

Now if any, in Proof of the outward Supper, shall Produce that saying in Mat. *26.26,27,28. And as they were eating* Jesus *took Bread and blessed
it, and brake it, and gave it to the Disciples, and said, Take, eat, this is my
Body; and he took the Cup and gave thanks, and gave it to them, and (page 45)
said, Drink ye all of it, for this is my Blood of the new Testament, which is
shed for many, for the remission of sins.*

I *Answer,* That this Figuratively pointed to the true Bread, I think,
very clearly; so likewise, that the Wine there figured out that Spiritual
Wine which was to come from him, will not be hard to make appear; so
in the very next verse, saith Christ, *I will not drink of this Fruit of the
Vine, until that Day when I drink it new with you in my Father's Kingdom.*
And that he did not mean, they should stay for this Wine, till they
came to Heaven (as some understand by the Word Kingdom) see what
himself saith in Mat. 16.28 Luke 17.20,21. *Verily I say unto you, There
be some standing here that shall not taste of death till they see the Son of Man
coming in his Kingdom. And when he was demanded of the* Pharisees, *when
the Kingdom of God should come? he answered them, and said, The Kingdom of God cometh not with Observation, neither shall they say, Lo here, or
Lo there, for behold the Kingdom of God is Within you.* And that this
Wine was drunk by the Disciples; see *Acts 2.* from the first verse to the
18th. When *(page 46)* the holy Ghost fell upon the Apostles, how full of
the new Wine of the Kingdom they were, to the astonishment of Beholders! And certainly this Wine of the Spirit, or Wine of the Kingdom (which is all one; for Christ's Kingdom is a Spiritual Kingdom)
must come from him; for he is the true Vine, as he calls himself, *John*
15.1. So that the Text alledged, doth not at all prove outward &
Elementary Bread and Wine to be of use after Christ's second and spiritual coming; for this he fulfilled before his Death, and the holy Ghost
was not given till after he was glorified, as you may read, *John 7.39.*

But possibly some may object, *It was practiced by the Church of* Corinth
*after Christ was inwardly come, after the Holy Ghost was given them, as
may be argued from* 1 Cor. 11.24,25. *where the Apostle repeating Christ's
words in* Mathew, *and This do ye as oft as ye drink it in remembrance of me.*

To whom I answer, on the behalf of the People whom I have undertaken to speak for; If any break outward Bread, and Drink outward Wine
with a sincere Intention, as believing it their *(page 47)* duty, that they
may the more be put in remembrance of the Body and Blood of Christ,
by the Remembrancer, the *Spirit* of *Truth* which is *appointed* by the
Father to lead the Saints into all Truth, they judge them not, but rather
hope that such will come further out of the Shadow to the Substance:

But to do it meerely, by Imitation or Tradition, as most do, is not to offer a Sacrifice to God in Righteousness; however, the outward Supper cannot be the Communion of the Body and Blood of Christ, Which the Apostle speaks of in 1 Cor. 10.15. and so on. This can be but a sign, to put us in Remembrance thereof; and therefore, though it was commanded to, and practiced by the Church of *Corinth*, yet that doth not perpetuate its continuance: For so was washing one another's feet, abstaining from things strangled, and Blood; anointing the Sick with Oyl, laid upon the Saints of old, which ye your selves judge not needful to be practiced now. But if any shall say, *The Apostle relaxt some of these, by saying in* 1 Cor. 10.25. Whatever is sold in the *(page 48)* Shambles that eat, asking no Questions for Conscience sake. Then it must be granted that there is no necessity for the continuance of the other; for the same Apostle saith, *The Kingdom of God is not Meat, and Drink, but Righteousness, and Peace, and Joy in the Holy Ghost,* Rom. 4.17. *Let no man therefore judge you in Meat or in Drink or in respect of a Holy Day, or of the New Moon, or of the Sabbath Day, saith he; wherefore if ye be dead with Christ Jesus, why, as though living in the World are ye subject to Ordinances? Touch not, taste not, handle not, which all are to perish with the using after the Commandments and Doctrines of Men,* Col. 2.16, 20, 21, 22. So here is as much said for the abolishing of this latter (as to any necessity) as can be alleged for the former; therefore those that can dispense with the one, have small reason to plead for the other. And yet I testifie, the communion of the Body and Blood of Christ the *Quakers* do own, as that which every one must come to know and witness, or they have no Life in them.

John 13.14.
Acts 15.28, 29.
James 5.14.

Now I appeal to the *Reader,* How then can it be said, that they deny the true *(page 49)* Institution of the *Lord's Supper?* Yet am I loth to leave the thing here, being willing to hope I write to some, who are Conscientiously scrupulous in this matter, who ('tis like) are ready to say, as my self (in Heart) have often said, viz. *To lay aside this Administration, were at once to cast off and count useless what so many Martyrs in the Marian-Days, so zealously contended for; yea, resisted unto Blood in striving to maintain:* And having this Opinion, I confess, I was much swayed thereby, as thinking it had been merely for the outward Administration that they suffered Martyrdom; but having since more seriously considered the Matter, I can truly say, I have received this from the Lord for Answer, viz. *It was not to maintain those outward Signs of Bread and Wine, but to bear Testimony against the Falshood and Foppery of* Transubstantiation, *that the Worthies of those days stood so stoutly against it, that they counted not their Lives dear unto themselves, that they might finish the Testimony they had received from the divine Spirit;* which indeed History is clear in (to them that read with Understanding) For the Question put to them was not, *Why do (page 50) you breake Bread and drink Wine, in your Sacrament, without Consecration?* But, *What say you to the Sacrament of the Altar, after the Bread and Wine is Consecrated? Is the Real Presence of Christ there, I or no?* This was the Interrogatory they were to answer; and bravely indeed did *Tindal, Philpot,* and others, maintain their Negation to their Question; which those that are acquainted with Martyrology, cannot but have a Knowledge of: Therefore the laying aside these outward Signs, to be used by way of Remembrance, when the Spirit it self is their Remembrancer, this is not to put to a slight upon the Sufferings of those Martyrs, who then were breaking through a Cloud of Apostacy and Errors, the bright side of which (blessed be our God) hath since more fully appeaerd.

To conclude this point: If any shall be offended at what I have written to vindicate the laying aside of this outward Sign, where the thing signified is inwardly come; if they will dwell upon the Figure of the Death of Christ without, and care not to come to know and witness his Resurrection and Life in *(page 51)* themselves, I'le leave them where they are; giving them to understand, I have not attempted a formal Confutation of Error, but a Vindication of the Truth.

CHAP. VI.

Touching Free-Will

Although I have heard say, *That the* Quakers *are* Free-willers; Yet this doth not prove them to be so, no more than People saying so, is proof that they deny the Scriptures: But since some are so willing to receive Reports against them, something I shall say as to this Particular in behalf of them, and that is this; They are not of those that slightly say, *Man may be saved if he will;* for they know right well, *'Tis not of him that willeth, nor of him that runneth, but in God that sheweth Mercy;* for we are not able of our selves, so much as to think a good Thought, but all our *sufficiency* is of God, who worketh in us *(page 52)* both to will and to do of his own good Pleasure: And therefore say we with the Apostle, Of *his own will begat he us with the word of Truth, that we should be a kind of first Fruit of his Creatures,* James 1.18. But since there is a

willing Faculty placed in Man, and this Will being corrupted, is naturally froward and averse to any thing spiritually good; whereby Man chuseth
that wherein the Lord delighteth not, and will not hearken to his Counsel,
nor return at the Reproofs of Instruction which are the Way of Life; but
obstinately pursues the sinful Desires and Lusts of the
Prov. 6.23.   Flesh, to his Soul's Ruin; and so his Destruction is of
himself, and God clear of his Blood, by the Free Ten-
ders of his Grace, and strivings of his Spirit within him. If this be granted,
then it will follow, if ever Man be saved, this stubborn Will must be
bowed and subjected, and brought into Obedience of the Lord Jesus;
for 'tis the Willing and Obedient to whom the Promise is made, *Isa.* 1.19.
So that Man must come to be freely willingto serve the Lord, and to take
up the Cross, and *(page 53)* bear the Yoke of his Son Christ Jesus, not
only of Necessity, but of a Ready Mind: And thus now, to have the Will
sanctified, and brought into the pure Obedience of him that sanctifieth
it, (which is an Effect of the Free Grace of God) here comes the true
Freedom of Will to be known, even to be made free from Sin, being
delivered from the Bondage of Corruption, into the Glorious Liberty of
the Children of God, which agrees to that of the Apostle, *Rom.* 8.21.
And here, as the Truth maketh free, Man comes to be free indeed, and to
receive Ability to attend upon the Lord without Distraction; and to do his
Will on Earth as it is done in Heaven, according to that Prayer which
our blessed Saviour taught his Disciples, as we read in the sixth Chapter
of *Matthew; After this manner pray ye,* (saith Christ) *Our Father, which art in
Heaven, hallowed be thy Name; thy Kingdom come, thy Will be done on Earth
as it is in Heaven, &c.* And yet how many are there that will plead for this
Platform of Prayer, who never expect to receive an Answer? *(page 54)*

**Can they think
that Christ would bid
his Disciples pray for
what he never meant
to grant? This were
to render him who is
Truth itself, an Im-
poster; and to tax
the Blessed Son of
God with Deceit: O
Horrible!*

*For say they, The Will of God cannot be done per-
fectly here:* I grant, where the Kingdom of God is
not come, there his Will can never perfectly be
done; but where the Kingdom of God is known
and witnessed to be within; that gives Power and
Ability, and makes willing to yield Obedience
unto his Requirings of us; so that here every one,
according to their several Measures, may perfectly
perform the Will of their Heavenly Father: Yet is
here a vast difference between the Natural Freedom of Man's Will, which some plead for; and
the Gracious Freedom thereof, maintained by the *Quakers*, for that is
quite another thing to what hath been slanderously reported of them.

(page 55)

CHAP. VII.

Concerning Inherent Righteoufnefs.

A S touching *Inherent Righteousness*, (as a *Righteousness of Self* is intended) a thing wherein this People have been falsly as well as foully aspersed, it having been given out concerning them, *viz*. That hereby they expect to Merit Heaven. Now seeing the Truth struck at with such a Soul-murdering Weapon as this, makes me (like *Crofus* his Dumb Son) to speak: What! Can their Adversaries wrongfully reproach them with nothing less than laying waste the very Foundation of the *Christian* Faith? Which stands in submitting to the Righteousness of Jesus Christ, and not in establishing any Righteousness of our own, as inherent in us, and of our selves. But be it known to the World, though it hath been reported that the *Quakers* hold this dangerous Tenet; yet the report will not hold true, when it comes to be examined: *(page 56)* For although I have heard others often charge it upon them; yet I never could find the Person that durst say, this was their own Confession, *viz*. That upon the account of Inherent, or Self-righteousness, they expect Salvation; (but if we will take the Confessions of these that are so forward to make Confessions for others, we may then believe the *Quakers* are as bad as they are pleased to render them to us: But we must not take things upon trust, but hear both Parties, if we will be Ingenuous) no, Reader, they have no such expectation; far are such Thoughts from them: For though they do reckon a Man must be made inwardly Righteous by the Power of Christ, that is meet for the Kingdom of Heaven. I think this amounts to no more than what I have heard asserted by a Teacher of your own, * (viz.)*That God bestowes his Grace upon Men and Women and afterwards rewards his own Grace in his own Children.* Which words plainly imply, the Grace of God to be free to all, and

*Namely, Loaves an Independant Preacher

to be tendred within, which whoso accepts thereof, *(page 57)* to be led by the same, do thereby receive the Spirit of Adoption, and so come to obtain the Reward of Children, which is a part in their Father's Kingdom, and this indeed is according to the *Quakers* Principle; for they know right-well, God's Grace is Universal, a proffer whereof he maketh unto all, by which they might be made a Righteous People, and in it come to enjoy Salvation: Therefore they believe that inward Righteous-

ness is wrought by Virtue of THE GRACE OF God, and is a necessary Quali-
fication to fit Man for Glory, which makes them chuse with the Apostle,
rather than talk of the Righteousness of Faith, to shew forth their Faith
by their Works; yet do they not expect to be saved, neither for their
Faith alone, nor by their Works, but by Christ who worketh true Faith.
For 'tis not Works of Righteousness, as done by them, nor only as Inherent in them, by which they expect to be accepted of God, and justified before him, but by and through Christ Jesus, the Author and Worker
of those Acts in them, and for them, whereby they know that they are
in him, and he in *(page 58)* them; and they hold him as their Head, into
whom all things are gathered together in one, even in him. *How comes
it about then* (it may be asked) *that this Report spread so far concerning
them?* Why truly, Reader, if I may give in my Answer, it must be this,
He who was an Enemy to all Righteousness, ever since the beginning,
seeing the Faithful among this People, not only Nominally, but Really
Righteous, throughout their Conversation; he hath been so inraged
against them, that he hath not spared any pains to put on his Instruments to Reproach and Vilifie them: Therefore have they been masked
with the most affrighting vizards of Self-righteousness and Self-suffi-
ciency, to bring about their own Salvation, that if possible, he might
fright People from having any converse amongst them; but notwithstanding the Wrath of the Adversary, their Innocency will appear with
its open Face; for the time is now a hasting, wherein it will be seen who
are but Nominally, and who are Really Righteous. Bear with me, my
Friends, to whom I Dedicate this little Tract: For though I rank't this
(page 59) Point amongst the Scruples of the Moderate, having heard some,
whom I esteem much, lay this Principle to the *Quaker* Charge. But now
being better acquainted with them, I find they have wrongfully Charged
it upon them, and therefore I can do no less but use some sharpness of
Speech, to refute the Falseness of this Opinion, that through a mistaken Zeal (I am apt to think) some have taken up against them: Well
may I say mistaken, for were the *Quakers* rightly understood, People
would find that they have as low Thoughts of any Humane Righteousness, as those that daily confess all their Righteousness to be but as
filthy Rags.

(page 60)

CHAP. VIII.

Concerning a Poſſibility of a Total fall from True Grace.

THis Doctrine being held by the *Quakers*, it hath been branded with the Approbrious Term of *Hetrodox;* which if so, I know not how the Apostles Doctrine can be accounted *Orthodox;* and yet I know the General Opinion of many Professors is, *Once in Grace, and ever in Grace,* (or, *Once in Christ, and ever in Christ*). But it is not Universality, if they had it, that can give a certainty; if this would have sufficed, our Ancestors needed not to have divided from her who stiled herself the Universal Church: Therefore, as we are not to follow a multitude to do Wickedly; so neither are we to receive an Opinion for Truth, because it is so received by many. Here I'll digress no further, but proceed to shew the Apostles Judgment in this matter: *(page 61)* Paul speaking of the *Jews*, (whom he calls the natural Branches of the true *Olive*) how that they were broken off; that the *Gentiles* (whom he compares to Branches of a wild Olive) they might be grafted in, saith the Apostle to them, *Well, because of Unbelief they were broken off, and thou standest by Faith; be not High-minded, but fear; for if God spared not the natural Branches, take heed also, lest he spare not thee. Behold therefore* (saith he) *the goodness and severity of God: towards them that fell, severity; but towards thee, goodness, if thou continue in his goodness, otherwise thou shalt be cut off,* Rom. 11.20,21,22. And the Author in his Epistle to the *Hebrews*, having spoken of *Israel* of Old, to whom God sware in his Wrath, *That they should not enter into his Rest:* He cautions them, saying, *Take heed, lest there be in any of you an Evil Heart of Unbelief, in departing from the Living God,* Heb. 3.12. And in Chap. 4, he exhorts both them and himself, saying, *Let us labour therefore to enter into that Rest, lest any man fall after the same Example of Unbelief.* And in Chap. 6 Verse 4,5,6. he shews them the danger of falling, for saith he, *'Tis (page 62) impossible for those who were once enlightened, and have tasted of the Heavenly Gift, and were made partakers of the Holy Ghost, and have tasted of the Word of God, and the Powers of the World to come, if they shall fall away, to renew them again unto Repentance; seeing they Crucifie unto themselves the Son of God afresh, and put him to an open shame.* And in Chap. 12. Ver. 15. he wishes them *to look diligently, lest any fail of* (or from) *the Grace of God, lest any Root of Bitterness springing up should trouble them, and thereby many be defiled.* Nor was this his Suspicion concerning others only, but his Supposition of himself; *For I keep under my Body, and bring it into subjection,* saith he, *lest that by any means, when I have preached to others, I myself should become a Castaway,* 1 Cor. 9.27. And in his Epistle to *Timothy* he speaks positively, *The time will come when they will not endure sound Doctrine, but after their own Lusts shall heap unto themselves Teachers, having itching Ears; and they shall turn away their Ears from the Truth, and shall be turned unto Fables,* 2 Tim. 4.3. 'Tis likewise said of *Hymeneus* and *Philetus, that concerning the Truth they have Erred, (page 63) 2 Tim. 2.17.* And this I have heard publickly asserted, by one Eminent in your own (a)Esteem, (viz.) *That there could be no Hereticks if some* (a) Dr. Annesly. *did not Apostasize from the True Faith;* which he Inferr'd from *Paul's* Advice to *Titus,* Chap. 3. Ver. 10,11. where he bids, *A man that is an Heretick after the first and second Admonition, reject; knowing that he that is such, is subverted and sinneth, being condemned of himself.* And this was the Exposition which he gave upon the Text, (viz.) *A Heretick is one that maintains an Error, contrary to the Light of his own Conscience, pertinaciously persisting in it, notwithstanding Reproof.* And without doubt the Text was truly exploited, may we understand him to intend the Light of Christ Jesus in the Conscience; (for 'tis Christ the true Light who lighteth every Man's Conscience, and that is the Light of Conscience) which if we may believe, he had regard unto, then it will follow from the foregoing words, *First,* That it is possible for People to turn from the true Grace of God, by sinning against the Light which he hath placed in their *(page 64)* Consciences: *Secondly,* That those are Nick-named (or Mis-called) who are called *Hereticks,* for acting according to the Dictates of their enlightned Consciences, (or, which is more clear, to say, For being guided by the Light of Christ in their Consciences:) *Thirdly,* It follows, that 'tis utterly impossible to prove a Man an Heretick, unless he be guilty of Heresie, and condemned in himself by the Light of Christ placed in his own Conscience, to shew him what is Error, and what is Truth. Thus much the words import; but it may be, some will refuse to confess to the Import of them, for fear of being counted *Quakers* herein: Howbeit, the Spirit speaks expressly, *That in the Latter Days some shall depart from the Faith, &c.* 1 Tim. 4.1. And such who have so done, we know that inward Condemnation doth attend them, according as the Apostle *Peter and Jud.* spake of some in their Day, as *had forsaken the Righteous Way, and were gone astray, following the Way of* Balaam, *the Son of Bofor, who* loved the Wages of Unrighteousness: These saith *Jude, are Wells without Water: Clouds carried about with a (page 65) Tempest, to whom the Mist of Darkness is reserved forever; for when they speak great swelling words of Vanity, they allure, through the Lusts of the Flesh, through much Wantonness, those that were Clean escaped from them who live in Error: For if after they have escaped the common Pollutions of the World through the Knowledge of the Lord and Saviour Jesus Christ, they are again entangled therein and overcome, the latter End is worse with them than the Beginning; for it had been better for them not to have known the Way of Righteousness, than after they have known it, to turn from the holy Commandments delivered unto them; but it is happened to them according to the true Proverb, The Dog is turned to his Vomit again, and the Sow that was washed to her wallowing in the Mire, 2 Pet. 2, 15, 17, 18, 20, 21, 22.* And hence in Chap. 3. Ver. 17. of his Epistle, the Apostle gives Caution to whom he wrote, saying *Ye therefore beloved, seeing ye know these Things, beware lest ye also being led away with the Error of the Wicked, fall from your own stedfastness.* For 'tis threatned by the Lord, That *when the Righteous Man turneth away from his Righteousness, and commits Iniquity, and dieth (page 66) in them,* [Mark, here is included a Total Fall] *for his Iniquity that he hath done he shall Die,* Ezek. 18.26. and 33.13. Wherefore we are exhorted to continue in the Grace of God, and to keep ourselves in the Love of God, because of the danger that there is of falling from his Grace; *for 'tis those that endure to the End that shall be saved;* these are Christs own words in Mat. 24.13. Mark 13.13. *'Tis to those that are faithful unto Death, to whom is promised the Crown of Life.* Rev. 2. 10. *Such as are implanted into Christ, and abide in him, they shall inherit the Kingdom. For if a Man abide not in me,* saith Christ, *he is cast forth as a Branch, and is withered,* John 15.6. And in Ver. 10 he tells them, *If ye keep my Commandmems[sic], ye shall abide in my Love, even as I have kept my Father's Commandments, and abide in his Love.* Thereby signifying, that if we keep not his Commandments, neither shall we abide in his Love; so then if we abide not in that which keeps us in the Love of God, we cannot abide in God, for *God is Love,* 1 John 4.16.

(page 67) See *Reader,* here is a whole Cloud of Witnesses, bearing Testimony, that 'tis possible, if there be not a diligent watching, for People to *fail of* (or rather fall from) that measure of the true Grace of God, which was once given to them. Therefore, what the *Quakers* hold in this Point is no New Doctrine: For if this could not possibly be, how could any do Despight unto the Spirit of Grace, or Resist the Holy Ghost? Yet do this People believe, A *Christian* may come to such a

growth and standing in the Grace that is in Christ Jesus, from which he cannot fall away, according to that Promise in *Rev. 3.12. Him that overcometh will I make a Pillar in the Temple of my God, and he shall be no more out, and I will write upon him the Name of my God, and the Name of the City of my God, which is* New Jerusalem, *which cometh down from Heaven, from my God, and will write upon him my New Name.* And they also believe, that such a one may come to be assured; that he is in such a state, even as the Apostle was, who said, *For I am perswaded, that neither Death, nor Life, nor Angels, nor Principalities, nor Powers, nor Things (page 68) present, nor Things to come, nor Height, nor Depth, nor any other Creature, shall be able to separate us from the Love of God, which is in Christ Jesus our Lord,* Rom. 8.38,39.

CHAP. IX.

Concerning Perfection

WHich Doctrine, though it be firmly founded in Scripture, yet it is rejected and set at nought, because 'tis believed by the *Quakers;* notwithstanding which they freely confess, that a Perfect Principle they plead for, and press the necessity and benefit of Man's believing and conformity to it: Therefore I ask their Adversaries, Is it any Crime to be *Perfect?* To which if they shall Answer, (as in effect they have said) *This is to be accounted Vile.* To such my Reply is, I hope that the Lord will enable his People to become, and be contented to be counted more vile: For to this *Abraham* was commanded *(page 69)* by God under the Old Testament, as 'tis written, *Gen. 17.1.* The Lord appeared unto *Abraham,* saying, *I am the Almighty God, walk before me, and be thou perfect.* And to this we are commanded by Christ under the New, whose words are thus recorded, *Mat. 5.48. Be ye therefore Perfect, as your Father which is in Heaven is Perfect.* Nor is it only commanded, but also promised; see *Rom. 6.14. For Sin shall not have Dominion over you.* And in 22, 23 Verses, there we find it experienced; for the Apostle speaks of such as were *made free from Sin, and become Servants to God, and had their Fruit unto Holiness, and the End Everlasting Life: For the Wages of Sin is Death, but the Gift of God is Eternal Life, through Jesus Christ our Lord.* And In *Rom. 8.2.* there *Paul* speaks his own Experience, *For the Law of the Spirit of Life in Christ Jesus, hath made me free from the Law of Sin and Death,* saith he. And therefore, he exhorts the

Corinthians, Having these Promises, dearly beloved, let us cleanse our selves from all filthiness of the Flesh and Spirit, perfecting Holiness in the fear of God, 2 Cor. 7.1. And in *1 Cor. 2.6.* 'tis *(page 70)* said, the Apostle spake Wisdom among them that were Perfect; and in *2 Cor. 12.9* the Apostle wishes their Perfection: And thus he concludes his Epistle to them in the 11th Verse of the same Chapter, *Finally Brethren, farewel, be perfect, &c.* And this was it the Apostle *James* desired, (*viz.* that those to whom he wrote might be perfect and entire, lacking nothing) *Jam. 1.4.* For it was the end of the Apostles Ministry, that they might present every Man Perfect in Christ Jesus, labouring fervently in Prayer for them, that they might stand Perfect and Compleat in all the Will of God: And in behalf of the   *Col. 1.28.* Thessalonians, *Paul* prayeth, *That the very God of Peace would Sanctifie them wholly; that their whole Spirit, Soul and Body might be preserved Blameless unto the coming of our Lord Jesus Christ,* (a) *1 Thes. 5.23.* And we find the Apostle *Peter* making the same Sup-

plication, even, *That the God of all Grace (page 71) would make them Perfect,* 1 Pet. 5. 10. For this being the very end for which God appointed Teachers in his Church, as 'tis written, in *Eph. 4.11,12,13. He gave some Apostles, and some Prophets, and some Evangelists, and some Pastors and Teachers, for the Perfecting of the Saints, for the Work of the Ministry, for the edifying of the Body of Christ, till we all come in the Unity of the Faith, and of the Knowledge of the Son of God, unto a Perfect Man, unto the measure of the stature of the fulness of Christ.* Yea, this seems to be the end of Christ's giving himself for his Church, that he might sanctifie and cleanse it, that he might present it to himself a glorious

(a) Upon which Text I heard a Preacher of your own thus Paraphrase; The Words, *saith he,* signifie a *Compleatness* in the subject, that nothing be wanting: For to be negatively Blameless, is to be without Crime, to be without Offence, to be without Fault; but to be positively Blameless, is to be in some measure Innocent; 'tis to be like *Adam* in his pure Creation; 'tis to make Christ our Pattern. *Now whether this doth not tantamount to Perfection, I'll leave the Reader to judge.*)

Church, not having Spot, or Wrinkle, or any such thing, but that it should be Holy and without Blame; see *Eph. 5.26, 27.* Therefore, those that deny Perfection to be attained by the Lord's People, *(page 70 [sic])* do in effect deny Christ the one Offering: For by one Offering he hath perfected for ever them that are sanctified, as saith the Apostle, *Heb. 10.14.* Wherefore, saith *John, Whoso is Born of God doth not commit sin, for his Seed remaineth in him, and he cannot sin, because he is born of God*, 1 John 3.9. These and many more Scriptures which I might have quoted, do abundantly speak forth a Man of God, or a truly Godly Man to be Perfect or Compleat in Christ: Therefore *Perfection* must needs be attainable even in this Life; and to shew that it is not altogether unfeasible to be attained, I shall bring in instances of some which have attained it: Noah *was a Just Man, and Perfect in his Generation*, Gen. 6.9. Job *was a Perfect and Upright Man, one that feared God and eschewed Evil*, Job 1.8. Nathaniel *was an Israelite indeed, in whom was no Guile*, John 1.47. Zacharias *and Elizabeth were both Righteous before God, walking in the Commandments and Ordinances of the Lord Blameless*, Luke 1.5,6. Indeed, this is the one thing needful; *for Circumcision is nothing, and Uncircumcision is nothing, but (page 63 [sic]) keeping the Commandments of God*, I Cor. 7.19. *This is that that hath the Blessing, and gives right to partake thereof; for 'tis written, Blessed are they that do his Commandments, that they may have right to the Tree of Life, and may enter in through the Gates into the City*, Rev. 22.14. And this is the Perfection the Quakers plead for, *viz*. That People may conform unto, and come to be guided by that perfect Principle of God, placed not only in their Consciences, but in the Consciences of all Men; which as they yield Obedience to, they will be inabled to keep the Commandments of the Lord, and so come to witness in themselves the fulfilling of his Determination, which is, To finish Transgression, and to make an End of Sin, and to bring an Everlasting Righteousness, as was seen in *Daniel's* Vision, Chap. 9. Ver. 24.

(page 64 [sic])

CHAP. X.

Concerning Infallibility.

ONE Charge more I have heard brought in against the *Quakers*, and that is *They own Infallibility, and this* (say some) *there is none own but the* Papists and them; therefore we know not how to distinguish them.

I Anfwer: (b)

(b) It is not at present laid upon me to discover all the Errors of *Popery*, therefore I shall say no more, than what is pertinent to my present Matter: But that the Papists

Because the *Papists (page 66 [sic])* say, *Their Church is Infallible* (which ye your selves affirm to be no true Church; so not the Spouse of Christ, but the Mother of Harlots, and all Abominations of the Earth) and because the *Papists* say, *Their Councils are Infallible*, (whom we know do miserably thwart and contradict one another) and because they say, *The Judgment of the Pope that's Infallible*, (though he speak never so much besides the Matter.) And now, because the *Quakers* say, *The Spirit of the Lord, that is Infallible* (which teaches to deny all Ungodliness and Worldly Lusts, and is always at Unity with its blessed self, and is the *Christians* Oracle for Advice in all Concerns) will there admit of no distinction between these? Certainly they want Reason as well as Faith, are far from Infallibility, (notwithstanding they pretend highly thereto) their difference in Doctrines (to which *Bellarmine* himself hath confest) with the Disagreement of their *Popes*, (one pulling down what another had set up) and the Dissention of their *Councils*, particularly about the *Popes* Supremacy, their Priests Marriages, and Worshipping of Images; wherein one Synod hath decreed what another hath disanulled) their own Writings witness against them; which those that have read anything of *Papal* Story, cannot but have a Knowledge of.)

who cannot judge how these may be distinguished: They place *Infallibility* in *Persons*; we in the *Holy Scripture* and in its *Teachings*.

But further, to clear the Matter, and wipe off this Scandal, of the *Quakers* being counted *Concealed Papists* (I think) *George Whitehead* and *William Penn*, their Declaration before the Parliament, at their Sessions, held in the first Month, *(page 66 [sic])* *Anno 1678*. together with the *Test* (containing several Articles, shewing the Doctrinal Differences between the *Quakers* and the *Roman Catholicks)* which was subscribed to by several Hands of such as are well known in this City, and then given in to a Committee of Parliament, requiring the same; and the Case was afterwards moved in the House: So that, as I said before, (I think) sure the Knowledge of this publick Discrimination, may very well serve any that are but willing to be undeceived, both to rectifie their Mistakes concerning the People called *Quakers*, and to give them satisfaction: For I must confess, it went far with me, in my own serious Thoughts about them, although then I was far from them; yet I could not but conclude, there was a Hand of Providence had wrought wonderfully for them, in giving them an Opportunity of clearing both themselves, and their Principle of that unjust Censure which had so long lain upon them.

But to conclude this Point: Though I have heard it said, *The* Quakers *hold Themselves Infallible*; I see now it is not *(page 67 [sic])* so: They hold not themselves Infallible, as they are Men; but only as they are guided by the Infallible Spirit, namely, the Spirit of the Lord, a Measure of which he hath placed in all Men; and this never failed any, who

were led by the same: Yet whatever can be said to evince the Truth of
the *Quakers* Principle, whereby the Innocent may be vindicated; 'tis no
wonder to have their Sayings wrong reported, and their Sence quite
perverted.

And now, my former Acquaintance, to whom I present this small
Treatise, you will not yield your selves Mistaken in the Reports you
have received? I freely acknowledge to you, for my part, I am willing so
to do, and that with shame taken to my self herein, my Lot having been
cast so near this Land of *Goshen*, that it may well be wondered at, why
I did not discern my Mistakes long e're this time: Now though it cannot be so said of you, that the Light has shone so clear about you, yet
know this every one of you, The Light hath shined in you, and that (I
am sure) as it is heeded, will make manifest to you; how falsly the People
called *Quakers* *(page 68 [sic])* have been accused: They have been looked
upon (like the Apostles in days past) as Setters forth of *strange Gods*;
they have been counted as *unknown*, and yet *well known*; they have
been reckoned as *Deceivers*, and yet *True*: for Truth don't use to suffer
under its own Name; but when Men can fasten the Name of *Heresie*
upon its Principle, then they think they have pretence enough to punish its Proselytes: And so it is with these, as it was with the *Christians* of
old; their Adversaries put Bear-skins upon them, and then set Dogs to
bait them. There were such, 'tis known, that were counted the filth of
the World, and as the Off-scouring of all things, who wandred about in
Sheep-skins and Goat-skins, being destitute, afflicted, tormented, of
whom the World was not worthy: And what if I shall say, such there are
now? Yet are they Slighted, Contemned, Derided, Reproached, Reviled,
Defamed, Slandered, Traduced, Malign'd, Vilified, and set at Nought,
as if the worst Term that could be given them, were even good enough:
One while, they are branded for *Illiterate Novices*; another *(page 69 [sic])*
while, counted so profoundly Learned, that they must needs be *Jesuits*;
though that order can boast of Antiquity, whilst these are looked upon
as a Novelty; yet are they found in the same Ancient Faith with Righteous
Abel in the beginning: But 'tis no new thing for Truth to be called an
Upstart, and then prosecuted under the Name of *Novilism*.

Thus, having shewn in several particulars how grosly People have
abused the Principle of the *Quakers*, I should nextly come to speak
concerning their Practices, to see if they find any more favour; but
remembring my Promise was, *not only to rectifie Peoples Mistakes concerning, but to inform them in the Principle of true Religion*, (for the Principle of Truth is but one) I shall therefore, according to the Manifestation

of the Spirit given unto me, endeavour to signifie, *What this Principle is, from whom it comes, and whereto it leads.*

PART II.

Concerning the
Principle of TRUTH.

What it is, from whence it comes,
and whereto it leads.

IT is a Principle of Divine Light and Life of Christ Jesus, placed in the Conscience, which opens the Understanding, enlightens the Eyes of the Mind, discovers Sin to the Soul, reproves for it, and makes it appear exceeding sinful; quickens such as accept and believe in it, though they were dead in Trespasses and Sins, makes them alive to God, and brings them into Conformity to the Image of his Son Christ Jesus, that he may be the First born among many Brethren.

(page 72 [sic]) That this Description accords with Apostolical Doctrine, see *Ephes.* 5.13. *All things that are reproved, are made manifest by the Light; for whatsoever doth make manifest is Light.* Therefore saith Christ, *John* 3.20,21. *Everyone that doth Evil, hateth the Light, neither cometh to the Light, lest his Deeds should be reproved: But he that doth Truth, cometh to the Light, that his deeds may be made manifest that they are wrought in God. Ephes.* 2.4,5,6. *But God, who is Rich in Mercy, for his great Love, wherewith he loved us, when we were dead in Sin, hath quickened us together with Christ, &c. Rom.* 8.29. *For whom he did fore-know, he also did predestinate to be conformed to the Image of his Son, that he might be the First-born among many Brethren.*

Thus in general have I briefly described the *Christian Principle*; but that I may make it further intelligible unto you, I feel it upon me to write more particularly; that so when you shall read it by a familiar Denomination, you may the sooner be prevail'd upon to yield to its operation.

§. II. In the first place, this *Principle*, of which I am now writing, 'tis *(page 73 [sic]) the Grace of God that bringeth Salvation, and hath appeared* to all men, teaching us, that denying Ungodliness and Worldly Lusts, we should live soberly, righteously, and godlily in this present World, as saith the Apostle, Tit. 2.11,12. Even that Word of his Grace which is able to build

Gal. 1.15.
Rom. 3.24.
Ephes. 2.8.
us up, and to give us an Inheritance among all those that are sanctified through Faith, which is in Christ Jesus; see Acts 26.18. By which Grace we are called, justified and saved. That is, if we believe in the same, if we receive it, and continue therein, grounded and settled, and be not moved away from the Hope of our Calling, nor from the Hope of the Gospel, which we have heard, and which was preached to every Creature which is under Heaven, according as its written Col. 1.23. But if we turn this Grace into wantonness, and so receive it in vain; then indeed it will not save us: However, this Grace of God, in itself, is able and sufficient to save all to whom it appears, and all that believe in it, and are led by it, are preserved; because it was by this Grace of God that his Son Christ Jesus should *(page 74 [sic])* taste Death for every Man: For there is no difference between the Jew and Greek; but the same Lord over all, is Rich unto all that call upon him: *For the Lord is Gracious and full of Compassion, slow to Anger, and of great Kindness. The Lord is good to all, and his tender Mercies are over all his Works*, as you may read, Heb. 2.9. Rom. 10.12. Psal. 145.8,9. All which are clear Proofs, that the Grace of God is both Free and Universal; which Grace of God is elsewhere called the Light of Jesus, he being that Gift of Grace, *given by God to enlighten the Children of Men*, as 'tis written of him; John 1.9. *He is that true Light, who lighteth every man that cometh into the World.* And this is he whom the Father promised by the Mouth of his Prophet, saying, *I will give thee for a Covenant of the People, for a light of the Gentiles*, Isa. 42.6. The same is again spoken of, Chap. 4.9.6. *It is a light thing that then shouldst be my Servant to raise up the Tribes of Jacob and to restore the Preserved of Israel; I will also give thee for a Covenant to the Gentiles, that thou may'st be my Salvation (page 75 [sic]) to the Ends of the Earth.* And the Prophet Isaiah, speaking to the Church, chap. 60.20. Saith thus, *The Lord shall be thine everlasting Light.* to which the Prophet David brings in his Experience, *The Lord is my Light and my Salvation*, saith he, Psal. 27.1. This is indeed the mighty Saviour, he upon whom the Father hath laid help, and who is able to save unto the uttermost, all that come unto God by him, whose appearance is Light, whereby he Discovers and Reproves Sin in Men; see therefore that none reject him.

Rev. 3.7.
For this is he, who hath the Key of David, that openeth the Understanding of his People, by which they understand the Scriptures when they read them.

This is he, who hath discovered himself to be God manifest in the Flesh; and also doth manifest himself in our Mortal Flesh in which we dwell.

This is he, who when he was on Earth, yielded both Active and Passive Obedience to his Heavenly Father in Life, Doctrine and Death; which I firmly do believe, was a Sacrifice acceptable unto God for the Sins of Men; *(page 76 [sic])* by believing in whom, and yielding *obedience* to him, *pardon* and *remission* of *sins* comes to be known: and so the Creature finds *acceptance* with the Father through the Son.

This is he, who Justifies by Faith in his own Name.

This is he, which imputes his own Righteousness to the Children of Men (without whose applicatory Act and Gift of Grace, in imputing of his own Righteousness unto us, all creaturely actings are but vain).

This is he, that hath laid down his Life for us, and took it up again; for saith he, *I have Power so to do*, John 10.18. And by the same Power that raised his own Body out of the Grave, doth and will He raise up the Souls and Bodies of Believers to glorifie his great Name.

For this is he, that Acquits his People of all Sin, old as well as new, taking away and cleansing them from the Sins of their first and fallen Natures, as well as pardoning (upon Repentance) those sins which some have at unawares, or through weakness, fallen into, after they have received the Knowledge of *(page 77 [sic])* the Truth: For he who is called *the Light of the World*, Joh. 8.12. Ch. 1.9. the same is called *the Lamb of God*, that taketh away the Sins of the World, vers. 29. And therefore was his Name called Jesus (a Saviour) for it was said he should save his People from their Sins, *Mat.* 1.21.

This is he, who baptizeth his People with the Water of Life and Regeneration, and sealed up his love to their Souls, by giving them his Flesh to eat, which is the true Bread that cometh down from Heaven.

This is he, that gives true freedom of will to his People, whereby they can cheerfully serve him, and keep the Word of his Patience, though in much Affliction; and he hath promised to keep such in the hour of Temptation, *Rev.* 3.10.

This is the Lord our Righteousness, and he of whom our Righteousness is (a) as saith the Prophet, which while we abide in him, we have a sure standing: But if any go out from him who is a God at hand, and whose Salvation is near to be reveal'd in all *(page 78 [sic])* that wait for him; then 'tis no wonder (a) Jer. 23.6. Isa. 54.17. and 56.1. 25.9.
if they fail of the Riches of that Grace which is treasured up in him.

This is he whose Works and Ways are all Perfect, and in him we are made compleat; that is, as we are guided by his Spirit, which he gives to lead the Saints into all Truth, according to his Promise, John 16.13; 14. *Howbeit, when the Spirit of Truth is come, he will lead you into all Truth; for he shall take of mind and shall shew it unto you,* saith Christ; and this his Spirit by which his People are led, is an Infallible Spirit: *Now if any man have not the Spirit of Christ* (which is Infallible) *he is none of his,* saith the Apostle, *Rom.* 8.9. And now if any Man have, and profess to be led by this Spirit of Christ, he is made a Scoff, even by the very Professors of his Age.

Thus I have again toucht upon the former Particulars, wherein I undertook to Vindicate Truth and its Followers, in all which Christ (the Light and Life of Man) is all in all unto his People: John 1.4. for *Christianity* doth not consist in the belief of so many Doctrines, Articles *(page 79* [sic]*)* and Principles (as some suppose) but in conformity unto that one Eternal Principle, to wit, the Light of Christ manifest in the Conscience, and yet leads into a heavenly Order, both in Doctrine, Principle and Conversation, according to the diversity of its Gifts, whereby Man comes not to be at liberty in his own Will, but bound again to God, which is the true signification of the word *Religion:* And this Light of the unerring Spirit (by which the Lord leads his People in the Way Everlasting) it shineth within, (mark) *It shineth in the Darkness, though the Darkness comprehend it not,* as saith the Apostle, *John* 1.5. It shines in the dark Heart of Man, though Man in his dark state cannot discern what it is, yet it is that sure Word of Prophecy whereunto we do well to take heed, as unto a Light that shineth in a dark place, until the Day dawn, and the Day-star arise in our Hearts, according to that, 2 *Pet.* 11.9. which is as much as if the Apostle had said, This is commendable, that you give diligent heed to the least measure of this Light, or Grace of God, which he hath dispenced to you, till he *(page 80* [sic]*)* shall see fit to bestow a greater measure upon you. For 'tis still but one thing that I am describing, although rendred by divers Names: In as much as the sure Word of Prophecy, and the Day-Star here spoken of, differ only in Degrees, not in Nature and Kind; both which Expressions denote to us, that one Gift of Light and Grace through Christ Jesus freely bestowed on all Men; and according to the Improvement that they make of their Measures, so an increase thereof is administred to them: It was by this Light that *Job* walked through Darkness, *Job* 27.3. And it is by this Light that we come to see our Darkness; but 'tis not that we should abide in Darkness, but walk through it, and come out of it by following the Light of Christ, that in his Light we may see more Light, and so come to receive the Light of Life, as 'tis written, John 8.12. *Then spake Jesus unto them, saying, I am the Light of the World, he that follows me shall not walk in Darkness, but shall have the Light of Life.* And praised be the Lord, there is a Remnant who have experienced it, and can say with the Apostle, this thing is true *(page 81 [sic])* in them, (viz.) *The Darkness is past, and the true Light now shineth,* I John 2.8.Which Light is a Light of the Spirit of the Lord dwelling in his People; and therefore whatever the World may think concerning them, 'tis no presumption in them to own they are made *Possessors* of the same; for saith the Apostle to the *Corinthians, Know ye not, that ye are the Temples of God, and that the Spirit of God dwelleth in you? For ye are the Temples of the Living God; as God hath said, I will dwell in them, and walk in them,* I Cor. 3.16. 2 Cor. 6.16. Now since God himself is said in Scripture to dwell and walk in his People, why should it be thought Arrogant for them to say, Christ in them is the Hope of their Glory, according to that of the Apostle, Col. 1.27. *To whom God would make known what is the Riches of the Glory of this Mystery among the* Gentiles, *Christ in you the hope of Glory?*

And let me tell you, this *(page 82 [sic])* was the Judgment of Dr. *Langly,*which I my- self heard from him, in a Sermon preach'd upon that text, (viz.) *That the great Gospel Treasure is the Lord Jesus Christ, and the Glory of that Treasure is Christ in us.* This was his Observation, and this I think is Confession clear enough to the Truth of our Assertion, (*viz.*) That in being guided by the

These Instances I bring to shew, how those that speak against the *Quakers* Principle, (which is Christ manifest within) are forced many times (by the power of the same Principle in themselves) in plain words to confess to the same.

Light (which is the Spirit of Christ) within us, hereby a sure Hope of Eternal Glory is given to us. However, we do not conclude Christ in our selves only, but we say a Measure of his Light (in order to shew the Way of Life) every Man is, or hath been enlightned with; nor yet do we include him in the fleshly Temples of Men and Womens Hearts, so as to exclude him from being any where else, but *as we know his Presence fills Heaven and Earth, so we believe,* that notwithstanding his Appearance in our Hearts, he is continually at the Right *Hand of* God, at the Right Hand of the Majesty on High, ever Living to make Intercession for us, and by his Spirit we feel the Signification thereof within us.

(page 83 [sic]) For this Grace of God, which is the Light of Jesus, 'tis a Measure of the Divine Spirit, and a Manifestation of it is given to every

Man to profit withal; see 1 *Cor.* 12.7. Yea, this Universal Principle, which
I am describing, it is a Measure of the quickning Spirit, even of that
Spirit which raised up Jesus from the Dead; by the Indwelling of which
in us, we come to be renewed in the Spirit of our Minds, and to have
our Mortal Bodies quickned, so as to capacitate us to serve the Lord with
our Spirits, and with our Bodies, which are his.

Now if any shall think I have raised this Principle too high, let them
read *Rom.* 8.11. and they will find the Apostle speaking expressly, *If
the Spirit of him that raised up Jesus from the Dead dwell in you, he that
raised up Christ from the Dead, shall also quicken your Mortal Bodies, by his
Spirit that dwelleth in you.* Therefore (as I said before) 'tis no Arrogancy
for the People of God to own, that they have the Spirit of God dwelling in them, for 'tis not the Light of Nature, nor the Dictates of a Natural Conscience; but a Spiritual Divine *(page 84[sic])* Principle, by which
Men and Women are raised from the Death of Sin, to serve God in
Newness of Life, and Obedience of Conversation.

Now *Reader,* let me tell thee, Nothing Natural will or can reach so
far, Nature cannot change Nature; it must be a higher Power, that can
cause to put off concerning the former Conversation, the Old Man,
which is Corrupt, according to Deceitful Lusts, by renewing the Spirit
of the Mind, so as to cause us to put on the New Man, Christ Jesus,
which after God, is created in Righteousness and true Holiness; and so
old Things are made to pass away; behold, all things are become New:
Lo here is a New Creature, as there is a putting off the Old Man with
his Deeds: there is a passing away of the first Heavens and the first
Earth; and then behold, New Heavens and a New Earth, wherein
dwelleth Righteousness: as there is a coming to this Law of the Spirit of
Life in Christ Jesus (which Law is inward, written in the Heart, and
engraven on the Inward Parts) there is a setting Free from the Law of
Col. 2.14.   Sin and Death: And *(page 85 [sic])* so we come to know a
Rom. 8.12.   *Blotting out of the Law of Commandments contained in Ordi-
              nances, which was against us, and contrary to us, our Lord*
having taken them and nailed them to his Cross. And thus, *He that believeth*
(in the Cross of Christ, which is the Power of God unto Salvation) *hath
a Witness in himself, the Spirit it self beareth them Witness that they are the
Children of God,* according to that in 1 *John* 5.10. *Rom.* 8.16. And as they
continue in the Faith, they come to be sealed with the Holy Spirit of
Promise, and to set to their Seals that God is true: For faithful is he that
hath promised, who also will do it; he hath promised to redeem us from
all Iniquity, wherefore let us hope in his Word, *and not grieve his holy*

Spirit, whereby we are sealed unto the Day of our compleat Redemption, according to the Apostle's Advice, *Eph.* 4.30. O! let us take heed that we do not vex and quench the Spirit of Christ within us, that so we be not of those (complained of by *Nehemiah*) *To whom the Lord gave his good Spirit, but they rebelled against it.* (And what then?) *so he (page 86 [sic]) became their enemy, and fought against them.* These were such of whom *Job* speaks, Chap. 24.13. saying, *They are of those that rebel against the Light,* (the Light and Spirit here spoken of, being one in Being, and not divided, but distinguished only in degrees of Discoveries;) for this Spirit is a Spirit of Wisdom and Revelation in the Knowledge of Jesus Christ, *which openeth and enlightneth the Eye of the Understanding, and giveth to know what is the Hope of the Calling of Christ Jesus, and what is the Riches of the Glory of his Inheritance in the Saints,* according to the Apostle's Prayer to God for the *Ephesians,* Chap. 1.17,18. And this was it that Christ promised, when he was about to leave his Disciples (as to his *Personal presence* amongst them) at which their Hearts began to be sorrowful, he therefore tells them, to comfort them, *he that dwelleth with you shall be in you,* John 14, 17. Thereby he meant himself, (who then was present with, but passing from them in the Flesh) *would come again unto them, and abide for ever with them, in the Spirit: For the Lord is that Spirit,* saith the Apostle, 2 Cor. 3.17. Wherefore he bids *(page 87 [sic])* them *Examine themselves whether they be in the Faith; Prove your own selves,* saith he, *know you not your own selves, how that Christ is in you, except you be Reprobates,* 2 Cor. 13.5. And hereby know we that we are not in a Reprobate state, because we witness the Spirit of Christ dwelling in us. For this Principle of which I write, 'tis the Unction which we have received from the Holy One, whereby we know all things: That is, this doth instruct us in all things that are necessary to be known by us. For 'tis that Spiritual Anointing that the Apostle *John* speaks of, which those who have received it (and in whom it abides) needs not that any Man teach them, but as the same Anointing teacheth them all things, *and is Truth, and is no Lie, even as it hath taught them, they should abide in him,* 1 John 2.27. that is, in Christ Jesus, from whom this anointing doth come: Now whoso is taught by the Anointing, the same is taught by God, as its written in the Prophets, *And they shall be all taught of God. Every man therefore that hath heard, and hath learned of the Father, cometh unto me,* saith Christ, John 6.45. For this was the *(page 88 [sic])* Promise of the Father, even the New Covenant which he made with the House of Israel, *After those days,* saith the Lord, *I will put my Laws into their Minds, and write them in their Hearts; and I will be to them a God, and they shall be to me a People: And they shall not teach every Man his Neighbour, and every Man his Brother, saying, Know the Lord, for they shall all know me from the least to the greatest,* Jer. 31.33, 34. This being the Tenure of the New Covenant, *That all the Children of the Lord shall be taught of the Lord, and in Righteousness shall they be established,* Isa. 54.13, 14. Which implies, that God will teach them so effectually by his Free Spirit, that they shall not stand in need of any other Prophet. But here I must obviate an Objection, before I can proceed.

Possibly some may ask me, *Why then do those People that thou art now gone amongst, keep up their publick Meetings to Preach, and to Teach People the Way of Salvation? What need is there of their Teaching, if every one hath a Teacher in them, able to Instruct them in the Way to the Kingdom?*

(page 89 [sic]) To which I *Answer: First,* Though I did say as much, as that every one hath a Divine Teacher in them, yet I did not say, that every one knows this Teacher in them: For this hath been the Misery of many Ages of the World, People have gone out after the many *Lo here's,* and *Lo there's,* to find Christ without them, in the mean time neglecting his Appearance *within* them, even as was *foretold by Christ* himself, when he was on Earth in the days of his Flesh; *In the Last Days,* saith he, *they shall say, Lo here is Christ, and Lo he is there, but go ye not out after them, nor follow them; behold, I have told you before,* Mat. 24.25. Luke 17.23. And now, since we upon whom the Ends of the World are come, have seen it so come to pass, that People are gone from this Gift of God in themselves, to the many outward Observations of Days, Times, and Superstitious Customs, thinking to find Christ in them, whilst they shut their Eyes against his Light, which shineth in their Consciences, to guide their Feet in the Path of Peace: Is it not high time for his faithful Watchmen, who see the danger of such a state, to Cry *(page 90 [sic])* aloud unto the People, that they may take Warning before it be too late; and therefore do they lift up their Voice like a Trumpet, to sound a Retreat to the Inhabitants of the Earth, who are without the Spiritual City of Refuge, that they may return in time, and lay hold of the Horns of the Heavenly Altar, and get into the Habitation or Tower of Safety, before the Enemy of their Souls take the strong Hold of their Hearts, and fortifie himself against them, and keep them without the Gates, till the Avenger of Blood (who once would have had Mercy on them) pursue and overtake them, and so they be destroyed: Therefore, right-glad are the Hearts of many that ever they heard this joyful Sound, [*Retire to the Inward Grace*] thereby signifying to them where Help is to be had, who were seeking Salvation from the Hills, and from the Mountains, yet laboured

but in vain, but in Returning, and in Rest, they have found themselves saved, according to the *Word* of the Lord by the Prophet *Isaiah* 30.15.

(page 91 [sic]) Secondly, Although I did say, That all the Children of the Lord are taught of the Lord, yet I did not say, that all are his Children; for 'tis they, and they only, *who are led by the Spirit of God that are the Sons of God:* For tho' the Lord hath given his Spirit, yea, his Son, to be a Leader and a Commander to the People, yet many   Rom. 8.14. there are who do not follow his Guidance, saying in their Hearts, (what the *Jews* spake with their Mouths) *We will not have this Man to Reign over us.* Now is there not need that some should seek to convince such of the Evil of their Ways, and the Error of their Doings, (who instead of walking in the Straight and Narrow Way of Righteousness, which leads to Everlasting Life, are going on in the Broad Way of Sin and Wickedness, which leads down to the Chambers of Death) that so they may be perswaded to leave off the Weapons of their Rebellion, wherewith they Fight against God, and wound their own Souls; and submit themselves unto his Ambassador of Peace, the Spirit of his Son in their Consciences, that *(page 92 [sic])* true Balm of *Gilead,* with which they may be healed?

Thirdly, That I may be rightly understood, let me acquaint my Reader; neither do I assert, that those who are set out as Travellers in *Sion's* Road, are at once so perfectly instructed in all the Paths thereof, that they need not to inquire of those that are gone before, which is the way thither, whose Experiences may be to them of use, for escaping the Snares which the subtil Fowler layeth to catch Souls in, both on the Right Hand and on the Left, that so they may walk right forward with their Faces *Sion*-ward, until they shall come to sit down in Heavenly-places in Christ Jesus our Lord.

Lastly, Nor is it altogether useless for those that are established in the Truth, to hear the things thereof declared, notwithstanding they knew the same before; yet may it be to the stirring up of their pure Minds by way of remembrance, of the dealings of the Lord with themselves in days that are past; and for the comforting and refreshing of their Spirits, to feel how the Work of the Lord prospers in *(page 93 [sic])* others of his People, and for the clearing and making glad their Hearts, to hear how Truth prevails and gets Ground in the Earth. This therefore is the end of all Declarations amongst us, (*viz.*) That the Ignorant may be instructed, that Gainsayers may be convinced, that the Weak may be confirmed, and that the Strong may be consolated; therefore do our Ministers labour in the Word and Doctrine, to Convert Sinners to Christ

Jesus, (the Gift of God) and to build up Saints in their most holy Faith, and to Edifie one another in Love.

Thus much in Answer to the Objection; so I return to the Point in Hand, which is further to *demonstrate* (as the Lord shall enable me) what this *Principle* is, that is Preacht up amongst us.

'Tis that *Divine Principle of Life* which brings the Glad-tydings of Salvation near unto all, by which they may be put into a Capacity of receiving the *Grace of God* in the *Gift* thereof, which he hath purposed in the appearance of the Son of his Love, to bestow upon as *(page 94 [sic])* many as shall believe: This being the Everlasting Gospel that *Paul* gloried in, *I am not ashamed of the Gospel,* (saith he) *for it is the Power of God unto Salvation, to every one that believeth,* Rom. 1.16. Yea, it is that Word of Reconciliation, which God hath committed to such as himself hath called, to make them Ambassadors for his Son Christ Jesus; by the Ministry of which, they turn People from Darkness to Light, and from the Power of Satan unto God, that they may receive Forgiveness of Sins, and Inheritance among them that are Sanctified, through Faith that is in Christ Jesus; see *Acts* 26.18. Thus these profit their Hearers; and so do not only Pray, but also prevail with Sinners to turn unto the Lord, that he may be a Father to them, and they his Sons and Daughters.

And this Word that reconcileth, is not afar off; 'tis not in Heaven, that any should say, Who shall go up for us, and bring it down to us, that we may hear it and do it? (a) Neither is *(page 95 [sic])* it beyond the Sea, that any should say, Who shall go over the Sea for us, and fetch it to us thence; but the Word is very nigh unto thee, in thy Mouth, and in thy Heart, that thou may'st hear it, and do it; as was testified by *Moses,* a Man of God, *Deut.* 30.12,13. and also by *Paul,* an Apostle of Jesus Christ, *Rom.* 10. 6,7,8: This now is the Word of Faith, which is again preacht by those whom the World in Scorn call *Quakers:* And though such Preaching be accounted foolish by the Learned Rabbies of our Age; yet let them know, 'tis by the Foolishness of Preaching that God is pleased to save them that believe, as 'tis written, 1 *Cor.* 1.21. So notwithstanding these use not enticing words which Man's Wisdom teacheth, yet do they preach in the Evidence and Demonstration of the Spirit, and in a way of Power, whereby they are known to be of God (as were the Apostles; see 1 *Cor.* 2.1,4.) And the Tendency of their Ministry is to direct People to the Teaching of Christ, the one Prophet, promised to *Israel, Deut.* 18.18. which Promise the Apostle repeateth.

(a) So then the *Indians* and *Americans* shall not perish for want of the Bible, which we have here in *England.*

Acts 3.22 saying, *(page 96 [sic]) And it shall come to pass, that every Soul that will not hear this Prophet, shall be destroyed from amongst the People,* Vers. 23. Thus do they commend themselves to every Man's Conscience in the sight of God, by turning them to the Light of Jesus (the Power of God manifest within) which, as 'tis yielded to and obeyed maketh free from Sin, which still is that one thing that I am writing concerning, (*viz.*) A Principle of Divine Light and Life in Christ Jesus, according to the Apostles Record, *John* 1.4. *In him was Life, and the Life was the Light of Men:* And this Light, I say, (however it may be called) 'tis the shining of the Son of Righteousness in Men's Consciences: *'Tis* not Conscience, which some have described to be a reflex Act of the Mind (whereby Men view their past Actions) the which accuses them for what they have done ill, and approveth of what they have done well; though this be more than some there are will allow in this matter, yet is this too short to express its noble Nature: For this Principle doth as well shew Men the Sin of their future Evil Purposes and Intentions, as set *(page 97 [sic])* before them the Iniquity of their former Actions: Therefore I say, 'tis not Conscience, for that is but a created Faculty; but that of God placed in the Conscience has its Being from all Eternity: *For he that sheweth unto Man his Thoughts, is the same that formed the Mountains, and created the Winds, whose Name is the Lord of Hosts,* as saith the Prophet *Amos* Chap. 4.13. And this is he who is without beginning of Days, or end of Life, the *Alpha* and the *Omega,* The First and the Last, the beginning of the Creation of God, the Image of the Invisible God, the First-born of every Creature, the faithful Witness and the First-begotten of the Dead, and the Prince of the Kings of the Earth. This is he who is the Resurrection and the Life, in all that do believe in his Light, as 'tis Recorded concerning him, *Heb.* 7.3. *Rev.* 1.11. *Col.* 1.15. *Rev.* 1.5. *John* 11.25. *Therefore whilst ye have the Light, believe in the Light,* (saith Christ) *that ye may become Children of the Light,* John 12.16.

And this Light is elsewhere called the Seed, even that Incorruptible Seed, *(page 98 [sic])* by which we are Begotten to God, and Born again by his Eternal Word, which liveth and abideth for ever; see 1 *Pet.* 2.3. This is the Promised Seed; yea, that Seed of the Woman, spoken of, *Gen. 3.15.* where the Lord said to the Serpent, *I will put Enmity between thee and the Woman, and between thy Seed and her Seed; it shall bruise thy Head, and thou shalt bruise his Heel.* This is the Seed of the Kingdom of Heaven; for Heaven's Kingdom is within (as Christ said, *Luke* 17.20.) Wherefore this Seed is sown in the Hearts of the Children of Men; as was set forth by the Parable of the Sower, *Mat.* 13. and the beginning; he spake many things to them in Parables; *Behold, a Sower went forth to sow; and when he sowed, some Seed fell by the Way-side, &c. some fell among Stony-places, &c. and some fell among Thorns,* Ver. 18,19. *Hear ye therefore the Parable of the Sower,* saith Christ; *when any one heareth the Word of the Kingdom, and understandeth it not, then cometh the Wicked One, and catcheth away that which was sown in his Heart; That is he that received Seed by the Way-side, &c.* And in the 31, 32 Verses, *(page 99* [sic] *)* Christ saith, *The Kingdom of Heaven is like to a Grain of Mustard-seed, which a Man took and sowed in his Field; which indeed is the least of all Seeds; but when 'tis grown, 'tis the greatest among Herbs, &c.* 'Tis truly so indeed; the Seed (or Grace) of God, is small in its first Appearance, (even as the Morning-light) but as it is given heed to, and obeyed, it will encrease in Brightness, till it shine in the Soul, like the Sun in the Firmament at its Noon-day height: But if People will despise the Day of small things, and will not believe in this low Appearance of the Light of Jesus in their Hearts; which though it discover to them their Sins, and reproves for them; yet because its Reproofs are soft and mild, and its Voice small and still, they out-clamour the sound thereof in their Consciences, whereby they reject the Son of God (in Spirit) as the *Jews* did (in Flesh) because he came to them in so mean a manner, they would not have him to be their Saviour: Will it not be just for Christ to say to these, as he did to them, *John* 8.24. *If ye believe not that I am he, ye shall die in your Sins; and then whither I go ye cannot (page 100*[sic]*)* come. For the Lord hath said, *His Spirit shall not always strive with man,* Gen. 6.3. He is a gracious and long-suffering God; but though he be Forbearing, yet he will not always bear; though his Spirit doth strive with some for a long Season, yet if they continue to resist the same, the time will come, when it will cease striving with them; and then Wo will be unto them; but right blessed are they that are prevailed upon by the strivings of the good Spirit of the Lord, (in the Day of their Visitation) to know and mind the things that concern their Everlasting Peace, before they are hid from their Eyes: But if People will shut their Eyes against the Light, how just is it for the Lord to withdraw its shinings from them, and to cause Darkness to overtake them? Wherefore hear ye, and give ear, be not Proud, for the Lord hath spoken; give Glory to the Lord, before he cause Darkness, and before your Feet stumble upon the dark Mountains; and while you look for Light, he turn it into the shadow of Death, and make it gross Darkness, according to the Advice of the Prophet *Jeremiah,* Ch. 13.15,16.

(page 101 [sic] *)* For though a measure of this Divine Light, is, or hath

been in every Man, in order to save them, yet it will not always abide
with them, (I mean, as to its saving Efficacy) it will continue no longer
than during the Day of their Visitation: Therefore saith Christ, *Yet a
little while is the Light with you; walk while ye have the Light, lest Darkness
come upon you,* John 12.35. *Again,* he limiteth a certain day, saying, in
David, *To day, after so long a time, as it is said; To day if ye will hear his
Voice, harden not your Hearts, Heb. 4.7.* True indeed, there is a day
wherein People may know the things that concern their Souls Everlasting Peace: But if they sin out this day, afterwards those things will
be hid from their Eyes; as Christ said, when he came near the City
Jerusalem, he beheld it, and wept over it, saying *if thou hadst known, at
least in this thy day, the things which belong to thy Peace; but now they are
hid from thine Eyes,* Luke 19.41,42. Be it known to you, (my Friends and
Acquaintance, to whom I write) Man cannot be his own Saviour, if he
will not be saved in the Day of the Lord's Power, he must perish for
ever. *(page 102 [sic])* And this is the day of the Lord's making bare his
saving Arm, and revealing his Power, even that time wherein he lets in
Light into the Soul; which not only discovers to Man his Sin, that
leads down to the Chambers of Death, but also shews him the way of
Holiness, which leads to Everlasting Life: But if Man pass this time
over without any regard to the Loving-kindness of the Lord extended
to them in this matter, 'tis just with him to turn their Light into Darkness in them; and then, as Christ said to some of old, *If the Light that is
in you be Darkness, how great is that Darkness?* Mat. 6.23. (Mistake me
not.) 'Tis not to be understood as if the Son of Righteousness (which is
the Fountain of Light) could in it self possibly become Darkness, but as
to those that have fast-closed their eyes, (or lost the true sight) lest
they should see by its Illumination in their Inward Man; when once
their Day is over, they may be as dark as if there were no Sun in their
Horizon; and so they put Darkness for Light: Hence it is that we see so
many that have been in some measure enlightned by this inward Divine *(page 103 [sic])* Principle, to see much of the Vanity of their former
Practices, and so have for a time forsaken many of the same; but afterwards having gone from this Principle, by which they were in some
measure saved from Pollution and Sin, they have again been intangled
and insnared by the Pleasures, Profits, Honours of this present World;
and so the latter End hath been worse with them than the Beginning;
and so these having left their Habitation (like Satan, (who abode not
in the Truth) envy and accuse the faithful Servants of the Lord, which
keep their dwelling in him; and like the Spies of old, *bring up an Evil*

Report upon the good Land, frighting others with the Giant-like Difficulties that lye in the way to be surmounted; thereby insinuating, *as if Israel's God were not able sufficiently to strengthen them against these Spiritual Anakims great and tall, that must be encountered with, before the Inheritance comes to be divided.* These are such whom the Apostle *Jude,* in the 12th and 13th Verses of his Epistle, calls *Clouds without Water, carried about of Winds; Trees, whose Fruit withereth, twice dead, plucked up by the (page 104 [sic]) Roots; raging Waves of the Sea, foaming out their own shame; wandring Stars, to whom* (at least they have cause to fear) *the Blackness of Darkness is reserved for ever;* unless they can speedily find a place for Repentance, before the Decree bring forth, before the day pass as the Chaff, before the Fierce Anger of the Lord *Zeph. 2.2.* come upon them, before the Day of the Lord's Anger come upon them: And with this I'll pass them, being mov'd to write (not much to those who have forsaken, but) to those who have not been acquainted with the Truth.

To whom I further say, Although there is a time wherein the Lord waits to be gracious, in which time he often expresses his Willingness to save Men from their Sins, and to gather them to himself; as Christ said to *Jerusalem,* O *Jerusalem, Jerusalem! thou that killest the Prophets, and stonest them that were sent unto thee, how often would I have gathered thy Children together, even as a Hen gathereth her Chickens under her Wings? but ye would not,* Mat. 23.37. Again, the Lord complains, *All the (page 105 [sic]) Day long have I stretched forth my Hands to a Disobedient and Gain-saying People,* Rom. 10.21. And thus the Lord expresses his Kindness towards all Men, in stretching forth his Arm to save them, even as a Man stretches forth his Arms to swim, by sending his Son unto them to knock at the Door of their Hearts, to see if they will open to him, that he and his Father may come in, and take up their abode with them; but if Men will not accept of Salvation while the Lord extends his Arm to save them: If they will not take hold of his strength while they may make Peace with him: If they refuse to answer his gracious Call, and to entertain his Son whom he hath sent, but keep him out till his Head be wet with the Dew, and his Locks with Drops of the Night: If People will *Acts 7.5.* make their Necks as an Iron Sinew, and will not yield them *Luke 7.30.* to the Yoke of Christ, being *Stiff-necked and Uncircumcised in Heart and Ears, always resisting the Holy Ghost, and doing despight unto the Spirit of Grace; setting at nought all the Counsel of God;* rejecting it (within) *(page 106 [sic])* against themselves, and will have none of his Reproof; and continue thus to slight him, till their Time and Season

be over, giving the Lord cause to complain of them, that he hath
stretched forth his Hand, but no Man regarded it: Will it not be just for
him then to Laugh at their Calamity, and Mock when Fear cometh
upon them? And most certain it is, that those who despise the Reproofs
of Wisdom, and hate the Knowledge of the Holy, Distress and Anguish
will come upon them; but whoso harkeneth thereunto, shall dwell in a
safe Habitation. For Wisdom is a Defence (Christ) the Wisdom of God
is a strong Rock, and a sure Foundation; he is that Foundation on which
God hath laid in *Sion*, even the Foundation Stone, that Tried Stone,
the Corner Stone, Elect Precious; who though he be to many a Stone
of Stumbling and Rock of Offence; yet as many as believe in him shall
never be ashamed.

Read here now what this Principle is, in which the Lord hath given
a Remnant to believe.

(page 107 [sic]) 'Tis the Grace of God: 'Tis the Light of Jesus: 'Tis a Manifestation of the Spirit: 'Tis the Glad tydings of Salvation: 'Tis the Word of
Reconciliation: 'Tis the Law written in the Heart: 'Tis the Word of Faith:
'Tis the Seed of the Kingdom: 'Tis that Stone which hath been rejected by
many a foolish Builder, but now it is become the Head of *Sion's* Corner.

These are all significant Expressions of that excellent Principle, which
I have undertaken to Treat on. But if any shall say, *They are Expressions
of so different a Nature, that they know not how to reconcile them, and make
them one together.*

To such I *Answer*; They might as well confess, they cannot understand how the Lamb of God can be the Lion of the Tribe of *Judah*, nor
how the Shepherd of *Israel* can be the Bishop of his Peoples Souls;
there seeming as much difference in these latter, as in any of the former;
yet do they all speak of but one thing, although it be exprest by divers
Names: For it will admit of *(page 108 [sic])* a manifold Description; though
(as I said before) 'tis still but one thing, if rightly understood in its true
Notion. And thus I chose to express it, because thus I have found it,
(*viz.*) A Principle of Divine Light and Life in Christ Jesus, placed in
the Conscience, which discovers both Sin and Duty to us; and not only
so, but it Reproves the one, and Enables to Perform the other: And this
I know, that a measure of the same is placed in the Consciences of all
Mankind, by which they might see the right Way, were but their Minds
turned thereunto. Therefore let none slight or undervalue this Light of
Jesus (manifest in their Consciences) by calling it (as some have done)
*A Natural, Created, Insufficient Light, which will lead men down to utter
Darkness.* Though sometimes again these very Persons will confess, *That*

the Light of Nature, (as they call it) *ought to be followed, as far as it will lead; for* say they, *Though the obeying its Dictates will never bring Men to Heaven; yet the disobeying them will certainly sink them down to Hell.* Hereby rendring the Lord Cruel to his Creatures, as if he required them to *(page 109 [sic])* follow a Guide that would certainly lead them amiss, or leave them short of the Place of Rest; and then would punish them for being misled, or for sitting down when they had no Guide to shew them the Way to walk in; and that from a purpose in himself, to leave the greatest part of Mankind without any other Guide to direct them in Matter of Salvation; but that *that is so Insufficient, that it must be a Miracle if it shew them the Way to Heaven,* according to their common Answer, when asked, how those must be saved who have not the Scriptures amongst them? (which these account the only Rule to Guide Men) *Why, we leave them to the Mercy of God,* say they, *the Lord may in an extraordinary manner bring some to Heaven, if he have any Elect amongst them; but whether any of them shall be saved or not, 'tis hard for us to determine.*

Thus they darken Counsel, by uttering words without Knowledge: They say, *The Grace of God is Free;* and yet they make it a Monopoly; so it shall not be Free to all; nor must all be sharers in it; neither will they allow *(page 110 [sic])* the Lord himself to dispence it; nor yet to Inspire his Servants to go forth and preach it: But arrogate to themselves a kind of Sacerdotal Right, to be Dispensers of the Grace of God, and Ministers of the Gospel of Jesus Christ, because of some outward Qualifications achieved by them (as External Parts, or Humane Learning) although they never were called of God to the Work of the Ministry, nor never had the Word of Reconciliation committed to them; yet would they have People come to enquire of them, the Way to the Kingdom, though they are so narrow-spirited, as to shut out the greatest number of Mankind, by absolute Predestination; not sticking to affirm, that God nor Christ never purposed Love nor Salvation to a great part of Mankind, and that the Coming and Sufferings of Christ never was intended, nor can be useful to their Justification, but must and will be effectual for their Condemnation. So being void of Universal Love themselves, they fondly imagine the Lord to be like themselves: Hence concluding, there is no Salvation to be had without the explicite *(page 111 [sic])* Knowledge of Christ's coming in the Flesh, and of the Scriptures; both which we know whole Kingdoms and Empires in the World are unavoidably ignorant of; and yet few or none of these will Jeopardize their Lives to preach amongst such; notwithstanding this was the Apostle *Pauls* Practice, to preach Christ where he had not before been named; for said he, *if I build upon another Man's Foundation, I make my Glorying void.*

But blessed be the Lord, he hath caused many Witnesses to rise up amongst us, who have given Testimony to the Truth as it is in Jesus, and have taught others (both in our own Country, and in Nations abroad) to take heed to that sure Word of Prophecy, nigh in the Heart, and in the Mouth, which if the true Grace of God, that is sufficient for us, not only (as some say) to leave Men without Excuse, and so to aggravate their Condemnation; but as 'tis received and obeyed, it will lead out of Sin, into Holiness, and in the end crown with Salvation.

And thus I am brought to the next thing promised, which was, to shew *(page 112 [sic])* whence this Principle of Grace proceedeth: I have (according to my Measure) shewn, *What it is;* now I come to shew, *From whence it comes;* to which I say;

§. III. It comes from God, (through Christ) as saith the Apostle; *God, that commanded the Light to shine out of Darkness, hath shined in our Hearts, to give the Light of the Knowledge of the Glory of God in the Face of Jesus Christ,* 2 Cor. 4.6. 'Tis Gods Gift unto us, and therefore well may we return Thanks unto him for his unspeakable Gifts: God is the Author of it, *who is Light, and in him is no Darkness at all;* for *he covereth himself with Light, as with a Garment;* and *dwelleth in that Light which is inaccessible, which no mortal Eye can approach unto; he is the Father of Lights;* and therefore hath he given a Measure of his own Divine Light to all Mankind, to reveal himself unto them; that so they may know substantially *What he is,* and not worship him as the *Unknown God:* And this knowledge of himself, the Father is pleased to dispence to Men, in and *(page 113 [sic])* through the Son of his Love, Christ Jesus, our Lord *who is come a light into the World* (saith Christ) *that whosoever believeth, in me should not abide in Darkness.* And therefore I believe, and am well assured, this is the one Faith, whereinto many thousands by the Lord have been gathered, *viz.* That the God of all Grace hath sent his Son into the World, a free Gift unto the World; and hath given a measure of his Light and Spirit, to manifest and reveal him unto all men: Thus hath his universal Love and free Grace appeared. For though God made Man *pure* and *innocent,* yet Satan and disobedient Man hath marred that Creation: *In the Beginning God created Man in his own Image, in the Image of God created he him,* as we read Gen.3.17. But Man soon defaced and stained this glorious Stamp, and by yielding to the Tempter, went out from his first Nature, and so his Beauty was turned into Defor-

1 John 1.40.
Psal. 104.1.
1 Tim. 6.26.
James. 1.17.

mity (I mean) that beauty of his inward Man wherein the Image of
God stood, in which he had Communion and Fellowship with his
Maker; through Disobedience this was lost and *(page 114 [sic])* so man
came to be without God in the World, being alienated from that divine
Life, Light Love, Grace, Goodness, Wisdom, Power, Holiness, Virtue,
Purity, Innocency, wherewith the Lord Invested him at the first in
perfect Beauty: but man going out from that first Divine Nature and
Seed, in which he stood before Transgression, here was his Fall and
Degeneration, and so he came by that unexpressible Loss of the Favour
of God and Freedom of Will, that now the Lord being angry with
him, he had no Power to do any thing to appease him; the Garment of
Innocency being lost, their Fig-leaf-Aprons could not hide their shame-
ful Nakedness from the Lord; which he seeing, and taking notice of,
compassionately made them Coats of Skin for their clothing; and them
he drove then out of the Garden of *Eden:* So here man was put out of
the Paradise of God for eating of the forbidden Fruit of the Tree of
Knowledge, and Cherubim placed at the East End of the Garden with a
Flaming Sword, which turned every way to keep the Way of the Tree of
Life, as may be read in the third *(page 115 [sic])* Chapter of *Genesis* at large.
Thus man being drove from the Presence of the Lord, Death came over
his Soul; though he lived outwardly, yet did he dye as to that
Inward Principle of Divine Life and Virtue which once he enjoyed,
and so the Threatning was fulfilled which the Lord had said, *In the Day
that thou eatest thereof, thou shalt surely Dye:* Here Man and Woman
having Transgressed the Royal Law of God, by breaking of his holy
Commandment, in eating of the Tree whereof he commanded them,
saying, *Ye shall not eat thereof,* by this they came to be separate from
him: So it was Sin that made the Separation, and it is Sin which makes
the Separation: For Man and Woman in their Primitive state (wherein
they were created) were good, as the rest of the Creatures of God;
for 'tis written, *God saw every thing which he had made, and behold it
was very good:* And God blessed Man and Woman, and they were in
Favour with him, till they became subject to Vanity, by reason of that
false Hope which the Serpent suggested to them; they hoped to have
been as Gods, to *(page 116 [sic])* know Good and Evil; but by going out
of God's Counsel, they became corrupted by the Evil one; and being
joyned to the Serpentine Seed, they were alienated from God: so that,
had not the Lord, out of his unmeasurable Lovingkindness and Compassion, opened a Way to restore them, they must have perished in this
Deplorable Condition.

And this Way of Restoration was by Christ, the *Light*, the *Seed*, the *Saviour*; for he, of whom God said unto the Serpent, *I will put Enmity between thee and the Woman, and between thy Seed and her Seed; it shall bruise thy Head, and thou shalt bruise his Heel*; He it was who was to be the Saviour of the World: So that now, considering the Sons and Daughters of *Adam*, as they are found in the Fall and Degeneration, having all sinned and come short of the Glory of God; herein (I say) hath his universal Love and free Grace appeared, to wit, in giving of his Son to be a Saviour unto them, as saith the Apostle *John; In this was manifest the Love of God towards us, (page 117 [sic]) because that God sent his only begotten Son into the World, that we might live through him,* 1 Epist. 4.9. And that he was sent to the whole World, see what *John* the Evangelist saith, Chap. 3.16. *For God so loved the World, that he gave his only begotten Son* (Mark) *that whosoever believeth in him, should not perish, but have Everlasting Life:* To which the Apostle testifies, 1 Joh. 2.2. saying, *He is the Propitiation for our Sins, and not for ours only, but for the Sins of the whole World.*

This was the free gift of the Father, that the Son of his Bosom should take Flesh upon him, come into the World, and lay down his Life for poor Sinners; for he came from God, and went to God again: So that though he laid down his Life of himself, having Power, and being willing so to suffer, according as 'tis written, *John* 10.18. Yet himself also said, *That his Body was prepared of his Father,* Heb. 10.5. In which Body he did the will of him that sent him: *Lo, I come to do thy will, O God,* (saith he) *for a Body hast thou prepared me.* Who now, that rightly considers this Dispensation of favour, but must needs cry *(page 118 [sic])* out, Oh! the Height, and Depth, and Breadth, and Length of the Love of God, and of Jesus Christ our Saviour, who took not on him the Nature of Angels, but took on him the Seed of *Abraham*, and was made in everything like unto us (only without Sin) that he might restore Fallen Men! Which thing I know will readily be granted; but 'tis the extent hereof that some would have limited; affirming, That Christ dyed for a certain definite number, and not for the whole Lump of Mankind, one as well as another: Nay, they speak as if none had any benefit by, no, nor so much as the Revelation of Christ (This Gift of God) whom to know is Eternal Life, but those who have the outward Letter of the Scripture: Yet do I believe, and so do Thousands more, whom the Lord hath called (*viz.*) That the Father of Lights, and God of   *Jame.* 1.17. the Spirits of all Flesh, hath given a measure of his own   *Numb.* 16.28. Divine Light and Spirit unto all the Children of men; to manifest and reveal *(page 119 [sic])* the Appearance of his Son in them (a) who is that same Saviour which shed his Blood for us, that he might

(a) Note, That I do not say Person-ally (as some suggest concerning us) as if we believe that very Body of Christ is in us, that was hanged upon the Cross; which were foolish as well as False to assert, but Spiritually; as he is the Word of God, the Wisdom of God, the Power of God; so he dwells in every Christians Heart: And so he dwells in us, by which Power he compleatly sanctifieth us.

wash us and cleanse us from our Sins; and was offered upon the Cross, not only as a Propitiatory Sacrifice, to make Reconciliation for the Trans-gressors; but that by his once offering up of himself, he might bring in Ev-erlasting Righteousness, and Perfect for ever them that are Sanctified and a measure (I say) of this his Power (which is Light) God hath placed in every persons Heart, in order to their

Sanctification, as they shall be subject to this his appearance in them.

True indeed, all are not Sanctified and made Perfect by him, although this was the end of his coming (that he might finish Transgression, and make an end of Sin) and this was the will of *(page 120 [sic])* the Father in sending him, to wit, our thorow Sanctification) but this is not because all have not a Knowledge and Manifestation of his Light (or Spiritual Appearance of him in themselves) but because all do not believe in, and obey this his Appearance: Now that People may attain to what Knowledge may be had of God by the inward Manifestation of the Light of his Son (which is a measure of his Spirit) in their Hearts; this is clearly proved by the Apostle, *Rom.* 1.19. *That which may be known of God,* (saith he) *is manifest in men; for God hath shewed it unto them.*

For the Lord of the whole Earth, who is the Preserver of Men, he is impartial in his Love to all Mankind; not only to them in *Christendom* (so called) who have the Scriptures amongst them, but his Love is ex-tended unto all People, in one Land as well as in another, for his Spirit is not inseparable from the Scriptures (as some suppose). Yet would I not be thought to undervalue the Scriptures any whit; for I have very Venerable Thoughts of them, and a Reverential Esteem for *(page 121 [sic])* them, as being Holy Writings: But I dare not confine all means for Man's Salvation to them, because the Lord hath not confined himself to them, but hath left himself a Witness in every Conscience; which Witness is a spiritual Manifestation of his Son, the Saviour of the World: And this the Scriptures plentifully declare of, which sometimes they call the *Word,* the *Law,* the *Grace,* the *Spirit of God;* at other times they call it, the *Light of Jesus,* the *New Covenant,* a *Light to lighten the* Gentiles, a *Rod,* a *Staff,* a *Shepherds Crook,* the *Word nigh in the Heart and in the Mouth,* the *Sure Word of Prophecy,* the *Manifestation of the Spirit;* a *Shield,* a *Buckler,* a *Strong Tower,* the *Armour of Righteousness:* All which have one in Nature, though diversly exprest, according to its distinct Operations in the Soul, as the Creature standeth in need; sometimes to lighten its darkness, at other times to lead it in the Way of Holiness: One while it Instructs; another while it Corrects: Sometimes it Counsels; other times it Consolates; and as its Counsel is heeded, and the Soul guided by it, it preserves and *(page 122* [sic]*)* defends in all Exigences and Straights: but I pass over its special use, intending to shew that in another place; only here may be seen the great Condescention and Matchless Love of him, who gives unto all Life, and Breath, and Being; in that he hath sent the Holy Ghost down from Heaven, with the Revelation of his *Son Jesus Christ,* in the Hearts of the Children of Men, that whosoever adhereth to the *Spirit* of his *Son* within them, may thereby know him not only as a Saviour and Redeemer, but also to be their Saviour and Redeemer; and that not only from the Punishment, but from the Power and Dominion of Sin, by setting of them free from the Bondage of Corruption, and bringing them into the glorious Liberty of his own Children: But as for such who will not believe in this Principle of God, but instead of owning it as his Power unto Salvation, say it is A *Satanical Suggestion;* and instead of owning it to be of the Divine Nature of God or Christ, they call it the *Dim Light of created Nature,* putting Bitter for Sweet, and Sweet for Bitter, counting Darkness Light, and *(page 123* [sic]*)* Light Darkness: Such may continue in their Bondage and Vassalage under the Prince and Power of Darkness, in the blindness of their Minds, hardness of their Hearts, and deadness of their Spirits, notwithstanding Freedom and Liberty, Life and Immortality is brought to Light through the Gospel; which it hath pleased the Father should be preached to every Creature, by his Son, *Sion's* Deliverer, who is his own Messenger; see *Rom.* 11.26. Mal. 3.2.

For this Principle of Light (of which I now write) 'tis something of the Nature and Being of God himself, who as he is a Spirit, so he is Light (as you may read concerning him, *John* 4.24. 1 *John* 1.5.) and therefore 'tis by his Light, with which we are enlightned: It proceedeth from him, he being the Ocean wherein the fulness thereof is contained, 'tis from him (through his Son Christ Jesus) that we come to be enlightned by the same: So 'tis in his Light that we see Light, even as the Natural Sun causeth its Beams to extend to the Ends of the Earth; so this Eternal Son of Righteousness (who is the Ocean and Fountain of Divine *(page 124* [sic] *)* Spiritual Light) causeth more or less of the streams thereof to descend into all Immortal *Souls* upon it.

Thus having shew'd the Nature and Quality, Original and Fountain of this blessed Principle, I come further to shew its Use and Extent, that so I may not only tell my *Reader, What it is, and Whence it comes,* but according to my Promise, write something *of What it doth, and Whereto it leads.*

§ IV. In the first place; it daily Reproves for Sin, even in all Men, and excites to Holiness, during the Time of their Visitation; though 'tis possible for Men to sin themselves into such a state (by drinking in Iniquity, as the Ox drinketh Water, when through custom and sinning, their Consciences become seared as with an hot Iron) that this Principle of God may cease striving with them, and so these may not know when they do Evil; yet there is a Time in which this Principle of God doth stand as a faithful Witness against all Unrighteousness and Ungodliness in the Hearts of Men and Women, and leads, draws, moves and inclines their Minds *(page 125* [sic] *)* to Righteousness, seeking to leaven them (as they yield thereunto) into the Nature of it self; whereby an inward, thorow and real Redemption may be wrought in the Hearts of all Men, of what Kindred, Nation or People soever; notwithstanding any outward Benefit or Priviledge they may Providentially be deprived of, yet is the Lord so gracious as to dispence such a measure of his Grace, Power and Spirit unto all the Children of Men, to Convince them of sin, to Reprove them for it, and to lead them out of it, that as they give up to the Operation thereof in themselves, it will thorowly sanctifie and make them clean, and so prepare them, and make them meet for his Heavenly Kingdom; yea, though they never had the Scriptures amongst them, nor never heard Christ outwardly named to them, (the Name of Christ being often put for the Power of Christ within) as in *Mark* 16.17. *In my Name shall they cast out Devils,* saith Christ of his Disciples. So in *Acts* 4.7. the High-priests and Rulers asked *Peter* and *John, By what Power, or by what Name, they have made the Impotent (page 126* [sic] *) Man whole?* For the Name of Christ which heals and saves, is his Power that maketh free from Sin. Now whoso knoweth this Name of Jesus to be given unto them, and effectually to have wrought in them, they can truly witness him to be the Arm of God's Salvation: However, we do say, That the Scriptures, in which we have a Declaration of what Christ hath done and suffered for us, those do much Facilitate Salvation through Faith in Christ Jesus; and therefore they ought thankfully to be received by us, and born witness to, whenever the Lord shall require us, so as that we may not be ashamed to own, nor afraid to confess him to be our Saviour; who they make mention of, to have been put to Death in the Flesh above Sixteen Hundred and Sixty years past, by the Hands of Sinners. For we do not believe that this Light, Grace and Power of God, which is sufficient both to sanctifie and save, and able to give an Inheritance among them that are sanctified, through Faith which is in Christ Jesus, (where Christ is not outwardly named) I say, We do not believe that this is given to any *(page 127* [sic] *)* without Christ; but we do believe it to be to the Purchase and Benefit of his Death, who tasted Death for every Man. And so we do freely confess all that is derived to us, to be in and by Christ Jesus, as a Mediator, unto whom we ascribe all, acknowledging him to be our Head, in whom all Fulness dwells. So that this Light, with which all Men are in some measure enlightned of God, 'tis no other, but a measure of that Divine Fulness that dwelt in the Son of his Love, when he was here on Earth, and now dwelleth in him, since he is ascended up to Heaven, where he was before, whence he descends the streams thereof into the Hearts of all the Children of Men, in order to bring them out of the Fall in the First *Adam*, and to redeem them up unto himself, the Second *Adam*; that as they have born the Image of the Earthly, so they may bear the Image of the Heavenly, and be restor'd unto that Grace and Favour of God again, which by Transgression they are fallen from.

But, *First*, Let me tell thee, whoever thou art that reads me, This effectual *(page 128* [sic] *)* Operation of the Spirit, (or Principle of God Within) is not, nor cannot be known without a being centred down into the same: For this I speak from good Experience, the Spirit's first work is, to Convince of Sin, (before it effect a Restoration) and this it doth even in all, (though all do not regard it) it doth first shew them what is Evil, and then it Reproves them when they do evil; which Reproofs, if they be despised, cause the fierce Anger of the Lord to be kindled; and such as despise Wisdom's Reproofs, which are the Way of Life, while they are so doing, they are treasuring up to themselves *Wrath* against the Day of *Wrath*, and Revelation of the Righteous Judgment of God: And as ever they would come to know Remission of their Sins, and enjoy Peace with the Lord, who is hereby justly incensed against them, they must submit to bear his Indignation against them, that so they may be Redeemed through Judgment, and brought to unfeigned Repentance; and then, and not till then, shall they know a blotting out of their Transgressions, according as 'tis written, Acts 3.19. *(page 129* [sic] *)* But, I say, before Remission of Sins comes to be known, there must be a centring down into the Manifestation of the Spirit of God within, which will bring down every exalted Imagination, and every high Thing, and lay it Low, even to the Ground; that so every Thought may be brought into Subjection to Jesus Christ: And here comes the Terrors of the Lord to be known, which cause Fear and Trembling; now doth the Soul exceedingly Fear and Quake under the Sence of the Just Wrath of the Almighty, who is of purer Eyes than to behold Iniquity, and whose Jealousie burns like Fire, and will so do, till it have consumed the Stubble that it meets with in the Heart of the Sinner: For he that long offered himself as a Guide, is now become a Judge in the Conscience of this Creature; and his Just Judgment against all Unrighteousness must be accomplished. True indeed, the Operation of the Word of his Power, (by which he judgeth) is diversly felt and experienced: In some 'tis a Hammer, to break the Rocks in sunder: In others 'tis as a Fire to melt down the Dross, and separate *(page 130 [sic])* it from the Silver: In all, 'tis as a Sword to divide Sin and their Souls asunder; yea, it divideth between the Soul and that sinful Spirit, which hath got into it and defiled it.

Thus the Lord deals with his Creatures, as the matter doth require; he considers their Nature and Temper, and lays no more upon them than he gives them strength to bear: For he knoweth our frame, he remembreth that we are but Dust; therefore he doth not retain his Anger for ever, lest our Spirits should fail before him, and the Souls which he hath made us: However, all that have sinned, must know a time of Sorrow; yea, even such who have not so rebelliously despised his Coun- sel, and slighted his Reproofs, and cast his Law behind their Backs, (as some there are which have) yet in as much as they have at any time not hearkned unto his Holy Spirit within them, his Judgments will over- take them, and in Righteousness will he plead with them; and then, I know, former things will come into their Minds.

This I write, as one having witnessed the Spirit to be given for a Remembrancer, *(page 131 [sic])* which was faithfully promised by the Lord Jesus, *John* 14.26. even that Spirit of Truth, which he told his Disciples, *it should bring all things to their remembrance;* and so indeed it doth call back things that are past, and set them in order before us, judging and condemning of us for what we have done amiss: And now, a Remnant having heard that (in our Hearts) that hath told us all things that ever we did, we know this to be the Voice of Christ; yea, the spiritual Appearance of the Christ of God. For this was he who saw us under the Fig-tree (when we had nothing but Leaves to cover us) although we saw him not, yet did he send and call us to himself, that he might cover us with his own Spirit, which when we came to be covered with, we then saw who it was that cast the Skirt of his Love over us, and said unto us, when we were polluted in our Blood, *Live*: And then was the time of his Love, even when he stood at the Door of our Hearts and knockt, that he might be entertained by us; yea, and sometimes in the silence of the Night hath he broken in upon us; I know it *(page 132 [sic])* in my own particular, when no Creature hath been near, this Invisible Oracle hath secretly communed with me, reproving of me, wherein I had done amiss; and shewing me what was right in his Sight: And at other times in Company, thus would the Lord cause his Voice to sound in my Heart [THE CUSTOMS OF THE PEOPLE ARE VAIN] by which I was brought off from many of those Vanities which before I had spent time in; and that by the Witness of God in my own Conscience, which testified against the same; although then I did not understand what it was that did so restrain me from sin; but now I know it was the Lord that girded me, though I knew him not. For I well remember, when I have been using the common Language of our Country (especially if after the now most usual strain) this Testimony from God would arise in my Heart against it, *viz.* [*I will return unto my (page 133 [sic]) People a pure Language.*] Whereby I was reproved in my self for using Flattering Speech (though such as was and is accounted of by many to be but Civil Language, or Expressions of Common Civility to Persons, according to their Quality) in which I had such a Care to keep within the Bounds of Verity, that I dare assert, I did steer as near the Compass of Truth-

Yet Truth doth allow of a Propriety in *Speech*, which may be put into a decent Stile; althongh [sic] it admits not of giving Flattering Titles to Men: Read *Elihu*, his Acknowledgment, *Job* 32.21,22.

speaking, as the Nature of such Speech would couch. But since it hath pleased the Lord by the in-shining of his heavenly Light in my Conscience, to let me see clearly into the Falshood and Folly of this corrupted Courtesie: I do not only Conscienciously, but Voluntarily decline the using such Flattering Speech; notwithstanding, I know 'tis to expose my self to be censur'd by some as a Person Unaccomplished, Unmannerly, and Ill-bred.

Praised be his Powerful Name, who hath made me willingly Renounce both giving and receiving that Honour that cometh from Man, that so I might partake of that Honour which proceedeth from himself alone:

For this is the Honour which all the Faithful in Heart *(page 134 [sic])* chiefly esteem, it being the Unbelieving who seek the Praise of, and Honour from Men: Which made Christ say to some of old, *How can ye believe, who receive Honour one of another, and seek not the Honour that cometh from God only? John* 5.44. Yet notwithstanding this, Christ did then require his Disciples to *render Honour to whom Honour,* and *Fear to whom Fear;* which Requirings of his, all his true Followers (in their Respective Places) are at this time careful to answer, how uncivil soever accounted by the World; yet have they learnt *Gospel-manners,* which is, *to give the Right Hand of Fellowship to whom it doth belong;* in *Honour Preserving one another, each Esteeming other better than themselves.*

And now, I say, it was by this Principle of Divine Light (which God hath placed in my Heart) by which he pleaded with me in days past, even when I knew him not; that is, I knew not that it was the immediate Act of his own Power and Spirit, though I felt such a Force in it, that as I did in the least yield thereunto (I must confess) I was overcome by it, but still it was as I was subject and obedient to his *(page 143 [sic])* Power; for I cannot say, *The Lord wrought in an irresistible manner;* although I know, and do declare, it was he who did subject me, and made me willing in the Day of his Power: And thus being prepared by him, then did he send his Spirit to convince me both of Righteousness and of Judgment, as well as Sin; yea, to convince me of that Righteousness and Religious Way of Worship, which I formerly walked in; whereby he let me see it was but a humane Righteousness, and an invented traditional Worship set up by the Will, and performed in the Spirit of Man, and derived to me by outward Instruction and Education; so that I had a Form, which the Power did not attend, for want of having regard to the Movings and Guidance of God's own Spirit, in which alone he delights to be worshiped: And therefore is he striving by this his Spirit in the Hearts of the Children of Men, to bring them out of all Forms of human establishing, that they may worship him in Spirit and in Truth, and serve him in the Gospel of his Son, that so they may be accepted through him; yet I do acknowledge, that while *(page 136 [sic])* I saw no farther, and did sincerely serve the Lord in the Way which I walked in before (hoping it might be *right,* because *reform'd in many things* to what some other Ways of Worship are) the Lord was graciously pleased often to administer some Comfort and Refreshment to my Soul, through the Ministration I then sat under: And in like manner I do believe his Dealings are with all the Upright-hearted, who are seeking after him in the divers Ways of Worship; which if they

continue seeking him in the Integrity of their Spirits, I doubt not but
he will seek them out (for his Seed's sake) and in due time bring them
to the Mountain of his Holiness, where his dwelling is: For this was
Christ's Promise, John 10.16. *Other Sheep have I, which are not of this Fold,
them also* (saith he) *will I bring, and there shall be one Sheepfold, and one
Shepherd over them:* And when Christ comes to fold them upon his holy
Mountain (which Mountain is within) then will they walk in the Foot-
steps of the Flocks of his Companions, and know a lying down where
he makes his Flocks to rest at noon: but *(page 137 [sic])* first they must
come to know a passing through Judgment, and their works must be
burnt (and they suffer loss) because the Lord of Hosts hath said, Zion
shall be redeemed with Judgment, and her Converts with Righteousness,)
Isa. 1.27. And Christ said, *I lead in the Way of Righteousness, in the midst of
the Paths of Judgment,* Prov. 8.20. And the Spirit of Christ was promised
to convince the World of Sin, of Righteousness, and of Judgment, John
16.8. by which the Spirit and Prince of this World should be judged,
and he cast out of his Throne in the Hearts of the Children of Men,
whereby every one, who comes to experience God's Righteous Judgments (in themselves) to be brought forth unto Victory, such may also
witness an Overcoming of the Prince and Power of Darkness, thorow
the spiritual Strength of his Son of Righteousness: Howbeit, while two
Spirits are striving together, the Soul cannot but be sensible of an hour
of Sorrow; I surely know, that day is a day of *Mourning,* of *Weeping* and
of *Lamentation, when* Zion *sits solitary with her Tears upon her Cheeks, clad in
(page 146 [sic]) Sack-cloth, covered with Ashes* (in a spiritual sense) *fearing and
quaking exceedingly before the Lord, and trembling in her self, because of his
fierce Wrath, and just Indignation, that burns as a fiery Oven against Sin:* Oh!
Then 'tis a time of heaviness and of great sadness with the Soul; *sleep
departing from the Eyes, and slumber from the Eye-lids, because of Grief in the Night-season;* it being truly the Time of   Jer. 30.7.
Jacob's trouble, even the time when the seed of *Jacob* is
travailing to bring forth; and therefore doth that Dragon, the Devil (as
in the general, so in the particular) seek to destroy this Birth; he is not
willing this holy Off-spring should be born, and therefore doth he raise
Wars without, and Fears within, stirring up the Wicked to revile and
smite with the Tongue; and causing cutting Calumnies and sharp Censures to come from more sober hands, hereby intending to encrease the
Commotions which are within, by threatening the Soul with this, That
now it must expect to be reproached with the Reproaches of Men. Thus
the Evil One in the Time of sore *(page 139 [sic])* Conflict, seeks to aggra-

vate the Soul's grief; and what he cannot do by Storm, he will attempt by Terror, secretly striving to make the Soul impatient under its Exercise, thereby to drive it into Dispair. But though it be a Day of Tryal (in which every ones Work must be tryed as by Fire) and of sore Exercise with the Creature, yet is there a secret Hope lieth hid under all this, which is as an Anchor to the Soul, sure and stedfast, founded upon that Rock which endures for ever; and this bears it up above those Floods of Persecution which the Dragon spues out of his Mouth to drown that heavenly Birth that the Power of God is bringing forth within; which when it is brought forth, and comes to have the Government in the Soul, it must, shall and will reign over Death, Darkness, Sin and Corruption, and all the Powers of Hell and the Devil.

I would have none think strange of what I have writ concerning this thing, though I know 'tis a Mystery to the Natural Understanding of the wisest of the Children of Men; and therefore since *Paul* was called a *Babler*, for *(page 140 [sic])* preaching such strange Doctrine to the *Stoick Philosophers*, Acts 17.18. I can expect no better from some, but to be counted a *Non-sensical Scribler*, for writing of the same; but this I am content to bear, knowing in my self I had no Previous Intentions to amuse my Reader; but having undertaken to describe (in measure) the extent of this Powerful Principle of God, placed in the Conscience of his Creatures, following the Foot-steps thereof for my Guide in this Matter: Before I can attain to the End of my Journey, I am necessarily brought hither, and as I stand here, I see by the Light of this spiritual Pillar of Fire, that though the Sea, with the Waves thereof, roar, yet is there a Way for the Ransomed of the Lord to pass over; and this Way is *Christ*, the *Light*, the *Lamb*, the *Grace*, the *Gift of God;* given by the Father to bring out of the Fall (which all Mankind are in by Nature) that whosoever believeth in him, layeth hold on him, and continueth to be led by him, should be brought into Fellowship with himself, and abide therein for ever; and this same is he, who leads in the midst of the Paths of *(page 141 [sic])* Judgment, and through the many Exercises that I have been writing of, before he brings to the Banks of Salvation, and puts Songs of Deliverance into our Mouthes, whereby we can sing of the Mercies of the Lord. And thus having brought out of spiritual *Egypt's* Land, and caused to drink deep of the River of Judgment, he then brings to *Shiloh's* Brook, and giveth to drink of the Waters of Refreshment: So 'tis the same Hand that wounded, which healeth; and that Arm which broke us, doth now bind us up; the same Power which killeth, reviveth; and he who once caused

Grief, now giveth Songs in the Night, *and appointeth*
to Zion's Mourners Beauty for Ashes, the Oyl of Joy for   Isa. 66.1.
Mourning, and a Garment of Praises for the Spirit of
Heaviness; & who will in due time bring all his true spiritual *Israel* out
of the Waste Howling Wilderness, into a Land of Everlasting Rest.

Thus it appears, that the Light of Jesus in the Conscience is no Natural
Insufficient Thing (as some have sought to render it) being something
of God's *(page 142 [sic])* placed in every Man, to witness against all Sin,
convincing and reproving for that which is Evil; contrary wise, prompting,
exciting and inclining to that which is good: So that as many as yield
to the Motives of it, it is sufficient, not only to condemn and destroy,
but also to justifie and save; being a measure of the living *Omnipotent*
Power of that *One Law-giver*, who is able to save, as well as to destroy;
see James 4.12. *which Power is Christ*, as saith the Apostle, 1 *Cor.* 2.23,24.
We preach Christ crucified, unto the Jews a Stumbling-Block, and unto the Greeks
Foolishness; but unto them that are called, *both* Jews *and* Greeks, *Christ the*
Power of God, and the Wisdom of God; Who as He was once Manifest in
the Flesh, so now is he manifest in Spirit, to be that Covenant of *Light*,
which the Father promised by the Mouth of his holy Prophet, *Isa.* 42.6.
And this Light, Power and Arm is (in measure) extended and reached
forth, at one time or other, unto all People, for the gathering unto him,
in whom the Election stands; that so as many as obey his Call, in yielding themselves to be gathered by this gathering Arm, *(page 143 [sic])* may
make their Election, and consequently their Salvation, sure in him: for
this is he who would have gathered *Jerusalem*, and saved
her from that Ruine and Destruction which afterwards came   *Luke* 19.44.
upon her, because she knew not the time of her Visitation:
'Tis the very same Jesus, and no other, whom we believe in for our
Saviour, who by his spiritual Appearance in the Hearts of the Children
of men, gives Light, gives Life, gives Power and Victory over sin (to as
many as follow the Leadings and Guidance of this Immaculate Lamb)
for 'tis given to the Lamb and his Followers to overcome; and whose overcometh
shall sit down with the Lamb on his Throne, and live and reign with him for
evermore, Rev. 3.21.12.11. *Even the same which was with his Church in*
the Wilderness, being that Spiritual Rock that followed them,
of which they drank by the way, and were refreshed in him,   Acts   7.38.
who is the Rock of Ages, the Alpha *and* Omega, *the Begin-*   1 Cor.10,4.
ning and the End. The First and the Last, the Ancient of   Rev. 22,12.
Dayes; whose Dominion (page 144 [sic]) is an Everlasting Do-   Rom. 7.13,14.
minion, which shall not pass away; and his Kingdom, that   Mich. 5.2.

*which shall not be destroyed, whose goings forth have been from of Old
from Everlasting. For he is the blessed and only Potentate,*
1 Tim. 6.15,16.   *King of Kings and Lord of Lords, who only hath Immortality and Eternal Life;* to whom be Glory and Honour,
Dominion and Power, henceforth and for ever.

Here now ye have a Description, and that in Scripture Dialect, concerning the Principle of our Faith; something I have writ as to the Nature
of it, which, tho' at first it causeth grief, and brings in sorrow upon the
Soul, yet doth this sorrow work Repentance, ever to be repented of; after
which cometh reviving: so that it was truly said, *Though Weeping may endure for a Night, yet Joy cometh in the Morning; for they that*
Psal. 30.5.   *sew in Tears shall reap in Joy; he that goeth forthWeeping,
bearing precious Seed, shall doubtless come again Rejoycing,*
bringing his Sheaves with him. And such shall truly say, *In (page 145 [sic]) the
Lord have we Righteousness and strength, for in the Lord shall*
Psal. 126.5,6.   *all the Seed of Israel be justified, and shall Glory* (in him)
not in Wisdom, Wealth nor Strength, but in this, *that
they know him to be the Lord, who exerciseth Loving-kindness, Judgment and
Righteousness in the Earth,* as saith the Prophets, *Isa.* 45.24,25. *Jer.* 9.23,24.
And this is he whom we acknowledge to be our Judge and
Isa. 33.22.   *Law-giver; yea, he is our King and he will save us;* for to this
end he hath appeared by his Light in our Hearts, and
for this end doth he appear in the Hearts of all Men, that as many as
bow down to the measure of his Appearance in them, may thereby see
and be enabled to forsake their Ways and Doings, which have not been
good, whereby they may be saved from sin; and by the same saving
Power and Spirit in their Hearts, come to be led into the Way of all
Truth, which Way of Truth is Christ, our Mediator and Intercessor with
the Father, through whom Man comes to be accepted of God, as he
cometh into him, in whom alone the Father is well-pleased: For 'tis no
other Jesus, concerning *(page 146 [sic])* whom I write, but the same that
was born of the Virgin, even the Lord's Christ, who hath made himself
known unto his Servants by such Peculiar Names, as suited the particular Circumstances of their *Souls:* and according to their several Experiences of him, so they reported concerning him, *Isaiah* describes him to
be as the *Shadow of a great Rock in a weary Land, a Refuge from heat, a
Cover from Rain and from Storms,* ch. 4. v. 6 and ch. 32.2. Again, he
speaks of his being to his people, *as a place of broad Rivers and Streams,*
chap. 33.21. *David* calls him, *The Shepherd of* Israel, *which leadeth* Joseph *like a Flock,* Psal. 80.1. He also calls him, *The Watchman of* Israel,

who neither slumbereth nor sleeps, Psal. 121.4. *Paul* speaks of his being our *High-Priest*; yea, *a Priest for ever, after the order of* Melchizedeck, Heb. 5.6. And likewise calls him *the Minister of the Sanctuary, and of the true Tabernacle which God hath pitched*, Chap. 8.2.

John the Evangelist calls him *the true Light that lighteth every man that cometh into the World*, John 1.9. The other *John* (or *John* the Divine) saith, *This is (page 147 [sic]) he which was, and is, and is to come*, Rev. 1.8. And now since he is come to a Remnant, and they have believed in his Light as manifest in them, they are not ashamed to confess That in the mind, which gives a discovery of Sin, to be the Power of God, the Appearance of Jesus, and that Light of the Lamb, which the Nations of them that are saved must and shall walk for ever in (according to *Rev.* 21.23,24.) Neither is this any new Doctrine, Opinion or Principle, other than that which *Abel, Seth, Enoch, Noah, Abraham, Isaac* and *Jacob*, with all the holy Patriarchs of Old, were led and guided by, in things declaring both to Faith, Life and Worship: For what else could be a Rule unto them, in matters of Salvation, but this Divine Principle; when as they had no written Laws nor Ordinances amongst them? Which Principle is Christ, the Light and Leader of People, in all Ages of the World, who is one in all, never was divided, though variously described; being the same, who by his Light sheweth unto the Wicked, and condemns them for, the Vanity of their Thoughts; who also by the same Spirit comforts *(page 148 [sic])* and consolates his Peoples Hearts, that so as many as whose minds are turned to this Light of Jesus, and stayed in it, though it be but small in its first appearance, yet shall they see a growth and increase of it.

Thus Reader, have I (according to the Gift communicated to me, from the dispensation of the Most-high) described what the Principle of Truth is, which is perfect in it self, and tends to the perfecting of those that are gathered into it.

And now my former Familiars, Neighbours, Acquaintance and Kindred in the Flesh, and all others to whom this may come, hereby I invite you all to turn in hither, even into the secret of your own Soul, to that which there reproves you for your Sins, witnessing for God against all Unrighteousness of men, both in Thought, Word and Action, striving in their Hearts to turn them from the Evil of their Wayes, and from the Vanity of their Conversations, to walk in the newness of Life, that so they may be redeemed and restored out of their fallen state of Degeneration, into the Image of God again, which hath been lost through Transgression.

(page 149 [sic]) O turn in, turn in, I say, before it be too late, lest you at last cry with them spoken of in *Jeremiah* 8.20. *The Harvest is past, the Summer is ended, and we are not saved:* Work while it is Day, while the Candle of the Lord shineth in your Tabernacle, be you workers together with God; for the Night cometh wherein no man can work; and who can tell how soon the Sun of Righteousness may go down upon you, and the Light thereof obscure it self from you: Therefore hear Instruction and be wise, while the good Spirit of the Lord is nigh to teach you;

Isa. 55.6. seek ye the Lord while he may be found, call ye upon him while he is near; and refuse not to hearken to his heavenly Oracle in your Consciences (whereby under this his spiritual Dispensation, he is pleased to speak unto the Children of men) lest he say by you, as he said by some of Old who regarded not his Counsel, *They shall call upon me, but I will not answer; they shall seek me early, but they shall not find me*, Prov. 1.25,28. For that in the Conscience which checks for Sin, and excites to Holiness, is the *(page 150 [sic])* Voice of the Son of God, by whom in those last days the Father speaketh unto us: Oh! be ye perswaded to hearken diligently unto him: *Hear, and your Souls shall live; and I will make an everlasting Covenant with you,* (saith the Lord) *even the sure Mercies of* David, *Isa.* 55.3. And then you will come to know that Faith which Jesus is the Author of, which stands in the Power of God; even in that Power which enables to resist Temptations, and overcome Sin, and to get Victory over the World, and the Spirit of it: So will you witness a dying unto Sin, and a living unto Righteousness, to the praise of his Grace, who is calling of you out of Darkness into Light, that you may be holy in all manner of Conversation.

So now since God's saving Arm is made bare for the gathering many People to himself before your Eyes; Beware therefore lest that come upon you, which is spoken of in the Prophets, *Behold you Despisers and Wonder and Perish; for I work a Work in your dayes, which you shall in no wise believe, (page 151 [sic]) though a man declare it unto you.* Read Acts 13.40,41.

But Friends, my Hearts desire and Prayer to God for you is, that you might be saved: And therefore have I (in the tender Bowels of his Love, which he hath shed abroad in my Heart by Jesus Christ) sent this Invitation unto you, that ye all may make ready, and come to the Supper of the great God, who hath spread his Table, and prepared a Banquet for you; whereof whosoever will, may eat abundantly, as long as the time of Visitation is extended unto you: For this I write in the openings of Life, and from the motion of the good Spirit of my God, do I declare unto ye (*viz.*). That none of ye were absolutely excluded from Eternity; well knowing that a measure of his Grace hath been freely tendred to every one of you: because his Love extendeth Universally, and he is crying, *Ho, everyone that thirsteth, come ye to the Waters of Life: And he that hath no Money, come ye, buy and eat; yea, come, buy Wine and Milk, without Money and without Price,* Isa. 55.1. Here is free Grace indeed, free Love indeed: O do you but yield your selves *(page 152 [sic])* the Subjects of his Love, and he will set your Souls at liberty, that Sin shall not have Dominion over you; only obey his Voice, and he will soon subdue your Enemies for you, and remove that which letteth out of your way; and that you may know when the time of Visitation is upon you, I'll leave this mark with you, even then when you feel the Son of God knocking at the Door of your Hearts, that he may come in and Sup with you; then I say is the time, when the Year of Jubilee is approaching to you, when those that are in Bondage may be set at liberty: which if you refuse to accept of it, and will not be set free when the year of God's Release is proclaimed unto you, how can you expect any other, but that your Spiritual Task-master will obtain leave to bore your Ears to the Posts of his Doors, and make you his Servants forever? Therefore bow down to God's Power in you, that ye may come in and set up his Judgment-seat in every Heart: *For Judgment,* saith he, *am I come into this World,* John 9.39. That so after you have felt his *Righteous Judgments,* for every Unrighteous thing, you may *(page 153 [sic])* find him to be near, which Justifieth your Souls: and that you may experience Christ's coming in your selves, with Power and great glory, to work redemption in you, as well as that he hath purchased Redemption for you. Wait for him (I exhort you) in the way of his Judgments; *For the Lord is a God of Judgment, and blessed are they that wait for him,* as saith the Prophet, *Isa.* chap. 30.18. So shall you feel your Souls redeemed out of the Earth, and out of the Earthly Nature, after which you will witness the Peace of God to be extended towards you, like a River: *But if you rebel against him, you shall dwell in a dry Land, and shall not see when good comes.* Howbeit when Calamity overtakes you, then shall you know that you had a Time, you had a Season, you had a Day of Visitation, in which you might have obtained Mercy; would you have turned unto God, he would have turned unto you, and put his fear into your Harts: and blotted out your Transgressions for his own Namesake; and become a Father to you, and you should have become the Sons and Daughters of the Almighty. And now once *(page 154 [sic])* more I invite you all to turn in to the Principle of God, which daily visits you in your inward parts, in order to bring you out of a state of Sin and Misery, and to make you partakers of his Righteousness and Felicity: Come, taste and see that the Lord is gracious, who long waiteth upon you, that he may be gracious unto you, because he delighteth in Mercy.

O Come, come away, haste out of *Babylon,* while the Deliverer is near you, so will he turn back your Captivity like Rivers in the South, and conduct you to *Canaan,* the Land of Everlasting Rest, where Praises shall spring up in your Souls, to the Glory of his Name, even to all Eternity. And with this I'le leave you, tho' much more might be said; yet when all is said that can be, 'tis the feeling sense of the inward Operation of this Divine Principle, that alone can satisfactorily inform ye: which that you may Experience in your selves, and so be happy, is the hearty Desire of your Soul's Friend, who writes this unto you.

(page 147 [sic]) Thus, having written my Experience of the QUAKERS Principle, I hall [*sic*] write something to detract the Erroneous and False Opinion, that is got up in the Minds of many, concerning the Way and Means by which People come to believe therein. *(page 157 [sic])*

PART III.

A Confutation of *P*eoples Falſe Opinions, concerning the Manner how we have been Convinced of the *P*rinciple of True Religion.

Many and various are the Reports that have been rumoured abroad, relating to the Manner and Practice of this People, in gaining upon others to *believe in the Principle of Truth,* which they bear witness of: The *Principle of Truth,* I call it; for so my Soul does witness it; although I am not unsensible, that such who do despise it, will not stick to scandalize it; and instead of calling it by its true and proper *(page 150 [sic])* Name, brand it with the opprobrious Terms of Heresie and Schism, Sullen Separation, and the Effect of a Melancholy Brain; some of whom not knowing the Way of the Spirit in themselves, and yet seeing the evident Change which hath been wrought upon others, by

Vertue of the Powerful Operation of this spiritual Principle, or Power of God in their Consciences, they have hereupon confidently affirmed the same to be effected by the Art of Witchcraft, and Diabolical Inchantment; which Affirmation, though false, yet may it truly be said to have been fixed as a *Scare crow*, or *Ghostly Apparition*, to affrighten People from so much as looking towards this Religion: But albeit it hath been so intended, yet through the Mercy of our God, there is a Remnant who have not been so affrighted as to flee from, but have drawn near to see and feel, whether there were any Substance in the same; and such have found, to their satisfaction, that the Substance of Life hath lain hid under this dark Reflection, which through the cloudiness of the Understanding, and Prejudice that hath been in the Minds of People *(page 159 [sic])* against the Principle of Light, they have enviously cast upon the Professors of it, as the means whereby they Convert and Turn People to it; alledging it as matter of Wonder, *that any should be so strangely altered, both in Countenance, Carriage and Communication, and that on a sudden too,* (as some have been observ'd to be) *unless it were by the Power of Sorcery, or some Satanical Possession:* And hence have they mocked at and derided that Godly Fear and Holy Trembling, that hath been made to appear in some, when the Terrors of the Almighty took hold on them by reason of Sin, as though this were occasioned through some *Frenzy Humour, being the product of Natural Weakness and Defect, or else produced by the invincible force of Magick Art, which the Creature can no ways resist:* So that this hath been a main Argument, why People should not adventure themselves so much as to go into a *Quakers Meeting,* for fear of the great Danger that some suppose there is, *of being Charmed into that Religion;* which fear hath so much affrighted the Hearts of some, that notwithstanding there are good Desires in them after Satisfaction in Matters of Religion, and *(page 137 [sic])* they have freely confest, (even in my Hearing) *That this seemeth to be the Way to attain the same;* yet they never were, nor do they dare to come amongst this People (to wit, the *Quakers*) *for fear of being forceably possest with the belief of their Principle;* which if they should receive, and walk herein, every one knows what will follow thereupon; this would certainly expose them to the World's Hatred and Scorn, which the Servants and People of the Lord in all Ages have born: So that, for these to be accounted *Witches* is no Wonder, since the Wicked have not spared to sling the same Reflection upon their Lord and Master; Christ Jesus himself, when he was on Earth, was Censured to *work his Miracles by Magick Art;* for when he cast out a *Devil* out of one possest, some said, *He did it by* Beelzebub, *their Prince:* And now, these having received Power from Christ, by their Ministry to effect the like in another kind, because the effect thereof hath brought some into Fear and Trembling; therefore they are judged to *deal with Familiar Spirits,* and to *work by Conjuration:* But how unjust this Judgment is, and how groundless the Surmise, *(page 157 [sic])* I shall not need to Answer; let the Reader but search the Scriptures, and they will give it on this Peoples side, *Psal.* 2.10,11. the Prophet *David* instructs *Kings and Judges of the Earth to serve the Lord with Fear, and rejoice with Trembling. Phil.* 2.12. the Apostle exhorts them, *to work out their own Salvation* with the like frame. Nor was this only their Advice, but also the Saints Practice; for *Moses* confesseth himself a QUAKER, *Heb.* 12.21.

(a) No doubt but *Habakkuk's* Countenance was altered, when his Lips thus Quiver'd; for 'tis true what *David* said, *Psal.* 39.11. *When thou, Lord, with Rebukes does correct Man for Iniquity, thou makest his Beauty to Consume away like a Moth:* If so, why should any think it strange when they see the like Change?

(a) *Habakkuk* likewise acknowledges that at the *Voice of God his Belly did Tremble, and his Lips did Quiver, Hab.* 3.16. Neither was this their Case alone; for we find the prophet *Ezra* meeting with a whole Assembly of them, *Ezra* 9.4. saith he, *Then were assembled unto me every one that Trembled at the Words of the God of Israel.* And the prophet *Isaiah* points at such as the *Lord's Peculiar People,* Chap. 66.5 *Hear the (page 162 [sic]) Word of the Lord* (saith he)*ye that tremble at his Word; your Brethren that hated you, that cast you out for my Name sake, said, Let the Lord be glorified; but he shall appear to your Joy, and they shall be ashamed.* And in the second Verse of the same Chapter, the Lord expresly Promises, *But to this Man will I look, even to him that is Poor, and of a Contrite Spirit, and that Trembleth at my Word.* And in *Jer.* 5.21. the Lord called by the Prophet, saying, *Hear now this, O foolish People, and without Understanding; which have Eyes, and see not; which have Ears, and hear not: Fear ye not me, saith the Lord? Will ye not Tremble at my Presence?* And so he goes on, expostulating the Matter with them, till at last he threatneth to visit them, and be avenged on their Nation, Ver. 29. And sure something of this King *Darius* was afraid of, when he made a Decree, *That all under his Dominion should Fear and Tremble before the God of* Daniel, *Dan.* 6.26. Certainly *Quakers* had a better esteem with him, than they have with this Generation; the Name being given them in Derision and Scorn; notwithstanding the Posture is that, in which the Servants of the Lord, backward from *Moses,* thro' *(page 163 [sic])* the Prophets and Apostles Days, till this very time, have been found. Thus it appears by Scripture, that *Christians* were exercised in Fear and Trembling, (together with Humility, Patience and Self denial) and that not from the Procurement of any Evil Art, but by the Living Sense of the Dealings of the Lord: For proof of which, see what God himself speaketh of his Church by his Prophet *Jeremiah,* Chap. 33.9. *And it shall be to me a Name of Joy, a Praise, and an Honour before all the Nations of the Earth, which shall bear all the good that I do unto them; and they shall Fear and Tremble, for all the Goodness, and for all the Prosperity that I procure unto it.*

Thus 'tis manifest how the matter hath been Misrepresented, to wit, *That the* Quakers *are Inchanters,* but this being mostly the Charge of the Rash and Inconsiderate, I shall say no more to take it off, but only add the words of Christ, Mat. 10.24,25. *The Disciple is not above his Master, nor the Servant above his Lord; 'tis enough that the Disciple be as his Master, and the Servant as his Lord; if they have called the Master of the House (page 153 [sic])* Beelzebub, *how much more shall they call them of his Houshold?*

But there are others, in many things, more Sober and Judicious, who yet have not been sparing in their Censures: Some of whom have given out, *That 'tis through Craft and Cunning Collusion, by which these People* (the *Quakers) gain over Proselytes to their Religion: They are Wise, they are Subtil,* (say they) *they have Reaching Brains; and so they can but Propagate their own Party, they will be at any pains.*

In Answer to whom, my *Reply* is, What Craftiness they mean, I must confess, I cannot tell; but what Craft I have ever found amongst them, is no other than that of which the Apostle writes to the *Corinthians,* 2 Cor. 12.16. *Nevertheless being Crafty* (saith he) *I caught you with Guile:* Which holy Craft and godly Guile hath appeared in them, as they have been careful to keep a Conscience void of Offence towards God, and towards all Men; taking the Apostle's Advice, *James* 3.13. *Who is a Wise Man, and endued with Knowledge amongst you,* (saith he) *let him shew out of a good Conversation his Works with meekness (page 141 [sic]) of Wisdom.* So likewise have they been careful to observe Christ's Counsel, *Luke* 10.3. who there said, *Behold, I send you forth as Sheep in the midst of Wolves, be ye therefore Wise as Serpents, and Harmless as Doves.* And thus sanctifying the Lord God in their Hearts, having a good Conscience, whilst falsly accused, it hath pleased the Lord many times to plead their Righteous Cause, even in their very Adversaries Breasts whereby he hath made their own words to become their Burden; and that they have intended to fix upon his People, by which

to render them Guilty of Deceit and Fraud, hath returned back upon
their own Heads, whilst Integrity and Inocency hath been the others
Armour of Defence, until such time that God hath wrought their more
full Deliverance.

But I must bring the matter a little nearer, that so I may write of that
which relateth to my own particular: This having occasioned some to
wonder, viz. *That I should be decoy'd* (as they call it) *after this manner!*
for so some have bespoke me, by shewing a seeming pity toward my
Person, whilst they have *(page 166 [sic])* manifested enmity against my
Principle; and therefore, that they might not bear too hard upon me,
they have laid the heaviest Load upon those about me; †as if for fear of
one, and to please another, I had hereby prudently
†*Who they are that* provided to serve my Superiours Humor: And so,
'tis supposed I should from them, my Friends have born the greatest
either fear or flatter, Blame, whilst I, in part, have been excused, con-
I need not name; sidering the many Tryals, Temptations and Snares,
for those to whom I whereunto they reckon I have been expos'd; which
write, may easily Consideration of theirs hath procur'd me some Al-
Understand. lowance, from such as are any wise Tender-hearted,
amongst my former Acquaintance; therefore I hope they will not blame
me, if I make use of this Allowance, as well to shew them their Mistakes herein, as to take off the Unjust Aspersions that have been cast
upon my Friends: Wherefore I say, the first Mistake is gross: for any
thing of *Force* (which is that that [sic] some conclude to be the cause of
my coming mongst the People called *Quakers*) *(page 167 [sic])* that, I do
declare, I never felt; nay, I now find it to be Diametrically opposit to
that Foundation Principle, upon which their Religion is built, which
Principle is Christ, the Prince of Peace, who utterly disallows of all
Coersive Compulsion, Force, Constraint or Violence to be used in
Matters of Religion; and teaches such who learn of him, in Meekness
to Instruct those that are ignorant of the *Way of Truth,* and then patiently to wait till he inclines their hearts to walk in it; so that having
their Dependance upon, and Expectation from the Lord alone, they
dare not attempt the Propagation of the Gospel of his dear Son by the
strength, and in the skill and time of Man, without being guided, directed and subjected by him, in whom is all their Help found: This as
to the first Mistake.

But the second mistake amounts to thus much (*viz.*) *That what could
not be wrought upon me by Constraint and Force, was otherwise attempted
to be brought to pass,* to wit, *by subtil Insinuations, and fair Promises, by*

which (it hath been said) *this (page 148 [sic]) People use to tamper with those whom they design to make their Proselites.*

In Answer whereunto I shall make this *Reply:* This Mistake is Obvious: For Promises of outward Advantage and Worldly good availeth nothing that can stand the Soul in stead: Therefore it were altogether imprudent, as well as utterly unlawful to propose any thing of such a kind upon this occasion, neither indeed was it outward advancement, that I sought after (although this is a Reproach I have been made to hear) the Lord is my Witness herein, who subjected me unto himself, and made me willing to be at his disposing, and to have my Lot cast by him. The truth is, Corn, nor Wine, nor Oyl I did not esteem, nor yet length of dayes to enjoy them; for (in my solitudes) the whole World seemed to me as a very little thing; my Soul desiring nothing but a part in God's Kingdom, which made me earnestly intreat him, that he would lead me in the Way everlasting; wherefore this was my frequent Suplication unto him (viz.) *O thou incomprehensible Majesty! who hast established thy Throne in the high and holy (page 144 [sic]) Heavens; yet dost thou graciously condescend to look down upon the Inhabitants of the Earth: Wilt thou now be pleased to suffer Dust and Ashes to plead with thee, and to admit Mortal Flesh to make request unto thee? This is it, O Lord! that I would most earnestly implore of thee, Even that thou wouldst cast up, cast up a Way for me, and remove all Letts and Stumbling-blocks from, and mark out a plain Path before me*, *in which I may walk straight forward towards thy heavenly Country; and that amidst the various Forms there are for worshipping of thee, my Soul may certainly know how to serve thee aright, and wherewith to bring an Acceptable Sacrifice unto thee.* So that this being the Prayer which the Lord often put into my Heart (as I then took it) to Pray unto him, when my Soul was seeking the Way to his Kingdom, Promises of outward Promotion (had they been proposed) could not have given me Satisfaction.

And as for that which hath been termed, *The* Quakers *subtil Insinuation;* I think it must needs intend their sincere and upright Conversation: For as to my own particular, I do declare, There *(page 170 [sic])* was no way by which they did insinuate into me, but by being found real in what they appeared to be: The Heart-searching God having then put my Soul upon search to find out a People with whom I might joyn as with a Communion of Saints; I looked here and there into many Assemblies, but alas! still I saw their Conversations so much contradicting their Professions, that I could heartily joyn with none of them: And then as to their Principles, some indeed I did believe, when I heard

them declar'd; but othersome, God's witness in my Conscience did so
testifie against, that them I could not receive. And thus finding no
People with whom I could joyn in every thing, I concluded my self to
be single in the matters of Religion, which made me many a time extend my Voice to the Lord in these Words, *Oh! my God, upon whom I
have been cast from my Infancy up: How long shall my Faith stand alone
upon the Earth?* In Answer whereunto (I must acknowledg) the Lord
was graciously pleased (even at those very times) to signifie unto my
Spirit, that he had many Thousands *(page 171 [sic])* (though I knew
them not) who were sincere and upright before him, unto whom he
had regard as to his own Children: But still I over-looked this People
(of whom I am writing) as if it had been altogether unlikely I should
find what I sought for amongst them, although natural Affection had
laid a Bond upon me to judge charitably concerning them: Howbeit, at
length there was a Way made whereby I was brought to search here
also, notwithstanding the many false Aspersions which my Ears were
filled with concerning them; for I could not tell but little *David* (the
beloved of the Lord) might lie hid under the Stuff, whom God hath
anointed to Reign in Self-seeking Souls stead; wherefore I then was
willing to look amongst this People (to wit, the *Quakers*) and turn up
the soul covering which others had cast upon them, under which I
soon saw a glorious One lie hid, the Form of whose Countenance was
like the Son of God: And now having not only sought, but found the
Lord and his People in the Earth, in their behalf do I here set my
Probatum Est (I have proved *(page 149 [sic])* them) in the thing which
they profess: They profess themselves the Disciples and Followers of
Jesus Christ, from whom they derive their Name *Christian*; which Name,
though it were given the Disciples in scorn at first in
Acts 11.26.   *Antioch*; yet did they, and so do these, esteem it as an
honourable Epitaph: And therefore have they laboured
to answer their *Christian* calling, with such a Meek, Patient, Holy, Harmless, Humble, Trembling, Self-denying Conversation, as may be most
conformable to the Pattern of Christ Jesus, the High-Priest of their Profession: So that now, I say, upon my search amongst them, I have found
those who are guided by the Principle of Truth in themselves; by which
they were called (for 'tis such only whose Cause I am Vindicating) very
careful to walk worthy of their High and Holy Calling; like as they have
been called by this inward Principle to be Saints, so by it have they led
Saint-like Life, that thereby they might reach to the same principle in
the Consciences of others: And by this their Innocent Life, I needs

must acknowledge, I felt *(page 145 [sic])* my own Conscience powerfully
reached for some time, before my Judgment was fully satisfied: But having those words of our Saviour imprinted upon my Mind (*John* 7.17.) *If
any man will do his will, he shall know of the Doctrine, whether it be of God,
or whether I speak of my self.* Then immediately I consulted not with
Flesh and Blood, but was made willing to give up to the obedience of
his Will revealed in my Conscience, and so I came to receive the Faith
of that principle which the *Quakers* do profess, and by it am I joyned to
them, not only in Head, but in Heart; so that this Faith, by which I am
united to them, is more than a meer natural Credential, that stands in
the bare assent to the Truth of a proposition, as propounded by man;
for it is founded and grounded upon Christ Jesus, who was the Author,
and I trust, will be the Finisher of the same.

But there hath arisen another Wonder; and that is, *That not my self
only, but also, my Brother and Sister should together, and that so quickly
too, become Converts to the Truth; at this,* say some, *we cannot but greatly
admire. (page 174 [sic])* To which, though it might suffice for answer, to let
them know, The Lord's Works are all Works of Wonder, and therefore
may very well be admired by Beholders; yet I must needs say, there is
little reason why such should wonder, that true Conversion should at
once pass upon three [sic], who talk so much of expecting a *Nation to be
born in a Day*; sure if their Faith can conclude the certainty of the latter, they need not be so incredible concerning the Truth of the former:
No doubt therefore but it was prejudice enough against the Truth, that
caused some to say, *It must needs be Hypocrisie which brought us all at
once into the Profession of it.* But the truth is, such neither know how
we came by it, nor can they tell what Progress we have made in it, how
far any of us do witness a real Change; my Soul is made to rejoyce
therein, and for this I bow my Knee to the God and Father of our Lord
Jesus Christ, *That he would prosper and carry on this his own Work more
and more in every one of our Hearts*; yet dare we not be found false Witnesses for God, in speaking of things beyond our Measure, or *(page 175 [sic])*
boasting of that which we have not attained; for though it may be
granted, we did feel an inward and effectual Call, much about a time,
to come out of spiritual *Egypt's* Land, yet must we travel through the
Spiritual Wilderness, before we arrive at the *Heavenly Canaan*: Therefore I would have none mistake, so as to think, that Conversion is
wrought in an instant; for it is a gradual Work, carried on by degrees in
the Soul, which is not presently Compleat and Perfect; although the
very first Motion towards it proceeds from a Principle which is *Perfect*

in it self; and which will in time perfect the Soul, as it follows the Leadings thereof: But if any shall sit down by the way, on this side the Mountain of true Holiness, notwithstanding they began in the Spirit, yet if they end in the Flesh, how far soever they have travelled on in their Journey, still may their Carcasses fall in the Wilderness. Howbeit, I write this not to Discourage any, but to provoke to Diligence, as well my self, as others, that after we have set out towards the Promised Land, and had a sight of it, none of us may grow *(page 152 [sic])* weary, nor faint in our Minds, and so fall short of the Everlasting Rest; for 'tis not a bare Convincement of the Truth in our Understandings, which may produce a change in the Judgment, Opinion and Profession, that will serve our turn, without a change of the Old Nature, without there be a change wrought in the Inward, as well as the Outward Man, whereby the Heart may be throughly Sanctified and made Clean, else there can be no real Conversion; yet may We say, since we have felt the beginnings of this Work in our Hearts, we have been made as Signs and Wonders in the Earth; whilst we have been Weaning from the Worlds Breasts, we have been made a Mock to the Scoffing *Ishmaels* of our Age: But be it so, we are not much concerned, having an Eye to the Hope set before us, we do not only despise the *World's Flateries*, but also contemn its *Scorns*, even as those Worthies of Old who after they were Illuminated, indured a great Fight of *Afflictions*, partly in being made a *Gazing-stock* both by *Reproaches* and *Afflictions*, partly by *(page 140 [sic])* being *companions* with them that were so *used*; yea, though they had Tryals of cruel Mockings, yet they esteemed the *reproach* of Christ greater *Riches* than the Treasures of *Egypt*; For they had an Eye to the Recompence of the Reward, and patiently they indured this with much more, as seeing him who is Invisible; which you may read in the 10th of *Hebrews* more at large: Wherefore we think it not strange concerning the fiery Tryals that are to try us, as though some strange thing happened unto us; when the Wicked reproach us, and speak all manner of Evil against us falsly for Christ's sake; in this we account our selves happy, yea, we secretly rejoyce that he hath accounted us worthy to suffer Shame for his Name, himself having said to our Comfort, *Blessed are ye when Men shall hate you, and when they shall separate you from their Company, and shall Reproach you, and cast out your Names as Evil, for the Son of Man's sake; Rejoyce ye in that day* (saith he) *and leap for Joy, for behold your Reward is great in Heaven; for in like manner did their (page 178 [sic]) Fathers to the Prophets,* Luke 6.22,23. So 'tis no wonder that the World hate us; for we know they have hated all the Righteous Generation that went before us; *They*

were defamed and made as the filth of the World, yea, they were accounted the off scouring of all things; by the Wicked of that Generation, and so are the Off-spring esteemed with such a   1 Cor. 4.13.
sort of People even at this present time: For the Seed of
the Righteous have alwayes been despised in the Eyes and reproached
in the Mouthes of the Proud Ungodly World; howbeit,
they have learned to put their trust in him, who hath   *Psalm* 31.20.
promised to keep them in a Pavillion from the Pride of
man, and to hide them from the Strife of Tongues: Yet Some there are
that say, *Their Tongues are their own, who is Lord over them?*
And such (I may say) have sorely railed on me both in   Psalm 12.4.
Word and Writing, wherein were Queries, which I think
not worthy to receive an Answer, because they came from a Nameless
Author: *(page 179 [sic])* Therefore I'll leave them with their remote
Questions; winding up all in this Conclusion, Let none no longer
inquire at a distance after the *Quakers* and their Principle, as *Nathaniel*
did concerning Christ, *John* 1.46. saying, *Can there any good thing
come out of* Nazareth? But let them remember the answer of *Philip,* who
bid him, *Come and see;* so shall they meet with satisfaction in that inward Principle of divine Light (and the Professors of it) which hath
made many, and now hath it made me, a Spiritual Traveller for Souls
Eternal Wellfare.

Elizabeth Bathurst

(page 136[sic])

An E P I S T L E to fuch of the *Friends of Chriſt*, as have lately been Convinced of the Truth as it is in Jeſus.

MY Dear Friends and Spiritual Relations, unto whom by Grace I am allied, in the Love of Truth I send you this Salutation: Often have you been upon my Mind, long before I found a place to write unto you: For though it was first upon me to write to my former Friends and Acquaintance, and Natural Relations; yet you being that *New Kindred,* spoken of by Christ Mat. 12.50. thus are you nearer to me by *(page 182 [sic])* the Union of his inward Grace, than any unconverted thereunto can be.

And now I tenderly admonish you, That as you are convinced of the saving Power of this Divine Principle (to wit, the Light of Jesus manifest in the Conscience) see you constantly keep therein. For, *Friends*, let me tell you, here lieth our strength in these times of Tryal; herein is our Safety this Day of Danger, in this you'd be sure and quiet, when Peoples Hands shall be upon their Loins, because of fear in the Night: Yea, though you may be come but to the dawning of this Day of God, where you can discern but the glimmering of its Light appear, which may at present shew you Trouble, and minister Condemnation to your Souls for your Evil Deeds, placing Judgment on your Heads, making you possess the punishment of your Iniquities that are past; so that instead of Peace, you may have great Bitterness; yet be perswaded to dwell in the Judgment; wait patiently upon God, who draweth near

Isa. 26.8. & 41.1.   to you in the way hereof, and I will assure, in this Light you shall see more Light, and in it Consolation and Salvation shall be enjoyed. Wherefore I now write unto you, little Children (in the spiritual stature, being my self one of that Number) by way of Exhortation, To cast away your Idols, and keep your selves from them; say unto them, *Get ye hence to the Moles and to*

Isa. 2.20.   *the Bats:* Friends, you know what I mean by them; turn in, and I am sure the Light will let you see them, and the sooner you part with them, the sooner will you find forgiveness with the Lord, for the Idolatry which he hath beheld in them: And when your Idols are utterly destroyed, then shall you be joyned to the Lord in a perpetual Covenant that shall never be broken: And here will your Bow abide in strength, wherewith you shall shoot at *Mystery Babylon,* and see her falling down; yea, *though her Archers may shoot sorely at you, yet shall they not be able to hurt you; for the Lord (the help of Israel) will be a Shield before you, and will turn back their Arrows into their own Quiver, so shall they hang by their sides, and stick in their Hearts, who privily intended to wound the Innocent (page 184 [sic]) without Cause.* Yet 'tis very likely the Wicked will be pushing at you, and casting scandalous Calumnies upon you; in which I cannot but tenderly simpathize with you, having my self lately passed those Piques of the Enemy: *Renowned of the Lord of Hosts, the Captain of my Salvation, which caused me to march through valiantly, and also given me the Victory;* so that, though I speak not boastingly, yet I can say, *The Revilings of the Ungodly do not at all dis-spirit me;* for now I can take their Reproaches for Christ's sake, and bind them as an Ornament unto me: *To God be all the Glory, who hath raised this Spirit of Courage and Christian-Fortitude in me, and now hath called me to call on others to wait upon him, that they may be thus strengthened with Might in their inward Man by him.* Therefore wait on the Lord, be of good Courage, and he shall strengthen your Hearts; wait, I say, on the Lord, as said Holy *David*, *Psal.* 27.14. so shall One chase a Thousand, & two put Ten Thousand to flight; (*Friends*, read inwardly, so you'll understand me;) I do not mean that you should avenge your selves on any with Carnal Weapons of War; *(page 185 [sic])* No, no: But as you stand and wait in the Light of the Lord, though you can handle neither Sword nor Spear, he will make you shew comely as *Tirzah*, and terrible to the Wicked, even as an Army with Banners: For though the Remnant of the Just (as to outward Defence) are left this day like a City without Gates or Walls) whom the Wicked will be plotting against; *yet God will laugh at him, for he seeth that his Day is coming;* and hath also given me this Confidence of Hope in him, to wit,   *Psal. 30.2,13.* *That he will not give his People into the Hands of cruel Lords, nor suffer Men of fierce Countenance to rule over them:* But they shall be as Standers in the Gap, and Stakes in the Hedge (though some may be but of tender growth) to stop the Enemy from laying waste our Countrey, and to stay the Lord's sore and terrible Stroke.

Ah *Friends!* it is not Pity, that Sin should make an *Aceldama* of our Nation, and this City? See therefore ye mind your inward Reprover, that ye may be no cause in Procuring the Nation's Misery. You Children of the *(page 189 [sic])* Light, arise therefore, and shine; for your Light is come, which will adorn your Conversation; let it now appear throughout your whole Behaviour, so shall your Words and Actions glorifie your heavenly Father: Thus shall the Wicked see our Rock hath not sold us; for stronger is he that is in us, than they that are against us: So though they may outwardly beset us, yet we have a Rock to shelter us, where the Enemy shall despair for ever at coming at us. Wherefore *faint not in your Minds, nor be discouraged in your Spirits, at the Tidings you hear abroad; but dwell within your Tent, and serve the Lord with Fear, every one in your Sphere, so shall you shine like Stars in their proper Orbs:* Yea, though some of us may be but of small Magnitude, as in the natural Firmament, one Star differs from another Star in Glory, yet as we abide in the Fear, being cloathed with Humility, so shall we be preserved in our Spiritual Station, while we are as strangers and Pilgrims on the Earth, to have our Conversation honest (and as much as in us lies inoffensive) amongst them that are *(page 187 [sic])* without; that whereas they speak against us as Evil-Doers, they may by the Good   *2 Pet. 2.11,12.* Works which they shall behold in us, *Glorifie God in the*

Day of their Visitation, so shall we convince the World of that Principle
of Light and Grace, that shineth in their Hearts, which if they turn in
to it, and obey it, it will teach (and enable) them, *That denying*
Ungodlyness and Worldly Lusts, they should live Righ-
Tit. 2.11,12. *teously, Soberly and Godly in this present World.* And by
this Grace shall we be to those about us, as Saviours in
the Hand of the Lord upon Mount *Sion,* as others have been to us,
when we were in Spiritual *Babylon:* Thus we being as a *City set upon a*
Hill for People to behold, this shall they confess, *Verily God is in us;*
when their Hearts shall fail them for very Fear of what Men are about
to bring to pass: But would the Inhabitants of this Island bow to the
Scepter of the Son of God in their Hearts, they should not need to be
afraid of any *Tripple Leagues* or *Conclave Consultations* to do them *(page*
188 [sic]) hurt; for yet would God arise, and break such Associations, and
take such wicked Wits in their own Craftiness, so that their Hands
should not find their Enterprizes; so should *England* become the *Re-*
nown of Kingdoms, and a *Mart of Nations,* maugre the strength of Hell-
ish Combinations. Therefore let them that read me, mark what I say;
for the Lord of Hosts hath determined, *That the Haughtiness of Man shall*
be humbled, and the Loftiness of Man shall be laid low, that himself alone
may be exalted in this Day: And mens Idols he will utterly abolish; yea, he
will famish the gods of the Earth, that People may worship him in his own
holy Place, as say the Prophets, *Isa.* 2.17,18. *Zeph.* 2.11. Again he saith;
I am the Lord, that is my Name; and my Glory will I not give to another,
neither my Praise to Graven Images, Isa. 42. 8. Wherefore such who will
not turn from their Idols, to serve the living God, so as to break off
their Sins by a real Reformation, he will be terrible unto them, and will
certainly visit them with Ruin and Destruction.

But you who know the Lord, and *(page 189 [sic])* are turned in to him,
do you put your Trust in him, who is Prince of the Kings of the Earth,
unto whom all Power doth belong, *and through God you*
Psalm 60.12. *shall do valiantly;* for he it is that shall *tread down all your*
Enemies. Friends, I mean chiefly as to the *inward;* yet am I
to exhort you as to the *outward* this day, *That you be in nothing terrified by*
your Adversaries, which will be to them an evident Token of
Phil. 1.28. *Perdition, but to you of Salvation from the Almighty;* for the
Shields of the Earth are his; therefore trust you in him,
whose Name is, *The Lord of Hosts* yea, *The Lord Jehovah, in*
Nahum 1.7. *whom is Everlasting Strength; who is a Strong Hold in the Day*
of Trouble; and he knoweth them that trust in him; so shall

Fear be far from you; and as for Terror, it shall not come near you: You
Meek and Harmless Ones, you shall increase your Joy in
the Lord, and shall inherit the Earth, and delight your   *Isa. 29.19.*
selves in abundance of Peace; for the Righteous God will
establish *(page 190 [sic])* the Just, when Bloody and Deceitful   *Psal. 37.11.*
Men shall not live out half their Days: You shall triumph
in Christ Jesus who will make manifest the favour of his Wisdom by you
in every place; so that though you may suffer, yet shall you not despair;
for in due time the Lord will be your Deliverer: Wherefore, lift up the
Eyes of your Minds this day, and look for the *Son of Man's* appearing,
who hath determin'd to destroy the Man of Sin by the Spirit of his
Mouth, and by the Brightness of his Coming.

   And now it rises in me to write a word to comfort you, you Friends
of the Bridegroom, that mourn for his Withdrawing, and eat
your Bread with Quaking, and drink your Water with Trem-   *Ezek. 12.18.*
bling, as those who find no comfort till you do enjoy him.
   Wait without Weariness, and you shall behold his Countenance, and
hear *(page 191 [sic])* his pleasant Voice, which will revive your Spirits; but
still be you mindful when you hear things unutterable, that you keep
low and humble, so shall you be kept from the Snares of the Devil. And
Friends, Let no Outward things over-set your Minds, but sit loose in
Heart from all that here you have, that nothing may be preferred like
the Favour of the Lord.
   And you of Tender Years, who are void of Worldly Cares, be ye aware
of Pleasures, Pride and Worldly Honours; for these may be your Snares:
I am sensible many are the Temptations to allure you unto Vanity; but
as you eye the Lord, they shall not overcome you; he will fight your Battels
for you, and lift up a Standard in you against your Souls Enemies; and
Satan and his Host shall fall like Lightning before you: Therefore stand
you still, and wait for God's arising, so shall all his Enemies be scattered
before him: And he will surely rise against our spiritual Adversaries,
and bring them down in us, that they may not insult over us: For the
Lord takes notice of the Kindness of our Youth, *(page 192 [sic])* and is well
pleased to have our first ripe Fruits holiness unto him; wherehe assures
us, that *as we continue in the well-doing, we shall always inherit his Blessing.*
Therefore you Weak and Feeble ones, put your Trust in
him; *For he giveth Power to the Faint; and in them that have no*   *Isa. 40.29.*
Might he encreaseth Strength. This our Spiritual Shepherd
hath a tender regard to the hindmost of his Flock; He gathereth his

Lambs with his Arms, and carrieth them in his Bosom, and gently
leadeth those that are young: And thus, as we follow the Son of God,
our Leader, Christ Jesus, our Captain and Commander, so shall we become as a well-disciplined Army, marching on in order, every one keeping our Ranks, and making War in Righteousness with the Prince and
Powers of Darkness; the Weapons of our Warfare not being Carnal, but
Spiritual, mighty through God to the pulling down the strong Holds of
Sin and Satan, and casting the Dragon, the Beast, and the False Prophet,
together with the spiritual Locust, into the *(page 193 [sic])* Bottomless Pit,
where they shall sink into the Lake of his Divine Wrath, so as never to
rise more to cover the Earth. For, *Friends,* we are this day as an Ensign
among the People, exposed unto many Spectators, and the Lord's Presence is amongst us (magnified be his Name) because his Glory rests
upon us: And as we wait on him, He will appear more and more in our
Meetings, and Crown our Assemblies, and make our Antients
Honourable, and our Young Men like *Eldad* and *Medad,* and our Dam-
sels like the Daughters of *Philip.* Yea, though we have not all the Gift of
Prophecying (vocally) bestowed on us, yet by our upright Carriage, we
shall every one become Preachers of Righteousness amongst our
Neighbours, whereby we shall reach to the Witness, that lieth slain in
their Consciences, and shall cause it to arise and stand upon its Feet,
and Prophesie in their Streets; so shall we raise up that in themselves
that will judge them for their Sins: Though the Love of God hath taught
us to be kindly affectionated towards all, and to be pitiful, notwithstanding we are *(page 194 [sic])* grieved to behold the sad and woful state of
the Wicked World; yet can we praise the Lord in Spirit, that he hath
turned us from Darkness unto Light, and from Satan unto himself; and
hath made us to turn our back upon the Glory of the Earth, before this
Day of Shaking came upon it; when mens Confidence in it shall be
shaken: and their Expectation from it disappointed; then shall those
who truly fear the Lord be abundantly satisfied.

    For Friends, I must acknowledge it often arises in my Soul, as a Return of
Thanks to God (*viz.*) The Remembrance which he gives me of the
Time of his Love, even when my Soul was secretly crying, *Where shall I find
true rest?* Then was the Lord pleased to bring me to the Mountain of his
Holiness, where a peaceable dwelling is, and that just before their Distur-
bances broke out, in this part of the World, where my lot is cast: Oh! praised
be his Name. For now he hath taken me into his Family, and makes me
to sit down with the Antients of his House, at the Table of his Blessing,
where he feedeth every *(page 195 [sic])* one with Food convenient for them.

And now *Friends*, let me mind my self, and you, *That we greatly Love and Esteem, and in Hononr [sic] do prefer those that were in Truth before us;* some of whom have been made as Trumpets (by the Breath of the Lord) to sound the *Everlasting Gospel* in our Ears; and others, on whom the Gift of *Utterance* hath not been bestowed, yet have they taught us to *Fear God* and *give Glory to Him,* by the Example which they have set before us: And thus respecting these as *Elders,* so shall Love regularly extend it self towards all others. I write this to you, *Friends,* only by way of Remembrance, as knowing, none need teach   1 *Pet.*1.1. us to love those who have received like precious Faith with us (much less need we any humane Teachings, to *Esteem such as held the same antient Faith before us*) For we are taught of God to *Love*   2 *Thes.*4.9. *one another,* and by this shall all men know, that we are the   *John* 13.5. *Disciples of Christ Jesus.* Thus as they behold our *comely Order,* while we live in Love together, like Children *(page 196 [sic])* of one Father, and in the inward union dwell, so shall they discern the *Splendor of the Truth* to shine in and amongst us, even like an *Orient Pearl:* And so shall we be bound up together in the Bundle of Love and Life in Christ Jesus, and shall grow up in him like Willows by the Water courses, and as tender Plants which God's Right Hand hath Planted; and our Natural Talents augmented, *to serve the Lord with faithfulness in our several places, where we shall be as Lights unto the World whilst our dwelling is here amongst them,* and then having improved our Talents to the Glory of God, and run well to the end of our Race, when our Course is finished, we shall lay down our Heads in Peace, and hear that joyful Sentence pronounced on us, *Well done good and faithful Servants, enter ye into the joy of your Lord;* where we shall receive the End of our Faith, even the final Salvation of our immortal Souls, which shall eternally live to sing and set forth Praises and Hallelujahs in the highest to him that sits on the Throne, and to the Lamb, Christ Jesus, *who hath redeemed us from the Earth,* unto whom *(page 197 [sic])* the Praise doth belong, for the Assistance of his Spirit is in this thing.

Given forth by one of the leaſt of the Flock of Chriſt whoſe outward Name is,

Elizabeth Bathurſt.

THE

SAYINGS

OF

𝔚omen.

Which were fpoken upon fundry Occafions, in feveral
Places of the Scriptures.

Briefly Colleted and Set together, to fhew how the Lord
poured out of his Spirit upon the whole Houfe of Israel; not only
on the Male, but also on the Female; and made them *Stew
ards of the manifold Gifts of his Grace;* and as those who knew
they must give an account of their Stewardfhip to the Lord.

So did all the Women that were wife in Heart, manage their
particular Talents, to the Praife and Glory of God.

London, Printed by *T. Sowle.* 1695.

(page 102 [sic])

The

SAYINGS

o f

𝔚omen.

First, WE find the Sayings of faithful *Sarah*, concerning her Son
Isaac, the Child of Promise, (to whom the Inheritance
belonged) when she saw *Ishmael* mocking of him, she said to *Abraham*,
her Husband, *Cast out this Bond-woman and her Son, for the Son of this
Bond-woman shall not be Heir with my Son, even with* Isaac. And God
commended her Care, and justified her Speech, saying unto *Abraham,
Let it not be grievous in thy sight, because of the Lad, and because of the*

Bond-woman; in all that Sarah *hath said unto thee, hearken (page 202 [sic]) unto her Voice, for in* Isaac *shall thy Seed be called,* Gen. 21.10,12.

2dly. We find *Rebecca,* the Wife of *Isaac,* speaking to the Lord, and the Lord answering her, Gen. 25.22,23. when she was with Child of *Jacob* and *Esau;* the Children strugling together within her, she went to inquire of the Lord, [not of Doctors] saying, *If it be so, why am I thus? And the Lord said unto her, Two Nations are in thy Womb, and two manner of People shall be separated from thy Bowels; and the one People shall be stronger than the other People, and the Elder shall serve the Younger.* And after the Children were Born, and come to Age, she spoke unto her Son *Jacob,* and instructed him how he should obtain the Blessing, which God had promised, Gen.27.6. and so on. And afterwards she took care of her Son *Jacob,* concerning his Marriage, saying to *Isaac* her Husband, *If* Jacob *take a Wife of the Daughters of* Heth, *such as these, which are of the Daughters of the Land, what good shall my Life do me?* Verse the last. And *Isaac* approved of her Speech, and called *Jacob* and blessed him, and said unto him, *Thou shalt not (page 203 [sic]) take a Wife of the Daughters of* Canaan, Chap. 28.1.

3dly, We find *Rachel* and *Leah* speaking unto *Jacob* in these wholesome Words, saying, *Now therefore whatsoever God hath said unto thee, do,* Gen. 31.10.

4thly, We find *Miriam* the Prophetess speaking to an Assembly of Women, *Exod.* 15.20, 21. when *Moses* had made an end of his Song of Praises to the Lord, for the Salvation and Deliverance of his People; then *Miriam* the Prophetess, the Sister of *Aaron;* took a Timbrel in her Hand, and all the Women went out after her with Timbrels and with Dances; and *Miriam* answered   *Psal. 68.25.* them, and said, *Sing ye to the Lord, for he hath triumphed gloriously; the Horse and his Rider hath he thrown into the Sea,* &c.

5thly, We find *Deborah,* a Valiant Mother and Judge in *Israel* (and she was also a Prophetess) speaking to *Barack* a Captain, who had Ten Thousand Men at his Feet, yet she instructed him how he should go up against *Sisera,* (Captain of *Jabin's* Army, the Children *(page 204 [sic])* of *Israel's* Enemy) and she said, *I will surely go up with thee, notwithstanding the Battel thou takest shall not be for thine Honour, for the Lord shall sell* Sisera *into the Hands of a Woman;* read *Judges* 4. throughout. And then we have her Song, wherein she magnified the Name of the Lord, and said, *Blessed be* Jael *above Women, the Wife of* Heber; *blessed shall she be in the Tent,* &c. *Judg.*5.24. And she made a large Declaration of the Righteous Acts of the Lord, in the foregoing and following Verses; for he it was that had avenged his People of their Enemies.

6thly, We find *Jeptha's* Daughter, saying to her Father, *As thou hast opened thy Mouth unto the Lord, so do unto me according to what hath proceeded out of thy Mouth, for as much as the Lord hath taken Vengeance for thee on thine Enemies, even of the Children of* Ammon, Judg. 11.26.

7thly, We find *Manoah's* Wife saying to her Husband, *A Man of God came unto me, and his Countenance was like the Countenance of an Angel of God, very terrible; but I asked him not whence he was, neither told he me his Name; but he said unto me, Behold thou shalt conceive and bear (page 205 [sic]) a Son; and now drink no Wine, nor strong Drink, neither eat any unclean thing, for the Child shall be a* Nazarite *to God from the Womb, to the day of his Death,* Judg. 13.7. And when *Manoah* said to his Wife, *We shall surely die, because we have seen God;* his Wife being more stedfast in Faith, wisely answered, and encouraged him, saying, *If the Lord were pleased to kill us, he would not have received a Burnt-offering and a Meat-offering at our Hands; neither would he have shewed us all these things.*

8thly, We find *Naomi* speaking concerning her own Adversity, saying to the People of *Bethlehem; Call me not* Naomi, *call me* Marah, *for the Almighty hath dealt bitterly with me; I went out full, and the Lord hath brought me home again empty, and hath afflicted me,* Ruth 1.20,21.

9thly, We find *Ruth,* the *Maobitess,* speaking comfortably to *Naomi,* her Mother, in her sorrow, saying, *Intreat me not to leave thee, nor to return from following thee; for whither thou goest, I will go; and where thou lodgest, I will lodge; thy People shall be my People; and thy God my God; where thou diest, will I die, and (page 206 [sic]) there will I be buried; the Lord do so to me, and more also, if ought but Death part thee and me,* Ruth 1.16,17. And afterwards, both these Women found Favour from the Lord; and the Women of the City blessed the Lord on their behalf, *Ruth* 4.14.

10thly, We find *Hannah* praying in the Temple, and pouring out her Soul before the Lord; and the Lord heard her, and granted her Petition, 1 *Sam.* 1. from Vers. 10. to 18. And when her request was granted, she made a fervent and large Speech, in magnifying and exalting the Lord, *Chap.* 2. from Vers. 1. to 10.

11thly, We find when *Saul* and *David* had made a great slaughter upon the *Philistines,* the Women came out of all the Cities of *Israel,* Singing and Dancing, with Instruments of Musick; *And the Women answered one another as they plaid, and said,* Saul *hath slain his Thousands and* David *his ten Thousands,* 1 Sam. 18.6,7. And as the Women were pertakers of outward Salvation and Deliverance, as well as the Men, by *David* in the time of the Law; so are *(page 207 [sic])* they partakers with their Brethren of inward Salvation and Deliverance from the Devil, by Christ, the

Captain of our Salvation: And therefore they ought to Praise and make Melody in their Hearts to the Lord, now in the time of the Gospel.

12*thly*, We find *Abigail*, the Wife of *Nabal*, speaking to King *David*, saying, *Let thine Hand maid, I pray thee speak in thine Audience, and hear the Words of thine Handmaid.* And so she went on, and preach't a large Sermon to him, as we find written, 1 *Sam*. 25.24,25,26,27,28,29,30,31. And *David* the King heard her patiently, and afterwards he said unto her, *Blessed be the Lord God of Israel which sent thee this day to meet me; and blessed be thy Advice, and blessed be thou, which hast kept me this day from coming to shed Blood,* Vers. 32,33. So we see this Wise Woman, by her Prudence and Inocence, saved her House from Destruction.

13*thly*, We find the Woman of *Tekoah* speaking to King *David*; yea, she communed with him, till she convinced him of the Matter she had to say unto him, see 2 *Sam*. 14.4. and so on. Though she spoke in a parable, yet by *(page 208 [sic])* her discretion she made Reconciliation between *David* and *Absolom*, and caused the King to call home again his Banished, which he had expelled from him.

14*thly*, We find a *Wise Woman* of the City of *Abel*, speaking to *Joab* the General, yea, she preached to him, and told him, *She was one of them that were faithful in* Israel, *and thou seekest to destroy a City and Mother in* Israel; (said she) *why wilt thou swallow up the Inheritance of the Lord?* 2 *Sam*. 20. from Vers. 16 to 20. So she convinced him, and preserved the City: And her Wisdom, Courage and Faith is recorded to Posterity.

15*thly*, We find a poor Widow speaking to the Prophet *Elijah*, saying, *I have but a handful of Meal in a Barrel, and a little Oyl in a Cruise, and behold I am gathering two Sticks, that I may go in and dress it for me and my Son, that we may eat it and dye,* 1 Kings 17.12. Yet in Faith she made the Prophet a Cake thereof first; and she found that her Meal and Oyl wasted not, as you read *Verse* 16. for the Lord gave in a supply, who had commanded her to sustain the Prophet, *Vers.* 9. So she had the *(page 209 [sic])* reward both of her Faith and Works.

16*thly*, *We find* the *Shunamite*-Woman speaking to her Husband concerning the Prophet *Elisha*, saying, *Behold! now I perceive that this is a Holy Man of God, which passeth by us continually: Let us make a Chamber, I pray thee, on the Wall, and set for him there a Bed, and a Table, and a Stool, and a Candlestick, and it shall be that when he cometh to us, that he shall turn in thither,* 2 Kings 4.9,10. Thus she was sensible of the necessity of the Prophet in his Journey; and according to her care, the Prophet was careful it might be recompenced to her; see Vers. 13. For she was a great Woman, and had no Child, therefore the Prophet told her, *She should*

have a Son, and she had so, according to his word: And when the Child
dyed, she had Faith to believe (and also told her Husband)
Heb. 11.35.   *That if she went to the Man of God, all should be well:* ()
And it was so; for by Faith she received her Dead raised to
Life again, as you may read, Vers. 23. and 36.

17*thly,* We find a captive Maid, who was brought out of the Land of
Israel, (page 210 [sic]) and waited upon the Wife of *Naaman* the *Assyrian,*
(who was a Leper) saying to her Mistress, *Would God, my Lord were with
the Prophet that is in* Samaria, *for he would recover him of his Leprosie.*
Thus she spoke from the sense she had of the Power of the Lord, which
he would shew through his Prophet; and it proved so, for *Naaman* went
unto him, and was healed, 2 *Kings* 5.23.

18*thly,* We find *Huldah* the Prophetess, which dwelt in the Colledge
in *Jerusalem,* speaking to *Hilkiah* the Priest, and *Shaphan* the Scribe,
and to the King's Chancellor, which he sent, and commanded to
commune with her; and to them, and those that came with them, she
made a large declaration in the Name of the Lord, as you may read,
2 *Kings* 22. from *vers.*12. to the end. Now here, neither King nor Priest,
despised a Womans Speech.

18*thly,* [*sic*] We find Queen *Esther* speaking to King *Ahasuerus,* in
behalf of the poor *Jews,* her People; *Mordicai* her Uncle having sent
unto her, she bid the Messengers return him this answer, *Gather together all the* Jews *that are present in* Shushan, *and fast ye for me; neither
eat (page 211 [sic]) nor drink three Days, Night nor Day; I and my Maidens
will fast likewise:* And (with Courage and Resolution she said) *so will I go
in unto the King, which is not according to the Law, and if I perish, I perish,*
Esth. 4.16. And by her discreet Behaviour she obtained favour of the
King, (God inclining his Heart) so that he held out the Golden Scepter to her, and said unto her, *What wilt thou Queen* Esther, *and what is
thy Request? it shall be given thee to the half of the Kingdom,* Chap. 5.2,3.
So again, Chap, 7.2: *Then* Esther *the Queen answer'd, and said, If I have
found favour in thy sight, O King! and if it please the King, let my Life be
given me at my Petition, and my People at my Request; for we are sold, I
and my People to be destroyed, to be slain, and to perish: But if we had been
sold for Bond-men and Bond-women, I had held my Tongue, although the
Enemy cannot countervail with King's damage. Then King* Ahasuerus *answered, and said unto* Esther *the Queen, Who is he? and where is he that
durst presume in his Heart to do so?* And Esther said, *The Adversary and
Enemy is this wicked* Haman, Vers. 3, 4, 5, 6. And Esther *spake yet again
before the King (page 212 [sic]) and fell down at his Feet, and besought him*

with *Tears*, to put away the mischief of Haman, *and his Device that he had devised against the* Jews. *Then the King held out the golden Scepter towards* Esther; *so* Esther *arose, and stood before the King, and said, If it please the King, and if I have found favour in his sight; and the thing seem right before the King, and if it be pleasing in his Eyes, let it be written, to reverse the Letter devised by* Haman, *which he wrote to destroy the* Jews, *which are all in the King's Provinces; For how can I endure to see the Evil that shall come upon my People? Or how can I endure to see the Destruction of my Kindred?* Chap. 8.3,4,5,6. And the King granted it. So by her Wisdom, Faith, and innocent Resolution, she saved her People, and became a Nursing-Mother in *Israel.*

20*thly*, We find Zeresh, the Wife of *Haman*, saying unto her Husband, (before the Queen had made complaint against *Haman*) *If* Mordecai *be of the* Jews, *before whom thou hast begun to fall, thou shalt not prevail against him, but shalt surely fall before him,* Esth. 6.13.

21*thly*, We find King Solomon's Mother, saying to her Son, by way of Instruction; *(page 213 [sic]) Give not thy Strength unto Women, nor thy Ways to that which destroyeth Kings. It is not for Kings,* O Lemuel, *it is not for Kings to drink Wine, nor for Princes, strong Drink; least they forget the Law, and pervert the Judgment of any of the Afflicted: Give strong Drink unto him that is ready to perish, and Wine to those that be of heavy Hearts: Let him drink and forget his Poverty, and remember his Misery no more: Open thy Mouth for the Dumb in the cause of all such as are appointed to Destruction: Judge Righteously, and plead the Cause of the Poor and Needy,* Prov. 31. from Vers. 3. to 9.

Thus we find many renowned Women recorded in the Old Testament, who had received a Talent of Wisdom and Spiritual Understanding from the Lord; as good Stewards thereof they improv'd and imploy'd the same to the Praise and Glory of God.

So likewise in the *New Testament* we find another Number of many Daughters, who as they were made Heirs of the Grace of Life, together with their Brethren; so upon sundry occasions they spoke and praised the Lord, who had bestowed Mercy on them.

(page 214 [sic]) And here, *First;* We find the Woman of *Canaan* speaking unto Christ in behalf of her Daughter, crying out, and saying, *Have Mercy on me, O Lord, thou Son of* David; *my Daughter is grieviously vexed with a Devil,* Mat. 15.22. And again, she came and worshipped him, saying, *Lord help me,* Vers. 25. But he answered her, *It is not meet to take the Childrens Bread, and cast it unto Dogs.* And she said, *Truth Lord, yet the Dogs eat of the Crumbs which fall from their Masters Table.* Then Jesus

answered, and said unto her, *O Woman! great is thy Faith; be it unto thee even as thou wilt: And her Daughter was made whole from that very Hour,* Vers. 27.28.

2dly, We find a Worthy and Noble Act recorded of a Woman, who having an Alabaster-Box of very precious Ointment, 'tis said, *She poured it on Jesus his Head, as he sate at Meat,* Mat.26.7. For which the Disciples reproved her; but when Jesus understood it, he spoke in her Justification, saying unto them, *Why trouble ye the Woman,* &c? *Verily I say unto you, wheresoever this Gospel shall be preached throughout the (page 215 [sic]) whole World, there shall also this that this Woman hath done, be told for a Memorial of her,* as you may read from Vers. 8. to 13. more at large. And *Mark* makes mention of it again, *Chap.* 14.3. and *John* likewise, *Chap.* 11.1. Now though there is no mention of what she said at that time, yet what she did is recorded; and she is commended by Christ her Lord, as worthy of Commemoration unto all Generations.

3dly, We find *Pilate's* Wife speaking in behalf of Christ, when her Husband was sate down on the Judgment-seat, she sent unto him, saying, *Have thou nothing to do with that just Man, for I have suffered many things this day in a Dream because of him,* Mat. 27.19.

4thly, We find the Woman, that was twelve Years diseased, and had spent all her Living upon Physicians and still grew worse and worse; her Faith in Christ was so strong, that she believed, and also said, *If I may Touch but the Hem of his Garment, I shall be whole,* Mark 5.25. and so on. And when Christ felt healing Virtue go out of him, he inquired, who it was that touched him? then the Woman came Trembling, and *(page 216 [sic])* fell down before him, and told him all the truth what she had done: And Christ did not reprove her for *speaking* to him, but he said unto her, *Daughter, thy Faith hath made thee whole, go in Peace.*

5thly, We find the *Virgin Mary,* to whom the Angel of God was sent, telling of her, That by the Power of the Most-high, she should bring forth a Son, whose Name should be called *Jesus,* and he should be the Son of the highest, and he should Reign over the House of *Jacob,* and of his Kingdom there should be no End, *Luke* 1.26. and so on. Now, though this seemed to her impossible, that such a thing should be, yet in Faith she believed, and said, *Behold the Hand-maid of the Lord; be it unto me according to thy Word,* Vers. 38. And then we have her Song of Praise, from *Verse.* 46. to 55. And *Mary said, My Soul doth magnifie the Lord, and my Spirit hath rejoiced in God my Saviour; for he hath regarded the low estate of his Hand-maiden: For behold! from henceforth all Nations shall call me Blessed; for he that is mighty hath done to me great things, and Holy is his Name, and his Mercy is unto them (page 217 [sic]) that fear him, from*

Generation to Generation; He hath shewed strength with his Arm, and hath scattered the Proud in the Imagination of their Hearts; He hath put down the Mighty from their Seats, and exalted them of low degree; He hath filled the Hungry with good things, and the Rich hath he sent empty away; He hath holden his Servant Israel, in remembrance of his Mercy, as he spoke to our Fathers, to Abraham, *and his Seed for ever.*

6thly, We find *Elizabeth*, the Wife of *Zacharias* the Priest, saying, *Thus hath the Lord dealt with me, in the day wherein he looked on me, to take away my Reproach among men,* Luke 1.25. This was when she was with Child of *John* the *Baptist*, the fore-runner of Jesus Christ; and when *Mary* came into her House, she was filled with the Holy Ghost, and spoke out with a loud Voice, saying, *Blessed art thou among Women, and blessed is the Fruit of thy Womb: And whence is this to me, that the Mother of my Lord should come unto me? For lo, as soon as the Voice of thy Salutation sounded in my Ears, the Babe leaped in my Womb for joy; And blessed is she that believed, for (page 218 [sic]) there shall be a performance of those things which were told her from the Lord,* Vers. 42. and so on.

7thly, We find ancient *Anna*, a Prophetess, a Widow, of about Fourscore and four Years of Age, which departed not from the Temple, but served God with Fasting and Prayer, Night and Day; when the Child Jesus was brought thither, she coming in at that instant, gave Thanks unto the Lord, and spake of him to all that looked for Redemption in Israel, *Luke* 2.36, 37, 38.

8thly, We find *Christ*, and *Mary* communing together, *Luke* 10.39. And when *Martha* would have called her away from sitting at Jesus's Feet, where she heard his Word; Christ reproved her for her cumber, and commended *Mary*, saying, *She hath chosen that good part, which shall not be taken away from her,* Vers. 42. And this is Chronicled and left upon Record, that all People might chiefly prefer the better part, and esteem the Word of Truth as the one thing needful.

9thly, We find certain Women, which followed Christ even to his Crucifixion; see *Mark* 15.40. giving Testimony *(page 219 [sic])* of his Resurrection: *Luke* 24.10. Its said, *it was* Mary Magdalen, *and* Joanna, *and* Mary *the Mother of* James, *and other Women that were with them, which told these things unto the Apostles;* to wit, that Christ was risen. And Vers. 22, 23, 24. One of the Brethren, named *Cleophas*, confest to Christ, that certain Women of their company made them astonished, which were early at the Sepulchre, and when they found not his Body, they came, saying, *That they had seen a Vision Of Angels, which said, that he was alive; and certain of them which were with us, went to the Sepulchre, and found it even as the Women had said.*

10*thly,* We find Christ, the head of the Church, discoursing with the Woman of *Samaria* concerning *living Waters* and Worship, John 4. from v. 7.to 27. as you may read at large *she desired living Water* (v. 15.) and by the Answer Christ gave her, *she perceived him to be a Prophet,* (v.19.) Then said she to him, *Our Fathers worshipped in this Mountain, and ye say, that in* Jerusalem *is the place where men ought to Worship* (v. 20.) Jesus saith unto her, *Woman, believe me, the hour cometh, when ye shall (page 220 [sic]) neither at this Mountain, nor yet at* Jerusalem, *worship the Father,* (v. 21.) and then he certified her, both of the place and manner of Worship; *But the hour cometh, and NOW IS* (saith Christ) *when the true Worshippers shall worship the Father in Spirit, and in Truth; for the Father seeketh such to worship him: God is a Spirit, and they that worship him must worship him in Spirit and in Truth* (v. 23,24.) (This se-cret Christ revealed to a Woman, and suffered her also to speak freely unto him.) The Woman said unto him, *I know that Messias cometh, which is called Christ; when he is come, he will tell us all things.* Jesus saith unto her, *I that speak unto thee am he,* (v. 25,26.) And upon this came his Disciples; and marvelled that he talked with the Woman; but no man said, *Why talkest thou with her?* The Woman then left her Water-pot, and went her way into the City, and said to the men, *Come see a Man, which told me all things that ever I did, Is not this the Christ?* v. 28.29. and many of the *Samaritans* of that City believe in him, for the sayings of the Woman, which testified, *He told me all that ever I did,* v. 39.

(page 221 [sic]) 11*thly,* We find *Mary Magdalen,* coming early to the Sepulchre on the first day of the Week, and finding the Stone taken away from the Sepulchre, she runneth to *Simon Peter,* and to the other Disciples whom Jesus loved, saying unto them, *They have taken away the Lord out of the Sepulchre, and we know not where they have laid him,* John 20.1,2. And ver. 11. we find her standing without at the Sepul-chre weeping, and as she wept, she stooped down and looketh into the Sepulchre, and seeth two Angels, which said unto her, *Woman, why weepest thou?* she said unto them, *Because they have taken my Lord, and I know not where they have laid him,* v. 13. And when she had thus said, she turned her self back, and saw Jesus standing, but knew not that it was Jesus; Jesus saith unto her, *Woman, why weepest thou; whom seekest thou?* she supposing him to be the Gardner, saith unto him, *Sir, if thou hast born him hence, tell me where thou hast laid him, and I will take him away.* Jesus saith unto her, *Mary;* she turned her self, and saith unto him, *Rabboni,* which is to say, *Master;* Jesus saith *(page 222 [sic])* unto her, *Touch me not, for I am not yet ascended to my Father; but go to my Disciples, and*

say unto them, *I ascend unto my Father and your Father, unto my God and your God:* Mary Magdalen came and told the Disciples this Message, *That she had seen the Lord, and that he had spoken these things unto her;* as you may read from *Vers.14. to 18.* how Christ conferred with *Mary,* and she with him; unto whom he first shewed himself after his Resurrection.

12*thly,* We find a certain Woman named *Lydia,* a seller of Purple, of the City of *Thyatira,* which worshipped God, whose Heart the Lord had opened, that she attended unto the things that were spoken of *Paul;* and she spake unto him, and them that were with him, saying, *If ye have judged me to be faithful to the Lord, come to my House, and abide there.* So she constrained them, *Acts* 16.14,15. And these her sayings, with the sayings and doings of many faithful Women more, were Chronicled by the Church for rare Patterns of Love to Christ, and his Disciples, to be Examples to their Childrens Children.

(page 223 [sic]) 13*thly,* and *lastly;* As to what I shall now write, we find a certain Damsel possessed with a Spirit of Divination, which brought her Master much Gain by Southsaying; the same followed *Paul,* and the other Apostles, and cryed out, saying, *These are the Servants of the Most High God, which shew unto us the Way of Salvation:* And this did she many days, *vers.* 17,18. of the 16th Chapter of the *Acts:* Insomuch that *Paul* was grieved for her, and had compassion on her, so that he turned, and said to the Spirit, *I command thee in the Name of Jesus Christ, to come out of her;* and he came out the same hour. From whence we may take notice, that she obtained the Reward of her Faith, and of her Testimony to the Truth; for as she believed and owned the Apostles to be the Servants of the Lord, so she was dispossessed of the evil Spirit by *Paul,* who spoke in the Name and Power of God.

Hereunto I might add divers others *instances* of believing Women, as that of *Dorcas,* who is call'd a Disciple of Christ Jesus, *Acts* 9.36. And likewise of *Priscilla,* who together with her *(page 224 [sic])* Husband *Aquilla,* took *Paul* home to their House, when he was first instructed in *Christianity,* and Expounded unto him the Way of God more perfectly, *Acts* 18.25,26. And afterwards were Fellow-helpers with *Paul* in Christ Jesus; as himself saith, *Rom.* 16.3.

And I might bring in *Philip's* four Daughters, which were Prophetesses, sent forth to encourage others.

And also *Phebe,* a Woman in Esteem in the Church of Christ, whom *Paul* commends, and calls, *Their Sister, and a Servant of the Church which is at* Cenchrea, *Rom.* 16.1.

And that Woman, to whom *John* the *Evangelist* sends his Epistle, ought not to be forgot, to wit, *The Elect Lady and her Children, whom I love in the Truth,* saith *John,* 2 *Epist. v.*1. But I remember I spoke of Brevity in the beginning, therefore I do but mention these Worthies in the latter end, because I find nothing said by them; thus I leave them, designing only to write out of Scripture the Sayings of the Women, and not to say much of them.

(page 225 [sic]) So I shall draw to a *Conclusion,* laying down this assertion, viz. That as Male and Female are made one in Christ Jesus, so Women receive an Office in the Truth as well as Men, and they have a Stewardship, and must give an account of their Stewardship to their Lord, as well as the Men: Therefore they ought to be faithful to God, and valiant for his Truth upon the Earth, that so they may receive the reward of the Righteousness, which is as they are faithful to their little, so shall they be made rulers over much: And as they patiently continue in well-doing, seeking Glory, Honour and Virtue, so shall they obtain a Crown of Immortality and Eternal Life, when they shall have passed through this Vale of Trouble and Tears; then shall that blessed Sentence be finally pronounced on them, *Well done good and faithful Servant, enter into the undisturbed Rest and Joy of your Lord.*

Elizabeth Bathurst

(page 226 [sic]) POSTSCRIPT

Although the *Woman* was first in Transgression, which brought in Death; yet was she made by the Power of the Lord, to bring in him *who is the Resurrection and the Life:* For this was the promise of the Father, *That the Seed of the Woman should bruise the Serpents Head,* Gen. 3.15. And it is long since fulfilled: For in the fulness of time Christ came, being born of a *Woman,* to wit, the *Virgin Mary,* as 'tis written, Mat. 1.23. So that it may be said, *As by Woman came in the Transgression and Degeneration; So by Woman also came in the Reconciliation and Restoration,* to wit, *Christ,* who came of the Woman's Seed; *He it is, who is the Healer of our Breaches, and restorer of our Paths:* And in him Male and Female are made all one, as saith the Apostle, Gal. 3.28.

THE END

LETTERS AND EPISTLES

Margaret Fell 1653, 1654

❦

Anne Gilman 1662

❦

Elizabeth Hendericks 1672

❦

Geertruyd Deriks Niesen 1677

❦

Mary Waite 1679

❦

Anne Whitehead and Mary Elson 1680

❦

Katharine Whitton 1681

❦

Dorcas Dole 1684

❦

Theophila Townsend 1686

❦

London Women's Meeting 1685

❦

Women's Yearly Meeting at York 1688

"WEAVING THE WEB OF COMMUNITY" LETTERS AND EPISTLES

by Margaret Benefiel

Introduction

Letters and epistles formed the backbone of the young Quaker movement. As a non-credal, non-hierarchical religious movement, ties between local worshipping communities were weak. Quaker ministers had no bishop to report to. Isolation, discouragement, and loss of vision constantly threatened to undo the movement.[1] Early Friends met this challenge partly by travelling in the ministry. However, travelling Friends could not cover all the the territory nor could they travel frequently enough to keep meetings current with each other's status and needs. Furthermore, during times of intense persecution, the travelling ministry was often severely curtailed. Letters and epistles supplemented travels, covered the large territory that travelling ministers could not, and got through in times of persecution. Through letters Friends offered encouragement and exhortation to individual meetings and also kept meetings in touch with one another. These letters and epistles wove the ties of community both within meetings and throughout the Religious Society of Friends.

Before examining these letters and epistles, some terminology needs to be addressed, specifically, the terms "letter," "epistle," and "community." Early Friends used the terms "letter" and "epistle" somewhat interchangeably. Although letters were most often addressed to individuals or small groups and tended to be more personal, and epistles were most often addressed to larger groups and tended to be more formal, the lines of distinction often blurred. For example, Margaret Fell's letters to individual Friends and epistles to groups of Friends shared an intimate, personal tone. And it was not unusual for a Friend, while corresponding with Friends, to refer to that correspondence as both a letter and an epistle.

Unlike the terms "letter" and "epistle," the term "community" is confusing not because early Friends varied their terms but because the term is used differently today than it was in the seventeenth century. The term "community," used broadly today, had a more specific meaning for early Friends. The women who wrote the letters included here had a strong sense of corporate unity with other Friends. For them, coming to

the Light meant not only a personal transformation, it also meant ini-
tiation into a group of believers. In fact, the personal transformation
could only happen, in their view, in the context of such a group. This
group was referred to by them as the body of Christ[2] or Christian community. Quakerism was not an individualistic faith. Quakers trusted
God's Spirit to draw each person into her place in the community and
expected her and her gifts to flourish in the context of being loved,
loving, and serving in that body. The individual became fully herself
only as she experienced her connection to the community. To be cut
off from the body was to lose one's source of life and to wither and die
spiritually. The letters included here conveyed this message and thus
served to weave the web of spiritual community among early Friends.

Margaret Fell

Foremost among the writers of letters and epistles was Margaret Fell.
Born in 1614, she grew up an earnest religious seeker. After she married
Judge Thomas Fell, she took a keen interest in the life of their Puritan
parish and "went often to hear the best ministers that came into our
parts . . . whom we frequently entertained at our house."[3] However, she
was dissatisfied until she heard George Fox preach in her parish in 1652.
She was convinced then and became a leader among Friends almost
immediately. Fell used her home as a center for communication, nurture, and support of Quaker ministers. Her letters kept ministers and
meetings in touch with one another.

Of the five early letters (1653-54) of Margaret Fell included here,
two address specific Friends in prison and three address Friends in general. Through her use of the image of the body of Christ and her sense
of the solidarity of all Friends with Friends prisoners, Fell drew her readers
into an awareness of their interdependence. For Fell, the
interconnectedness of spiritual community was palpable. In these
letters, she understood her task to be calling Friends back to their
initial powerful experience of the "Light of Christ:" "walk in the
Light, where the Fellowship and the Unity is."[4] As they lived in the
Light daily, as they were faithful to the "measure of Light" they had
been given, Fell taught that Friends would see the invisible God made
manifest, which occurred primarily in community.

In her letters to Friends in prison, Fell set their experience in
the context of God's larger work in the world. By placing imprisoned Friends in continuity with such biblical figures as Daniel,

Fell transformed the images of imprisonment and freedom. Imprisoned Friends were portrayed as suffering in solidarity with all those who had suffered for their faith in ages past as well as with other Friends of their day. She described them as God's underground agents, challenging the unjust political and religious order, in the vanguard of God's movement for change in the world. Friends, as characterized in Fell's letters, were no longer considered dangerous criminals or the castoffs of society, but respected, faithful heroes, leaders in the community of Friends. In fact, Friends' freedom in Christ made those Friends in prison freer than those outside prison walls, who were "imprisoned" by their idols and appetites. Fell's images connected imprisoned Friends to the past, to one another, and to other Friends, stressing the interdependence of the body of Christ.

In her letters addressed to Friends in general, Fell again called Friends back to the Light which would in turn illuminate their interconnectedness in spiritual community. For example, in the second 1654 *Epistle to Friends* included here, Fell uses Paul's image of the body of Christ. As individual Friends responded to the Light, they would begin to "see the whole Body full of Light"[5] and see the invisible God made manifest in their community. The Light-filled body was the manifestation of God's presence. As Friends experienced more and more of the love and respect for different members and saw various members freed to live into their part of the whole, they would be experiencing God more fully. Furthermore, the body included Friends beyond their locale. Fell reminded Friends that some members in other places bore the "heat of the day" in persecutions and imprisonments and that those members deserved respect, prayer, encouragement, support, and love.

Fell was not the only writer whose letters wove together the Quaker community. Others, like Anne Gilman, Elizabeth Hendericks, Geertruyd Direks Niesen, Mary Waite, Anne Whitehead, Mary Elson, Katharine Whitton, Dorcas Dole, and Theophila Townsend wrote in the same vein. Samples of their writings are included here in chronological order to demonstrate both their contributions to community and how such contributions changed over time.

Anne Gilman

In 1662, Anne Gilman (d. 1686) wrote *An Epistle to Friends: Being a Tender Salutation to the Faithful in God Everywhere*. Written during the

renewed persecution of Friends under the newly-restored monarch
Charles II, this epistle emphasized the message of hope, a present hope
which arose out of living with the present Christ. Though little is known
about Gilman, her writing exemplifies her deep faith in the power of
God and the courage which came from that faith. Besides writing to
Friends, she wrote *A Letter to Charles, King of England* (1662), exhort-
ing him to stop the persecution of Friends, and *To the Inhabitants of the
Earth* (1663), inviting them into the truth discovered by Friends.

Elizabeth Hendericks

Elizabeth Hendericks (fl. 1655-78) wrote *An Epistle to Friends in England
To be Read in their Assemblies in the Fear of the Lord* from Amsterdam in
1672. She had been one of the first four Quakers to arrive in Amsterdam
from England in 1655 (the other three were also women). Later, she
visited Princess Elizabeth of Bohemia twice. In 1678 she travelled in
the ministry with Geertruyd Deriks Niesen in the Rhineland, where
the Duke of Holstein censured her for preaching in public.[6] This epistle
urges Friends under persecution to "keep yourselves close to [God's]
Light"[7] so that they might feel God's power, be judged and purified,
know God's will and counsel, and be brought into unity with other
Friends, thus strengthening the Quaker community. Hendericks wrote
five other epistles, most of them to Friends in Holland and Germany.

Geertruyd Deriks Niesen (also Gertrude Dirrecks)

In 1677, Geertruyd Deriks Niesen (d. 1687) wrote *An Epistle to be Communicated to Friends, and to be read in the Fear of the Lord in their Men and
Womens Meetings, and other Meetings; only among Friends, as they in the
Wisdom of God shall see meet and serviceable.* Deriks was a Dutch woman
who settled at Colchester. Women's and men's meetings had been set
up for nearly a decade by this time, and Deriks viewed them as prime
audiences for her message. Deriks wanted to call Friends back to the
high standards by which she believed earlier Friends had lived. Her
principal concerns lay in two areas: children and trading. She urged
Friends to take seriously their child-rearing responsibilities, above all
exhorting them to be good examples to their children.[8] Second, she
pointed out the economic injustice which resulted from financial over-
extension in trading, and called Friends to just trading practices.[9]

Mary Waite

Mary Waite (d. 1689) wrote *A Warning to All Friends, who Professeth the Everlasting Truth of God, which he hath Revealed and made manifest in this his Blessed Day, (whether on this Side, or Beyond the Seas)* in 1679. A native of York, Waite labored with her husband (the local distributor of Quaker books and tracts), to advance Quakerism in her area. She frequently appealed to the authorities to stop the persecution of Friends, and she herself was imprisoned in York in 1684. Like Fell and Deriks, Waite wanted Friends to stay close to God and maintain high standards of conduct. Writing during a time when persecution had lessened, Waite warned Friends against "lukewarmness."[10] She exhorted Friends to allow the Light to cleanse and purify them, so that God's life and works might shine forth powerfully through them.

Anne Whitehead and Mary Elson

In 1680, Anne Whitehead (1624-86) and Mary Elson (c. 1623-1706) wrote *An Epistle for True Love, Unity and Order in the Church of Christ.* Convinced in 1654 in London, Whitehead travelled in the ministry as one of the earliest Quaker women preachers. She spent time in prison and later worked with Rebecca Travers and Sarah Blackborow to establish women's meetings.[11] She remained an influential London Friend for over three decades, until her death at age sixty-three. Mary Elson, convinced by Whitehead in London in 1659, helped her, Travers, and Blackborow to set up women's meetings. One of the London Quaker meetings met in Elson's home. In this epistle, Whitehead and Elson exhorted younger Friends to observe the advice and counsel of the elders. They also defended women's meetings against their detractors, outlining their history and the needs which they fulfilled.[12]

Katharine Whitton

In 1681, Katharine Whitton (fl. 1670-92) wrote *An Epistle to Friends Everywhere: to be Distinctly Read in their Meetings When Assembled together in the Fear of the Lord.* A York Friend, Whitton was fined in 1670-71 under Charles II's Second Conventicle Act.[13] Active in the York women's meeting, she signed their epistles in 1686, 1688, and 1692. In the epistle included here, Whitton delivered a message of judgment, claiming that the Day of the Lord was coming soon and that Friends needed to allow

God to cleanse and purify them now so that they would be able to stand in the day of judgment. Though the purpose of the epistle is to warn of judgment, the theme of hope stands out more strongly. Whitton uses more references to and images of hope than of judgment. According to Whitton, the judgment was merely a short (albeit intense) preparation for something much more glorious. For example Whitton believed that "the time is come wherein [God] is pouring of his Spirit upon his Sons, and upon his Daughters, Servants and Hand-maids, and enduing them with his Heavenly Wisdom."[14] In addition to this epistle, Whitton wrote a testimony for Robert Lodge (1691) and a testimony for Sarah Beckwith (1692).

Dorcas Dole

In 1684 Dorcas Dole (d. 1716) wrote *A Salutation of My Endeared Love to the Faithful in All Places That Bear their Testimony for the Lord, and Keep in the Lowliness to Truth as it is in Jesus* from Newgate prison in Bristol where she was incarcerated from 1682 to 1685. A Bristol native imprisoned during the last serious persecution before the Toleration Act of 1689, Dole wrote all her publications from prison and addressed all but this one to Bristol inhabitants. Here, Dole emphasized hope in suffering. Like Margaret Fell when she wrote to Friends in prison, Dole stressed the freedom and joy available in persecution and suffering, and viewed suffering Friends as heroes and leaders in the Religious Society of Friends, not as the outcasts that society made them out to be. Dole reminded Friends that "[the Lord] delights in such Instruments that stand up Valiently [sic] for his holy Name on the earth."[15] Dole also wrote to the Friends children of Bristol, who continued to meet for worship when all the adults were in prison, in *A Salutation and Seasonable Exhortation to Children* (1682).[16]

Theophila Townsend

Theophila Townsend (1656-92) wrote *An Epistle of Love to Friends in the Womens Meetings in London, &c., to be read among them in the fear of God*. An inhabitant of Gloucester, she was imprisoned there in 1681 for preaching, nearly died in prison several times, and remained there until 1686, the year she wrote this epistle. In it, Townsend praised the London Women's Meetings for their service of God, consoled them in their recent loss of their pillar Anne Whitehead, and exhorted them to remain faithful to the Quaker testimony of simplicity. Townsend felt

that the London Women's Meetings had drifted from their earlier commitment to simplicity in dress and consequently were losing their zeal
for God. Since the London Women's Meetings served as an example to
women's meetings all over England, Townsend urged them to return to
their earlier seriousness.[17]

The London Women's Meeting

Besides letters and epistles written by individual women, seventeenth-
century Friends produced epistles written by groups of women. These
also served to build the Friends' community. For example, the London
Women's Meeting whom Theophila Townsend addressed in 1686 had
written *A Living Testimony From the Power and Spirit of our Lord Jesus
Christ in our Faithful Womens Meeting and Christian Socity* [sic] the previous year. Signed by Mary Foster, Mary Elson,[18] Anne Travice, Ruth
Crowch, Susannah Dew, and Mary Plumstead on behalf of the other
members of the London Women's Meeting, this epistle demonstrates
the importance of women's meetings to the work of weaving community among Friends. Many early Quaker women used Paul's image of
the body whose head is Christ, with many parts but one purpose, to
testify to their experience of this unity amidst diversity even among
themselves. Their strong sense of the inter-connectedness of all believers modeled a faith community among themselves and held up a vision
of it for other Friends. They upheld each other and the vision by faithfully carrying out the tasks that came to be associated with women's
meetings. As delineated in this epistle, these tasks included helping
poor families, overseeing marriages, supporting newly-married women,
supporting mothers of young children, and caring for the sick: all es-
sential tasks in the building and sustaining of the Quaker community.
Finally, like Elson and Whitehead, these women defended the importance of women's meetings against their detractors. They claimed that
God's Spirit empowered the women's meetings and that their work in
them was as much ministry as Spirit-led speaking in meeting for worship or powerful public preaching.

The Women's Yearly Meeting at York

Like the London Women's Meeting, the Women's Yearly Meeting at
York also issued epistles. Included here is the 1688 epistle, interesting
partly because the women at their yearly meeting decided to append to

it Mary Waite's 1679 *A Warning to All Friends*.[19] Signed on behalf of the meeting by Katharine Whitton,[20] Judith Boulby, Elizabeth Sedman, Frances Taylor, Mary Waite herself, Deborah Winn, Elizabeth Beckwith, and Mary Lindley, this epistle begins with an account of the mighty power of God these women experienced in their gathered meeting. They claimed that God "filled our meeting with his living presence, . . . and opened the fountain of life unto us, and caused the streams of his love freely to flow among us."[21] Like the London women, these women testified to their experience of spiritual community and held that up as a vision for all Friends. With Mary Waite, the York women felt that with the decrease in persecution (persecution had diminished rapidly over the previous few years and the Toleration Act would come in 1689), Friends had become lax in their behavior. Like Fell, Deriks, and Waite, the York women wanted to call Friends back to the high standards and the self-denial that they believed had been present in the early days.

Conclusion

Letters and epistles, then, both those written by individual women and those written by groups of women, performed the important task of weaving together the Quaker community. During times of persecution, this meant offering hope, encouragement, and support. Fell's early letters of solidarity with Friends prisoners and of interconnectedness with all other Friends, and Gilman's and Hendericks' epistles of hope in suffering and of unity with Christ and with other Friends, illustrate this. During the late 1670's, when persecution had lessened, the focus shifted. Warning against "lukewarmness," women like Deriks and Waite saw the task of building Friends community as one of calling Friends back to earlier high standards. Whitehead and Elson, as well as Whitton, continued in this vein. Dole, who wrote from prison in 1684, returned to the theme of hope in suffering. Townsend and the Women's Meetings, writing in the few years following, in a context in which most Friends were free from the immediate threat of persecution, again emphasized seriousness in the faith and high standards of conduct. Friends women took seriously their roles as weavers and menders of the fabric of community.

Notes

1. This was especially true during times of persecution. For example, during the mid-1660s when the Clarendon Code (a group of laws designed by Lord Chancellor Clarendon to enforce conformity with the Church of England) was in full force, many Quaker leaders were in prison and local meetings were suffering severe persecution. Morale was low and Friends felt isolated from one another. The movement among Friends was in danger. For a further discussion of this period, see John Punshon, *Portrait in Grey* (London: Quaker Home Service, 1984), pp. 82-85.

2. Friends appropriated Paul's image of the Body of Christ from I Cor. 12.

3. Margaret Fell, *A Brief Collection of Remarkable Passages and Occurrences* (London: J. Sowle, 1710), p. 2.

4. Fell, *A Brief Collection*, p. 48.

5. Fell, *A Brief Collection*, p. 56

6. Maureen Bell, George Parfitt, & Simon Shepherd, eds., *A Biographical Dictionary of English Women Writers, 1580-1720* (Boston: G. K. Hall & Co., 1990), p. 103. I am indebted to Bell and Parfitt for much of the biographical information on other women in this introduction, as well.

7. Elizabeth Hendericks, *An Epistle to Friends in England* (n. p.: n. p., 1672), p. 6.

8. Geertruyd Deriks Niesen, *An Epistle to be Communicated to Friends, and to be read in the Fear of the Lord in their Men and Womens Meetings, and other Meetings; only among Friends, as they in the Wisdom of God shall see meet and serviceable* (N. p.: n. p., 1677), pp. 3-4.

9. Deriks, *Epistle*, pp. 5-8. Deriks Niesen also wrote two other epistles: *A Letter to Friends* (written in Dutch to Dutch Friends in 1680) and *An Epistle to Friends in Holland, Friesland, the Palatinate, etc.* (written in Dutch in 1682).

10. Mary Waite, *A Warning to All Friends, who Professeth the Everlasting Truth of God, which he hath Revealed and made manifest in this his Blessed Day, (whether on this Side, or Beyond the Seas)* (York: n. p., 1679), p. 11.

11. On women's meetings, see Mary Garman's introduction to this book, pp. 1, 5, 6, 9, 10, 16.

12. Whitehead and Elson also wrote *For the King and Both Houses of Parliament* (1670, with others) and *A Tender and Christian Testimony to Young People* (1685).

13.   The Conventicle Act (1664) had outlawed religious meetings of more than five people other than those of the Church of England, fining those who disobeyed. The Second Conventicle Act (1670) increased the penalties in an effort to ruin financially nonconformists. In addition, it made preaching at or harboring a conventicle illegal, and encouraged informers against Friends and other nonconformists. For more on the Conventicle Acts and related legislation, see John Punshon, *Portrait in Grey* (London: Quaker Home Service, 1984), pp. 82-90.

14.   Katharine Whitton, *An Epistle to Friends Everywhere: to Be Distinctly Read in their Meetings* (London: Benjamin Clark, 1681), p. 8.

15.   Dorcas Dole, *A Salutation of my Endeared Love to the Faithful in all places That bear their Testimony for the Lord, and keep in the Lowliness to Truth as it is in Jesus* (London: John Bringhurst, 1685), p. 2.

16.   In addition, Dole wrote *To You that Have Been Professors of the Truth of God in the City of Bristol, etc.* (1683); *A Salutation of My Endeared Love in God's Holy Fear and Dread, and for the Clearing of My Conscience once more unto you of that City of Bristol, amongst whom My Soul Hath some Years Travelled Many a Dreadful Exercise* (1683, with Elizabeth Stirredge); and *Once More a Warning to thee, O England, but more Particularly to the Inhabitants of the City of Bristol* (1683).

17.   Townsend also wrote *A Testimony Concerning the Life and Death of Jane Whitehead* (1676), one of the testimonies in *Some Testimonies of the Life, Death and Sufferings of Amariah Drewet* (1687), *A Word of Counsel, in the Love of God the Persecuting Magistrates and Clergy, for them to Read and Consider, but Chiefly to those of the City and County of Gloucester, etc.* (1687), and *An Epistle of Tender Love to all Friends that are Tender Hearted* (1690).

18.   Co-author of *Epistle for Love, Unity, and Order* (1680), see p. 447.

19.   See p. 447.

20.   Author of *An Epistle to Friends Everywhere* (1681), see pp. 447, 502-12.

21.   *Epistle from the Women's Yearly Meeting at York* (York: n. p., 1688), p. 530.

An Epistle of M. Fell's *to Friends, 1653.*

FRiends, whose Minds are turn'd to the Light, which comes from Jesus Christ, which never changeth, whose Light enlightens every one coming into the World; in it abide, and in it walk, and to it be faithful and obedient in your Measures, that with it your Minds may be guided up to God, who is the Father of Lights, that you may bring your Deeds to the Light, to try whether they are wrought in God.

(page 48) My Dear Hearts, God is Light, and in him is no Darkness at all, the work that he works, is in the Light, which is pure, and leads to purity; which Light testifies against all Sin, and all the deeds of Darkness, and all Earthliness, Lust, Pride, and Covetousness, which is Idolatry; whose Minds turns from the Light, turns into the Idolatry, and into the Sorcery, under the dark Power, and into the Witchery, where the Devil hath Power.

Therefore if you love your Souls, which is Immortal, abide in the Light, and love the Light, and walk in the Light, where the Fellowship and the Unity is.—For if you walk in the Light, and abide in the Light; which is Low and Meek, and wait in Silence and Faithfulness, and Obedience, wait Patiently, and you shall have the Light of Life. Who hath Life, hath the Son, and who hath not the Son, hath not Life. And be still and low, that you may receive the teachings of the Lord; and learn of him, who is Low and Meek, and hearken diligently, and keep your Minds to the Light, that so your Souls may live. And the Light which comes from Jesus Christ, which is the Messenger of the Living God, sent from God, may bring your Souls out of *Egypt*, and out of the Fall, from under the Curse, which Disobedience hath brought upon all Men. Dear hearts, this is the Day of your Visitation, and Salvation, if you be faithful and obedient, for the everlasting God, which is the Life, Light and Substance of Life, is risen, and arising, and raising up the Dead to hear the voice of the Son of God, and they that hear do live. And the dead Bones is coming together, and standing up; yea, the Earth is giving up her Dead, if you be faithful to the measure of God's Spirit, by which he hath quickned you, this ye shall see, and witness; therefore

(Page numbers of original document appear in text as *page _.*)

go not forth, nor look out to them, that say lo here is Christ, or loe there is Christ, for no other Name under Heaven, but by this Name Christ Jesus, who is the Light which *John* bears witness to, which is *(page 49)* come a Light into the World, and lighteth every Man that cometh into the World; this is the Light that shines in a dark place, which you may do well to take heed unto, until the day dawn, and the day star arise in your hearts; and this you will witness if you be faithful to the Light; but if you turn from the Light, and hate the Light, then the Light makes you manifest that your deeds are evil, and that is your Condemnation, the Light that is come into the world, which you can never flee from, but wherever you go, the Light, that is the condemnation of the World will pursue you, and that of God in your Consciences will be your Condemnation. And this is your Teacher, and is always present with you, if you keep down to it, and close to it, it will keep your Minds low, and humble, and tender, and it will quicken you; and so you will come to know the pure Law, the righteous Law of God, which is the School-Master until Christ. And this is not the Letter without you, but this is the faithful Promise of God, which he hath promised to those who are taught of him, which is the substance of the New Covenant which he hath made; who hath said, *I will put my Laws in their hearts, and write them in their inward parts*. Therefore with the Light in you, which lighteth the Candle of the Lord in you, with which Candle he searcheth *Jerusalem*, let this Light search you, and try you, and mind whether you have receiv'd the New Covenant, which is everlasting, which never shall be broken, which is the Law written in the Heart; which Law is pure, which Law is Spiritual, Just, and Good. So examine and try your own selves, for if you know not that Christ is in you, you are Reprobates.

So dear hearts, mind your Eternal Teacher, which is the Preacher of Righteousness, which speaks to the Spirits in Prison, for you cannot hear without this Preacher, nor any can speak to the Spirits in Prison, but he who is sent of the living God, which *(page 50)* is now made manifest, he that is anointed to preach glad tidings to the Poor, is come; he that gives liberty to the Captives is come, he that sets the Oppressed free is come; they who are faithful and obedient shall witness Redemption, and *Zion* is arising, for her Light is come; *Arise Zion, for thy Light is come*—So here is your Teacher, and your Preacher, and your Redeemer, and your Saviour, if you be obedient and faithful to the measure of this gift of God, as it ariseth, and as it teaches, and as it makes the will of God manifest, and as it moves; if you be faithful and obedient to this, you shall eat the good of the Land. So the Lord God Almighty of Life and Power, keep you faithful and obedient to your measure made manifest, and preserve you in that of him, which is arising and quickning you, to his everlasting Praise; and so you will come to witness for the Lord in your measure, and by the invisible eye (which is the Light) and if you standing single in the Light, and if your eye be single in it, you will see the whole Body full of Light, and this leads to the invisible God; and by your measure of this is the invisible God made manifest; and this is the invisible eye which sees God, that no mortal eye can behold or reach unto; and here is your Teacher if you never hear Man speak; and here is your Teacher, if you be faithful to the measure of God, and to the leading and guiding and moving of it, you will come to witness Christ the Shepherd of your Souls, and the fat Pastures; and it will lead you to God, the Father of Lights, which all the World, and all the Ministry, and all the Worships of the World, which are out of the Light, are ignorant of; nor any that ever took upon them to teach from the Letter without them, or from an outward Call, can ever say they saw God, or knew him, or ever heard his Voice. So Life and Death is set before you; and if you be obedient to the Light, which never changeth, it will lead you out of death, and out of the fall from under the Curse, into the *(page 51)* Covenant of Life, if you be faithful and obedient unto the Death: And the everlasting God of Life and Power, strengthen, nourish and refresh you, to his everlasting Praise and Glory; and so wait for the living Food, to come from the living God,

M. Fell.

(page 51)

A Letter to Francis Howgill, *and others, when they were Prisoners at* Appleby, 1653.

DEar Brethren, *Francis Howgill,* with the rest with thee who are Prisoners of the Lord, called Faithful and Chosen, abiding Faithful in the will of God, and there stand, you have Peace, you have Joy, you have Boldness, and you stand over all the World, standing in Righteousness; and there is a pure discerning, springing, which is refresh'd by you. I do see the secret Work of God going on in Peoples Minds; look not at the hard Rocks, nor look not at Bryars, nor look not at the Thorns, nor at the Mountains, nor the Coldness, for well it may be so; for there have been no Vine-dressers, nor no Plow-men; there's none to Dress the Ground, no Seeds-men to sow the Seeds, and therefore these Seeds-men sow'd in vain. The true Seeds-men must not regard the Weather, the Winds that blow, they sow the Seed before the Winter, There is a Winter, and there is a Summer; there is a time to sow the Seed, there is a time to reap, so the Lord give thee an understanding in all things, and the glorious God keep you in his Glory, and in his Love, keep you wholly in his Power to himself, for there is never no fainting, but to that Mind which goes from the pure within, that will faint, which runs for a while, and hath a joy in the Earth. The Earthly Mind is in the Earth, and so it faints, but I know *(page 52)* there is that in you which is Eternal, and stands in the will of God, being guided by that which is Eternal, unto God which is Eternal, out of your own wills; and you will see how all the Plotting of their Minds which are Earthly, and with their Earthly Portions, and Earthly Wisdom which will be broken in pieces; for that which is Earthly, holds for that which is Earthly, above the Seed of God; and that which Prisons the Seed in the particular, that makes a bond to Prison them where it is risen, but no Earthly band can hold, but what is Eternal will stand, and the other will be broken to pieces. Oh therefore wait, for the Lord is doing great things; for this Darkness, and this Heathenish Ministry and dark Power hath long reigned. Now God hath raised up his glorious Light, and brought the Life and Immortality to light in your Understandings; therefore wait on the Lord alone, and rejoyce that you are made worthy to suffer for his sake, and be faithful in what you know, treading and trampling over the deceit, and the Lord God of Power keep you faithful, bold, and pure, every way in his Power, to his everlasting Praise. And I am well, praised, praised be the Lord. The Lord keep all Friends that way in savouriness, to discern the voice of a Stranger, from the voice of our Lord Jesus Christ, that they may be kept clean from the pollutions of the World, and out of the Mire and Clay (up to God who is pure) for all must be accounted so, in respect of him, the God and Father of our Lord Jesus Christ, to whom be all Praise, and Glory and Honour for ever and ever.—So with my Love and Prayers to God for you all, I rest, blessed be the God and Father of our Lord and Saviour Jesus Christ, who keeps you, and preserves in his Power, for his own work; therefore look not at your Liberty, nor at Men, nor at Time, but at the Lord, who will be your Portion Eternally. Your Reward is in the Lord, the Lord hath a secret Work there amongst you, there must be a great deal of plucking *(page 53)* up, and casting down, and the wild Beasts driven out of the Field; therefore look at the Lord alone, see him present with you, in his Spirit and Power lifting up your heads above all your Enemies; to whom, be Praises, Honour and Glory for ever, whose Mercies endure for ever.

M. Fell.

(page 53)

An Epistle of M. Fell *to Friends,* 1654.

TO all my Dear Brethren and Sisters who are in the Light, which Christ Jesus hath enlightned you withal, I Warn you and Charge you from the Lord God, that you be faithful and obedient unto the measure of Grace which he hath given to every one of you to profit withal, and that the Light of Christ Jesus in every one of you, lead you, and guide you, that with it, you may see all that which would lead you out from it, and that with it you may see the Thief, and the Betrayer, which draws back from it. And beware that ye be not too hasty in going before the Light, and acting those things which are to be condemned with the Light, but bring all to the Light to be proved, and tried, that there be no works of Darkness among you: But that you may be kept in the fear of the Lord God, and abide in that which keeps in his presence, the Light; for Dreadful and Terrible is the Lord God to the Disobedient, and those that will not that he should reign over them, must be bound in Chains, and cast into utter Darkness.

Therefore, my Dear Hearts be Faithful every one in your particular measure of Gods Gift which he hath given you, and on the invisible wait in silence, and patience, and in obedience to that which opens the Mystery of God, and leads to the invisible God, which no mortal Eye can reach unto, or behold. Therefore as you tender your own Souls, *(page 54)* and your Eternal Good, keep in the fear of the Lord, and be low, that the Plant of the Lord may take Root downward in you: And that none of you fly up above your Measure, and so the airy Spirit get into the Imagination, and there rest, and make an Image like Truth; and so you eat that which is forbidden, and break the Command of the Lord, and so betray the Simplicity, and vail that which is Pure of God; which, if you are constant in Obedience to it, it will preserve in the Simplicity, and lead out of the Pollutions of the World, and the Filthiness of the Flesh; in that which is pure, you worship God in Spirit and in Truth: And now is the Lord seeking for such Worshippers in this his Day; which Day makes manifest, who turns out of the Eternal and Invisible, into the Imaginations, or Images or Forms, though it be of the Everlasting Truth; if it be only a Form, or a Colour, it cannot stand, but it is seen, and discover'd, and known, where the Lord rules.

Therefore all Friends, let the Eternal Spirit search and try every particular, and see what you are cover'd withal; yea, let the living Principle of God in you all, examine what ye enjoy and possess of him, who is Eternal; and what is of him, will stand in his Presence, who is a Consuming Fire to all that is not of him: And what ye do enjoy of that, which is Eternal of God, begotten of him by the Immortal Word, abiding, and being faithful in that, ye shall witness a Growth in the Eternal, in the Inward Man, according to your Measures. He that is in the Light, if he walks in the Light, and is Faithful to it, he shall have the Light of Life; and they that can witness the Life really and in truth, to them the Babe is born, the Son given: For, *he that hath the Son, hath Life; and he that hath not the Son, hath not Life.* And those that can witness this, wait to be made free with the Son; for, who the *Son makes free*, they are *free indeed.* So to the Measure of God's Grace in every one of you I speak, that with it you may *(page 55)* search and try where you are, and what you can really and truly, in the presence of God, witness born up in you; that you do not deceive your Souls, and worship the Works of your own Hands; for God is not worshipped, but in that which is Spirit and Truth.

And I warn you, and charge you, in the Presence of the living God, that you beware of Strife amongst you, and of that Spirit which exalts it self: For, *he that exalts himself, shall be brought low;* the Lord hath said it: And your Lord and Master, Christ Jesus, knows that Spirit, and will bring it down to the Dust. Therefore, in the Fear of the Lord God stand, and be low and humble; for he that brings down, and humbles that Nature, which would be up, he shall be exalted. So learn of him, who is Low and Meek, who makes clean the House in every particular. And beware of Hastiness, or Forwardness, in speaking many Words, except it be from a pure Discerning, of a pure Moving; and that you discern what you speak from, and what ye speak to; and who speaks here, is a Minister. For your speaking Words at random, when the Power moves, under pretence of a Burthen; which Burthen is the Earthly Part in your selves, and the Words that you speak belongs to your own Particulars: This being spoken out to others, and not from a clear discerning what it is to, then others take it, and Judge it. So I warn you to be silent, and to wait low in the Silence, until the Word be committed to you to minister: And none to strive for Mastery, but each to esteem others better than themselves; and that there be no Deadness, nor Dullness, nor Slothfulness amongst you. And likewise I warn you from the Lord, who are so forward and rash in Judging your Brethren and Sisters, to beware of it, lest ye be found the Hypocrites; and that ye be sure, that that which you judge in another, be cast out in your selves. For whoso-ever judges another, and hath not the Beam cast out, is an Hypocrite, and *(page 56)* shall not escape the Judgments of God; it is that which Christ Jesus abhors, who is the Judge of the World; and the Apostle likewise testifies against it. And it is speaking in the Imaginations of Truth, both in your Speaking and Judging, that causes Divisions and Strife among you; and all this is cursed from God, and shut out of the Kingdom for ever. Therefore in that which is Pure and Eternal, which is one in all, which leads into Love and Unity, dwell and abide faithful, and constant, and obedient, and ye shall eat the Good of the Land: And here is no Strife nor Wrangling; yea, this leads to Purity and Holi-ness, without which none shall see the Lord; and to the Church of the First Born, which is in God, where he is one, and his Name one. My dear Hearts, you are in the way to this, if you keep in the strait and narrow Way, which leads to Life; and be faithful unto the Lord God, in your Measures, unto the end, you shall come hither.

So to you I have cleared my Conscience of the Burthen that lay upon me: And the Lord God Almighty, of Life and Power, keep and preserve you all Faithful, in your particular Measures, to the Lord God. And I warn you, and charge you, in the presence of the Living God, that all Flesh be silent before the Lord, until the Eternal Power rise in you, and speak.

Your dear Sifter in the Truth of God,

M. F.

(page 56)

An Epistle to Friends, by M. F., 1654.

TO all my dear Brethren and Sisters, who are in the Light, Children of the Light, who are Obedient to the Light, which is the Head of the whole Body; in which Light, every particular, dwell and stand single, and you shall see the whole Body full of Light: For this leads into the Unity *(page 57)* and Oneness, which is in the Body, though many Members. So my dear Hearts, in that which is the Light of the whole Body, which leads into the Unity, to that be subject and obedient, that you may be serviceable to the whole Body; and give freely up to the Service of the Head, which is one, and but one in all; and who are faithful, the one Spirit makes subject: Even so are ye called in one Hope of your Calling, where there is one Lord, one Faith, one Baptism, one God and Father of all, who is above all, and through all, and in you all.

So all my dear Brethren and Sisters, in this which is Eternal, and leads into the Unity and Oneness, be Faithful and Obedient; be of one Mind, and live in Peace: For the Promise is but to one Seed; and you are all one in Christ Jesus, who have Faith in him, to whom all the Promises are *Yea* and *Amen*. And now is the Lord's Day made manifest, wherein he requires of you, in your particular measures, to be serviceable to the Body, in your respective places: For there are many Members, and but one Body; and the Head cannot say to the Feet, *I have no need of you;* for every one, in their measures, may be serviceable to the whole Body, in what is called for, and required; and who dwells in the Light, it makes subject, to be serviceable to the Body. And now, that nothing may be kept back, but as you have received freely, so freely you may administer, in Obedience to the one Eternal Light; you may be serviceable to the whole Body. And as the Lord hath loved you with his Everlasting Love, and visited you, and hath made manifest his Eternal Light in you, which is the Way that leads to the Father, and hath raised up the Eternal Witness in you, of his Everlasting Love. So let that Love constrain you to love one another, and be serviceable to one another; and that every one may be made willing to suffer for the Body's sake, and that there may be no Rent in the Body, but that the Members have the same Care one over another; and where *(page 58)* one Member suffers, all the Members may suffer with it: And here is the Unity of the Spirit, and the Bond of Peace. And that you cannot be unmindful, nor are you ignorant of the present Suffering and Service of many Members of the Body in this our Day, who are in Bonds and Imprisonment, and hard Persecution and Cruelty, which is acted in the Will of Man, upon the Righteous Seed, which is of the Body. And others there are, that are sent forth into the Service of the most high God, as Lambs among Wolves, who are made willing and subject to give their Backs to the Smiter; yea, to lay down their Lives for the Body's sake: And great and hard Persecutions have been suffer'd for the Testimony of the Lord Jesus.

Now, that every particular Member of the Body may be sensible of the Hardship and Sufferings of others, and be willing and serviceable in their places, in what the Lord requires; and to remember those that are in Bonds, as bound with them; and them that suffer Adversity, as you being your selves also in the Body; and that you may bear one another's Burthens, and be equally yoked in the Suffering. Our Friends in *Westmoreland* have born the Heat of the Day, and many have been sent forth into the Lord's Service from thence, and that hath caused the Burthen to lie heavy upon the rest of the Friends thereabouts; and most of all on our Friends at *Kendal*, who have been very serviceable in their places to the Truth, to the whole Body, to those who have been sent forth into the Ministry, and to them that have suffer'd Imprisonment, and for dispersing Books, and several other things that have been needful, wherein they have been serviceable to the Truth, I bear them record.

I see in the Eternal Unchangeable Light of God, that all and every Member, who are of the Body, ought to be serviceable in their places, and to administer freely, according to their Ability, as they have received of the Lord freely: For *Jerusalem,* *(page 59)* which is from above, is free, which is the Mother of us all; and who are here, are one. So, my dear Brethren and Sisters, let Brotherly Love continue; that every one, as the Lord moves you, and opens your Hearts, you may administer; that you may come into the Oneness in all things, and in that abide, which dwells in Love and Unity, which is one for evermore. And so you come to the fulfilling of the Scriptures, in your measures, and the Practice of all the Saints in the Light, that ever went before.

So, God Almighty of Life and Power, preserve and keep you in his everlasting Love and Unity.

Your dear Sifter in the Everlafting Truth,

M. F.

(page 59)

An Epiſtle to Friends, that were Priſoners in Lancaſter-Caſtle, by M. Fell, 1654.

Ear Brethren, in the unchangeable, everlasting, powerful Truth of God; my Love salutes you in the Heavenly Union: I am present with you, who are obedient to the measure of the Eternal Light, which never changes, and who abides in the Oneness of the Spirit, and in the Bond of Peace, which never can be broken, nor taken from you: Here is Freedom, which the World knows not; to the Measure of God in every particular made manifest, and obeyed, and lived in, doth my Love flow freely to you. My dear Hearts, be faithful in every Particular to your own Measure of Grace, made manifest and enjoyed; and in that which is Eternal, wait continually, I charge you in the Presence of the Living God, that you do not neglect your several Measures, which the Lord God of Life and Power hath given you to profit withal; that so you may come to receive Living Vertue from the Living God, and be fed *(page 60)* with the Living Bread, and drink of the Living Water of the Spiritual Rock, which they drank of in the Wilderness. And be subject and patient and do not look out, nor be weary, neither be of a doubtful Mind: for the same God you Suffer for, and by the same you are Preserved, which *Daniel, Shadrach, Meshach* and *Abednego* was; and by the same Spirit ye are preserved, which they were preserved by; therefore stand faithful and bold for the Truth upon the Earth, which strikes at the Foundation of all Deceit and Idolatry. And in the pure Eternal Light of God abide: which is the Stone cut out of the Mountain without hands; which strikes at the feet of the Image: which the Disobedient part, which look'd out from the Eternal, and is shut out from God, the Will of Man hath set up; and in that which is Eternal and Invisible, which overturns and brings down all Foundations, doth your Strength, and Victory, and Conquest stand, which is the Condemnation of the World? and this is that which must sanctifie you, and justifie you, and present you pure and holy in his Sight; and here is your Safety, and here is your Peace and Joy, and Eternal Inheritance which never fades away: And the Lord God of Power keep you, and preserve you Faithful and Bold to his Eternal Glory, to whom be Eternal Praises for evermore.

M. F.

AN

Epiſtle to Friends;

Being a Tender

SALUTATION

To the FAITHFUL in God everywhere.

ALSO, A

LETTER

TO

CHARLES, KING of *England*, &c.

By *ANNE GILMAN*.

LONDON,   Printed in the Year, 1662.

(Page numbers of original document appear in text as *page _.*)

(page 2)

An EPISTLE to FRIENDS, &c.

Ear Friends, to whom this may come do I send greeting. Grace, Mercy and Peace be multiplied, in and amongst you; who are of the Family of God, and of the houshold of the Faithful, in the Eternal God of my Life doth my Soul salute you, who are kept in the Faith, In which there is no shadow of turning: to you which are made partakers of an endless Life, which is hid with Christ in God, is my Life drawn; and I am even constrained to let forth my Love unto you, which know the washing in the blood of the Covenant, and are made partakers of an everlasting Inheritance, who have the Witness in your selves that you are his Children; and not only Children, but Heirs, and Joynt-heirs with Christ: For, as we *suffer* with him, we shall also *reign* with him; and though in the world we pass through great Tribulations; yet abiding in Him which overcomes, here is our Peace and safety known: for he hath chosen us to be a People for his Praise, and his Honour to dwell in; and this is the reason we are called into the Vineyard, even to know the Work and the Reward thereof: for now is the day known, wherein the time is to be redeemed, because the dayes are evil: Therefore, dear Friends, be not slothful; for the Lord is taking notice of the *standers idle* this day: for it is required of every one, according to your measures as you have received of the Lord, to clear your selves concerning this wicked Generation: for the Beast is let loose out of the bottomless pit, and his fury is very great, because he hath but a short time to reign; therefore doth he roar after his prey with a devouring voice. Therefore, my Friends, keep upon your watch; for this is the day wherein he is in subtilty transforming himself into an Angel of light: But dear Lambs, keep to that which doth discover him in his appearances; for that is the Anchor you are to know, and there you are to be staid even in the Power over Hell and Death, for these are the last *(page 3)* enemies we are to conquer: but blessed be God who is mighty in his appearance, and hath made himself known to be the Captain of our Salvation, and hath displayed the Banner of his Love over us, who in all our Afflictions is afflicted, and the Angel of his presence is known to support in the time of our need; and this is the reason that I am constrained to call upon you to keep to your watch: and if any Lamb among you be suffered to go astray, the Shepherd's Crook is to be known to catch them to the Fold. Understand what I say, my Friends; for I write to the Faithful that can reade with a single heart; who have known the Clouds pass over, and the Vail taken away, and the Partition-wall broken down; even they know what I say, and can feel me in the endless Life, and in the invisible Fountain of Love; for herein am I united unto you; And this is the day wherein the Lord is making up his Jewels, therefore are we made to speak oft one to another, and a Book of Remembrance is to be written thereof: Therefore, dear Friends, think it not strange concerning the fiery Tryals, which are to try you, as though some strange thing happened unto you: for, as Gold, must you be tryed and purified in the fire: and this is the reason that he is making Vessels fit for his Honour to dwell in; for there is nothing can stand before him but that which can endure the fire; even fire within, and fire without. Abide it, dear Friends, and keep close to the Lord; for there is none can wear the Crown but they that endure to the end: For the mighty God is arisen in strength, as with an Army, to support all those that trust in him, and are weak and little in their own eyes, being kept low in his Fear; for such doth he wonderfully uphold. And here is no need of sheltring one under another, for the Lord is the shelter of those that put their trust in him, and walk before him with an upright heart: for it is the heart he requires, which is redeemed out of the Form, and kept single to himself. Let them that reade, understand it, for this is the Key of *David*, which shutteth, and no man openeth, and openeth, and no man shutteth; yea, God Almighty it is, who is the strength of all those that in a pure heart wait upon him, in the undefiled Life which keeps blameless. And in an unspotted Conscience, the well-springs *(page 4)* of Life are set and known, which run most pleasantly unto all those that fear the Lord, and walk humbly before him. Wherefore fear not, little Flock, for it is the Father's will to give you the Kingdom: and this is the reason that none of you can be pluck'd out of the Father's hand, because your Lives are hid with Christ in God; and it is your meat and drink to lie down in the Will of the Lord. And this in my measure am I made a Witness of. And this is the reason that the Lord is pleased to unloose my lips, and untye my tongue, that his living Praises should be sounded forth amongst the Heathen: for wonderfully hath he wrought in and amongst you; therefore is his Name to be exalted above all the gods of the Heaven: for he is wonderful, and wondrously doth he work, for the scattering of all that is contrary to himself; that whatsoever is standing in any, that is not of himself, may be brought to nothing, that his eternal living Truth may be known in every particular. Oh you Prisoners of hope! for you do I oft pray, and am made sensible of the answer of my Prayers, because you are kept out of the murmuring, and out of the desiring after *Egypts Flesh-pots*. Oh let the Works of the Lord never be forgotten of you, who have tasted of his loving-kindness; for, of his goodness there is no end.

Therefore, my Friends, keep to that which gives you the Victory, and keep to your Dominion, that sin may not reign in your mortal bodies, and here you will find peace and rest for your souls, as your minds are singly staied upon the Lord; and your eyes kept in your head *Christ-Jesus*. Then will there be a watching over one another in love, and in the spirit of meekness, as becometh Saints who fear the Lord, and give glory to his Name: Such cannot watch with an evil eye, but are made to watch against that, because it is for Judgment. So to the *hidden Word in the heart* do I commend you, which gives victory over all that which arises contrary to it self, that noble Warriors you may be over all Corruptions and divers Lusts; for you are to triumph over all that which is contrary to the Lord, and then all things will work together for good: and nothing it is can separate you from the Love of God, which is made known to you that abide in his Fear; *(page 5)* which Fear is the beginning of Wisdom; and as we abide herein, we meet together as Children of one birth, and are refreshed in one banqueting-house of his loving-kindness: and here is no vain jangling, but all agree together, and can lie down in the Counsel of the Lord; and as we are kept to this, there is no place for the Enemy to enter. Oh, dear Friends, did our Enemies but know what we injoy, who are gathered into Faithfulness, surely they would cease Persecution, and own their Condemnation, concerning us; but it is hid from their eyes, and therefore can we say, *Father, forgive them*, because our love runs to our Enemies: For we who have been made partakers of the large Love of the Lord, desire that all might have part with us in his Fear: But alas, alas! our lamentation is taken up for them who slight these precious enjoyments; but to us is he risen with healing under his wings, and therefore can we thankfully take the Cup of Salvation, and praise the Lord amongst the Heathen: and this is the large Love of our God, and it is marvelous in our eyes. O Praises, Praises, Glory and Honour be given to God, who worketh all our works in us, and for us.

And here I am your Fellow-labourer
in the Vineyard of our Lord.

ANNE GILMAN.

(page 6)

A LETTER to CHARLES, KING of ENGLAND, &c.

Incline thine ear (O King) and slight not the precious Warnings of the Lord, which daily are made known unto thee, by that of God in thy own Conscience; and large and many have been the Warnings of the Servants of the Lord unto thee, but they have been cast behind thy back: And now is our God risen in his Mighty Power, to make Inquisition for innocent Blood; therefore, prepare, prepare, to meet the Lord, and consider what account thou canst give of the Innocent Blood which cryes in the ears of the Lord for vengeance, it is the voice of thy Brothers righteous blood which thou art to give an account of this day; and this is required at thy hands by him, who hath the hearts of Kings in his hands, and turneth them as the rivers of waters whither he pleaseth. What have we done (O King) that such usuage we should receive from thy hands, and by thy orders, that Souldiers should come into our peaceable Meetings in a warlike manner, as if some great enemies were to be conquered, amongst the People of God, whom by scorners are called *Quakers*, who cannot hold up a weapon against any? I say, What have we done that we should be haled, many of us, out of our Meetings, and cast into stinking Prisons on heaps, where, for want of air and room, many have sealed to this Testimony with their death, before they can deny to Worship God as they are perswaded in their own Consciences? for, if thou shouldest prepare, in the room of Prisons, a fiery Furnace, or a Lions den, we can as contentedly lye down, in the Will of our God, as we can suffer our bodies to lye in Prison: For the same Law which took hold of the Saints of God in the dayes of old, doth take hold of us at this day: for we cannot bow to the imaginations of men concerning the Worship of our God. And before we can own any man to be our Teacher, we can suffer death: for our Life cannot be taken away, it is hid with Christ in God; for those that *(page 7)* will live godly in Christ Jesus, must suffer Persecution: And therefore (O King) we are not careful to answer thee in this matter, for our Confidence is in the Lord, and our Strength lieth in him, who is God Almighty, and doth save his People from their sins, and from the wrath of our Enemies; and he giveth us courage and boldness, so that our lives, or any thing we do enjoy, is not near or dear unto us, for our Wills are freely given up into the hands of the Lord, that he should do with us as seemeth good in his sight; for this I know, that all things shall work together for good to those that love God, and are called for this purpose to suffer for his Names sake, who comes through great Tribulations, their Garments are washed in the Blood of the Lamb. And this is the Reason we cannot Conform to the Idol shepherds, which preach for Money, and divine for Hire, and seek their Gain from their Quarters; our Souls abhor such Teachers, for we are Redeemed from their mouths; and we should know it to be a yoke of Bondage, to turn to them again. And be it known unto thee (O King) that the Lord is risen, who is the Mighty God of *Jacob,* in strength, as with an Army, and is scattering to pieces all the deceitful workers of Iniquity; for though his loving kindness hath been plentifully known amongst his People, yet this will not excuse thee, when the great God shall render unto every one according to the deeds done in the body; and though God is pleased to preserve his People in the hollow of his Hand, and hide them under his Pavillion, because his hand is not shortened, but his arm is stretched forth still, because to us he is known a Deliverer in the time of trouble, therefore can we stand still and see his Salvation.

And therefore am I bold to declare, That the Lord is risen for the Redemption of his People, and is making way for his ransomed Ones to pass over; but *Pharaoh* and his Host are to be cast into the Sea of God's wrath: for those that fear the Lord, are his Promises made known unto, and his Secrets are made known to those that fear his Name; but to the proud, and haughty, and to those that forget God, and turn their backs at his Reproof, and will none of his Counsel, such will *(page 8)* our God sweep away with the beesom of destruction; for the worker of Iniquity will not be able to abide his Presence in that day: Therefore (O King) consider what thou art doing, for the Lord hath long waited upon thee to be gracious, and many precious Warnings have been handed to thee through the Servants of the Lord; yet that doth not clear me in the sight of my God: therefore (O King) return, return, and repent, and harden not thy heart, as in the day of provocation, against that secret witness of God, which reproves thee secretly when no mortal eye seeth. Therefore, if they were to be cast into utter darkness, who did not visite the Servants of the Lord, and who did not cloath them, and who did not feed them when they were in Prison; what will become of those who cast them into Prison, and cause them to go hungry through their hot Persecution? I say, it were better for a millstone to be hanged about their necks, and they cast into the midst of the Sea, than that they should offend one of the little ones that put their trust in the Lord.

Therefore (O King) lay it to heart, for these Warnings are not come forth in vain; for to that of God in thy Conscience do I defer my Cause, and let it plead for us when we are out of sight: for if Fire should be for us prepared, the ashes of our bones would rise as a witness against thee to plead the innocency of our Cause before thee. Therefore in love to thy Soul are these lines given forth, that a stop may be put to the Persecution of the Saints; And so whether thou wilt hear or forbear, I have cleared my self in the sight of my God concerning thee, *&c.*

ANNE GILMAN.

THE END.

AN

EPISTLE

TO

FRIENDS

IN

England,

To be Read in their A S S E M B L I E S in
the Fear of the *LORD*.

By your Friend in the Truth *Elizabeth Hendericks.*

Printed in the Year, 1672.

(Page numbers of original document appear in text as *page _.*)

(page 3)

AN

EPISTLE

TO

Friends, &c.

FRIENDS,

YOU unto whom the Lord hath appeared in this his day, in his eternal, inexpressible Love, and hath given you the knowledge of his Truth, and streched out unto you the Arm of his Power, and made known unto you the Way of Salvation: You it is, whom my endeared and unfeighned Love is flowing forth unto, which doth not consist in any thing that's visible but in that pure unchangable Love of God which he hath shed abroad in our hearts. And so in that, you are often presented before me, and often do I remember you with a deep sense of your conditions, and of the unspeakable Love of God to you-wards, and withal, of the manifold Temptations and Trialls you daily come to meet withal; and then is my heart poured out before the Lord with breathings and supplications, that you may persevere in faithfullness and stedfastness, and that you may be preserved in and through them all; and there is a certain assureance in my heart, that the Lord will do it unto all those that abide in the Faith, waiting upon him continually in his Light; and that he will not leave them, nor permit to come upon them beyond their abillity, nor yet more then will tend to their good. *(page 4)*

So dear Friends, keep close [sic] to the Light, and feel the Power of God, and abide in it, and let it be your daily care to remain in the Awe and Fear of God continually; that so you may come more and more to feel the leadings and guidings of the Lord in his Light, and that you wait at all times to know his Will and Counsel, and to feel his leadings therein: That so none may run before the Lord his Leader, but to feel Him go before, and to lead in the Way you should walk in, and in those things that concerns the Truth of God; that so you may still be preserved in that, in which the Peace of God truly comes to be felt. For *Friends*, This is a thing of great weight, and far surpasses all that is visible and transitory, so that you all may be kept waiting continually in the Light, upon the Lord, to feel the Power and Virtue of it daily and to enjoy it, and that you may come to dwell in it in steadfastness without wavering: And this is that for which my labour is, and for which my desire often times with deep Sighings and Breathings to the Lord is, that you may be kept and preserved in those dark places of the earth, where you have your Callings, and that you may be an Honour and Praise to him in your Generation, and that you may be refreshed and consolated by his Living Presence more and more.

Oh *Friends*! How pretious [sic] it is to feel the presence of God unto Refreshment and Consolation, but his presence is terrible unto those that are found in Iniquity and Unfaithfulness. Therefore *Dear Friends*, take heed of all that, that would draw you out from the constant and diligent watching in the Light, and to have a strict regard thereunto; and of that Spirit that would run out into visions and openings of the Truth, before the Leader; for that is that which is Impatient, Rash, Hasty and Unstable; and so that cannot hold out long but is soon weary, and quickly offended and troubled, when things doth not allwayes fall out according to that mind; and so there is no perfect satisfaction, but it is wearying it self, now in this, and then in the other thing, and this cannot stand in the day of trial. But *Friends*, Dwell low in the feeling of the pure measure of God, and feel the Spirit of the *Lamb* that bears and suffers, and hold fast the Faith in the Light, and cleave unto it with your whole hearts, that patience may possess your Souls, that so you may feel the plentious peace and satisfaction therein. And *Friends*, Take heed of many consultations and thoughts, concerning things which you cannot see through nor *(page 5)* comprehend, for if that gets place in the heart, that brings a burthen upon the mind, that darkens and vails, and greives the Righteous Seed of God, but in all things be careful that your minds may be kept continually out of all such things in that that opens the understanding, and makes the heart tender; for that is that which must preserve in that state. And so *Dear Friends*, there is an enemy near, against whom it is greatly needful to watch continually, that so the mind may be kept Single, Pure and Clean; and so that you may feel more and more these things, and to enjoy the Comfort and

Consolation in your selves, when the mind is kept single and clean of all Incumbrances, and Reasonings, and Consultations about things which you cannot discern nor under stand, and leave it to the Lord who is onely Wise, and knows every ones Condition, Sate [sic], and Capacity; who watcheth over his own, as a Father doth over his Children, teaching and instructing every one according to their growth and abillity, of those things that are his Will concerning them. And *Friends*, Take heed of that Spirit that still will seek to excuse himself, and to diminish and hide that which is not well, and to lay the charge and fault upon another, to clear himself by so doing; this is the Spirit of the world, and is out of Truth, and by the Truth, and Light of God it is condemned. This is he that appeared in *Adam* and *Eve* in the beginning after the Fall: And so *Friends*, You who are called to come out of the Fall, let nothing that is of that spirit and nature be cherished nor regarded, but that all may be judged in the Light, which is springing forth of that Ground, the cursed Ground in which the Thorns and Briars, and the Weeds growes, and let the Fire consume it: So *Dear Friends*, keep nothing back, nor excuse nothing, nor diminish it not, that cannot stand in the Light and Truth of God, but is Condemned and must be so for ever.

And *Friends*, Take heed of that, which when there is any thing done or spoken as in a sence of Truth, that will to much be seen and lookt upon in it, and boast in it; this is that which seeks self, and not the honour of God; but give you no place to that, for that will run when the Lord sends not, and will be doing of that which the Lord requireth not; so there ought to be a continual watch against that: And you still abiding in the true sence and feeling, you come still to feel what the Lord requires, and what he leads you unto; and so there Consolation and Peace is felt, *(page 6)* and this doth not lift up but keeps low and sensible of the goodness of God, and that breaks and tenders the heart, and overcomes it.

And so this is that which every one ought to wait for in himself, to feel it, that so you may be as obedient Children, that are minding the instructions and directions of the Father continually. And *Friends*, Watch against that which would be striving to comprehend and know, and understand much, before it be the Lords time and pleasure; for that is the same Spirit that is in the World, but wait low in the feeling of the Light and the Power, and dwell in it; that so what you know and understand of the Truth, and the things of it you may know in the Light, by the Revelation of the Lord therein: And this is that which is lasting, though never so little; and though such be as little Children, that as it were know nothing at all, yet it is pretious [sic] to keep in that state, and not to run, not to be busie, not to will, but to be quietly waiting upon the Lord, to feel his Power, to feel his Arm, to preserve and to lead, and to know him to be the Guide and Leader, who leads gently the little-ones, and bears the Sucklings in his Arms, and keeps and preserves them from that which would bruise and hurt them.

So *Dear Friends*, Your Strength, your Preservation and Salvation is in the Lord, and therefore keep your selves close to his Light, and imbrace it with a perfect heart, and cleave unto it with your whole strength, and let it not go, neither let any thing have place in your hearts that is against it; and where there is any thing yet remaining in the heart, which is felt not to be in unity with it, give your selves no rest, till you feel the Judgement of God set a rop [sic] over it in your hearts, and then let it be freely refined up unto the Judgement, that so, not an enemy to the Truth and to your own Soules, may be left alive in the house.

So *Dear Friends*, This is in true Love unto you, from one who hath experience of these things concerning which I have wrot unto you, as in a weighty sence that hath been upon my heart for a considerable time, and I could not well forbear longer, but must communicate it unto you, in a fresh and living sence of the Love of God, and of Love unfeigned; which often floweth forth to you-wards, as an overflowing stream, who are called of the Lord, and to whom the Lord hath stretched forth his Arm of Mercy and *(page 7)* Love. Oh *Friends!* Dwell in that which preserves Love and Unity amongst the Children of the houshould of God, that so there may be no place amongst you for discord, or any thing of that nature; neither let any thoughts enter the heart, which you dare not declare in words; for is it such as that you dare not make it known? Then they are things that ought to have no place in the heart, though many times such things may present themselves in the thoughts, but it ought to have no place, for it will hurt, though it may appear with some shew of Truth or Good in it, or of a good tendency, but the end is seen in the Light that it doth not proceed out of the Light: And so *Friends*, waiting in the Light, you will daily more and more, come to see the subtil workings of the enemy in the heart, which is the desire of my Soul, and that you may be preserved and kept out of his Snares.

So *Friends*, I have no other thing to which I can commit you, but to the Lord, who is able to preserve you and to keep you out of all the cunning devices of Sathan [sic]; yea, and I am perswaded that he will do it, to all those that perseveres in the Faith, in his Light, in faithfulness, stedfast unto the end; so that you all may be preserved and established in the everlasting Truth, and may endure to the end, that so none hav-ing put his hand to the Plough may look back, that is the earnest long-ing and desire of my heart.

So the Lord God of Power, who alone is our Strength, Power and Refuge, establish your minds more and more in his Light, and your hearts more and more in the Faith, and continually to wait upon him in his Light, and to confirme your confidence in him; that so, *you may run and not be weary, and walk on and faint not:* That so Peace, Rest, Comfort and Consolation may be multiplyed amongst you from the Lord. To whom be Glory, and Honour, and Praises, for ever.

From your true Friend in the Truth,

Amsterdam, the 19th.
   of the 6th Moneth,
      1 6 7 2 .

Elizabeth Hendericks.

THE END.

An *Epiftle* to be Communicated to Friends, & to be read in the Fear of the Lord in their Men and Womens Meetings, and other Meetings; only among Friends, as they in the Wifdom of God fhall fee meet and ferviceable.

FRIENDS,

Hereas it hath pleafed the Lord in the unfpeakable Riches of his Mercy, to vifit the Remnant in his Love, and to meet with us in a Way where we expected him not, when we were wandring from Mountain to Hill, and chufing our own Ways, feeking the Living amongft the Dead; yea, when we had long thus wearied our felves, and almoft difpaired of finding what we fought, but were faying in our felves, *Who fhall ascend up, or descend down for us to bring that to us, without which our immortal Souls can find no Rest?* Even in that time is the Lord appeared, not as a God afar off, but a God near, even in our Hearts is he appeared through the Light of his Son, and thereby open'd he our Hearts and Underftandings, according to his divine Wifdom, who knew every ones State and every ones Neceffity; and he became as a Pillar of a Cloud by Day, and as a Pillar of Fire by Night unto all fuch as imbraced and received his Appearance, and followed him faithfully; yea, he became as a *wall of fire* round about them who did wholely *(page 2)* put their truft in him. And thus hath he gathered us to be a people, who were once as fcattered Sheep that knew not the true Shepherd; and hath made us as Firftlings upon his holy Mountain, that we might be as Lights and Leaders to the next Generations; and many are fo in the Sight of the Lord and his Appointed, and are fo felt and known among his People.

And feeing we are called to be as Firftlings and Examples to the Generations that are coming after us, it is highly needful that we watch diligently in the Fear and Wifdom of God, that nothing may be, nor remain among us as an Old Leaven, to grieve and burden the Redeemed, nor to be an Occafion of Evil Example to the Young Ones that are

(Page numbers of original document appear in text as *page _.*)

coming up after us: And considering that it is every ones Duty to be faithful in their Measures, and not to put that under a *Bushel* which is manifested from the Lord, but to bring it forth in the true Love of God, and Faithfulness to each other, to the edifying and building up, and to the Amendment and Admonition of those concerned, and that all Causes of Stumbling might be removed, and that we might not leave a Hoof in Egypt, but might all follow the Lamb as the Redeemed of the Lord together; and being Washed, Sanctified and Born again, might come to sing the New Song, with the New Name in our Foreheads, and Hallelujahs in our Mouths, *Amen, Amen.*

For these good Ends it is in my heart to signifie these two things, that at the present are principally upon me, which I have born a weight concerning for several years, and did hope that some elder and fitter might feel the like Weight, and bring forth a Testimony concerning the same, whereupon I have forborn as long as well I durst; but now finding that I am not cleared *(page 3)* of the Matter, but that in a fresh living Sense it is renewed in me, I dare not longer forbear to write the things that are upon my Spirit in these two Particulars, and recommend the same unto God's Witness in all Consciences.

The *first* thing that lies before me is, concerning the *bringing up of our Children*, which is a very weighty Concern; and every one that hath the bringing up of Children will have very much to answer for, if they do not quit themselves as before the Lord in all Diligence and Faithfulness; they are God's Creatures, and given to Parents as a Gift from him, upon whom they are to improve their utmost Diligence, that they may grow up in the Fear of God; and that Parents should not over-look things in their Children through fond Affection, which they know by the Light of Jesus to be evil and bad; neither speak to them in a *slender Reproof*, as *Eli* did to his *Sons*, but from their youth upwards to set before their Eyes the Weight & Danger of their Iniquity, and that in a Holy Zeal, as for the Lord, and in a deep sense of his holy Power, seeking in their young years to reach the Witness of God in them, and above all things, to be a Good Example to them in all things, or else we break down in them that which we seek to build up; for how can we build them up in the Faith, except we so stand in the Faith as to obtain the Victory in our selves? and how can we bring their Minds to the Light of Jesus, except we walk in it? Neither ought any one to be bitter to their Children, nor to require more of them then we know they are of Ability to perform; and when they fall short of their Duty, not to Correct them in our own

Wills, nor in a Wrathful Angry Mind; for that Mind is it self for Correction; but on the contrary, to help them with *(page 4)* the Rod of a gentle Chastizement, in the Fear of God, to bow their own stubborn Wills, and so comes the Witness in them to be reached, and they grow sensible in themselves *that the Rod hath been a Help to them*, and come to feel, a *Love* and *unity* with them that have so helped them, while their Minds are kept to the Truth.

And seeing we are as a *City set upon a Hill*, and as *Fore-runners* and *Leaders to the next Generations*, where and in what should the Pattern of our Godly Lives more appear and shine forth, then to the Innocent Children of our own Birth and Generation, which are committed to us as a particular Charge and Ministry, from their time of greatest Innocency upwards, to whom we are bound by the Band of *Nature*, and by the Ordinance of *God*, to take Care over, and to bring up in his pure Fear, in all Wisdom, Discretion and Watchfulness, *that we may be a good Savour in them and to them, whether it be unto Life, if they be Obedient, or unto Condemnation, if they become Rebellious?* But alas! (with a great grief of spirit I write it) here is a great *want* and *shortness* in many professing *Truth* (I speak not of all) for *first*, they receive not their *Children* as from the Lord, in the Faith, as his Gift, neither do they offer them up again to him in their *hearts*, as being his, but seeing their own Likeness brought forth, imbrace it as their own, and nourish it up in the *self-love*, and their *lives* being bound up in the *children*, every Appearance of *sickness* or *death* is as a *death to the Parents*; and accordingly if the Child grow up till its perverse and crooked Will begins to appear, then is the Father (and for the most part, most of all the Mother) afraid to give it due Correction, fearing lest the Child should be grieved and vexed, and perhaps grow sick; yea, perhaps dye, if it should be corrected to the breaking of its stout and stubborn Will; and what is this but Unbelief *(page 5)* and Self-love in such Parents? but when Parents receive & possess their Children in the Faith, then the Light rules in the Parents, and that gives daily *wisdom* to rule the Children in *God's wisdom*; but when *fleshly affection* rules, what miserable *disorder* doth it bring forth, even amongst them that profess *truth?* and many times their *children* grow worse then many in the *world;* and that which is most to be lamented it happens sometimes, *that the Parents have not quit themselves as they ought, nor fully clear'd themselves of their Blood,* so that there lies a Guilt upon the Parents, and an Offence and stumbling in the minds of the Children, when they come to years, and to see how their Parents *Care* was not over them as it ought to have been: Oh, that none among us might be found guilty in this matter, but that every Friend would be diligent to keep a Good Conscience in the sight of God, that our Children may have a blessed Remembrance of us when we come to be taken from them, and they come to be in our state and condition, and that the Remembrance of our dealing with them may be as a good Pattern to them, and so from Generation to Generation, to the Honour and Glory of him who first called us, and to the edifying of them in the Faith, and to our Joy and everlasting Comfort, *Amen*.

The second thing that lies as a weight upon me, and have done for several Years, is concerning the *manner of Trading* that is practiced by several professing the pure Principle of Truth, both Merchants and Shopkeepers, and other Trades-men, who take too much Liberty in getting and borowing Money of others to inlarge their Trading in the World, beyond what Truth allows: When I first felt the weight of *(page 6)* this matter upon me, I presently examined my own Affairs, and took such a course as to prevent all peril of any Body suffering by me, however things might happen; and the same course did our Brethren take, who lived in those parts, they feeling the weight of the matter upon them as well as I; so that we came to sit every one as under our own Fig-tree, being satisfied that if we came to suffer loss in our outward things, whether for our Testimony, or by War, or by Sea, we should lose but our own: But many I find to be other-wise minded, who out of a greedy, though uncertain Hope of Profit, gets that which is other Mens into their Hands, and when they see things goes not according to their Expectations, but that Losses and Crosses happens in their Trading, are not so faithful and open hearted to let their Creditors know thereof, but rather goes on, setting themselves at Ease, and takes a large Liberty in their Housekeeping and Expences, as if all that is under their Hands were their own; and this lasts a while, until not only their own, but other mens Estates are spent also, and all the while under a shew of Profession, although all uprightness, and fear of God, and regard to make a righteous Account with men be lost; these are a stink among men, and a shame to their Profession: And this Evil increaseth daily in some parts of this Nation, where many young Ones, brought up among us; and hath little to begin withal, upon the Reputation of Truth dares to adventure upon, and get Credits, and set themselves in a high posture of Trading, House-keeping, and Expences. And some that are Ancient Professors of Truth, and should watch over them, and Counsel and Bridle them with the Bridle of Truth and Righteousness, in the

Power and *(page 7)* Wisdom of God, they are so incumbred with great Dealings, and great Debts, and Credits, and Adventures, both of what is their own and other mens, that they are not without Peril and Danger of falling short at one time or other, if loss at Sea, or spoiling of Goods for their Testimony should happen to themselves; & in the mean time that Godly care and jealousie is not taken by such over the younger sort as it ought to be; but some runs on without fear of God, or upright Communication of their State and Condition unto sound and faithful weighty Friends (and especially to such, whom they have made to be concerned in their Concerns) as they ought to do from time to time, that it might stand in their choice, whether they would be longer concerned with them or not; which is but a righteous and just thing, that every Creditor ought to keep, not only the Propriety, but the Command of what is his own, to ask it and receive it, when he sees cause, and not to be beguiled by great shews, as if the Debtor were in a good Condition as to his outward Estate, when indeed its very bad: But such do like this World, first seek the Kingdom of this World under a Profession of Truth: But if the Kingdom of Heaven were first sought, as it ought to be, then every one would sink down in the fear of God, to feel him leading them and ordering their Trading and Merchandize in sujection to his Will, Jam. 4.13,14,15. *Go to now, ye that say to day or to morrow, We will go into such a City, and continue there a Year, and buy and sell, and get Gain; whereas ye know not what shall be on the morrow: For what is your Life, it is even a Vapour, that appeareth for a little time, and then vanisheth away. For that ye ought to say, If the Lord will, we shall live and do this or that.* And not to go on *(page 8)* in their own Wills, adventuring the Estates of others without their knowledge or consent; when they themselves knows well enough, that if the Adventures fail, their Security must fail also. Oh! how many Widdows and Orphans, Old and Weak are there oppressed and wronged by these things? Doth not such think and believe that the Want, Poverty, and Cry of these will bring down Vengeance from the Righteous God? or think they not, that God will visit for these things for his pretious Truth and Names-sake, and for the Cry of the Oppressed? yea, assuredly he will plead their Cause, and will disburthen and clear his Truth and People of them, & their unrighteous Deeds together.

Is it not our duty, both Old and Young, to set our Affairs in such a posture, as that we may be out of danger that any Body should suffer by us, while we in the mean time only aim at our own profit & advantage. Oh, let the Truth here be judge, and then I know the Elder Friends will labour to quit themselves in this matter, and so have power to put a stop and bridle to such young Ones as takes this course, or else the peril and reproach of both will lie at their Door in a great measure. Oh! that a holy Zeal may increase in many Hearts for the Removing of this great Evil, and let go the eager desire of great profit; and every one to be content with his own, and serve the Lord and his Truth therewith according to his Ability. (and if he please, he will increase it) And take care of the younger sort, and become good Examples to them in this matter, that the stink of offences in this kind may be stopped, and the Truth of God may prosper and flowrish more and more, *Amen.*

Colchester the 29th of the 9th Mon. 1677. } *Geertruyd Deriks Niesen.*

A WARNING

To All Friends

Who Profeſſeth the Everlaſting Truth
of God, which he hath Revealed and made
manifeſt in this his Bleſſed Day, (whether
on this Side, or beyond the Seas.)

By Mary Waite

Dear Friends,

IN Tender Bowels of love, do I feel (from the Lord) a warning
Spring in my heart to you, that you all may be kept low
in his humble self denying Life, where safety is to be found.
For assuredly, the great and Notable day of the Lord is at hand, in
which he will arise in the greatness of his strength, to plead the cause of
his suffering Seed, with all its enemies, whether within, or without.

So all Dear Friends be faithful under your several dispensations, For
in our Fathers house are many Mansions, Keep in the low valleys; For
there will be your safety, there will the green pastures of Gods love be
partaken of, and with such will he delight to dwell. So all Friends keep
to your watch, that the day of the Lord come not in an hour you look
not for it, and so you receive the unfaithful Servants Reward, for indeed Friends my soul is in a great Travel for the Prosperity of Sion, that
her walls may be builded, her breaches Repaired and made up. For,
many months *(page 2)* yea some years, hath my spirit been bowed down
and groaned under the sense of an easeful, selfish, Lukewarm Spirit,
that hath crept in upon many for want of watchfulnesse, and Keeping
to the Dayly Cross of Christ Jesus, and in the Narrow way, and Savoury
life, that only will bring honour and praise to the Name of the Lord.
And how to be eased of these weights and burdens I did not know, my

(Page numbers of original document appear in text as *page _.)*

cry was to the Lord that he would give me wisdome, and strength to do his will. And it pleased him to lay his hand upon me and bring me near to the gates of Death (so far as I saw) and was pleased to hide himselfe from me, and my Soul was in a languishing condition, and my cries was great unto the Lord that he would not hide his face from me, but let me feel of his wonted goodness, and mercy, by which I had received daily comfort and satisfaction from him in his unerring path, in which he had been pleased to lead me. And at length the Lord appeared, and said he would be my Phisition and cure my disease, and came in and comforted my Spirit, with his overcoming love, which greatly revived me. And in the openings of the bowels of his endlesse love, he shewed me, a Terrible day drew near, (even as one may say at the doors.) And laid it upon me, to goe warn his people in this City (and elsewhere) to Depart from all filthinesse both of flesh and Spirit, from all Lukewarmness, from the fashions, customes, and friendships of this world, from Pride, Covetousness and every sin that separateth from the Lord, and brings drynesse, barronnesse, and deadnesse, upon many, and made as unsavoury salt, that was good for nothing, but to be cast forth and trodden upon.

And to warn them not to delay time, but come into the true humility, lowlinesse of spirit, and selfedenying life, that the Lord might be a hiding place to them, for terrible will that day be to all the unfaithful and disobedient. All the sinners in Sion shall be afraid, fearfulnesse shall take hold on *(page 3)* the Hypocrite. Dread and horror shall surprise them. O whither will you unfaithful fly! would you not be glad that either Rocks or Mountains could hide you from the presence of the Lord, and the wrath of the Lamb. O this will be a terrible day indeed, unto all those that have had a form of Godlinesse, but denyed the power, that would have saved them out of all defilements and pollutions of this world.

For long hath the Spirit of the Lord been grieved with these, who have long come and sitten amongst Gods people, as if they had been of them, but never came to sink down to the heart searching Light of Christ Jesus in them, that by it they might be cleansed, from all secret and open sins, from every Dalilah that lodgeth in the bosome, as Pride and Covetousnesse, which often the one attends the other, Covetousnesse (saith the servant of the Lord,) is the root of all evil, and advised them to fly from it, but who abide not in the spirit of judgment, and of Burning, which God hath prepared to purge away the filth of the daughter of Sion, their filth hath not been purged nor done away, which causeth many miscarriages, blots and staines, and great Reflections have such brought upon the blessed truth; and much dirt hath been thrown upon the pure holy undefiled way of the Lord, which he hath cast up, for the Ransomed to walk in, and so through the un-faithfulness and uneven walking of such, the name of the Lord hath been greatly dishonoured, his Spirit grieved, and the hearts of the Righ-teous made sad. And many a wounded Soul there is amongst the Lords people, who are bowed under these weights and pressures, but assuredly the day hastens that every one must bear their own burden, and the Lord will ease his Innocent ones, who have been bowed down before him, and have mourned and groaned under these things: yea, the day hastens, that the unfaithful and disobedient shall *(page 4)* bear their own burdens. And the Lord will arise for his own Name and Glory sake, and will ease him of his enemies, and avenge him of his adversaries, and take to himselfe his great power, that he may Reign and Rule in the hearts of his, that (faithfully labour in his work, and) ordereth their conversations aright before him; his glory shall rest upon them, for he will not give it to another seed, or birth, but to Christ Jesus the seed of the woman; who was given to bruise the Serpents head; he hath born the iniquities of all, and been pressed under them as a Cart with sheaves, his face hath been more marred then any mans, and his voice not heard in the streets, no beauty nor comlinesse seen in him. And because he hath been a man of sorrowes, and acquainted with griefs, therefore hath he been passed by and not regarded, but the Lord will make him the joy of many Generations; and his Sion the praise of the whole earth.

Therefore Dear Friends, love him with all your Souls, and be you delighted in him, above all injoyments whatever, that you may lye down in the bosome of his love, and be nourished by his side, as Children of our heavenly Father; begotten by the Immortal word of life, to Live and Reign hear with him (in it,) and when time shall be no more, enter into that blessed rest, prepared for all them that have obeyed his glori-ous Gospel: and though as yet we be but as the gleanings of the Vin-tage, yet the Lord hath many to gather, yea, the numberless number shall be gathered. And great will be the work of our God, which he is bringing to pass in this his blessed day, it cannot be declared, as it is seen and felt in the spirit.

So Friends be faithful in the work of your day, be valliant for the Lord and his blessed truth: Come up in the Nobillity of his life, and stand faithful witnesses for him; for we are the City set upon a hill, yea, battle Axes in Gods hand, Though our weapons are not carnal, but

Spiritual, and *(page 5)* mighty through the power of God, to the pulling down the strong holds of sin and Sathan [*sic*]: Friends, we are they whom the Lord hath raised to hold forth Christ Jesus, whom he hath given for an ensign to the Nations, unto whom all the ends of the earth must come for salvation;

So Dear Friends, let your light shine forth before men that they may see your good workes and gloryfie your heavenly father, so that by your godly life and holy conversation many may enquire the way to Sion.

All Friends be faithful, and keep your meetings, in the fear of the Lord, be dilligent in his work, for the woe and Curse belongs to them that do the Lords work negligently (or with careless minds,) and it is come on some allready, and will come more upon others, if by speedy repentance they return not unto the Lord. So be Zealous for the Lord and his truth, and as much as in you lies gather orderly together as neare the time as possible; that the meeting is appointed at, for Disorderly comeing hath been a hurt and burdened the faithfull who dare not be negligent, in the Lords work; and often they have waited a Considerable season and Gods power hath been felt, and the manifold grace of God been dispensed amongst us, and then others comes in: and misses of the Counsels, Admonitions, and Refreshments which the Lord by the operation of his blessed spirit hands forth to his people, and so for want of Zeal in comeing duly to meetings (especially on the week dayes) truth hath not grown in them, but such have long travelled in the wilderness: and many Carkasses fall'n there, and so for want of Zeal and faithfulness the enemy hath crept in, and darkned many minds, where once there was tender good desires raised after God, So all have need to be faithful and wait *(page 6)* dilligently every oppertunity the Lord gives you to feel your strengths renewed, for in the world is many Incumbrances and Intanglements, some on one hand, and some on another to draw the mind from God, (and but one to draw it to him,) so there is great need of holy zeal and dilligence, in observing the time to wait upon the Lord to feel your strength renewed; to help through the many things and his power to strengthen and support, that in your families and all your undertakings you may be a good savour to the Lord, being guided by his wisdome to rule and order your Children and Servants, and he will give Authority to Stand over every thing thats contrary to his witness, And in the feare of the Lord I warn and Exhort all parents not to winke or Connive at any sin in your Children, as you tender their Everlasting well being, let no sin go unreproved or uncorrected, but take the wise mans counsel who saith; Folly is bound up in the heart of a Child but the rod of Correction must drive it out, And he that corrects his Child shall deliver his Soul from Death: So friends Traine up your Children in the Blessed truth and fear of the Lord, So may you have hope they will not depart from it (when they are old.) And take heed of giving way or suffering them to get into pride, and the vain and foolish fashions, which are a shame to Sober people, and a great inlet to many evils, for they are prone to that by nature, and it may soon be set up, but hard to get it down; So Friends keep the yoak upon that Nature thats Proud, Stubborn, or Disobedient to Parents, break that will in them betimes which comes from the evil one, and bend them while they are young, least when they grow up you cannot. And then you may sorrow greatly when it is too late, for by your over looking their Folly, or Pride, the wrong Nature *(page 7)* growes in them to a strong head, whereby you have helped them forwards in the broad way which leads to destruction, and their blood (may come) to be required at your hands. Ah Friends, friends, as much as in you lies keep down the evil, and the good will arise, then their will be Room for the tender seed to grow up in them, and they will bless the Lord on your behalfs, for your love and care of their Immortal Souls.

And all Masters and Mistresses of Families, Keep in the Dominion of Truth, that in it you may Rule over every unclean thing, and wrong Spirit, that is contrary to the Lord, that you abiding in him who is the highest power, (and higher then the powers of darkenesse) may in it keep in your Authority in your Families, and look that all be kept sweet and clean, out of the Condemnable state, first in your selves; and then in your families to see that all Wildness, Wantonness, and Rudeness, be kept under by the power; yea every thing that would blot or staine the precious truth. And then if the Lord Require any Service or Testimony of any of you, (for this name and blessed truth,) that all may be cleare in your selves and justified by Gods witness, that you have stood in his Counsel and Authority in your families and been good Examples in life and conversation, by keeping your own houses in the good Order, and Ruleing their for God, then may you openly with boldness appear for the Lord, and thresh down sin and every evil way, in the power and Authority of his life, that none may have any thing to accuse any of you, (on the accounts above mentioned,) And deare Friends all keep in the savory life; but more especially you who are drawn forth to beare publick Testimonys for the Lord and his blessed truth, keep you to the watch that at all times, Places, and on all *(page 8)* occasions your lives may preach for God, by a clean unspotted Conversation, which is the Crown of all the faithfull, who labour in the worke of the Lord, and are upright before him, his Glory shall rest upon them and their Reward is sure.

Now unto all you young people Sons and Daughters, Apprentices, Men or Maids, Servants, all that are convinced of Gods truth and the way that leads to everlasting life and happiness, be you all faithful to Gods witness in you, and mind the motions and opperations [*sic*] of it, that thereby you may be changed, and all judge out whats contrary to his pure witness, let not your minds wander neither look out at the vani-ties in this world, for Christs Kingdome is not of it, nor to be found in Pride, wantonness and lusts of the flesh; The Fashions, Customes, and friendships of this world, for the Devil is the King of pride, and all its attendants that leads to the gates of Hell and everlasting destruction, where is the Woe and Misery and that for evermore, there the worm never dyes, the fire never goes out, so all you young and tender ones, where desires are begotten after God, keep you low in his fear, and to the daily Cross that all the contrary may be crucified, and all the Enmitie slain upon it. For every one that will be a disciple of Christ Jesus, must come into the selfedenying life, (you cannot have two Kingdomes,) So my advice to you all is, stoop to Christs appearance in you, he who Invites all to come and learn of him, who is meek and lowly and you shall find rest to your souls. So all be faithful in your several places and the exercises you may be under, that you may grow in grace and in the feare and wisdome of God, let not your eyes look out at others, but mind your own Conditions for if you do it *(page 9)* will Spye many faults in others, and may be over look more at home, This hinders the grouth of many, so all waite low within to feel your grouth in the Blessed truth, and know how the work goes on, and whether thou feel Gods love, mercy and goodness Renewed to thee day by day, or not, for your ac-counts will be for the deeds done in your bodyes, and not for others, so every one is to labour to know your calling and election made sure.

And you that are Apprentices keep in the truths love and obey it, for it will keep you faithful in your places and (out of every deceitful way) performing them not with eye-service but, with singlenesse of heart, as unto the Lord, from whom you must receive a Reward. And if the en-emy entice, consent not. Though he come in with never so fair pre-tences; that thou may'st deceive thy Master, and it will never be known &c. Or purloin or waste his Goods, believe him not he is a Lyer and the Father of lies, for there is an Eye that sees in secret, which will bring all the hidden deeds of darkness to Light and every worke to judgement, So as thy worke is shall be thy Reward. But fear the Lord and obey his voice in thee, and he will deliver thee out of every unclean way, and polluted path, by his dear Son Christ Jesus whom he hath given for a high way of Holyness, and a Restorer of paths to dwell in, Glory to his Name for ever, saith the Redeemed, who is now returning unto Sion with Songs of deliverance in their mouths; and everlasting high praises is founded unto him, by those whose garments are made white in the blood of the Lamb, for Sions Redeemer is come, the taker away of sin and iniquity is made manifest, the mourners in Sion comforted, The weary Travelers are Refreshed, the Feeble knees are *(page 10)* strengthened, the broken Spirit bound up, and the wounded Soul hath oyle poured in, who can but rejoyce and be exceeding glad, for he hath put a new Song in our mouths, he hath given his people beauty for Ashes, and in stead of heavinesse the spirit of praise, all that know him will speak well of his name, for all the Noble Acts he hath brought to pass for his Children. My soul is greatly affected in the Remembrance of the Lords numberless mercyes (to me) and a little Remnant whom he hath pluck't as Brands out of the fire, to shew forth his praises and declare of his goodnesse in the Land of the living, to hold forth Christ (the way to the Father,) To the Nations, that his scattered seed may be gathered from all the ends of the earth.

> So I have cleared my Spirit of what hath long lain upon me, and discharged my Conscience in delivering the Lords Message faithfully, according to the abillity he hath given me. And so am clear in my Spirit: The Lord set it home upon every heart whom it may concerne, and that it may be Received, in the same bowels of love it was given forth. Then shall I have my reward; and the Lord his Glory. And so shall return to my Tent, and enter into the hole of the Rock, where safetie is to be found, till the indignation be overpast, and in the endless unchangable love of God, do I Salute you, and bid you Farewel in the Lord.

> *Mary Waite.*

Yorke 10th. 2d. Month, 1679.

> Let this be Read in Friends meetings, when they are gathered together, in the fear of the Lord, and in his weightie savoury Life.

AN
EPISTLE
FOR TRUE
Love, Unity
AND
ORDER
IN THE
Church of Chrift,

Againft the Spirit of Difcord, Diforder and Confufion, &c.

Recommended to Friends in Truth, chiefly for the fake of the Weak and Unftable Minded, for Information and Encouragement in our Chriftian Unity and Society, held in the Spirit of Chrift, both in Faith and Practice.

By two Servants of the Church, according to our Meafures,

Anne Whitehead, Mary Elfon.

But God hath tempered the Body together——that there fhould be NO SCHISME *in the Body, but that the Members fhould have the* SAME CARE *one for another,* 1 Cor. 12.

LONDON,
Printed by *Andrew Sowle,* and are fold at his Shop in *Devonfhire* New-buildings, without *Bifhops-Gate,* 1680.

(Page numbers of original document appear in text as *page _.*)

(page 3)

AN

EPISTLE

FOR TRUE

Love, Unity & Order, &c.

Dear Friends ;

Whom the Lord hath called out of the World's Ways and Manners, and chosen to himself, and found faithful according to the Proportion of Faith, and Measure of his Grace received, how to walk, Oh! let us hold fast that which we have received, that none may take our Crown: Oh! let us keep to our first Love, let us do our first Works, and be rightly zealous for the Lords Honour; and so with a good Conscience towards God, and in the sweet Spirit of Peace, seeking good one toward another, as good Examples and wholesome Paterns in our Practices. Oh! let us keep our good Order in the Truth, and Unity of the Spirit, even as we received of Christ Jesus in the beginning, that we should walk *1 Joh. 1.7.* in the Light, as he is in the Light (so shall we have fellowship one with another) which *light* is one in us all, & the one only true & living Way, leading to the Knowledge and living Obedience of the one, true and living God, that in his own living Spirit of Truth, we might Worship him, and in all wholesome Service hold forth his Holy & Reverend Name to be One in us all, who are gathered into it, serving the Lord with one Heart, one Soul, one Mind and one Consent. _____ And in the beginning of our Day, you that were then born and brought forth in the Truth, you know the Harmony of our Unity was our Beauty and Comliness, yea, our Strength and Compleatness, so far as we had obtained then; and so 'tis now, blessed be the Lord, can we with one Heart say, who by his heavenly Power have been from *(page 4)* the beginning kept upon his Everlasting Foundation of true Unity, held in his Spirit, which is the Bond of our Peace, to this very Day and Time, in which the Lord hath suffered Blindness, in part, to happen to some, through their own Neglect of Watchfulness, and declining their first Love by the Enemy's Subtilty prevailing, who came out amongst us,

and had a part in the Belief and Discovery of the Way of Truth; but
now, some only have the Sheeps clothing, and others have lost that
too, who through a prejudiced Mind are alienated from that Unity of
Spirit and Bond of Peace, in which we keep our wholesome Practices,
which we have received in the Unity and Order of the Gospel of Peace,
and Truth of Christ Jesus, in the fellowship of the Spirit, in Bowels of
Mercy, being like-minded, and of one accord, in what-

2 Phil. 1.4.   soever things are True, Just, Honest, and of good Report; not that we should think of them only, but be in the Practice of
them, (as we are) and feel the God of Peace with us therein, who are

1 Cor. 1.6. &   confirmed in the Testimony of Christ Jesus, the one
10.   Guide, Way and Rule we are to walk after, where all
speak one thing, that there be no Dissention amongst
us, but to be knit together in one Mind and in one Judgment; this we
have received of Christ Jesus our Lord, King and only Law giver, that
we might walk so in subjection to his Rule and Government, that all
things might be done Decently and in Order; for our God is the God of
Order, in all the Churches of his Saints, and not the God of Confusion,
blessed be his Name; but to our burden and grief, we find among some,
a contrary Spirit that will not subject to Unity in wholesome Practices
amongst us, and that will needs interpose to destroy Unity in some
places, and obtrude it self to confound our wholesome Order and Practices received amongst us, as a Church and People. And through this
contrary Spirit, the prejudiced Mind, the Accuser of the Brethren is
broken out, under a specious pretence, crying out, *Liberty of Conscience,
Liberty of Conscience*, in opposition to those needful, convenient and
wholesome Practices exercised amongst us, in outward things, to which we
are called, as a People that are distinguished from the World's dark Ways
and Corrupt Manners, in keeping our Consciences void of Offence towards God and Man, in keeping both in the Power and Form of Godliness.

(page 5) Now that the Simple may not be ensnared, nor the Weak
unstable minded deceived, nor the Unwatchful at unawares overtaken,
through the crafty Insinuations of this accusing, opposing, dividing
Spirit, that is at work in this our day, to confound Order, against the
peaceable Government of Christ, amongst his People; therefore in Duty
to the Lord, and to clear my Conscience, for the sake of those before
mentioned, are these few Lines writ; Wherefore in Humility of Soul, as
before the Lord, I beseech you, tender Ones, in seriousness, and fear
towards God, weigh the Matter: This Dividing, Accusing, Prejudicial
Worker, would introduce a Belief, *That an* Apostacy *is entring, and we*

are gone from the Beginning, or first Principle, and the Power lost; and now Forms are setting up, and Imposition on Consciences, and the like: And amongst whom is all this, say they, *but amongst us who are in Unity of Spirit, both in Faith and Practices,* with sincere mind towards God, are preserved in subjection, peaceably in Unity, and wholesome comely Order that speaks forth our God to be the God of Order; and 'tis amongst these, and such that they imagine this Fearful Imposture, and Arbitrary Rule, imposing Prescriptions and Laws on the tender Consciences of the Weak, is now gotten up to Exercise, and so the Liberty of the tender Conscience is lost: And you say, They are entangled with a yoke of Bondage again, who would divide the Heritage of God at this day. Pray Friends, let us in this consider whether these in this Blindness, which God hath suffered through their prejudiced Mind, justly to happen in them, by which are they now putting Darkness for Light and Light for Darkness, while they are striving in the stifness of their Wills to rule, placing their own Wills for Conscience, and would have a Liberty therein, which Christ never set free to any that are in a Perverse, Gainsaying, Opposing, Willful Spirit, void of the Reason of Truth, and the Fellowship that is in it, and so are led by a Mis-guided Conscience; for we never understood that Conscience to be rightly guided, that was not renewed and regulated by the Light of Christ Jesus, which is one in all Consciences, and leads into the Sameness of Mind,   *1 Cor. 1.6.* not only in Faith, but also in sound Judgment and Practice (and so the Testimony of Christ Jesus hath been confirmed in us) the true Rectifier and Guide of the Conscience void of Offence; but now where Self-will is put for Conscience, *(page 6)* 'tis sensibly felt to be a gross Mistake. And such are (in Christian Charity) to be pitied and better informed, and indeed much Travel hath been for that, so that the Mis-led in a contrary Judgment might be helped and reduced back into Unity and our peaceable Fellowship, in our wholesome Practices, in the outward Affairs of Truth; but that which adds to our Sorrow, that though they still cry, *The tender Consciences,* yet woful Experience demonstrates it far otherwise, where Prejudice hath so hardned, that there is not so much softness left for the Reason of Truth to take Impression, or to receive that which pertains to Love and good Works, which is one end and product of our Meetings, distinctly and respectively the Men Friends, who discharge their places, to whom the Godly Women always give the Pre-eminence, as Brethren; and Women Friends in their places, not seeking Rule over one another, but that we may be Furtherers of one anothers Joy, and be each others Crown of rejoycing in the

Lord, meets in the Fear of the Lord, as in the Light of Christ Jesus in our Consciences, we received, so to walk and do according to the Order of his Spirit, in which Christ is Present in our so meeting together; and the faithful can seal to the Testimony of it, to the Glory of his Name forever.

But wherein doth this great and heavy Imposition on tender Consciences consist? One thing is, say some, *Womens Meetings are imposed: Why do you compel any contrary to their Freedom?* No; all are left to the Measure of Truth in them, which is one and the same in all Consciences; but Informing, Instructing and Exhorting, that every one be found in the Unity of our Duty, according to our Measure of the Light of Christ Jesus, received to walk in it, as Members of his Body to discharge our Office, and Servants in Christs Family to do our Service, as the good Women of old were Helpers in the Work of the Gospel, in such things as are proper to us, as visiting and Relieving the Sick, the Poor more especially and Destitute amongst us, that they be helped, as also the Poor Widdows, and Fatherless Orphans, that the Distressed in all things be rightly answered, the Children at Nurse be rightly educated, and well brought up, in order to a future well-being in the Creation. Again, we being met together, the Elder Women to instruct the Younger to all wholesome things, Loving their own Husbands and Children, to be Discreet, Chaste, Sober, keeping at *(page 7)* Home, that the Word of God we profess be not Blasphemed, &c with many other Matters pertient to us, as a Meeting whom the Lord blesseth with his Power and Presence, to sustain and bear us up against all our Opposers.

Again, It is Imposition (saith the Workers of Dissention) *for Marriages to offer their Intentions to the Consideration of the Womens Meeting.* But pray consider, in the Reason of Truth, a Marriage hath an equal Concern in the Woman, as in the Man; and 'tis as reasonable to consider the Women may have as near a Concern in that matter with the Woman, as the Men on the other Part. And farther 'tis said, *'Tis Imposition to go more than once to the Brethrens Meeting. But say we, that are in our wholesome Practices in these Matters, and our Consciences bear us witness in the sight of God, our Eye is to the Honour of his Truth therein, therefore cannot encourage or allow People we are concerned with, to hasten or run together in Marriage, without due Care and Weightiness, and that we are satisfied they are clear in all things touching their Marriage, as they ought to be, and for which end there ought to be a special care over Young People, to whom the Aged had need to be Examples, both of Gravity and good Order, that Christ's Yoke be not cast off by either, nor any false Liberty of the*

Flesh set up, encouraged or soothed among us; wherefore when they have proposed their Intentions to one Meeting, for them to consider, 'tis but reasonable they have time to make Inquiry and Search into the Matter, so as they may be satisfied, that all things are sweet & savoury, that so far as we can, we may be approved of by all in such publick Affairs. *Yea, But you will have such to come the second time, who are known to be clear.* Yea, 'tis but reasonable that such should manifest their Patience and Subjection, as good Examples to others, in these Needful and wholsome Practices, that are of good Report. And therefore we cannot approve such in their willful Endeavours, to confound the Unity of our Order in this matter, under pretence of a burden to their Conscience; for it was no burden to come once; for that Meeting in it self being Good, Just, Honest, and of good Report, answering the Light of Christ Jesus, which is one in all Consciences, as well in the Ignorant, Blind, Mis-guided and Erring, because they will not be informed, the Light is the same there to reprove and inform, as it is in the Conscience ruled and guided by the Light: Therefore pray consider how that can contract a *(page 8)* burden, (viz.) the going twice to such a Meeting, as before mentioned, how it can cause a burden on the Conscience that is rightly informed, though it may be weak, but rather contradicts the Self-will that brings Bondage, and blinds the Consciences: And are not such rather by their opposing Will justly under the Reproof of the Church, and that Endeavours may be, that the Understanding of such be opened, and brought to a better Information in their Consciences? For from the beginning we believe God's Witness in all Consciences is one, and its Reproofs of one Nature and Tendance, and its Instructions tending to one and the same end, and leads all, as they are guided by it, into one Way which allows of no false Liberty. *Yea, but you are gone from the Beginning; for you had not this Way in the Beginning,* say the Opposers. Pray consider, above twenty six Years ago, in the South Parts we were a very little handful of People, gathered into the Belief of the Light of Christ Jesus; so as it is that very Principle of Life in us, that we through Obedience to it might come to know God, as it is Eternal Life to know him, and rightly to worship him in his Spirit, and to be led by him into all Truth, and in Testimony of his own Spirit, in these our Practices, which since the Lord hath called us to, as we are a People called and gathered by the Lord. Pray Consider, I speak the Truth of my Knowledge, and my Conscience beareth me witness in what I have or shall say in this Matter, according to my small Portion and Measure, in the Unity of the Grace received (I give God the Glory, in Humility of Soul

before him, for my Preservation to this Day) for pray consider, through
the smallness of Number in the beginning, we were not so capable as
now for Order in outward Affairs, nor was there then such occasion as
now, but then the Grace of God grew amongst us, and the mighty Arm
of his Power was manifested, by which many were gathered to believe
in the Light of Jesus Christ, it being that, and no other Name given
under Heaven, by which men must be saved. Now in our little measure
of Faith, in this One Way, One Name, One Truth, we were as in a
threefold Cord of God's Love, joyned together; and as we encreased in
Number, then occasion begun of Services, of several kinds, which we
were called in the Truth to consider of, which are not so proper here to
mention, but this one of Marriage. Before we were or could be gathered
into the Order of Men & Womens *(page 9)* Meeting: Upon the weight of
the matter, a necessity did appear, that Friends in the Unity of the Spirit
and Wisdom of God should consider of a Way wherein this matter might
be transacted among our selves, in wholesome Savoury Order, as the
Truth might in no wise be Scandalized, but the Testimony of Truth
born in it to the World: The most convenient Method then seen, for
Truth's sake, was, that Persons declared their Intentions in our publick
Meeting; after Friends were satisfied in their Marrying, they took each
other in the publick Meeting: But after our Meetings grew more Numerous, and also disorderly Spirits began to get up, which were not
subject to the Truth, such would intrude in to our Meetings, to take
each other; so then a Necessity in Truth required a further Method, for
a more particular and strict Care in this case: In all which we are not
gone from the Light and Power of God, and first Principle; but in these
and other things we have been in our good Order and Practices, and
sweet Fellowship managed by it; and I hope the tender in Conscience
will consider, that are impartially Minded, that 'tis no Imposition to
inform and perswade the Ignorant and Willful to subject in this or any
other matter, that is Honest, Just, Savoury and of good Report, and
lawful to conform to, in the Unity of Love to practice, being no other
but what is consonant to the Conscience, swayed and regulated by the
Light of Jesus Christ, in which is the true Liberty of the Conscience,
whether weak or strong: For I hope all will conclude, that if the weak,
in their little measure of Light, be kept Conformable to the Truth, that
by the Light they cannot be led in their little measure to oppose the
strong in their greater measure; and may see further, that 'tis not reasonable in Truth; for the Light cannot contradict it self, and 'tis
the same in the strong as in the weak; But 'tis greatly to be lamented at

this day, that to any that have known the Lord, and at any time fellowship among his People, the Cross of Christ should become so ineffec-
tual, that such Blindness is happened, that they should put
Self-opposing-will for a tender Conscience: I do not say, they know it;
but whether they do or no, I pray God open their Understandings, and
subdue that perverse wilful Spirit and cross Selfish humor, that works
in opposition to a General Good and Peaceable Subjection amongst
the People of the Lord and Church of Christ. Surely *(page 10)* these,
though they may cry, *Liberty of Conscience*, and pretend for tender Consciences too, yet they are not fit Subjects for that Liberty that Christ
redeems to, and sets free in, to serve him with a Conscience purged
from Dead Works; nay, they that set themselves, in their wilful prejudiced Opposition, against our Peaceable practicing in the Church of
God; *Whatsoever things are true, whatsoever things are honest, whatsoever
things are just, whatsoever things are pure, whatsoever things pertain to Love,
whatsoever things are of good report*, Phil. 4.8. In which the God of Peace
is with us now; that which is opposing our Unity therein, would affright
the simple Ones with amazing expressions of Imposition, &c. on weak
Consciences, and going from the Spirit of Life and Power into the Form;
but blessed be the Lord that we have kept our Habitation in the Power,
and held our Unity in that Spirit that gives us Life, thereby to live to
God, and not to our selves, to serve him in that Form of Godliness,
which the Power hath brought forth amongst us, to live in the Unity
of, and in his Spirit, the Foundation of our Preservation, in Peace and
Consolation to this very day; and the Faith of such remains firm in
God's everlasting power, even as we received in the beginning of the
breaking forth of the Day of the Lord, in which his ancient Arm and
excellent Everlasting Name was revealed, which is above every Name,
into which a Number was gathered to believe and meet in, and the
Lord was there, and is to this very day in the midst of them, as Thousands, and ten Thousands can speak to the Testimony of it; Oh, Glory,
Obedience, and everlasting Dominion be ascribed to his honourable
and everlasting Name over all forever; For the Kingdom of our God
and his Christ, on whose Shoulders the Government is laid, shall prevail through all Clouds of opposition, and Mists of thick Darkness, that
have risen out of a misguided understanding, through a Prejudiced mind,
even to ensnare the weak and simple, and deceive the unstable Soul,
drawing from our *Christian* Unity, which is purely held in the Spirit.

And so, inasmuch as the Envious Worker is suffered to proceed, that
would even raze out the Foundation of Christ's Kingdom and Govern-

ment, under which his Subjects do only own their *Christian* Freedom and true Liberty of Conscience; and whatsoever may be insinuated to the contrary, by the Enemy of our Souls Well-fare *(page 11)* in the particular, and the Churches Peace in the general, which God may Suffer,it is for the Tryal of our Patience, and Manifestation and Confirmation of our Faith and Love one to another, and that it is in the Election in Christ Jesus which cannot be deceived, whereby we are strong in the Lord, and in the Power of his might is our confidence, that all shall work together for good to thee Called, Chosen and Faithful, according to his purpose in Christ, and effectual working of his Grace; And that the Lord in his Power and due time, will arise to clear the Innocency of his People, and Confound and lay Waste all that which works in Opposition to the Prosperity and Unity of his Truth, and peaceable Government of Christ in his Church, which is formed in the Power of God.

So all Glory we afcribe to the one pure Power, in which we believed in the beginning, as the Foundation of Chrifts Government and Kingdom that fhall never have end.

Anne Whitehead.

(page 11)

A true Information of our bleffed *Womens Meeting* (For we are bleffed, and the Lord hath bleffed us, praised be that Everlafting Arm of Power, that gathered us in the beginning to be a Meeting) betwixt 3 or 4 and twenty Years ago.

THus it was, after the Word of eternal Life and Salvation, and Light of Christ Jesus in the Conscience, had been Preached in this City, for some time, many there were that received the Report, and was Convinced of it, many Poor as well as Rich; and offtimes Sickness and Weakness came upon many Poor Ones, and *(page 12)* many Distressed and troubled in mind, when the Judgments of the Lord were upon them; and they would oftentimes desire the Servants of the Lord to come unto them, such that had a Word in season to speak to them:

And our dear Friend *George Fox,* that man of God, for so he is, the Lord has made him a Blessing in his Hand to many, praised be the Lord forever, he was many times sent for to many that were Sick and Weak in this City, and when he came to behold their want of things needful for them, some scarcely Clothes to cover them, or Food to eat, or any one to look to them in their Distresses and Wants: The consideration of it was weighty upon him, and he was moved of the Lord to advise to a Womans Meeting; and in order thereunto, he sent for such Women as he knew in this City; of which there are many living to this day, that can testifie to the same, who keep the Meeting in the Faith of that Power that gathered us together; Blessed be the Lord forever who makes willing, and gives strength to answer his Requirings in all things. And when dear G. *Fox* declared unto us what the Lord had made known unto him by his Power, That there should be a Womans Meeting, that so all the Sick, the Weak, the Widdows and Fatherless, should be minded and looked after in their Distresses, that so there should be no Want amongst the Lords People, but that all Distressed ones should be minded and looked after: I can truly say, we had an answer of God in our Hearts to his Testimony, and my Soul was refreshed at that time, and my heart tendred, with many more of my Sisters, in the sensible feeling of that everlasting Life and Power of the Lord, and his Universal Love that had moved in his dear Servant, to call us to this Work; and we joyned with him in the Power of God in it: and so we appointed a Meeting, and after we had met for some time, we considered which way we should answer the Necessities; and it arose in the Hearts of some Friends, *That we should have a conveniency, that so all the Faithful might offer us unto the Lord, not knowing what one another offers; that so from him they might expect their Reward;* and it was concluded upon accordingly by the Meeting. And these were found among us some that were unworthy, that we could not relieve out of that which was provided for the Faithful; and yet they were such that frequented our publick Meetings, and looked unto us for Charity; and we could not send them empty away; So we *(page 13)* considered, and had a Weekly Gathering for them, that it might be fulfilled, as it is written, *Do good unto all, but especially to the Houshold of Faith.* And after some time of our meeting together, their came two of the Brethren from the Mens Meeting to us, when we were met together, expressing their Unity with us, and also did declare the mind of the Mens Meeting, (viz.) *That they would be ready to help and assist us in anything we should desire for them for Truth's Service:* And so in some time it was agreed upon, in the Unity of the Truth, that the Men Friends should pay the Poor Friends Rents, and find them Coles, (such as we Relieve, that were faithful) and put out such poor Friends Children, as we should offer to them; And this has been done almost from the beginning of our Meeting to this Day; besides many other Services that fall in by the way, that cannot be omitted by us: And thus the Work of the Lord has been carried on and prospered by the Arm of his everlasting Power, *Magnified be his Name forever, who has found us worthy, and made us willing to answer whatsoever he requireth of us, according to the measure received of him.* And this I do declare, that it was the same everlasting quickning Power that first visited us by the Spirit of Judgment and of Burning, and wrought in our inward parts mightily, even as the little Leaven in the three Measures of Meal, to purifie and to cleanse, to purge out and put under all that was contrary to the Lord, and to make us Habitations fit to do his Will, that gathered us and made us a Meeting, and the same has been with us to this very day, blessed and magnified be his Name forever.

And I have a Word in my Heart to say unto you all *Back-sliders, Obstructors, Opposers* (& such as countenance them secretly) of this our heavenly Order of Men and Womens Meetings, which the Lord by his Power has set up, and hath given Wisdom according to true Knowledge, to act in the Church of Christ: you that have despised Dignities, and speak Evil of the Servants of the Lord, such that faithfully have laboured amongst us from the beginning, which the Lord hath found worthy of double Honour, giving some of them odd Names; Alas poor People! what will become of you, except you Repent? Consider and see, whether some of you could not once have plucked out your Eyes to have done them good? Oh what is the matter now! Has not the Serpent deceived you, and *(page 14)* made you to eat of the forbidden Fruit, and let in the Spirit of Enmity that sows Dissention, and makes Division in the Heritage of God; I do say, the Lord's Controversie is with you, and your End will be Miserable, except you come to Repentance; which my Soul hath often desired for you: For I do well know, and the Lord hath sealed it upon my Heart, That the Spirit which hath opposed the blessed Unity and Order of Truth, in these our Men and Womens Meetings, shall never prosper, nor they who are in it, inwardly to God, without Repentance; although outwardly they may make never so great a shew with high Words and Notions. But saith the opposing Spirit, *We are not against your Meetings in* London; *but we have no such need in the Countries.* Doubtless Christ's Churches in the Countries are one and the same as in the Cities, of which he is Head of his Churches there as in *London;* and surely his Members have the same Office and Service in kind and quality, although it may be not so much in quantity, which is reasonable for the Impartial minded to consider.

And now, my Dear *Friends* and *Sisters,* in the blessed Truth of our God, you that have kept this our Meeting for many Years, and some of you from the first Day the Lord gathered us together, and made us a Meeting, I do believe that you with me can truly say, *That we have felt the drawings of the Father's Love from time to time to this our Meeting, and his Blessing is amongst us;* Insomuch as we, dared not to suffer any of our own Occasions to hinder us from this our Service, to which the Lord hath called us, but many times have pressed through the croud of much Business; and many things that would have hindred, but we dared not to give way unto it, but in faithfulness answer the Lord's Requirings: The Lord hath been with us of a truth from time to time, his Living Powerful Presence has been truly witnessed amongst us, to the refreshing of our immortal Souls; which is a true Confirmation to us, that the Lord owns us in this our Service. And I can truly say, I had true Breathings to the Lord in the behalf of our younger Women, as they come to be settled in the World amongst us, that they may be affected with the Work and Service! of our Meeting as truly as we have been, and are to this day, and that they may be Heirs of the Grace of God with us. And this I can truly say, I have felt the Zeal of the Lord to arise in my heart, sometimes in a Meeting, and sometimes *(page 15)* upon my Bed against this wicked Spirit, that hath sought to lay waste and bring to nought our blessed Meeting and heavenly Society and Order, which hath been set up amongst us; and a true sence hath been upon me of our dear Friends up and down the Nation, of their great Tryal and Exercise that hath been upon them, because of this wicked dividing Spirit, and especially in my Native Country (viz.) *Wiltshire:* And this was the first moving cause in the Power of God in my Heart, to cast in my Mite as my Testimony to that everlasting Universal blessed Power, which the Lord hath made me a living Witness of, according to my measure: And this I can say, the more Opposition we have had against our Womens Meeting, the more we have increased in the Power of the Lord, and he hath blessed our Endeavours and Services; and therefore *Friends,* be not discouraged, but go on in the Work and Service of the Lord in his Power, to his Glory, who hath honoured his Daughters of *Abraham* and *Sion,* in his heavenly Work; and therefore we cannot but serve the Lord in our Generation, and be Valiant for his Truth upon Earth, and our desires are, that all our fellow Sisters in the Lords Truth may do the same every where throughout the whole Earth, where the Lord hath gatherd them, so that all may live to the Praise and Glory of God, *Amen.*

And though we are Abfent in the Body, yet Prefent in Spirit with all the Faithful, with the Spirit joying and beholding your fpiritual Order in the Spirit, and ftedfastness of your Faith in Chrift Jefus, the fecond Adam, the Lord from Heaven in whom our Peace and Reft is.

Mary Elfon.

THE END.

AN

EPISTLE

TO

FRIENDS

Every where :

To be Diftincly Read in their

MEETINGS,

When Affembled together in the
Fear of the Lord.

By a Friend of Truth, and a Lover of Righteoufnefs,
Katharine Whitton.

LONDON
Printed for *Benjamin Clark* Bookfeller in *George-
yard Lombard-ftreet.* 1681.

(Page numbers of original document appear in text as *page _.*)

(page 1)

AN

EPISTLE

TO

FRIENDS

Every where.

Dear Friends,

IN bowels of tender love to all Friends every where, am I constrained and pressed in Spirit to give forth this Testimony, under which I have lain for a long time bowed in Spirit, in a deep sense of the Fatherly care of our God over all his Lambs, and little ones, which he would gladly have all gathered unto him, that he might preserve them from the evil of the day which is approaching; for he hath shewed a terrible day near to break forth; yea, a day that will burn as an Oven, and all the proud, and they that do wickedly, will be as Stubble which cannot endure the Fire; for it will be as a flame, and serve as a fire to consume the counterfeit Mettal, and reprobate Silver, that the pure Gold may appear; yea, that the precious Sons and Daughters of *Sion* may come forth as Gold seven times tried, and shine in their Beauty and Lustre. For saith the Lord, *I will burn the Chaff with an unquenchable fire, but the Wheat I will gather into my Garner.*

And Friends, this is no Reflection, but comes for discharging a duty, from one whom God in measure hath placed as on *Sions* Walls; and who seeing the Sword come, dare not but give warning to such as are not upon the watch: For saith the Lord, *If they take not warning, if the Sword come and take them away, their blood shall be upon their own heads: But if thou do not warn them, if the Sword come and take any person from amongst them, they are taken away in their Iniquity; but their blood will I require at thy hands.* And *(page 2)* Friends, with many Tears and Cries unto the Lord have I been bowed down many a time, that I and every one whom God hath concerned may be clear of the blood of all: And that the House of *Israel* may be spoken to, least sin be upon us. For saith the Lord, *Cry aloud and spare not, lift up thy voice like a Trumpet, shew my people their transgression, and the house of* Jacob *their sin*. Yea it is a warning from the Almighty, to all and every one of the backsliders in *Israel*, and lukewarm ones, and careless daughters of *Jerusalem*, and Women at ease in *Sion*, yea an Alarm is sounded out of the Holy Mountain, that you may hear and be awakned to righteousness, and stirred up to holiness, to meet the Lord in the way of his pure Judgments; for woe will be to those that are at ease in that day that is a coming; yea the sinners in *Sion* must mourn, fear will overtake all the unfaithful and disobedient; yea terror will surprise the hypocrites, and woe and misery will be to all those, except they repent, for it is a warning in my heart unto all such from the Lord, that they may all turn unto him by true repentance, whose mercy is proffered, and observe his Commandments to do them, and keep Covenant with him, and see that every one be wise in heart, and travel in spirit, and make it their concern to bring glory unto the Lord in this his day; for he keeps Covenant with, and extends mercy unto them that love him and keep his Commandments, and he hears the Prayers of his own children, and hath heard them in every Age, and hath not forgot his word Spoken by his Servants of old; where he saith, *If you transgress I will scatter you abroad amongst the Nations, but if you turn unto me and keep my Commandments, and do them, though there were of you cast out into the uttermost parts of the heaven, yet will I gather you from thence, and will bring you into the place that I have chosen to set my Name there*. And surely Friends, we are the people for whom the Lord hath done great things, since the day that he hath opened our eyes, and let us see our miserable and wretched state, and the great need we had of him to help us out of that condition.

Oh! the many tears, with deep sighs and bitter groans in that day, can never be forgotten; and blessed be the Lord who hath heard the cries of the poor, and regarded the groanings of the needy, and hath met us in the way of his Judgments; and hath brought in the Ministration of Condemnation, which was glorious in its time, and placed it upon the head of the transgressor in us, whereby he *(page 3)* hath judged and condemned the transgressing and rebellious part, that would not that he should reign, and in his infinite love, and bowels of tender compassion, which yearned towards his own pressed Seed that groaned to be delivered, hath he ransomed and redeemed his own in measure, and led the same as he did *Israel* of old out of *Egypts* darkness, and from under *Pharaoh's* taskmasters, to sacrifice unto him, and praise him in the land of the living.

And my dear Friends, a remnant through Gods mercy can truly say, he hath visited us as with the day-spring from on high; and are witnesses that refreshment from his presence is come, and though sorrow endur'd for the night, yet joy came in the morning, the day being dawn'd, and the morning Sun arisen; yea the Winter is now through mercy, with many far spent, and the storms in measure over, and the spring time come, and the singing of Birds, and the voice of the Turtle is heard in our land. O! the glorious day that is dawn'd upon us, where the morning Stars do sing together, and all the Sons of God do shout for joy. Oh! the wonderful works of our God, and the noble Acts that he hath done; he hath made us to see his wonders in the deep, and as *Israel* of old, to sing his praises: Oh his tender dealings can never be raced out of our remembrance, he hath printed them in our hearts, and his engaging love constraineth us to speak well of him, and to make mention of his Name, and speak of his loving kindness and tender mercies which endureth for ever!

And dear Friends, after all this and much more of the Lords dealing with us, and kindness and mercy bestowed upon us, hath the old adversary and enemy of mankind bestirred himself; who in every Age hath gone about to insnare the simple, as in *Israel* of old, when he prevailed over *Achan* to covet the wedge of Gold, and the *Babylonish* Garment, for putting his hand to which, the whole Camp of Israel was troubled, until *Achan* was found, and *Babylon's* Stuff thrown out, and burnt without the Camp. And other some [sic] taking strange Wifes, mixing with the Heathen, loving their Gold, and learning their ways; for which *Ezra* in his bitter Lamentations, *plucked the Hair from his Head and Beard;* and *Jeremiah* wished, *that his Head were Waters, and his eyes a Fountain of Tears, that he might weep day and night for the slain of the Daughters of his people!* And dear Friends, in our Age many hath been the temptations and allurements this enemy hath assaulted the children of the Lord with, *(page 4)* sometimes transforming himself as into an Angel of Light, to deceive if it were possible the very Elect: But blessed be the Lord who hath preserved a remnant out of his snare alive unto himself, yet hath he prevailed upon some, drawing them into divers disorders whereby the worthy Name of the Lord hath been blasphemed, his precious Truth evil spoken of, and the simple insnared, to the sorrow of a remnant, and sadding the hearts of the righteous, which hath caused many tears and secret cries unto the Lord, that he would appear in his wisdom more and more for his own glorious Names sake, and Truths sake, to preserve the simple, and frustrate the enemy of his end: And blessed be the Lord who still hears the cry of his own Seed and being zealous of his own glory, hath appeared in his Faithful Messengers, to gather and encourage men and womens Meetings, whereby he is stopping the enemy in his progress, by placing judgment on his head, and condemnation to that part over which he rules; and in his work the Lord hath engaged Sons and Daughters, putting his spiritual Sword into their hands, for the beating down strong holds of sin; in which the mighty Prince of the power of darkness hath his place: neither dare they do his work negligently or over look, or connive at any of his practices, or proceedings in whomsoever they appear, but in Truth, and Righteousness, judge and condemn the evil, under whatever pretence the same do appear, at which the evil one is troubled; and likes not this way, neither would be thus dealt with, but under pretence of Truth pleads for more liberty and freedom of Spirit; and so transforming himself to betray the simple, and defile the Temple of God, and sit as God, yet he is the Serpent, and he cannot save his head, for the Seed of the woman is brought forth, and a bringing forth, and the enmity is placed between the two Seeds, and her Seed must break his head; and he is now a receiving Blows, at which he rageth; and raileth against the work of the Lord, and the instruments he imployeth: But the determination of the Lord is to disthrone him; and bring him down, and take his own possessions and reign in his own Temple, whose right it is to rule, and happy will all such be, who in submission do meet him in the sway of his Righteous Judgments; for they are always mixed with mercy, and they shall find it who submit unto him, but such as will not that he should reign, he will bring them to naught.

Therefore dear Friends, let us keep our Women's Meetings in Gods *(page 5)* pure fear, and wait upon him to feel his power and heavenly wisdom, and that will allow of nothing whereby the worthy Name of the Lord is blasphemed, his precious Truth evil spoken of, or good Spirit grieved either in the particular or general, but by his power and wisdom it will be judged and disowned, without respect of persons, whether by words or actions, Meats, Drink or Apparel, let the pretence be what it will; neither can this sowe pillows under the arm-holes of any, nor speak peace to the wicked; nor heal the hurt of the Lords people deceitfully; but search the wound, and pour in the pure oyl, to the comfort of the wounded: Tha[ ] that may be raised which delights to do its Fathers will, and honour him in all things (*i.e.*) both in life, practice and doctrine, that so in this holy life we may shine as Lights in the World, in Gods wisdom, having our Lamps trimmed, our Lights burning, and in our Centers the sweet Incense, which gives a good Savour, both to God and man, having the Savoury Salt in us with which every word and action may be seasoned, that others seeing our holy lives, and good conversations may glorifie our heavenly Father.

And dear Friends, let no difference be, but in the unity of one Spirit let's be a people of one heart and mind, serving the Lord with one consent, seeking his glory unanimously, working the work to which he hath called us, which work is to stop the enemies work (as I said before) in what pretence soever he come; for Friends, he will ask no more then to have footing amongst us, under pretence of Truth, putting a fair vizard on every action, calling pride decency, covetousness carefulness, Nicety and Curiosity in the forms of Meat, Drink, or other things, a point of good Housewifery; for every thing he will have a covering like Truth, that he may keep his Interest in the hearts of men and women, which is the principal part: But the Heir is brought forth which must take his Inheritance, and the true Light now shineth that discovers him in every action, not one corner he can shelter in where he is not seen, his coverings are all too narrow, the vail which he hath spread over him and his actions, must by the power of the Lord which is risen, and rising in the bosoms of a remnant, be rent in twain from the top to the bottom; so my dear Friends, whom God hath engaged, every one discharge your duty, be zealous for the Lord, and valiant for his Truth, and as the valiants of *Israel*, every one have on your Spiritual armour and weapons in readiness, for woe will be to those *(page 6)* who do the work of the Lord negligently, or with a careless mind; But they will with *Jael* be blessed, who put their hand to the work, and their right hand to the Workmans hammer, to the wounding of *Israels* enemy, for he must bow, yea he must fall, and Songs of Triumph over him, as in *Deborahs* days there must be: Therefore Friends, let us to the work, every one to the imployment to which we are or have been called; and while the Light shineth that lets us see every Corner, let all that's unclean be rid, and swept out; yea let us make clean work, for to be truly arrayed in the White-Linen which is the righteousness of Saints, is very decent, and to have this house (to wit, our hearts and inward parts) clean swept, and all its furniture of righteousness set in good and comely order, in carefulness, is very commendable and consistent with good Housewifery too: And I do not doubt but those who are careful in the matters before mentioned, will not as to outward things come short (according to their abilities) in any thing that is needful, necessary, comely, decent and of good report; as it is not fit they should exceed, so I hope they will not come behind, what may be of good example, and tend to edification, and to those things whereby Truth is honoured. So Friends let us be Faithful to the Lord, and careful over his household and family, not as the bad Servant, who smiteth his Fellow, but as the good Servant, giving them Meat in due season. Feeding the Hungry, Cloathing the Naked, Visiting the Sick, binding up the broken-hearted, healing the wounded, and let it be with *Gileads* Balm, and blessed shall all such be when their Lord cometh whom he shall find so doing; and greatly hath the presence of God to his praise appeared to the owning, carrying on and blessing of this his own work, and large hath been his love and Fatherly care over all Lambs and little ones, and very weighty is the work and great the concern, to strengthen the weak, and confirm the feeble, and gather all those that's scattered by the wiles of the enemy to him, that is and always was the ancient Rock and refuge of the righteous in every Age, that so if possible, not one may be left behind, but all be gathered: And it is the travel of my Soul, and desire of my Spirit, that none of those may slight the day of their Visitation, whom the Lord hath in any measure touched, or that they had their faces turned *Sion*-wards, but that they may be exhorted and admonished, and dearly intreated to hast unto the Lord who long hath hovered over us, as sometime he did over *Jerusalem* of old, and fain would *(page 7)* have all gathered under the shelter of his wings, that ever made mention of his Name; and many hath seen his Warnings, and Invitations by his Servants and Messengers, and still stands as with open arms, ready to receive all those that come unto him in humility of mind, and brokenness of heart. So dear Friends, let none stick in the World, its evil ways, vain Customs, or foolish fashions; be not partakers with them of their pleasures, lest such partake of their plagues; but be ye Separated, *touch no unclean thing, and I will receive you, saith the Lord:* so in this self-denying life, and by the ancient power by which we were gathered in the beginning, let us hast with speed to our God, who is our refuge and sure hiding-place; for the storm approacheth, and certainly will overtake the negligent & careless, who are gone from the Shepherd. So dear Friends, let no pains be spared, or means neglected, whereby the work so needful may be hastned, for it is Gods work, and not mans, though as I said before, it laid on the ancient and honourable in *Israel*, to put the work forward; for the Elders that rule well, are worthy of double honour, as the Apostle said, and also esteem them for their works sake. And as

Deborah said, *my heart is towards the Governours of Israel;* and I can truly say, many a time when I have viewed in my mind their sufferings, tryals and tribulations they went through in the beginning, my heart hath been broken, and I have secretly said, They have broken us a way through the Thickets, and trodden us a path through the Desarts; they have born the burden in the heat of the day, and what can I now do, or suffer for the Truth? am I not as one born out of due time?

But living praises to the Lord, who in every Age is ready to reward the faithful, in what hour soever they labour in his Vineyard; and there is not one Member, though never so little, if in the body, nor Instrument, though never so weak, if prepared of the Lord, but all needful and useful in their places, to the dressing of the Vineyard of the Lord, and for the plucking up of those hurtful weeds that cumber the tender Plants. And dear Friends, let this be done in Gods pure fear, and heavenly Wisdom, with a tender care over every weak Plant, that it may be nourished within good ground, that it may bring forth Fruit to Gods Glory; For *thereby saith he am I glorified, that ye bring forth much Fruit.* Then is the labour of love which the faithful bestows answered, when the Plants prosper, and the Lord is glorified; so in this labour, as co-workers and fellow-helpers, Male and Female, for which we were raised up by the Lords Power, let us put our hands to the work, and none look at their own weakness, for the Lord hath been pleaded with *(page 8)* touching the weightiness of the work, and the weakness of the Instrument he choosed; and his Answer hath been in the bosom of such (*i.e.*) I have chosen the weak things to overthurn the strong and Mighty, and the foolish things to confound the Wisdom of the Wise, and things that are not, to bring to nought things that are; and it is the travel of my Spirit, That none that puts their hand to the Plow may draw back or be dismayed, whatsoever the opposition be, for living praises to our God; the time is come wherein he is pouring of his Spirit upon his Sons, and upon his Daughters, Servants and Hand-maids, and enduing them with his Heavenly Wisdom, and sitting and strengthening them to perform every duty and service he hath called them unto, how feeble soever we have appeared to be: As he did the ancient *Jews,* when they had the walls of *Jerusalem* to build, though it was then said of them, what will these feeble *Jews* do? but mark what Courage they received from the Lord to carry on the work with one hand, and with the other hold their weapon and praises to the Lord; we have no cause to complain, for his ancient power hath been with us thus far, and his Heavenly presence hath accompanied us hitherto, whereby we are encouraged to the work for which we are appointed, even to labour in the Lord, for the repairing of the waste places of *Jerusalem*, and making up of the breaches in *Sion*, whom the Lord is making and about to make the praise of the whole Earth, for her Beauty must shine forth, that many seeing it may have their faces thitherwards, and beholding *Jerusalems* glory, may desire to dwell within her walls.

And dear Friends, let us diligently view *Jerusalem*, that we may count her Towers, and mark well her Bulwarks, that we may tell it to generations to come, and that those who succeed our day, may have those Testimonies left upon Record, what God hath done for us, and been unto us; that his Faithfulness may be declared from age to age, and from one generation to another. O praises, praises to our God for evermore, for he hath had regard to the low estate of his Hand-maids, and hath remembred our many tears, when we mourned apart for him as silly Doves without Mates, and hath visited with his love, & owned with his presence, which is better then life it self; yea he is the beloved of our Souls, he is altogether Comely, there is no Spot in him, he is Amiable in our eye, he is the chiefest of ten Thousand, there is none like unto him, nor worthy to be compared with him, he is our beloved, and he is our Friend, and hath given us cause to say, our lot is fallen in a good Land, and that we have a large possession; yea let this song be sung as in the *(page 9)* land of *Judah*, we have a strong City, Salvation hath God appointed for Walls and for Bulwarks, and will keep in perfect peace all those whose minds are staid upon him; but he will bring down those that dwell on high, yea the lofty he will lay low, but the way of the Just is uprightness, the most upright doth weigh his paths, yea in the way of his Judgments have we waited for him, and the desire of our Souls hath been to his Name, and to the remembrance of it; yea with our Souls have we desired him in the Night season, and with our Spirits within us have we sought him early; for when his Judgments are in the Earth, then its Inhabitants learn Righteousness. O living Praises unto him who hath appeared in our age, and brought forth Judgment into victory, and ransomed, redeemed and raised by his ancient power, his own suffering Seed, which in every age hath found acceptance with him from the beginning, as was manifest in righteous *Abel, Enoch,* (and also *Noah* whom he preserved;) though he destroyed the old World: and though *Sodom* was destroyed, yet *Lot* escaped, by flying out of it and getting into *Zoar*: And dear Friends, it is upon me yet once more to entreat, if any there be in any measure guilty of any of those Evils for which the Lord is angry with this Nation, the land of our Nativity, that

such by true Repentance, while mercy is proffered, would return and
get out of the same; for the Angel of the Lord hath warned, therefore
linger not, but I say get out of every thing wherewith the Lord is displeased, for he is a holy God, and of purer eyes then to behold Iniquity,
and without holiness none can come unto him: Therefore saith he, *be
ye holy as I am holy,* So dear Friends, in this holy life let us fly unto the
Name of the Lord, for it is our strong Tower, in which he will preserve
the Righteous, until his indignation be over and past; for he is angry
with this Nation, because of the many & gross evils which hath
abounded in it, with the oppressions of his people, because of all which
he is grieved, and is preparing as a man of war to cut down the workers
of iniquity, and sweep the Nation of Evil doers, and will finish Sin, and
put an end to transgression, and bring in everlasting Righteousness,
that the knowledge of his glory may cover the Earth, as the waters
cover the Seas, for he hath taken notice of his suffering Seed, and hath
remembred the afflictions of *Joseph*, and will set his Seed and heritage
free, and bring the prisoners out of the prison-house; for *Joseph* came
forth to answer the end for which he was appointed, (though he was
afflicted from a Child) to be a Saviour and preserver of much People;
for the promises of the Lord to our father, faithful *Abraham*, stands sure
for ever, who said, *in blessing I will bless thee, (page 10) and in multiplying I
will multiply thy Seed as the Stars of Heaven, and as the Sand on the Sea
shore which cannot be numbered,* in whose Seed also all the Nations of
the Earth shall be blessed. So dear Friends, in the blessed Seed let us
daily wait upon the Lord, to feel its breathings, and travels, and wrestlings
of the Almighty, for *Sions* sake; yea let those Spiritual Prayers ascend
up unto him, which in every age is his delight, and avails much with
him for *Sions* prosperity, and for *Jerusalem's* welfare; and not only so,
but for all that have their faces *Sion*-wards; and desire to Inhabit within
Jerusalem's walls; for good is the Lord, *slow to anger and of great mercy,*
willing to shew kindness to all *Sions* wel-wishers. And so dear Friends,
let us give our Attendance in all heavenly obedience upon him, in his
own pure life, begotten and brought forth by him, that so by his own
off-spring he may be honoured, and in that may sway the Righteous
Scepter, and lift up his Standard, and display his Ensign, that the Nations of those that must be saved by him, may flock unto him; that so
many there may be from the *East*, and *West, North* and *South*, that may
come to sit down with *Abraham, Isaac* and *Jacob*, to praise him in the
beauty of holiness, unto whom all praises, honour and renown belongeth,
and to him it is given and returned, saith my Soul.

Dear Friends, this hath long laid upon me from the Lord; but I would have hid my self, and have been as one unconcerned, but his hand was heavy upon me, and gave me no rest, until with many tears I cryed unto him that he would help me, and enable me to do my duty, and discharge my Conscience, and deliver his Message; and then I gave up, and in obedience found peace: and according to the ability he hath given me, and as he opened in my heart, have I delivered it, desiring it may be received in the same bowels of love in which it is given forth, and its end answered, which is only and alone that the Lords People may be preserved, and he over all glorified, who is God, worthy for ever and for ever, and for evermore.

From a Traveller in Spirit for Sions *profperity, and your true and loving Friend, in the univerfal and unchangeable love of our God, in which I bid you all farewell.*

Catharine Whitton

A
SALUTATION
OF MY
Endeared Love
TO THE
FAITHFUL
In ALL PLACES,

That bear their Teſtimony for the Lord, and keep in the Lowlineſs to Truth as it is in J E S U S.

T He Blessing of the Lord is with you that have given up your all to the Lord as an acceptable Sacrifice; and if you keep to that pure unchangable Power, that gives dominion over Sin, the Lords multiplying Hand will attend you, as it did Faithful *Abraham*, and make you a blessing among the people, and so you will feel the Lord nearer to you then when you first believed, and Truth more pretious to your Souls then ever; for your beloved will be yours, and you will be his; then in the sence of what he hath done for you, you will be willing to endure whatsoever the Lord *(page 2)* permits to come upon you for the tryall of your Faith, Knowing that the tryall of it is more precious then Gold that perisheth; and therefore have we great cause to count it all Joy, that he hath counted us worthy to suffer for his name; for it is those that have fellowship with the Death and Sufferings of our Lord Jesus that come through the great Tribulations, and are found worthy to walk with him in white, such have Right to eat of the Tree of Life: There-

(Page numbers of original document appear in text as *page _.*)

fore, my dear Friends let us be wholy given up in our Souls and Bodies
to serve the Lord Joyfully and willingly; for it is the free-will Offerers
that God accepts at this day, as in Antient Time; when the governours
and people of *Israell* [*sic*] Offered themselves willingly, the Lord Accepted of them, and prospered their undertakings, to the Reviving of
their hearts, which caused them to prayse the Lord, and Rehearse his
Righteous Acts, in the sence of the great deliverance they had Obtained from him alone; and then they also called to mind what great
thoughts of heart they were once in for them that staid behind, &c.
who came not forth to the help of the Lord against the wicked; but the
Lord had no need of the help of man at that day, to get himself a name
above every name, neither hath he in these latter days, yet he delights
in such Instruments that stand up Valiently for his holy Name on the
earth, and they shall wax Valient with Spiritual weapons; before their
faces many shall be much pained, for the Lord will rore out of *Sion* and
utter his Voice from his holy Habitation; and thou Oh *Israel* that hast
been faithful, and kept to thy first Love, shalt have a Habitation in
him, the Rock of Ages, and shalt be as a Royal Diadem in the hand of
thy God, and he delights to appear for thee and in thee, because thou
(page 3) hast delighted to appear before him, and to wait for him in the
way of his Righteous Judgments, and Kept them till they were brought
forth into victory; and though thou art very few in number, and least
among the Nations, and dare not medle with *Carnal Weapons*, yet Great
will the Holy one of *Israel* be in the midst of thee when he marcheth
through the Nations to plead with the *Heathen* round about for thy
sake; and the Spiritual Battel is already begun in the Nations, in which
the great and mighty God will plead with all Flesh as in the Vally of
Jehoasphat [*sic*], which is the Vally of Judgment, for the honour of his
great Name, and deliverance of his people, which is as near to him as
the Apple of his Eye: Therefore let us be Incouraged in our God, as
David was when *Ziglag* was taken, and burnt with Fire, and the living
carried away Captives by the hand of the Spoiler, and his Friends that
should have stood by him talked of Stoning of him, because of the
great distress of mind that was on them, which came only for the triall
of their Faith; but great was *Davids* Faith and Confidence in God, and
in the same he called upon him in the time of trouble, and the Lord
heard, and Answered, and delivered him out of all his Distresses, both
on the right hand and one [*sic*] the left, and all the living that the
enemy had carried away captive was recover'd again by the help of the
Lord to Praise him, neither did he miss anything; for the great Creator

of all things was with him, and gave him Victory over his enemies, and so he divided the Spoil; and he is the same to the Faithful this day that have put their trust in him in the midst of difficulties; for he is the same to his people as ever he was, God Almighty and Unchangeable, without Variableness or shadow of *(page 4)* turning, therefore my dear Friends let us be ingaged to follow the Lord Fully as *Joshua* and *Caleb* did, that so we may press through all Difficulties, and hold out to the end, that so we may be Saved; for this is my hearty desire to the Lord for my own Soul and all the Faithful, *that we may be Preserved to the end.*

And so dear Friends, keep in true Wachfulness against the enemy, that Seeks to defile and hinder the true access to God, and watch unto Prayer; for the Lord delightes to hear the Prayer of the Faithful, and it prevails much with him, and it shall reach to Heaven and draw down a blessing in abundance, when all *Babels Builders* shall be thrown down, that have sought to reach Heaven in their vain Imaginations, even like *Capernaam*, who was exalted on high till the Lord cast them down to Hell, and now the day of the Lord is going over the Nation to break down all Images & pleasant Pictures of Religion that are not of his own Appointing and Setting up, & he will dash them in pieces as a Potters Vessel; *for he will not give his Honour to any Idol, nor his Glory to Graven Images:* and blessed are all those that have a place in the munition of Rocks, while those things are bringing to pass; for they shall be glad to go together to the House of God, as *David* was, where the Lord does teach his people of his wayes, and gives them power to stand still and see his great Salvation brought to pass for their deliverance from all oppression; for it is but a very little while and all those that keep to the word of Patience will be delivered out of all Temptation; and my Prayer to God is, *That he will preserve my Soul in Faithfulness among the living in the Heavenly* Jerusalem *to the End.*

(page 5)

ANd now I have also a deep concern upon my Spirit, as a Faithfull **Warning** to you in all places that have slighted the Assemblies of the Lords People, and in so doing have neglected your duty to God both in Private and in Publick; for I know right well that those that keep their hearts with all diligence to the Lord, to feel the Issue of life in the Secrets of the heart, dare not neglect their Duty to God in Publick, but must come forth in their places, and stand as

Landmarks, that cannot be moved for fear of Man; and for this end did the Lord mark us out; *that we should bear his Name in our Foreheads*, and appear to others as Living Monuments of his Mercy; Oh? therefore have a care, you Careless Ones, that have slighted your own Mercyes, which you have in a large manner been Pertakers of among the Faithful; for it is those that keep in a living Sence of Gods Dealings with them that do prize it, and receive it with Thanks-giving, and to such the Sure Mercies of *David* are continued and multiplied Morning by Morning: Oh therefore be concerned for time to come you that have been negligent in the work of the Lord, and work while you have a day; for the Night is hastning upon many, in which there can be no work done for the Lord, for the work of the Lord is to be done while the Light shineth, which gives a true discovery of the Deeds of Darkness; therefore bring your deeds to the Light, that they may be made manifest whether they are wrought in God or no; *for the Just Mans Path is a shining Light, that shineth more and more to the Perfect day*; so in tender bowels of true love my heart is open to you, that have tasted of the good Word of God, and the powers of the World to come, to perswade you to persevere in the work of the Lord, and to wait diligently upon him, that he may perfect his own work in you to his own prayse, that so you may Sanctifie his great name in the sight of the *Heathen*, and appear to be in deed what you have made a long Profession of; and for this end did God Manifest his unspeakable Love unto us, and give us a Manifestation of his good Spirit that we might profit therewith *(page 6)* and be Perfected by it, that so we might come to witness, as the Apostle said, *that we are able to doe all things through Christ that strengthens us*; and as it was said of old, by one that had seen the end of all Perfection, that the commandements of the Lord were exceeding broad, so it is manifest to the faithfull this day, and they can keep them with great delight, and they are not grievous to them; for it is such that are in the true profession of the true Faith that shall hold fast the Profession without wavering, and they do shine as a City set on a Hill, that cannot be hid, and dare not hide their Candle under a Bushel or under a Bed, nor rest in a bare knowledge of the Truth, but are willing to be faithful in their measure to what God Requires of them, that so they may feel the increase of Gods Love to their Soules, to preserve them; though there be no need to say to some **know the Lord**, yet there is great need to say to some **Obey the Lord**; for *Obedience is better then Sacrifice, and to hearken to the Voyce of God then all vain Oblations*; and for want of **Obedience** many are become vain in their Imaginations, that were once Enlightned, and their Understandings again Darkned, and the Ear that was once open to hear the Voice of the true Shepherd, is again stopped by the *Philistian* nature; so though the Lord speak once, and again, yet they Regard it not; for the Abomination is yet standing in the hearts of such which are not Faithful to the Lord, and therefore they cannot hear the Voice of him that calls for purity and holiness; this hinders the work of the Lord; that so their Calling & Election is not made sure, but Excuses are made by such, *that they are not to be too forward to goe in a Trying time to offer Sacrifice*, and so cause the dayly publick Sacrifices to Cease, and see not so much need of the continuance of it as the Apostle did when he spake to the Church in the sence of what Christ had done for them, to offer up Spirituall Sacrifice through him to God; and they were exhorted, *not to forsake the Assembling of themselves together, as the manner of some were,* that saw not the necessity of it; for those that know the blotting out of Sin, and passing by Iniquity, saw they had as much Need to wait upon the Lord to feel Refreshment from his Presence, and their strength Renewed in him, as they had before to gather together to wait for him in the way of his Judgments; and the travel of my Soul is, that it may be so with all who make a Profession *(page 7)* of his name at this day, so that we may press forward toward the mark of the high Calling in Christ Jesus, that the Enemy do not betray us from the Simplicity of the Gospel, that so in the end we may say as the Apostle did, *that in Simplicity and Godly Sincerity we have had our Conversation in this World*. So blessed are all they that do order their Conversation aright, the promise is to them, *that God will shew them his Salvation;* for he that hath called us to cease from man, whose breath is in his nostrils hath also commanded us to live in the Spirit and power of holiness, and obey him in all things, lest we be cut off from the True Vine, and cast out as Fruitless Branches, fit for nothing but the Fire; wherefore seeing and knowing these things, let us take the more heed to our wayes, and consider what manner of Persons we ought to be in all our conversation, to the end if we are Christs Disciples the offence of the Cross is not to be ceased from, but a dayly taking it up is to be known by all them that follow the Lord fully, because it crucifies the world to them, and they to the world, and this is the Saints Glory, for they dare not to glory in any thing saving in the Cross of Christ, but must forget what is behind and wait upon the Lord for dayly strength to go forward to perform our reasonable service to him, seeing we can do nothing without him that is acceptable in his Sight, we have great Reason to Wait at the heavenly *Jerusalem*, to be indued with power from an [sic] high, that we may be carried on in the ark of safety, Christ Jesus, who Vanquished the Tempter when he tryed him with various Temptations, and when he had overcome in all things the Angels Ministred to him, and in the power of the Spirit he was carried into Galile [sic] and all places to do his Fathers will, and it was his Delight to please his Father in all things though through Deep Sufferings, and though a Son, yet learned he obedience to his Father and his Father Delighted in him, and gave him that testimony that in all things he was well pleased with him; and it was for our sakes that he gave the only begotten Son of his love to Suffer for us, that we might be redeemed to God through his name, and find acceptance to the Father by him who is the only propitiation for our Sins; and as we live in obedience to his power we shall Receive an answer from God that he accepts of us and our doings, because we live and move and are acted by *(page 8)* him in whom his Soul takes pleasure, and therefore hath he made him heir of all things, and put in subjection under him, and anoynted him with Oyle of Joy above his Fellows, that the Virgin Daughter of *Sion* may love him, because of the preciousness of the Oyntment that proceeds from him, who is the Husband of the true Church, and therefore is her desire after him, and those that do live in the sence of the great love he hath bestowed on them, will prize it, and walk worthy of it; and they are of the same mind the Apostle was when he said, *but who so keepeth his word, in him is the Love of God perfected; hereby know we, that we are in him; he that saith he Abideth in him, ought himself also to walk even as he Walked.* So in true love to all that make a profession of the Truth my Soul is inlarged beyond what Ink and Paper can demonstrate, desiring the prosperity of *Sion* and welfare of heavenly *Jerusalem*; and my Prayer to God is *That all might be gathered into that faith that works by love, and gives Victory over the World*; for they shall prosper, that Love *Sion*.

So having Cleared my felf of what lay upon me from the Lord I am a Friend to all that love the Appearance of our Lord Jefus Chrift.

Dorcas Dole.

Prifoner to *Newgate* in *Briftol*
  for the Teftimony of Jefus,
  the 17th of the 12th Month,
  1684.

THE END

LONDON, *Printed by* John Bringhurft *in* Leaden-hall, 1685.

A N

Epiſtle of Love

T O

Friends in the Womens Meetings in London, &c.
To be read among them in the fear of God.

Ear Friends and Sisters in *Christ Jesus* to you is the
salutation of my true and sincere Love, in the ever
blessed pure and precious truth of our God: and to
you is my Heart open, in the tender love of our heavenly Father, who hath reached unto us, and lifted up the light of
his countenance upon us, and caused with ever blessed light, of his
everlasting day to shine among us; and hath made known the riches of
his grace unto us, in order to fit and prepare us for his own work and
service: To you my wellbeloved in the Lord, doth my Love and Life
reach at this time; to you that are given up to serve the Lord his Truth
and People; with chearfullness of Heart and readiness of mind, according to the measure of his grace committed unto you; and the breathings
of my Soul unto the God of my Life is, that he may enrich you all with
his heavenly Gifts, and Graces, that you may be strong in the power of
his might, and made able to perform the work and service of the Lord,
in the Church of *Christ* in this your day, and serve up your Generation
in faithfulness unto the end: *Oh!* my tender Friends, and wellbeloved
Sisters in the Lord, having a sence of your great Loss, in parting with
one so dearly beloved of the Lord, and well esteemed among his people
Anne Whitehead, who was a worthy Instrument, and faithful Labourer
in the Church of *Christ,* one *(page 2)* whom the Lord had furnished with
his heavenly Wisdom, and so filled with divine vertues, that she was
able and ready to be helpful in all concerns in the Church of *Christ,* both
Spiritual and Temporal; this I was sensible of by that acquaintance I
had with her: She was indeed one of the Lords worthies; who hath
taken her unto himself; and he was right worthy of her; who had made

(Page numbers of original document appear in text as *page _.*)

her worthy of so blessed a work, and honourable a service in the Church of *Christ:* who blessed her labour and made it effectual for good (as is well known to you that have been Eyewitnesses, and conversant with her) as by the many living testimonys from the faithful Brethren and Sisters is demonstrated, and I had true unity with you in it, and I was refreshed, and my heart was truely tendered, and broken before the Lord; and I was affected with your care and diligence to leave it upon Record, that her worthiness may not be forgotten, nor her faithfulness be Buried in the Grave of Oblivion; I say my heart was affected in the reading thereof, and the desire of my Soul is, that we that are left behind, may walk in the same Path, and that her past publick testimony that she bore among you, may not be forgotten by you, but that it may be had in remembrance; for it was seasonable, and needful, *viz.* Against Pride and Vanity and superfluity in many of the younger sort that profess the Holy Truth: which is a grief to the righteous to see how it abounds among such in the City of *London,* and some other places: My spirit have been long grieved, and my Soul bowed down under the weight of it: but considering how many worthy Instruments attended your Meetings; and not doubting but the Lord hath put it into their hearts to testifie against it, I was willing to be silent, and bear the burthen and mourn in secret to see how Pride and Vanity notwithstanding hath taken place in many that profess the truth; so the true desire of my Soul is, that those concerned may lay it to heart, and be bowed down, and cast of [*sic*] that which causeth the weights, and brings the heavy burthens upon the honest hearted, and grieves the Holy spirit of the Lord, which is the Sin that so easily besets, to wit Pride, and is so delightful to the young people, that the Enemy hath captivated many and taken many in that Snare, to the dishonour of God and his precious truth which they profess; and that to the hurt of their own Souls; therefore in bowels of tender Love, I exhort you all whom it may concern, to whom this may *(page 3)* come in the City of *London, &c.* To incline your hearts to seek the Glory of God and the peace and welfare of your own Souls; and the advancement of the Holy truth that you profess, and are convinced of, which the God of all our mercies hath made known unto you: let your adorning be that comely ornament of a meek and quiet spirit, like Holy women professing godliness with good works: Oh! that I might prevail with you to follow the council of the Lord, and his servants, and mind the light of *Christ* in your own hearts and Consciences, to be guided by it into plainness and humility of mind, that you might not be evil examples to others round about you; for the Eyes of many in the Nation are upon you, and those that are inclined to take liberty in Pride and vanity, and superfluity, take strength by you; and when such have been cautioned and admonished to plainness as becomes the truth, they turn it upon us, and say, This is little to what Friends wear in *London:* (which is too true on some) therefore I intreat you to deny your selves, and take up the Cross and follow *Christ Jesus,* in the streight and narrow way that leads to Life and peace: And you that are Elders in the Church and Mothers in *Israel,* I intreat you watch over the younger for good, and be good patterns and Holy examples to them, and use all diligence to admonish, and counsel, with much tenderness in the wisdom and power of God, and judge down Pride and vanity, especially in your own Families, and give no liberty to your Children to please them in any thing that is contrary to truth: when they shall say to you such a one have a Chain of Gold why may not I? or any other needless thing that may give occasion to the enemies of truth, to point at it, and say the Quakers are as ready to run into any new fashion as we, and so cause the weak to stumble, and turn the simple out of the way: therefore my dear Friends and Sisters, you that have a concern upon you for the Church, and are Elders in the Family of God, stand up in the power and Holy authority of God, to find the Babilonish garment, and the wedge of Gold, that hinders *Israels* prosperity, and put it out of the Camp; away with the naked Necks and Backs, the needless pinches and Ruffles, the high dresses upon the Head, and tiring the Hair wanton Eyes walking and mincing as they go, and all superfluity that dishonours God and *(page 4)* his truth; least instead of a Girdle he send a Rent; and instead of well-set Hair Baldness, and instead of a Stomacher a girding of Sackcloth and burning instead of beauty, except you repent: therefore, I intreat you, receive it in Love, as a warning to you, laying aside all superfluity, and receive with meekness the ingrafted Word which is able to save you out of all those things (which grieves the good Spirit of the Lord:) and build you up in that most holy Faith which purifies the Heart, and gives Victory over the World. These things have been a grief unto me, and lay as a weight upon me for a long time: and when I heard the testimony of our dear Sister, which may be taken as the Dying words of so worthy an Instrument; it, I say, was more to be observed, and minded by those concerned. And it arose in my Heart, in the openings of Life, now it is a seasonable time for me to ease my Spirit, and clear my self, to back or revive, this the last publick testimony of our dear Sister, that it may not be forgotten by any that are concerned: so my dear Friends, I have this to say to you that love the Lord above all, and are given up in his service, in the works of Piety and Charity; you are the Chosen Vessels of the Lord, who will be with you, notwithstanding he hath removed and taken away such a faithful Labourer, and fellow helper from among you, yet the Lord is with you my tender Friends, yea, I say, *Israels* God is among you, and he will give you wisdom and strength, as you wait upon him; therefore be incouraged in the blessed work of the Lord, unto which you are called, and be bold and valiant for the truth, to withstand all the false pretenders to love and unity, and are in a dividing Spirit, and secretly endeavouring, to disturb the Churches peace. And stand up on the strength of the Lord, and in the power of his might against all such which would destroy your comly Order (into which the Lord hath gathered you) and bring all into Confusion as they are: and as your Hearts are inclined to this good work, the Lord who is rich in mercy and goodness, he will fill your Qivers with pollished Arrows, and cause your Bow to abide in strength, and so furnish you with his heavenly vertues to inable you for his work and service, that he calls you to; that hard things will be made easie unto you; Ye beloved of the Lord, Gods power will surround you, and his Salvation will be as Walls and Bulwarks about you, and his pure Powerful presence will uphold *(page 5)* you, and preserve you unto the end, Amen. So to the grace of God, I recommend you, that is able to keep both you and me, and all his Flock and Family everywhere, in the unity of the Spirit, which is the bond of true peace, and in the Holy fellowship of the Gospel of peace: where there is no seperation, for we have large experience of his goodness and mercies and favours; for our God hath done great things for us even beyond utterance; what Tongue is able to declare, his notable Acts, and his wonderful doings among his faithful people? Oh! who can but praise him, and magnifie his glorious name and return thanksgiving with *Hallelujah* over all, for he is worthy saith my Soul, who am your Friend and Sister in the Lord *Jesus Christ,* and have thus far cleared my Conscience and eased my Spirit.

Theophila Townſend.

Bear with my plainneſs and homely expreſſion
Charity make way for it, for the truths ſake.

A Living
TESTIMONY
From the Power and Spirit of our 𝕷𝖔𝖗𝖉 𝕵𝖊𝖘𝖚𝖘 𝕮𝖍𝖗𝖎𝖘𝖙
in our Faithful
𝔚𝔬𝔪𝔢𝔫𝔰 𝔐𝔢𝔢𝔱𝔦𝔫𝔤
AND
C H R J S T I A N S O C I T Y [sic].

Given forth in the Univerſal Union, and Approbation thereof, according to our ſeveral Proportions of Faith and Life, in the ſame Spirit.

T He Spirit of *Grace* having freely visited all *Mankind*, the Lord hath had regard unto the low estate of his *Servants* and *Handmaids*, notwithstanding the *Enmity* and *Subtilty* and *secreet Smitings* of that Spirit which seeks to *Divide* and lay *Waste* the *Heritage* of God, whom he hath Quickned, and Raised up *Heirs* of Life together, in the *Fellowship of* the Gospel of Peace, which stands in the *Unity* of that Spirit which gives *Life*; and our *Life*, *Peace* and *Joy* is increased in the Lord one toward another, whereby *(page 2)* we are made *Living* Members of that Body which Christ Jesus our Lord is *Head*, Glory to our God forever.

And we being turned to the Spirit of *Grace* and *Light* of Christ do believe in the Light, and are become *Children* of his Light, of his Day, and so *Members* of his holy Body, of which Christ is the Living and Eternal heavenly Head; and by the Spirit of Grace we are come into

(Page numbers of original document appear in text as *page _.*)

Favour with God, and into the Order of his Gospel, and are his *Daughters, Servants* and *Handmaids;* and we have a Heavenly propriety in the *Light, Power* and *Spirit* of *Grace,* and the *Gospel,* being *Heirs* of the same; so by Grace we are called into the Work and Service of God and Jesus Christ, that they require of us in our Age and Generation, and we have our Wisdom from the Lord Jesus Christ the Rock of Ages, and the Foundation of many Generations, who is made unto us Wisdom; and he hath enlightned our Spirits, which is the Candle of the Lord, which is his heavenly divine Light, which is the Life that is in Christ, the Word by which all things were made, that we might all see and know the Will of God, and do it, and know our several Works and Services the Lord requireth of us in his Church, we are not to put our Candles under a Bushel, nor to hide our Talents in a Napkin, as the sloathful do; but we are to have Oyl in our Lamps, like Wise Virgins to the Lord; and our Lamps are to burn, and our Lights are to shine, that we may all see clearly our Work and Service; namely, To help Families that are Poor, and have Children, and to see that they are diligent to improve things to the best; that they are not slothful in their business, no Wasters, and that they put their Children to some Imployment, as soon as they are capable; for the Truth hath a lively operation, it brings People to be diligent in all things, serving the Lord. For we which have been Mothers of Children, and Antient Women in *(page 3)* our Families, do know, in the Wisdom of God, what will do in Families, in Truth and Righteousness, and according to the Families; and so are able, through the Wisdom of God, to instruct such as want Instruction, and so are Helps to them in their Families: And as the Apostle saith, *The Elder Women are to be Teachers of good things, and instruct and teach the Younger to be Sober, and love their Husbands and Children, and to be discreet, good and chaste, that the Word of God be not blasphemed.*

So here is a great charge and care lies upon these Aged Women in the Truth, who are to teach these good things that the Younger be trained up in that which is good, sober and discreet, chaste and virtuous; so to be kept before they Marry, and after they are Married, sober, and to love their Husbands, and Children, and bring them up in the fear of the Lord, that the Name of the Lord be not blasphemed. Here we Aged Women in the Truth, have a Gift to be exercised in; and such a care lieth upon us, that the Church of Christ be not scandalized.

And we have a concern, as in *Tit.* 2. relating to Marriages, both before and after they are Marryed; and such Elderly Women in the Truth, are to be intreated as Mothers, and so not to be Railed upon; and the

Younger, as Sisters, with all Purity, and Widows, that are Widows indeed, are to be honoured; and if they have Children or Nephews, let
them learn first to shew Piety or Kindness at Home, and to requite
their Parents and Kindred; for this is good and acceptable before God.

Now this is a good Lesson for the Widows, to instruct their Children
and Nephews to Practice. And so we may see such holy Women, that
were taken into the Number and Society in that day, were to be well
reported for good *(page 4)* Works, *Lodging Strangers,* and *Relieving the Afflicted,* and if she have diligently followed every good Work; these were
of the Number of *good Women,* that were taken into the Number for
their *good Works* and *Service* in the Church of Christ, and that were
recorded for their Works and Service to the Lord.

Now here is a diligent Practice and Exercise in the Power and Spirit
of God, and to be diligent in every *good Work* and *Service, To relieve the
Afflicted, and to bring up Children in the fear of God; and to be Teachers of
good things, and be Instructors of the Younger, that the Name of God be not
Blasphemed.*

So here you may see the Apostle was of another Mind than those
perverse corrupt Minds, full of *Envy* and *Strife, Railing* and *evil Surmizing,*
and some that wilfully, scoffingly, maliciously and revilingly call the
Womens Meetings an *Idol* and an *Image;* but such Raging Waves of the
Sea have but foamed out their own Shame, and manifested they are
erred from the Spirit of Grace, which God poureth forth upon *Daughters, Servants* and *Hand-maids,* which have received as well as Sons,
and are to improve their Talents and measure of the Gift of God, and
not to grieve nor quench the holy Spirit, nor *walk despightfully against the
Spirit of Grace,* as some do, whereby we are sealed to the day of Redemption.

And concerning *Marriages,* it being God's joyning, and his Ordinance, we Women in the Spirit and Grace of God, being living Members of the Church of Christ, do see with the Spirit of God, our Service
concerning Marriage, that both Young and Old that profess Gods Truth,
may go together orderly, first having their Relations consent; for many
times we having seen, and do see more in the Young People and Widdows
State and Condition, than some of the Men, because we are more
amongst them; so in that we *(page 5)* dare not neglect our Gift in the
Spirit of Wisdom and Grace, but exercise and improve it to this glory
and honour, and in that we are meet Helps in the *Spirit of God,* to the
Men, our Brethren; knowing that *Male and Female are one in Christ; for
the Unity* and *fellowship* of *Sons* and *Daughters, Widdows* and *Servants,*

stands in the *Spirit of God*, and we in the same Spirit know our *great Service* to look after and *visit the Sick* that want *Nurses* to help them, and sometimes assisting the Men, our Brethren, to the placing out our [sic] *poor Friends Children to Apprentices*, and other good *Services* that the *Spirit of God* leadeth us to, and into the practice of the *pure Religion*, and that all such as do profess the *Grace of God*, may live and walk *godly, righteously* and *soberly in their Lives and Conversation*, all such as profess the *Word of God* may be *Doers* of the *Word of God*; for all that *fear God and work Righteousness, are accepted with God*. And so, the *Aged Women in the Truth* were and are to be Teachers of such good things; but such *wanton Women or Widdows, that are Tale-carriers and busie Bodies, that speak things they ought not*, and such Men that are in *Envy and strife, and are puft up with high swelling Words of Vanity, and vain unruly Talkers, Despisers of them that are good, having got into the form of Godliness, but not in the Power:* Such were in the Apostles days, as well as now, reproved by the Spirit of God, and turned away from; and we cannot receive their Chaff and Husks for the *Seed, Wheat,* or the *Bread of Life;* neither their *Earthly sensual Wisdom* for the *Wisdom of God;* and therefore have several of such unruly Spirits printed and written so many slanderous reproachful Books against us, and made disturbance against our Meetings, under a false pretence, as though they would call us to our *own, as it was in the beginning;* which if they themselves had kept to that that first convinced them, they would have shewed forth a *quiet and meek Spirit,* who under a pretence of *calling People to their own,* have drawn People from their *(page 6)* own; for we are come to our *Light, Spirit, Grace* and *Word of Life,* and *Anointing within,* which is our own, which at first convinced us, and which doth teach us to be *Doers* of the *Word of God,* and to *live Righteously,* and to practice the *true Religion;* and them that do not, the spirit of the Lord moveth us, and teacheth us to admonish and exhort them to *forsake the Evil, and cleave to the Good;* and them that oppose the Practice and Care, in the Spirit and Grace of God, of Men and Women in their Meetings, had they kept to the *Light, Grace, Truth* and *Spirit of God,* and *Unction within them,* they would have been one with us in the same, and in the practice of the *pure Religion,* and in the *Godly Care for God's Honour;* but many of them are turned Mockers, Scoffers, Writers and Printers against us, and are become *vain Talkers.* But we leave them to the Lord, to deal with according to their Words and Works: And we right-well know our *Services,* which the Spirit of Grace hath led us to in the Church of Christ.

And as to our orderly proceeding toward *Marriage*, we say and affirm, the *Man* and *Woman* both ought to appear at the *Monethly Meetings*, and Meetings for such Services, where we and the Men may hear what both have to say, that Men and Women may not be wronged of their Children, and that they are clear from all other Persons, that the Meeting, and all others concerned, may have satisfaction, in that *Life*, *Grace*, and *Spirit* of *Christ*, in which is our Unity, and may be *Faithful Witnesses*, both to God and Man, in our own *Gift of Grace*, in which God hath, and doth own us: And all that *write*, and *print*, and *speak* against our *Practice* (which the *Spirit of Grace* hath led us to in the *Church of Christ*) reach us not, neither are they of any credit with us: For we have *put on the Breast-plate of Faith and Love, and for an Helmet, the Hope of Salvation.* And so our desires are, *That whatever things are pure, vertuous, lovely, sober, honest, and of good Report, (page 7)* and that every one may follow that which makes for *Peace*, and that they may study to be *Quiet*, and do the Lords Business in his Spirit and Power, and their own in Truth and Righteousness, and walk as Children of the Light, in the day of Christ, and in meekness instruct them that oppose themselves, *If God per adventure may give them Repentance to the acknowledgment of the Truth; Greet one another with a holy Kiss of Charity; Peace be with you all that are in Christ Jesus, Amen,* Rom. 16. 1 Cor. 16.20. 2 Cor. 13.22. 1 Pet. 5.14.

Now this holy Kiss of *Charity* is wanting, and not to be found, nor expected from them that do not walk in the Spirit of God. And the Apostle saith, *I intreat thee, true Yokefellow, help these Women which laboured with me in the Gospel, with Clement also, and with others my Fellow-Labourers, whose Names are written in the Book of Life,* Phil. 4.3. *There is one God and Father of all, which is above all, and through you all, and in you all by his Spirit.* So all may see with his Spirit the Lord is near unto all to teach them to know their Service; and if these do lack wisdom, to ask it of God, who giveth liberally, and take counsel of him who is nigh unto you, and walk worthy of the Lords mercies, being faithful in every good work; for to do good & communicate, is a Sacrifice well pleasing to the Lord, and we who are made the Sons and Daughters, Servants and Handmaids, by the Spirit of God, in the same Spirit we have Unity and Fellowship, though we be absent in body one from another, yet we are present in the same Spirit, and by the spiritual Eye do see and behold, and rejoyce in our spiritual Order, and one anothers stedfastness in Christ Jesus. And so we have a communion in the Holy Ghost, both Sons and Daughters; and if any thing the Men do see that is more proper for the Women to do, and to look into, they do let us know of it, as Sisters in the Truth; and if any thing we see that is more proper for the Men, than for us, then we let them know as our Brethren in the Truth; so in this we do (page 8) assist each other in the Spirit and Truth, and are meet helps in the heavenly spiritual, Union and Communion, and Fellowship and Society, and do know the unity of the Spirit of Christ, which is the Bond of Peace, and in this heavenly Spirit that reaches through all, and over all, and is in you all, our dear Sisters every where, in Christ Jesus, 'tis you we visit, to whom we recommend this Epistle, *Farewel.*

Postscript.

W E have been a People that have sought the Lord, and now we have found him, we are willing to obey him in his Power and holy *Spirit, that he hath given us to enable us so to do; and though we are perse-cuted in spirit, and other ways, by unruly Tongues that have not power with their hands; such that are Sayers of the Word of God, and Talkers of the Grace of God, and of the Righteousness of Christ, but not Doers of the Word, nor walkers in the Righteousness and Grace of God, their ungracious Languages and Words, that they have spoken and Printed against us, shew the Trees and their Fruit, whom we desire may come to the Light of Christ, that with it they may see themselves, and repent; for we desire the Salvation and Eternal Good of all.*

Signed by us, in the behalf of the reſt of our ſincere Minded Members of our Meeting,

London, from our Womens Meeting,
gathered out of the City and
Suburbs, the *1st of the 4th Moneth,*
1685.
}

Mary Foſter,
Mary Elſon,
Anne Travice,
Ruth Crowch,
Suſannah Dew,
Mary Plumſtead.

THE END.

EPISTLE

FROM THE

Womens Yearly Meeting at York, 1688.

AND

An EPISTLE from *Mary Waite*.

(Page numbers of original document appear in text as *page _.*)

(page 3)

A T E S T I M O N Y *for the Lord and his Truth,*
given forth by the women friends, at their yearly
meeting, at York, being a tender ſalutation of love,
to their friends and ſiſters, in their ſeveral monthly
meetings, in this county, and elſe where, greeting.

Dear friends and ſiſters,

WE, being met together in the fear of the Lord, to wait
upon him for his ancient power, to order us, and, in his
wisdom and counsel, to guide us in our exercise relating to church
affairs: It hath pleased him to break in among us in a glorious manner,
to our great satisfaction, and he hath filled our meeting with his living
presence, and crowned our assembly with his heavenly power, and
opened the fountain of life unto us, and caused the streams of his love
freely to flow among us, and run from vessel to vessel, to the gladding of
our hearts, which causeth living praise, and hearty thanksgiving to be
rendered unto him, who alone is worthy. And, friends, we hereby signify to you, that there hath been many living testimonies delivered
among us from the divine openings of the spirit of life, in many brethren and sisters, whereby we are fully satisfied that the Lord is well pleased
with this our service, and doth accept our sacrifices and free-will
offerings, *(page 4)* and returns an answer of peace unto our bosoms, which
is greatly our reward. Here hath also been brought several testimonies
in writing from divers of our monthly meetings, to our great satisfaction, touching the care of friends for the honour of God, and prosperity
of truth in one another. And, dear friends, in that unchangeable love
and precious truth of our God, we dearly salute you, wherein our relation and acquaintance with him, and one with another, in spirit, is
daily renewed, and our care and concern for his honour, and one
another's good, is still continued; and therein we see there is as great
need as ever to watch over one another for good; tho' it hath pleased
God, in his infinite mercy and love, to give us a day of ease and liberty,
as to the outward, and hath broken the bonds of many
captives, and hath set the oppressed free and hath opened the prison
doors in a great measure: living praises be given him for ever! And now,
friends, it is our desire that we all may make a right use of it, and answer

the end of the Lord in it, and neither take nor give liberty to that part
in any which may give the Lord occasion to suffer our bonds to be
renewed, but in his fear and holy awe walk humbly before him, in a
holy and self-denying life, under the cross of Christ Jesus, *which daily
crucifies us to the world, and the world to us*, and teacheth us to deny
ungodliness, and worldly lusts, and to live righteously and soberly in
this present world, that by our holy lives and righteous conversation,
others, seeing our good *(page 5)* works, may glorify our heavenly Father,
and that, by our truth-like and Christian behaviour, and upright dealing in all our affairs among the children of men, we may walk as becomes the truth. And, dear friends, join not with any sort of people
further than will stand with truth's honour, and reach God's witness in
every conscience, but as much as in you lieth live peaceably with all
men, and do good unto all, especially unto the houshold of faith, and so
daily fulfill the royal law of love, in shewing to all men that you are
Christ's disciples, by loving him and one another. And, friends, we cannot but warn you of the separating and quarrelling spirit which leads
unto strife, contention and jangling, and would thereby lay waste your
concern for God's honour, and one another's good; this is that old adversary and enemy of mankind, who, in all ages, *went about like a roaring
lion, seeking whom he might devour*, and, as a ravenous wolf, sometimes
gets the sheeps cloathing, and never wants specious pretences to ac-
complish his design, and bring about his end, which is to divide, rend,
tear, destroy and separate from God and one another; and would lay
waste the heritage of God, and make spoil of his plantation, and leave
his tender plants without care, in the briars and thorns, and every hurtful weed to wrap about them to hinder their growth, and draw them out
of their order, by reason of which, as in the days of old, the way of truth
might be evil spoken of. The Lord disappoint him of his purpose, and
frustrate him of *(page 6)* his end, is our prayer, and keep him livingly
sensible, that the end of the Lord, in all his fatherly corrections, gentle
chastisements, and kind reproofs, hath been to preserve us from the
snares of the enemy. Therefore, dear friends, be concerned for the preservation of one another in every of your respective monthly meetings,
and be faithful in performing your service and duty to God, and to one
another, as he opens it in you, and lays it upon you, in exhortation,
admonition and reproof, in tender love, for so it will be as the balm of
Gilead unto those who are wounded by the wiles of the enemy; for, dear
friends, it is the very end of our travel and labour of love, *that the hungry
may be fed, the naked cloathed, the weak strengthened, the feeble comforted,*

and the wounded healed. So that the very weakest, and hindermost of the flock, may be gathered into the fold of rest and safety, where no destroyer can come, where the ransomed and redeemed by the Lord have the songs of deliverance and high praise in their mouths, giving him the honour, who alone is worthy for ever. And, friends, let us ever remember the tender dealing and mercies of the Lord to us, and it was not for our deserts, nor any worthiness in us, but his own good will, and for his seed sake, in which he heard our many cries, and had regard to our tears, and helped us through many exercises and trials inwardly and outwardly, and hath been our rock and refuge, and our sure hiding place, in many storms and exercises; and yet preserves in perfect *(page 7)* peace all those that trust in him, who keep his new creation full of joy; and the voice of thanksgiving and melody is heard in our land, and the Lord becomes unto us the place of broad rivers, and makes us before him as well watered gardens, and affects our hearts with his divine love to praise his name. And now to you young women, whom our souls love, and whom the Lord delighteth to do good unto, and hath visited with the tastes of his love, be you ordered by him in all things, that, in your modest and chast behaviour, your comely and decent dresses in your apparel, and in all other things you may be good examples to others, not only those that are without, but to some professing of the faith, that in the line of life, and language of truth, we may speak one to another and say, *Arise, ye daughters of Sion, shake yourselves from the dust of the earth,* put on the beautiful garments, even the robes of righteousness, the saints cloathing, the ornament of a meek and quiet spirit. And be not too careful for preferment on riches in this world, but be careful to know the Lord to be your portion and the lot of your inheritance. Then testimonies will arise as in the days of old; our lot is fallen in a good ground, we have large possessions. And, friends, be not concerned in reference to marriage out of God's fear, but first wait to know your Maker to become your husband and the bridegroom of your souls, then you will come to know that you are not your own, but that he must have the ordering and disposing of you, in *(page 8)* soul, body and spirit, which are all his; for he, being the only one unto you, and the chiefest of ten thousand among you, will be your beloved and your friend. Oh! friends, this state is happy, and blessed are they that attain it, and live in it; the Lord is not unmindful of them, but in his own time, if he see it good for them, can provide meet helps for them; then will your marriage be honourable, being orderly accomplished with the assent of parents, and the unity of friends, and an honour to God, and comfort to your own souls: then husbands and children are a blessing in the hands of the Lord, and you will arise in your day, age and generation, as mothers in Israel, as those holy ancients whose living testimonies reacheth unto us, and blessed memories liveth with us according to our measures; as Lydia open hearted to God and one to another, as Dorcas careful to do one another good, as Deborah concerned in the common wealth of Israel, and as Iael zealous for the truth, who was praised above women. And you, friends, who are under the present concern, and in your day's work, do it not negligently, not with careless minds, but be you diligent in every of your womens meetings, and order two faithful women in every meeting to take the care upon them, and so far as may answer truth, do you endeavour that nothing be practised among you, but what tends to God's honour, and one another's comfort; let nothing be indulged or connived at in any, whereby truth is dishonoured, and let that be cherished and encouraged in all *(page 9)* wherewith truth is honoured; and these our testimonies cast not carelesly into a corner, but some time peruse them, and mark well the wholesome advice therein; that our travel may be answered, the Lord honoured, and you reap the benefit; and let a record be kept from month to month, and from year to year, of the Lord's dealing with us, and mercy to us, to future ages; that from age to age, and one generation to another, his own works may praise him, to whom all praises do belong, and be ascribed both now and for ever.

From our yearly meeting at York, the 28th of the 4th month, 1688.

Signed on the behalf of the meeting by

Catharine Whitton	*Mary Waite*
Judith Boulby	*Deborah Winn*
Elizabeth Sedman	*Eliz. Beckwith*
Frances Taylor	*Mary Lindley*

See page 482 for Mary Waite's epistle.

INDEX OF PERSON AND PLACE NAMES

HIDDEN IN PLAIN SIGHT

was set in Goudy Old Style, a desktop Computer typeface from Adobe Type Library. Display pages were set in Adobe Caslon and Goudy Text.

Goudy Old Style was designed in 1915 by Frederick W. Goudy, his twenty-fifth type face and his first for American Typefounders. One of the most popular typefaces ever produced, its distinctive features include diamond-shaped dots on the i, the j, and punctuation marks; the upturned ear of the g; and the base of the e and the l.

Goudy Text, a modification of the blackletter types of Gutenberg's 42-line Bible, was completed in 1928 for Lanston Monotype.

In 1722 William Caslon released his first typefaces, based on seventeenth-century Dutch old style type designs. Used extensively in England, Caslon's designs became popular throughout Europe and the American colonies; printer Benjamin Franklin hardly used any other typeface. The first printings of the American Declaration of Independence and the Constitution were set in Caslon. For her Caslon revival, designer Carol Twombly studied specimen pages by William Caslon printed between 1734 and 1770.

The book was composed on a Macintosh Quadra 650 using Adobe Pagemaker. Fifteen hundred copies were printed in the United States of America by Thomson-Shore, Inc., Dexter, Michigan in October 1995. It was printed on 60# Gladfelter Supple Opaque, an acid-free recycled paper from the Gladfelter Company.

Book Design by
Eva Fernandez Beehler and Rebecca Kratz Mays